THUMBS UP

Thumbs Up

The Life and Courageous Comeback of White House Press Secretary Jim Brady

Mollie Dickenson

William Morrow and Company, Inc.
New York

Library of Congress Cataloging-in-Publication Data

Dickenson, Mollie.
Thumbs up: the life and courageous comeback of White House press secretary, Jim Brady/Mollie Dickenson.
p. cm.
Includes bibliographical references and index.
ISBN 0-688-06497-3
1. Brady, James S. 2. Presidents—United States—Staff—Biography. I. Title.
E840.8.B7D53 1987
973.927′092′4—dc19 87-17385
CIP

Printed in the United States of America

2 3 4 5 6 7 8 9 10

BOOK DESIGN BY CONRAD CARLOCK

For Jim and Sarah and their families,
Especially Dorothy, Frances, Bill, Missy, and Scott

And for my family

Acknowledgments

It was inevitable that there would be a book written about White House press secretary James S. Brady. This particular one came into being because Jim and Sarah Brady entrusted to a relatively unknown writer the challenge of chronicling their dramatic experiences. "We want an honest book," Sarah told me. My first and largest debt is to them. And in writing this book I found that the names Jim and Sarah Brady, and the esteem with which they are regarded, opened all doors to the interviews and material I needed. I won't attempt to name the interviewees here—their names are in the index—but I am indebted to each and every one of them because each provided pieces of the mosaic that makes up Jim Brady's life. If I have left anyone out it is with regret, and only because of the large amount of material I acquired, and the need to cut and mold it into a readable account.

There are a number of medical people who treated Jim who gave me a great deal of their time. I am especially grateful to Dr. Arthur I. Kobrine; and also to Dr. George Economos and Dr. Ed Kornel, as well as to therapists Cathy Wynne Ellis, Susan Marino, and Arlene Pietranton.

Jim's secretary in the White House press office, Sally McElroy, cheerfully answered my queries, as have Jeanne Winnick and Florence Taussig, also of the press-office staff.

I am indebted to Washington attorney Ed Weidenfeld for his advice and help; and to U.S. attorney Roger Adelman and FBI agent Frank Waikart for their invaluable assistance.

Many close Brady friends in Washington have given me endless encouragement along the way: Bob and Suzi Dahlgren, Debby and Jerry File, Wendy and Ernie Baynard, Jan and Otto Wolff, Linda and Kent Watkins, Jean and Ken Klinge, Estelle and Michael Sotirhos, Pam Jacovides, Lou Economos, and Cindy Kobrine. The same is true of many mutual friends:

Don and Marian Burros, Dick and Germaine Swanson, Bill Plante and Robin Smith, Steven Neal, and Gary Schuster. In addition I have received enormous goodwill and encouragement from the writing and journalistic community of Washington, especially from Kate and Jim Lehrer, Nick and Mary Lynn Kotz, Barbara Matusow and Jack Nelson, John Mashek, Myra MacPherson, Elizabeth Drew and David Webster, Marianne Means and Warren Weaver, Bill Kovach, John Fox Sullivan, Susan Shreve and Tim Seldes, E.J. and Roger Mudd, Bob Woodward, Edward Fouhy, Mark Shields, Al Hunt and Judy Woodruff, Finlay Lewis, Chuck Conconi, Story Shem and Michael Evans, and Charlie Peters.

Many others have supported me with their friendship and solicitousness about the progress of the book, among them Barbara Fouhy, Anne Shields, Linda and Bill Daisley, Willee Lewis, Barbara Pryor, Barbara Eagleton, Carrie Lee Nelson, Nancy Schoenke, Beverly Sullivan, Grace Gottlieb, Lynn Kovach, Sandra Berler, Sherley Koteen, Ann Culver, Sarah Mashek, Beth Peters, Carla Cohen, and Concepción Ramirez. And I will always treasure the warm reception and help I received from Jim's many friends in Centralia, Illinois.

Two TV cameramen, CBS's Charlie Wilson and NBC's Shelley Fielman, took extra time to allow me to view their videotapes. And Jane Brooks at ABC graciously made arrangements on several occasions for me to view tapes or read transcripts, as did CBS White House correspondent Bill Plante.

Many of my husband's colleagues at *The Washington Post* have given time and shown their interest; and I thank Executive Editor Benjamin Bradlee for allowing me access to the *Post*'s clipping files, and for his kind interest.

Sheila Harvill typed the manuscript, often with short notice. She accommodated my writing schedule with unfailing good humor and kind words. Editorial assistant David Means and copy editor Joan Amico at William Morrow have been equally kind and helpful.

I am grateful for the encouragement of my mother, Norma McCauley, and my children, Beth Oxley and John Lerch. And above all I am grateful to my husband, Jim "Dick" Dickenson, who supported me in every way possible throughout this project.

Finally, my gratitude goes to my editor, Lisa Drew, at William Morrow, who always thought there should be a Jim Brady book, and whose confidence in and support of me have made it a reality.

June 25, 1987 —MOLLIE DICKENSON

Preface

This is a biography written before its time. The subject, Jim "Bear" Brady, was only forty years old when his life was almost ended and irrevocably changed by John Hinckley's bullet to his brain—a bullet meant for the president of the United States. Backed by the goodwill of the entire country, Jim, just two months before, had launched what promised to be a brilliant sojourn as the president's press secretary. Many Washington observers thought Jim was better qualified, personally and professionally, than any of his predecessors in the job. Jim had every intention of influencing as much as he could the course the Reagan administration would take. We will never know what Jim's commonsense counsel and high intelligence would have meant to Ronald Reagan; nor what hijinks and high good humor Jim surely would have treated us to; nor what the next stage of his career in public life would have been. Only one thing is certain: His tragedy and losses have also been ours.

When I first met Jim and Sarah Brady I was three years into a career of free-lance writing. My husband, veteran newspaperman James R. Dickenson, had covered the 1980 John Connaly and Ronald Reagan presidential campaigns for *The Washington Star,* and came to know Jim Brady in the process. So I had the great pleasure of meeting this enormously attractive man who listens carefully to and focuses intently on whoever is standing next to him, and I sensed immediately that standing next to Jim Brady was where any sensible person would want to be. It was obvious that he was one of the good guys of the world and his appointment reflected well on Reagan and the new administration. Many of us felt that with him as White House press secretary, things couldn't get too far out of hand or off base. I ran into Jim and Sarah three times before John Hinckley cut his life out from under him.

On March 30, 1981, I sat with a neighbor before the television set, along with the rest of the country, and wept when it was announced that Jim had died, hoping fiercely that it was not true, wondering if it was even right to hope for that, considering Jim had been shot in the head. I read avidly the accounts of his progress from then on. From time to time my husband sent messages to Sarah inquiring after Jim, and in September Sarah felt Jim was well enough to see us. "Hi, Mollie," he said, when I walked into his hospital room, and then with glee he reached out his hand to my husband. "Jimmy Leroy," he laughed, recalling a nickname bestowed on my husband by NBC's Don Oliver on the campaign trail.

When Jim left the hospital we met him and Sarah for dinner occasionally, and the next year I wrote an article for *Family Circle* about Jim's progress, followed by an expanded article on him in *Washingtonian Magazine*. It was out of these articles that the book came.

"I've told my friends to 'tell all,' " Jim told me. " 'Tell all,' I tell them." I began work in October 1983 and finished in April 1987, three and a half years later. There were times when Jim thought I would never finish it. "Are we going to have a book in this decade?" he'd ask me. I always said yes. "So, we *are* going to have a book?" he would say and fix me with his eyes. At a party once he asked me, "Why aren't you home writing?" And another time he said, "Give *me* your goddamned notes and *I'll* write the thing." But another time he said, "Coon and I think you are doing it just right." Recently he told me, "The book be good. It be good."

Jim was always there with the right perspective on everything. On the day I interviewed President Reagan I suddenly found myself very nervous and I phoned Jim to see if he had any questions to suggest. "So, you're going to see 'His Cootship,' are you?" Jim said to me. That took the edge off my nervousness and on my drive to the White House I laughed all the way at Jim's easy irreverence.

Sarah said when I started the book, "I want this to be a fun project," and that it has been. Being involved with the Bradys has been one of the greatest experiences of my life. They haven't stopped living fully for one moment. In fact, one of my difficulties has been that there is always something new in their lives to add to the book. And so I have cut it off, knowing their story will go on and that Jim and Sarah will be heard from for the rest of their lives, making contributions to those near and dear to them and to the society at large.

Jim's courage and good humor in the face of pain and sorrow are so low-key and natural that it is easy to forget that every day is a struggle for him. Longtime Brady family friend Jim Wham, a fellow Sigma Chi and distinguished attorney in Jim's hometown of Centralia, Illinois, has summed it up succinctly. "After eight years as Reagan's press secretary, Jim could have done anything he wanted to—run for senator or governor of Illinois. Reagan couldn't have picked anyone better than Jim to represent him. Nothing could have stopped him from reaching great heights. He had such potential—then, wham!—back to zero for a while. It was a tragedy for the country because Jim is able to get strong positions across in an acceptable way, so that opponents don't take it personally. But the glory of Jim Brady is the way he has handled himself since the shooting. That is the glory of Jim Brady. There is no stopping him. He will make it. He will always be great in the people's mind."

Contents

PART ONE

March 30, 1981

CHAPTER ONE

"Shots Have Been Fired. . . ."

Monday morning came too early for Sarah Brady that next to last day in March 1981. And when she looked outside, it was rainy and gloomy. Jim Brady customarily got up at 5:30, "with the chickens," he would say, and he was up early today as usual. He sometimes liked to go upstairs to get his little two-year-old son, Scott, from his crib and bring him back down to his and Sarah's bed for some cuddling; they could hear Scott talking in his bed. But this morning Sarah was exhausted. "Oh, Jim, please let him stay there for a while. I desperately need another hour of sleep." But Jim was insistent. "No, I just want to see the weiner beaner," he said; "I don't get much time with him anymore," and he padded off toward the stairway to fetch him.

Jim's schedule since he had been appointed press secretary to President Reagan had been fierce, and he rarely saw his little boy these days, leaving home as he did at 6:15 and returning usually long after Scott was in bed. Later that day, Sarah, waiting fearfully at George Washington University Hospital for word of her husband's condition, would cast her mind back frequently to the early morning interlude, fervently hoping that the incident didn't have an ominous meaning—hoping it didn't mean that fate had arranged for Jim to see his little son one last time.

Jim Brady dandled and played with Scott for a few minutes, then showered, and dressed in his brand-new three-piece blue pinstripe suit and a white shirt, he walked out to his yellow Jeep waiting in the driveway. He started off on the ten-minute drive to his office in the White House, just across the Potomac River from their home perched on the side of a hill in Arlington, Virginia. The first thing on his agenda those early mornings was breakfast in the White House mess.

"That," claims Sarah, "is one reason why he left so early. He just loved the breakfasts in the mess." By now it was a well-known fact that Jim Brady loved breakfast—*and* lunch, *and* dinner, and anything in between. He loved to eat good food. But he also very much needed to get an early start on his day, every day. He hadn't completely gotten a handle on the press operation in the three months since he had been appointed White House press secretary, although he was getting very close to feeling he had it under control.

At the intersection of Fifteenth Street and Constitution Avenue that morning, Jim saw his good friend Lou Gerig, whom Jim had brought into the White House as director of media liaison. He yelled, "Hey, Lou. Come on, jump in," and together they rode to Jim's parking spot, number 26, on West Executive Avenue inside the iron gates of the White House compound.

Sarah, meanwhile, was getting a slow start on the day. She and Jim were invited to a reception that night given at the Watergate Hotel by Charles Z. Wick, Reagan's USIA director. But for now, she puttered around the house, enjoying the quiet and the time with Scott. She prepared a chicken for the Crock-pot—Monday was always chicken-in-the-pot night. Adhering to his long-established Washington ritual, Jim had had lunch on Saturday with good friends at Nathan's in Georgetown, and afterward, as he always did, he stopped by Mr. Dysart's farm truck on M Street to buy brown eggs, homemade country sausage, and a chicken for the pot. As she relaxed at home in jeans, a blue sweater, and penny loafers, Sarah cast her mind back over the busy weekend. She was truly tired—exhausted, but very happy. Ever since President Reagan's inauguration on

January 20, the Bradys had been living life in the fast lane, and they were loving it. They were on everybody's "A" list, and invitations to dozens of parties, political and social, were flooding Jim's White House mail.

Among them was a glittery party at the Georgetown home of Katharine Graham, owner of *The Washington Post*. As Sarah described it, "Gosh, I'd never been to a party any fancier than those where you throw your coat on a bed upstairs. At Mrs. Graham's we were given a coat check, and a check for our car as well when we drove up. We had had another engagement for that night, but when the invitation came in, Jim said, 'Well, as press secretary, that's one we simply cannot miss.' Mrs. Graham said she was just having a few people drop by, but when we arrived it was an elegant sit-down dinner for eighty people." Jim Brady walked into his home one night after a particularly glamorous round of parties and said to Sarah, "Isn't this the way to live? But don't get too used to it," he added.

This had been even a bigger weekend than usual. In a way, it was a culmination of Jim's new job, for it had been Gridiron weekend. On Saturday night, the sixty-member Gridiron Club of Washington, a press club, had put on its ninety-sixth annual, off-the-record spoof of the new administration. It was a theatrical event and white-tie dinner that required members of the Reagan White House to respond in kind with, hopefully, humorous speeches. Political reputations, if neither made nor broken here, could be enhanced by a good performance or damaged by a poor one. Founded in 1885, the Gridiron is the most prestigious press organization in the country, and invitations to the annual dinner are coveted by politicians and government officials. Press moguls from all over the country angle to be invited—it is a major press gala.

All the takeoffs of the Reagan people were sung by the members with the help of a few professional singers, accompanied by an orchestra conducted by Marine Corps Band director Colonel John Bourgeois. Lyrics were written by Gridiron members and they had Presidential Counsellor Edwin Meese's stand-in singing about his boss, the president, to the tune of "Something Wonderful" from *The King and I*. The lyrics captured the image of Reagan that the traveling press corps had formed and liked to joke about during the 1980 presidential campaign.

He will not always say
What you would have him say
But now and then he'll say . . . something won-derful!
Just put it on a card
He cannot dis-regard,
Then ev'ry time he'll say . . . something won-derful!

He knows a thousand things that aren't quite true.
You know that he believes in them
And that's enough for you.
You'll always go along
And help him be less wrong
And even when he's wrong
He is—wonderful!

He'll always need Ed Meese,
He needs to heed Ed Meese,
And when he heeds Ed Meese—he's more wonderful!

For Jim Watt, Reagan's secretary of the interior, who had immediately become the administration "heavy" because of his antediluvian views on conservation, they concocted words to the music of "Home on the Range."

Oh, give me a home—where no buffalo roam
And the ranchers and dam-builders play,
Where seldom is heard—the song of a bird,
But the oil rigs are pumping all day.

Home, home on the range.
Where no deer and no antelope play.
Where Smokey the bear breathes in toxic air
And the cattle chew nuclear hay.

But for Jim Brady, the Gridiron song was more of a valentine than anything else. Prior to his appointment as press secretary there had been a story circulating in the press that Nancy

Reagan wanted a press secretary who "was reasonably good-looking," a story Mrs. Reagan vehemently denies. "I never said anything of the kind," says Mrs. Reagan. "I liked Jim a lot. He was good and he was funny." Somehow, as these things in Washington have a way of doing, the "not good-looking enough" epithet became attached to the dapper clothes-conscious Jim Brady. Thus, the Gridiron lyrics for Jim set to music from *My Fair Lady:*

> **She's grown accustomed to my face,**
> **My ruddy cheeks and double chin.**
> **She digs the cavalier finesse**
> **With which I con the press,**
> **No sweat, no fuss,**
> **Hooray for US!**
>
> **I'm second nature to her now**
> **I've won her over with my grin**
> **And as I deftly shape the image of her leading man—that's Ron—**
> **She is more than willing that we let by-gones be-gone.**
>
> **She's grown accustomed to my looks,**
> **My sand and gravel voice,**
> **Accustomed to—my face.**

It had been an evening of fun and mostly good feeling. A few vestiges of the honeymoon between the press and politicians remained and there was still excitement in the air. The hardest work still lay ahead, although Reagan's budget director, David Stockman, had already fired off the first salvo in Reagan's battle to reduce the welfare state, saying on ABC's *Issues and Answers* the Sunday before, "I don't believe . . . that almost every service that someone might need in life ought to be financed by the government as a basic right. . . . We challenge that. We reject that notion." A few days later, at a lunch with *Newsweek* reporters, Jim Brady convulsed the group with a description of the lugubrious Stockman: "He sleeps in the closet hanging upside down with his wings folded over his eyes."

The next afternoon, Sunday, the Bradys attended a luncheon given by Walter Ridder, president of Ridder Communications, an annual post-Gridiron affair, at his home across the Potomac in McLean, Virginia. And then, in the evening, the Gridiron Club repeated its show for wives, friends, and hundreds of others who had not been in on the festivities of the night before. Jim and Sarah, who attended both functions, came rushing into the Capital Hilton Hotel a few moments before the show was to begin, and they were surrounded by reporters and guests. A funny and charming story about Jim's gourmet tastes and cooking ability had just appeared in *The Washington Post*, giving the press more grist for jokes about the newly popular couple. They wanted to know, for instance, why Jim called Sarah the "Raccoon." "Because I have dark circles under my eyes, and little tiny hands which I use to get the food to my mouth very quickly," she readily explained. And "Jim," they asked, "what again is that recipe for Captain Bear's Magic Nighty Night?" This latter is Jim "Bear" Brady's concoction of Lapsang souchong tea, bourbon, and sugar. The revelation in the same article that Jim and Sarah were, to each other, the Bear and the Raccoon had come as a delightful surprise to the hovering news throng. Even better, they called each other "Pooh" and " 'Coon" for short. The large, powerfully built and overweight Brady would say, "Well, just look at me and tell me I'm not a bear. I am a North American brown bear." Jim had, and has, the propensity to nickname everybody, and for that matter, everything, that is part of his world.

This Gridiron crowd was Jim Brady's bailiwick, the other half—with the president—of his constituency. They were his people, at least, most of them. They liked him and from all appearances, the feeling was mutual. Although he was the president's press secretary, Brady's axiom about the press was: "I see myself as the press secretary for the Nation. People say you can't serve two masters. That's right. I have only one master—that's the President. But I serve the President best by serving the press best. Where that comes out is that if you serve the President and the press, you serve the nation best."

There could have been no more perfect marriage of man to job than Jim Brady as press secretary. It was, as he said two years later, still struggling to recover from his injury, "a dream of a job. And as he would say in 1985 on *Good Morning America,* "I'd come a long way. Had probably *the* best job in the free world—a job that I'd been trained for all my life. And there it was. And I had it. I had it."

The Gridiron Club replay show that Sunday ended at eight o'clock and as the Bradys slowly made their way out of the Hilton, they once again greeted and were being greeted by members of the press and other guests of the club. Sarah and reporter Ann Blackman of the Associated Press chatted about their small children as they walked out—each had a two-year-old. Jim told Ann that life had settled down for them and they were enjoying the new job—and such social events as this evening.

Jim and Sarah were still in the mood to celebrate and, not having arrived early enough to have a drink or hors d'oeuvres, they decided on the spur of the moment to stop at the Portofino, an Italian restaurant at the bottom of their hill in Arlington. It was an old favorite of theirs and the same restaurant they had taken over for their wedding-rehearsal dinner almost eight years earlier. They were in a gay and loving mood, as they talked about all the exciting and lovely things they were both experiencing. When it came time to pay the bill they discovered that neither of them had any money, nor even a credit card. Sarah left Jim there as "hostage," sipping Fra Angelico, while she drove the five blocks home to get her wallet so she could settle the bill.

Home again, the babysitter paid and driven home, they piled into bed at twelve thirty. Tired but contented, they felt on top of the world.

The next day, Monday, Sarah was happily thinking about the weekend. At ten o'clock, she and Scott went to play group at the Methodist Church at the bottom of the hill, and on the way home at twelve-thirty they picked up Frances McKnight, Sarah's cleaning lady. Taking advantage of an unusually peaceful afternoon at home, after lunch she settled Scott with his toys in the basement, then she settled herself near him on the couch, and began to get involved with one of her favorite soap operas, *As the World Turns,* which came on at one-thirty. Until Scott was born, Sarah had always worked and daytime television was still a novelty to her.

* * *

A little less than four months earlier, on December 6, 1980, before Reagan was inaugurated, Jim and Sarah had been invited to another Gridiron event, the winter meeting of the Gridiron, a smaller and more casual affair, which that year was held in the restored colonial village of Williamsburg, Virginia, 120 miles south of Washington. Although Brady had not yet received an appointment in the new administration, he was "East Coast transition spokesman," and he got together with other Reagan appointees James A. Baker III, Vernon Orr, Richard Allen, and Dean Burch, to put on a little show of their own. With the help of the Marine Corps Band director, Colonel Bourgeois, they made up words to two songs, intending to needle the press with some biting ditties. But that was the game. They expected to be lampooned themselves, so they wanted to be sure they gave as good as they got. Besides, they had won the election. With their wives, the men rented a camper to make the journey to Williamsburg so they could all be together in order to rehearse their numbers. To the tune of "This Is the Army, Mr. Jones," the five men came on strong, singing the song of the winners they felt themselves to be.

We are the Reagan Transit Team,
Sturdy, upright and so clean. . . .
You are the ink-stained wretches we
Deem worthy of obscurity. . . .

At this point, Jim Brady was still quite sure he would receive another appointment, if not to the White House, then as spokesman to the Department of State, the Department of Defense, or the Treasury Department. Caspar Weinberger, secretary-designate of defense, and Donald Regan, secretary-designate of the treasury, had each spoken to Jim and each wanted Jim as his press secretary. "It was beyond my wildest dreams that he would get the White House appointment," says Sarah. "Jim would say, 'Maybe I could get Hodding Carter's job.' " (Carter was press spokesman at the Department of State in Jimmy Carter's administration. Secretary of State-designate Alexander Haig did ask Jim to become assistant secretary of state for public affairs.) When, a month after the winter Gridiron meeting, Brady was finally appointed White House press secretary, Colonel Bourgeois wrote him a congratulatory note and included new lyrics to fit the occasion, telling him that along with "Ruffles and Flourishes" for the president, he would now have to start playing "Hail to the Bear." Brady, naturally, loved the idea and framed the new lyrics. Months later when Bourgeois first saw the wounded press secretary again, Brady said to him, "Hi, John, Hail to the Bear."

For Sarah Brady, the Gridiron winter meeting provided the first taste of life to come under the Reagan administration. It was exciting, and life would be even more heady as the Bradys began to receive all the best invitations in town. For this occasion Sarah invested in her first designer dress, a two-hundred-dollar off-white Albert Nipon. Sarah had worked for the Republican National Committee on Capitol Hill until their son was born on December 29, 1978. She and Jim agreed that she would stay home to raise Scott. And now she was free also to take part in all the activities of the new administration.

As December wore on with still no word on who would be Reagan's press secretary, the Bradys went about their business, but hanging over them was the frustration of not knowing how it would all turn out. "The anxiety factor was really up there," says Jim. "I was twisting slowly in the wind. They tried their damnedest to make damaged merchandise out of me but they couldn't." Two weeks after the election, during his press briefing, a reporter asked Brady when the press office was going to be staffed. To laughter, he replied, "I don't know. I keep reading about that."

The Bradys celebrated Christmas with their families, then Scott's second birthday on December 29. It was toward the end of December that the rumor surfaced that Mrs. Reagan wanted a "reasonably good-looking press secretary." During his briefing on December 31, New Year's Eve, Jim began as he usually did: "Good morning, Breakfast Clubbers." Then he went on to say, "It is with a great wellspring of professional pride that I come before you today as, not another pretty face, but just here out of sheer talent."

Jim then introduced Richard Allen to the press to brief them on some international events. Allen took the podium saying, "I think you're a reasonably good-looking man." "Thank you," said Brady.

On New Year's Eve their good friends and neighbors, Brandy

and David Cole and Otto and Jan Wolff, gathered at the Bradys' house in Arlington. "I don't go out on New Year's Eve," Jim always said. Jim grilled salmon steaks outside; they drank champagne and danced to Jim's collection of fifties and sixties records. In addition, to the great amusement of his friends, Jim performed the University of Illinois Indian dance he learned while in college there. This was a dance traditionally performed at half time of Illinois football games—a thrilling and graceful "ballet" in which Chief Illiniwek covers the entire football field with such speed and grace that anyone seeing it for the first time realizes that there is a heretofore unknown scope to Indian dancing. Jim had mastered the entire dance and with all his 250 pounds (20 of them acquired on the campaign trail), he performed it with utter grace. "Jim was the best dancer in the whole world," says Sarah. "You can't imagine how good he was." It was the last time he would ever dance it for his friends.

On New Year's Day the Bradys attended a party at the Georgetown home of journalists Marianne Means and Warren Weaver. Brady took a good deal of twitting about not being "good-looking" enough to be press secretary, although most press insiders felt the charge was probably aimed not at Jim Brady but at the rumpled and untidy Lyn Nofziger, who was Reagan's press secretary until he resigned the job on November 30. After the election, Reagan spent most of his time, from election day, November 4, 1980, to inauguration day, January 20, 1981, in California, although he made several trips to Washington where he stayed at Blair House. But he maintained two transition offices as he had done during the campaign: one in Washington, where Jim Brady became the spokesman; the other, the primary office, in Los Angeles, where Nofziger, also a Californian, was press secretary, as he had been in the campaign. (When Nofziger resigned, Reagan press aide Joe Holmes filled in on the West Coast.) A former newspaperman himself and liked by most of the press, Nofziger was also a longtime Reagan loyalist and staunch conservative. He is a puckish man who invents puns and delivers wisecracks instead of information when he feels like it, which is often. Meeting with reporters on the day he resigned, he was asked if the Reagan people had a political litmus test for prospective Cabinet officers. "Absolutely," he said. "If they don't turn purple we don't take them." Saying he expected Reagan to talk to former president Richard Nixon from time to time, he was then pressed to describe the Reagan-Nixon relationship. "Man and wife," Nofziger cracked. Refusing to discuss upcoming Cabinet appointments, he said that Reagan's secretary of state would be Alger Hiss.

Jim Brady calls Nofziger "The Merry Punster," and remembers a particular 7:30 A.M. staff meeting the morning after Reagan chose George Bush, over ex-president Gerald Ford, to be his running mate. It had been a close call with a potential for bad feelings on the part of Ford supporters. Jim Baker, Bush's senior adviser, asked, "What should our demeanor be toward the holdout Ford delegates?" "Da meaner da better," cracked Nofziger, ever the partisan.

It could not be said, however, that Lyn Nofziger cared much about his appearance. His uniform was a saggy blue-checked blazer, Oxford-blue shirt stretched to the limit by his ample paunch, and a Mickey Mouse tie; he often appeared coatless, or in a cardigan sweater; in short-sleeved shirts; tieless, or with his Mickey Mouse tie loosened (one reporter mused that he couldn't recall ever seeing Nofziger wear any other) and top shirt button unbuttoned; his hair, sparse as it was, was usually wafting about his head in unruly wisps. Reporters interviewing him might find him padding around his office in his stocking feet. And his public style probably left something to be desired, too. Former White House press aide David Prosperi recalls that at the end of one of President-elect Reagan's first press conferences, Nofziger came out in his blue cardigan sweater, waving his arms, and shouting, "That's all, that's all, that's all." "It was a bit much," says Prosperi. All of this was highly attractive to the "ink-stained wretches" of the press, but probably less so to Nancy Reagan. It is interesting, however, that Reagan had chosen two such colorful and loose-lipped men—Nofziger and Brady—to represent him to the media. Nofziger told Reagan before the election that he did not want the job of press secretary and he resigned on November 30, leaving the post wide open.

"My assumption is that had I wanted to be press secretary, I could have been," says Nofziger. "But I'll tell you, after the campaign was over, I didn't want the damn job. I don't like government, and I don't think the job of press secretary is fun anymore. The press does not allow it to be fun. They have become personally nasty, personally vindictive—the press as a whole. But Jim liked it and was doing a good job. You can turn away a lot of problems in this business with a quip and a smart remark." Nofziger wanted and expected to be part of the inner policy circle, and in January he took the job of the president's assistant for political affairs, which he held for exactly one year, leaving when he found he couldn't breach Michael Deaver's and Jim Baker's tightly held grasp on Reagan's schedule and agenda. "People like to guard their turf over there," he says. "The funny thing is that the White House is big enough for everybody. You know," he mused, "the White House is not a very fun place and it ought to be. It'd be a far different place if Jim Brady'd been there. He was growing in the job—it was interesting to watch—he was showing more confidence, and he was more and more on the inside with Reagan."

At his daily briefing, a reporter asked him, "Jim, there is some feeling that Lyn's departure is really at Nancy Reagan's insistence. Can you confirm that?" "No, not at all," said Brady. "It was not. Lyn went through the whole campaign with an 'I love Nancy' button on and I notice clips from Pacific Palisades and places like that showing Lyn and Nancy walking arm in arm." "Oh, is *that* why he's leaving?" said another irreverent reporter.

But it is still a good guess that Mrs. Reagan had Nofziger in mind when word leaked out that she wanted "a reasonably good-looking press secretary." Somehow, over the drawn-out process of choosing a press secretary, that notion got transferred to the Brooks Brothers-attired Brady. After Jim was appointed, Mrs. Reagan tried to set the record straight by dubbing Jim "the Y and H" (youngest and handsomest) but the charge seemed to stick. "The Y and H" was a play on "the O and W," a nickname her husband acquired on the day he announced his candidacy in November 1979. Congressman Jack Kemp introduced Reagan as "the oldest and wisest candidate running." The campaign press immediately picked up on it and from then on they referred to Reagan as "the O and W." Some of the more irreverent members of Reagan's staff, certainly Jim Brady, also adopted the phrase.

The Bradys were at home the evening of Friday, January 2, relaxing and recovering from the hectic holiday season. Jim was decked out in his 'BAMA T-shirt, a souvenir from his days on the John Connally campaign when Connally made a courtesy call on Alabama Coach "Bear" Bryant. The phone rang after dinner—it was Jim Baker calling for Jim Brady. Jim looked at Sarah. He knew the press-secretary decision was going to be made that day and had been feeling strongly that he would be the one. Baker had earlier asked Brady, "If they offer you the job, will you take it?" Jim assured him he would. And now Baker told Jim the president would be calling in a minute. They hung up and Jim sped to the kitchen and the refrigerator to grab a bottle of champagne someone had given them. He popped the cork and the phone rang again. It was Ronald Reagan. "Jim, I'd be very pleased and honored if you would be my press secretary." "Of course, Mr. President," said Jim. "We've already opened a bottle of champagne to celebrate." "Well, then, it's done," said Reagan. Mrs. Reagan came on the line to congratulate Jim.

As to why the decision to choose James Brady as press secretary was put off for so long, Lyn Nofziger recalls, "There was no immediate rush to Jim—they were looking around—it just became clear there wasn't anybody better, or even as good. Brady wasn't being looked over closely by Ronald Reagan, believe me." Reagan customarily accepted his senior staff's recommendations for appointments, although, one of them says, "Once in a great while, Reagan will say, 'I just don't think this fella is right for the job,' but this rarely happens." "Brady," continues Nofziger, "was very good, very smart. He had a great knowledge of people and issues and how the system works—which, I must say, most of these guys don't understand. I spent eight years as a reporter and three with the Nixon administration. It always appeared that Jim knew a lot more than I did."

On the other hand, any resistance to choosing Brady, says Nofziger, probably was fueled by the perception that Brady and Reagan came from "different parts of the Republican party [Brady was perceived as a moderate] and from different generations." (Brady was just forty, Baker, Meese, and Nofziger were all in their fifties, and Reagan himself would turn seventy on February 6, 1981.) Brady had been John Connally's press secretary and only joined the Reagan campaign after Connally dropped out. In addition, says Nofziger, "Jim had great rapport with the press, but Jim is, as I am, a bit of a wiseass.

There was a time or two he was talking when he should have been listening—yes, such as the 'Killer Trees' incident.* But it was a funny remark and Ronald Reagan is capable of laughing at funny remarks, even if they're directed at him. My philosophy of press relations is: Do all you can for the media but never forget who you're working for. There was a time early on in the campaign when there was a feeling he was talking to the press about things he shouldn't have talked to the press about. Although," adds Nofziger, obviously of two minds about it, "everybody was talking to the press. It was an open operation—which was a good thing. And it *wasn't* a good thing. It's fun to talk to the press but some people forget that the purpose of the campaign is to win an election, not to give reporters stories."

However, Bill Plante, who covered the Reagan campaign for CBS News, recalls that "Jim Brady was often accused of leaking stories to us, when, in fact, the leaks were coming from senior staff people."†

Jim Brady was regarded by the press, and ultimately by the Reagan people as well, as a talented PR professional, not an ideologue. The two men primarily responsible for choosing the press secretary, Michael Deaver and Chief of Staff Jim Baker, aren't ideologues either. But, Deaver says, "we kept looking for a Jody Powell [that is, the ultimate insider, with unquestionable personal loyalty to Reagan]. Baker and I were talking it over one day and it hit us. Why are we looking around? We know Brady, his strengths and his weaknesses. Baker at one point suggested that I take it. 'Are you crazy?' I said. 'I thought you were my friend. No one in his right mind wants that job.' But we were looking for something that didn't exist. There is no Jody Powell here, we finally realized. And Brady has done this good job in the campaign and in the transition—he's not an empire builder—he will be satisfied with the job. If he had stayed active, he could have become an insider. The president was very fond of him and trusted him in more and more meetings. Furthermore, on the campaign we had developed a fun

*A reference to Reagan's claim that trees create more pollution than automobiles do, prompting Jim Brady to yell, "Killer trees, Killer trees," to reporters as the Reagan campaign plane flew over a forest fire.

†Senior staff on the campaign plane were Michael Deaver, Edwin Meese, Lyn Nofziger, William Clark, Paul Laxalt, Richard Wirthlin, Stuart Spencer, Martin Anderson, Richard Allen and William Timmons.

relationship—Brady was a lot of laughs. In a campaign there is a crisis an hour, but Brady was always solid. He just never took himself seriously, whereas everybody else on the campaign was very serious about himself. And he never resented any of the rest of us talking to the press as long as we briefed him on it afterward. In fact, he would suggest or encourage us to talk to the press. He was not jealous of his turf."

Members of the Reagan campaign press lobbied for Jim to be press secretary. "Whenever any of us were asked," remembers Bill Plante, "we would say we hoped that Brady would be their press secretary."

And Jim Brady was very happy to have the job. As soon as President-elect and Mrs. Reagan had rung off, Jim Baker called back and he and Brady talked for thirty minutes about the new position. The only precondition Baker and company laid on was that television newswoman Karna Small, whom the Reagan people had known in California, be one of Jim's deputies. Beyond that, Jim was free to choose his staff. "I knew what the job should be and that's what I told Baker I was accepting," says Jim.

Jim and Sarah excitedly began calling their families with the news. Sarah called her mother, Frances Kemp, who lives nearby. Jim called his parents in Centralia, Illinois. In the middle of their next call Blair House interrupted the line. Jim Baker came back on to ask them not to tell anyone for a few days.

This was a tall order, of course, but their parents were duly cautioned and the Bradys canceled dinner with newsman Gary Schuster and his wife, Barbara. "I just don't think I could spend a whole evening with Schuster without spilling the beans," said Jim. No word of Jim's appointment leaked for several days until an enterprising reporter, who had heard a rumor that Jim had been chosen, called Dorothy Brady and ensnared her with the leading question, "Well, Mrs. Brady, how's it going to feel having your son be the president's press secretary?" Mrs. Brady, assuming the announcement had been made public, gushed right back, "Well, it's pretty wonderful—we're very proud of him." The news went out around the country that Jim Brady's mother had confirmed the story and Reagan and his staff's hands were forced. For this indiscretion, Mrs. Brady earned the title of "the Leak in Centralia" from her son. But she couldn't help it. "I'm as proud as a peacock," she told a friend. Sarah was at Elizabeth Arden that morning about to have her hair cut, when she received a phone call telling her to come immediately to Blair House, the president-elect's temporary domicile across from the White House on Pennsylvania Avenue.

At transition headquarters Larry Speakes, one of Brady's press aides, alerted reporters to the impending announcement. "The Breakfast Clubber is en route to Blair House for a meeting with the president-elect this morning. Those who are prudent will be at Blair House at ten-thirty or ten-forty-five for the announcement of additional White House staff. And I think you know what that is. . . ." (The reference to Brady as The Breakfast Clubber referred to the way Brady customarily began his press briefings.)

A reporter asked, "Is there any reason why the president-elect would not announce his own Cabinet personally but will announce Brady?" And Speakes replied, "No one has said that he will announce Brady yet, but I think that if that takes place that will indicate the feeling that he has for"—he paused, not wanting to name Brady—"and the importance of the job of press secretary, and that if indeed, if he does walk down the steps of Blair House with Jim Brady this morning it will indicate that he feels that it is an important job and one that he should do himself." And though Reagan had not appeared at the announcements of any of his other high-level appointees, he did indeed walk down the steps of Blair House to present James S. Brady and Karna Small to reporters as his press secretary and deputy press secretary. It helped dispel the rumors that he was planning to downgrade the importance of the job in his administration—and also helped to thaw any frostiness Brady might have felt while waiting in the cold for so long.

Mr. Reagan began:

> I have an announcement to make. My part in this will be very short. I will leave Jim Baker, our chief of staff, with you, and the two people that I'm about to announce to you, our press secretary, Jim Brady, and his deputy, who will be Karna Small. I think that I have a meeting inside and I shall leave them to your tender mercies here.

Q: Governor, is the new press secretary going to actually have access to you? Will he talk to you daily or will he just only see your aides?

The President-Elect: I've never run an administration in which people didn't have access to me.

Q: We will know that he'll speak for you and really know what you're thinking about certain things?

The President-Elect: I guarantee you. They can both see me.

Q: When will you have your first press conference and how often?

The President-Elect: I'm going to leave all those questions to Jim Brady and to Jim Baker here and to Karna and get back into my meeting now.

Q: But you will have regular news conferences?

The President-Elect: My idea has always been to have regular news conferences.

Q: Are you going to conduct some of the briefings in the briefing room?

The President-Elect: Well—

Mr. Brady: We'll keep that a surprise.

The President-Elect: Yes, yes.

Q: What do you consider "regular"?

The President-Elect: That, I think, has to be worked out. I think it's a matter of—I think it's got to depend on what the time element is. After all, I'm just starting out so I don't know what some of the chores are going to be.

Then, taking advantage of a chance to question Reagan about the spate of stories about Brady's appearance:

Q: Do you think Brady's good-looking enough? [Laughter]

The President-Elect: Let me, let me—this will be my closing answer to a question and then I will leave you all there. That question leads to a story that has been written concerning Nancy which was a total invention out of whole cloth and there have been several more of those and I am getting to be an irate husband at some of the things that I am reading, none of which are true. [Reagan paused and smiled.] And Nancy couldn't be more delighted and thinks he's absolutely handsome. [Laughter]

Mr. Brady: Thank you, Governor. Thank you very much.

Q: What were the other stories about your wife that weren't true, Governor? [Laughter] What were the other stories written about her?

The President-Elect: There are a number of them and I think some of you are aware of some of them.

Mr. Brady: Thank you, Governor.

Q: Thank you, Governor.

[Pause—as Reagan leaves]

(Reagan probably also had in mind two articles that had appeared in *The Washington Star,* both giving unflattering physical descriptions of Mrs. Reagan, not the sort of thing any husband would enjoy reading, and certainly not the devoted Ronald Reagan.) The assembled reporters continued with the press conference:

Q: Could you elaborate about meeting with him regularly?

Mr. Brady: We'll meet no less than once a day and anytime that's appropriate.

Q: What does "regular press conferences" mean and when will the president hold one?

Q: Yes, when's the first press conference?

Mr. Baker: With appropriate frequency.

Q: When's the first one? Can you give us a date today?

Mr. Brady: We don't want to make an announcement on that here today.

Q: Mr. Baker, the president-elect said you'd answer questions. I'm not sure on what subject.

Mr. Baker: You have to ask me a question.

Q: Well, how do you feel today?

Mr. Baker: I feel very well. Thank you very much. I'm very pleased with this arrangement.

Q: Tell us, if you can, exactly what the arrangement is between the governor and the press secretary about how much access he will have and who he will be speaking through and for and so on?

Mr. Baker: He will meet with the president no less

often than once a day. He will have complete access to the president and he will be able to speak for the president.

Q: In other words, if we ask Mr. Brady a question and he gives us an answer, it won't be off the top of his head or it won't have to go through you or through some paperwork?

Mr. Baker: He will not have to go through me to give you an answer to a question, no. The normal reporting channel will be through me, just as Jody Powell's normal reporting channel is through the chief of staff in the White House now. Now that's, as a matter of fact, not the way it works in practice and we would hope that ultimately ours would work the way that arrangement works over there. We expect that to be the case.

Q: Can we ask you kind of a stock question in front of the microphones and that is to what extent you would feel that you couldn't tell us the truth if it somehow was an injurious statement to the president or national security? I mean, just how honest are you going to be?

Mr. Brady: First of all, Sam, I wouldn't tell you something if it wasn't the truth. I don't have to answer every question but I could tell you I know and I'm not going to tell you.

Q: Well, you'd never have a situation where you thought you'd have to deliberately lie for some purpose?

Mr. Brady: No, I don't think that's part of the job.

Q: Ms. Small, do you feel the same way?

Ms. Small: I absolutely feel the same way. I agree with Jim.

Q: Are you satisfied with the access that you'll have to the president?

Mr. Brady: I've always been satisfied.

Q: Mr. Brady, are you going to divide your responsibility between the two of you or how's it going to work?

Mr. Baker: Let me answer that question for you because I'm probably in a better position, perhaps, to do it. There is not going to be any downgrading of the press secretary. The press secretary is going to function as press secretaries have in the past. There will not be four separate press secretaries for various areas of substance and

Jim Brady and Karna Small, for that matter, will have complete access to the president and will be able to speak for the president when they brief you.

Q: Are you a Republican?

Ms. Small: [Nods yes]

Q: And what are going to be the salaries?

Mr. Baker: The salaries will be those salaries which are fixed by law. The press secretary is an executive level II person and I believe that person is $59,000* a year.

Q: Is that enough money for you, Brady? [Laughter]

Mr. Brady: Well—

Mr. Baker: Thank you very much. Jim, congratulations.

Q: What are you doing next?

Mr. Brady: Well, we're going to get our picture taken. Thank you.

Before the reporters left and with television cameras still whirring, Brady suddenly felt moved to go into his Nixon imitation—hunching his shoulders and thrusting his hands into the V for victory sign, he announced with his jowls shaking, "I am not a crook. I am not a crook." His popularity with the assembled reporters, most of them veterans of the campaign trail, assured him that they would not use this bit of mischief in their stories or nightly reports. Every incoming press secretary deserved a honeymoon period with his adversaries, this one in particular. However, says Dean Reynolds, then with United Press International, "If it'd been a slow day, we'd probably have nailed him with it."

The question of "access" raised in the press conference is a crucial one for a presidential press secretary. Meeting with reporters on the day he resigned, Lyn Nofziger observed, "I don't think you can do the job of press secretary unless you have access to the president." With regard to Brady's appointment, it was the question that most worried the White House press corps. How reliable is the information I am getting? How much of an insider is Brady? Will he really see the president before he comes out here to brief? Or is he spoon-fed the company line by the president's aides? The reliability of the press secretary's word bears directly upon the integrity and reliabil-

*With a raise in executive salaries it was $61,600.

ity of the reporters who cover the president.

"Brady was good in the White House," says Gary Schuster, former Washington bureau chief of *The Detroit News*. "He gave the Reagan people a sense of direction about Washington. Most of the players had no idea how it worked. Brady knew Capitol Hill—Reagan's people knew what was good for Reagan. The commingling was good for everybody. And he was beginning to get into the inner circle. He had insisted on full access to Reagan as a condition for accepting the job, and he did have it. He could see Reagan when he wanted to, and he had won over the White House press corps because they knew he had access to Reagan. They took what he said as policy. And he was honest with them—when he didn't know, he said so."

Another press colleague, James R. Dickenson of *The Washington Post*, says of Brady, and presidential press secretaries in general, "A guy can be the most savvy guy in the world, but if the president doesn't see or confide in him, there is no way to overcome the lack of access. You had the sense that Brady knew how the world turned. He was not a witless ideologue who tried to convert us to the candidate. Good press secretaries like Brady know better than to operate like salesmen for their candidates. Most press secretaries are afraid of either the president or the press, but a press secretary serves *two* constituencies—the president *and* the press—and the press cannot be a distant second. Jim is a professional—he has been in Washington for ten years—he was good to deal with—you could trust him. And his personal identity did not rise or fall on his association with Reagan. The press understood that and respected it, and when deadlines were met you knew you could have fun with Jim Brady. He clearly would have been an asset to Ronald Reagan."

The question of access would come up over and over, however. During the transition, when he was clearly not an insider and had little information on who Reagan's Cabinet selections were, Brady announced, "I'm going to continue the Brady doctrine of running a dry creek as to process or people. I might let you know that I've gotten so bad on giving out information on Cabinet selections and people process that the IRS, and you will all be interested in this, has promulgated a new ruling, that lunches with me as a source are not deductible anymore."

As press secretary, his biggest problem during his short tenure was balancing his time between meetings with the president and other government officials, and meeting with members of the press, many of whom felt they didn't yet know him because they hadn't been on the Reagan campaign plane. The job had conflicting pressures. There were no conflicts, however, the next morning at 9:45 A.M. when Jim Brady held his first press briefing as President-elect Reagan's press secretary in transition headquarters.

"Good morning, Breakfast Clubbers."

"Good morning, good-looking" was the rejoinder.

"Thank you very much," said Brady. "We're going to commit a little news here today," and he launched into announcements of more staff nominations, and a rundown of the president-elect's schedule, including a luncheon with Democratic senators. Asked why a meeting with Democratic senators, Brady said, "I imagine we need their help." Brady described to them his staff of forty-two, which included the photographic office, advance, media liaison, and the news summary. "Will you have Jody Powell's office?" "I will have Jody Powell's office. "Do you know where the Class Reunion is?" To laughter, Brady said, "Yes, I knew where that was before Jody did." The Class Reunion was a media and White House staff hangout just two blocks from the White House, and indeed, Jim Brady had been a regular there for years. Jim said that he would be doing the briefings every day, but that Karna Small would also brief so that "she will not be a second-class briefer. She's going to have access. She's going to go to the meetings. She's going to be interchangeable with me and that way I don't have to go down every day and do this."

"You mean on the tough days she'll come out?"

"That's right, that's right. She may be even better."

Three months later, however, on this Monday morning, March 30, 1981, it was with considerable confidence that Jim Brady bounded into the West Executive entrance to the White House at 6:30 in the morning. Lou Gerig* headed for his office in the Old Executive Office Building across the way, but before they parted, he and Jim planned to have breakfast to-

*Jim never bothered to nickname his friend Lou Gerig. "I thought Lou Gerig was enough," he says. (Gerig is not related to Lou Gehrig of baseball fame.)

gether when the mess opened at seven. That gave them each half an hour at their desks. But first Brady went downstairs to the Situation Room to check out the latest international cable traffic. Back upstairs, Jim walked into his office. His desk, chaotic as usual, was piled high with messages, reports, briefing books. He lit a fire in the fireplace, as he always did, no matter what the weather. Perched on the mantel was his "Chicago Cub," a stuffed bear who served as a hat rack for Jim's Chicago Cubs hat, and who, says Jim, "oversaw the office." He shuffled through the messages that were continually piling up, and gave the morning papers a once-over to get a handle on the day's news so he could begin to think about the questions the White House press corps would throw at him today during his daily briefing.

The headline on the front page of *The Washington Post* this morning was POLISH LEADERS ENDORSED IN STORMY MEETING ON CRISIS. The threat of a labor strike in Poland was imminent and the Soviet Union was viewing the situation with alarm, as well as moving its troops within and toward Poland. On the editorial page the Evans and Novak column announced, THE HONEYMOON IS DEFINITELY OVER, as they predicted a Democratic versus Republican free-for-all over the coming social-welfare budget cuts. Clayton Fritchey argued in his column that foreign policy should be articulated through one voice, preferably that of Secretary of State Alexander Haig, instead of the cacophony of administration voices that had been making foreign-policy pronouncements these first two months.

Jim began reading the National Intelligence Briefing (the NIB) and the President's Intelligence Briefing (the PIB), the two compendia of national news that are prepared each day for the president and senior White House staff members by the CIA.

Jim's office was a large room, carpeted in navy blue, with, says Brady, a stickler for detail, Williamsburg Tavern Blue walls. It had a high ceiling and dark wooden bookshelves along two walls. Three big windows faced north on to the White House driveway and Pennsylvania Avenue beyond. A couch, a coffee table, and two comfortable chairs were along one wall, a round table and four Windsor chairs in one corner, and Jim's circular desk (his desk chair completing the circle) was in the farthest corner. "Jim Hagerty [President Eisenhower's press secretary] liked that desk," says Jim, "because *they* [the press] couldn't get behind him and read his notes or whatever he had on his desk." Behind the couch on the bookshelf was the model of the U.S.S. *Constitution* that John F. Kennedy had had in his office. Jim had asked for it when he moved into the White House. "I thought it would be nice, because I think I conducted my office much the way he conducted his office—Camelot, and the New Beginning, I mean." He added, "Only this time we do it right." Hanging in the closet was the bulletproof vest left to him by President Jimmy Carter's press secretary, Jody Powell, a legacy to Powell in turn from Ron Nessen, press secretary under President Gerald Ford. Pinned to the vest was Powell's note: "Dear Jim, It's not the bullets that get you in this job, it's the ants and the gnats."

Sometimes some of the more enterprising reporters would catch Jim at his desk at this early hour. "Helen Thomas [White House reporter for United Press International] would peck on my window from outside," says Jim, "and I would yell through the window, 'Woman, have you no shame?' " And then he would shout, "Get yourself in here!" When she reappeared at his office door, he would repeat his question. Her answer always was "No, do you think I'd have gotten this far if I'd had shame and piety?" Jim only lavishes such insults on people he regards with affection and respect, and, says Jim, "Helen Thomas is a wonderful person, a professional's professional."

At two minutes to seven, Jim buzzed Lou Gerig. "Hie thee over here, boy, and let's go down for breakfast." They were the first ones in the mess that morning as Jim often was. The steward liked to kid him. "You want your usual, Mr. Brady?" The "usual" was waffles and sausage, and yes, he wanted his usual today. Brady and Gerig talked about the NCAA basketball final between Indiana and North Carolina that was going to be played in Philadelphia that night. Gerig was from Indiana and had tickets for the playoff. He told Jim that a young friend of his, Mark Lubbers, was going to come by the White House and he would like to have him see Jim's noon briefing for the press. "No problem," said Jim. "By all means bring him by." Other staffers began to drift in to sit at the round table, including Karna Small. Jim's secretary, Sally McElroy, dropped by. They all chatted about the day's news, in order to get a grip on what questions reporters would be asking that day.

After breakfast, at 7:30, Jim headed back upstairs to his office. He checked over the president's schedule to see what meetings he thought he should attend. Reagan had an 8:30 breakfast meeting with 140 sub–Cabinet-level administration officials, his regular National Security Briefing at 9:45, and at 10:30 a meeting with a group of Hispanic supporters. Jim didn't usually attend the president's security briefing, but he thought he would drop in on the other two meetings. But he couldn't decide whether or not to go with Mr. Reagan when he addressed the convention of Building and Construction Tradesmen at the Washington Hilton Hotel at 1:45. Maybe he'd send Larry Speakes on that one. He had plenty to do at his desk.

Then, as he often did, Jim took off for the press room to "troll" among the early birds among the White House press corps, to see what their questions were, what they were likely to ask in the press briefing. He had figured out long ago that knowing what the press was concerned about helped him deliver information to them and helped his boss's image at the same time.

Jim firmly believed in communication—that it was worthwhile trying to explain complex ideas of government in ways that were understandable to the American people. "The only thing we have to sell is service," he says, "to try to answer their questions, or at least tell them we will 'take' a question, meaning we'll take it to the president and try to clear it up. That's a nicer way of saying 'I haven't the foggiest idea.' "

Back at his desk Jim spent a few more minutes reading and preparing for the regular eight o'clock meeting of the president's senior staff.* They would get together to pool their knowledge of the day's upcoming events.

At the same time the senior staff was meeting, Jim's press office staff met in Jim's office, and Deputy Press Secretary Larry Speakes led them through a discussion of what issues would most probably be raised by members of the press that day, and what photo opportunities there would be for the photogra-

*White House senior staff: Chief of Staff James Baker III; Deputy Chief of Staff Michael Deaver; White House Counsellor Edwin Meese; White House Counsel Fred Fielding; Director of OMB, David Stockman; National security, Richard Allen; press secretary, James Brady; staff director, David Gergen; congressional liaison, Max Friedersdorf; public liaison, Liddy Dole; Ed Harper; presidential personnel, E. Pendleton Jones; intergovernmental affairs, Rich Williamson; political affairs, Lyn Nofziger.

phers and television. They tried to anticipate questions, the best indicators being the morning papers and the morning network television shows. Speakes assigned various chores to the staff. Mort Allin was to call the State Department about the trouble in Poland and the Department of Defense to see what they were saying about it. The whole effort was meant to coordinate the various spokesmen of the executive branch of government so that they were all saying the same thing about the subject. Jim usually tried to join his own staff's meeting toward the end, so that he could make further assignments and suggestions, fill them in on matters brought up in the senior staff meeting, and coordinate his inside information with what Speakes had set in motion.

Jim had gathered together his press-office staff from friends and co-workers he liked and respected from his eight-year career in Washington as a press-relations specialist; at HUD and the Pentagon, on Capitol Hill, with the John Connally presidential campaign.* As the meeting began to break up, Jim reminded his staff that at 4:00 that afternoon they were all to meet with the Secret Service to be briefed on what they were to do in case there was ever a crisis. The agenda wasn't totally clear, but "we figured," says Lou Gerig, "that it must have to do with war and/or assassinations—the big two." There had never been time for such a meeting until now—they had all been working too hard getting the reins of their various jobs in hand.

While the Bradys were getting their early start that morning, the man in Room 312 of the Park Central Hotel, just two blocks west of the White House, still slept. Twenty-five-year-old John W. Hinckley, Jr., had checked into the hotel the day before at 12:30, just after lunch, after a two-and-a-half-day bus trip from California. He had left Denver, Colorado, four days earlier, flying to Los Angeles with the idea of trying to sell some of his songs to the record industry, an idea he had tried and failed with before. Deciding once again that his efforts were futile, he turned

*Press-office staff: Deputy Press Secretaries Larry Speakes and Karna Small; Kim Hoggard, Mark Weinberg, Robin Gray, Sally McElroy, Lou Gerig, David Prosperi, Connie Romero, Flo Taussig, Betsy Strong, Jeanne Winnick, Kathy Ahern, Mort Allin, Sue Mathis, Bob Dahlgren.

around the next day and set out to take a bus back to Colorado, he said. By chance he learned that for just two dollars more, he could go clear across the country. So he booked himself to Washington, D.C., hoping to go up to New Haven later to contact his idol, actress Jodie Foster. He thought the two-dollar deal allowed for a change of destination, but he learned somewhere mid-country that it did not. It would cost another twenty dollars to go to New Haven where Jodie Foster had enrolled at Yale. He was annoyed as hell. His funds were low. He had always been able to get enough money out of his parents, often lying to them about his needs, but his parents had all but cut him off. This time they meant it, he thought. And the trip had been hard. He hoped he could at least sleep in that morning.

When he woke up at 7:30 he asked himself: Why can't I go back to sleep? He got out of bed, turned on the television set, and watched one of the morning shows until 9:00, and then pulled on his clothes. He took the elevator downstairs to the small Art Deco lobby, walked out the front door of the hotel, turned right, and walked up to K Street. He had had a hamburger at the Burger King at Sixteenth and K streets the night before. This morning he turned left on K and walked two blocks to Crown Books, where he browsed for a while but left without buying anything. He crossed the broad street to McDonald's and breakfasted there on an Egg McMuffin. As he ate he debated whether to stay in Washington and try to get some sleep, to go on up to New Haven, Connecticut, or to "get it all over with." He was contemplating suicide as his third option, he said later.

He had been turning these questions over in his mind for some time, years in fact. In 1976 he was captivated by the film *Taxi Driver* in which Jodie Foster, then thirteen, played a child prostitute whom Robert De Niro, as cab driver Travis Bickle, was determined to rescue from her pimps. Hinckley saw the movie over and over, and became infatuated with the real Jodie Foster. When she entered Yale University in the fall of 1980, he read about it in *People* magazine. At last he knew how he could find her, and by now, March 1981, he had made ten trips to

New Haven, leaving notes and poems and other writings at her door, or in her mailbox, even talking to her on the phone (and taping the conversation). It was through that conversation, the previous September, with the giggling of her roommates in the background, that he got the message that she didn't want anything to do with him. And he began to think about doing something desperate to win her, or at least impress her.

As Travis Bickle had stalked a politician in *Taxi Driver*, he began stalking President Carter. In Dayton, Ohio, in early October he found he could get within one foot of the president and could have shot him if he'd had a gun with him. The next week when Carter was in Nashville, he had the same luck, but once again, he did not act. He wasn't psychologically ready for it. In his last-minute rush to catch his plane out of Nashville, his two bags were X-rayed as carry-on luggage; it had been too late to check them at the ticket counter and still get them on the plane. As the bags went through the machine, his three guns were detected. He was arrested and jailed for half an hour while he and his guns were checked for previous violations. Finding none, the airport police fined him $62.50, and sent him on his way. Hinckley was enormously relieved they didn't read his diary and its record of his criminal intentions. Four days later he was in Dallas, Texas, where he replenished his arsenal with two .22-caliber Röhm revolvers, guns that were assembled in Miami out of German-made parts to get around the legal ban on the manufacture of Saturday night specials.

The election in November changed Hinckley's focus to Ronald Reagan, and in late November and early December he made two trips to Washington where he mingled with the tourists who were watching President-elect Reagan come and go from his interim residence, Blair House, across Pennsylvania Avenue from the White House. Sometimes he had his new gun with him and could easily have taken a shot at Reagan or some of his Cabinet members, but he still wasn't ready.

On December 8, Mark David Chapman murdered John Lennon in New York City, and Hinckley was deeply affected by it. He was an avid fan of John Lennon and his songs. But at the same time he was struck by the similarities between himself and Chapman. They were the same age almost to the day, and even looked alike, with their pudgy round faces and turned-up noses. He began to think more and more about killing the president in order to impress, maybe traumatize was a better word, Jodie Foster, and he bought a .38-caliber revolver like Chapman's and began to target practice two or three times a month. Back home in Colorado, he wrote to Jodie and outlined his intention to kill Carter or Reagan. He signed the letter, but didn't put his address on it. So here he was, in Washington, more or less by accident, but not really. Mostly he felt tired, and with no resolution in mind about what his next step would be, he left McDonald's and walked back to the Park Central Hotel.*

At 9:15, Jim Brady dropped in on the leadership meeting of Reagan-appointed sub–Cabinet-level officials being held in the East Room. The president quoted Thomas Paine to them, "We have it in our power to begin the world over again." Back at his desk at 9:30, Jim continued to read the intelligence briefings, the papers, take and return phone calls, and parry reporters' requests—mostly in preparation for his noon briefing. He went by the Cabinet Room where Reagan was meeting a group of Hispanic supporters.

Although the time varied ("sometimes I'd just nose over there to see when I was on"), Brady always met with President Reagan in the Oval Office every day to be sure he had the president's own personal view of the day's events, so that he could put the correct spin on his own remarks and responses. "Did the president want to clarify this today—it is apt to come up? Do you have anything you want to say about this?"

Jim was almost ready to give his briefing, to enter the fray. He was almost psyched up for his entry into the press room, just down the hall from his office, where the members of the White House press corps worked, read, ate, lounged, slept, groused and, on slow days, just milled around. "It's like a ti-

*Hinckley's thoughts and activities are taken from *United States* v. *John W. Hinckley, Jr.*, trial-transcript testimony of those who interviewed him after the assault.

ger's cage," says Jim with understanding and some fondness for the inhabitants of the cage. Jim believes there should be a little sign above the press-room entrance saying, "Abandon hope, all ye who enter here."

Even though the press area was greatly enlarged in the seventies, even taking over the space formerly occupied by an indoor swimming pool, it is an extraordinarily tiny place for the one hundred or so journalists who are accredited to the White House. And, even more so, for the fifty to sixty working journalists who are assigned tiny cubicles with just enough space for a phone and a typewriter, and who actually perform their jobs there. The "lower" White House press office, just next door, which houses part of the press secretary's staff, is small and cramped as well. As close together as they are, it makes for an unusually close mix of people who have conflicting missions.

On the one hand reporters are competing fiercely with each other in their attempts to squeeze news out of the White House. But, on the other, the effect of this competition is to make them into a single force, which batters away at the doors of access to the president and his closest aides.

For its part, Jim's press-office staff is trying both to help reporters get information through press releases and other factual material and to help them with their logistical problems of covering the president, such as travel arrangements. But at the same time the staff is trying to thwart the press's discovery of anything unflattering to the president and his administration. It is correctly described as an adversarial relationship.

Even though the press corps labors only thirty or forty feet away from the president in the Oval office, they rarely get to see him day to day except for brief moments as he comes and goes from the White House, or at formal picture-taking sessions with visiting dignitaries, where questions from the press are discouraged. Since the essence of their work is to report on and interpret the president's actions and thoughts, this lack of access to him causes enormous frustration, and is responsible also for the shouted questions and seemingly rude behavior that the public deplores as too undignified to be addressed to the president.

In a way, the daily briefing serves as an escape valve for

some of that frustration because it is the one place where White House reporters have the chance to get at someone who is connected to the object of their highly competitive journalistic endeavors, the president of the United States. "Very little news comes out of the briefings," says former NBC White House correspondent Judy Woodruff. "Often they are used by the administration for announcements they want to make. But occasionally news stories are advanced by something the press secretary doesn't say or refuses to say." Most important, the briefing is the reporters' daily contact with the official White House—it is their daily feed, and for people whose reports are often made up of nuance, the barest of crumbs, and the twentieth-century equivalent of reading of entrails, the briefing becomes a tense struggle every day. There can be a fair amount of bitter back and forth between the press secretary and reporters, too, as well as occasional high hilarity.

Most White House correspondents are well-known, respected journalists who represent the major news organizations of the country, but sprinkled among them are a few people who, says one veteran political writer, could almost be described as "the twisted, the moonstruck and the damned." Strange as it may seem, the White House press corps harbors a number of harmless but rather offbeat individuals who occasionally put a peculiar twist on the nature of the news operation. All accredited White House correspondents do have to go through a thorough security clearance, of course, but eccentricity is not something that disqualifies them. These few are the ones who ask the off-the-wall, ideological questions at press conferences and who keep the press-office staff in turmoil with their insistent demands. "It keeps you humble," says Jody Powell.

At 11:50 A.M. Jim Brady, ready for his briefing, left his office and turning left went down the ramp to the lower press office and through the sliding door of the press room. He stepped up on the podium and "let the jackals have at me," as it amuses him to say.

He began the March 30, 1981, briefing, his final briefing, with a series of personnel announcements—the Reagan people were still filling jobs in the executive departments. He announced who would be in the press pool for Reagan's trip to

Springfield, Illinois (Jim's home state),* the next day. He read the president's schedule for the day with "a courtesy visit by David Rockefeller, George Bethoin, and Watanabe of Japan to discuss trade relations between the U.S., Japan and Europe." Jim added, "Nofziger is the travel pool on that." There was a burst of laughter, at the reference to longtime Reagan aide and staunch conservative Lyn Nofziger. The reporters knew that David Rockefeller and the other two men really would be there representing the Trilateral Commission, an internationalist and moderately liberal discussion group founded by Rockefeller, which meets periodically to discuss international economic and trade matters. But on the president's published schedule of the day there was no mention of the Trilateral Commission. The Trilateral Commission had always been anathema to conservatives, especially to Sunbelt and western conservatives such as Nofziger, who suspected it of being effete, elitist, eastern, and too liberal.

That Brady was doing a little needling of the Republican right wing, as well as of his predecessor Nofziger, is testimony to his personal confidence and continued irreverence on the job. A reporter asked why the president's schedule hadn't said that Rockefeller and the other two men were representing the Trilateral Commission, knowing full well that Ronald Reagan was doing a little political fence mending after the campaign but didn't want to rile the conservatives. Brady replied, "It should have; they call it the Omission of the Commission." "Yes, the Trilateral Commission," added the reporter. "We don't have those keys on the typewriter here," said Brady. Asked if there would be a photo opportunity at the meeting, Brady cracked, "We'll have Nofziger's surveillance footage we'll be making available for the press." To laughter he was asked, "Are these the people who are secretly running the world?" "Depends on who you talk to," said Brady, proceeding on with more announcements, and more detail on Reagan's Tuesday trip to speak to the Illinois state legislature. Brady told them that President Reagan and West German Chancellor Helmut Schmidt had talked by phone that morning and agreed that if

*Jim's mother, a woman who had spent her life involved in Republican politics, was planning to drive to Springfield the next day to try to catch a few moments with her son.

there was suppression in Poland of the Solidarity trade union, or movement of Warsaw Pact forces into Poland, they would each find it impossible to render further economic aid to Poland.

After considerable back and forth on Jim's characterization of the conversation between Reagan and Schmidt, with Brady holding firmly to saying only what he had originally said, he was asked about a story from Tass that said U.S. use of economic aid to Poland as leverage in the situation was interference in Poland's internal affairs. Brady replied, "Well, I think the differentiation on that, Leo, is that it's our money and it's basically an internal decision what we do economically. We can either give it or not give it and that's an internal decision of our nation. What is closer to our nation than our own money?" he added to laughter. "In this administration, nothing apparently," a reporter suggested sarcastically.

Jim was then asked about an allusion Caspar Weinberger, secretary of defense, had made the day before on *Face the Nation* to the possibility of an American military response if there was external (meaning Soviet) intervention in Poland. (To show administration disapproval of Soviet troop movement, Jim himself had canceled out of a party the previous Friday night because Russian Ambassador Anatoly Dobrynin was to be there.) Could he elaborate on that? No, he wouldn't elaborate. Try as they might, they couldn't get Jim to comment on Weinberger's statement. "Whatever he said, we'll stand on," he said. Someone asked, "Does that go for the neutron bomb, too?" "No, that was the Gridiron, Saul," replied Jim (a reference to Weinberger's stand-in at the Gridiron Club, who sang, "Thank heaven, for neutron bombs, / They blow up in the most constructive way. / Thank heaven, for neutron bombs, / They save our cities for another day.")

Jim next dealt with a question about Japan's export of automobiles to the United States. Attempting to show his insider's knowledge, and also to give some "deniability" to the Reagan administration to protect the delicate nature of the negotiations, Jim said that in none of the meetings he was in with the president and the prime minister of Japan did it come up that the United States had asked for voluntary restriction of a *specific* number of cars exported. He danced around the question of who had told whom what, but at the same time it was clear that a figure had been thrown out to the Japanese by someone, somewhere.

Jim says, "You get in there and they're clawing at you, they try to get you down on the floor and put their knees in your back to get you to answer the question. The president would make a statement sometimes that you didn't want to take on, or answer piecemeal or indirectly until you checked with him. It's fear and loathing time, but there's no way to get away from standing up there and taking it. Most executions down there are public." Jim's motto is: "You never win an argument with someone who buys ink by the barrelful."

There were several more questions on the reporters' minds—the first, a complicated political question asking if the Reagan administration was willing to put off, as Senator Howard Baker had said he understood it was, the social-issues agenda (abortion, prayer in the schools, etc.) in order to get its economic recovery and tax plan through Congress. Brady, a confirmed supply-sider himself, who truly believed in the tax cut's benefits to the economy, gave as his reply:

> Well, it's not something within our power to dictate to Senator Baker [the order in which Congress would deal with the Reagan program], John, as you know. Clearly, our most immediate priority is to get the president's economic recovery package through the Congress to have an opportunity for the medicine to begin to work on the nation. And that, by no means, should indicate that there's not great sympathy in our willingness to go ahead at the appropriate time with the social agenda, with other things in the economic area and with other initiatives.

It had become clear that the package of highly emotional social issues would interfere with the passage of the Reagan economic plan, but the Reagan people didn't want to come right out and say so for fear of angering the conservatives. It was a delicate line for Jim to walk. Someone asked if that delay would mean the president wouldn't support a bill this year against abortion if congressional hearings could determine when human life begins. Jim fudged. "No, I think we have to look at that—when it becomes in being." ". . . the appropriate time being when the economic package is in Congress?" asked the reporter. "Yes," said Brady.

The briefing's last question of substance had to do with the legality of Israeli raids into Lebanon, and the use of American weapons in the raids. Jim referred the legality question to the State Department, first saying, "We deplore violence in the region while at the same time recognizing the right of Israel to protect its borders." As to the use of American weapons, Jim said, "I don't know whether we have an opinion on that or not."

There was one last try at getting Jim to say whether the president was considering any military response in the event of Soviet attacks on Poland. "Pat," said Jim, "we're not going to comment on any specific options."

The briefing ended on a light note. A reporter quoted Vice-President George Bush, who was in Texas that day, as saying that President Reagan, "while he may be a Californian in name, is pure Texan at heart." "Do you agree that it is somehow better to be Texan than Californian?"

Diplomatically deflecting the question, Jim answered, "Sarah would," referring to Sarah McClendon, the venerable and feisty reporter for a number of small and medium-sized Texas dailies.

The briefing ended in laughter at 12:15 P.M. "Fortunately, it was a slow news day," says Jim Brady today, in one of the all-time ironical statements. Before going back to his desk Jim stopped by Larry Speakes's office, which was near his own in the upper press-office area. It was the first time he had ever dropped in on Speakes. Usually he called his staff into his office. Speakes was dictating to Connie Romero and they were both taken aback by the sudden appearance of Brady. Romero sensed that Jim had something on his mind and left the room. But, "Jim just plopped down," says Larry Speakes. "We just chatted about things. One thing we talked about was which one of us should go to the Washington Hilton that day with the president." "You want to have lunch?" Jim threw out after a while. He and Speakes had not had lunch together since coming to the White House. "Sure," said Speakes. He was pleased. He had been working very hard, and he felt that Jim's invitation was a sign that he thought he had been doing a good job. "We were just beginning to enjoy ourselves," says Speakes, "to get our feet on the ground." They agreed to go down to the mess at one o'clock. And Jim went back to his office to whack away at the clutter on his desk.

Back at the Park Central, John Hinckley bought *The Washington Star* from a dispensing box in front of the hotel, and took it up to his room. It was 11:30. Room 312 was an interior room overlooking an air shaft, and he kept the blinds closed. It was furnished with twin beds, a nightstand, a desk and chair, two lounge chairs, a bureau, and a color television, and there was a full bath. The bed coverlet's large brown and white flowered print matched that of the drapes—the carpeting was brown and the walls painted cream. On the nightstand was Hinckley's travel alarm clock and the current *TV Guide*. One of his suitcases was on the luggage rack near the door, the other on the bureau.

Hinckley still thought he was tired. The bus trip had been a long one and he felt as if he hadn't gotten enough sleep. He tried to sleep but he couldn't, and he browsed through *The Washington Star*. Prominently displayed on page 3 was President Reagan's schedule of the day. Hinckley had been in Washington a number of times recently. He knew the *Star* carried the president's schedule. He read it over carefully. It appeared the president would be making a public appearance at the Washington Hilton Hotel at 1:40 in the afternoon before the Building Tradesmen of the AFL-CIO. Hinckley decided to get cleaned up—to shower, shave, and change his clothes.

Now, as he showered, he had a specific option to ponder. Should I make a little detour to the Washington Hilton Hotel, or go on up to New Haven? Should I go over to the Hilton and take my "little pistol" and see how close I can get, he thought—just see what the scene is like? His mind started to turn. He took a Valium to calm himself down.

Dressed now, in a navy-blue sport shirt, khakis, and his brown-tweed sport coat, Hinckley took out his gun, a German-made .22-caliber RG 14 Röhm revolver. He took out his cache of bullets—there were forty-three of them—thirty-five hollow-point bullets, two round-nosed bullets, and six Devastator bullets designed to explode on contact to cause maximum injury. He unscrewed the pin that held the cylinder in place and drew it out of the revolver. He clicked the cylinder to the side, then loaded the six Devastator bullets into it, leaving the less lethal ones in their boxes. He had been saving these Devastators since he bought them in June 1980. He snapped the cylinder back into place, reinserted the pin, and screwed it back in. He put the bullet boxes back in his suitcase and slipped the loaded gun into his right jacket pocket. He then sat down to begin work on a letter to Jodie Foster at Yale. He dated it 12:45 P.M., March 30, 1981, and began:

Dear Jodie,

There is a definite possibility that I will be killed in my attempt to get Reagan. It is for this very reason that I am writing you this letter now.

As you well know by now, I love you very much. The past seven months I have left you dozens of poems, letters and messages in the faint hope you would develop an interest in me.

Although we talked on the phone a couple of times, I never had the nerve to simply approach you and introduce myself. Besides my shyness, I honestly did not wish to bother you. I know the many messages left at your door and in your mailbox were a nuisance, but I felt it was the most painless way for me to express my love to you.

I feel very good about the fact you at least know my name and how I feel about you. And by hanging around your dormitory I've come to realize that I'm the topic of more than a little conversation, however full of ridicule it may be. At least you know that I'll always love you.

Jodie, I would abandon this idea of getting Reagan in a second if I could only win your heart and live out the rest of my life with you, whether it be in total obscurity or whatever. I will admit to you that the reason I'm going ahead with this attempt now is because I just cannot wait any longer to impress you. I've got to do something now to make you understand in no uncertain terms that I am doing all of this for your sake. By sacrificing my freedom and possibly my life I hope to change your mind about me. This letter is being written an hour before I leave for the Hilton Hotel.

Jodie, I am asking you to please look into your heart and at least give me the chance with this historical deed to gain your respect and love.

I love you forever.

John Hinckley

It was getting close to 1:15. He had been working almost half an hour. John Warnock Hinckley, Jr., was watching the time. For once, the first time in a long time, he had a deadline to meet, he had an agenda today.

Suddenly, someone knocked on the door. It was Sue Kondeah, the room maid. Her record showed that the man in Room 312 was scheduled to check out and she had come by several times to see if he was gone so she could ready the room for the next guest. "Are you going to check out today?" she asked the polite young man. He was drinking a Pepsi. No, he said, he was planning to spend the night. Kondeah asked him if he had checked that with the front desk. No, he said, but that he would. He had pulled the spread back on the bed farthest from the door. A pair of trousers was stretched neatly across the near bed. His suitcase was open. He told her that, yes, she could finish cleaning the room while he was there, and he took up a position near the bathroom door, standing there the entire time she was in the room. She had to say, "Excuse me, please," before she could get past him to clean the bathroom. When she finished she told him she didn't have any more towels on her cart and that she would return shortly with a supply of them for him. As soon as she left, John Hinckley patted his jacket pocket, put his letter to Jodie in his suitcase, grabbed his tan rain jacket—it had been misting earlier—and left the room. Downstairs and outside the hotel he hailed a cab. "The Washington Hilton," he said to the driver.

A few minutes later when Sue Kondeah went back to Room 312, the young man was no longer there—the room was neat—everything was in order.

Several years later, when Jim Brady was told that

Hinckley had gone back and forth, weighing the two options of assassinating the president or committing suicide in New Haven, Brady said, with his characteristic poker face, "The latter would have been preferred."

At one o'clock Jim Brady, accompanied by Larry Speakes, sailed across the West Lobby toward the stairway to the mess. "Hi, Mrs. Fillmore," he called out to Nell Yates, the receptionist in the West Lobby. Mrs. Yates had worked in the White House since 1955, longer than anybody else there, and Jim liked to tease her about it. Sometimes he would say, "Hi, Mrs. Lincoln," or "Hi, Mrs. Buchanan"—whatever struck his fancy that day.

The presidential entourage was due to leave the White House at 1:45, and Jim and Speakes didn't have much time to eat. The staff in the mess tried to hurry up their sandwich orders, and they could hear the two men discussing who should go with President Reagan to the Hilton. Speakes urged Jim to let him go with the president. He knew that Jim was feeling torn between having access to President Reagan and being in on the top policy meetings on the one hand, and on the other hand, spending enough time with the press, answering requests for interviews and information, and just returning phone calls. Jim considered having access to President Reagan every day to be his number-one priority if he was to secure his reputation for integrity and reliability with the White House press. As a relative outsider when he was appointed, Jim, in his first two months as press secretary, spent so much time "having access" to the president that he was now being criticized for not being available to the press. "This access is killing me," he told Dean Reynolds, now with ABC, when Reynolds mentioned that there were complaints about not being able to see him. "If anything," Jim says today, "I had too much access. I couldn't get the job of press secretary done because I was so busy having access. You can't tell the president, 'I can't come to your meeting because I have this press briefing.' There were real conflicts."

The joke began to be that Reagan had access to Brady instead of the other way around. But Jim was enjoying the job immensely and he knew he was up to its challenges. And always there was his humor, which enabled him to gloss over some of the administration's gaffes, and to defuse its severest critics. At a press breakfast two weeks earlier, Jim had just sat down when he caught a tough question about Secretary of State Alexander Haig and the "crisis management" flap that had erupted between Haig and Vice-President George Bush. "Whatever happened to foreplay?" Jim queried.

So now, Jim was trying to use his time more productively, and one of the things he was beginning to hand off to Larry Speakes and other members of his staff was the routine accompanying of the president on such cut-and-dried occasions as the one today. But even so, Jim was planning to go with Reagan. The truth was, he enjoyed it—it was a situation reminiscent of the 1980 campaign, which he had loved—the movement, the action, bantering with the press. Over lunch, however, Speakes managed to change Jim's mind and they decided that Speakes, after all, would go with Reagan. Gulping down their last bites, they dashed upstairs to check in at their desks once more. Then Jim, changing his mind again, stuck his head in Speakes's office and said, "Catfish,* I think I'll go on the traveling circus today after all," and he hurried out to get into the senior staff car, which was the third car behind President Reagan's limousine in the lined-up motorcade. Press aide David Prosperi hurried after Jim, asking, "Are you going to need someone with the pool† since Larry isn't going?" "Yeah, come along," said Jim, and Prosperi headed for the press van, which was second to last in the fifteen-vehicle motorcade, an ambulance bringing up the rear. From inside the press van, wrote NBC White House Correspondent Judy Woodruff, "I watched the President walk . . . to the 1972 black Lincoln Continental limousine emblazoned with presidential seals on the doors and

*Larry Speakes was from Marigold, Mississippi, and Jim had decided that "Catfish" was an appropriate nickname for him.

†A press pool always accompanied the president to and from all events just to make sure that no public moment of the president's would go uncovered. Among themselves, they call it the "deathwatch," a terrible admission that if something happens to the president en route to or from an event, they want to be sure they have it covered. Reagan himself once referred to it as "the awful awful" in a conversation with Mrs. George Bush. Their grim vigil would pay off today.

The White House press pool is made up of representatives from one of the three television networks, both of the wire services—UPI and AP—one radio network, one major newspaper, one weekly magazine, and photographers from the wire services and one of the weekly news magazines.

decorated with an American flag and a President's flag on the front fenders."

Labor Secretary Raymond Donovan rode along in Reagan's car in order to brief the president on the labor group he was going to address. Secret Service Agent Drew Unrue drove the limousine and in the right front seat was Jerry Parr, special agent in charge of the Presidential Protective Division. With two police motorcycles leading the way the motorcade set off promptly at 1:45, out the northwest gate, up Jackson Place to Connecticut Avenue and the Washington Hilton Hotel, just over a mile away.

John W. Hinckley, Jr., was already there—waiting for them. "Just let me out here," Hinckley had said to the cabbie when the cab stopped at the light across the street from the Washington Hilton Hotel at the intersection of Connecticut Avenue and T Street. He was nervous—not quite ready to breach the Hilton property line quite yet—and he crossed Connecticut Avenue to the Holiday Inn where he browsed in the lobby and used the men's room before crossing back to the Hilton. "I didn't know what I was going to do," said Hinckley. "I had my little gun. I thought I'd see how close I could get." Police, at the direction of the Secret Service, had set up a barrier on the sidewalk, a theater rope stretched between two stanchions, to keep press and public away from the president. And Hinckley found he could get almost up to the rope.

He stood there waiting with the others, press and onlookers.

NBC cameraman Sheldon Fielman was there with his substitute partner whom he had told that morning, "It's a piece-of-cake day. We'll go to the Hilton and then go get some Mexican food."

Reagan had made similar trips to the Hilton several times since assuming office, as had presidents before him, and each time a great deal of time and thought had gone into the security arrangements at the hotel. The week before, representatives from the Secret Service, the White House Advance Office (which plans the president's exposure to the press and public from a political point of view), the hotel's security force, and convention officials held a meeting to coordinate their security plans. In addition, the District of Columbia police would be on hand to help with crowd control out in front of the hotel for those brief seconds when Reagan would be exposed to an unscreened public.

On the day of the event, the hotel was cased for possible security problems. A counter-sniper team and an intelligence team were stationed at predetermined sites. A thorough search in and around the hotel for any possible threat was conducted, and the convention hall itself was swept. It and all areas that Reagan would visit were sealed off by Secret Service agents. The conventioneers were required to pass through metal detectors and to have any bags or parcels searched.

Suddenly, out of nowhere it seemed to Hinckley, the presidential motorcade pulled up, and the president's limousine stopped at the VIP door built discreetly into the curving wall about halfway up the hill between the lower and upper public lobbies. Secret Service Agent Tim McCarthy, riding in the follow-up car behind Reagan's, went quickly to the limousine's right rear door and opened it. Reagan stepped out, and in gestures that were almost second nature to him after all his years in public life, he waved, first to onlookers across the street, and then toward the police line where John Hinckley stood. Hinckley felt Reagan's eyes fall on his, ever so briefly, and he waved back. He was startled, and thought maybe it was just his imagination that their eyes had met. The president was about thirty feet or more away—just out of range of his revolver—it was most accurate at close range, ten to twenty feet. Lead advance man Rick Ahearn was at the door to meet Reagan, and surrounded by Secret Service agents, the president was ushered into the hotel. As he disappeared, Hinckley, along with the rest of the crowd, walked into the Hilton's lower lobby to wait. He would have twenty-five minutes in which to contemplate his next move. He was still nervous. He used the men's room again. "If I was gonna have to wait more than five or ten minutes," he said, "I was going to go back to the hotel. I just wasn't that desperate about it. I just wasn't that desperate to act that afternoon. That plan wasn't my plan. It was raining, misting. I wasn't going to stand around in the rain."

Meanwhile, outside, the police and Secret Service reorganized the positions of the cars in the presidential motorcade as they routinely did here at the Hilton. They backed Reagan's limousine down out of the ramp about twenty feet, and nosed it out toward T Street to facilitate a quick getaway. They moved the stanchions and rope back a few feet until they were just about even with the bumper of the car. The driveway running by the VIP door was actually a one-way ramp going in the other direction, and it would have been impossible for the car to exit by way of it.

Inside the hotel, Reagan worked a receiving line of labor leaders, and then waited in the VIP holding room with Donovan, Deaver, and Brady before ascending the dais to be introduced to the convention. Off to stage right of the dais, Jim Brady stood with the press pool. The NBC camera crew was teasing Jim about his appearing on Friday in his Chicago Cubs hat at the White House, and as Reagan began his speech, the bantering was still going on. The White House had honored the All Star members of the Old Timers baseball team that previous Friday, including Ernie Banks and Jack Brickhouse, players of yore on Brady's beloved Cubs team. Jim had worn his cap into the Oval Office when they met privately with Reagan, as well as sporting it all during the large and gala luncheon in the State Dining Room, "and waving signals at reporter-pals like he was a third base coach," wrote Raymond Coffey in the *Chicago Tribune*. The newsmen were teasing Jim about his undying loyalty to the unwinning Cubs, and Jim was giving it back to them.

Reagan finished his speech—some thought it was given without his usual conviction, but he made a strong appeal for organized labor to join him in his economic recovery plan, and made a ringing statement of support for the workers in Poland, calling them, "stalwart sentinels of freedom." He also mentioned the issue of "crime in the streets," saying that "violent crime had surged ten percent, making neighborhoods unsafe and families fearful in their homes."

To applause, the presidential party made its way out of the ballroom and up the stairs to the VIP door where they had entered just half an hour before. The Secret Service agent-drivers of the cars and limousines of the motorcade had been alerted and had already started their engines for a quick takeoff.

Hinckley, hearing the commotion of the press coming into the lobby behind him, preceded them outside and positioned himself at the front of the police line. He saw that Reagan's limousine was now considerably closer to him. "I thought, 'Boy, has security fouled up.' I didn't really think it would work out. I thought the police would keep us back too far." He looked around and identified the Secret Service agents and observed that they weren't looking at him.

"It was my job to get the press outside so they could observe the president as he emerged from the hotel," says David Prosperi. "There were some complaints from them that there were bystanders in the press area."

The press came tearing out of the lobby yelling, "Press. Press. Let us through!" and Hinckley said to them, "No, we were here first," meaning himself and the others who were already there. At last he had the chance to end the roller-coaster ride he was on and he didn't want anybody in front of him. He maintained his position to the right of cameraman Fielman. Several Secret Service agents came out of the VIP door. Agent Dennis V. N. McCarthy (no relation to Agent Tim McCarthy) came out and walked straight toward the crowd and Hinckley, checking around him as he went. At the police line he turned right and stationed himself between it and the rear bumper of the limousine.

Now Agent Tim McCarthy, as part of the president's inner security perimeter, strode out to the car to open the door for Reagan. Just ten feet behind him, and walking briskly now, the president exited onto the sidewalk. He was surrounded by Agents Parr and Shaddick and Green, White House aides Michael Deaver, Jim Brady, and Rick Ahearn, and military aide Major Jose Muratti.

Mike Putzel of the Associated Press, who was standing behind the rope, called out a question to Reagan about the situation in Poland. Out of the side of his mouth Deaver told Brady, "Go deal with it," as the others went toward their cars.

Hinckley said to himself, "Should I? Should I?" He saw Reagan wave across the street as before, and then start to wave toward him again. "I never let him get all the way around," said Hinckley. The president was close enough, he realized, that he didn't even need to move forward—an action that surely would have been stopped. "I will never get a better opportunity," he thought. As he pulled his gun out of his right jacket pocket, it flashed through his mind, "I can't go back now. They've all seen the gun."

Hinckley dropped into a combat crouch, as he had practiced doing. He stretched out both arms, cradling his right hand and the gun with his left hand and he aimed the revolver at the president. Moving his hands and body from right to left Hinckley tracked Reagan, as he rapidly, within two seconds, fired off all six bullets. "I could see him flinch at the shots," said Hinckley. It was 2:27.

He had done it. He had linked himself with Jodie Foster for the rest of history.

"He never even got a date with her," says Brady today. "I mean, talk about a failure. He tries to waste the president, shoots me, gets a cop and a Secret Service agent, and doesn't even get a date with her."

Jim never heard the gunshots. When he was eight feet away from the press line, the first bullet out of the gun tore into his forehead and he pitched forward, coming close to hitting Hinckley as he fell, his two hundred fifty pounds slamming his face partly into the sidewalk and partly into a metal grate that crossed the sidewalk—the grate soon becoming a conduit for the blood from Jim Brady's wounded brain. In his left hand he still held a felt-tip pen. Jim always carried pad and pen for note-taking. This would be the last useful function his left hand could ever perform for him. He had been the president's press secretary for only eighty-four days.

The bullet hit just above the middle of Jim's left eyebrow. It exploded upon impact, the only one of the six Devastator bullets to do so, and burst into twenty to thirty fragments, the largest four or five of them continuing on to wind up within the brain itself. The other tiny pieces lodged in the flesh surrounding his eyes and over the bridge of his nose. The four or five fragments that entered the bullet hole and splintered into tiny pieces as they plowed through the tip of the left frontal lobe of Jim Brady's brain, crossed the midline and continued on through a large portion of the right lobe, the largest fragment ending up in an area of the brain just above Jim's right ear.

Metropolitan Police Officer Thomas Delahanty had just turned to look at the president exiting from the VIP door. It was a fluke that Delahanty was on duty at the hotel that day. He was a canine handler with the District of Columbia Police Department and normally he would be working with his dog, Kick. But Kick was sick today and Delahanty had pulled the duty to protect the president at the Washington Hilton. He had been there for over an hour waiting while the president came and went. Upon the president's arrival Delahanty had stopped the White House press pool from entering the VIP door behind Reagan as they came running from their van. They had clearance to be with Reagan but Delahanty didn't know that. As he stood now facing the crowd, he took a quick look behind him to see where the president was, and as he did so, he took the second bullet in his upper left back. It hurled six inches toward his spinal cord to be stopped by the bony spinal column. His hat flew through the air, his knees crumpled, and he fell forward onto his face, away from Hinckley. He lay there groaning in agony, his legs and Jim Brady's legs intertwined.

After the slightest millisecond of a pause, Hinckley fired again, and again—four more bullets left the gun, and, although it was empty, still he kept pulling the trigger.

Special Agent Timothy J. McCarthy had been on the Reagan Presidential Protection detail of the Secret Service ever since Reagan had announced his candidacy in 1979. Today as usual he was part of the inner security perimeter that the Secret Service maintained at about ten feet in all directions from the president. Riding in "Halfback," the Secret Service code name for the car behind the president's limousine, he was out first to open the door for Reagan upon his arrival at the hotel. He preceded him into the hotel, and following Reagan's speech, preceded him from the VIP door. He had just reached the limousine door and opened it for the approaching president when he heard the press shouting questions at Reagan. He turned to face him, then turned to survey the crowd thinking that the president just might go toward them. Suddenly he heard the sound of gunfire, and the six foot two inch McCarthy instinctively, according to his training, turned full front to face the shooting in order to block the president with his body. And the third shot hit Tim McCarthy in the chest and lifted him, spinning, to his right. He crashed onto the sidewalk on his right side, his feet just six feet from Delahanty's head. The bullet hit McCarthy between his fifth and sixth ribs on his right side, went through his right lung, through his diaphragm, through the right half of his liver and lodged at the tip of his eleventh rib at his back, a total of twelve inches.

". . . when the shooting started," says President Reagan, "I thought it was firecrackers and I remember starting to say, 'What's—you know—what is that?' "

Special Agent Jerry Parr lunged toward the president, Reagan's smile fading suddenly from his face as Parr grabbed him and began folding Reagan's body beneath his own in order to shield him and to shove him into the limousine. As he did so the fourth shot hit the car window, and had the window not been bulletproof, the bullet would surely have hit Reagan.

"In fact," says Reagan, "I got a glimpse of [Hinckley] as I was thrown into the car. He was so close. He was right there between the cameramen and the front line of the press corps . . . and I saw everybody running and everything."*

But the fifth bullet hit its mark. In an ironic twist of fate, it ricocheted off the right rear panel of the car, through the one-inch opening between door and car, and sliced into the chest area under Reagan's still raised left arm as Agent Parr shoved him into the limousine. "I've seen the bullet," says President Reagan, "and it was like a coin—it was flattened out and had black paint on it from the car." The president's chest landed on the transmission hump, with Jerry Parr on top of him, and Agent Ray Shaddick pushed their feet into the car and slammed the door. "Take off, take off!" Shaddick screamed.

*From an interview for this book, May 23, 1985. (Reagan had told *Time* magazine's Larry Barrett, for a book published in 1983, however, "I never saw the man with the gun.")

". . . it was only then that I suddenly felt very paralyzing pain," says Mr. Reagan. "So I thought something had happened that—I interpreted it as that I'd maybe broken a rib or something from the location of the pain."

Inside the car Parr was yelling to driver Unrue, "Haul ass, let's get out of here!" Although he would have liked to have Agent Shaddick in the car with them, Parr didn't want the limousine opened up again. He didn't know whether there were other guns waiting to go off out there. Ray Shaddick jumped into the follow-up car behind them.

The president felt as if he'd been hit by a hammer. "Jerry, get off me. You're hurting my ribs," he said to Parr,* thinking that the hard landing on the car floor had injured him.† Neither man suspected at that moment that he had been hit. But in 1.8 seconds, and with six shots, Hinckley had hit four people. The sixth shot went over the limousine and hit a window in the Universal Building across T Street. An instant after the motorcade left, Jerry Parr's wife, an attorney whose office happened to be in the Universal Building, came running over, distraught and terrified that her husband had been one of the gunshot victims. Her fears were immediately assauged by Agent Don Higgins, who was kneeling by Jim Brady, and she ran back as quickly as she had come.

White house photographer Michael Evans, who had been to Reagan's right, kept advancing and taking pictures. "Until I caught sight of Jim on the pavement, I thought the gunshots were firecrackers under the limousine. I had never heard a twenty-two before."

Hearing the first two shots, Police Sergeant Herbert Granger, who had been standing next to the VIP door, looked to his left and immediately spotted Hinckley shooting, crouched in what he recognized as the "combat position."‡ At the same

*It was reported that Reagan had said to Jerry Parr, "You sonofabitch, you broke my ribs." But both men say that is not true. "The president doesn't talk that way to the people around him," says Parr. "I had no resentment at all," says Reagan. "I knew why he had dived on me, and what he had done." (From personal interview, May 23, 1985.)

†Four years later, in April 1985, when Jerry Parr retired from the Secret Service, Reagan honored him and his family with a ceremony in the Oval Office. But before he began, the president said to Parr, "Now you're not going to throw me over the couch or anything, are you?"

‡The combat position, taught and used by the police and the military, gives

time, Granger saw a man behind Hinckley raise both fists as he was about to pummel the back of Hinckley's head. It was Alfred Antenucci, a Cleveland labor official who was attending the convention. ("I hit him in the back of the head as the second shot went off," says Antenucci. "I was in a rage.") Granger took off and lunged for Hinckley, who was steadily squeezing off rounds as he carefully tracked the president's moving position, lowering his hands as Reagan was lowered and shoved into the car by Jerry Parr.

Agent Dennis McCarthy, stationed just to the left of Hinckley between the police-line stanchion and the limousine's rear bumper, wasn't sure what it was when he heard the first shot, but at the second shot he knew it was a gun, but where was it? Suddenly he saw it start to come out of the crowd as people fell away from the sound, and he dove through the air over the fallen Jim Brady and came down on top of Hinckley, his right arm around Hinckley's head. Sergeant Granger reached Hinckley just an instant later, and he grasped Hinckley's hands in his right hand, pushing them and the gun down. McCarthy, Antenucci, and Granger all went down together. Other agents and policemen piled on top. All the bullets had been fired but Hinckley was still pulling the trigger as they went down. A Secret Service agent yelled at Hinckley, "You motherfucker!" Antenucci had his hands around Hinckley's neck, choking him. "Let him go," shouted McCarthy. "Let him go." And he struck Antenucci.* Agent McCarthy reached for his handcuffs, which were looped over the back of his belt, and put one cuff on Hinckley's left wrist. Although Hinckley was offering no resis-

the weapon holder a solid foundation, reduces his size as far as being a target himself, and aids in gunsight alignment. Hinckley planted his feet about two feet apart, went into a semicrouch, held both hands and the gun straight out in front of him, and sighted over the top of his hands. With body and gun he tracked Reagan's movement, thus giving the lie to his later claim that he had aimed only at the limousine, not at the president.

*That afternoon, after being questioned by the authorities, Alfred Antenucci was hospitalized at Georgetown University Medical Center with an irregular heartbeat.

The Building and Construction Trades Department of the AFL-CIO happened to be the same group President Gerald Ford had just addressed in 1975 in San Francisco when he was fired upon by Squeaky Fromme. When Reagan met with members of this group several years later he said, "Gee, if I'd known you were the same group Ford had spoken to, I'd never have gone."

tance, his apprehenders were struggling so fiercely to keep Hinckley's arms spread apart that it took a few seconds for McCarthy to pull Hinckley's right arm close enough to be manacled. "Have you got his fucking gun yet?" somebody yelled. "No," came the reply. As one by one they stood up, Hinckley's gun appeared under Officer Granger, and Secret Service Agent Thomas Lightsey came up to secure it, not touching it, but picking it up with his handcuffs. Pulling Hinckley's raincoat up over his back to further restrict his movement, agents hustled him into a police cruiser, and they took off for District of Columbia Police Headquarters. Officers would find in Hinckley's wallet a truncated version of the Second Amendment to the Bill of Rights: ". . . the right of people to bear arms shall not be infringed."*

"I ran to find a phone to call the White House," says David Prosperi. "The only phone available was a credit-card phone. So I charged the call to my home number." Florence Taussig answered in the press room. "Let me speak to Larry right away. It's an emergency," Prosperi told her.

"What's up?" asked Speakes.

"The president's been shot at and Brady's been shot."

"Jim was?" said Speakes. "Okay, thanks a lot. Stay there and keep us informed." And Speakes ran to Jim Baker's office.

"Ed Meese's top aide, Craig Fuller, came into Meese's office," says Mitchell Stanley, a close Brady associate, who was then a Meese assistant. "He said, 'I have some real bad news.' Meese looked up. He sensed something of the most incredible proportions. He turned white, jumped up, and ran to Baker's office. He seemed to know something unearthly had happened.

"It was raining. I remember looking out of the window at a tree on the White House lawn and thinking, 'What would it have been like to have been here another couple of years without this horror.' "

Rick Ahearn, the president's lead advance man, who walked out a few steps behind Reagan, thought the first shot was a firecracker. When he heard the second shot, he knew it was

*"A well-regulated militia being necessary to the security of a free state, the right of the people to keep and bear arms shall not be infringed."

gunfire. He took a running step toward the president, but one of the shots shattered glass on Reagan's limousine and sprayed fragments in Ahearn's face. He fell back for an instant. Agent Jerry Parr pushed the president into the car, and it took off.

Ahearn ran over to Brady. "His legs were kicking and he was moaning. I put my face down next to his and then I saw the wound. I shouted to him, 'Jim, don't move—we're going to take care of you. Can you hear me?' " "Yes," Brady moaned. He tried to get up. Ahearn tried to stanch the flow of blood with his handkerchief—it was quickly soaked. "Anybody got a handkerchief?" he called. Several were offered by agents and press. A U.S. Park police officer had dropped his revolver, a .38, and it lay next to Jim's head, and the photographers were snapping close-ups. Ahearn didn't like the juxtaposition and he pushed the gun away. "I tried to keep his legs still—I was afraid Jim's movement might make the bullet move and make his injury worse." Agent Jim Very was checking Tim McCarthy for wounds but couldn't find anything at first. "Well, then," McCarthy reportedly thought to himself, "you might as well take out my revolver and shoot me because why am I lying here on the ground?"

Suddenly Ahearn became aware of a man in a rugby shirt kneeling at the side of fallen policeman Tom Delahanty. He shouted that he was "here and now establishing triage [a battlefield term for giving the highest priority to the seriously wounded who had the best chance of survival] and this man gets the first ambulance." He meant Officer Delahanty. "No," shouted Rick Ahearn, "this man goes first. He has a head wound." Ahearn knew from his previous police training that it was imperative to treat Jim immediately. Brady kept trying to push himself up with his right hand, and kicked his legs up in the air, too, in the attempt to get up, but he could not and he lay back down, his head turned, left cheek down now to the harsh pavement. Ahearn and Rugby Shirt shouted back and forth, expletives flying, for several seconds, until an ambulance pulled up, siren screaming, and its medic hurried over. Ahearn ordered him to pick up Brady. Medic Bobby Montgillion quickly assessed the three wounded men, and he agreed with Ahearn. Quickly they lifted Jim onto a wheeled stretcher, removed his tie, opened his shirt, and loaded him into the ambulance. An oxygen mask was clamped to his face. "Jim was aware of what we were doing," says Montgillion, "but his head was swelling so fast I was afraid he'd lose his airway before we got him to the hospital." They were ready to take off, when another furious argument erupted, this time between Ahearn and the ambulance driver. The driver insisted that his orders were to take the patient to the Washington Hospital Center, four miles away through difficult city traffic—a trip that would take at least twenty minutes.The driver refused to change his course, then, suddenly, unaccountably, admitted he wasn't sure he knew the way to Washington Hospital Center. Hearing this, Ahearn, with the backing of Agent Don Huggins, prevailed, and the ambulance sped off toward George Washington University Hospital with Huggins directing the driver on the fastest route. That decision saved Jim Brady's life. Ahearn kept talking to Jim, who was making semicoherent responses, trying to touch his head with his hands. Ahearn tried to assure Jim that he was there with him, and that they were doing everything they could as fast as they could.

Another ambulance had arrived just seconds after the first one, and it took off with Tim McCarthy just ahead of Jim's. And not long after that another ambulance arrived for Thomas Delahanty.

"Jim Brady would not have survived the trip to Washington Hospital Center," says Dr. Arthur I. Kobrine flatly. Kobrine is the professor of neurosurgery who took charge of Brady's case. "He was getting ready to die when they wheeled him into the emergency room. His brain would have soon herniated, that is, the swelling would have forced the brain stem, which is the center of cardiac and pulmonary impulses, through the bottom of his skull, constricting it so that it could no longer function. Everything would have come to a halt—his breathing, his heart." As it turned out, Jim Brady was in the emergency room in well under ten minutes.

The scene of the shooting was run over and over by the networks throughout the day, the next week, and dozens of times thereafter, whenever there was a profile of Jim or a reprise of any aspect of the assassination attempt.

"Jim Brady never completely lost consciousness," says Jerry Parr, who saw him brought into the emergency room.

CHAPTER TWO

"Inside His Head"

In "Stagecoach," President Reagan's limousine, Jerry Parr rolled off Reagan: "I'm sorry, sir," he said. Parr got to his knees. Quickly he pulled Reagan up and shoved him into the right corner of the backseat. Parr glanced to his left and saw the bullet mark on the window; then, over the president's shoulder, he saw three men down on the sidewalk as the limousine made the turn onto Connecticut Avenue. The president moved to sit on the edge of the seat. "Sit back," said Parr. "I can't," said Reagan. "It hurts too much. I think I've broken a rib." Kneeling on the floor of the car before him, Parr quickly ran his fingers over the president's chest, then up his sides under his arms; next, he bent him forward to feel all over his back under his suitcoat and the back of his head. He could find no wound.

Parr had broken his radio in their fall into the car. "Give me the mike," he said urgently to Drew Unrue who passed the car's mike through the sliding bulletproof window. Parr radioed Ray Shaddick in the car behind his. "Rawhide [Reagan's code name] not hurt. Repeat. Not hurt." Shaddick radioed Secret Service headquarters in the White House. "Shots fired. Men down. Rawhide returning to Crown [the White House]."

Reagan dabbed his mouth with a paper napkin he'd taken from the convention-hall lectern. "I think I've cut my mouth," he said to Parr. Parr was startled but from his training he knew the instant he saw the bright-red oxygenated blood on the president's lips that he had suffered a lung injury. "I think you've hurt yourself—maybe broken a rib or something. We're going to the hospital." Sitting uncomfortably forward on the seat, the president nodded his assent. "I'm having a little trouble breathing," he told Parr. There was no panic in his voice. It didn't occur to either man that it could possibly be a gunshot wound.

"And just then I coughed," says Reagan, "and I had a handful of blood and so my diagnosis then was that I'd broken a rib but it had also pierced my lung. I used my handkerchief, and then I used up his. My first reaction was, okay, you've heard of that happening—a broken rib pierced the lung and that's why I'm bleeding. But it panicked me a little. When you have a feeling that you're getting less and less air, you think, 'What do I do if one of these times I take a deep breath—and no air comes in?' "

By this time the motorcade was going close to sixty miles an hour down Connecticut Avenue. The entire avenue had been blocked off for Reagan's return to the White House at this exact moment anyway, and the avenue was entirely clear. Parr told Unrue, "Let's go to the hospital." In the mike to Shaddick he said, "We're going to G. W. Hospital." He added, "Let's hustle." "I did not indicate to Shaddick the president's condition," says Parr, "because the press monitors our channels all the time and I didn't want them to hear it and get in our way. But I gave Shaddick a clue when I said, 'Let's hustle.' "

When the limousine reached Pennsylvania it turned right to head for the hospital just six blocks away instead of going through the White House gates. (Police motorcycles and two of the lead cars sailed right into the White House grounds, not having had radio contact with Parr.) "Agent Mary Ann Gordon, who was driving the third armored car, whipped around us and got in front of us to lead the way. I looked back at the follow-up car and saw both agents had their machine guns out—they were following the trained course of 'extreme response.' "

Washington restaurateur Dominique d'Ermo, at home in his apartment on Washington Circle, was on the phone to his mother in France. Suddenly he saw SPECIAL REPORT flashed on his television. *"Tiens, Maman,"* he said, and as he took in the first report of the shooting, he heard sirens. He dashed to the window in time to see the president's car speeding around Washington Circle toward the hospital.*

When Charge Nurse Wendy Koenig picked up the white phone ringing on the emergency-room desk, the voice said, "The presidential motorcade is en route to your facility." "A call on the White House phone always alerts you," says ER nurse Kathy Paul Stevens. Until they received the elliptical phone call, it had been a normal day in the emergency room of George Washington University Hospital. Normal by their standards, anyway.

At 2:25 in the afternoon, there were almost twenty patients checked in, who were either being examined or waiting to be seen. They had ailments ranging from sore throats to asthma to pelvic inflammation to chest pains. There was one serious trauma: A woman who had suffered cardiac arrest had been brought in by a policeman. The emergency-room staff was working on her in ER Bay 5A, the bay that had the most complete array of emergency resuscitating equipment.

When the special phone rang with its message, Judith Whinerey, who was senior to Wendy Koenig, took over as charge nurse (nurse in charge). She in turn called her superior, emergency-room Head Nurse Jeanne Marquis, who was in her office across the street. "Something is terribly wrong," Whinerey told her. "Get over here right now."

"We all assumed the worst, that we might be getting the president as our patient," says Whinerey. "We thought his limousine wouldn't be coming here without him in it." "But at the same time, we could hardly believe it was happening," adds Kathy Stevens. "We started to prepare for the worst."

"I paged the trauma team, and I decided we needed specialists as well," says Whinerey. "I wanted the 'attendings' there [the university hospital's senior staff physicians]. I put out a 'stat' page call to Giordano [chief of Emergency Medicine and of the Trauma Unit.]"

The policeman who had brought the cardiac patient in was

*Dominique is sure that his mother was the first person in Europe to be told the president had been shot, because her son immediately made that correct assumption—a fact that nobody in the outside world yet knew.

still standing by. His radio had been crackling steadily, and now he started to listen to it. "Oh, my gosh," he said, "there's been a shooting at the Hilton, and a policeman has been hit." Wendy Koenig and Kathy Stevens were already setting up Bay 5A with IVs of saline and lactose solutions, and the other lifesavers of emergency medicine. "We got out *all* the trays," says Stevens.

From the telemetry communications system in Jim Brady's ambulance they then received word that another shooting victim was on his way. The message was "Trauma Code," meaning every possible body system shut down, including cardiac arrest. Working furiously now, the nurses moved the cardiac patient to another bay and continued setting up 5A and, now, 5B.*

The president's limousine had whipped around Washington Circle and now was pulling under the emergency-room porte cochere. The trip from the Hilton had taken three and a half minutes. No one was there. Jerry Parr threw open the door and leaped out. "Get me a wheelchair," he shouted at Ray Shaddick right there behind him, and then he looked down at the president. "I could tell it was important to him that he walk in," says Parr and so, surrounded by agents from the backup car, Reagan walked toward the entrance.

The emergency-room double doors suddenly burst open. By coincidence Secret Service Agent Fred White was in the ER with a fellow agency employee who had taken ill. He looked out in time to see the president's car pull up, and he ran to prop the doors open. Nurse Kathy Stevens was there, too, just in time to see the president of the United States step out of his limousine. She went quickly forward to meet this unlikely band of men, and to see why they were there and how she could help. Then she heard Reagan say, "I can't breathe. I feel so bad—I can't catch my breath." "His face was ashen," she says. Just before they entered the second set of doors, Reagan collapsed. "He dropped like a piece of lead," says Parr. Together, Nurse Stevens and Agents Parr, Shaddick, and White

*A doctor from Coronary Care was called to come down to the emergency room to take care of the patient, a woman in her sixties. Her heart resumed a normal rhythm and she survived.

Emergency-room Attending Physician Robert Shesser came to the ER with Head Nurse Jeanne Marquis, and they either admitted to the hospital or discharged the waiting emergency-room patients.

caught him and carried him back to Bay 5A.

The security of the president was uppermost in Jerry Parr's mind. As they carried Reagan into the ER, Parr barked to Agents Miller, Gordon, and McIntosh, "Start setting up a perimeter," and he told Dale McIntosh to station himself at the front entrance of the emergency room. There were eight agents at the hospital already, from the three presidential cars there, and in minutes the entire area would be swarming with agents and police, and each entryway would have an agent guarding it.

Parr looked at the nurses. "Who's in charge here?" he asked. "I am," said Judith Whinerey. "I've got to keep things tightly secure," said Parr, "and you've got to help me decide who needs to be here and who doesn't." Physicians from all over the hospital, medical students, nurses, and hospital personnel were converging on the ER, having heard the urgent pages or their own beepers going off.

As fast as they could, Nurses Koenig and Stevens were cutting Reagan's clothes off with their heavy-duty, blunt-tipped "trauma scissors." ("They will cut through anything, including coins," says Whinerey.) If there was an instant of awe at who their patient was, it was gone in a flash as they swiftly went through the trauma protocol for which they had been so intensively trained. Time was of the essence here. Lives can be saved or lost in minutes—sometimes seconds—and the president was looking very bad indeed. Wendy Koenig took Reagan's blood pressure. "I can't get any," she said. Then she tried again. "I can't *hear* it, but I can *feel* it," she said. "It's sixty." (Normal systolic pressure is 120.) Jerry Parr listened with shock to her reading. "It was so low I feared we had lost him right there," he says.

But the president's physician, Dr. Daniel Ruge, who traveled everywhere with the president, was standing unobtrusively at the foot of the stretcher, monitoring Reagan's pulse by holding an artery in the president's foot, and he could feel a strong and steady heartbeat. Medical technician Cindy Hines started an intravenous line in the president's right arm. From his appearance, the immediate assumption by the medical crew around the table (which now included two surgical residents and an intern), was that the president had had a heart attack. They would need more than one IV line in order to push medications and blood enhancers into him. As Koenig stretched out his left arm to insert the second IV, the small wound suddenly became visible.

"We all thought, 'Oh-oh. He's been shot,' " says Kathy Stevens. For an instant, when he saw the wound, Jerry Parr, still certain that the president had not been exposed to gunfire, thought maybe Reagan had caught his side on the corner of the car door. The ricocheted bullet had been flattened to about the size and shape of a dime, and the wound it made was more like a knife wound. Reagan was bleeding internally—into his left lung cavity. Overall, he would lose more than half his total blood volume, a life-threatening amount. Had he gone back to the White House instead of coming directly to the emergency room, it is distinctly possible that the president would not have survived. The deprivation of blood and its life-giving oxygen to Reagan's vital organs could easily have put him into a state of shock—irreversible shock when the blood loss was as great and swift as it was. Jerry Parr's decision to go to the hospital was an inspired one, one that probably saved President Reagan's life. "I was thinking with the right side of my brain on that one," says Parr. "I call it 'creative adjustment.' " Dr. Joseph Giordano says flatly, "If ten minutes had gone by, the president would not have survived. My feeling is that the secret hero was Jerry Parr, who recognized the origin of that bright-red blood and got the president to G.W. immediately." Parr was enormously relieved to see that "as soon as they started the glucose in one arm and the blood in the other, his blood pressure went right back up."

Anesthesiology resident Judith Johnson was nearby in the operating-room area when she heard the hospital speaker and her beeper go off simultaneously. She headed immediately for the emergency room and went straight to the side of the patient in 5A to check his oxygen. A tall man she had never seen before was holding an oxygen mask over the face of the man on the stretcher. She took the mask in her hand to check it out, and asked the patient, "Are you getting enough air?" "I'm not sure," he said. "Are you having trouble breathing?" "Yes, I am," said the man. She took over holding the mask from Dr. Ruge, who resumed monitoring Reagan's pulse through his foot. Dr. Johnson saw Dr. George Morales, chief of anesthesiology, come in and she relinquished the mask to him. It was only as she backed away that she realized that she had been treating the president of the United States.* "The room was filling up with men in three-piece suits and it was getting very crowded," says Johnson. "I was about to leave when attending physician Dr. Joyce Mitchell told me there was another gunshot victim due to arrive. I moved over to Five-B to get ready. I picked up a laryngeal scope and an endotrachial tube. I checked the tube."†

Jeff Jacobson, a junior resident in neurosurgery, was talking to a group of medical students on the fifth floor. "I heard them announcing all these surgeons' names over the paging system," he says, and "I called down to the emergency room, and got Judith Whinerey." "Do you need me?" he asked. "Yes," she said, "get your tail down here. The president has been shot." "As I was running in," says Jacobson, "I was tackled by a Secret Service agent." Whinerey identified him to Jerry Parr and Jacobson went in to examine Reagan briefly for any neurological damage. The trauma team of surgeons and nurses was preparing to make an incision into Reagan's pleural cavity to release the large volume of blood building up within. Dr. Giordano came up to the table in time to do the surgery. Only three or four minutes had passed since the president's arrival in the emergency room.

The hospital paging system had summoned all the members of the shock-trauma teams. Numerous doctors on the staff were paged individually as well. They were all in house and available, a lucky circumstance of the time of day. It was well after the lunch hour and still within regular hospital hours of 8:00 A.M. to 6:00 P.M. After 6:00, the trauma staff is reduced by half. In another lucky break, a shift change was due to take place soon, at 3:30, which would double the nursing staff because those who were needed would remain on duty, working double shifts. In addition, staff nurses and doctors with appropriate specialties who heard about the shooting on the radio

*For his part and even under these extreme circumstances, Ronald Reagan noticed the beauty of Judith Johnson. His private joke with Jerry Parr after that was that "there was this beautiful nurse taking care of me for a few minutes, and I never saw her again." He and Parr would speculate from time to time about where she had gone.

†An instant later Agent Tim McCarthy arrived and was wheeled to ER3—just a few feet away from President Reagan. Officer Delahanty had been taken to the Critical Care Tower of Washington Hospital Center—where Jim Brady was originally slated to go.

came to the hospital in case they were needed.

Now, Jim Brady's ambulance, siren screaming, pulled up to the emergency-room door. Rick Ahearn and medic Bobby Montgillion helped orderlies unload Jim's stretcher and they rolled him swiftly through the two sets of double doors, into the emergency room toward Bay 5B. He looked hideous. His entire head had begun to swell, and blood and brain tissue, oozing toothpastelike from his wound, were dribbling down his face. He was propped up at an incline to help relieve the pressure inside his head, and his head was lolling over toward his left shoulder. Nurse Kathy Stevens turned away from Reagan to work on this new arrival. "I found out later who he was," says Stevens. Jeff Jacobson saw Jim Brady roll by. "At this point, I didn't know who he was. Someone shouted out that he was part of the same thing. It was obvious to me that he had been shot in the head and the general surgeon released Jim to me because it was obviously a neurosurgical problem. Jim was conscious—delirious, but conscious. He was moaning and groaning and flailing around." That in itself was unusual because, says Jacobson, "Most gunshot cases to the brain come in with no neurological functions at all—thanks to the efficacy of the high-velocity weapons on the streets these days."

Mike Deaver was on the phone to Jim Baker at the White House. "Oh, my God," he cried. "They've just brought Jim in and he just looks awful."

Carefully and swiftly, orderlies and nurses transferred this mountain of apparently mortally wounded man to the hospital gurney in Bay 5B, which was only six feet from the one Reagan was on. The curtain between the two men was partially pulled as Kathy Stevens began cutting all of Jim Brady's clothes away. "He was still able to move his left leg at that point," says Judith Johnson. She asked him, "Are you getting enough air?" "Yes," said Jim. But he was trying to remove the oxygen mask. "No, you've got to leave that there," she told him. "Okay," said Jim, and he put his hands down.

"His blood pressure was extremely high—two thirty over one eighty," says Johnson. "I said to Jeff Jacobson, 'We're going to have to go ahead,' " even without a staff doctor there. "Absolutely," said Jacobson. An intravenous line was put into his left arm. Through the line, says Johnson, "I gave him sodium pentothol to anesthetize him. It also helps decrease the brain's metabolism—it quiets the brain down." Then she injected 10 milligrams of Pavulon, a derivative of curare, to paralyze him for the delicate procedure of "intubating" him, so they could flood his brain with oxygen—make him hyperventilate—crowding out the carbon dioxide so that his blood pressure would go down. An extremely uncomfortable procedure on a conscious patient, intubation is the inserting of a ¾-inch plastic tube, 8 inches long, down the windpipe to the lungs. When attached by its mouthpiece to a respiratory machine, the tube does the patient's breathing for him. It has a small balloon at the end, which inflates at the bottom of the trachea to hold the tube in place. "It was a frightening situation," says Johnson. "Everything I was doing could make him worse. Jim was heavy and he had a thick neck. In the roof of his mouth there was swelling and blood. It was difficult, but I was lucky—I got it in on the first pass."

Intubating Jim could have taken several tries, using up valuable time. "This was perhaps the most important procedure performed on Jim Brady in the emergency room," says neurosurgeon Arthur Kobrine, who would soon assume command of Jim's case. "If she hadn't gotten it in on the first pass, he might have gone several minutes without breathing. Meanwhile the CO_2 was building up. Also coming in as he did with a full stomach, the procedure could easily have made him vomit, drawing some into his lungs, which would have been terrible. He could so easily have herniated and died right there in the emergency room. It was a gutsy thing she did. Not all residents could have handled that, and they would be perfectly within their rights to say, 'I'm just not confident doing that,' and call for an attending physician." But Judith Johnson did it, and through the tube "pure" (100 percent) oxygen began surging into Jim's lungs and from there to his brain by way of his bloodstream. As the priority organ, the brain controls blood flow, and when it received the pure oxygen, it signaled his rapidly beating heart to slow down, thereby reducing the pressure within his brain.

And it is this swelling and the resultant enormous pressure that kills most brain-injured patients. "Only one in ten survives," says Arthur Kobrine. "Brain cells expand when they are injured. The automatic regulator that supplies just the right amount of blood to the brain goes to pot when there is a brain injury, and it becomes engorged with blood. Then the little blood vessels become injured by the increased blood pressure and they release blood serum, which leaks out into the surrounding brain cells."

It is almost as though our physiological nature defies medicine to save us under these circumstances. And, in fact, it was only *time,* and the understanding of everyone involved that *time* was of life-and-death importance in Jim's injury that allowed him to survive to this moment in the emergency room. It had been only ten minutes since the shooting, and now he was stabilized.

Judith Johnson injected lidocaine (of the novocaine family) into Jim's IV line for additional help in reducing intracranial pressure. Continuing the protocol for dealing with severe head injuries, Jeff Jacobson called for the injection of other medications into the IV line: one hundred grams of Mannitol, which acts as a brain diuretic, shrinking brain tissues by drawing water out of them. "I refilled the syringe with Mannitol eight times," Kathy Stevens remembers. Then Stevens injected steroids, including Decadron, which is believed to protect the nervous system; and antibiotics to counteract infection from the wound and for the surgery yet to come. Also a tetanus shot. Neurosurgical resident Rod Clemente joined Jeff Jacobson at Brady's side.*

By this time there were almost fifty Secret Service agents and policemen in the emergency room, some with handguns drawn, as well as many medical people "standing by" in case they were needed. Charge Nurse Judith Whinerey was floating between the two tables in order to help her two nurses because it was impossible for them to move away from their patients through the crowd to get supplies from cabinets just ten feet away. "Get me more Mannitol," or "Get me more syringes," they would call out to her, and these would be handed, fire-brigade style, from hand to hand back to them. All the intensive training of the emergency-room staff had come into play. The room was full of noise and confusion, yet in its midst were two islands of tranquillity, one around the table holding the president of the United States, the other around James Brady.

*Jacobson and Johnson were carrying out the protocol for dealing with severe head injury designed by Dr. Arthur Kobrine and in use at George Washington since 1975.

The portable X-ray machine just used to X-ray Reagan's chest was now wheeled over to Brady, and pictures were taken of Jim's head, front and side views. Then they propped him sitting straight up for a preoperative chest X ray. "Oh, my God," gasped Kathy Stevens when she took a look at him in that position. "He looked so terrible, I can't tell you."

Arthur Kobrine, who was nearby reviewing one of his patient's X rays, heard the commotion in the emergency room. His beeper was going off as well, and he took off toward the noise. Tall and athletic, the thirty-eight-year-old Kobrine had a reputation for brilliance and an intensity that included a willingness to display his temper if he thought his patients weren't receiving the care he had ordered for them. Staff who knew him best appreciated his perfectionism. They knew it was aimed at his number-one priority—the best possible patient care. Kobrine was the staff neurosurgeon on call that day. Neurosurgery resident Ed Kornel saw Kobrine coming and told him that the president had been shot. Together they raced down the hall. Coming up to one of the hospital administrators who was in charge of administering staff, Kobrine said, "Are there any head injuries? Am I needed in there?" In the confusion, Kobrine was told that there were no head injuries in the ER, and that he and Kornel were not needed. The fact of the matter was, of course, that Jim Brady lay only a few feet away from them, and an attending neurosurgeon *was* needed to go any further in the authorization of Jim Brady's treatment. But suddenly, Kobrine saw Dan Ruge, the president's physician, coming out of the ER. He was walking toward Mrs. Reagan, who had just arrived at the hospital.

The two men knew each other well. Ruge, also a neurosurgeon, had been professor of surgery at Northwestern University when Kobrine took his residency in neurosurgery there. (In addition, Ruge had been a partner in practice with Dr. Loyal Davis, Nancy Reagan's father.) To Kobrine, he said, "You'd better get in there. Someone has been shot in the head." "Is it the president," asked Kobrine. "No, the president's going to be okay. I think it's the president's press secretary. And, Art, I think you should handle it." As Kobrine turned to leave, Ruge asked his former student who should be the thoracic surgeon to operate on Reagan if that became necessary. Kobrine told him it should be Dr. Benjamin Aaron, chief of thoracic surgery at the hospital. Ruge stepped toward Mrs. Reagan, putting his arm protectively around her and began briefing her on her husband's condition. "Mrs. Reagan looked anguished and terrified," says Ed Kornel. "I wanted to tell her her husband looked okay, but I didn't feel it was my place."

In the emergency room, Kobrine came up to the group working on Jim Brady. From that moment on, Arthur Kobrine would direct Jim's medical care with his neurosurgical residents Ed Engle, Ed Kornel, Rod Clemente, and Jeff Jacobson acting as his liaisons. "Have you taken X rays yet?" he asked Jacobson. "Yes, the pictures will be back in a minute." By this time, only three or four minutes had passed since Jim's arrival in 5B, but the external swelling of his head was so great that Kobrine was unable to open Brady's eyes. "Were his pupils reacting to light when he first came in?" asked Kobrine. "Yes," said Jacobson, "and he was breathing on his own." Both were good signs that it was not yet an irreversible injury. Kobrine lifted the four-inch-square gauze off the wound. Even he, with all his experience, was taken aback by Jim's appearance. "I have never seen a face on a patient that grotesque and ugly," he said. "Jim's face was purple. His eyes were purple. His left eye was the size of an egg. His nose was swollen and his lips were swollen. He had abrasions all over his forehead and cheeks. He had bruises on his knees. His appearance made me even more pessimistic about his chances than I thought I would be." The entrance wound itself was small, about the size of the eraser on the end of a pencil. It was located just at the middle of his left eyebrow. There was a raised "abrasion collar" around the opening, and injured brain tissue was oozing through the hole.

A radiology technician brought Jim's X rays to Kobrine, and they showed, as expected, his fractured skull and multiple fragments from the bullet, but also that the bullet had crossed from the left to the right side of his brain. Kobrine outlined his options to his residents. Most gunshot victims who have had both sides of their brains penetrated are not good candidates for surgery. There is almost no hope for them. But there were other considerations, most important the fact that Jim was conscious when he came in and breathing on his own. Furthermore, Jim Brady's fame put additional pressure on Kobrine to undertake what he thought was a hopeless endeavor.

Dan Ruge, having gently broken the news to Mrs. Reagan that her husband had indeed been shot, then led her into the ER to see him. "Honey, I forgot to duck," Reagan gamely quipped. She kissed him, and reluctantly left him to await word of the next step. Now, Dan Ruge was back at his post with his hand on the pulse in Reagan's foot. He called out to Kobrine, "What do you think about your patient, Art?" Kobrine looked at him. "It's a terrible injury. I don't think he has a chance," said Kobrine. "I don't think he's going to make it, but I think we should try. He is still breathing and we will operate." "Well, do what you have to do," said Ruge.

Kobrine sent a clerk to the CAT-scan room to hold it open for Jim, while Judith Johnson went to help set up an operating room for the coming brain surgery.

No more than fifteen minutes had elapsed since Jim Brady's arrival. Swiftly, Kobrine wheeled Brady to the CAT-scan room, accompanied by Jacobson, Kornel, and Rod Clemente, who were making sure that Jim's oxygen was uninterrupted and his head remained stable and propped up, as well as monitoring his heart rate and blood pressure.

A sophisticated X-ray process, the CAT scan displays a series of horizontal slices through the skull and brain. After several pictures through the area of the injury, Kobrine told the radiology technician to stop the test. "When I saw the track of the bullet, the bone fragments, plus this enormous blood clot, I didn't need to see anymore," says Kobrine. "I had seen enough to plan the surgery, and I didn't want to spend another twenty or thirty minutes completing the study."

"He's in big trouble, isn't he?" said Dr. David O. Davis, chairman of radiology, to Kobrine. "We could see there was a great deal of blood in the right hemisphere, and a lot of 'mass effect'—the distortion of the brain—as a result. I fully expected he would not survive. I assumed Kobrine was on a doomed course."

Kobrine outlined to his residents the procedure he intended to follow for the next several hours. "We decided we wouldn't do things any differently than we normally would do them," says Ed Kornel. They wanted to avoid succumbing to the VIP syndrome, which it is often tempting to apply to well-known patients but which often results in medicine by committee, and sometimes even faulty care. And although Jeff

Jacobson was junior to resident Ed Engle, and Rod Clemente junior to Ed Kornel, they were both on the schedule to assist in any neurosurgical operations that day. All four residents would be on hand, however, in order to observe and to be ready to lend a hand. Kobrine himself needed to scrub and get into his greens. But first, he needed to find Jim Brady's wife—to tell her what he was going to do.

Just thirty minutes earlier, *As the World Turns* was ending, and Sarah looked over at her little son, Scott. He was still playing happily on the floor, near his toy box. Sarah decided to indulge herself further with *The Guiding Light*.

Suddenly, on the screen, flashed the notice CBS SPECIAL REPORT. "This is a CBS Special Report," the announcer said. "From Washington, here is CBS news correspondent Richard Roth."

> "Good day," began Roth. "Shots have been fired at President Reagan. According to initial reports, the president was not injured. He has been returned to the White House. The shooting occurred outside the Hilton Hotel in downtown Washington where the president had spent the past thirty minutes addressing an AFL-CIO meeting. As the president emerged from the hotel there was the sound, according to witnesses on the scene, of pop, pop, pop. According to one account, five shots were fired. The president was immediately hustled into his limousine by Secret Service agents and sped away. Again, according to the initial reports, there has been no injury to President Reagan. However, according to reports from the scene, three people were wounded in the shooting.
>
> "Repeating: Shots were fired this afternoon at President Reagan as he emerged from a Washington hotel after addressing an AFL-CIO meeting. According to initial reports the president was *not* injured. More details as they become available."

Sarah listened, stunned, to the news. "Frankly, it never occurred to me that Jim might be anywhere around. I was just shocked to think anyone would shoot at President Reagan." Before she had time to react the phone rang, and in a slip of the mind, assuming it was her mother, who regularly watched the same show, Sarah answered with, "Did you see that? Did you see that?" But her mother, as Sarah well knew, was visiting relatives in Arizona, and it was her good friend Jan Wolff on the line. "Yes, I did," said Jan. She was crying. "Sarah, do you want me to come take care of Scott?" Sarah was puzzled. "Why, Jan," she started, "why would you want to come take care of—Scott—?" Jan realized that Sarah didn't yet know that Jim had been shot. She couldn't speak. But from her silence, the truth hit Sarah. Sarah felt a surge of panic. "Oh, my God, Jim's dead, isn't he?" she screamed. Jan found her voice. "No, Sarah, but I think they have taken him to the hospital." Sarah said, "I've got to hang up and call the White House."

She called the signal operator at the White House. "This is Sarah Brady. I understand my husband's been shot. Can you confirm that?" "No," he said, "hang up and I'll call you right back." Within thirty seconds the operator called back to say it was true. "Is he alive?" asked Sarah. "Yes," he replied. "Is he stable?" "Yes," came the reply. They rang off, but then Sarah realized she didn't know what hospital Jim was in, and she called Jim's secretary, Sally McElroy, at the White House. "He's at George Washington University Hospital," said Sally. "I'm on my way," said Sarah. But Jim's old friend, White House press assistant Bob Dahlgren, called her right back from the press office. "Sarah, don't drive yourself in," he said. And Sally McElroy called to Bob across the room, "Tell her that Mark Weinberg and I will be right out to get her in a White House car."

Sarah ran upstairs to get her purse. Frantic now, she called to Frances McKnight, who was cleaning up on the second floor. "Frances, come quick. Jim's been shot." Settling Scott with her, Sarah left to go out to the street through the basement. She took another look at the television. CBS was running its first raw tape of the shooting. She saw her husband lying facedown, but he was trying to get up. "Oh, my poor baby." She wept. But, she says, "He was moving and that reassured me. I didn't think he'd been hit in the head for sure." Sarah saw that Rick Ahearn was kneeling beside Jim. "I'm glad Rick is with him," she thought. "It eased my mind a little bit." She ran outside to wait for the car.

Her neighbors began to gather, Joyce Velde from across the

street, the two men from next door. A woman drove up, rolled down the window and called out, "It's Jonathan's mother. Can I do anything to help?" "Jonathan?" thought Sarah. "Who is Jonathan?" Much later she remembered Jonathan was her paper boy. Jan Wolff's husband, Otto, pulled up. He had left his office in the Commerce Department the minute he heard the news. "Sarah, is there anything at all that I can do?" "I don't know, Otto, I just don't know," she said. Then she said, "You could go with me to the hospital."

Sarah was beginning to think the car would never come. She had been waiting in the light rain at the curb for less than five or six minutes, but it was beginning to seem like an eternity. Now she could see the car speeding up the hill. She and Otto jumped in, and the driver, Sam Sampsell, took off "fast," says Sarah, "into the mist" toward Washington.

Sarah asked Sally McElroy what had happened, and Sally and Mark filled her in on what details they knew about the shooting. At that point no one knew very much. But, still, it was several minutes before Sarah asked where Jim had been hit. "I knew she didn't know he was hit in the head," says Sally. "I just assumed he had been winged in the arm or something," said Sarah. "Sarah," said Sally, who had been dreading the inevitable question, "the reports are that he was hit in the head." "Oh, no," Sarah cried. "Not in the head!" Her mind went into a spin. "Oh, no. That's how Kennedy died. Oh, please." She wept, then she turned to Otto. "Oh, my God, Otto, do you think he's already dead?" "Of course not, Sarah," he said. "He's too goddamn tough to die."

The driver picked up speed and "began to provide a very good diversion from our trauma," says Sally McElroy, "as he took Memorial Bridge Circle on two wheels," honking as they went through red lights. The car sped up Twenty-third Street toward the hospital, but as they got closer they could see that the streets were filling up with traffic drawn to the area by the terrible news of the shooting. In front of the hospital they could go no farther. The car could not get around the corner to the emergency-room entrance, where they had been instructed to go. In a panic Sarah jumped out and ran through the front door, with the others following closely behind. "We have Mrs. Brady with us," said Sally to a hospital representative who escorted them—they were all running—through the hospital toward the emergency room.

Sandra Butcher, head of social services at GW, saw them coming, saw their faces, and she knew. "Are you Mrs. Brady?" "Yes," said Sarah. "Come with me," said Butcher who was there specifically to aid the families of the shooting victims. "Sarah, in her jeans and sweater, looked like a teenager," says Butcher. "I took her over to the CAT-scan room and sent a nurse in to get Dr. Kobrine." Butcher had asked earlier where he would be. "Families want and need valid information immediately," she says.

Kobrine came out to meet Sarah Brady. Sarah rushed toward him saying, "I'm Sarah Brady. How's my husband?" He was surprised to see someone so young. From Jim Brady's appearance he had assumed he was a considerably older man. He drew her off to a corner where they could sit, and he began: "Mrs. Brady, your husband has been shot above the left eye." Sarah closed her eyes—her head dropped forward. It was true. Kobrine plunged ahead. "The bullet went through his brain and is lodged in the right hemisphere of his brain. His condition is extremely serious. We are going to operate and the operation will take four to six hours. It will begin immediately." "May I see him?" asked Sarah. "No," said Kobrine. "We are worried about time. We have got to get started." He went on; Sarah was listening carefully. "If the operation is a success, your husband will wake up tomorrow with little use of his leg and no use of his left arm. Eventually, he may be able to walk. In fact, he may walk out of this hospital someday. However, I want you to know that he could easily succumb to this operation." "Was he conscious when he came in?" Sarah wanted to know. "Yes—not fully conscious, but moving," he said. Kobrine stood up to leave. Sarah looked at him. "You've got to save my husband," she said. "My two-year-old little boy needs his father."

"I had to look away," said Kobrine later. "I did not think Jim Brady would survive the operation." He went back to the CAT-scan room to get his patient. Kobrine was shaken. He told Ed Kornel, "She told me we had to keep him alive—that they have a two-year-old son who needs his dad." Kornel, in turn, was shaken, too. They all knew how terrible the injury was, how little chance for survival there was, or should that miracle happen, how great the possibility for the brain damage to totally debilitate and depersonalize Jim Brady. "We'd better get to the OR right away," said Kobrine. "We've just got to try." And he wheeled Jim Brady out of the CAT-scan room toward the suite of operating rooms that were near the ER and the radiology complex. He had asked the nearest Secret Service agent to clear a path through the crowded halls, and told them and his medical team, "We are not going to stop for anybody." But halfway there, the stretcher was suddenly blocked by people up ahead. "I said we are not going to stop for anybody," exploded Kobrine. "Well, that is the president, sir," said an agent, "and he has priority."

The president's party had entered the operating suite through a different door, and Kobrine had heard before he left the ER that they weren't going to operate on Reagan. But Reagan continued to lose blood and Dr. Aaron knew he had to get to the source of the bleeding. The president's stretcher was surrounded by agents dressed in surgical greens carrying Israeli-made Uzi submachine guns. Mrs. Reagan, walking alongside the stretcher holding her husband's left hand, caught a glimpse of Jim Brady behind them. "Jim's head was swollen out to here," she said, later, holding her hands six inches from each side of her own head. "Being a neurosurgeon's daughter, I knew when there is a head injury the swelling begins immediately. But it was a terrible thing to see."

The president's three top aides, Edwin Meese, Michael Deaver, and Jim Baker, were in the hall waiting to see their chief go into the operating room. When Reagan saw the three of them standing there together, he asked, "Who's minding the store?" The gag swept over the worried throng like a fresh breeze, giving them all a sense of relief and hope. When Reagan was first wheeled into OR 2, the cardiac-surgery operating room, he looked around at the roomful of doctors and nurses and said, "Please tell me you are Republicans." His surgeon, Ben Aaron, a liberal Democrat, replied, "Today we are all Republicans, Mr. President."

Arthur Kobrine and his residents resumed their short journey and pushed Jim Brady into OR 4, just across the hall from President Reagan. Following close behind, Tim McCarthy's stretcher was wheeled into OR 5. In OR 4 scrub nurses Randy

Hawkins and Joanne Chong were already opening the packs of sterile craniotomy tools. They transferred Jim from the cart to the operating table. It would take several minutes of shaving and washing Jim's head to prepare him for surgery. Kobrine had decided that Jim's entire head should be shaved, and when he and Jacobson finished shaving "whatever hair he had left," says Jacobson of the balding Brady, Kobrine told the scrub nurse, "I think you had better scrub his whole head." He didn't know whether or not he might have to open Jim's head in more than one place, and he wanted the entire head sterilized so that he could enter it anywhere.

Kobrine and his residents went off to change and scrub while Randy Hawkins began preparing Jim, using sponges and soft brushes and Betadine, a soap with disinfecting iodine in it. He scrubbed around Jim's left eye, then all around the head at top-of-the-ear level. Jim's head was draped with sterile sheets to expose only the disinfected area. His body was maneuvered into the "supine" position—his legs were flexed and his upper body raised at a thirty-degree angle. His head was stabilized by laying it on a "doughnut," fashioned from a sterile towel rolled into a circle. Circulating nurse Gael Fuentes started another IV line into his radial artery at his left wrist. A line was started into his foot as well. They needed to know there were plenty of ways to get drugs or blood into his system, and fast. Fuentes transferred Jim to the OR's oxygen system. Resident Rod Clemente inserted a Foley catheter into his bladder to drain it.

Anesthesiologist Dr. Don Lee and resident Judith Johnson checked Jim's breathing and prepared to monitor Jim's vital signs throughout the operation. Lee had been at home when he heard about the shooting, and he came right in to the hospital. Jim had already had sodium pentothol, but Lee "carried" him with Phentanyl, a narcotic. "We had to keep him deep," says Johnson, "and be mindful of his high blood pressure at the same time. We did countless studies during the case to check on it." Jim's heartbeat could be seen on the EKG monitor. His heart was racing and the beep, beep, beep could be heard throughout the OR, reminding everyone there of his perilous condition and of the need for immediate action.

As he quickly changed clothes in the locker room nearby, Kobrine debated with himself just how to approach this injury.

It was a difficult one. He could open a window over the bullet entrance area to take care of the damage there, and then make another opening at the site of the bullet above Jim's right ear. Or he could open up the entire front of his head and then open another area only if it became necessary. He decided on the second course. It would give him the most flexibility. Dressed now in sterile greens, he went through a shortened scrub, using brushes and Betadine to scrub his hands and arms up to his elbows not for the prescribed ten minutes but for four or five minutes. He needed to get inside that head.

On CBS, Bill Plante was saying from the White House, "There is a vigil going on here in the press room and upstairs in Jim Brady's office. . . . There is incredible concern for Jim Brady . . . intense concern and tears on the part of those who were close to him."

Residents Jacobson, Kornel, and Clemente were in the operating room in sterile garb when Kobrine entered. An operating headlight was strapped to his capped head. Putting his hands through the sleeves of the sterile gown being held for him, then his hands into sterile gloves, he said to Jacobson, "I think we need to make a bi-coronal incision." Starting above Jim's left temple, Kobrine guided Jacobson's incision. Holding gauze sponges tightly to Jim's scalp to stanch the bleeding, they cut into the half-inch-thick scalp, going straight up over the top of his head, then down to just above his right temple.

At the same moment, Mansour Armaly, professor of ophthamology, began to cut the ligaments on the outer corner of Jim's left eyelid to release the tremendous pressure on the orbit. While Jim was still in the CAT-scan room, Kobrine had asked Dr. Armaly to take a look at the enormous hematoma (blood clot) that had formed over Jim's left eye. Kobrine knew that left untended, the pressure would have destroyed the optic nerve and Jim's vision in that eye.* Armaly and his partner had scrubbed and were ready to work on either Jim or the president if needed. "Art told me to feel free to do whatever I needed to do for the eye," says Armaly. He put two drains in the incision to get rid of the blood and fluid that had collected there. Later, after Jim was told of his operation, he always referred to it as "my episiotomy."

*"It always amazes me," says Sarah, "how clearly Art was thinking. He saw to it if Jim lived his eyes would be fine."

Meanwhile, as Kobrine suctioned the blood away, Jacobson clamped plastic Rainey clips on to both sides of the incision to stop the bleeding of the highly vascular scalp. Carefully, Kobrine and Jacobson rolled the scalp away in both directions to expose the bone, cutting it loose from its attaching fascia and muscle. Along with the scalp they rolled the skull covering, the periosteum. Kobrine planned to use it later.

As Armaly worked, Jacobson began drilling dime-sized holes in Jim's cranium with the "bone-biting" rongeur attachment to the craniotome, which has a pressure clutch to prevent the bit from entering the brain. As he started the second hole, Kobrine took over from his resident. "Maybe I'd better be doing this," he said, partly because of who Jim was, partly because of the difficult nature of the injury. A row of four holes was made, two on top and one on either side of the head. In addition, they drilled off the edges of the bullet hole. It was considered a "dirty wound"—a possible source of infection.

Dr. Armaly was called across the hall briefly to check the president's left eye. Before he was put under, Reagan had told Dr. Manganello that he wore a contact lens in his right eye but not in his left eye. Dr. Aaron decided he wanted to be sure that was true so there would be no damage done to the president's eye in case a lens was still in it. Armaly brought in an ultraviolet light and put drops into his eyes. The president was not confused. There was no lens in the president's left eye. Reagan wears a lens in his right eye for reading, and uses his lensless left eye for distance. Later, after the president awoke from the anesthesia, he saw in a mirror what he thought was blood in his eye. He was assured that it was only the residue of the orangeish-colored dye.

Armaly finished draining Jim's eye, putting in two Penrose drains, as Kobrine and Jacobson carefully rolled the thick skin flap farther down to just below Jim's brow line. Now the bullet hole in the skull was exposed. It was about three eighths of an inch in diameter. They drilled two more holes—one above each eye. Kobrine changed the attachment of the craniotome to the cranial saw, which has a footplate which is inserted into the drilled hole. The footplate prevents the saw from going into the tough brain cover, the *dura mater* (literal translation, "hard mother"). The footplate also separates the dura from the skull, where it adheres in places. Kobrine worried that he still didn't know if he was going to need to get into the back area where the bullet was. With the saw, they connected the holes—up across the top of his head, then across the brow. The large bone flap was free from the rest of his skull, and they removed it in one piece, setting it aside to be wrapped in a wet sponge (gauze) for its replacement after the operation. "We were in his head within an hour of the shooting," says Kobrine.

Kobrine looked at the dura mater that covered Jim's brain. It was intact except for the ragged hole made by the bullet. The dura is about as thick and as tough as chicken skin. "I took the scissors and opened the hole up to expose the left frontal tip of the brain. There was a little necrotic [dead] tissue and chips of bone and bullet in the frontal tip. I cautiously debrided [sucked out with a pen-sized instrument] the area of obviously dead and detached brain tissue and several bone fragments. I barely moved the brain, however, just enough to see that the bone floor beneath was shattered." The entire brain is encased in bone of varying thicknesses, the bottom plate being the thinnest, and the explosion of the bullet had shattered it. "I would estimate that the brain loss from the left frontal tip was, in volume, the equivalent of two walnuts," says Kobrine, "half of it forced out by pressure; half of it I debrided."

"A craniotomy is not something you get used to," says Jeff Jacobson. "It is important to have a healthy fear every time you look into someone's brain. If you become too blasé"—he paused—"well, the brain is a very unforgiving organ."

Kobrine inspected everything, trying to determine what was viable tissue and what was not, making every effort to be conservative in what he took out. It was important not to be overly aggressive—not to manipulate or even move areas of the brain that he had already adjudged from the CAT scan to be all right.

Putting some cotton pads over the left brain, Kobrine moved to the right side of the head and once again with scissors opened up the dura in a curved line so the dura could be "flapped" down. "The brain looked normal on the surface, but I knew I had to get inside, to the bullet damage. I picked a spot that was avascular [without blood vessels] and as I was about to make an incision, this huge blood clot burst spontaneously to the surface, like a geyser, sending blood two inches into the air and opening up a cavernous, really, hole for me to work through. It also immediately relieved most of the pressure—it was serendipitously fortunate to say the least."

Kobrine looked up and saw Dr. Ruge watching him from the door. "Dan, you should see this. It's incredible," he said, referring to the bursting blood clot. "No, but thank you very much," replied Ruge, who was going back and forth between the two operating rooms, "you carry on." "Dan Ruge is one of the unsung heroes of that day," says Art Kobrine, "not because of what he did but because of what he didn't do. He monitored the president but he didn't try to interfere—he stayed out of our protocol as well. But his presence was felt there in the OR, and it helped me immensely throughout Jim's case to have a senior neurosurgeon with whom to bounce ideas and problems around.

"I suctioned out the huge blood clot and four or five bone fragments," says Kobrine. "The bullet had cut two arteries—two major arteries—they had been the source of the blood clot. We cauterized them, electrically, cutting them off.

"The lack of oxygen to the brain caused by the bullet's severing these arteries, plus the bullet's damage to the brain tissue itself, are the two factors responsible for Jim's disabilities today. Those were two very important arteries and the brain death caused by their severing is the reason Jim is so weak on his left side.

"Injured brain gets gooey," says Kobrine. "It loses its integrity as a structure. You have to be very gentle. You touch it or even put a sucker *near* it and, as the jokes go in neurosurgical circles, 'Whoops, there goes high school. Whoops, there goes college.' "

It was five o'clock; they had been operating for an hour and a half. Scrub nurse Joanne Chong relieved Randy Hawkins. Now Kobrine was on a search for the largest bullet fragment. Kobrine carefully put his finger in the hole opened up by the bursting hematoma. He was feeling much better about his patient. Jim's heartbeat had slowed down to within a normal range—the sound of it on the monitor was almost soothing. Even more important, Kobrine and his residents found themselves saying to each other, "The brain looks good." "It's a sense you get," says Rod Clemente, "of whether the brain looks healthy or unhealthy. When it 'looks good,' it pulsates gently." "A healthy brain," says Kobrine, "is a pinkish color and it pulses to the heartbeat, as well as rising and falling to the slower waves of the respirator." Jim's brain was looking good.*

In OR 5, Dr. Paul Colombani found the bullet that had pierced Tim McCarthy's chest, going through his right lung, his diaphragm, and then his liver. When a Secret Service agent looked at it, he realized it was a .22 and not a .38-caliber bullet, as they had been told. The news was rushed to Ben Aaron, who was working on the president in OR 2. Aaron was relieved that the bullet showing up in the X ray was the entire bullet. But he was having trouble finding it. He ordered another X ray done, and saw that he was searching too low. The bullet had ricocheted higher and closer to the president's heart than he had thought. Finally he felt it within the lung tissue, and he worked it out of the lung through its incoming path.

The atmosphere in all three ORs had settled down to a gentle hubbub. There was a collegial going back and forth to exchange notes from operating room to operating room on the part of the many medical personnel who weren't directly operating. Secret Service men in greens were everywhere, guarding the president, and Brady and McCarthy, too. In addition, they were gathering evidence for the shooting investigation, taking copious notes, as well as standing by to confiscate the bullets, or pieces of bullet in Jim's case, when they were extracted from the three victims. "You could tell which ones were Secret Service," says Ed Kornel. "Each one had some piece of his OR garb on wrong."

Kobrine probed for the main piece of the bullet. He knew where it was and soon he had his finger on it. Keeping track of it with his left index finger, he reached in with a slender forceps to retrieve the piece of metal. An agent held out a cup and Kobrine dropped it in. Kobrine began the delicate, painstaking search for dead brain tissue, bone fragments, and more of the bullet. He came across the tiny canister that contained the charge that exploded the Devastator.

Plastic surgeon Jack Fisher, Kobrine's good friend, stuck his head into the operating room to say, "Hey, Art, the radio just said your patient is dead." "Well," said Kobrine, "no one

*An "unhealthy brain," one that is in trouble, looks inflamed and swells malignantly from sources of unseen and unknown pressure. "When that happens," says Kobrine, "you sometimes literally have to suck out healthy brain tissue in order to replace the bone flap and close the head."

has told that to Brady or me." Things were looking so good at the moment that the news that their patient was "dead" struck the OR team as funny. What is going on out there, they wondered? They hadn't had an instant to reflect on just what had happened to send these wounded men to their care. Little by little, information began to filter in from the outside. They heard the name Hinckley for the first time. There was speculation as to whether the shooting was a conspiracy or not. "There was a lot of talk going on," says Kobrine.

Earlier, after Arthur Kobrine briefed Sarah Brady on the operation he was about to perform on her husband, she had watched him disappear down the hall as she sat weeping where he left her; Sandra Butcher stepped in again and led Sarah and Otto to the small ER staff lounge nearby. Sarah asked her, "I wonder if you could get me a Valium or something like it?" "Why?" said Butcher. "You are doing marvelously." It hadn't occurred to Sarah that she was "doing marvelously," but now she realized that she seemed able to face whatever might come. And Butcher's positive assessment of her emotional state had a calming effect on her. She decided to do without any artificial aids.

Moments after they were ensconced in the staff lounge, Nancy Reagan, Michael Deaver, and Jim Baker came in to see Sarah. "We all hugged each other," remembers Sarah, "and I could feel Mrs. Reagan shaking. At this point I had no idea the president had been shot."

"I am so scared," said Sarah.

"So am I," said Mrs. Reagan, and in that instant, without being told, Sarah realized that the president must have been shot, too.

"They're going to be fine," she said to Mrs. Reagan. "They are both strong men."

Alone again with Otto, Sarah's fear began to overtake her. She was terrified Jim might die before the operation began. "You know," she tearfully said to Otto, "Jim insisted on seeing Scott this morning before he left for work—he almost never gets to see him anymore. I sure hope that doesn't mean anything." Otto, who knew how much pleasure Jim Brady took in his tiny son, broke down and cried for the first time upon hearing that.

"I've got to keep busy," Sarah said to herself, and she began to make phone calls. She called her mother in Arizona. "Mom"—she was weeping—"Jim has been shot." "I know, darling, I know," said Frances Kemp. "Will you come home and take care of Scott?" "Honey, I'm on my way," said Mrs. Kemp who had started packing the minute she heard the terrible news.

Sarah called Jim's parents in Centralia, Illinois. "Shall I come?" asked Dorothy Brady. "Please come," said Sarah. She too said, "I'm on my way." Sarah tried to reach Missy (Melissa), Jim's daughter from his first marriage, who was in college at Colorado State University in Fort Collins, Colorado. But Missy had heard the horrifying news about her father and, with a friend driving, was already on her way to the Denver airport to catch a plane, first to Chicago to meet her mother, then to Washington. Mrs. Kemp and old friends Bill and Charlene Greener were on the same plane. "I didn't know how to think," says Bill Greener. "I was scared he'd live and scared he wouldn't."

Sarah called her home and reached Jan Wolff. "How is Scott?" she asked. "Scott's just fine," said Jan. "It seemed to comfort Sarah to know what was going on at home," says Jan, and Sarah called Jan periodically. One time Sarah asked Jan to have someone take Frances McKnight home. Another time she told Jan she could find dinner cooking in the crockpot.

Mike Deaver came to the lounge to tell Sarah that Mrs. Reagan was in the chapel nearby. "Otto and I went there, too," says Sarah. She wanted the comfort of being there with Mrs. Reagan, and they found Jim Baker in the chapel with her as well. They all prayed together—Sarah and Nancy Reagan holding hands. Mrs. Reagan told Sarah that the president had been shot in the chest and was in surgery, but she didn't tell Sarah that she had seen Jim. She was afraid she would give away how hopeless she felt about him at that point.

Back in the tiny lounge, "word came in that there was a priest outside, a Mr. Guernsey," says Otto Wolff, "but Sarah didn't recognize the name." He was turned away, but Sarah soon learned that Mr. Guernsey was the name of the associate minister at the Bradys' church, Christ Church in Alexandria, Virginia. "Soon he and minister Mark Anschutz joined us and we prayed together."

Jim's Catholic aunts in Jacksonville, Illinois, sent a Catholic priest to the hospital, leading to some confusion in the press as to what Jim's religion was. And the appearance of a Catholic priest who was quoted saying "I have been asked to come" added weight to the erroneous ("and premature," says Brady) reports that Jim had died. Being super-cautious the next day, the press labeled a picture of Guernsey and Anschutz "Bradys' Alleged Ministers." Jim and Sarah enjoy that little joke to this day, teasing the two men, their "alleged ministers," whenever they see them.

At five o'clock, when her staff had left for the day, Sandra Butcher suggested moving Sarah and her friends to her own larger and more comfortable suite of offices. Butcher reminded Sarah so much of one of her old friends, Bobbie McGraw, that she called her in Chicago. Both my sons were really shaken by the shooting," says Bobbie McGraw. "You know, Mom," one said, "When I was a little kid, no matter how many people were around, I always felt I was important to Mr. Brady."

They hadn't been in Butcher's offices long when Otto called his wife at the Bradys' to check in. Jan was weeping, and she told Otto, "They have just announced on television that Jim has died." "Rubbish," said Otto to his wife, and he hung up on her. But a heartrending drama had just taken place at the Brady home, where Jan Wolff, who was taking care of Scott, had been joined by Brady friends David Cole, Scott's godfather, his wife, Brandy, and Dennis Thomas. Thomas (who, Jim Brady always says, "is the only person who doesn't drink that I trust") had been in his office in the Treasury Building when he heard of the shooting.* The four friends and Scott were sitting before the television in the Bradys' basement watching and listening with horror to the news of the unfolding story, when at 5:10 CBS's Jed Duvall broke in on Dan Rather to say:

> "Dan, we've just gotten some news that is *not* good news, that from congressional sources and our correspondent Phil Jones up on the Hill, that Jim Brady is dead. The press secretary. James Brady. Forty years old. Shot in the head, in one of the—apparently one of the first bullets, if we've looked at the videotape enough now. Yes.

*Thomas was administrative assistant to Treasury Secretary Donald Regan.

That's what we have, Dan. From congressional sources—that Jim Brady has not survived."

Immediately, Dan Rather, anchoring in New York, came on:

> "Let us hope in this case we are wrong on that story. We emphasize that the report of James Brady, White House press secretary's being dead is unconfirmed from official sources, but we have reason to believe from congressional sources that Jim Brady did not survive the attack this afternoon. We'll see as time goes along whether that is officially confirmed, and if so, how soon. It has certainly been considered to be not a good sign that we have had no report on Jim Brady's condition as the afternoon wore on. He was obviously badly hit, we could see that in the videotape from the scene itself."

Three minutes passed, then Rather, repeating the report to the watching public, said:

> "CBS News has been told by sources on Capitol Hill that James Brady did not survive. I repeat, there is no official confirmation on that."

In the very next breath, however, Rather went on:

> "It is now confirmed that Jim Brady has died. I'm just handed a note saying that it's confirmed that James Brady, forty years old, serving his country as press secretary to the president of the United States, died of gunshot wounds suffered just outside the Washington Hilton Hotel as the president himself was wounded. Under the circumstances, I suggest, uh, that we take a moment in James Brady's memory."

Rather sat silently for ten seconds while a smiling picture of Jim Brady was displayed over his left shoulder. And out across the nation, millions of Americans bowed their heads in prayer for the press secretary they were just beginning to know.

In the *Washington Post* newsroom, reporters gathered around the TV fell silent. "I just felt enormously sad," says Jim Dickenson, who had covered the Reagan campaign for *The Washington Star.*

At the White House Jim's friend Bob Dahlgren heard the news and, distraught, walked outside to Executive Avenue where staffers parked their cars. There he saw Jim's yellow Jeep. "Get it out of here," he yelled. "Get that thing out of here."

In the Brady basement, little Scott saw his father's picture suddenly displayed on television. "There's my daddy, there's my daddy," he exclaimed. Dennis Thomas folded his arms around Scott and carried him upstairs out of view of the television. "I suddenly had a permanent sense of what that loss means. I thought, God, what Scott is going to miss. Then, I thought, what I am going to miss—Jim Brady was an important part of my life. For me it had the effect of putting things in perspective as to what is important, and I have never lost that feeling."

At the hospital, Otto, without saying anything to Sarah, found Sandy Butcher and told her what he had just heard from his wife. "Was it true?" he wanted to know. "Not that I know of," she answered, "but I will check," and she sent a nurse into the OR to find out. The word came back: "There is nothing to report. Surgery is proceeding."

Sandy Butcher returned to her office. Sarah looked at her face as she came in. "She looked perturbed," says Sarah. Butcher said, "There is no news, but they are still operating." Sarah was startled. "What do you mean, 'they're still operating,'" she said. "Why wouldn't they be? He's alive, isn't he?"

"Yes, he is," said Butcher. Then she explained to Sarah that television and radio had reported that Jim had died, but she emphasized it was not true—that she had just confirmed with Kobrine that it was not true.

"How in the world did that happen?" asked Sarah.

"The White House announced it," said Butcher. Sarah, by this time, had full confidence that she was getting accurate information from the hospital, and she laughed, "Well, they really do need a press secretary over there, don't they?"

The announcement that Jim Brady had died was the result of a human error that quickly mushroomed into an event that ultimately resulted in a great deal of finger-pointing and hard feelings within news bureaus in Washington and New York, as well as between the press and its adversaries. To many, particularly Reagan supporters, it was just more evidence of press irresponsibility.

But, innocent and inadvertent as the error was, it did not begin with the press. The truth is that the first report that Jim had died came from a Secret Service agent at the hospital, who phoned it to his boss, Secretary of the Treasury Donald Regan, who was in the Situation Room in the White House basement, along with other members of the Cabinet, including Secretary of State Alexander Haig, Secretary of Defense Caspar Weinberger, and National Security Adviser Richard V. Allen, who was the unofficial chairman of the gathering.

At 4:55 P.M., fifteen minutes before CBS's death announcement, Treasury Secretary Regan told Allen quietly, "It has just been reported to me that Jim Brady is clinically dead." Allen sadly announced to his colleagues, "Jim Brady has died." The announcement stunned the roomful of already shaken government chiefs. "It was an awful, awful moment," says Deputy Press Secretary Karna Small. "Everything stopped. We were all near tears—Cabinet officers and everybody." Then Dick Allen said, "Can we have a moment of silent prayer for Jim?" And they all bowed their heads.*

"It was Dick Allen, from the beginning," says Karna Small, "who kept interrupting the procedure all the way through to say, 'Wait a minute? Where's Sarah? Is she taken care of?' And then, 'Where are Jim's parents? Locate them, and send a plane for them.' He was seeing to down-to-earth personal concerns while everybody else was saying 'Where are the Russians?' or 'Are we on alert?' he was the thoughtful, humane, even religious person throughout the whole thing."

And earlier, at the first news of the shooting, it was Dick Allen who did a walk-through of the White House, bucking up the morale of the staff, and checking on the security of the building.

But in the meantime, the false news of Jim's death began wending its way to the public. From the Situation Room,

*When White House speechwriter Ken Khachigian called home to California that evening, "My ten-year-old daughter was crying over the phone. 'Daddy, you come home right now,' she said. She knew Jim and I were friends. It made you think it wasn't all worth it, believe me."

Congressional Liaison Max Friedersdorf phoned Republican Senator and Majority Leader Howard Baker with the bad news. Baker in turn told his press secretary, Ron McMahan. McMahan and Baker held the news for several minutes, but being in direct contact with the press and under a great deal of pressure for any news—the White House was giving out no word at all—McMahan told Phil Jones, CBS Capitol Hill correspondent, and Albert Hunt of *The Wall Street Journal* of Brady's death. Ron McMahan has such a reputation for integrity with the press that Jones did not doubt McMahan's assurances to him of what Baker had been told and, of course, McMahan had every reason to believe his information was, sadly, accurate.

In the CBS newsroom in Washington, Jed Duvall was told while he was momentarily off the air by producer Brian Healy that Phil Jones had called in to inform them that Jim Brady had died—that Senator Baker's office was saying that his brain scan showed him dead. Duvall didn't want to go with it, although Producer Shad Northshield authorized Duvall to go ahead. "I made up my mind not to announce it. I knew he was married, and had parents. I wanted to go by the 'old' rules, which were that you only announce a death on the official word of the doctor or, in this case, the White House." And Dan Rather had, just moments before, explained to his audience the difference between CBS sources and "official" sources such as White House announcements, after he reported some medical news about President Reagan (which later proved to be wrong). "I do think it is important that we emphasize that our information on that has come from congressional sources," said Rather.

But now there was a report that Jim's death was being talked about on Secret Service radio channels. And then, another report that White House press aide David Prosperi had confirmed it to members of the press, although Prosperi says that he did not, that it was a case of mixed signals. At this point, CBS Washington Bureau Chief Edward M. Fouhy, who knew Ron McMahan and his track record for honesty in his dealings with the press, gave Duvall the go-ahead after talking to Phil Jones again, who expressed his confidence in it. Fouhy said, "We've got to use it." "That was enough—that was what I needed," says Duvall. "Ed Fouhy and I had worked together for a long time, and I trusted his judgment. I said, 'Okay, we'll go down together.' " But it was painful for Duvall, who covered the White House on weekends and was getting to know Jim Brady well.

"I'm glad we were wrong," says Ed Fouhy. "But that incident underscores the hazards of news gathering on live television. Had we not been live, we would not have made the mistake. In the normal course of a story, we get a lot of false leads, which get sorted out and discarded. In this case, there were the additional factors of having enormous competitive pressure, very little time, and then, we considered the source, Ron McMahan, whom I considered to be impeccable."

NBC followed CBS closely with its own grim announcement, with ABC several minutes behind. All three networks had undergone their own agonizing appraisal of the story.

At ABC Frank Reynolds was reluctant, but he said, "We have a report that Jim Brady is not doing well. We have it from two sources, no official report yet, but I am told Jim Brady is not doing well." ABC was the first network to come on the air at 2:45 P.M. with both the news and film from the shooting scene, but it was the last to report Brady's death.

One minute later, Reynolds said, "We are being told that Jim Brady has passed away. I am reporting this live. Gentlemen, I trust your information is accurate. The White House according to Bill Greenwood is now confirming that James Brady is dead. James Brady, a likable, affable fellow, thoroughly engaged in the give-and-take with reporters in the briefing room. And so, a murder has been committed now." Then, ABC's Bill Greenwood at the White House, with David Prosperi as his source, confirmed that Brady did not survive, and added, "Jim Brady was a very popular press secretary. He was a big, jovial man who was known as 'The Bear' because of his size." Frank Reynolds, speaking to Greenwood, said, "I see in the background the podium he used to brief the press from. The unthinkable has occurred and he has been struck down."

At CBS, meanwhile, a eulogy to Jim had begun.

Rather: Jed, uh, in a shocking development that has thrown a lot of us off stride—it's now confirmed that James Brady died of his gunshot wounds. Only forty years old, who took the job as press secretary to President Reagan after serving with John Connally in the Connally campaign. Brady had quickly established himself as a pro's pro in that job. It's well known that when he first came to the job that Mrs. Reagan wasn't all that certain that James Brady was the right man for her husband in that role as president, we are told, but that in recent weeks that Brady had won over Nancy Reagan and, oh how he had won her over. That she had changed completely and felt he was just doing a tremendous job as I gather did most of the reporters in Washington. I believe that Brady had established himself early as a person who had good access and good communication with the president himself.

Brady was last seen—I saw him at two dinners this last week in Washington. Perhaps you'd seen him earlier in the day, Jed, I don't know. I know you saw him regularly in your role as White House correspondent.

Duvall: No, the last I saw him was Saturday, Dan, and the questions were about Poland, and the White House line was—just don't say anything about Poland. . . . And we pressed him and pressed him and pressed him. And he just stayed with it. "Can't comment. Can't comment." he said, "You can't bother the old Bear with that." "Bear" was Brady's nickname. He liked that a lot, and used it some. I was just looking over some of the articles about Brady in the past. He was a new celebrity in Washington, and, just very quickly, find adjectives—"bright," "articulate," "seasoned." I wanted to add "patient" to that because, you know, Dan, a White House press secretary gets more questions, more often with a higher ratio of strange and sometimes obnoxious questions than most of us, than most *people* do. And he handled them with extraordinary patience and with clear and clean language. I know you know Brady that well."

Duvall paused.

Duvall: We have here further confirmation from the White House, one of the White House aides has told reporters that Brady has died.

I first met him in the Connally campaign in the latter part of 1979. After that campaign ended, he was out of sight for a while, then reappeared in the Reagan campaign. And I think you know, Dan, he is very well known for the "Killer Trees" joke that apparently got him into hot water with the Reagan staff. As you remember, the candidate Reagan at one time, perhaps inadvertently, blamed trees for a lot of pollution, and one time, landing somewhere on the campaign, Brady looked out the window of the plane and hollered: "Killer trees. Killer trees." That's the one he's best known for. The joke I remember is—MEGO. We were sitting in the White House Press Room a couple of weeks ago and Brady was giving us a lot of budget information and a lot of that is heavy stuff—percentages and numbers, and it kind of gets dull after a while. And Brady said, "This stuff is MEGO." We said, "Whaddya mean?" He said, "My eyes glaze over."

Back at ABC, suddenly Frank Reynolds said, "I'm being told now that there are conflicting reports. Oh, my goodness. I must apologize. I hope what we've been reporting is wrong. I hope it's true—we all hope it's true." Then Reynolds, somewhat emotionally, delivered himself of these words: "Let's get it nailed down. *Somebody.* Let's find *out.* Let's get the *word* here and report it accurately. Lyn Nofziger says that it isn't so."*

Bill Greenwood again affirmed that White House aide David Prosperi said that Brady had died. Prosperi and Greenwood have agreed to disagree permanently on whether Prosperi confirmed Jim's death. Prosperi is adamant that he did not; Greenwood equally adamant that he did.

Ted Koppel came on the air: "We have a report from one nurse on the floor that Mr. Brady is still in surgery." This was the first television report of Brady's being in surgery. Koppel said that the wire services and all three networks had reported Brady's death. However, UPI never did report that he had died.

Ron Cohen, managing editor of UPI, who was transcribing what the networks were reporting says, "We got word from the networks that Brady had died; then we got a phone call from a former employee who was getting the same story from Howard Baker's office. Under normal circumstances I would have

*"My father's big thing," says son Dean Reynolds, "was—'what if Brady's mother heard me say he is dead?' It was a combination of keen embarrassment at the mistake, but also of an overriding feeling about Jim's mother."

believed her, but I just felt we needed stronger stuff—the confirmation from a doctor. We normally put on the wire what the networks say and then go to work to get the story on our own. But in this case I just didn't want to put anybody's death on the wire. I called our correspondent at the hospital, Peter Brown, and told him to try to confirm or deny this. In the meantime we are getting all kinds of callbacks from our subscribers. It was a real pressure situation.

"It seemed like an eternity, but in ten or fifteen minutes Peter Brown called to say that Lyn Nofziger, who was at the hospital, had told him Brady was alive. Brown told me he saw Nofziger in the hall and he had said, 'I just came out of there and I can say for sure Brady's not dead.'

"The networks are generally so good," says Cohen, "that if they've got it, it must be right. I would be shocked, for instance, if they were wrong about an election projection.

"It was just a gut feeling I had. It's gotten to the point now that there are so many stages of death that I wanted to get it from a doctor. But getting it from Nofziger was good enough for me—he was a name at the scene."

Cohen's UPI colleague, political editor Clay Richards, sat next to Jim at the Washington Press Club dinner the next January. Fellow Sigma Chis, they had met on the campaign, and Jim told Richards, "Thanks for not killing me off." Richards had been as determined as Cohen to hold the story.

On ABC Ted Koppel said, "Lyn Nofziger has emphatically denied that Brady has died."

Frank Reynolds: "We are happy to be able to report that despite earlier reports of Jim Brady's death, he is still alive."

At 5:25 P.M., fifteen minutes after Jed Duvall's first report of Jim Brady's death, Duvall went on with other news reports and words of condolences from Tip O'Neill, but Rather broke in to say that Larry Speakes was briefing from the White House: "The doctors, in a preliminary report to Mrs. Reagan, have just assured her that the president's condition remains 'good,' " said Speakes. "As far as the report about Jim Brady. It is untrue. And he is in serious condition. Thank you." Speakes immediately walked off the podium.

Rather wasn't sure he had heard it right. He looked to his left, offscreen, than scanned the New York studio for help. "Well, some confusion here, uh, that, I believe that I heard

Larry Speakes say that the report about Jim Brady is untrue. Jed Duvall, check me on that—better still, Lesley Stahl, you're at the White House. Did Larry Speakes say that the report about Jim Brady is untrue, not true?"

Stahl, slowly weighing her words, said:

> He said it is *not* true. He said the reports about Jim Brady are *not true.* I . . . but that he is in very serious condition. I must tell you, Dan, that the last time I went back into the White House I saw several aides dissolved in tears. I was about to come out and say that, based on that, it appeared to be true. So, I don't know if, uh—I guess what's happening is that most aides in the White House are watching television, and there are very few people here who really know what's happening at the hospital. And, we're all as much in the dark as anyone in the country *here* at the White House as close as we are. Larry Speakes did say, however, Dan, that the president is in good condition, and the reports that James Brady has died are *untrue.*
>
> **Rather:** Well, we again need to try, for our viewers and listeners, to put in some perspective. It is of course, live television. We're still waiting for a full report on President Reagan's condition. You just heard Larry Speakes say briefly that Mrs. Reagan had been told that her husband, having undergone the surgery, continued to be in good condition. We hope to have more details shortly. We'll, of course, be on the air here at CBS News at least until we have a full report on the President's condition. . . .
>
> However, dealing with live television you have to see this reporting on two tracks. One is official sources and official statements. Larry Speakes speaks for the White House and he says that Jim Brady, while in serious condition, is alive. We had on the other track other sources during the afternoon—a number of other sources—and we were told about fifteen minutes ago that it was confirmed that James Brady had died. Now that's where that situation stands. That's the best we can say to you. It's the best available information. We are having to pass along to you the best available information. Now, if you're confused on

the point of whether James Brady is or is not dead, then know that your confusion is matched by our own.

Jed Duvall broke in. "Dan, Dan . . ." "Yes, Jed."

Duvall: Well, you saw Speakes and I saw Speakes and I can't think of anything I'd rather be wrong about more than this. To have Speakes right about it would be very, very good news. Unfortunately, we've heard from Senator Howard Baker's office, the majority leader of the Senate, that Brady has not survived. The Secret Service reported and this apparently is a quote from the Secret Service that "President Reagan was wounded in the left side of the chest and Brady was wounded in the head and Brady subsequently died at George Washington Hospital."

Well, we'll just have to, I guess, keep putting chips of paper against chips of paper. I'd like to be wrong about this. I hope we are.

Rather: Well, so would we all. And I do think anyone with memories of the two assassination attempts on President Ford's life—the successful assassination attempt on President Kennedy—in these first hours there is always an irreducible minimal amount of confusion.

Rather then, as he had done periodically throughout the day, launched into a rundown of the day's events, winding up with a description of the four gunshot victims' conditions to that moment. About Brady he said:

And then James Brady, the White House press secretary who was at the scene, believed to be hit by at least one bullet in the head—there is a wide and growing body of sources in Washington, including Senator Howard Baker and the Secret Service, who say that Brady did not survive his wounds. The White House itself, Larry Speakes, said a few moments ago that those reports were untrue. So, you now know as much about the Brady situation as we do. That is the situation at the moment.

At 6:00 P.M. a news report was put in front of Rather and looking down he started to read, "An unconfirmed report is that President Reagan is undergoing—" Rather paused and said, "Well, I'm not sure we want to report that at the moment." Looking around, he said, "Are we absolutely certain we want to do that?* Well, frankly, I don't like to do that but, I was handed a note—I think that maybe what I want to do is to go to our correspondent in Washington, Jed Duvall. Jed, is there anything you feel confident enough to report at the moment?"

Duvall: Dan, we have had a report from our people at the hospital that two priests have been summoned there by the Brady family; that a doctor on the neurological staff of George Washington University Hospital has done a scan on Brady; that he is seriously injured; that he is on a life-support system; that he is in the intensive care unit. . . . I'd just like to repeat that apparently the Brady family has requested two priests to the hospital and that a doctor there has Brady on a life-support system and in the intensive-care unit.

Rather: Jed, Lyn Nofziger, a White House aide who arrived at the hospital about the same time as President Reagan, I'm told, has just said the following: "There has been no, I repeat *no,* open-heart surgery performed on President Reagan (contrary to rumors)." . . . Lyn Nofziger also says that James Brady, the White House press secretary, is still alive. He describes Brady's condition as being serious, but Brady, says Nofziger, is still alive.

And more than an hour after the first report that Jim Brady had died, Dan Rather summed it up again:

The question mark at the moment, in terms of the overall afternoon, is the condition of James Brady, the White House press secretary. We've had these conflicting reports during the afternoon. There were what seemed to be confirmed reports that Brady had not survived the gun attack. However, the White House officially said through Larry Speakes, its spokesman, sometime after that, that James Brady remained alive. . . .

*It was an erroneous report that Reagan was undergoing open-heart surgery.

As expressions of shock and distress from heads of state all over the world were read, from Moscow came a dramatic report from Walter Cronkite:

> . . . I am feeling a little like being in another world, perhaps on another planet sitting here this night looking out a window on the lights of Moscow as the news comes blaring out of the radio and rattling across the teleprinters. There's no way to know what the reaction or feelings of the Soviet leaders may be at this hour of the night, but this correspondent can say that if there's anything more despairing than watching and listening to the horrible news on television and radio at home tonight, it's sitting in a foreign capital, and particularly one where the rivalry with everything American is particularly acute, and knowing that a few hours from now, on the morrow, one is going to have to face a lot of Russians who are going to ask with their eyes if not their voices, "What sort of society is it that our democracy has built in the West?" As one whose reportorial career has now included an unsuccessful attack on President Truman and the assassination of President Kennedy, it's a difficult question to answer.

At evening-news time, CBS was still announcing both that there were reports that Jim Brady had died, and that the White House had said those reports were "untrue."

During the newscast Dan Rather and Lem Tucker discussed the original report that President Reagan had *not* been shot.

> **Rather:** I don't think it can be stated too often or forcefully enough that in the immediate wake of something such as this, when it happens, that there is confusion even among the most experienced and best-intentioned persons. And that among other things in part explains why an official White House spokesman, after the shooting, said that the president had *not* been hit. She was operating under the best available information she had at the time. She had every reason to believe that was true. It turned out after he got to the hospital that he had indeed been shot.

Three years later, Sarah Brady viewed the television tapes for the first time and said, "If I'd known there was this much confusion, I'd have gone out and given a press conference myself. No one was speaking for my little Jim."

Soon after the death announcement, Brady friends began coming to the hospital—many of them in tears—some sobbing uncontrollably. Senator Strom and Nancy Thurmond came in, and White House National Security Adviser Richard Allen and his wife, Pat. Friend "B" Oglesby brought Dorothy Brady to the hospital.* They all expected to find a distraught Sarah, but they found instead that she was able to comfort them in their own grief.

Between visitors, Sarah turned to Sandra Butcher and asked, "He *is* going to be all right, isn't he?" Butcher responded, "We certainly hope so. I know they are doing everything they can." Butcher knew it was better for Sarah to have the truth and not just have her feelings assuaged by false hopes. Butcher looked at the clock and realized the hospital cafeteria would be closing in a few minutes. "I think I will order some hamburgers for you all," she said to Sarah. "Oh," said Sarah, "we couldn't possibly eat anything." But when the food came it was consumed on the spot.

In OR 4, Kobrine was still working on the severely traumatized right side of Jim's brain. Kobrine asked his senior resident, Ed Engle, to help now, and Engle gently held the healthy brain back so Kobrine could debride the dead and disconnected tissue. For over an hour they worked on Jim's right hemisphere, carefully suctioning out dead brain and bone fragments. It was important to get out all the bits of bone that were embedded in the brain; overlooked, they would provide an altogether too perfect medium for infection.

Now, Kobrine went back to look at the left frontal lobe. He pondered about it. "Hell's bells, I'd better not do any more over here," he thought. "I still didn't think Jim would survive at that point, but I knew that if I mucked with it anymore, he'd be a vegetable if he did survive. I didn't want any reporter doing independent research and then writing an article about how Brady had been lobotomized," says Kobrine, "and Jim is

*"The first person I met was Nancy Reagan," says Dorothy. "She stopped and kissed me. She started crying and I cried too."

very definitely not frontal lobish. The inferior surface of the left frontal lobe [for a right-handed person] is the most important as far as one's social skills go, and Jim's social skills are very good. The very, very tip of the left lobe you can get by without, although it may have an effect on such things as initiating, attentiveness, spontaneity, and caring about one's own image. The entire left hemisphere is mostly language (speech, reading, writing, and also understanding what is being said) and knowledge—where one's education is stored. It was virtually undamaged. The left side also controls all motor functions (movement) on the right side of the body." But from the X ray, Kobrine knew that there was a bullet fragment in Jim's left lobe that had gone straight back from the wound. "It would cause too much brain damage to go after it," says Kobrine, "and eventually scar tissue would grow around it and encapsulate it." But before that happened, it would cause Jim a great deal of additional pain and misery in terms of violent seizures and convulsions that would once again threaten his life.

Two more procedures remained to be done on Jim Brady's tortured head. Upon its entry, the bullet had gone through Jim's left frontal sinus, a cavity within the bone just above the eye. Knowing that the shattered sinus was a potential cesspool of infection, Kobrine packed it with muscle taken from over Jim's temple and an antibiotic powder, Bacitracin. Then, to isolate the sinus from the brain, he sutured the thin layer of skull covering, the periosteum, which was still attached to the scalp, over the sinus. He kept his fingers crossed that he had solved that problem. Kobrine felt there was no way he could make the dura watertight however. Over the three openings in the dura (the bullet hole and the two incisions) he placed sheets of Gelfoam, an artificial collagen sponge which acts as a matrix for new tissue to grow through.

It was almost eight o'clock—they had been at it for four and a half hours. Kobrine believed he had done everything he could do for now. It was time to close Jim Brady's head and to hope for the best. Over the last hour, Dr. Dennis O'Leary, clinical-affairs director of the hospital, had periodically sent nurses into Kobrine's OR to ask him just what could be said to the public about Jim Brady. "All I can say is we're still working and he is still alive. There isn't any more to say at this point."

O'Leary had held off a meeting with the press until he could get more definitive word of Jim but now he needed to brief the nation on the president's condition. The president's surgery had ended at 6:30, and by 7:30—now in the nearby recovery room—he was coming out of the anesthesia. Dr. Aaron and the OR team were immensely pleased with Reagan's condition. On television Reagan's son Michael said he'd been told his father had come out of surgery in good shape and in good spirits. "My dad has been in good spirits for seventy years," he added. Secret Service Agent Tim McCarthy too was out of danger and recovering in the intensive-care unit (ICU) on the fourth floor. O'Leary would have to go on television without the specifics of Jim Brady's condition. "What could I say at that point?" says Kobrine. "I still felt strongly that he could die at any moment—or wake up a vegetable."

Kobrine told Engle and Clemente they could start putting the bone flap back in, and then to continue the closing procedure. In brain injuries as serious as Jim's, the bone flap is sometimes left out to allow for further swelling. And Kobrine was still thinking this case could go either way. But he was thinking that if Jim died, and the Brady family held a wake, that without the bone flap Jim would look too grotesque to his loved ones.

On the other hand, Kobrine also had well in mind how "good" the brain was looking. It was worth the chance to have Jim wake up looking pretty much like a whole human being. "Put the bone flap back in," he told them. Someone stuck his head in the OR to say that O'Leary was still on television answering medical questions about the shooting victims. Kobrine walked out of OR 4 and down the hall to the lounge to catch the last few minutes of O'Leary's briefing.

During the afternoon, Lyn Nofziger and Jim's White House press staff had set up a press operation in Ross Hall, a university building across Twenty-third Street from the hospital. At eight o'clock Nofziger had introduced O'Leary to the assembled press and O'Leary began to brief them and the nation on President Reagan's condition, giving them the first real news they had had all day. O'Leary gave a complete description of the operation done on Reagan and in answering their numerous questions, he came out with such comforting statements as "He is physiologically very young," "He was at no time in any serious danger" [erroneous], "The prognosis is excellent" and "He is an excellent physical specimen." O'Leary informed them, "The bullet was distorted and we believe it was distorted when it struck the seventh rib." (It was distorted when it hit the limousine.) He also gave the startling news that Reagan had received five units of blood before surgery. It was later determined that Reagan had lost 3,300 cc of blood, almost half of his body's blood volume.

At last, O'Leary answered questions about Jim Brady, but with a minimum of detail. "Mr. Brady is still in surgery," he said. "His condition is critical. . . . We have no further information at this time. . . . He was shot in the side of the forehead—the bullet did pass through his head and came out the other side [erroneous]. . . . Dr. Arthur Kobrine is operating on Mr. Brady. K-O-B-R-I-N-E." He spelled it out for them. "He is an associate professor of neurosurgery." To the question "Is Brady on a respirator?" O'Leary said, "Almost anyone undergoing brain surgery would be on a respirator."

There were more questions about Brady. Just exactly what is being done? "Very simply, he is having a craniotomy, which is an exploration of the inside of the head. One tries to remove damaged tissue, but tries to leave any tissue that has the remotest chance of recovery. This is not a good injury—it causes a lot of damage."

As O'Leary briefed the press, Jim Brady was indeed still lying on the operating table in OR 4 of George Washington University Hospital, but the operation was essentially finished. Neurosurgeon Arthur Kobrine had "broken scrub" and had left the room, leaving to his surgical staff the tasks of replacing the piece of Brady's skull they had removed four and a half hours earlier, and of suturing his scalp back together. He had done all he could for this big man who had come in with a gunshot wound that had plowed through from one side of his brain to the other. Kobrine, his greens covered with Jim Brady's blood, sat in the physicians' lounge watching the end of the press conference.

When it was over, Kobrine went back to OR 4 to watch Ed Engle finish suturing Jim Brady's scalp. Then, for cosmetic appearances, Kobrine cut out, or "ellipted," the bullet hole from Jim's eyebrow and sutured that incision together. Soon it was done. It was time now to take Jim to the recovery room and to wait it out—to see what the next twenty-four hours would bring. Kobrine wanted his patient to be out of the operating room and safely hooked up to all the machines in the recovery room before he met again with Sarah Brady.

The president was already in one corner of the recovery room and Jim was taken to the opposite corner. Kobrine stayed with Jim for twenty minutes to see that his vital signs remained stable. And, miracle of miracles, all his signs were good. Kobrine was relieved that he would have some good news for Sarah Brady and for Jim's mother.

But first, the Secret Service wanted to huddle with him. Would it be all right, they wanted to know, to move Jim to the intensive-care unit on the fourth floor? Security for the president dictated, they felt, that he be the only patient in the recovery room. Kobrine could think of no objection. Jim's care would be every bit as good in the ICU as in the recovery room. If, God forbid, they needed to get back "in his head," they could get him downstairs plenty fast. Kobrine, still in his bloody greens, went to find Sarah.

Sarah saw him come into their waiting room. She fearfully searched his face, but she could tell by his eyes that it was good news. "I am very happy with the operation," he told her. "I have had your husband taken directly to the Intensive-care unit instead of the recovery room." He cautioned that there were still some hurdles, the biggest being brain swelling and infection, which would keep Jim in danger over the next three days. "I don't want you to think that we are out of the woods, but it looks awfully good."

Dorothy Brady was at the hospital in time to hear Kobrine's report to Sarah. At home, Sarah's mother and aunt, Jim's former boss and friend Bill Greener, Jim's daughter, Missy, and her mother, Sue Camins, had arrived too. "I was feeling almost joyful by this time," says Sarah, "with Jim out of surgery. We had the TV on, and felt we could relax a little bit." Sandra Butcher arranged for her to spend the night near Jim, and Sarah called home to have her nightclothes, a change of clothing, and a bottle of Mount Gay rum sent to her.

Jim Brady had beaten the odds by surviving the first hour of his terrible wound. Only one in ten survives such a gunshot wound to the head. Time was the saving factor—the fact that only ten minutes elapsed between the shooting and the relief of potentially fatal pressure on the brainstem.

And he had survived the surgery. But these were only the first steps on his amazing and dramatic journey to recovery.

PART TWO

The Illinois Years

CHAPTER THREE
Centralia, 1940–1958

What roads had Jim Brady traveled over his life's journey of forty years so that at that crucial moment, just six hours earlier, he was at the side of the president of the United States as his press secretary in one of the most important jobs in the country? And now he lay wounded, perhaps fatally, in a Washington hospital. How could it happen that the president, Jim Brady, and two other men would that day be meeting the agenda of an unhappy, privileged son of a wealthy Republican family from Colorado, instead of their own carefully drawn-up schedule?

The next day, the president was to have made a flying trip to Springfield, Illinois, to make a speech to a joint session of the Illinois state legislature; a contingent of Jim Brady's family and friends were planning to drive the eighty miles from Jim's home town of Centralia to cheer on their favorite son.

Instead, tonight, at the tiny Centralia airport, newsmen were doing a live interview with Jim's mother and father, Dorothy and "Big Jim" Brady, both looking pale and small as they sat in wheelchairs waiting for Governor Thompson's plane to arrive. "You must have a strong spirit, Mrs. Brady," one of them observed. "That's what it takes to get by now," she said. Asked about her husband sitting silently beside her, she said, "He's taking it pretty hard. He's had a stroke, you know, that's why he's not going with me. When Sarah called—" Her voice broke momentarily and CBS cut away.

Even when he was in the White House, his thoughts often strayed to Centralia. In his mind, Jim Brady was never very far from home, always planning his next visit, sometimes using the White House signal line to call his mother and his friends—like his exuberant schoolmate Betsey Kourdouvelis who remembers that Jim had called her just the week before the shooting. When she answered, Brady shouted at her, "Wild." "Hi, Jimmy," she said. She knew who it was. Jim has a propensity to nickname everybody, and he always called Betsey "Wild" because she tended to greet any conversational offering with "Wild! Simply Wild!" "I'm sitting here in the White House," he said, "planning a dinner party, and I need your shrimp recipe."

Centralia and the southern Illinois countryside have a permanent hold on the boy who went off to find fame and fortune, but who always came back to his roots. And his appointment as White House press secretary was probably the biggest thing that has ever happened to Centralia, a visit by astronaut John Glenn in the 1960s being second. Not that life is dull here—it isn't. Centralians are caught up in their personal relationships, in their long-term and lifetime friendships, in the very real pleasures that a small town affords, and of course, in their jobs. They don't pretend that Centralia has everything—although it is pointed out that St. Louis, with all its cultural charms, is only an hour away. It is only with gentle affection, however, that they poke fun at their town. "Have you seen the new Carillon yet? It's the tallest structure in town." (Fourteen stories high.) Centralia with its population of 15,100 (18,300 if you count its two suburbs of Central City and Wamac) they will tell you is a "good place to live," to "bring up families." Even in the 1980s it maintains the atmosphere of an earlier day which is almost turn-of-the-century in its sweetness—like the fabled River City in *The Music Man.* Jim Brady's college-age daughter, Melissa, who spent her childhood summers here "with Gram," thinks of Centralia, and towns like it, as "the real America." "You can do everything there—there's Raccoon Lake, the parks—you can walk to everything. And everybody is watching out for everybody else."

The land of southern Illinois lies between the two largest rivers on the North American continent—the Mississippi and the Ohio. Southern Illinois has been called "Egypt" by its inhabitants ever since 1832, when the combination of a late spring and an early frost ruined the year's corn crop and caused "the great corn famine" in northern Illinois. A steady stream of wagon traffic began going south for the plentiful and cheap corn there. The people of that era, being well versed in the Bible, knew the story in Genesis of ten of Jacob's sons going down to Egypt for corn, and they began to say that they "were going to Egypt for corn for ourselves and our little ones." From Cairo, Thebes, and Karnak at the southern tip of Illinois, up to Centralia, many place names are taken from the Egyptians. Centralia itself has its share. The newspaper, the *Centralia Evening and Sunday Sentinel,* bills itself in its logo as "Egypt's Greatest Daily," and it is housed in an exotically beautiful building of Art Deco Egyptian design. Jim Brady throughout his high school career was on *The Sphinx Weekly* and *The Sphinx Annual.* The town is home to the Egyptian Concrete Company, and the Egyptian Wholesale Florist, plus the Little Egypt Pancake House and the Little Egypt Club. Centralia's athletic teams are named the Orphans, however, a result of a basketball team's showing up late due to a snowstorm for a game in a Chicago suburb, and dressed in a conglomeration of old uniforms. Their appearance inspired a Chicago sports reporter to refer to them as "appearing like orphans from the storm," and they have been "the Orphans" ever since, or "the Orphs," for short.

Centralia is on the same latitude as Louisville, Kentucky; Charleston, West Virginia; and Richmond, Virginia. "Much of our culture is southern," says Red Schwartz, who is in the insurance business there. "Our winters are mild—it doesn't stay cold here very long." Centralia is so flat that its residents like to say that when it rains the water just beads up—there's no place for it to go. Just south of town in Walnut Hill was the Creed Mansion, where legend has it that slaves were bought and sold. "The upper attic rooms still had rings and shackles on the floors and walls when it was torn down in 1978," says Schwartz. But Lincoln's Illinois was Union, and Union forces stretched a chain across the Mississippi above Cairo to control the river. Links ten feet by ten feet were found when the river was dredged years later. "Grant's first order was to secure the railhead at Cairo," remembers Jim Brady.

Early in the nineteenth century, the stagecoach brought Scottish and Irish settlers looking for land and timber, and German and Dutch settlers as well, who came for the farming. The discovery of coal and oil in the twentieth century brought an influx of Irish, Italians, blacks and Poles. There is a Polish community in Centralia where Polish is still spoken: Fifteen percent of the population is black; ten percent is Catholic. "School buses pick up the parochial kids, too," says Schwartz. "No one has a majority rule here. As a result, what we have done here in Centralia is that we desegregated the public swimming pool long before the Supreme Court decisions of the sixties. There is a very active and involved community of Jews here, and we also have a black Masonic Lodge and a black Elks Club, which is pretty unusual. Women have been members and officers of the Chamber of Commerce for years, and a woman heads the recreation department. There is a black on the school board."

The lake Jim's daughter enjoyed as a child is Raccoon Creek Reservoir north of town. Raccoon Creek flows northwest out of the reservoir to the Kaskaskian River, which then runs west into the Mississippi. The Kaskaskian was named after the Kaskaskian Indians, a farming tribe of the Illini Indians attracted to the "land between the rivers," whose culture left a stamp on the hearts and minds of Centralians. Jim Brady as a youth was heavily into Indian lore and Indian dancing, learning the authentic steps—his mother making authentic costumes for his dancing troupe. He was so good at it that as a student at the University of Illinois, he was the backup for Chief Illiniwek, the football mascot who at half time does the startlingly beautiful Indian dance described earlier.

Taken over in 1851 and virtually invented as a railroad town by the Illinois Central Railroad, Centralia later became known for its huge coal reserves, and in 1947 for one of the worst mining disasters in history, which took 113 lives. In 1939 oil was discovered, in the town itself and in the surrounding countryside. It is not unusual to see oil pumps working in the backyards of Centralia. The town had its rough side in those days. It was a melting pot, and railroad crews stayed overnight in the hotels near the station and fronting the tracks. There were oil crews and construction crews, too. There was a lot of illegal gambling among them, and "sporting houses" flourished as late as 1975, a fact that did not go unnoticed by the town boys. One of them remembers a determination by himself and a friend to march themselves up to the Hilltop Tavern, "and see just what ten dollars could do. The door opened and the guy recognized us—called us by our first names as a matter of fact, and said if we didn't get home right away he was going to call our mothers." There were as many taverns then as there were churches, which is not true today. The boom days of itinerant workers living the bachelor life are over, and the town has settled for the most part into a comfortable life of stable or at least predictable relationships.

Centralia like many other towns is struggling to survive the effects of urban renewal. Broadway and Poplar streets, the two intersecting main streets, are always in danger of losing their business to the shopping center built by Ohio developers west of town. "It just makes me sick," says Jim Brady's Aunt Louise who has an antique shop at the western end of Broadway's business district, across the railroad tracks.

But most important of all, certainly to the Brady family, Centralia was a railroad town—a hub for the Illinois Central (now the Illinois Central Gulf), the Burlington Northern, and the Southern railways. In 1851 Illinois legislators, including U.S. Senator Stephen Douglas, were interested in establishing a north-south line that would bypass St. Louis and preserve the importance of Chicago as the Midwest's premier trade center. To begin the Chicago branch line, the Illinois Central Railroad Company picked a tiny settlement fifty-five miles east of St. Louis and called the railhead Centralia, after the railroad company.

Jim's father was a railroad man. And except for a tour in France in World War I in the 78th "Lightning" Infantry Division, Centralia and the Burlington Northern Railroad came to be as much world as he wanted. Harold James Brady was called "Jim" by many people though he was "Harold" to his brother, three sisters, and a number of others. He was the fourth generation of Bradys named Jim. And when his son came along his family called him "Big Jim" to differentiate the two. Big

Jim's father was James Linus Brady, originally of Jacksonville, Illinois, and a railroad man, too, an engineer on the Beardstown run of the Chicago, Burlington and Quincy Railroad.

Dorothy and Jim had been married seven years when Jimmy was born. They had known each other for seven years before they married, but Jim was ten years older than Dorothy and neither family was thrilled about the age difference nor about the difference in religions, the Bradys being Catholic, Dorothy Davidson a Protestant. In addition, even as a bachelor in his thirties, Harold "Jim" Brady was in no hurry to give up his freedom. He had already been married once briefly and it didn't agree with him. "He was a devil," says Dorothy, "he liked all the girls." Born in 1896, he was thirty-seven when they married in 1933—and Dorothy was twenty-seven. When her son became famous in 1980, Big Jim was eighty-four years old and it was often assumed by the press that Dorothy was in her eighties, too. (Big Jim died in 1981, the year Jim was shot.) In 1982, when Jim and Sarah returned to Chicago for their first visit back to the home state after the shooting, Jim told Chicago columnist Irv Kupcinet, "I want you to know my mother is getting damned tired of being called eighty years old by the newspapers."

Dorothy Davidson Brady was born in 1906 and raised in Odin, Illinois, eleven miles north of Centralia. Salem, Illinois, nearby, is the birthplace of William Jennings Bryan, and "we once figured out," says Jim, "that Mother was his fifty-second cousin or something." Dorothy's father, Scott Davidson, was a mortician; her mother, Margaret McGee, "was a Christian lady," says Dorothy. "I never heard her say a bad word about anybody, ever." She was "Grandma Davy" to her grandchildren, and, says Dorothy, "Mother thought there was nobody like Jimmy."

Dorothy was next to youngest of five children, the only daughter. When she was growing up she often accompanied her father on his undertaking rounds. (A prominent citizen, Scott Davidson's name was on the cornerstone of the County Courthouse built in 1910.) There wasn't a high school in Odin, and so the three Odin girls of high school age traveled daily by taxi "with curtained windows," says Dorothy, to Centralia Township High School. When she graduated in 1924 Dorothy took a secretarial course at Brown's Business College in Centralia, then was hired as a secretary at Central Illinois Public Service Company. She immediately started night classes at Centralia Junior College and continued taking courses for many years after—at the University of Illinois in the summers, after she was married, at Southern Illinois University in nearby Carbondale, at McKendree College in Lebanon, Illinois—until she earned enough credits to be certified as a social worker in 1968 at age sixty-two. "Everybody in class was always younger than I," she says.

Dorothy Brady still remembers the exact time her only child was born. It was 7:05 in the evening, on August 29, 1940, and he weighed seven pounds, eight ounces. Dorothy and Jim named their baby James Scott Brady (Scott, after Dorothy's father) and immediately nicknamed him Jimmy. A protective mother, the first time she took her baby out was on New Year's Eve, and even then, "I had to go check on him every two minutes. I believe in rocking kids when they cry." He was colicky for the first six months, and susceptible to allergies, and she understandably worried about him. His Christmas vomiting attacks made them realize he was allergic to pine needles; strawberries made his ears turn red. He outgrew some allergies and grew into others.

And he was precocious. Jimmy's first word, at age one was "Bang!" ("I don't know where he got that," his mother says. "Maybe I was thinking of Hinckley," says Jim.) At his third Christmas he could go through his parents' basket of Christmas cards and tell whom each one was from. He was enchanted by the proximity of the railroad tracks just four blocks away, and at 5:00 P.M. every day "he just had to watch the Panama Limited, a crack train, go through." One evening his parents had him downtown for the occasion dressed in a tan tuxedo coat, and a cap with a little bill on it, when they ran into Aunt Helen. "What's my darling boy doing?" she said. Jimmy, who already knew he had his aunt wrapped around his little finger, hinted hopefully, "He's a-lookin' in the dime store."

As it happened, Jimmy Brady was the only grandchild of James Linus Brady, who had had five children, and Jimmy was their "darling boy," say his doting aunts Helen Brady Cain and Margaret Brady Burke. "We idolized him." "We are just an unusual family, we are so close," says Aunt Helen, or Aunt

He-wen as Jimmy called her, and still does. "We just don't want to be very far away from each other."

And they never were very far away from each other or from Jimmy. Shortly after his birth his parents were asked to vacate the Hocdeffer Apartments across the street from St. Mary's Hospital where he was born, because of a "no children" policy. They moved to a house on Maple Street just one block away from his Grandmother Brady and his two aunts, where they could keep in close touch with the only Brady of the next generation.

Jimmy Brady lived all his life in Centralia in the house on Maple Street—a modest one-story white frame house with a little front porch, a parlor, three bedrooms, one bathroom, a dining room, which doubled as Dorothy's office, a commodious kitchen, and a tiny back porch—and Dorothy lives there to this day. The house is on a quarter-acre lot. They were one door in from Broadway, the main street, and just across the street from the Catholic school, St. Mary's, which Jimmy attended through the eighth grade. When he wasn't in school he spent a lot of time playing on the school grounds. "That schoolyard was like a magnet to me," he remembers. Two blocks west on Broadway, the business district began with the Green Grill, a restaurant and bar, which became, as he grew older, Jimmy's father's afternoon haunt where he "liked to meet his cronies and cure the ills of the world," says brother Ed. Big Jim would say to his son, "Well, I'm going to mass now," and head off to the Green Grill for his daily ration. In his later years he was a quiet man, but in his prime he cut a wide swath. He was an absolutely dazzling dancer, a tall, handsome ladies' man. "He was a Catholic union man," says Jim, "a member of the Brotherhood of Railway Clerks." That pretty much defined his life. Big Jim worked all his life at the train yard about a mile south of his house. He walked to and from work every day—leaving home at 6:30 and arriving back at 3:00 P.M.

One block east of Jimmy's house, on Broadway, was the Centralia Public Library where Dorothy Brady was a board member for many years. It is a handsome Carnegie library in the center of two acres called Library Park. And Centralia High School, when it came time for that, was a "distant" seven blocks away. It was a small world for Jimmy Brady—a veritable paradise of freedom and adventure for a small boy. There was a stage in Library Park and in the summer there were band concerts. "People came with their blankets, and all of us kids came to listen and eat ice-cream bars," remembers King "Butch" Betz, one of the kids on Jim Brady's block, now of the Home Federal Savings and Loan Bank. All summer they would make stilts, roller-skate around the block, play kick the can, capture the flag, and have scavenger hunts. Muses Betz, "Of course, we had our block fights, too. The Peifers would come down the alley on their bikes with slingshots and rocks, and we'd be all barricaded in along the alley."

Dorothy Brady remembers the time Jim and the Peifer boys dug up the Brady backyard into a mound with a cave in it and poured water over it all to harden it. In the same backyard Jimmy had a sandbox in which he spent hours positioning his two hundred metal soldiers. "He never gave me a moment's trouble," says his mother, contemplating her son's early childhood, forgetting momentarily the inevitable scraps and scrapes of boyhood and adolescence.

"Jimmy could always entertain himself," remembers his Aunt Louise. He liked to draw and his father would bring home rolls of Teletype paper for him. He'd start at one end and cover the paper with detailed drawings of boats and cars."

Jimmy's year from age four to five included a serious case of whooping cough, so Dorothy kept him out of kindergarten. But in August 1945 when he turned five he was raring to go to school. His plans were sidetracked, however, by a freakish accident that left him seriously injured and took two months of recuperation. Playing two houses down on Maple Street he was hit in the head by a brick thrown by a hapless boy who was, says Jim, "actually trying to hit some chickens with bricks, which as I look back on it I think also lacked charm." Jim remembers a sizable dent in the back of his young, still soft skull. He recovered completely though, and by early November he was eager to enter first grade at St. Mary's across the street. Dressed in a mackintosh and cap, he said, "Bye, Mom," and was out the door.

Jim's class was a closely knit group of sixteen boys and only four girls who went all through school together. The Felician Order of Sisters ran the school and, though not strictly a Polish order, it was tradition that in Centralia they all be Polish. Some of them, as in all schools, became legendary for their strictness, and some of them introduced Polish idioms into their English. Students learned how to say, "Good morning, Sister. Jesus, I love you," in Polish, and began the school day that way. Jim remembers one of them would say, "Make off the lights," which he had the poor judgment to correct one day. "Don't you mean, turn off the lights, Sister?" "My God in heaven," she responded, "This is a pack of fools, everlastingly talking. This is the worst class I've had in thirty years of teaching, just everlastingly talking, all the time. I'm going to call the Father Pastor." The nuns all had their master's degrees, however, and in spite of some of the silly things the children remember, they were well educated. One of them Jim describes as "feisty" because of her frequent incursions into the boys' lavatory "to make sure you only gave it three shakes—otherwise you were playing with yourself." When the school was remodeled in the sixties, old bricks from the original building were sold to raise money. Betsey Kourdouvelis sent a brick to Jim with the message "Remember the Nuns."

Jim could mimic the nuns perfectly and did so for the private amusement of his friends, including Mike Zibby. For public consumption, Zibby recalls, Jim would reel off a Jonathan Winters takeoff on Sam Spade. "My name is Sam Spade, Private Eye, Ears, Nose and Throat. My office overlooks the blue Pacific which is rather difficult since my office is in New York. . . ." This talent did not go unappreciated by the nuns and fathers of the school. They thought it so remarkable and funny that they sent Jim around to all the classes to give his Sam Spade spiel. When an Italian father joined St. Mary's parish he was amazed to discover that Jim Brady could chant the entire mass perfectly in Latin. His steady service as altar boy and his photographic mind had made it second nature to him.

Jim remembers that they were instructed to greet the priests of the parish, "Praise be to Jesus Christ, good afternoon, Father." But one day "we cornered Father Fix as he was coming out of the Green Grill—me, 'Jake the Snake' [Jim's best friend, Mick Scheriger] and Buddy Conaway, and we greeted him, 'Praise be to Jesus Christ, good afternoon, Father Fix.' " Father Fix allowed as how that was a good practice when they were around the school but "when he was out drinking in the town it could be dispensed with," says Jim.

Dorothy Brady was a Methodist and attended the Methodist church on Broadway, but her husband was a Catholic and Dorothy raised her son a Catholic. "She, *and my aunts*, raised me Catholic," Jim interjects. "We all want to go to the same place," Dorothy says, "heaven." There were no conflicts for Jim over religion—neither with his mother nor within himself. "Mother didn't care as long as I was a good whatever-I-was-going-to-be." And he liked the idea for himself. "That's the real me," he says, "being tolerant." Jim was an altar boy all through lower school and through public high school as well. He and Mick Scheriger served together and pulled 6:00 A.M. duty one week out of ten.

But on occasion of a Sunday morning, admits Jim, "I'd be going off to church and I'd look down the alley and see Mick on his bicycle heading off to church, and we'd go off somewhere—like to the Westside Community Center to shoot baskets."

Another neighborhood friend, Danny Griffin, lived three houses down and across the alley. He attended the public school. "I was younger and smaller, and Jim always used to take care of me. He always found a place for me in his endeavors." Jim included Griffin in the weekly trips to the 15¢ movies. They often had evening meals at each other's houses and "Jimmy would spend the night with me or I with him."

One thing Griffin remembers is that Dorothy and Big Jim kept some change in a silver teapot in the dining room. "That was Jimmy's source of revenue. He took what he needed, but he never abused it.

"The year Eisenhower was running for president [1952]," says Griffin, "Jimmy and I passed out Eisenhower literature. We did it because we wanted campaign buttons, but we wound up getting up as early as we could, got on our bicycles, and worked diligently from early morning until dark. Twice we got jobs helping to set up the carnival that came to town for the Fourth of July. Scouting was a big influence on Jimmy and on me, too.

"But the most interesting thing I remember which we did together was to study Indian lore. In Jimmy's garage, without any adult supervision, we formed the Indian Dance Clan and Jimmy was the chief. It was Jimmy and me, Mick Scheriger, Johnny Branch, David Heick, John Hollaran, Bob Dunbar, and Jack Tyler. We would go to the library and study a certain tribe of Iroquois. We learned the drumbeat and the Iroquois language. We used an encyclopedia and got some material from the Boy Scouts too, which told us why they danced and how to pronounce their language. We bought costume kits and spent hours making costumes and headdresses. We studied and learned the dances of the Iroquois, several Apache tribes, the Navajo, Sioux, and Arapaho. And Jimmy was the driving force, he was the leader."

In 1953, when Centralia had its centennial, we had a place in the pageant, which was called "Thrills of a Century."

Griffin's father, Herman, ran Centralia Candy, "and we had our warehouse in the backyard," says Griffin. "Jimmy and I often helped out there in the packing of candy. He was just involved in everything we did, as I was with his family."

The boys collected tropical fish. "We'd go to the library and read up on them and breed them and trade them. Jimmy probably had eight or ten aquariums. He always wanted to do things better than anybody else and he was willing to devote as much time as it took. He always had a high level of reasoning power and drive. Those two combined to make up Jim Brady."

Their study of Indian lore got them "involved in shooting bows and arrows," says Griffin. And they once laid siege to Louis Dipert's grocery at the end of the alley, and sent a few arrows sailing into the store. " 'Let's go pester Louis,' we'd say," says Griffin. "Once we rubbed some Limburger cheese on Louis's engine to make it stink when he started it. But he chased us down and rubbed it on our faces and noses."

St. Mary's schoolmate David Heick remembers, "We played a lot of sports—from about fourth grade on. That was about all we did—basketball, baseball, and football. I would ride my bike to Jim's house and we would go across the street to play in the school yard."

"When we bought Jimmy his ten-speed Schwinn," says Dorothy, "I got on it and rode it into a tree."

When Jimmy was six and seven, he and his mother began taking summertime fishing excursions; first a fishing trip by bus to nearby Crooked Creek north of town, packing a bucket of worms and sandwiches. Using their railroad passes they trained to Colorado for fishing and horseback riding one year, and to the Ozarks for trout fishing the next. "Jimmy caught a trout," says Dorothy, "and he had that fish in and out so many times showing it to people that by the time he got it home it smelled to high heaven." They took trips to Memphis to visit Dorothy's mother, Grandma Davy, and her brother Gerald. "Jimmy and I did so much together," says Dorothy. "Big Jim just didn't want to go on these trips—he'd say he could drink his beer just as well in Centralia as anywhere else."

"The sun rose and set on Jimmy for Dorothy," observes Mick Scheriger. "As he got older, Harold was always kind of in the background." It was Dorothy who encouraged her altogether willing son into all the activities he joined. "He has a drive that is just unbelievable," says Scheriger.

When he joined the Cub Scouts at age eight, Jimmy began the scouting career that became such an important part of his youth. He joined a troop across town because there wasn't one in his neighborhood, and over the next three years he earned the webelos rank—the highest. Dorothy decided when he was ten that he was old enough to go to Scout camp, but only after she and Aunt Margaret drove over to Clayton, Missouri, to check out the camp's sanitary conditions. Sunrise Ranch was a delight to him—no homesick problems there. "Jimmy was too busy to be homesick," says his mother. His postcards home (preaddressed and stamped by Dorothy) are testimony to his confidence. "Wright [sic] me more letters and don't forget about the $10 worth of fireworks," said one. He asked about Biddy, the chicken, and "How is Junior and Sarge and Tiger and the ducks?" (Junior and Tiger were the cats; Sarge, the springer spaniel.)

There were always animals at the Bradys' house. When Jim was five, there was Sarge, and when Sarge died, Jim, then fourteen, bought with his own twenty-five dollars a beagle named Mike, "the dumbest sonovabitch I've ever seen" recalls Brady. Biddy, the Plymouth Rock hen, had free run outside, but was kept in line by the dog next door, who would push her back with his nose into the Bradys' yard when she strayed. And there were always cats. Bootsie the cat had one hundred ten kittens over her lifetime, "all in my bedroom," says Dorothy. "We always managed to give them all away." "Damn cats," Big Jim would say, but as he got older feeding them every day was part of his ritual. One night he brought home a reluctant cat he thought was theirs, but wasn't.

Jim's father was a man of few words, "but they were the

right words," says his son. "Jimmy could do no wrong in his eyes," remembers Mick Scheriger, "but Harold was firm with him, too. I've seen him knock the shit out of him when we came in at three A.M." Jim remembers the corporal punishment, too. "The worst time was when he caught me halfway up a tree and I couldn't get the rest of the way up, and he was whaling away at me with a piece of lath." "But Harold didn't worry too much about anything," says Scheriger. "He was forty-five when Jimmy was born and by the time his son had grown up, I think Harold thought that he had lived a full life. He liked his little Thirty-six Buds [a seven-ounce can] and then after his heart attack [1970], when the doctor told him he couldn't drink anymore, he'd still go to 'mass' and drink orange juice. But he'd still buy his round. He was a member of the VFW and the Elks and in the fifties and sixties he played the slot machines there. At the Bradys' frequent parties Harold would pull Mick into the kitchen, "Hey, Mick, come back to the kitchen—I don't want to talk to all those people." "I treated him like my own dad." Scheriger remembers that he taught the boys how to stand up for themselves. One day, when some other boys threatened Jimmy and Mick away from the St. Mary's playground, he said, "You go get something from your toybox ['An equalizer,' says Jim, 'like a baseball bat'] and tell those kids you're going to play there, too," then watched over them from the Brady front porch.

Centralia attorney Jim Wham says of Harold James Brady, "Everybody liked him a lot—he was a very gentle person." Big Jim always had a cigar clenched between his molars. "I don't recall ever seeing him without one," recalls Red Schwartz.

He sometimes took Jimmy to his place of business, the train yard. Brady was chief clerk of the "Q" (as, notes Jim, "trainmen called the Chicago, Burlington and Quincy"). "We'd go out and hitch a ride on a switch engine and run it up and down the tracks—maybe take it as far as Waltonville or Christopher." Father and son would shoot the breeze about "how the Cardinals were doing and why," says Jim. Harold liked sports on television—"We were all to keep quiet when the Gillette fights were on." "He had his routine," says Aunt Louise. "He got up very early, took the garbage out, and opened the garage door for Dorothy. He always fed the cats and the squirrels, then walked to work. He depended on Dorothy for all business transactions. Thank goodness he had to go first," she adds, "he'd never have made it by himself."

In 1941 Dorothy bought their first car—a used Oldsmobile for six hundred and fifty dollars. By that time, Big Jim had given up driving altogether, and so Dorothy became the teamster in the family. She kept the Olds for almost twenty years, until 1960, when she bought a red and white Chrysler, the family's first new car. "I let Jimmy pick it out," she says. Jim remembers his dad's advising her—"Now don't get a radio in the car, it's just a fad"—a statement he wasn't ever able to live down.

At age eleven, Jimmy was eligible to join the Boy Scouts and for him there was no hesitation. This time there were enough of his own school pals to make a patrol and they converted the Brady garage into a Scout clubhouse, complete with stove and refrigerator, knot board, "and weights so we could pump iron," adds Brady: They were part of Boy Scout Troop Number 259—the Mohawk Patrol—"The Mighty Mohawks" they called themselves. Jim went at scouting with the same fervor and commitment he would attack everything in life. He wound up as an Eagle Scout at age fourteen, having won thirty-seven merit badges when only twenty-one were required, which won him, in addition, a silver palm. "My mother came close to losing her eyesight sewing my patches on," says Brady. He attained the highest possible rank as a Boy Scout.

Through scouting Jim learned to enjoy camping out, and he and Mick liked to take their sleeping bags to nearby Foundation Park for overnights. Dorothy would wrap steak and vegetables in foil for them to cook on the fire. One memorable night at a father-son camp-out, Jim and Mick had gone to bed but could hear their dads sitting around the fire talking late into the night. "I'm sure they had gone into town for some beer," says Scheriger. In the morning the boys awoke to find that all the cans of cocktail sausages had disappeared overnight, a treat that the boys themselves had been earnestly counting on. "Who ate the teeny weenies?" the cry went out. Small boys were looking high and low. It seemed hard to believe their own fathers could be such poor citizens. On those father-son weekends they would all go into town for 6:00 A.M. mass "so the rest of the parishioners wouldn't have to put up with us," remembers Scheriger.

Jim came home from camp at the end of the summer before his freshman year to find that Dorothy had redecorated his room, plus, wonder of wonders, she had bought him a stereo set. "I just *knew* you were going to do this," said the immensely pleased boy.

Dorothy Brady always worked outside the home and held a number of different jobs over her lifetime—as a secretary, a saleswoman, and later as a social worker—but the most interesting job she would ever hold was as business manager to Mrs. Lottie J. McAdams, her landlady, who lived next door in a mansion that fronted on Broadway. She held the job from the time she moved there in 1940 until Mrs. McAdams died in 1957 at the age of 104. The McAdams fortune came from the production of railroad ties in the nineteenth century, and there were farms to oversee, employee accounts, and Mrs. McAdams's personal affairs to manage. The elderly woman kept, in addition to Dorothy, three nurses, a yardman, a cook, a personal maid, lawyers, and doctors on retainer—among others. It was somewhat heady stuff for the Bradys living on modest incomes next door. "Jimmy would come home from school and often would eat Mabel's cooking over there," says Dorothy. In high school he fired the coal furnaces in the winter. Big Jim did a number of personal favors for Mrs. McAdams—including occasionally taking a dinkey up the rail line to her farms in central Illinois to pick up farm produce for both households, and other items. The Bradys' lives were entwined to a degree with the demands of the McAdams household. Jim always said he wanted to buy the McAdams house if he returned to live in Centralia.

When the old lady died, Dorothy spent months inventorying the estate, and in her will Mrs. McAdams left Dorothy the modest white frame house behind her own that the Bradys had been renting all those years. She also left ten thousand dollars to Jimmy Brady, but the will was contested and he never received it.

When Mrs. McAdams's death ended Dorothy's job next door, she went to work at the Smart Shop, a ladies' dress shop two blocks away on Broadway, for thirty-five cents an hour. Later, after years of study, she was certified as a social worker and she worked for the Illinois State Welfare Department. Money was sometimes scarce, but growing up, Jimmy was never aware of it. Big Jim believed that money was to be spent—on immediate pleasures if at all possible—a characteristic he handed on to his son. "If Jimmy had a hundred dollars," says Mick Scheriger, "he'd spend a hundred dollars and one cent." "It was frustrating at times," allows Dorothy, "but I never felt that having money was all that important. It doesn't impress me." Lack of money never stopped the Bradys from living fully in Centralia. One of the benefits of small-town living is that like-minded people easily find each other, and neither financial nor social status stands in the way of friendship. The Bradys counted among their many friends the well-to-do of Centralia, including the Anheusers of Anheuser-Busch, who for many years had a brewery there, as well as people from all walks of life. To Jimmy's friends it appeared that Dorothy ruled the roost. "She was the one who was involved, in politics and in everything else," says Butch Betz.

Dorothy and Big Jim "were really kind of gay blades," remembers Jim's friend Bill "Porpoise" Crain (Jimmy gave all his friends animal nicknames), now an attorney in Centralia. "And Dorothy is the princess. You can't help but like Dorothy Brady. I always thought there was a real enjoyment between Dorothy and Jimmy. They kept things stirred up—and Big Jim, almost elderly by then, was allowed to sit around and be amused by them. He and Jimmy were *both* observers, though. Big Jim would sit back and watch other people's foibles."

"Big Jim was quiet but he had a wry sense of humor," says another Centralia friend, Kent Watkins. "He liked what she did and supported her. I never saw her treat him condescendingly. It was a very tender relationship."

"Harold was real proud of Jimmy and real proud of me, too," says Dorothy.

There is no doubt that Dorothy Brady is a force in Centralia. "I used to see her at the Elks Club Christmas party and I always wondered—who is that lady directing people here and there?" says Dewey Kessler who moved to Centralia in the sixties. "Above all," says friend Kay Warner, "Dorothy never forgets her friends."

Dorothy came to politics naturally. Her father was elected to the Marion County Board of Supervisors and served on it most of his adult life. Every time he thought about not running, he would reconsider, saying, "Nope, they'll just elect some

Democrat." He was a Republican and Dorothy inherited both his political activism and his party. As a young woman, before she married, she had the distinction of being the first woman ever to be president of the Young Republican Club. Later she was the first woman ever appointed to the Board of Review, which required her to judge real-estate assessments of land and buildings. "I climbed through barbed-wire fences and went all over the county in that job," she says. But throughout, she was active as a volunteer in every political activity there was. "She was always able to be a ward chairman," says Kent Watkins, "and from there she knew how to use the network—from local to state to national. And the library board, of which Dorothy is still a member, was a mirror of local politics."

Typically, in 1980 when she was seventy-four, she worked for the election of Ronald Reagan. She recruited other volunteers, sent out campaign packets, phoned voters, and drove them to the polls—all the volunteer activities that both parties depend on so heavily. When he was growing up, Jimmy would go with her on some of these errands and to special events like the annual Lincoln Day dinners where he picked up the flavor of and the feel for grass-roots political endeavor. When he entered politics himself, he had no illusions about the hard work involved.*

As busy as his mother, Jimmy Brady got involved in almost everything. During his years at St. Mary's, in addition to scouting, he played third base on the Church League baseball team, he participated in the Annual Water Carnival in Fairview Park, where he was a big hit one year doing a synchronized swim event entitled "Davy Crockett." He started a collection of model trains, which filled his bedroom, and he displayed them for a Scout merit-badge show at the Community Center. He received a chemistry set one Christmas and concocted vile potions in the garage while his mother lived in fear that "he was going to blow the place up."

Growing up was not without its pain and hard lessons, too.

*Perhaps the biggest political visitation in the town's history occurred in 1952 when Richard Nixon, campaigning as the vice-presidential candidate on the Eisenhower ticket, made a whistle-stop tour through Illinois and stopped at the Centralia depot. Centralia political insiders remember the event chiefly because an elderly, slightly senile Centralia lady managed to get on the train and was halfway to Chicago before she was discovered missing.

One afternoon when he was nine years old and his mother was still at work next door, he accidentally fired his BB gun through the screen door, and the pellet hit playmate Dick Peifer. He didn't mean to hit him, he said later. The pellet hit the lad in the lower rib cage—doing no real damage, only leaving a tiny bruise—but scaring him, of course, and infuriating the boy's parents. All hell broke loose and Mr. Peifer stormed over to demand, "I want that gun, and I want it in pieces." Big Jim took his ax and whacked the gun in two and handed it to him. "I never wanted him to have that thing in the first place," says his mother, "and he didn't have it for long, I will tell you." Looking back on it, Jim says, "Let's say it was a vote for gun control in that it was obvious I wasn't going to handle a gun ever again."

On the receiving end of an accident, too, Jimmy came home one day with a thoroughly bloodied face and a broken nose. Playing baseball across the street, he had taken a direct hit in the face from a batted ball.

Scouting continued to give reference to the activities of his young life. He went to Scout camp every summer. In July 1953, at age twelve, Jimmy went off to the National Boy Scout Jamboree, at Irvine Ranch near Santa Ana, California. His parents drove him to St. Louis to catch the Missouri Pacific Streamlined Special, and drove back a week later to pick him up. His mother remembers his return—"When he got off the train he was wearing a big sombrero and a serape, and had the dirtiest face and hands you ever saw. But was he happy!" Jim gave a report of his week at the Jamboree on a local radio station.

At age eight Jimmy had started to collect armed forces insignia, beginning with one of his father's from the 78th "Lightning" Division. Over the years his father's friends at the VFW gave him many more of them, and Jimmy advertised in the VFW magazine for others and began trading duplicates as well as making a number of pen pals out of the project. Dorothy had a bed coverlet made for him using his collection of over four hundred insignia—which Jim still has.

In February 1954, as an eighth grader, Jim was awarded the Ad Altare Dei Award in a ceremony at Belleville, near St. Louis. It is the highest award presented by the Catholic Committee on Scouting, and represents "attainment of superior achievement according to rigid requirements of spiritual activity as outlined by the national and the diocesan committees."

In 1952 when Jim took up Indian dancing as part of his effort to earn a badge in Indian lore, he studied with the Sypoie (Turtle) clan of Belleville for two weeks. This was an activity at which he shone, having inherited his father's love of dancing. He and his troop performed for the VFW Christmas party, for the American Legion, for the PTA, for the "Blue and Gold" Scout banquets in the area. In addition, he taught Indian lore and Indian dancing to Cub Scout leaders at the Community Center. The troop was part of Centralia's centennial in 1953, and they also danced at the Baptist Orphanage.

As an Eagle Scout working for a merit badge in soil conservation in the summer of 1954, Jim also tried to win an award sponsored by the New York Zoological Society. *The Centralia Sentinel* published his article on forestry conservation. The Illinois state forester for the Southern District of Illinois, Martin Anderson, saw the article and wrote Jim, complimenting him on it and for his interest in conservation.

In June 1954, Jim's eighth-grade class graduated from St. Mary's and prepared to enter Centralia Township High School—"Home of the Orphs." And Jim went, too, although his aunts wanted him to go to Mater Dei in nearby Breese. It was not a difficult adjustment, Mick Scheriger remembers. "We integrated very easily. We had all come from schools all over town—eleven in all." They were very "cool." "We always wore our collars up as freshmen," says Jack Tyler, who moved near the Bradys when the boys were in the eighth grade.

In October 1983, when Jim went back to Centralia for the first time since the shooting, there was a big party for him at the Elks Club. One of the guests that night was Vera Goessling who was the librarian and an English teacher at Centralia High School while Jim was there. "Surprise," he said upon seeing her. "Jim went with a crowd that was very active—he was popular with the boys *and* the girls," she says, "but the fight he and I always had was over library books. I would say, 'Jim, you have a book overdue.' 'Oh, no,' he'd say. 'I don't have a book overdue—I didn't know till now where the book was—that's different.' Every time he would try to argue me out of the library fine—the point being that Jim was very vocal—he argued for the fun of it—he always wanted to win the argument." At the Elks Club that night, her former students were still trying to twit Vera Goessling. When she remarked that Chet Allard's hair was a little bit too long, Mike Zibby said, "Now, Vera, you're not going to tell the bank president he needs a hair cut, are you?"

Miss Goessling was known as a strict disciplinarian, "and I *was* to the *n*th degree," she confirms, "but you can't study without the right atmosphere." She was on to all the tricks—the pin in the front of the shoe, the squirt gun hidden in the hollowed-out book, pitching pennies in the back of the room. She always confiscated the coins, saying with elaborate gratitude, "I want to thank you so very much for the pennies because I use them in the parking meters." Jim Brady and his pals got the better of her one day in study hall, however. "They were all at one table, talking and talking, until finally I said, 'That whole table over there will go to the principal's office right now.' " The boys looked at each other and in unison they picked up the study table and marched it out of the library.

Jim Brady went out for track all four years of high school. He played tennis and entered the Centralia Open Tennis Tournament, and won it. He was on the B squad football team his sophomore, junior, and senior years. During the summer of 1956 before his junior year, he was a lifeguard and swimming instructor at the Centralia Municipal Pool, earning $470. He was on the Southern Illinois District Swimming Team for the three years the team won the Southern Illinois championships, winning four firsts, five seconds, and three third-place ribbons. And Jim was on the cross-country team his last two years of high school.

Dorothy and Big Jim would go out to Foundation Park to watch him train. His favorite memory and perhaps his finest moment as an athlete came when he ran the cross-country as a senior, for which he earned a letter.

"Jim and I were probably both above average as athletes," says Jack Tyler. But that wasn't quite good enough. "Centralia had a very advanced and well-organized athletic program, and the natural athletes, not Jim or me, were picked out early for extra training and encouragement." "He was a better swimmer than anything else," says high-school friend Rod White, now the track coach at Centralia High School. "But," says Mick Scheriger, who starred at basketball, "in football Jim was a professional grass picker." His high-school coach, Jim Evers, always said, "Well, he wasn't very good, but he always showed up." Brady himself says, "I played end—end of the bench." Physical confrontation and contact sports weren't Jim's forte.

On the other hand, says Scheriger, "he has this unbelievable drive. He's tough, he's mean. I remember Brady's being hit in the face with a baseball and he hardly flinched as the blood spurted out." And when Scheriger saw the first footage of the shooting on March 30, 1981. "I recognized that old bald head of his when CBS flashed the first pictures on, but when they came on and said that Jim had died, I said, 'That isn't true.' I didn't believe it for a minute. He's too tough. I never once had the slightest doubt that he'd make it."

As for scholarship, "Jimmy got mostly As and Bs," says his mother. Although he was on the honor roll his sophomore year, he was too busy with all his activities to do that the next two years. A quick study, he had the facility for getting good grades with very little effort. That left him time to enter into all the extracurricular activities he loved and where he shone. The number of activities in which he was engaged was truly astonishing. He was on the school paper (*The Sphinx*), the Student Council Decorating Committee, the Student Council Facility and Clean-Up Committee; he was in the Pep Club all four years of high school, on the Class Fund-Raising Committee, and on the school annual (also called *The Sphinx*), into which Jim says they managed to slip: "It's not the school we don't like, it's the principal of the thing." In addition, he was in French Club, and in Pogo Club, which Jim and his friends founded. "We had a very gifted teacher of English literature in high school, Sarah Bush, who could really motivate you to want to read and learn," says Jim. "She had Pogo books and Pogo records and we had meetings of M.A.S.O.P.O.O. at her instigation (Mutual Admiration Society of Pogo of Okefenokee)." The credo of the club was "to develop, encourage, promote and enjoy a sense of humor; to foster and keep alive the ability to laugh at one's self as well as laugh with other human beings. To further advance the knowledge of Pogo's doings and find the deeper meaning of the Pogo stories of Walt Kelly."

And then there were the contests. Jim Brady was in contests in Centralia all his life, beginning when Dorothy Brady's good friend Ruth Sanders thought he was such a pretty child that he should be in a baby contest. Dorothy demurred but

Sanders entered him anyway and he won. Later, in high school, he won prizes in the annual citywide Halloween window-painting contests—he took third prize in the Voice of Democracy contest and third in a VFW essay contest. They were all chronicled in the *Centralia Sentinel* and for most of them he received a small stipend. In one of his many mentions in the *Sentinel* it was announced—"Jim Brady having won first place in the Halloween picture contest now has a window decorating job at the Smart Shop for the Christmas season." "I had a good press agent," says Jim. "Mother would come with all these entry forms—she was as bad as Brooke Shields's mother—and say, 'Here, enter this, dummy.' "

In 1958, his senior year, Jim entered the Youth Leadership Contest sponsored by the Benevolent and Protective Order of Elks. For this contest he submitted a lengthy documentation of his activities and accomplishments, and included letters from several adults who had known him all his life.

Superintendent of Recreation Howard Cooksey wrote that Jim always volunteered to "help me organize the activities for his age group and has since childhood." Former Centralia mayor O. W. Wright said Jim was "so outstanding in all his actions and attitudes . . . and personality, likeableness and general worthwhileness."

And Father Barry Jones wrote, "He is one of the most amazing and mature young men I have ever met. He has the talent, the personality, the moral judgment, the enthusiasm and the ability to command humbly."

Dorothy enclosed her own letter in Jim's application; it perhaps described her son better than all the rest. "I would say we are an average American family," she began, and after briefly describing Jim's activities and interests, ended the letter by saying, "Jim likes people and that is what makes him a good leader." Jim won the boys' division of the Youth Leadership Contest of the South District of Illinois, which carried a prize of $200, and then went on to win the boys' division of the Illinois State Contest and its prize of $500.

Rod White remembers, "You'd go over to his house and he'd be in his room listening to classical music. He read political books and books on philosophy. He spoke two or three languages." (Not really, but it may have seemed so. Asked if he took French in college, Jim said, "No, it took me.") White remembers that Jim had started playing chess. "He could converse on any intellectual matter under the sun. I wasn't surprised when he was named press secretary, and it wouldn't have surprised me if he became president. There aren't many teenagers then or now who can handle adults and adult matters as well as he could. He could be as comfortable talking to the lowest hick in town, or to the president of the United States.

Jim doesn't claim quite so much for himself, however. "I was a partial wiener [his term for a goof-off-cum-smart-aleck]—I didn't always mind my parents," he says, meaning it as an understatement. Looking back on his high-school days he allows as how "humility and I were not on a first-name basis," and he believes he suffered a little from a swelled head—a problem, he would soon find, that people at the University of Illinois would be more than willing to help him correct.

"Jim was a super guy," says Jack Tyler. "He was a little more thoughtful than the rest of us, though. He was funny, yes; but not a clown or anything. We just told jokes on each other, that sort of thing. We were all really nice kids. We didn't pull any dirty tricks on anybody. You can't get into too much trouble in a town like Centralia because everybody knows who you are. I have often said if everybody grew up in a town like Centralia, the country would be in much better shape."

Jim was popular with the girls in high school. He had girls as friends, and girlfriends. And he and Scheriger tried looking for romantic adventure in Centralia's outlying suburbs and smaller towns nearby. Asked if he got serious with anybody, Jim says, "I got as serious as I wanted to get." "There was nothing un-American about him in that respect," adds Scheriger.

JoAnn Bain says, "I did go out with Jim, not as an official date, strictly as friends, and I felt no pressure from him. It was just to have a good time." Years later, Bain teased him, "Jim, you have kissed me more since I've been married than you did all through high school." Bain's middle name was Charlotte, a name she hated. So Jim tried to use it as much as possible. When she visited Jim in the hospital he greeted her, "Hi there, Charlotte."

"Jim was always at the church youth group on Wednesday nights," says Bain. "Well," says Jim, "I was president of CYO one year, and when you're president, the priest drops by your house to pick you up and says, 'Your flock awaits you,' so you go. Those of sufficient patriotism could go down to the Lady of Perpetual Health novena first. Afterward, we danced, played pool, shot baskets" in the Knights of Columbus Hall.

Rod White says that "Jim probably had more black friends than any of the rest of us." The Brady house on North Maple was just a few blocks from "North Town" (as whites call it, or "The Ville" as blacks now call it), one of the two black living areas in Centralia, where the town's housing projects are located. Jim always brought his friends home, including his black friends. "When he was in high school he liked to go to Lonnie's Place in North Town," says White, "to have what I suppose you'd call soul food—ribs, fried chicken. He had no prejudices and no inhibitions either."

Along with school activities and sports Jim was always pursuing other projects, many of them to earn more merit badges. He was an Explorer Scout now, working toward new goals. As a freshman he and a friend built plywood figures of the Nativity for his parents to display at Christmas, and display them they did for many years. That same year he and other Explorer Scouts, for the second time, took over the city government for Citizenship Day. It was all duly noted in the *Sentinel* and Honorary Finance Commissioner James Brady was quoted as saying rather grandly, "I think Mr. Besant [Centralia's Finance Commissioner] has civic improvement in mind, but I think it would be a hindrance not to help the airport. The field is not in good enough shape yet, but it would be a boon to the community if it was large enough for a commercial airline. And if the money will be borrowed on a self-liquidating basis, it's not hurting the taxpayer, so why not go ahead?" The same spring, on April 12, 1955, Jim, at age fourteen, became an Eagle Scout, a not inconsiderable accomplishment—only 2.5 percent of scouts achieve that rank.

In the summer of 1955, before his sophomore year, Jim spent nine weeks in nearby Salem, teaching Indian dances to Scout leaders, "so they in turn could teach their groups," he says. And at the end of that summer, Jim studied for a week at the Lake Villa School of Conservation on Fox Lake, north of Chicago. Dorothy had entreated the Illinois Department of Conservation to allow him to attend, even though policy dictated that students attending be of junior or senior standing. But he was also recommended to the school by the Marion County superintendent of schools, and was sponsored by Ferrin Elevator of Ferrin, Illinois. As a result he won a merit badge for conservation. "I was going for the big quinella [Eagle Scout]," says Jim. "I really wanted it, and I enjoyed doing it."

When he returned after a week's course he gave a talk on his experience to the Optimist Club of Centralia—his first public speech. The *Sentinel* reported on the speech which covered all of the topics he had studied at Lake Villa. "Brady closed by saying, 'It took one thousand years for nature to produce one inch of topsoil,' and he asked the members to do their part in conservation."

Added to everything else, Jim often helped Dorothy with her Republican political projects, stuffing envelopes or whatever was needed. "I'd come over," says Jack Tyler, "and they would have pamphlets and stuff spread all over. Jim enjoyed working with his mom.

"Dorothy seemed to be a strong person," Tyler adds, "and had high aspirations for Jim. And Jim was just a little bit different from the rest of us. It was clear he wanted experiences beyond Centralia. I always thought he'd be in law or politics."

In the spring, Jim, once again the only sophomore among juniors and seniors and, this time, college students, journeyed to Washington, D.C., for the Cherry Blossom Festival. It was a program begun by Centralia High School history teacher Charlotte Spurlin, and the students were carefully chosen for the trip.

Jim Brady turned sixteen the summer of 1956 before his junior year. He had been working at the municipal pool all summer, partly so that when he turned sixteen he could buy his first car. It was an old Chevy he picked up for sixty-five dollars, and not a fine specimen, either. It spent most of the time in the Brady garage. While working at the pool that summer he entered a tennis tournament in City Park and won a medal for singles in his age class.

Jim's junior year was as full of activities as ever. There was, of course, the Explorer Scouts where he was now den chief. And, in school, he was chairman of the Constitution Committee, chairman of the Junior-Senior Prom Decorating Committee, president of French I. There was the annual and the school paper, for which he mostly covered sports. He went out for football in the fall and track in the spring. At church he was captain of the Church League basketball team. He was also president of the Knights of Columbus Organization at St. Mary's. Throughout the year he and Jack Tyler put on Indian dances for "Blue and Gold" Scout banquets in Centralia and surrounding towns.

At Christmastime Jim was pictured in *The Sphinx* helping decorate the school Christmas tree. He was wearing his white letter sweater.

With his Chevy dead in his parents' garage, that spring Jim bought a 1931 Model A Ford. He had big dreams for this car and first he put a 1948 Ford V-8 engine in it. Then he tried to remodel it into a convertible by cutting the top off it. Dorothy warned him that would ruin it, which it did, and it was ultimately sold for junk. "Everybody kept cutting their hands on it getting in and out," says Jim.

In July Jim began work as a volunteer, collecting data for the International Geophysical Year, which ran from July 1957 to July 1958. He subscribed to *Sky & Telescope* and had read about the need for volunteers. A year earlier his parents had given him a telescope for Christmas, a Unitron 2.4 Refractor. It was something he had wanted since he was ten when he first became interested in astronomy. As a sophomore he joined an astronomy class at Kaskaskia Junior College for field trips. In a writeup in *The Sphinx,* headlined MAN OF MARS SHOOTS STARS AND BITES THE MILKY WAY, it was noted that Jim was working in cooperation with Dr. C. W. Gartlein of Cornell University: "Jim is participating in the aurora and air glow program, in which he sends special reports to the aurora data center in New York. The most interesting things Jim has seen through his telescope are the ring nebula in Lyra, Jupiter and four of its moons, the rings of Saturn, and the phases of Jupiter (and the screw on Mickey Scheriger's television antenna)."

In an article in the *Sentinel* (complete with a picture of Jim and his telescope), he was quoted as saying, "When you get interested in it, it grows on you, kind of like a fever. You want to know more." And, indeed, he would take a night class in astronomy at the junior college in the fall of his senior year.

But, first, that summer of 1957 was to hold Jim's biggest

adventure to date. He had been accepted as a junior counselor at Camp Foley, a Catholic boys' camp in Pine River, Minnesota. Once again the rules were waived and he was allowed to go at age sixteen instead of seventeen (his seventeenth birthday would come at the end of August). He packed up his telescope, his sky charts, and several huge boxes of Indian costumes. He would teach Indian lore and nature at the nine-week session of Camp Foley.

It was while he was there that Jim discovered he loved cooking and eating. "While everyone else was out trying to climb a mountain, we were back in camp trying to cook beef Wellington in a reflector oven. I thought, if you can make things taste this good out here, what could you do in a kitchen? That's when I began to seriously think about 'chefifying.' " Aunt Louise remembers when Jim started to cook at home that fall. "He'd go up the alley to Dipert's store for provisions, and when Dorothy came home from work her kitchen would be a solitary mess."

Jim started working on a chili recipe in college, which he ultimately named Goat Gap Chili. According to Bill Crain, a neighbor and friend who is a gourmet cook and gourmand himself, "The original Jim Brady Chili was functionally inedible—it was so hot. Most people don't cook because there's always the possibility of there being a disaster. If Jim had a disaster—fine! Great, in fact! It was all part of the fun."

In 1980, during his last visit to Centralia before the shooting, Jim took Betsey Kourdouvelis to O'Neill's Place, a black tavern, and on the menu, she says, "we see snoot. What is snoot? Bring us an order of snoot. We want snoot." Jim didn't tell Betsey until fork was to mouth that "snoot" was pig's nose—a cut of meat the idea of which was a bit more than she could handle and she dropped her fork to the table. "Jim would hold court in those situations," says Bill Crain. "It was always fun to watch him with Betsey."

Dorothy had a surprise waiting for Jim when he came home from Camp Foley that summer. She had bought him another car, one that worked. That fall as a senior Jim organized and was vice-president of a hot-rod club, the Pumas. The entire club was pictured in the *Sentinel* along with Chief of Police L. C. Peters, who was elected an honorary member. "The Pumas," said the story, "are dedicated to safety and courtesy on the road. . . . Club meetings will all be held regularly at Jim Brady's home. . . ." "Everybody had a hot-rod club in those days," says Jim. "We had plates that hung under our license plates that had a puma on it."

In October Jim helped build a winning float for the annual Halloween parade. Over the years Halloween had become a celebration that involved the whole town.

Dorothy remembers the year she dipped dozens of apples in caramel, and in the process got it all over the cats and the beagle. Jim, today, still talks hopefully about getting back to Centralia for Halloween. The float he worked on his senior year had as its theme "Teen-Land" and was a typical scene out of the fifties. A nine-foot facsimile of the Dot-label record "Jailhouse Rock" by Elvis Presley, stood as a backdrop to a jukebox and dance floor beyond which was a soda-shop booth. Two couples danced to the jukebox while another couple sat with Cokes in the booth. Jim, of course, was one of the dancers. Jim says his dad latched on to the record title, saying "it was appropriate since that's where I'd be unless I hewed to the straight and narrow. He didn't let the logic of that event pass me by."

The previous year Jim had lobbied for a place for teens to gather and dance in the Community Center (they called it the Attic Club), then worked hard to raise a hundred dollars for a jukebox. When he reached his goal, the *Sentinel* pictured Jim Brady and Jeanne Cooksey presenting the money for it to Mayor O. W. Wright.

Jim began taking flying lessons at the Centralia Airport in the spring of his senior year. The lessons were a Christmas present from his parents, and as a treat for them, or so he thought, he arranged to fly them, accompanied by his instructor, to Chester, Illinois, for the ceremony of his winning the Elks Youth Leadership Contest. Big Jim and Dorothy were terrified but resolute in keeping that information from Jimmy. "I have a horror of small planes," says Dorothy. Big Jim sat silently chomping on his cigar with greater determination than usual, never uttering a word. The elder Bradys arranged for ground transportation for the trip back to Centralia, giving Jim vague excuses to save his feelings. A few weeks later Jim came bounding into the house, thrilled because he had soloed that day for the first time. And he had undergone the pilot's ritual of having his shirt ripped to shreds by his fellow students and other pilots. Dorothy recognized the torn shirt as the sign that he had soloed and was just grateful she had not known about it ahead of time.

CHAPTER FOUR

Champaign, Springfield, and Chicago

In his senior year at Centralia High, Jim applied to Georgetown University in Washington, D.C., as well as to the University of Illinois at Champaign-Urbana, about 135 miles from home. His dream was to go to the Edmund A. Walsh School of Foreign Service at Georgetown and to law school there as well. If he went to a Catholic college (Georgetown), his aunts, ever concerned about Jim's religious life, told him they would help him. But although he was accepted at Georgetown, the realities of the tuition (and not being sure he wanted to be an East Coast "stripey pants diplomat," as he puts it) forced his decision, and he went off to the University of Illinois in the fall of 1958. Also, Jim had won a Marion County academic scholarship, which paid his tuition, and the legislative scholarship from his county, too.

Before making his decision, Jim had talked to several attorneys in Centralia who advised him, he says, "that going to the state law school would hold me in good stead. I would know attorneys in all parts of Illinois, and know them well enough so I'd know which ones I could go up against and beat, and which ones to avoid."

It was a happy decision. Mick Scheriger, and other friends from Centralia were going too. One bonus Jim had was a railroad pass for travel to and from school, through Big Jim's position with the "Q." While Jim rode in style, on the *Panama Limited,* Scheriger pounded the highway in his vintage Chrysler. "One thing that always bugged me—just frosted me," says Scheriger, "was that he always got a free ride on the railroad, while I had to drive that highway with his clean or dirty clothes in the backseat."

As a freshman Jim pledged Sigma Chi, probably the most prestigious national fraternity. "The ideals of Sigma Chi were a very, very important part of Jim's life," says Scheriger. Ideals as basic as good manners, he said, but it was the loftier principles he had in mind. Scheriger joined Sigma Chi, too, a year later.

"It wasn't a sleep and eat club," says Jim. "It's a lifetime proposition. They are long on ideals and qualities." Jim felt he was in the right place. "They got the right man," he says.

They studied hard, worked hard, and played hard at Illinois. They hung out occasionally at a bar called Cam's Pharmacy where they were able to get their checks cashed. Scheriger's grandfather told him, "I want to see this pharmacy you've bought."

Throughout his undergraduate years Jim took a full load of courses for the degree in political science and communications he had set his sights on. As a freshman he was as attracted to a career in journalism as to one in politics until he learned how poorly it paid.

Schoolwork aside, Jim immediately plunged into a multitude of extracurricular activities. He played intramural football and joined the Dolphins, a swim team Jim describes as being as social as it was athletic. He was Chief Illiniwek's substitute for half times at Illini football games, although was never called upon to perform the dance except to amuse his friends. He was vice-president of the journalism fraternity, Sigma Delta Chi, and wrote for the satirical *College Tumor.*

He joined the Young Republican Club and was its president one year, and later a district governor. He was a member of the Illini Union and its president in his junior year, and he joined the Conservative Club. In his senior year he received the Sachem Award for his extracurricular contributions and the Taft Young Republican award. His energy and high achieving drive hadn't slowed a bit.

Every now and then on a Friday night he and Scheriger would drive thirty miles east to Danville to pay their respects to Lil's Jockey Club and other honky-tonk and topless dives. Scheriger, after a spree in Danville one night, woke Jim up at the fraternity house and pulled an old canard. "Jim, Jim," he said excitedly. "There's a drunk in the dorm!"

"Who, Mick, who?"

"It's me, Jim, it's me."

"When Mick did that," says Jim, "there was nothing to do but throw his mattress out the window. Then, as he was out on the lawn picking it up, we called out sweetly, 'Oh, Mick.' He looked up and we threw a garbage can full of whoop-de-doop ice-cold water on him." Brady loves that memory, particularly of Scheriger looking up innocently at the sound of his name.

Dick Church, a high-school senior from Catlin, Illinois, whose path was destined to cross Jim Brady's several years later, remembers meeting Jim on a pre-pledge tour of the Sigma Chi house. "This is my beatnik roommate," said Dan Taylor as they went into Jim's room. Jim had a basement room in the new section of the house, a special plum because, says Church, "those rooms had ground-level windows and you could get your date in and out of the house easily." (In the early sixties, girls were not allowed in fraternity houses.) "Jim was stretched out facedown on a small mattress in the middle of the floor," remembers Church. "A few minutes later he stirred to life and put on some godawful-looking jean cutoffs and a T-shirt." Jim rambled around the room, then indulged himself in a little bravado and proceeded to tell the story of his previous night's activities. "It seems he had attended a party at Kickapoo State Park and there was some sort of altercation, in the middle of which Jim said he broke a beer bottle over a picnic table and said, 'All right. Which one of you sonsabitches wants to be first.' " Jim Brady had caught eighteen-year-old Dick Church's attention. Church joined Sigma Chi that fall.

Jim had a number of part-time jobs while in college. "I did dishes," he says. "I was the houseboy at a girls' dorm. They would call me over to change the light bulbs or something like that, and then they had to search the house to be sure I was gone," he adds.

In communications class, Jim was required to have on-air

TV experience on the university station, WILL, and he drew the position as host of a Saturday morning TV children's show. Coming on as "Trader Jim," and dressed in a pith helmet and bush jacket, he conducted games, did magic tricks, and told stories "about being in the wilds of Africa," he says. It was a job Jim didn't tell his fraternity brothers about, and they might never have learned of it had not Centralia friend Kent Watkins gathered them all together one morning, saying, "Hey, let's tune in to Channel Three at eleven this morning."

When the frat house tuned in, of course, there was Trader Jim. "We hung a 'Welcome Home, Trader Jim,' sign across the Sigma Chi house," said Watkins. "He was chagrined and embarrassed, but not angry at all."

Jim denies that. "Watkins made sure that my Saturday morning slot was well advertised. He told all the girls, 'Have you seen Trader Jim's new show?' It didn't help my image."

Kent Watkins, who was four years older than Jim, had moved to Centralia with his parents when Kent was in college. He first met Dorothy Brady through his political activity, but several years later, when he returned to Centralia to work for the largest employer, Lear Siegler, he and Jim became good friends. At one point Jim and Watkins toyed with the idea of starting a diaper service. It was going to be "Tops for Bottoms," and they were going to get a loan from the Small Business Administration. Watkins sometimes drove to Champaign for the weekend and double dated with Jim and the beautiful girl Jim had met in his junior year, Sue Beh. "Jim and I would at times sit around and talk about how we wanted to marry the right woman," says Watkins. (Dorothy Brady, meanwhile, had gone back to school in social work. "She'd get all As and we would kid her about it," says Watkins.)

Sue Beh was a Kappa Kappa Gamma and Inter-Fraternity Queen one year. "She was stunning," says Watkins, "the center of attention wherever she was. She was the epitome of the all-American girl—cashmere sweaters and social graces." And Jim had fallen head over heels in love with her.

"Jim was chairman of the Illini Union publicity committee," says Sue, "and I signed up to work on it. We met that way. He loved to party, told lots of jokes, and was the center of attention at any party. He asked me to wear his pin."

They were married on campus in the winter of 1961, during

Jim's senior year. But the difficulties of married student life began to overtake them almost immediately—money, or the lack of it, being the most serious. In addition, Jim was president, or consul, of his fraternity elected in a last-minute campaign, says Mick Scheriger, who engineered the election, "because the other two guys running didn't fit into my program. I didn't want to get slapped with a fifteen-dollar fine if I came in at three A.M." He had several roles to juggle—husband, father, student, president of Sigma Chi. He and Sue lived in a duplex nearby, where Jim was the maintenance man for the other units to defray their rent expenses.

In June 1962 Jim graduated with a bachelor of science degree in communications and a 3.8 grade-point average. "I was a student of fair ability with ambitious purposes," he says.

That summer Jim worked as a field representative for Senator Everett M. Dirksen, and he and Sue moved to Centralia to live with Dorothy and Big Jim. Dirksen, sixty-six, hired five or six college students as "promotion assistants" to manage parts of Illinois for the campaign for his third term in the Senate. It was largely through Dorothy's political connections that Jim got the job. "Each of us had three or four congressional districts to manage," says Brian Whelan, who was an undergraduate at Loyola. It was Brady, Whelan, Tom Corcoran, Perry Roberts, and Alan Drayzak, and they came to be known as The Group among Young Republican campaign workers. And they were out to change the world.

The job required a good deal of travel (Sue went with him when it was feasible) and "two or three of us would meet often for an exchange of war stories," says Whelan. "We had very little money," (a hundred dollars a week and expenses), and Jim had learned where all the good cheap restaurants were. I remember he touted a smorgasbord in Bloomington on Route Sixty-six, but warned us, 'Skip the Jell-O salads. Go right to the meat and potatoes.' "

"Jim loved working for Dirksen," says Dorothy Brady. She once fried up five chickens when The Group descended on Centralia one night. "Doesn't Dirksen pay you enough to eat?" she asked them.

"Jim was extremely smart and street-wise for his age," says

Whelan. When Dirksen at the last minute couldn't show up for a long-scheduled Republican dinner in Tazewell County (near Dirksen's own hometown of Pekin), Jim saw to it that someone else told that fact to the county chairman. "Jim was always adroit enough not to be the bearer of bad news." Jim remembers the poor soul to whom the task fell pointing into the air and saying, " 'S-S-Senator D-D-Dirksen is in that pl-pl-plane going over us right n-n-now,' " says Jim, "as if the people could get excited about hearing the sound of Dirksen's plane." Dirksen gave all the money back, Whelan adds. That same summer Jim also worked for the election of Bill Scott for Illinois attorney general. Both of his candidates won their elections.

"Jim was totally at ease with anybody. And he was a natural promoter," says Whelan. "He was always thinking. And he absolutely reveled in this opportunity he was given at age twenty-one. More than any of us Jim relished every aspect of the campaign, and the people involved in it. He is a total natural political animal." Describing his work that summer, Jim says, "We checked in with each county chairman to see what they needed and thought and what events Dirksen should attend and why, then wrote up reports which we sent to Louella [Mrs. Dirksen]. She knew more about what was going on in that campaign than anybody."

There were so many characters out there among the county chairmen and party people," says Perry Roberts. "It was a laugh a minute."

Roberts recalls one time in Alton, Illinois, "when I picked up the candidate, from Jim, I believe, and Dirksen, campaigning alone, had been to four chicken dinners and had eaten them all. He lay in the backseat of my car and moaned and groaned. Here I was, a nineteen-year-old college student and I thought a United States senator was about to die in my car." Dirksen spent the night in the hospital and the news release mentioned "nervous stomach."

But the young men of the Group all thought Dirksen was "just great," says Roberts. "He was never out of character, and his voice (described once as mellifluous) never changed from morning to night." At one stop they had him standing on a manure spreader to speak to the crowd. "Here I am, a Republican, standing on a Democratic platform," Dirksen intoned. Senator Dirksen had been minority leader of the Senate since

1959 and was a national figure with his pompadour of gray curls and his famous voice.

Roberts swears it was Brady who planned an appearance in Harrisburg, Illinois, which had Dirksen standing on one side of the highway delivering a speech to a crowd on the other side. "And the cars and trucks were whizzing back and forth between them," laughs Roberts. "Hell, we've done worse than that," says Brady.

Jim remembers that Dirksen had trouble recognizing any but his closest staff members. "If he remembered who you were, which was rare, he didn't remember what your function was. I closed down a press conference once, saying, 'The senator has time for just one more question.' And Dirksen in his slow, majestic voice said, 'My pilot says I have to be going now.' "

"If I'm your pilot, Senator, you're in trouble," Jim told him.

"We had a pool every morning on how many times you'd meet him that day," says Jim. "We'd be in a shopping center with him and he'd come and shake your hand and say, 'Hi. I'm Everett McKinley Dirksen, your senior senator from Illinois.' And we'd say, 'I'm Jim Brady—or Brian Whelan—or whoever—and I'm on your staff, Senator.' He'd apologize, 'Oh, Jim, I'm sorry. I just meet so many people,' but it didn't even slow him down," says Jim. "He'd do it all over again on the next stop."

Such are the funny memories of that campaign, but there was respect, too, for what they considered Dirksen's statesmanship. Perry Roberts says, "In 1962, Dirksen was talking prophetically about what he called 'Vet Nam,' saying we were getting into trouble there. We shouldn't be sending in all these advisers, and that the Kennedy administration was handling it all wrong."*

Dirksen's opponent was U.S. Representative Sidney Yates, who put up an impressive fight. Jim says that Dirksen's back was close enough to the wall that he felt it necessary to announce that " 'religion never has been and never will be an issue in this campaign,' to alert people," says Jim, "in case they didn't already know that Yates was Jewish."

*Dirksen died in 1969 at the age of seventy-three. Speaker of the Illinois House Ralph Tyler Smith was named to fill his post until the election of 1970 when Smith lost the seat to Democrat Adlai E. Stevenson III.

Jim was a leading member of the group of Republican student activists who were constantly involved in campaigns. "We all did it," says Susan Bryant, a Knox College student and Republican volunteer. "We just barely went to class—then went out to the campaign office. We worked nights and weekends. Looking back on it, we were nuts. There's never been another bunch like us. We were special."

One thing they all learned during that campaign was that they and their friends in the Illinois Young Republican College Federation were all willing and able to work a lot harder for Republican victories than their older, more established counterparts in the Illinois Young Republican Clubs.

"Jim became one of two or three forces that transcended their local bases—their own home districts," says Whelan. "He became a minor celebrity in statewide Republican politics; probably knew more people than any senior Republican officials. Not only knew them. He knew their stories and where their skeletons were hiding."

Whelan could never tell just what Jim's personal political views were. "When I first knew him I'd say he was a moderate conservative. At the University of Illinois he was a member of the Conservative Club. But Jim is so pragmatic. I never knew that much about his views. He wasn't one to talk political philosophy. He was always absorbed in practical considerations. He was a doer. He wouldn't let ideology get in the way of the goal."

If he had to guess, Whelan says, "Jim is a typical Illinois Republican. He came from a Republican family. He's a Robert Taft Republican—just right of center politically."

In the fall Jim entered law school as planned, and soon after, on October 17, Sue and Jim had a baby girl, Melissa Jane, a beautiful child whom they loved and enjoyed. "She was the most adorable little baby," says Sue, "with dark brown eyes and dark hair."

That spring, says Mick Scheriger, "Brady and I spent a night in jail together. It was a Sunday, and at one o'clock in the morning Brady called, woke me up, and said, 'Would you help me move?' "

Jim says, "I was taking a mattress down from Sue's house in Evanston for our house."

"We finished setting up the bedroom at five in the morning," says Scheriger, "walked outside and there were cop cars all around."

"They took us about ten blocks to a woman who said, 'Yeah, that's the one,'" says Jim. "She accused us of running through her yard at night. Not that I'm above that but we didn't do it. I told 'em I was working for Dirksen and was just moving a mattress. And Scheriger was talking fast but not getting anywhere. The cops said, 'Book 'em.'"

Jim and Scheriger got one of their fraternity brothers to bring bail money, "but there was only enough for one, so I had to sit there all night," says Scheriger. "To this day I have a criminal record and I still don't know what the crime was."

As for Jim, he says, "I have since had it expunged from my record."

Jim had told Scheriger, "Don't tell 'em anything or they'll never let you out. Keep something back as a bargaining tool."

The next summer, Jim applied to be a summer intern in the Antitrust Division of Robert F. Kennedy's Justice Department. Just a few law students out of several thousand from all over the country were chosen, and he, sponsored by Everett Dirksen, was among them—working for "The Brothah," as Jim puts it, mimicking the Kennedy accent. He moved to Washington for the summer and lived with Kent and Linda Watkins. "In a closet," says Watkins, "where he threw a mattress on the floor." Later, when Sue and baby Missy came out to be with Jim, they moved to a small apartment on Capitol Hill. "Missy was a campaign baby," says Jim. "We'd take her over to Dirksen's office and she'd reach up and wool his hair all up." "Why, Missy," Dirksen would say. Jim told friends they were so poor that summer he and Sue picked up returnable pop bottles to get enough money to squeeze by on. He also sold encyclopedias door to door in suburban Virginia. "Our group wrote a book that summer on antitrust law from 1956 to 1962," says Jim, "for the Commerce Clearing House."

Kent Watkins had moved to Washington to be legislative assistant to Democratic Majority Leader Carl Hayden of Arizona. Hayden was eighty-five and failing noticeably. One day Brady and Watkins chanced to be in the same Senate elevator with their respective senators, and Dirksen was chatting pleasantly to Hayden. When Dirksen got out, Hayden turned to Kent and said, "Who was that nice young man?"

It was the summer of Martin Luther King's March on Washington, and Jim and Sue were there on the mall for those emotional ceremonies.

Back in Champaign-Urbana for his second year of law school, Jim's schedule began to overwhelm him. "Law is a jealous mistress," says Jim. And with his complicated life he wasn't able to give the law his all. "Being a young daddy and all the rest took its toll on the law school," he says. He dropped out of school and he and Sue moved to Centralia.

It was a low period for both of them. They didn't really want to be in Centralia at this point in their lives, Sue especially. They had left too much unfinished business out in the world. "It was like pulling your tail in, putting it between your legs and slinking back," says Jim. "As I recall, Sue would rather have eaten razor blades."

It was to be the first of many reverses in Jim's life. At the same time there was no doubt that Jim loved Centralia and southern Illinois. It was home and he was comfortable. He often talked as the years went by about moving back.

Through a friend of his parents Jim quickly got a job in the accounting department at Lear Siegler, Inc., manufacturers of heating and air-conditioning units. "Mother told me," says Jim in his wry way, "that Walter Ullman [president of Lear Siegler] would be extremely grateful if I went out and applied for a job."

"Accounting wasn't his bag and he had no training for it," says Scheriger.

In addition to his job, Jim hoped to use his law school credits to get a master's degree in public administration, and he enrolled in Southern Illinois University in Carbondale, just eighty miles south of Centralia. "He drove his little Cutlass down to Carbondale after work every day," says Dorothy. He also had the position of Teaching Fellow and happened to have Perry Roberts, a member of The Group from the Dirksen campaign in his constitutional-law class. "He was terrible," says Roberts. "I don't think his real concern was teaching. He was focused on Illinois politics and in class he advanced the more practical and political approaches and theories of the American system."

At the end of the quarter Jim knew the academic life wasn't for him. Besides, he had landed the job of managing the campaign of Wayne Jones, an attorney from Paris, Illinois, who was planning to run for the U.S. House of Representatives in "the old twenty-third," Jim's home district, which took in a large area of southern Illinois. Jones was taking a flyer at incumbent Democrat George Shipley who had first been elected in 1958 (and who would safely hold the seat until 1978 when ill health would force him to retire).* Now this was something Jim could sink his teeth into. He was hopelessly hooked on practical elective politics. And undaunted, Jim would involve himself in several tries with different candidates to unseat Shipley.

"Jim directed the field operation for Jones," says political activist Susan Bryant who volunteered in the Wayne Jones campaign. "Jim was married, which made him different from every body else. He dealt with the county chairmen and all the party people working at the grass-roots level. And he also kept tabs on all the Young Republican organizations all over the Twenty-third District."

In 1964, she says, "out of thirteen hundred students at Knox College, eleven hundred belonged to the college Young Republicans. It was an accepted organization for idealistic people who really believed this was the place to get training for a future in political careers. The organization was strong throughout the Midwest in those years." It was conservative Barry Goldwater and his run for the presidency who was inspiring this perfervid participation in national politics.

"At Knox they were extremely conservative. But they had a problem with me. I wasn't going to sell the post office or the national parks; therefore, I established my credentials as being crazy (in their minds), but I became important enough they had to pay attention to me." One year later Bryant was president of the club. "Also, I was female. They didn't know how to cut deals with females.

"Jim Brady was an alumnus of the University of Illinois, which was believed to be a communist school by people at Knox College." She says, "Being from Centralia, Jim should have been a male chauvinist pig, but he is one of the most liberated men I've ever met. He is just fabulous. It never

*In 1972, the twenty-third District was redistricted and in 1982 its number was eliminated altogether when Illinois was reduced to twenty-two districts.

dawned on him that being female should make you less competent. He likes women—loves women—but his relationship to me was that of big brother."

Meanwhile, Jim had helped Sue Brady find a job in the Department of Public Aid, working with the county's hard-core poverty cases. But the bottom was falling out of their marriage. That spring after a fight, Sue left Centralia abruptly, with Missy, and she did not return. "Jim took it very hard," says Brian Whelan. "I've never seen him as troubled. But I never heard him speak ill of Sue. I didn't know what their problems were, but Jim probably wanted to be a politician and on the go, and didn't really want to stay home."

Talking about it today, Jim sings a phrase from *Camelot*—"If ever she would leave me, how could it be in springtime?" "But she did," he finishes. "I think Sue thought he ought to grow up and get out of politics," says political friend Don Udstuen. "But we loved our politics! The idea that we'd get paid for it was an afterthought." "We were politicians first, before anything else," confirms Jim.

"Our problem," says Sue, "was that we were very young, and we didn't know how to communicate with each other."

"After Sue left," says Scheriger, "Jim had a real hard year. I know because he started smoking cigarettes."

For the Jones campaign, Jim recruited Perry Roberts from The Group, Don Udstuen, and Jack Schaeffer. Brady, Roberts, and Schaeffer were all from the Twenty-third District and they had all worked in Dirksen's 1962 campaign, and Udstuen had worked as a volunteer. Jim snatched Roberts from another, nearby congressional campaign when it "became clear," says Roberts, "that my candidate was a major loser."

"Come on up here and help us," Jim told him. "We've got a winner here." "He took me to the Centralia House," says Roberts, "filled me with good food and Manhattans. Then he broke it to me how I was going to live for the next few months."

Jim's grand plan was that the four of them would all live together in his apartment in Centralia. "We lived there for the entire campaign," says Roberts, "and earned a hundred dollars a week, plus expenses." (Jim, as manager, earned more.) "We would shoot out in all directions for three or four days," says Don Udstuen, "going to county fairs, talking to county chairmen and other party people, then meet back in Centralia for a couple of days. Then we'd shoot out again in different directions. It was a very big congressional district."

Their candidate, Wayne Jones, was "a high-quality guy with high standards," says Roberts. "But it wasn't to be. It was 1964 and Republicans got killed everywhere." "It was Jones's first and last contact with politics," says Udstuen.

"But it was a very well run campaign," says Roberts. "There were no bases left untouched. And it was well financed. Jim loved to work with the media, going into TV stations and newspaper offices. He was good at it. He liked the flashy stuff—the big stories and the big guys. He had very little regard for Republican organizations as such. He felt they were going to do their own thing regardless of our needs and he felt he could make some major accomplishments through the media."

The summer of 1964 was an especially hot one in southern Illinois, and the ninety and hundred degree temperatures put an extra strain on the living arrangement in the apartment. "There was only one air conditioner and it was in the bedroom," says Udstuen. "There were two twin beds in there and Jim got one, of course. The first man to get there got the other one. The two of us who were trying to sleep in the living room lay awake hoping the guy in the other bed would go to the bathroom so one of us could grab it away from him."

Throughout the summer and fall, it was evident that Jim was suffering over the breakup of his marriage, says Roberts. "He was a nervous wreck."

The Wayne Jones campaign attracted TV celebrities Fess Parker and James Drury. Parker presented special challenges. "He would only ride one kind of horse, an Appaloosa" says Jim, "and he was a vegetarian, so we had to provide nuts and berries and fruits and such."

"The only decent meals we got that summer were the ones Mrs. Brady cooked," says Don Udstuen. "We were always so delighted to get an invitation from her. The rest of the time it was just hamburgers."

Udstuen noted that Brady liked to live well although he didn't have much money. "He always owed people money. And he would charge things, then get this stack of bills which seemed to surprise him and which he always was late in paying. But that's just Jim. It was like it was beneath him to respond to bills."

"From time to time we all had to go to Chicago," says Roberts. "Jim was notorious for registering himself for a room with two double beds to save money. To cut down on luggage, he'd make us all pack our stuff in his attaché case—one shirt apiece.

"He was very good at cutting back on expenses in the big city, but not so good at cutting back in the district. He searched out the finest dinners, and good entertainment, most of which was to be found at various roadhouses. From time to time, yes, we even found time to pursue people of the female persuasion," says Roberts.

But all the hard work of this merry little band couldn't overcome the fact that 1964 "was the worst year in the Republican party," says Udstuen. "We were all devastated at the size of the defeat. We thought we'd all be able to get on some other Republican's staff but they *all* lost. It was a damn good thing we were all young."

While running Jones's campaign, Jim and the others were also promoting the entire Republican ticket, from Barry Goldwater for president to Charles Percy for governor and on down. And in July Jim went to San Francisco for the Republican convention. "When I heard Goldwater say," Jim says, " 'Extremism in the defense of liberty is no vice' I said to myself, 'We're goners—that's it.' " The Goldwater campaign adopted the slogan "In your heart you know he's right," but, says Brady, moderate Republican operatives were muttering gloomily and crudely to each other, "In your butt, you know he's a nut."

"But we gave Shipley a hell of a run," says Jim. Shipley acknowledged that to him once, he says. "Every time I turned around there was that damned campaign car of yours," Shipley told him.

They were all down and out and to top it all off, Jim lost the lease on the apartment for nonpayment of rent. Completely dispirited they wanted to go their separate ways, but they were all dead broke. Brady and Roberts and Udstuen moved to the tiny, unheated rustic cabin on Raccoon Lake that Brady and Roberts were buying together. There they pondered their bleak futures. "It was a badge of honor to be out of work and beaten," says Jim.

After a month of pondering and eating beans out of cans, Udstuen left them to live with ex-candidate Wayne Jones for a while, and they were joined by another out-of-work political compatriot, Mike Mehan, and soon, they formed the PR firm of Brady, Roberts, and Mehan. "I was the breadwinner for this enterprise," says Roberts. "I went to work for the local radio station while Brady and Mehan went around philosophizing and figuring out what this magnificent PR firm was going to do." Roberts, Schaeffer, and Udstuen all went back to college in January. And Jim went back to work for Lear Siegler, this time as assistant to the president.

"I prepared talking papers for President Siegler," says Jim, "and did whatever else they asked me to do. Lear Siegler had companies all over the world and there was a constant need to communicate with them. The president and vice-president lived there in Centralia." Jim moved back home to save money, where, Dorothy says, "he'd often cook up batches of stuff for the three of us."

Kent Watkins saw Jim whenever he came to visit his parents during those two and a half years Jim was in Centralia. "He was always fun, always perceptive. We'd go see Willie Joy* and talk about what we were going to do in life." Kent's impression of Jim at that point was that "on a continuum of intellectualism at one end and the macho, social fraternity gung-hoism on the other, Jim was heavy on the latter end. We decided to get into the Elks so we could stop into Elks Clubs around the county if we ever ran for office. We got Jim's dad to sign for us.

"I never heard Jim talking about ideas or intellectualizing," says Watkins. "He might throw out the names Sartre or Heidegger, and enjoyed juxtaposing different phrases. He could tie things together and make a witticism about them as opposed to making an analytical statement about them. He wasn't a reader; he was a listener and a talker—a product of the TV generation. He was really up on pop culture. And at that point I think he accepted the ideology of the YRs."

Politics remained Jim's abiding interest. "It was a passion he inherited from his mother," says Watkins. "Although I harangued him about finishing law school—to his annoyance. But I think he just hadn't been raised in a law-school type family."

Jim continued to be as heavily involved in Illinois politics

*The publisher of Centralia's newspaper, the *Centralia Sentinel*

as ever and in the off year 1965 The Group made their first serious try to take over the leadership of the state's Young Republicans. Frustrated with his attempts to get good volunteer help from the older established Young Republicans in 1964, Jim joined Brian Whelan and his other college YR colleagues in the attempt. "The organization had grown tired and wasn't doing the campaign work people thought it should," says Whelan. Many members had left in disgrace or disgust after the 1964 Goldwater debacle. As the Group expanded and gathered other enthusiasts around them, they began calling themselves, and being called, the Syndicate. They believed it was their hard work and organization that was making a difference in Illinois politics and not the YRs. So during election years they worked strenuously to elect Republicans and during the off years they collaborated on taking over the Illinois YRs. "Jim was the principal downstate person involved," says Brian Whelan.

By 1966 Susan Bryant was working statewide for a number of Republican congressional candidates as, of course, was Jim. "Jim took me under his wing as he did many people," says Bryant. "We met any number of times in somebody's backyard, where Jim would bring us up to date as to what we should be doing. Jim was the kingpin among college YRs. Every now and then he'd tell his secretary, 'Call Susan. Let's get together and have a little steak and see how she's doing.' In the northern part of the district it was my parents who fed us and in the southern part it was Dorothy."

Although Jim took on the management of yet another doomed go at Congressman Shipley in 1966, with the campaign of candidate Les Jones, this time he didn't quit his job. Nor did he see the election through. "It was a hopeless cause and Jim didn't stay with it very long," says Don Udstuen.

Jim, as usual, was working for the full slate of Illinois Republican candidates and there was one big winner that year. Having lost his bid for the governorship in 1964, Charles Percy ran for the U.S. Senate and defeated Democratic Senator Paul Douglas.

"Brady was involved in the Percy campaign, too," says Scheriger. "He conned me into voting for Percy. And I've never forgiven him."

"I still don't like him," he told Brady several years later.

"Yeah, but now he doesn't need you," Brady replied.*

Another candidate Jim helped that year was Thomas F. "Tom" Railsback who was elected to his first term in the U.S. House of Representatives.

The Vietnam war was raging furiously in Southeast Asia, and before he turned twenty-six that year, Jim was called by his draft board for his physical. But "they didn't want me," says Jim, "because I had asthma." His view of the war at that time was "We were in there, let's try to win it."

Jim didn't see Les Jones's campaign through, mainly because he had been touted on to the job of handling public relations for the Illinois Medical Society by Cliff Raber, who was leaving the job. And Jim was ready to leave Centralia. He moved to Chicago (where Missy and Sue lived also) and began his career in public relations—as director of legislative and public affairs for the medical society. "Missy's being in Chicago was a big plus," says Jim. He would divide his time between Chicago and Springfield, the state capital—"Springpatch," he and his cohorts called it. Many of his old friends in politics had by now caught on with Richard Ogilvie, who, having been sheriff of Cook County (Greater Chicago), had run successfully for president of the Cook County Board of Supervisors—a very powerful position in Illinois.

"It was Jim's first real job," says Don Udstuen, "with a good salary and an expense account. He did really well, having a gift of gab second to none. With the advent of Medicare and the other socioeconomic issues that increasingly affect doctors," adds Udstuen, "they found themselves becoming a special-interest group. They had to hire people like Jim who know how to stay on top of and handle the issues."

Jim moved to an apartment in one of the round twin towers of Marina City in the heart of downtown Chicago. Marina City was a haven for young, upwardly mobile professionals. Jim was plunging into big-city bachelorhood with a flourish.

He spent that fall in Chicago learning his new job. "They sent me throughout the state to meet the heads of the various medical groups," says Jim. And beginning in January 1967 he spent four days a week in Springfield during the legislative session, which ran from January 1 to June 30, going home to

*Percy was reelected in 1972 and 1978, but was defeated in his bid for a fourth term in 1984.

Chicago on the weekends. In Springfield Jim used the modest bedroom and bath attached to the medical society's office.

"I wrote their newsletter and had their legislation introduced," says Jim. "I was active in keeping the chiropractors out of their knickers. The head of the Health Committee was a chiropractor, and he'd load up a bill and send it through. If I couldn't kill it in the House, I'd kill it in the Senate." Fellow University of Illinoisian Marion Brown "B" Oglesby was House Speaker Ralph Taylor Smith's* executive assistant and they worked together. "We had a series of telephone signals set up to signal if a bill was coming up. If I couldn't derail it, I'd fatally amend it, saying that all chiropractors had to wear green hats or something."

Tom Railsback, who was elected to the Illinois legislature in 1962 and 1964 from Moline on the western edge of Illinois, describes what life was like in Springfield during the six-month legislative session. "You would be in Springfield for two or three nights a week, often two or three of us would room together, and go home from Thursday to Monday. It was like a fraternity. The legislators, the news media, and the lobbyists formed kind of a community. You would work together and you would 'recreate' together. You might fight a lot of battles and be on opposite sides, but after work when you'd go out to eat together, the party lines blurred.

"I met Jim in 1966 when I was running for Congress and he was extremely helpful to me. He introduced me to the public-affairs people—the political people—in the big corporations, some of whom contributed a great deal of money to my campaign. Jim knew all of them. He is very bright and quick on the uptake. He's got a twinkle in his eye; he's just a lot of fun, and a very warm guy."

Coincidentally, fellow Sigma Chi Dick Church, whom Jim had met briefly, now newly married to Jerilyn "Jeri" Howell, had moved to Springfield and was working for the telephone company as a marketing representative, "which means," he says, "I sold telephones to businesses. I called on the Illinois Medical Society office and they told me they would have a new lobbyist in town during the legislative session named Jim Brady." Church left his business card and "Jim called us up and took us out to dinner. He was a walking party, you couldn't

*"Through him the majority speaks."

have bought better entertainment. Within three days of his arrival he knew everything about Springfield, knew all the legislators, all their stories, their nicknames, the right bars to go to, and the bars not to be seen in." One source of advice for Jim was another lobbyist (for Illinois Bell), "a real pro," says Church. "Norm Billington, appropriately nicknamed 'Tingaling.' Jim learned a lot from him."

Jim had a particular love for piano bars, and one of their favorite hangouts came to be the Boardroom, where the gimmick was that the closing figures of the stock market were up in lights behind the bar. "Jim knew all the Big Ten fight songs, all the piano-bar songs, and all the songs from all the Broadway musicals. And he had to sing them all. We frequently closed the place."

Jim, Dick, and Jeri became a threesome. The Churches often had Jim over to dinner. "I was just learning to cook," says Jeri. ("That's for sure," her husband interjects.) "We usually sat on the floor around the coffee table eating off my brand-new china." Soon college acquaintance "B" (a.k.a. "Beaver") Oglesby, who had been a Phi Delta Theta at Illinois, entered their orbit as well.

By chance, "B" Oglesby had worked for Illinois Bell prior to entering politics and his first job was in Centralia where he often encountered Big Jim Brady at the Green Grill. "He was a nice, friendly man—someone whom people obviously liked," says Oglesby. Oglesby is from nearby Flora, and as he and Jim got better acquainted they discovered they had many friends in common.

Dick Church visited Jim at his office one day and found him going through "this enormous stack of papers and receipts."

"Roger told me I had to do my expense account or he'd fire me," said Brady. It was Church's first glimpse of what would become one of Jim's trademarks. The famous Brady desk: always piled high with paper, phone messages, old newspapers, anything and everything, none of which he ever threw away. And he never wanted anyone to clean up his clutter. He claimed he knew exactly where everything was.

Church accompanied Jim on a trip to Washington, which provided further revelations. It was his first commercial airline flight and Jim told him, "Now you want to go to the rear of the plane because that's where the stewardesses are going to be."

Riding around Washington, says Church, "Jim'd have the cab stop a couple of blocks from our destination. He had memorized the boundaries where the fare changed." It was one of the economies he'd learned when he lived in Washington as an impoverished student and which, uncharacteristically, stuck.

It was this trip to Washington that was the genesis for an expense-account boondoggle "which still reverberates around Springfield," says Don Udstuen. "Jim took his medical-society clients out to dinner, and when it came time to order a bottle of wine he ordered one that cost four hundred dollars."

Jim began bringing dates along to the Churches'. "He always had some gal on the string," says Dick. "He would convince himself there was some legitimate purpose to this endeavor. That's how he'd justify his expense account to his boss, Roger White." Church remembers one date who, Brady claimed, was important because she set the headlines for a local newspaper. "There were also one or two girls whom he saw regularly and whom he cared about," says Dick. "I'm not sure he spent very many nights alone," he adds.

At his medical society room, the two secretaries, Gloria Evans and Betty Kararo, mothered him and took care of him, as did the Churches. And when he went home to Centralia or to Chicago, Evans and Kararo often cleaned up his apartment after him. "He looked after us, too, like we were his little mothers," says Evans.*

One winter weekend Jim and a girlfriend drove through a snowstorm from Chicago to visit the Churches. They got within thirty miles and called to say they couldn't make it any farther—news the Churches received dubiously; they arrived at noon the next day and over the course of the afternoon and evening, the four of them drank a memorable fourteen bottles of wine.

Dick and Jeri didn't realize in those early days just how wounded Jim had been by his separation from Sue. "It took me several years to figure out," says Dick, "that a lot of his quirks and his womanizing were directly related to having failed in his marriage. He had a tremendous need for acceptance."

At the same time Brian Whelan saw another side to the

*Evans is now Illinois Governor Jim Thompson's personal assistant. Kararo is in the legislative office of the state's Department of Transportation.

freewheeling, fun-loving Brady. "Jim is so extraordinarily complex, he is hard to analyze. He was known as someone who was glib and extremely talented. I really think he is also a deep person, not just a complex personality. As a young, newly separated bachelor living it up in downtown Chicago, totally immersed in his business, he sometimes took the time to stop in with me at Old St. Mary's Church at the south end of the Loop—to hear the Paulist choir. In fact, he and I thought of making a record of them we thought they were so spectacular. At the end of every Mass they sang 'The Star Spangled Banner.' "

"B" Oglesby says, "Jim could be moody, too, and quietly reflective. But even then he is comfortable to be around. Brady can fall asleep on the couch in front of you and you're not offended."

"Jim is puckish; he likes to stir the pot," says Bill Crain. "If a situation is scabbed over, he likes to pick it open. He has a power of concentration of about thirty or forty seconds."

With Jim there was always something brewing. That fall of 1967, he organized his Springfield friends—Dick and Jeri, Oglesby, and a few others—for an outing at the Covered Bridge Festival just across the border in Rockville, Indiana, one hundred fifty miles away. "When you were with Brady you were a participant in the event," says Oglesby. "Hell, we were working the crowd, "Hi, how are you,' introducing ourselves."

The Brady crowd made the rounds of the festival stands in the town square, and found persimmon ice cream, homemade sausage, "and they had big chunks of beef steaming in the ground (which wasn't all that good)," adds Oglesby. They also took note of what looked like a sorority house there that had the letters KKK on its portico, and "figured since it was Indiana, it must be 'the Klan sorority,' " says Oglesby.

Another time, Jim and Oglesby went out of their way to stop at the Elks Club in Paris, Illinois. "They had turnips in the steam table, and you don't get many turnips in Chicago," says Oglesby. "We stayed and ate turnips until we cleaned them out."

Jim was elected president of the Illinois Young Republicans one year. "The swearing-in took place in Decatur," says Dorothy, "and I took hors d'ouevres up for it." Jim saw all his political colleagues at Republican party events. "And we kept in touch regularly," says Udstuen, who succeeded Jim as lobbyist for the Illinois Medical Society. "Jim's apartment in Marina City was a gathering place for all of us. It was the most unneat apartment you could find." They all retreated to Jim's after the first year's Christmas party in Chicago, but Gloria Evans and Betty Kararo of the medical society made sure they got to Chicago early the next year so they could clean it up, "they'd been so embarrassed by it the year before."

"Jim continued to be really interested and involved in all of Illinois's political activities," says Brian Whelan, who by this time was working for Richard Ogilvie and living in Chicago. "By virtue of his job with the medical society, it meant he was instrumental in the largest political-action committee in the state. Jim Brady became a very important person to political candidates because he was holding the purse strings" to the large contributions the medical society was able to make.

Whelan had introduced Jim to Ogilvie, a talented moderate Republican who was now preparing to run for governor in 1968. And Jim began selling big-city Chicagoan Ogilvie to his own dubious downstaters. "It just shows how wise Jim is," says Whelan. "He saw Ogilvie as electable, and therefore promoted him downstate."

It was an off-election year again in 1967, and time to gear up for The Syndicate's biennial stab at wresting control of Illinois's YR Clubs away from their complacent caretakers. Susan Bryant says, "They wouldn't let us do anything. It was a lesson we learned—to let the young people in. They have more energy, they have ideals, and they'll get in anyway. Brady put together the YR Convention, and our faction won and took control. We would play a major role in Ogilvie's primary fight against John Henry Altorfer," says Bryant.

John Kolbe, a 1961 graduate of Northwestern University, joined them. "We were this group of radicals who were trying to keep the party out of the hands of all these 'dangerous' moderates," he says. "How serious we all were then and how funny it seems now. In certain Republican circles we became legendary."

Brady and Whelan had talked "B" Oglesby into becoming the downstate candidate for Illinois's national committeeman to the YR Convention and he won. As a concession to the opposition he withdrew from the post at a propitious moment, and that sealed The Syndicate's victory over the establishment. The entire exercise served as a rehearsal for the upcoming Ogilvie campaign. "Having gone through the process of organizing our various counties, it was easy to move on and organize the state for Ogilvie," says Susan Bryant.

Jim, a downstater, was taking a chance by allying himself with them in the takeover. "But Jim was ambitious," says Whelan. "He was setting himself aside from the downstate old-boy, Republican organization which was saying, 'Let's go along,' and at the same time allying himself with the Chicago faction, which was anathema to downstaters."

Jay Bryant, a college YR from Northwestern University, one of those who helped in the takeover, had met Susan Bryant (her own surname) through their political activity and they married in 1967. "Barry Goldwater's presidential campaign in 1964 energized a lot of young idealistic people on the right," says Jay. "Goldwater's libertarian ideas—less government, an emphasis on individual liberty, that sort of thing—had a great deal of intellectual significance for all of us."

And in Illinois they had coalesced around the T. Richard Ogilvie campaign. "Ogilvie had always been a sponsor of this group of kids, finding them jobs and scholarships," says Susan.

"Jim Brady was one of the leaders of the group," says Jay Bryant. "He always had this great good humor and sharpness. And he was always a very practical-minded person." A much needed ingredient, because, says Bryant, "we also had some very flaky people in the group. There was some resentment of Jim because he had a job. People felt his loyalties weren't absolute toward Ogilvie. He knew you had to cut deals and B.S. with county chairmen and so forth."

After the takeover, Susan and Jay Bryant moved back to Jay's home state of Maine. Susan was pregnant. "We told each other we weren't going to be in politics," she says. "We were going to be hermits in Maine." Just two weeks after their arrival, Jim Brady was on the phone asking, "Who should we get to organize Shelby County [Susan's home county] for Ogilvie?" Susan suggested her brother and the Bryants settled in for a long winter.

Meanwhile that fall of 1967, Jim, still with the medical society, continued to be heavily involved behind the scenes lining up recruits for the Ogilvie campaign, as was Brian Whelan.

Jim himself took the job of campaign manager for Bob Dwyer, the Republican candidate for lieutenant governor. Candidates for lieutenant governor of Illinois at that time ran separate campaigns from the gubernatorial candidates. It was the dawn of the age of campaign consultants and the beginning of the multibillion-dollar campaign industry that has since developed. Dwyer, a wealthy Chicagoan, was enamored of the idea, even though he had no primary opposition. He signed up with the California firm of Whitaker Baxter, who in turn hired Jim as executive director of the campaign in December 1967.

A few nights later the Bryants got another phone call. "Boom-boom"—as Jim called Susan—"how fast do you think you could get back to Illinois?" "Jim, you talk to Jay and I'll go pack," she said.

"It was forty degrees below zero in Maine," says Susan. "Are you ready to come back?" Jim asked. "Yes. It is so cold and I am so bored." (Susan called Jim "James" or "Jay Bird.") "Jim Brady gave us our first paying political jobs," says Jay Bryant, who handled scheduling for Dwyer. Susan worked until their baby was born in May. "That was a big deal in the sixties. People didn't work when they were pregnant. Jim had a baby shower for me at Maxim's," says Susan. "All men, and we drank all afternoon. Brady ordered brandy milk punch for me, saying, 'Susan has to have her milk.' "

It didn't take much to get Dick Church into the Dwyer campaign, either. "It was probably the biggest break I've ever gotten in my life. I am really Jim's protégé. I had the chance to get to know all the people who were going to run Illinois politics." (Dick and Jeri Church are now managers of several trade associations and keep track of their political needs.) Dick Church hired on as Bob Dwyer's "driver and gofer," he says, "to advise and take care of the candidate."

He moved to Chicago and, until Jeri could transfer there, too, four months later, he bunked on Jim's living-room couch. Living with Jim provided more revelations to Church. "Jim is, first of all, the messiest creature on the face of the earth. His kitchen was always a mess, even though Jim had just won the Chicago bachelor-recipe contest with his 'Stuffed Pork for Stuffed People.' So the apartment just built up. The apartment floor was black tile and there were dust balls large enough to lose yourself in.

"He had a huge walk-in closet but you couldn't get in the door of it. Jim just took off his clothes and threw them all, suits too, into the center of the closet. Jim had this theory about dirty clothes; after they had sat long enough they'd become somehow more clean, and if he needed underwear, say, he'd reach under the bottom of the pile for some." Church called the closet "The Org."

"Dick, on the other hand, is a neatnik," says Jeri. Jim and Dick were the odd couple. "Finally," says Dick, "I had a cleaning crew come in and clean the place. I counted Jim's dirty shirts and sent out *fifty-four* shirts to the laundry. What was amazing to me is that Jim always looked so neat. I finally figured out that rather than having his shirts laundered he would just go out and buy a new one.

"We never had a working phone," says Church, "because Jim didn't pay the bill. I don't know whether he couldn't pay it or whether he just never got around to it."

Once, to get in touch with Dick, Jeri had to phone the Marina City doorman and ask him to go up and tell Dick to phone her. "That was the time we agreed I just simply had to move," says Dick.

"We worked long hours on the Dwyer campaign," says Susan Bryant, "often late into the night, always on weekends. Jim wouldn't get A-pluses for proper office demeanor, but he made it so you couldn't wait till you got to the office in the morning." And, very important to Susan, "Jim respected my advice. He took it as fact if I said 'You've got a problem in Cornwallis.' He'd listen and act on my information."

"Jim was always very much on top of everything," says Jay Bryant. "It was great fun working for him." "I've never thought of Jim Brady as a genius," says John Kolbe, "but through his humor, and you had to know him to catch it, he had this very instructive way of viewing political situations as to what might be done and what ought *not* to be done. He has a very savvy political head. There was always a laugh a minute." "He had enormous energy. Sleep was not one of his priorities," adds Susan, "and humor *was* a high priority."

Dwyer's campaign car, a black and white Cadillac Eldorado, driven by Dick Church, became a hilarious symbol of the campaign for Dwyer's minions. "After depositing Dwyer for the night," says Dick Church, "I then drove Jim around in it so he could make an entrance somewhere."

Throughout it all, there was always a party brewing, often planned and given by Jim, who was still "living at about a hundred forty percent of his income," points out one of the group. "It was always a great treat to go to his apartment for dinner," says Jay Bryant. "There was usually a diverse group of people there," says Whelan. "There wasn't much furniture. Here he was, living in one of the luxury buildings in Chicago, and with no furniture. It wasn't a high priority for him. He was just on the go so much."

"Jim was just completely irreverent about everything and everybody," says John Kolbe. "He would deflate everybody's candidate in jokes that would make as much fun of our guys as of the opposition. We'd have a party and sit around telling candidate and campaign stories. You always wanted to be around Jim when things were tough. He would bring some light into your life."

"Jim was kind of a prowler," says Whelan. "You'd have dinner at one place, then go to four or five different bars. And he'd know everybody."

Sometimes Mick and Polly Scheriger visited Jim from Centralia. Once or twice Sue joined them. Although Jim and Sue were separated, neither of them moved to get a divorce until 1970. Jim saw as much as he could of his daughter, given his schedule. "He adored Missy," says one friend. "Sue would send him some of Missy's artwork and he would show it proudly around."

On the campaign front, "Whitaker Baxter had convinced Dwyer he could raise a million and a half to run the campaign," says Church. "In fact, he wound up raising pennies, and spent a ton of his own money. And he had no opponent in the primary! No opponent!"

"But Jim had been hired to implement the decisions of Whitaker Baxter," says Susan Bryant. One of the firm's executives kept a room at the Drake Hotel and flew in and out of Chicago.

The campaign had a press secretary, too, Roy Olson, the cigar-smoking political editor of *Chicago Today*. "So we had all this PR firepower, but no opponent and therefore no issues. We were putting out two or three news releases a day—on nothing!" says Church. "John Dreiskie, a columnist for the

Ritchie Studio

One-year-old Jimmy Brady, Centralia, Illinois, 1941

Dorothy Brady pinning the Eagle Scout award on fifteen-year-old Jim, as his father, Harold "Big Jim" Brady, poses proudly, 1955

Jim in his senior year at Centralia High School, 1958

The Kappa Kappa chapter of Sigma Chi
at the University of Illinois,
plus sweethearts (Jim circled), 1961

The political
team from Jame
and Thomas,
Chicago, 1969

im as Chicago's Bachelor of the Year,
971

Wedding Day, July 21, 1973: from left,
Stanley Kemp, Frances Kemp, Sarah, Missy, Jim,
Dorothy Brady, and Big Jim Brady

Jim Lynn, Jim Brady, and Mayor Richard Daley
in Chicago on a HUD trip, 1974

Jim at a White House reception
with President and Mrs. Gerald Ford,
1974

Jim taking off for a trip with Secretary of Defense Donald Rumsfeld, 1976

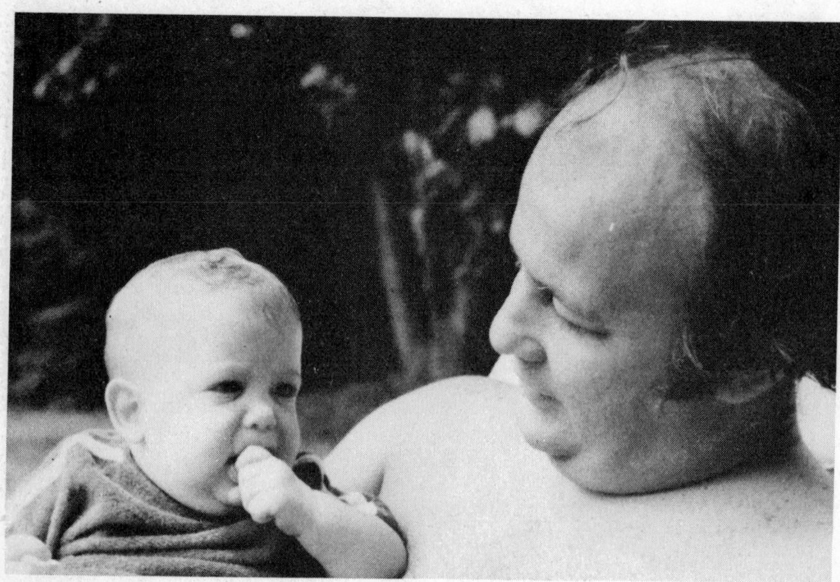

Jim and eight-month-old Scott, 1979

Taking notes on Jim Baker's call:
"Will you accept the job of press secretary
if it is offered to you?" January 2, 1981

Jim celebrating with Dom Pérignon after
Reagan's phone call asking him to be
his press secretary, January 2, 1981

Jim and President Reagan on the day he was announced as press secretary

Margaret Thomas—*The Washington Po*

Inauguration Day. Standing behind President Reagan: from left, Michael Deaver, James Baker III, Edwin Meese, James Brady, Richard Allen

White House Photo

Chicago Sun-Times, finally accused us of peddling pap." And Church remembers that "Jim was zooming all over the place trying to figure out how to handle" that low, but accurate, blow.

The campaign office was in a suite of rooms in the La Salle Hotel. "Jim took the largest room and rented the largest conference table he could get in the door," says Church. "That was his desk and from the first day on you never again saw the top of that table." "Don't touch it," Jim invariably said, "or I'll never be able to find anything."

At the end of August Jim instituted a campaign appearance for Dwyer and others at the Hambletonian trotter races at the Du Quoin State Fair south of Centralia. "The Hambletonian was beautiful," says Jeri Church, "a really nice thing. It is like the Kentucky Derby in importance to trotting races."

It also coincided with Jim's birthday on August 29, and became an annual event, campaign or not. But for now it was a perfect excuse to get everybody down to the center of the universe—Centralia. "He was always telling us about Centralia," says John Kolbe. The day began with a big party in Big Jim and Dorothy's backyard. Then they caravaned by car to Du Quoin sixty miles away.

It was all a great merry endeavor for Jim and his crew, but in September, with huge campaign debts mounting, Dwyer fired Whitaker Baxter, and Jim and most of the others included. (Jay Bryant was safe; he had shifted to the Ogilvie campaign after the primary. And Dick Church, originally Dwyer's driver, became his campaign chairman.) And in November, although Ogilvie won, Dwyer lost the election to Democrat Paul Simon (elected U.S. senator in 1984), which meant that for the first time in Illinois history, a governor and lieutenant governor of different parties held office. The Illinois constitution was subsequently changed so it would not happen again.

Being let go by Dwyer, and Dwyer's subsequent defeat, were, of course, blows to Jim. He had staffed the Ogilvie and Dwyer campaigns with many of his friends and acquaintances, and here he was out of a job before the election. But with great good humor he would say, "Yep, we elected a Democrat in that campaign." Those who were in Ogilvie's campaign all got important positions. "All these kids who'd been working in politics since 1962, and who were still for the most part under twenty-five," says Susan Bryant, "were made top assistants."

There was, however, still a sense that wives shouldn't work, says Susan, "but we were poor, we had college loans, a new home, and I needed to work from a psychological standpoint as well. I called Brady. 'I need a job, Jim. Do you have any ideas?' "

Jim told her he knew of one job and maybe some others—and Susan got the job of secretary to the Illinois Funeral Directors Association, "probably because Jim highly recommended me. It tided me over until a better job came along.

"Political people usually don't want to ruffle the waters or buck anybody for their friends," says Susan, "but Jim had established the code of the group: You were always loyal. You help each other, because they will help you, too."

Jim himself quickly caught on with the Chicago public-relations firm of James and Thomas, handling their political clients, but also working with nonpolitical clients, too. At James and Thomas, Jim was executive vice-president. The firm was named for its two founders, James Dunniker and Thomas Bertsche.

"I don't think a job in government was Jim's goal at all," says "B" Oglesby. "I think he was much happier doing the political consulting work, and working with his other clients." Perry Roberts agrees. "I don't think not having a job in Ogilvie's administration disappointed Jim. I felt he probably had found his niche doing PR in Chicago."

"Jim came highly recommended for the job he had done for Ogilvie downstate," says Tom Bertsche. For James and Thomas, Jim handled politics in season, and consumer accounts after elections. But they often began working on campaigns a year before elections, and earlier if the candidate had a primary fight in March.

"I ran the firm and supervised everything, for better or for worse," says Bertsche, "but we would all review whatever everybody else was doing so everything was done right. Jim would make suggestions about my campaigns as I would his." They made up large flow charts, calendars really, working backward from election day, which showed what needed to be done on what date in order to achieve the results they wanted; when brochures needed to be written and the artwork finished; the candidate's speaking itinerary; fund-raising. All the elements that went into a well-run campaign.

At work, says Bertsche, "Jim was very laid back, very calm—slightly disorganized, but as long as he had the flow chart everything got done. But he was a very hard worker and a conscientious worker. He kept me on an even keel at times."

Jim invited Bertsche and his wife to his apartment in Marina City "for Dungeness Crab," says Bertsche, "and we sat cross-legged on the floor. I told him next time I would be glad to sit cross-legged on the floor but I would be naked. We were covered with butter from head to foot."

Jim also took the Bertsches to see the musical *Hair*. "He had to show me how the other half of the world lived.

"He was a fabulous person. I never met anybody who didn't like Jim. I might get madder than hell at him. But he's a lovable guy—like a huggy bear. And there is nothing Jim wouldn't do for you. He always wanted to do something for you."

James and Thomas represented Chester T. Padgorski in his run for the Chicago Board of Supervisors. "His name wouldn't fit on any of our campaign posters," says Jim.

Jim signed up Republican candidate Bert Hopper, who would have this year's go at the indomitable George Shipley. They also represented Speaker Ralph Tyler Smith. Among their other clients were Honeywell, Prudential Insurance, the Wick Building, and Maywood Park.

In the fall of 1969, shortly after Senator Dirksen's death, Dick and Jeri Church were celebrating their third anniversary by spending the weekend at the Playboy Club in Lake Geneva, Illinois. But after one night there, they were lonely. They missed Jim. "Wouldn't it be fun if Jim came up here?" they said to each other. So they called him to come join them for their second night. The problem was that the Playboy Club had a two-night minimum, and even so, it supposedly was sold out. "By then I had developed some of Brady's habits," says Dick. "I called the front desk and told him I had kind of a unique problem. I said, 'I am involved in interviewing candidates for Senator Dirksen's replacement, and one of them, Illinois State Senator Brady, is able to join me here for his interview tonight.'

" 'No problem, Mr. Church,' said the front desk. 'We can accommodate Senator Brady. Just have him call me from the front gate when he arrives.'

"Pretty soon," says Church, "here comes Brady. We had

told him he was Senator Brady, et cetera. So he drives up in his little red VW Bug with the top down—some *bimbo* beside him. He was in his cutoffs, his flip-flops and a T-shirt and had a huge Styrofoam cooler full of beer in the backseat. I was afraid he had blown it. But the bellboy carried all this crap up into his room, and I'm damned if they didn't give him a suite with a big round bed and mirrors everywhere. They even sent him champagne."

That fall, Jim took in another protégé, Joe Anderson, son of Illinois Republican Majority Leader Ray Anderson, who had been Dwyer's downstate chairman. Young Joe had just graduated from Knox College and moved to Chicago. "I didn't have a place to stay so I moved in with Jim and slept on his couch." Later Anderson got his own apartment just down the hall. "We became good friends, best friends, over the next four years. I had a car and he didn't. He had a little black book filled with names of single women and I didn't."

Anderson thinks of those four years as "The Yah Hah Years." "We didn't sit around and say, 'I'm going to be doing this or that in ten years.' It was—'Who can we get a date with Saturday night?' " One of Jim's girlfriends called him Roo-Roo, for Roué. Anderson guessed at that time that Jim would stay in the private sector. He was having too good a time there.

An informal social group formed on two floors of Marina City, says Anderson, "and we got together on a weekly basis to dine, if you can call it that." They held potluck suppers, "and Jim was always the big hit at these affairs," says Anderson. "At that point we were gourmands instead of gourmets, and we used one apartment for coats, one for drinks and hors d'oeuvres, and one for dinner and so on. All the management people at Marina City detested Jim and me because they were trying to foster the image of a downtown sophisticated address." And Jim and Joe weren't living up to the image.

They made friends with the parking-garage attendants, however. "We used to take their bets to the track [Arlington Park] for them." If Dr. Fager was running, "we'd bet on him anytime. He was probably the premier horse of that period.

"We did everything to excess," says Anderson. "We bet, ate or drank up every cent we took out to the track. And sometimes we had to drive home on the back streets of Chicago because we didn't have enough money left for the tolls."

Jim was dating a United Airlines stewardess or two, among others, shuffling everybody around a lot, playing the field. He once stole one of Joe Anderson's girlfriends. "I was mad," says Anderson, "but I couldn't stay mad because it's impossible to stay mad at Jim. People have always forgiven Jim Brady his peccadilloes because down deep he's such a generous, kind person. Every now and then he'd make a mistake, but he had high ethical standards. He'd apologize and give you a look like a big puppy. It was irresistible.

"Every Saturday noon we would invite people in to have brunch. Especially the members of the group we called the Order of the Walrus. We picked that name because the walrus is a fat, lazy animal that lies around and eats. We'd cook and cook and cook. We'd eat. Then collapse. And all we could do then was to roll over, turn the TV on and watch football."

Jim and Joe joined the Carry On Club—a club for "white-collar junior-executive types," says Anderson, "and a prime source of dates, good bars, new restaurants. Jim kept his ties to the YRs, too."

By the time Joe Anderson arrived in Chicago, Jim had received so many parking tickets the city had impounded his car. He paid them off and retrieved it, but it was eventually impounded again for nonpayment and his driver's license was taken away. Big-city traffic brought out the worst in the competitive Brady, as it does in many people. "Driving gives me a nosebleed," he says.

"One night when we were out carousing in my car," says Anderson, "a cab came up fast behind us and passed us on the right. 'Don't let him do that,' yelled Jim, and he browbeat me into chasing the cab. Jim was hanging out the window and screaming at the top of his lungs. We finally caught the guy at a light and Brady jumped out of the car to chew him out. I pulled over and when I got there, here was the cabdriver with a gun, and Jim had his hands up and was backing up slowly. We ran, jumped in the car, and took off."

On occasion, says Anderson, "we'd call in sick and catch the El out to Wrigley Field to see the Cubs play. Jim knew Dickie Nye, a Cubs pitcher, and Nye would leave us tickets at the box office.

"We both shared an interest in model trains," he adds, "and Jim had every possible car there was—perhaps a hundred of them." When hometown friend Connie Mann came over to visit Jim once, there was the model train covering the entire floor of his apartment.

"Jim Brady never sat still," says Anderson. "I would describe him as extremely active. He was also very passionate about anything he did—to the extreme. If he was going to play golf he had to have the best golf clubs."

Through those years, Anderson says, "he was a terrific father to Missy. He was always borrowing my car and taking her places."

"We did a lot of things together, the zoo, the art institute, just going around the town, eating out," says Missy. Missy's mother, Sue, married Harvey Camins when Missy was seven. "I'm probably just as close to my stepdad as to Dad. In Chicago Dad was the bachelor. I was 'The Porcupine.' We'd always do some fun, crazy things. He used to throw his Christmas tree into the Chicago River from his balcony. He used to tell me there was an alligator in the river and when I was little I'd stand there for hours throwing down food. But that's what makes him so much fun, you know."

"Jim was crazy about Missy," says her mother. "He didn't see her that often, but he was good to her. He took her to Jamaica once, and on skiing trips. It was from Jim she developed her interests in adventure, in astrology, wildlife and growing things. She is very much like him."

Joe Anderson found he could always get Jim's goat by telling him he looked like a famous balding television newsman. "That was the thing that set him off the worst. Jim was going to turn thirty in 1970, and he didn't want to come to grips with the facts that (a) he was getting older; (b) he was getting fatter; and (c) he was losing more hair."

Throughout these post-college years in Springfield and in Chicago, Dorothy and Big Jim visited Jim several times a year. Jim always threw a party for them. "I can see him right now, out in the kitchen fixing smoked salmon canapés," says his mother.

And Jim went home frequently, and always for the now-established Hambletonian and the big party Dorothy gave for his birthday beforehand. He brought all his friends to the Hambeltonian at one time or another. "Jimmy really liked to come home," says Dorothy Mann. "He was always very thoughtful of his parents and went out of his way for them."

Bill Crain saw Jim on one of these visits walking through Foundation Park with a spectacular blonde. "She was dressed in what looked like the American flag—red, white, and blue," he says, "and I saluted, I'll tell you."

Jim came home for a party that Bill Crain and Red Schwartz put on for Schwartz's son Rick's high-school graduation. They engaged the Block House Tavern for drinking and Herb Haywood's Centralia House for food, establishments that were just across the railroad tracks from each other. "Herb Haywood made ears and tails sauce, and Red and I stayed up all the night before cooking two hogs," says Crain. "We hired seven bartenders and had a rock band and there were three hundred people. It was a smashing evening.

"Brady and Al Perfansi would walk back and forth between Herb's and the Block House, but on one of these trips, Al lost Jim. When he went back he found he'd fallen into a construction pit. Jim wasn't worried. He just wondered when someone was going to come and get him out. We were going to put a memorial to him there."

Herb Haywood bought and refurbished the legendary Centralia House in 1969 (it had been a hotel, a brothel, and a gambling house at various times in its day), and Jim always dropped by the kitchen when he was home. "He'd sit in the kitchen with me and watch me cook," says Haywood, "and we'd nip on a bottle of wine. Sometimes he'd turn his hand to some creole dish I was cooking."

"The first time we ever went to Centralia with Jim," says Jeri Church, "he got us involved in a pyramid scheme called Holiday Magic." "I think we invested two or three hundred dollars in it," says Dick. "Jim's role was to hustle people like us so he could get his own money back. He got one of his girlfriends, 'Rabbit,' into it and we even had a training session in St. Louis for it."

"The way it works," laughs Jim, "is that the distributor brings nine thousand pieces of crap over to your house and you have like a Tupperware party and you tell all the ladies how great they look. Bill Crain told me if he ever saw me again with some scheme he'd kill me."

For the 1970 off-year elections, meanwhile, James and Thomas had contracted for Jim to manage several Republican candidates running for the U.S. House of Representatives: Dick Wathen in Indiana; Jay Wilkinson (son of football coach Bud Wilkinson) in Oklahoma; and right-wing, anti-abortionist Phyllis Schlafly, who was running against none other than George Shipley in Jim's home district. "My job with Phyllis Schlafly was to teach her how to be a mainstream Republican instead of a right-winger," says Jim. "I had to teach her how to speak Republican. I had to caution her and say, 'No, you had better say it this way.' I could usually talk sense into the woman's head." "Jim complained about her being cold and distant, and too ideologically oriented for the old Twenty-third District," says Jay Bryant.

In Indiana "Dick Wathen didn't have a prayer against a Democrat in a Democratic area," says Anderson. "It was making the best of a bad situation, and that was Jim at his best, because Wathen made a real decent showing for himself. Jim was real good at handling money. The political-advertising field is filled with indecent people, and a lot of people would come in and hire a Chicago firm, hoping that would do the trick. But Jim wasn't like that. He put his own time and a great deal of effort into his campaigns and produced a high-quality product. He worked hard for his people."

Jim's *modus operandi* was that he always rose to whatever challenges his current position presented to him. "From the very first day I met Jim," says Brian Whelan, "I've considered him one of the most naturally talented people I've ever known. Jim could be good working two hours a day. I believe to reach the place he ultimately reached is partly attributable to the fact that, one, he had mentors, or, the job was such it utilized all of his talents and pushed him. He always measured up to the expectations—it just depended on how high they were."

In March 1970 Jim was in Washington, D.C., for a national conference of campaign managers when he met a young woman named Sarah Jane Kemp, for whom, albeit slowly, he would put the Yah Hah Years behind him.

PART THREE

A Year of Recovery

CHAPTER FIVE
The Long Journey Begins

At 9:30 on the night of the shooting, Sarah and Dorothy went up to the fourth floor to the intensive care unit to wait for Jim's arrival. There, Sarah met Alison Griswold, a senior staff nurse who had been assigned to care for Jim. Sarah was anxious to see her husband, but Griswold told her, "I want to get him in here, assess him, and clean him up a bit; then you can come in, okay?"

"Sarah was tearful but composed," says Griswold. "I told her that we were going to break the rules because of the severity of the situation. 'If you want to be with him, then you can stay as long as you like. If it's too difficult—it's up to you. I don't know how things are going to go but we will work it that way.' " The two women hit it off immediately—they knew they were going to get along, and Sarah and Dorothy Brady retired to a room two doors down from the one Jim would occupy.

Alison Griswold had been given a very pessimistic report on her new patient. She didn't expect very much from this grievously wounded man, as he arrived with his head swathed in a huge turban bandage, still intubated, with IVs and catheter tubes going in or coming out of various limbs and apertures. "There was a lot of blood on his face and bloody secretions were coming out of his nose and mouth," remembers Griswold, "and his face was puffy from all the medications he had received." She checked his blood pressure, his pulse, his pupils. "He didn't show signs of intracranial pressure." Then she checked his responses. "His right hand responded to pressure and his left hand was still responding, but weakly." She noticed that his college ring was cutting into his finger, and called the ER for a tool to cut it off. "There were no bad signs. Things looked good—I was encouraged." She recorded all her observations, then set about cleaning him up. He was beginning to come out of the anesthesia. At 10:30 Alison went to the door of Sarah's room to call her in.

Sarah's first look at Jim frightened her. There were so many lines into him and monitors throbbing, but she went to his side and took his right hand. "Jim, it's the Raccoon. We're all here, don't be afraid." She looked at Griswold. "I know he's going to be fine. He's squeezing my hand." Griswold was astonished that he was able to respond in any meaningful way. She and Sarah began talking to Jim—asking him to wiggle his hands, his toes. "Do it for the Raccoon," Griswold told him. He did everything they asked him to do. "Way to go, Jim, way to go. Looking good," they encouraged him. They spent most of the rest of the night that way, Sarah going to her room from time to time. When Sarah came back into his room, Griswold would say, "Bear, Raccoon is here," and Jim would squeeze Sarah's hand. "Any response is a good response in a head injury," says Griswold. By dawn, Jim was moving his right arm and his right leg on command, and Griswold was convinced that Jim had been improving all night. She gave Jim a wad of gauze to hold and squeeze with his right hand.

Sarah encouraged Jim's mother to go in to see her son, but the sight of her beloved only child was almost more than she could bear. That all the years of nurturing and love could come to this, she thought. She prayed for strength, and for help with her grief.

Word came in that U.S. Senator Charles Percy of Jim's home state of Illinois was in the hospital. Dorothy Brady spoke with him, "but I was too hyper to sit down," says Sarah. Sarah had told her own mother, Frances Kemp, not to come to the hospital. "I left my TV on all night," says Frances. "I was horribly upset and worried. It just about broke my heart; I don't know how Dorothy Brady has gone through it. I really don't know.

Emotionally, it crushed me to see this happen to Jim. They were so happy and Sarah was so crazy about Jim. It was like I was in a dream."

Later Dick Allen and his wife, Pat, came up to the ICU. "Come on in and see Jim," said Sarah. "I was really moved by it," says Allen. "His head was all wrapped up, he couldn't talk with that tube down his throat, and he was having tremendous spasms on his left side and was twitching. Sarah bent down and said, 'Bear, it's Dick and Pat.' I remember grabbing his right hand and he squeezed it. He held on and squeezed. I felt an enormous sense of awe at the strength of Jim Brady."

Sarah called home to tell them about Jim's squeezing her hand. "It was a very emotional call," says Jan Wolff. At the Brady house, chaos reigned. "The phone rang continuously," says Jan, "and we set up a list of callers. Everybody they ever knew called, as well as people they didn't know and Washington's elite. Flowers and plants started coming. Neighbors dropped off notes and mail piled up. The press was coming up and peering in the windows and knocking on the door. We pulled the curtains closed. Bill Greener arrived and handled the press." Jan asked Sarah what she should do about Scott. "Do what you think is best," Sarah said. "I just can't make those decisions right now."

Jan took Scott home with her for the night, along with a pile of Jim's shirts. "It made me feel so good, washing and ironing ten of Jim's shirts. I was convinced if I did, Jim would be sure to wear them again."

At the White House, working until after midnight, White House Counsel Fred Fielding went out to his car on West Executive Avenue. "Jim's yellow beach Jeep was the only car left sitting there," he remembers, "as though everybody else had gone home, but he hadn't."

Good friends Bob and Suzi Dahlgren came by the hospital very late that night after leaving the Bradys' house. "I told Bob," says Suzi, " 'We just have to go to the hospital.' And we were able to get in because of Bob's White House pass. But when we got there, I said, 'I just don't think I can handle seeing Sarah, I'm going to burst into tears.' And Bob told me, 'You be strong, because Sarah's being strong.' And when Sarah came out of Jim's room to see us she had a grin that went from ear to ear." "He's going to be all right," Sarah told the Dahlgrens as she hugged them. "Jim just squeezed my hand." "Sarah and I both started crying," says Suzi.

"Bob and I went home and stayed up till three or four talking about how positive Sarah was, how she could find Jim's squeezing her hand a positive sign."

"Here he had been pronounced dead just a few hours before," says Bob Dahlgren. "Sarah Brady is one of the very few people I've known in my life who can find the glass is half full. Always. She cheered *us* up! That was the only thing that got us through the night. And it was just the first of many times. When I was feeling down about it, we had only to talk to Sarah and she could always find that the glass was half full. It was never half empty. Never. No way."

At 6:30 in the morning Art Kobrine and his residents came by to make early morning rounds and Alison Griswold told them what Jim had been doing. They simply couldn't believe her. "Alison," said Kobrine, "don't get your hopes up too high. This patient's chances are very slim." She then tried to show them, but at first Jim didn't respond. "It's been a long night, Alison," said one of the doctors. "You may be getting a little too emotionally involved," said another. "It wouldn't have surprised me if it had taken a week or ten days for Jim to even regain consciousness," says Kobrine.

Angry now that she couldn't convince them that Jim could hear her, she went to Jim's side. "Jim, shake your fist," she said, shaking her own fist in frustration. Lo and behold, Jim raised his right hand in a fist and shook it. "Now, give them the thumbs-up sign," she said, and Jim signaled "thumbs up." Kobrine and the residents broke into broad grins. They could hardly believe what they had seen. But Kobrine cautioned Griswold that a dangerous road still lay ahead for Jim. "A lot of head-trauma patients die after surgery," says Kobrine, "because of continued swelling. That's why I didn't mind sucking away necrotic-looking tissue because I knew the brain would continue to swell like crazy for five hours or more after the trauma."

There was so much commotion and excitement in Jim's room that Agent Tim McCarthy, next door, was alarmed and he sent his nurse out to see what was going on. And every time Sarah heard "Way to go, Jim," she hurried over to see what new feat Jim was able to do.

There were guards at Reagan's and McCarthy's rooms, but not at Jim's. Sarah asked one of the detectives, "Why does everyone have protection but Jim?"

Before dawn, President Reagan had been brought up to the ICU after passing a successful night in the recovery room. All night he had kept up a steady patter of one-liners, writing them out at first while he was still intubated. "I am—am not—alive, aren't I?" he wrote after waking up from a nap. "I'd like to shoot the whole scene over beginning at the hotel," he said in another. While doctors were suctioning out secretions from his lungs, he wrote, "All in all, I'd rather be in Philadelphia," borrowing W. C. Fields' epitaph. To head recovery-room nurse Denise Sullivan, he wrote, "Does Nancy know about us?" Four years later, in an interview for this book, Reagan said, in answer to a question about his good humor before and after his surgery, "Well, I thought, with all that crowd standing around, somebody ought to entertain them some way."

But when Reagan asked, "Was anybody else hurt?," his nurse told him that two others had been hit (she hadn't heard about Delahanty), but weren't injured seriously. Dr. Ruge thought that it was too soon to tell the president of the seriousness of the injuries of the others, especially Jim's.

At 8:30 in the morning, Griswold, who had worked through two shifts, was relieved by day nurse Ann Neureiter. Otto Wolff came by to see Sarah. "By then, she was almost mechanically saying, 'He's going to be fine; oh, I'm fine,' " says Otto. Sarah had had no sleep all night. It was not until that second night that she was able to relax enough to sleep for several hours.

The daytime routine was an enormously busy one, filled with doctors' rounds, nurses' rounds, lab tests, baths, meals, extensive updating of charts, CAT scans. Dr. Armaly came in and removed the drain from Jim's eye. There wasn't much time to test for Jim's alertness or improvement, but still, Jim was getting obstreperous in his bed, moving about and constantly trying to get at the endotracheal tube in his windpipe. As a result, his right hand and right leg were tied down and restrained with pieces of cloth.

Jim's former employer U.S. Senator William Roth, came by to see Sarah. "He's going to make it," she told him. "There was never the slightest doubt in her mind," says Roth. It was just a great testimony to her fortitude and bravery."

During the day, when it was clear that Reagan was doing very well, Ruge decided it was time to break the news about Jim Brady and the others to the president. Nancy Reagan said, "I want to be with you when you tell him," and she held his hand as Ruge recounted the victims' stories. "I told him Jim's injury was very serious—a brain injury and he was still in a coma." "Oh, dear," he said, "I didn't want a supporting cast," his eyes filling up with tears. "That means that four bullets hit. Good Lord." He wanted to see Sarah.

"He looked wonderful," remembers Sarah, "but he was very, very upset." "I just feel terrible, Sarah," said the president. "I feel like it's my fault that Jim was hit, too." Sarah quickly tried to assuage him. "Don't worry, Mr. President," she said. "Jim is going to be fine. And I want you to know that he loved that job more than anything else in the world. He was right where he wanted to be." Reagan and Sarah held each other's hands. "He grasped onto everything I said," says Sarah, "in the way of reassurance that he should bear no guilt for what had happened."

Dan Ruge continued to keep Reagan informed about Jim's recovery and one night, several weeks later, having dinner in the White House with the Reagans and Loyal Davis, Mrs. Reagan's neurosurgeon father, Ruge explained to Davis and the Reagans the problems of the operation. "To let him and the Reagans know how serious Jim's injury was—to avoid future recriminations—that the floor of the skull was literally destroyed and that only by the grace of God would he not wind up with meningitis and death.

"Art carried a horrible burden in having to deal with this," says Ruge. "He did what he had to do in order to save Jim's life, and at the same time not to destroy his brain. That's really the mark of the surgeon—a judgment of how much to do, and how much *not* to do. I knew as time went on people would make comparisons."

Cindy Kobrine, Art's wife and an RN as well, says, "If Jim had died on the operating table, people would have understood. But having survived one hour, one day, it became more and more important to Art that he not die. He didn't want this patient to go. As time went on, he became more determined that he wouldn't let anything happen to him. Art agonized over every decision, wanting to be sure they were the right ones. Art sometimes used me as a sounding board to talk things out and help bring things into perspective."

Art Kobrine, who had made rounds on the president and Tim McCarthy, as well as on Jim Brady, said, "I was impressed at how professional Baker, Deaver, and Meese were. They just didn't let this thing interfere with the running of the country's business." When the three of them walked into Mr. Reagan's room the morning after the shooting, the president greeted them with, "Hi, fellas. I knew it would be too much to hope that we could skip a staff meeting." And they had some business for him, too—the signing of a bill that canceled an increase in dairy price-support payments. "And he did sign it," says Kobrine, "probably partly because Baker, Meese, and Deaver wanted to show his ability to function."

His nurses knew, however, that Reagan had been given thirty milligrams of morphine for pain since his surgery, and they wondered how he could understand what he was signing. (Four years later, for his surgery for colon cancer, and again in 1986, for prostate surgery, morphine was injected into his spine so that it would not reach his brain.)

That morning Jan Wolff took Scott to Sarah's mother "who really needed to be brought up to date on how her daughter was holding up," says Jan. "She wanted to know where Sarah was when she found out about Jim. She was crying but she was happy to see Scott." Jan took Scott and her own daughter out to lunch. "Our waitress told us she belonged to a prayer group which had stayed up all night praying for Mr. Brady." Jan didn't tell her who the little boy with her was.

At 3:30 that afternoon, Alison Griswold was back on duty. "Jim was more awake than when I had left," she says. "I checked him out, and in doing so, took off the hand restraint but held on firmly to his hand. Suddenly, Jim put his hand to his mouth and with it he literally pulled me up on top of him. He got his hand on the tube and pulled it halfway out." Griswold called out to Jeff Jacobson who was just outside Jim's room. "Jacobson, get in here and help me." Jacobson helped her ease the tube out of Jim's throat. "He was determined to remove that thing," says Jacobson. ICU doctor Bill Knauss checked Jim over and said, "Well, he is probably ready to breathe on his own." But they stood ready to reintubate him if necessary, and they continued giving him oxygen, but through nasal prongs.

Anesthesiologist Judith Johnson, who had intubated Jim twenty-four hours earlier, came in to check on his breathing. "I was checking his hand," she says, "and Jim hauls off and gives me a knee in the ribs. But he obeyed all my commands. 'Squeeze my hand. Pull away from me.' And his ventilation was fine."

Jim's throat was sore from the tube, and his mouth dry from all the medications to prevent brain swelling. Griswold tried to relieve his discomfort by wiping his mouth out with a wet cloth. She observed, "I thought that Jim had perked up a little more since that morning. He seemed more purposeful in that he seemed to understand that he was in the hospital, and that he was in a bed, so his restless behavior was less. He began to acknowledge my presence, and when told that Sarah was in the room, he would know to put his hand out toward her. Stimulation helps in the recovery," she says. "I have seen it help." Griswold asked Sarah to bring in some tapes and her recorder, and she played music for Jim on her shift thereafter. "It helped to know what kind of a person he was and I could perceive his sense of humor, even though he maintained a poker face. I felt that trying to reach his mind was like digging into a long, dark tunnel."

By Tuesday afternoon, the mood of George Washington University Hospital was jubilant. The president was doing well. He had been moved to a private room on the third floor. Tim McCarthy and Officer Delahanty were out of danger. And Jim Brady was amazing everyone. "There was almost a party atmosphere," says Sarah. She and Carol McCarthy, Tim McCarthy's wife, split a bottle of wine and stayed up for hours talking, "almost like schoolgirls in a dorm," remembers Sarah fondly. Sarah's brother, Bill Kemp, had arrived, too, after an overnight flight from Portland, Oregon. Missy came to the hospital to see her dad for the first time and came every day. They held hands and Missy tried to stimulate him by talking to him.

At 11:30, night nurse Elizabeth Ann (Betsi) Horwath joined Jim's case. She found Jim's room guarded by two Secret Service men. In fact, there were Secret Service agents at every door. "They were very protective of Jim, almost questioning whether we nurses were doing the right thing. At times they got a little hyper, because they didn't really know anything, and they'd call for us, saying 'Hey, he's moving—things like that."

"When I was at Jim's side caring for him that night," says Horwath, "he would put his hand in my pocket and put two fingers on my scissors—then open and close them." This ability to recognize things by feel is called stereognosis, and it is a significant ability of the brain. Horwath was impressed with Jim's enterprise and she made up a ball of gauze and tape for him. He squeezed it at first, but an hour or two later, "he was bouncing the ball on the bed," says Horwath. "Hey, Jim," she said, "throw me the ball." Jim reached back, wound up, and threw it across the room toward the sound of her voice. His eyes were still swollen shut. " 'I can't believe this,' I cheered. 'Yay, Jim.' Sarah heard the noise, came over, and the three of us played ball for two hours. Except for our boisterousness, the ICU was eerily quiet, though," says Horwath. "There is so much activity that usually it's very noisy. But we had had a bomb threat the night before and outside there were armed men on every rooftop and searchlights plying the sky."

When Kobrine made his rounds early the next morning, Horwath told him, "You won't believe this but Jim has been playing ball with us." Kobrine chastised her. "Betsi, this isn't funny. I know you are a hopeful thinker, but after that injury, Jim Brady just couldn't be doing anything like that." "I'm not making a joke," she said, and she called out, "Hey, Jim, throw me the ball." Jim threw it across the room to her. "Oh, my God," said Kobrine when he saw the windup and the pitch. "We were all, like, literally crying," says Horwath. Then Kobrine said, "Jim, what do you have there in your hand?" "Ball," said Jim, very deliberately. It was the first word he had spoken since being put under anesthesia in the emergency room, and it surprised them all. Kobrine said, "Gosh, the way he is throwing that ball, maybe he won't have the flattened affect of a frontally-lobish person." "It was then I knew that his computer hadn't crashed," he adds.

Bill Kemp joined in, too. "Jim would count as he threw," says Bill. "When he got past twenty he'd get a little confused, but he'd try to keep going higher. He'd say 'twenty-four, twenty-eight, thirty-two, wait, twenty-three?,' and he'd try to finesse the fact that he was making errors. That's when I figured he'd be back at work, maybe after six or eight weeks."

It was the vim and vigor with which he was delivering the ball that gave them so much hope. Kobrine was amazed. "This is great," he enthused. "This is marvelous. This is just great." Kobrine then asked Jim to stick out his tongue. Jim complied. "Anybody who can't do that," says Horwath, "will have trouble speaking. It is an important motor function controlled by the brain." Kobrine asked Jim to count. "One, two, three," said Jim. "Jim was both good and not good at the same time," says Kobrine. "And it was a mixed blessing because people, even Sarah, began to hope and assume he'd be perfect and, of course, I knew he would not be perfect."

Sarah and Jim's nurses tried in vain to get him to speak again. But the next afternoon Sarah was holding Jim's hand and she asked him, "Jim, do you know who this is?" "Raccoon," he said quietly, but firmly. "From then on," says Griswold, "if there were a moment of silence, he'd ask for 'Raccoon.' He was one surprise after another. Asked how he was feeling, Jim gave the thumbs-up sign and said, 'Fine, fine.' He started speaking one word at a time. He began to ask for 'water' or 'drink.' We were 'keeping him dry'—dehydrated, that is—to keep down the swelling, and he was very thirsty. It was frustrating for him. Also, he was allergic to some of his medications, and he was itching like crazy. He would say 'scratch' and 'feet, feet,' meaning he wanted his feet scratched." "He did that before he was hurt," says Sarah, "and it used to drive me up the wall. He always wanted me to scratch his feet. But it sounded pretty darned good to me when he said it for the first time in the hospital."

The four days Jim was in the ICU, a steady stream of high administration officials came by Jim's room. Mrs. Reagan came each day, as did Vice-President George Bush and Richard Allen. Jeff Jacobson gave the vice-president a rundown of Jim's condition, adding that Jim would survive, "but the quality of survival we weren't sure of." Bush also visited Delahanty at Washington Hospital Center. The president's troika, Baker, Meese, and Deaver, came by after seeing the president, and Senator Roth and Mrs. Roth. Secretary of Defense Caspar Weinberger came, too, and Sue Block, wife of the secretary of agriculture, brought Sarah doughnuts the first morning after the shooting.

"For the first few weeks," says Sarah, "my brother Bill, and Kathy Ahern [Jim's personal assistant at the White House] came every single day and Bob and Suzi Dahlgren were there often."

The president's son Michael Reagan and his wife, Colleen, came to see Jim after visiting Reagan, and Sarah received a handwritten note from Richard Nixon.

A mountain of mail began to flood the hospital and the White House for Jim and the first of three hundred teddy bears of all sizes began to arrive. A man in Toronto rented a truck in order to haul a huge stuffed bear to Washington. "As the bear collection grew they just added on another bookcase," says Jan Wolff.

Sarah knew she didn't want to leave the hospital until the three-day period of danger Kobrine warned her about was past. And during the third day Jim was strangely quiet, not moving much, and not talking. Kobrine rushed Jim downstairs for a CAT scan, but he could see nothing too ominous in the photo. There was air inside his brain but Kobrine was not surprised at that. With great relief he concluded that Jim had worn himself out with almost constant activity. That evening, Sarah left him for the first time and went to her mother's for an hour to see Scott.

As a result of the scare, Kobrine kept Jim in ICU an extra day. The next evening Jeff Jacobson noted on Jim's chart: "First eye open. Unswollen enough to see I don't wear glasses or have a moustache. Spontaneously answers questions; alternates between rest and agitation."

On Saturday, April 4, Kobrine moved his patient to 5E, the neurological ward on the fifth floor—to a private room at the end of the hall. Susan Deyo, one of Jim's new nurses, describes his arrival. "Jim loved people. When they brought him up he was waving to everybody as he went down the hall." Jim was still on an IV for food—he wasn't alert enough to swallow liquids or solids. "No sedation since surgery," said his record. "Oriented as to city, person, and time." To the question, where do you work?, Jim answered, "The White House" or "My office." Asked what his job involved, he said, "I answer questions." "Who for?" "Anyone who asks them." Nurse Deyo says, "His left hand was flaccid—it had no tone at all. He had this huge bandage on his head, and I could see a few sutures.

I gave him gentle stimulation to increase his alertness—like asking him to open his eyes and tactilely rubbing his limbs with a dry washcloth. He became agitated and restless later on, but he was cooperative."

Several hours after his surgery Jim had stopped all voluntary movement in his left hand and left foot. Kobrine had predicted this would happen, and already Jim's left-hand muscles were contracting in a painful way. Before he left the ICU, hospital occupational therapist Susan Marino came to evaluate Jim's muscle flexion. "I was a little frightened at what I thought would be a gory scene. But it wasn't gory. It was just this very large man, lying in bed, barely alert." Marino ordered a splint that would keep his hand in as nearly normal a relaxed position as possible. She began working with Jim, positioning and stretching his limbs on the right side to preserve muscle tone, and on the left side to reduce the flexion—the imbalance of muscle tension caused by the brain injury—the broken connections to his brain. Many connections had been broken.

Sarah was frightened to have Jim moved out of the ICU. "I almost felt that there was no way anything could happen to him there with his nurses watching constantly over him." For their part, Jim Brady had been a special patient. Betsi Horwath says, "I cannot tell you how much respect, gratitude, and love I have for Sarah. It was an emotional, rewarding experience, both fearful and exciting. And Jim had a warmth about him—he has that energy. I never got tired of taking care of him. Sarah was so very, very grateful. You felt that she totally trusted you."

There were enough small glitches to justify Sarah's fear the first few days and to keep her edgy and on her toes, however. A junior resident said callously in her presence, "Yeah, he's doing pretty good for someone who's supposed to be dead." A homicide detective showed up every day for a while to see if Jim was still alive—"almost as though he was hoping it would turn into a murder case," says Sarah. "That unnerved me, you might say. I was afraid he had heard something that I didn't know." The first day on 5E one of Jim's new nurses gave him the choice of having liquid or solid food—"as though he knew what was good for himself at that point," says Sarah, "which he didn't." Jim, lying flat on his back, opted for solid food and he choked badly on it. Kobrine, who had ordered liquids for him, hit the ceiling, and the nurse was reassigned.

As much as the hospital tried not to single out its famous patients, a certain amount of extra attention was inevitable. Sandra Butcher remembers, "Yes, it has been a special case. The Bradys are the warmest, brightest people. And, rarely, do you ever work with anyone that well known. Never, however, did they make me feel that I was working with someone famous."

Sarah slept in Jim's room the first two nights. "But," she says, "it soon became ridiculously clear that I didn't need to do that. Besides, Jim's night nurse was a male nurse, George Speese. George would get Jim ready for bed, and tuck him in, then he turned to make up my bed. Then," Sarah laughs, "he would sit in the room with the two of us all night." Jim had round-the-clock RN care for almost two months and George Speese was his "primary care nurse." Jim called him "Jorge, My Primary Care Nurse." Sarah soon adapted to the hospital rhythms, however, for a struggle that was just beginning. But it was a strong beginning, and she was full of hope. She brought their son to see Jim. Scott climbed immediately and happily into bed with him. Scott visited Jim every Saturday and Sunday and while he was there he visited *all* the other rooms nearby and climbed in bed with all the patients who would let him.

Whenever Sarah left the hospital during the first few weeks, brother Bill took her place in Jim's room. "Sarah felt a member of the family should be with Jim at all times," says Bill.

"Jim was not real clear about where he was, what date it was and so forth, right at first," says Speese. But he observed that Jim was able to figure out a way to take care of a very basic problem, that of scratching his itchy feet. "He worked his big toe and second toe out from under the covers and slid them along the bedrail to scratch them. I thought it was a good indicator for the future," says Speese.

At first, Jim slept most of the time, and when he was awake he would just watch what was going on around him. But he had been told what had happened to him and he was able to take it in, saying "The Bear certainly was in the wrong place that time!" and "Not a bad job, Doc" to Kobrine. But hearing about what had happened to him also terrified him. "They told me only one in ten [head-wound victims] makes it," says Jim. "That scared me. I thought I was going to die." He began sitting up in bed, drinking water, and started eating solid foods, and the bandages were removed from his head exposing his angry red scar. On Monday, April 6, one week from the day of the shooting, physical therapist Cathy Wynne joined occupational therapist Susan Marino in Jim's room to begin to organize Jim's rehabilitation. When they walked in, there were two doctors and two nurses struggling to help Jim get from his bed to the chair. He was extremely heavy and almost a dead weight. "All of us were nervous because he had such a serious injury and because he was such a famous patient," says Cathy Wynne, "but there was no time to get nervous. Sue and I plunged in and helped them transfer Jim to the chair, and I began a brief evaluation of his physical condition.

"I checked for head control and he appeared to be able to hold his head up real well, which is important." She checked his ability to move—his body in general—then his left arm and left leg, his ability to roll over and to sit up. "I noted what an incredibly muscular man he was, with huge legs."

Jim was completely exhausted by that little bit of activity, and Marino and Wynne decided they would work on him in his bed at first. The muscles on his paralyzed left side were getting tight and needed stretching. Marino and Wynne tried to figure out what kinds of splints to put on his left hand, which was also painfully contracted. But he continued taking his meals sitting up in a chair.

The next day, Wynne started working on Jim's sitting balance on the edge of the bed, getting him to use his "head righting" and "trunk righting" reflexes. She asked him to lean forward, backward, and from side to side. "He would work with me," she says, "but he was very quiet. He had a very flat 'affect'—a blank emotional look, and I started facial exercises for the paralysis on the left side of his face." Wynne had read about James Brady's appointment as press secretary, and "I thought at the time that it seemed very unusual that such a neat guy was being named to such an important position. When Brady was shot," she says, "I felt terrible. I felt like I already knew him, and I liked him." Although he had had flashes of liveliness with family and friends, Brady was initially unresponsive with Wynne. She tried without success during that first week simply to get Jim to talk to her. One day in the second week Wynne mentioned to Sarah that she needed to buy a bottle of wine to take to a dinner party that night. Brady immediately chimed in, "Get Jordan, Cabernet Sauvignon, '78. You can get it at Eagle Wine and Liquor. Ask for Doug Burdette" (wine consultant and Jim's friend). "I almost fell off my chair," says Wynne. "He even told me how to get there. Sarah and I were so thrilled with this show of memory, I can't tell you."

Wynne and Jim's relationship developed quickly. A few days later, Wynne asked Brady to stick out his tongue. He complied with a cartoon sequence, slapping the back of his head to trigger his tongue out, "pulling" it to the left by tugging at his left ear, to the right via the right ear, tugging at his throat to pop it back in. Wynne was impressed and delighted. "He was purposefully being funny. That took a lot of initiative, considering his situation. It let me know there was a lot going on in there. If there were a lot of left frontal-lobe injury, he wouldn't have done it. It was a real good sign—a hopeful sign for the future."

While Reagan was still in the hospital, senior White House staff continued to stop by Jim's room occasionally to check on his progress after looking in on the president. Jim Baker came several times, and Ed and Ursula Meese dropped by twice. Meese asked Jim, "Can you hold up three fingers?" When Jim dutifully complied, Meese said, "Well, you've come a long way, Jim. You could never do that before." Jim laughed. Dick Allen had seen Jim briefly the night of the shooting. "The next time I saw him, he still had bandages on and he was black-and-blue. It shook me. I knew he knew me, though. When he talked it sounded a little like he was crying, but he wasn't. He was laughing, and I said to myself, 'That doesn't bother me, because it sounds like he's laughing.' Every time I saw him I was enormously encouraged by his progress."

Sarah's friend Pamela Jacovides, from the International Club—a women's club Sarah belonged to—and her husband, Andrew, ambassador of Cyprus, came to see Sarah. The Dahlgrens and other friends came to sit with her. Jim was too sick to see many people yet.

Mrs. Reagan came by twice. "On her first visit she came by with an entourage about nine or ten P.M.," says George Speese. "It had been a long day for Jim, of visits from Kobrine, Dr. O'Leary and others, and Jim had finally dozed off and was resting well. So I asked Mrs. Reagan, 'Could you possibly come back another time?' And she was more than understanding about it." Speese received a little flak about it around the hospital, but, he says, "I have thought about it since and if I had to do it over again, I'd probably do the same thing." Mrs. Reagan sent Jim flowers from the White House, and candy. When the president made his next trip to his California ranch, Mrs. Reagan brought back cookies made for Jim by their housekeeper, Anne Allman, who had taken a shine to Jim at their first and only meeting.

Sue Block brought homemade chicken soup one time and baklava another. Marge Guarasci, proprietor of Finesse Caterers, sent a huge Easter basket of goodies—cold lamb, soup, cold pasta, chocolate mousse. "It was one of Jim's first meals," says Sarah. Barbara Bush, Vice-President George Bush's wife, popped in one day to find Sarah reading a book at Jim's bedside. "What are you reading, Sarah?" she asked. "I hope it's a good dirty book. That's what you need."

Wynne believes the officers in the Uniformed Division of the Secret Service guarding Jim at the hospital helped him tremendously, too. "His interactions with them showed insight and memory. They were a White House connection, and they knew him. They would come into his room and tease him—Frank Slattery would get Jim on the 'mike' to talk to the guys at Secret Service headquarters. They would tease me, too, saying, 'What is this woman doing in your room again?' "

"They were wonderful to Jim," says Bob Dahlgren. "They went way beyond the requirements of their jobs. They took such pride in protecting him and had such personal feelings for Jim." The officers took over the job of turning Jim in his bed, something that had to be done every two hours to keep his blood circulating well.* And at night they would play games of catch with Jim in his room. "Jim would crack jokes about all the attention he was getting," says Frank Slattery. " 'Here I've got my 'protective' turning me over,' he'd say. Jim Brady's determination to come back made a lasting impression on me. It was amazing to us, too, how Sarah was able to keep herself up

*Throughout his eight months in GWU Hospital Jim was protected at all times by officers of the Secret Service Uniformed Division. The regulars were Frank Slattery, Gene Michinski, Frank Lopez, Clemmie Griffin, and Mike Bamber. Later, when Jim went to physical therapy or into surgery, Frank Slattery, who had the day shift, was always with Jim there, too.

day in and day out. We would all talk about that among ourselves."

On Saturday, April 11, President Reagan, smiling broadly, walked stiffly out of George Washington University Hospital to return to the White House. Leaving his wheelchair at the elevator, he said, "I walked in here. I'm going to walk out." Before he came downstairs, Sarah had joined Mrs. Reagan, Michael Deaver, and Patti Davis, to meet with the president. When he saw her, he said, "Sarah, tell Jim that 'Hell, he didn't have to do this to get a vacation.' " Reagan didn't see Jim before he left the hospital, but it was evident to onlookers that he was still suffering considerable discomfort. "What are you going to do when you get home?" a reporter asked. "Sit down," the president replied.

On the same day, District of Columbia police officer Thomas K. Delahanty also left the hospital for home. "I feel good. I'm ready to go," he said.

Ten days after the shooting Jim made two phone calls—to his deputy at the White House, Larry Speakes, and to Peter Teeley, Vice-President Bush's press secretary and an old PR friend. Speakes and Brady talked about the running of the White House press office. Speakes said later, "For all of us here in the White House, this is nothing short of a miracle." With Teeley, Jim picked up on an old joke they shared about fishing for sharks. Brady always claimed they would want to use dynamite instead of rod and reel. "It wouldn't be any fun without it," Brady told Teeley in his phone call. "To tell the truth," says Teeley, "I never was quite sure whether Brady was serious about shark fishing with dynamite or not, either before or after he was shot."

But, joking aside, Jim was becoming quieter. "I think," said Kobrine at the time, "the impact of what's happened to him is registering. His cognitive functions have improved to the point where he's aware of his injury and the impact his injury will have on his life. He is probably angry as he now fully realizes the gravity of his wounds. He is still talking to us whenever we go in the room—it's just that he was so bubbly for a couple of days—the tendency is for all of us to want him to go right back to work. . . . That's unrealistic." The good news was that Kobrine felt Brady was showing very little of the emotional sluggishness or apathy typical of lobotomized patients. "It would have been an entirely different ball of wax if the major part of the injury had been to the left frontal or dominant lobe," says Kobrine. "That would have left him unable to speak and radically altered his personality."

"For the first two weeks," says George Speese, "we would check several times a day on Jim's orientation to see if there were any problems of swelling or bleeding, and he got real tired of the same old questions. Who are you? Where are you? Who is the president of the United States? He'd look at me funny and say, 'George, I've answered that twelve times today.' So we began to vary them. Who was president before Reagan? What day will it be three days from now?"

At about the same time, Jim began scanning the newspaper and watching television. "The one thing he was intent on was reading the morning paper," says Ed Kornel. The White House later installed a "squawk box" in his room so he could listen in on the press briefings, and he had a White House signal telephone line with access to every corner of the earth. "He probably wasn't taking in much of the news at that point," says Kobrine, "but I wasn't worried about his mental capabilities. I was just so afraid of all the other physical dangers."

The days on 5E were as full of activity as they had been in the ICU.

The nursing team that shared the eight-hour shifts every day included Joan McKinney, Carolyn Prichett, George Speese, Jane Tiller, Cathy McAndrews, Ernie Brown, Abdulia Elvelna, Cathy Conroy, and Susan Deyo. Head nurse on 5E was Pamela Campobianco.

After the first week, Susan Deyo, who had just graduated from nursing school but was not yet a licensed RN, became Jim's day-care nurse, staying with him in his room at all times throughout her shift. During Jim's medical crises she worked double sixteen-hour shifts. "I once worked double shifts eighteen days straight." Jim called her Flash, "because she's a flash—she's fast," he says.

"I did everything for him except administer his medication," says Deyo. "It took Jim awhile to warm up to me, but soon he did, and then we talked all the time. He taught me a lot about politics. We watched the evening news together and he'd tell me the nicknames he had for people at the White

House. When reading the newspaper he'd take a black marker and mark out much of the story he was reading, then tell me, 'Now, what's left are the true facts.' "

Sarah told Deyo how comfortable she felt when Deyo was with Jim. "I can't emphasize enough how close we became, Sarah, Jim, and I," says Deyo. Jim and Deyo developed their own language. The painful lumbar punctures, which Jim hated so much were "B.F.s—big fuckinneedlesticks."

"Kobrine's bedside manner was very important to Jim," says Deyo. "He spent a lot of time talking to Jim. They'd exchange political ideas and talk about baseball and the Cubs." (Kobrine was from Chicago, too.)

In addition to the normal hospital routine, says Deyo, "we tried to teach Jim to do things like shave himself, feed himself, or bathe himself—all the things he would now have to do with one hand. It took a lot of time."

The Dahlgrens came by to see Sarah one night about two weeks after the shooting, and she asked them, "Are you ready to see Jim?"

"He really looked different," says Suzi Dahlgren. "Dramatically different. But he spoke first. He said, 'Hi Francesca,' he always calls me Francesca, and, 'Hi, Boobie,' his nickname for Bob. Bob cried the whole way home—sobbed—saying, 'That was my friend,' and 'Jim, Jim.' It was the first time in my life I'd ever seen Bob cry. But it was an incentive to keep going back, because every time we saw him again he was a little bit better, there was a little more wit."

Jim continued to sleep much of the time, but when he was awake, he often would respond in a random way to all sorts of noises and conversations. "He wanted to respond to everything, all the time," says Susan Marino, "to a conversation being held outside in the hall, or to laughter out there, or he would respond to the television instead of me. Once Sarah was on the phone talking to a mechanic about her car, and Jim was answering her questions." Another aspect of his brain injury—perseveration—showed itself. He would repeat things for no reason, an act, a word, a gesture. When eating, for instance, at first he might continue to fill his mouth with food, and not swallow, until he choked. He had to relearn the complicated act of swallowing food. When given pen and paper, he wrote 'Racoocoon," or "Bob Woodwardard." He drew a portrait of

Ed Kornel with thirty buttons down the front of his jacket. He drew a self-portrait of himself with the top of his head lopped off. "At first," says friend Ken Adelman, "Jim would write things out. He wrote *Ken Smith* and *John Adelman* over and over." Perseveration affected almost everything he did. He couldn't help doing it. He would just get stuck on something and be unable to turn it off. It was one of the many problems he would spend years on, trying to overcome.

Jim would get lost as to what time frame he was in, and went back and forth in the past, particularly thinking he was still having the intense experience of being on the Reagan campaign plane. "Where are we heading for today?" he would say. In his jottings could be seen the efforts of a mind turned topsy-turvy, desperately trying to impose some order on itself. He would jot down phrases as he watched television news. "Economic program." "Economic chaos." There was a poignant little note to his son: "Dear Scott, Here's your autograph. JSB 1:59 P.M. "I think I was so drugged that I didn't really know what to think, I just know that I was one hurtin' unit," he says today.

He floated in and out of reality as he began to recover and to relearn almost everything he had ever done. "Jim was very, very sick for a long, long time," Sarah has said over and over. And Sarah spent all day, every day, by Jim's side, monitoring every nuance in his condition, giving endless encouragement to every tiny scrap of improvement. "Jim, you're doing beautifully," she'd say soothingly. Her days began at 6:30 in the morning when she awoke and pulled the phone over so she could check on Jim's night, and they ended at 11:00 at night when she went home to bed.

But out of the miasma of his mental turbulence, Jim's sense of humor, his intellect, and his interest in the people around him, shone through. In the important things he was the same man he had always been, but he had specific deficits, and they would be extremely difficult to improve. His physical state was pretty well defined almost from the beginning. He had some movement left in the quadriceps of his left leg—the heavy muscles on the front of the thigh—which allowed for some movement in his left hip, but virtually none anywhere else in his left leg. His left arm had only the slightest voluntary movement left in it and his left hand was useless to him. Neither he nor Sarah was prepared to accept these limitations and Jim would work ceaselessly to make what he had left work for him.

"Without Sarah, Jim would never have done as well as he did," says Susan Deyo. "There's no doubt in my mind about that. She gave her all. She knew everybody who was taking care of Jim, and she cared about everybody and knew all about them. She stayed on top of everything that was being done to Jim and had a say about everything. She is a very smart lady. She'd ask for explanations of the procedures we performed, and asked questions until she completely understood."

"I would see her come home from the hospital those nights," says her mother, "at ten or twelve, then stay up to do the laundry and her other chores. She was leading an awful life."

"Sarah was very, very worried about Scott in those days," says Jan Wolff. "I just feel so awful not being there," Sarah told her. "She would come home to spend an hour or so with him and then go back to the hospital."

Jim's mental deficits were less easy to define than his physical ones, but they were serious. But Kobrine told Sarah that his brain could very well heal and improve its functioning—finding and making new neural pathways—over the course of the next seven to ten years. That knowledge gave her great hope. It also dictated the cautious statements made about Jim to the media. Art Kobrine wanted to give his patient every chance to heal without the stigma of his early condition becoming widely known. He also wanted to give Jim Brady himself all the hope he could that he would be able to recover substantially from this terrible wound. "I didn't dissuade him from that. I felt I needed to hold that out to him to make him work it out, and to keep him working."

Kobrine himself was under enormous public pressure. "I knew when I walked out of the operating suite at midnight, March thirtieth, that we were in store for all kinds of complications with those eggshell fractures on the bottom of his skull. Either you are lucky and things go well, or you are unlucky and have terrible problems. I felt at that moment it was likely he would remain as unlucky as he had been to be in the wrong place at the wrong time to have caught that bullet. And he was. I knew I was going to have to take the long-term overview of this." Kobrine himself snatched a few hours' sleep and was in the OR again at 7:30 that morning. It wasn't until 3:00 A.M. on April 1 that he went home, showered, slept until 6:00 and went back to the hospital.

In the first few weeks Sarah allowed only their closest friends to come to see Jim. He was conscious, but hardly in control. Still, he pulled himself together to greet his old friends. He greeted Otto Wolff as he usually did. "Wolfie!" he said. "Herr Wolff, does the Führer know where you are?" "But," says Otto, "I cried after I saw him." "Otto came home so upset and emotionally shaken," says Jan. A week later Jan went to see him, wearing kelly-green culottes and a strawberry-pink top. "You look like a Talbot's catalog," Jim told her. Kent and Linda Watkins came by during the first week, and were stunned to hear Jim say, "Hi, Linda. How are things in St. Paul [Virginia—Linda's hometown]?" "My reaction was," says Watkins, "he is making a conscious attempt to prove he is able to remember things like that." But also it was Jim's personality as well as his career as a political professional to remember names and places—to focus thoroughly on the person before him. It was one of his many attractive traits. "He didn't talk much and his conversation didn't track but what he said had that spark of humor. I was very shaken by his loss of weight and his very red and visible scar. His head had been completely shaved," says Watkins. Bob and Suzi Dahlgren brought their daughters, Jordan and Sarah, to see their "Uncle Jim." To Sarah Dahlgren, Jim said, "Hi, have they named a country for you yet?" It was an old joke between them—Jim had always teased that "Jordan" was a funny name and he liked to razz the girls about it.

"I saw Jim before the end of April," says Dick McGraw. " 'Hi, Dickie,' he said and grinned. He had a firm grip. Sarah had tried to prepare me, and physically he looked okay. But the lack of emotional control and the impediment to his speech—those things were very disconcerting. It was depressing, saddening. But every time I saw him thereafter, there was improvement—more each time.

"One can have nothing but admiration for Sarah," adds McGraw. "She must have been strong before the shooting, but it just wasn't apparent—Jim was so dominating in conversations."

Sarah tried to prepare friends Brandy and David Cole, but "David was a lot more upset than I was," says Brandy. "He wasn't prepared for what he saw." Jim said to her, "Hi, kid, how are you?" And to David, "It's good to see you, Señor Cole." "I was very nervous," says Brandy, "but what I saw was that Jim did everything he could to put us at ease, and I thought, 'That's Jim Brady for you.' What upset David the most was the wail. The other thing was, his attention span was absolutely zero."

Newsman Jerry O'Leary saw Jim about two months after the shooting. "Well, if it isn't the old colonel coming in to see me," Jim greeted him. (O'Leary is a recently retired Marine Corps Reserve colonel.) But "his face no longer had any expression," says O'Leary. "When I walked in and saw what *was* his marvelously expressive, round, ursine face, always twinkling with good humor—and he had no control over his voice. That was the great shock of all time to see him unable to express himself, knowing he could think perfectly well. There were long silences. Unless you said something to him, he'd not say anything."

Jim began developing a leak of cerebrospinal fluid from his brain into the forehead flap that had been rolled down for surgery. "It was getting pretty awful looking," says Sarah. "The fluid had distended his forehead, and would roll back and forth as he moved." "I may not look all right on the outside," said Jim, "but I'm a carnival on the inside." At the worst stage of this new development, Richard Allen and *Detroit News* Bureau Chief Gary Schuster walked in unannounced. "Their eyes widened in amazement," says Sarah, "and I was mortified that a newsman would see Jim in this condition." She was afraid he would describe it in his newspaper. But not a word came out. The next day Kobrine asked Jacobson to tap the fluid off, "and something very funny happened," says Jacobson. "I had to be very careful about inserting the needle, and I told the nurse to hold Jim's head tightly, that she was not to move. Hearing this, Jim then reached up and slipped his hand onto her breast. 'What'll I do?' she shrieked. 'What'll I do?' " Jacobson told her, "Well, you can enjoy it, or not enjoy it, but don't you move!" Obviously, this lack of inhibition was due to brain damage. "At first," says Jan Wolff, "Jim had no inhibitions. It used to embarrass Sarah." His worst trick, Sarah thought, was his "flashing" the room by waving his hospital gown. All hands went flying to stop that behavior.

Jim's head flap filled up again, and Kobrine decided to wrap his head with gauze to try to force the reabsorption of the leak. The result was an unexpected and unwelcome one. Cerebrospinal fluid started leaking out of his nose. That worried Kobrine even more.

There was no doubt that for Kobrine Jim Brady was a special case. But he had a regular roster of other patients as well to whom he was giving conscientious treatment—operating and following through with postoperative attention. In addition, the intense public interest in Jim's progress brought about often vexing media pressure. "Dan Ruge helped me with the press," says Kobrine. "I'd come back to my office and there would be thirty-five pink message slips from the press on my desk." Ruge told him, "The way you deal with that, Art, is to take all those pink slips and throw them in the wastebasket. And once you have done that, then you've dealt with 'em." "I would talk to science reporters, as opposed to sensational reporters, from time to time, but we pretty much decided that, at first, Dennis O'Leary would be the only outlet to the press.

"There were interviews on television with doctors who had zero knowledge of the president's case or of Jim's," continues Kobrine. "It was upsetting to me, but Ruge would explain that, in the long run, the truth will come out. I used to run by him everything I was doing with Jim, and we would toss it around. He gave a lot of support to what I was doing." At his first press conference three days after the shooting, Kobrine realized that every time he moved his head, the cameras would click and whirr. "Every move I made was scrutinized, and I had to make decisions that were unpopular. I didn't think it was anybody's business to know every little thing about the case. It just made sense to me that everything I said be cautious."

Then on Thursday, April 16, came the first of a series of setbacks. Jim's temperature started to rise and he developed a rash. "Fever to me meant infection, unless proved otherwise," says Kobrine. They did a spinal tap and the fluid "grew out" bacteria. "We changed antibiotics and added more of them." The temperature went up and up and Susan Deyo gave him alcohol baths to try to lower it. Kobrine and infectious-disease specialist Dr. Carmen Tuazon figured the rash was probably an allergic reaction to Dilantin, Kobrine's first-choice antiseizure drug. "It has the fewest side effects and works the best," says Kobrine. They took him off Dilantin and his high-blood-pressure medicine, substituting phenobarbital and Tegretol instead. But the fever raged on for two days, reaching 104 degrees before it finally broke two days later, the afternoon of April 18. Sarah and Susan Deyo, who had been keeping the vigil, embraced tearfully. "Susan was afraid that Jim would go into seizures and that would be it," says Sarah. "We were so relieved and thankful," says Deyo.

Jim began to be alert enough that he started nicknaming the regulars who were caring for him. Jeff Jacobson was "Jeffie J.," Ed Kornel became "Dr. Princeton." Day nurse Susan Deyo was "Flash" or "Florence Nightingale." RN Jane Tiller was "Nurse Jane Fuzzy Wuzzy" or "Jingle Jangle Jane," because of the large set of keys she carried. He addressed Art Kobrine as "A.K." and Kobrine in turn called him "J.B." Jim also called Kobrine "Dr. Goodknife."

Jim's playful nature emerged more and more in ways that some hospital people thought were indicative of his injury. Sarah kept telling them, "No, no, you don't understand. He was that way before." Jim had a little hand puppet he called "Mingo." Early on, Mingo served as Jim's alter ego, who would tell his nurses, therapists, and doctors things he didn't want to tell them himself. Mingo would say, "Go away, I'm tired," or "Stop it, you're hurting me." "We would talk to Jim through Mingo, too," says Deyo.

Jim remembers very little of the first several weeks of his hospitalization. "I was drifting in and out," he says today. "And I'll tell you, if it wasn't for the honor of it, I'd just as soon skip it." Sarah adds, "But if it had to happen, we were surely surrounded by good people and in a good place." "Yeah," says Jim, "but the next time, I think I'll pass."

Jim had no more recovered from his allergic reaction when, four days later, on April 22, doctors and nurses noticed he wasn't talking as much. In *The Washington Post* that morning was a White House story saying that Jim was doing so well he would begin walking with a cane the next week and be back at the White House in a few months. "He just didn't seem right to me that day," says Kobrine, who had seen him in early morning rounds. "It was hard to get him to talk."

Later in the afternoon Cathy Wynne went in to work with him. "I noticed he was extremely compliant and very quiet," she says. "So I called Dr. Kornel." Kornel was alarmed to see Jim even more quiet than in the morning. In addition, Jim's nurses reported that he had had a sneezing fit. Kornel called Kobrine, who rushed over from his office. "Jim had started sneezing again and got more sleepy," says Kobrine. Kobrine was telling Jim to try not to sneeze, "and Jim thought I meant not to sneeze at all—obviously a physical impossibility. So he was sneezing, but suppressing the sneezes. And I was yelling at him, 'Don't do that.' " Kobrine felt pretty sure there was air in the brain ventricles instead of the cerebrospinal fluid that is made there and bathes the brain. He thought there might be a hole in the dura.

Sarah was waiting in the hall, chatting with CBS newsman Bill Plante, who had come by for his first visit with Jim. First, Jane Tiller came out crying. She had come under the famous Kobrine temper. When he found out he didn't have the equipment he needed, Kobrine chewed her out in no uncertain terms. Then suddenly, out of Jim's room burst Jim on a stretcher with Kobrine once again at the helm, about to embark on an all too familiar journey. Downstairs to the CAT scan room, where Kobrine viewed a few pictures to confirm the suspicion he dreaded. Then back to his hospital bed where Kobrine prepped him for the cranial tap. He put two needles carefully through the top holes made less than a month earlier by the craniotome. "Air came hissing out," says Kobrine. "Jim immediately opened his eyes and looked around—talked and joked." Kobrine was appalled. It was clear that there had to be a significantly large hole to allow that much air to build up—a condition called tension pneumocephalus, air in the brain—the pressure of which would begin to destroy brain tissue unless soon relieved. Kobrine went out to talk to Sarah. "There is a problem, Sarah," he told her. "Is Jim going to die?" she said. "No, but he needs another operation," said Kobrine. Kobrine took his patient to the operating room to begin a full-fledged, formal craniotomy, only three weeks after the shooting and the original craniotomy, tracing over the original incisions in the scalp, bone, and dura. Ed Engle, Jeff Jacobson, and Ed Kornel assisted Kobrine.

"I think for Art it was very hard," says Kornel. "He was on the line. And it was a much longer operation, much more difficult, because the trick this time was to repair the leak without doing any damage to the Jim Brady who had survived the first operation." "Eighty-five percent of leaks stop by themselves," says Kobrine, "but it was obvious that the hole was large enough to be life-threatening. And I knew we had to go in and fiddle around with his dominant lobe."

"We found a hole in the bone and the dura, almost as big as the bullet hole, just an inch or so down from the entrance wound in the roof of the left eye orbit," says Kobrine. It was a hole opened by the original explosion of the Devastator bullet, which Kobrine had not discovered because of his reluctance to fool with Jim's left frontal lobe while it was in its runny, injured state. Now, just three weeks later, Jim's brain had regained its firmness and integrity and could be gently moved without damaging his brain. The dura on both sides had completely healed together, too. "I saw fracture lines emanating from the hole, and the fractures in the cribriform plate [the floor of the skull] I had seen before. I didn't try to correct these—I just hoped they would heal with a little luck." Nor was there any need to reopen the right lobe. Kobrine repaired the newly found hole in the skull with a piece of tissue from Jim's temporalis muscle, taken from above his left ear. He packed the dura with a piece of Gelfoam. Six and a half hours later, Kobrine crossed his fingers that he had solved the air leaks, "but I wasn't at all convinced it would solve the problem of CSF [cerebrospinal fluid] leaks, having had a really good look at all the cracks in the bone beneath the brain."

Jim recovered more quickly from this operation than from the first one since he wasn't suffering from the enormous trauma of brain swelling this time. But he developed another rash, a reaction to the latest antiseizure medicine. And Sarah began to notice a "wailing" when Jim talked. He also had difficulty swallowing and seemed to have to relearn the eating process. "It was a setback, too, as far as physical therapy was concerned," says Cathy Wynne. "He couldn't sit up. He had to be on his back with his head back."

Kobrine told Jim all about what he had gone through and Jim had questions about it, but to Jim the worst part of the whole thing was that he couldn't eat solid food because he was having trouble swallowing. When he was taken off intravenous feeding, he was put on a diet of high-nutrient puddings. Dr. Tuazon promised him she would bring him a Philippine meal when he could eat again. "Oh, a Luzon lunch," said Jim. "Where is my Luzon lunch?" Jim would ask her whenever he saw her. Ten days later, Sarah, the Kobrines, the residents, and other staff gathered in Jim's room for chicken and pork adobo, noodles pansit, BBQ pork ribs. "We got to be very big fans of Philippine food," says Sarah. One of Jim's nurses, Abdulia Elvelna, also from the Philippines and nicknamed "the Mongoose" by Jim, brought more Philippine food in to him.

A White House medical bulletin said: "Mr. Brady is quite alert and there remains no evidence of infection thus far. Yesterday, Mr. Brady engaged his neurosurgeon in a game of 'thumbsies,' and won, in what Dr. Arthur Kobrine describes as a fair match." Jim came back well enough that two nights later Sarah took her first evening out away from Jim and went to the annual White House Correspondents' Dinner. The White House Correspondents' Dinner is an annual press party in Washington similar to the Gridiron Club, and usually the president attends. But this year he and Mrs. Reagan were at Camp David, the presidential retreat in Thurmont, Maryland, where Mr. Reagan was still recuperating. However, in a special phone call made to the assembled throng and played over the sound system, Mrs. Reagan said to Sarah Brady, "I remember those days in the hospital when you and I had many conversations and we both agreed that you and I had a bond that was very special, that nobody could break." Then the president proposed a toast to Jim: "There isn't an hour when he isn't in our prayers," he said. "Why don't we raise a glass to the Bear—and Sarah." The eighteen hundred guests stood, glasses aloft. Sarah Brady was alone in the spotlight, with tears in her eyes.

A few days after his surgery, the hospital received a bomb threat. There had been numerous threats since the shooting, but this was the first one aimed at Jim. Policemen and dogs, and Secret Service agents swarmed through the hospital—meeting first to case Jim's room. Jim himself slept through the whole thing, "even the dogs," says Sarah. But Jim's loyal friend and personal assistant Kathy Ahern happened to be coming down the hall at that moment. Seeing the profusion of police in and around Jim's room, she immediately assumed he had died and she collapsed against the wall and sobbed.

Five days after his second craniotomy, Jim's medical chart read: "Continues to talk with more than a yes or no—sometimes needing no prompting." He was starting to talk much more spontaneously. The next day he spent two hours sitting up in a chair, the longest he had been out of bed since being wounded.

But that evening, Jim had a sneezing fit, and four drops of cerebrospinal fluid leaked from his nose. A CAT scan revealed a new pocket of air and another area of possible trouble that couldn't have been exposed in the craniotomy without doing damage to his brain. This time, Kobrine's tack was to keep Jim in bed and to elevate his head at a 30-degree angle for ten days. In that position, the pressure inside and outside Jim's head was in balance. Kobrine ordered Jim's diet be reduced to high-calorie puddings, which could be easily eaten in that position without his chewing. "I hoped that would solve the problem," says Kobrine.

Two of Jim's former bosses came to visit him: Donald Rumsfeld (Jim had been assistant to the secretary of defense when Rumsfeld held that post in the Ford Administration from 1975 to 1976) and Governor John Connally (for whom Jim had been press secretary and political adviser during Connally's unsuccessful bid for the Republican presidential nomination in 1980). "Jim's great value in our campaign," says Connally, "was in having a deep understanding of government and its functions. We asked him his judgment constantly and his judgment was unerringly good. He had amazing mental equilibrium. If he was ever angry he never showed it." It was when Connally dropped out of the race in March 1980 that he highly recommended Jim Brady to Edwin Meese on the Reagan campaign, which resulted in Jim's joining the Reagan team. On his first visit to the hospital, Connally left with tears in his eyes. "I was absolutely sick when I first heard the news, and pretty upset when I saw Jim. The second time, Nellie [Mrs. Connally] came with me, and he was much more vocal and lucid." Jim greeted him with "Hello, Governor." "It literally ripped your heart out to talk to him. His voice reflected an emotion in a way and made him speak in a sobbing voice. If you'd known him as we had—it was very hard for us to accept. Nellie and I always called him Friar Tuck. His appearance, his loyalty, his dedication—all the attributes that Friar Tuck showed. I kidded him and I told him I could sympathize with him." (Governor Connally himself had been shot and seriously wounded—by Lee Harvey Oswald—as he rode in the same car when John F. Kennedy was assassinated in Dallas in 1963. The rifle bullet went through his back, blew two ribs out the front of his chest, cutting his lung in half, went through his wrist, breaking all the bones in it, and into his leg. "I knew I'd been hit," he says. "It was like someone had come up behind me and hit me with their fist as hard as they could." The exit wound from Governor Connally's chest was as big as a tennis ball. "They told me I would have died from loss of blood if the hospital hadn't been five minutes away, just as Reagan would have.") "Having been through an assassination," says Connally, "I have a sympathy for him the average person can't possibly feel, because I appreciate more fully than most what an enormous tragedy it is. We see Sarah, see her devotion and what heartbreak and tragedy she endures. I attribute much of Jim's progress to her care."

Don Rumsfeld says, "I will never forget the first hospital visit to see Jim. He always called me Boss, and he greeted me with 'How ya doin', Boss?' But for me there was a gap between the news stories and my expectations. You'd read about his 'miraculous recovery' and you'd go in and you couldn't see it." But while in Jim's room, Rumsfeld brought up an old friend of his whom Jim had also met once on a Department of Defense trip he and Rumsfeld had made to Hawaii. The man was a pilot and legendary for his ability to enjoy himself. "I said to Jim and Sarah of my friend that he was heavily focused on beer, broads, and boobs, when Jim interjected, 'And not necessarily in that order.' It was tremendously encouraging to me to have this humor pop out of his mouth. It gave me a lot of hope."

"Jim always came alive when people from his work world came around," says Susan Deyo. "They had things to tell him, the latest gossip, what was going on outside. Once he learned about our hospital world and its gossip, he became a part of that, too."

At the end of April Jim's secretary, Sally McElroy, came by for the first time to see Jim and to bring gifts and letters that had come to the White House. "Hi. Got some work for me?"

he asked her. "He looked so good," she says. "I felt positive he would make it. I was so happy I walked all the way back to the White House."

On May 3, Jim was awarded the Significant Sig Award on the occasion of the 100th anniversary of the Kappa Kappa Chapter of Sigma Chi by his fraternity brothers at the University of Illinois. It was a decision that had been made before the shooting, but now it became a huge emotional event. Seven hundred people turned out, including university president Dr. Stanley Ikenberry, and Jim listened to the ceremony on a telephone hookup as Grand Consul Jack McDuff announced the award. Centralia, Illinois, attorney Jim Wham told them, "The story of Jim Brady is the hallmark of Sigma Chi. His courage in adversity—his humor, even on a bed of pain—his resolve to live and write yet another chapter in the ongoing saga of freedom. It's a lesson unsurpassed in the annals of Sigma Chi. From these bonds of brotherhood tonight, a mighty chorus of regard, concern and love rolls out across the land to you, Jim Brady and Sarah. As you wait together through the healing hours, you shall not tread the winepress alone, for we are with you. We know you shall return to even broader lands and better days."

Sarah responded for Jim, ". . . I see the look in his eyes and the emotion that he's expressing, and he's so thankful for this award. . . . I don't know of any other honor that has ever brought such emotion upon him. He is thrilled with it . . . he has loved his association with Sigma Chi, and this is a very deep and important moment for him, and we both thank you from the bottom of our hearts."

Then, as Jim listened, his old friends and fraternity brothers regaled him with affectionate words of tribute, beginning with Dick Church. "Our thoughts are almost constantly with you, Jim. Knowing me as you do, you know I don't do much praying, but I have been praying very hard for you and your recovery." Then Jim Redpath reminisced about Jim's pledging him to Sigma Chi in the fall of 1961. Bob Cornelisen said, "You have a lotta guts, guy, to pull through this thing. I know Ronald Reagan is anxious to get you back on the job. You're too darned valuable." Another said, "Thanks for your courage, Jim. It's a fabulous example to all of us." Then Jim's friends began to remind him of shared youthful escapades. "Remember that night in Springpatch," asked Dick Church, "when the piano player was cross-eyed and kept getting more cross-eyed all night? And the time we consumed thirteen bottles of wine and our bar tab only came to thirty dollars?"

Dick Church was one of Jim's friends who went out of his way to look in on him. As a trade-association manager, he often had business in Washington. But beyond that, says Church, "I made sure I had business in Washington that year, if you know what I mean." Jeri, his partner in business, came with him, too, when she could. They had been in close phone contact with Sarah, who was always very positive and optimistic, says Church.

"Before my first visit Sarah sat me down and prepared me for what Jim was like. Prepared me to the extent that I was relieved, honestly, when I saw him because he looked better and acted better than I expected. He was still bruised, slightly swollen, and had a bandage around his head, but when you consider I originally had thought he was dead, I was relieved to see him as good as he was."

"Hi, Weenie," Jim greeted him on his first visit in early May, Weenie being a nickname Church had been given during the Illinois campaign. Jim occasionally confused Church with White House policeman Frank Slattery and bestowed the name "Weenie" on Slattery from time to time.

"Dick would come in on the weekend and spend a whole day with Jim in the hospital," says Sarah. "He kept up with Jim almost better than anybody."

"I spent a lot of time playing catch with him with a Nerf ball," says Church. "And Sarah stressed working on his past memory so we spent the days reminiscing about Illinois campaign stories to help stimulate Jim's mind.

"At first I thought things weren't functioning correctly. His conversation was mostly responses to things I had said." But as time went on, says Church, "I was never quite sure if he wasn't conning me a little bit. His reaction to my remarks was such that I felt he was going to say something coherent and cogent.

"He always had something to say—some big story to tell. He'd never say, 'I don't know.'" Church watched Jim persistently call a nurse by the wrong name, then when she left the room, laugh about how funny her reaction was. "He puts you on. He plays dumb when he knows really what you are doing."

It bothered Church that too many people were too easy on Jim. "I try to treat Jim very normally and irreverently. I call him names, 'Dum Dum' when he screws up—things like that. I've always felt he responded best to that."

Sarah began to feel she could relax her vigil a little. But on May 4, one week after the last crisis, asleep at home, Sarah woke suddenly at four in the morning. She called the hospital. "I cannot believe you are calling," said Jim's nurse. They had just discovered that Jim was having trouble breathing. "We are worried he may have thrown an embolus [blood clot]." Kobrine had been called at home, and he rushed in to view the lung scan he had ordered. The scan showed numerous small blood clots—fortunately, for a large clot could have been fatal if it blocked the pulmonary artery. The clots had developed as a result of Jim's inactivity. There was pressure on Kobrine from the disease group of physicians and some of the radiologists to prescribe heparin for Jim (a blood thinner). Heparin, it was true, was the most effective of its class but it carried with it the danger of causing bleeding elsewhere, "like in the head," Kobrine was thinking. And furthermore, if he had to operate again, he would have to wait for the heparin to clear Jim's system. Radiologist Ed Drury supported Kobrine, and also recommended a new device that could be implanted surgically to catch and strain blood clots—a device that had been doing a much better job in patients than the older "umbrellas" or blood strainers, with which they were all familiar. Kobrine asked vascular surgeon Hugh Trout to enter the case and Trout also recommended installing the new "Greenfield umbrella" in Jim's vena cava. (Blood clots generally form in the legs, and the vena cava is the large collecting vein that drains the blood from the legs and lower trunk.)

"That was one of the scariest days of all," says Sarah. "At any moment he could have thrown a killer blood clot and died." And for a while Trout and Kobrine couldn't find one of the new umbrella devices. They were about to send a helicopter to Richmond, to get one from its inventor, when their phone calls turned up one at Mt. Vernon Hospital in nearby Alexandria, Virginia. In the meantime, they had injected Jim's bloodstream with a dye so they could watch for any large clots. Had one formed they would have operated hurriedly to try to catch it.

In a three-hour operation under local anesthesia, Dr. Trout, through an incision in Jim's right groin, threaded the umbrella (two and a half inches long and half an inch in diameter) along a wire up to a point in the vena cava just above the navel. Ed Kornel joined them in the OR. "I just wanted to be there," he said.

It was another problem solved, they hoped. But one problem seemed to lead to another. They had treated the CSF leak with bed rest, but blood clots formed as a result. Jim had so little reserve, says Kobrine, that "when there was a setback, it just started a cascade of events, and everything that was being held together with baling wire just fell apart. For the longest time he was potentially ill." And Jim himself began to worry about his blood clots and the CSF dripping.

Art Kobrine brought his wife, Cindy, around to meet Jim for the first time. "We were going out and the nurse called Art about another patient, so we went by the hospital on our way." When Art introduced Jim, he shook her hand firmly and said, "Hi, Cindy. It's great to meet you. Your husband and I have been a little close lately. I know him really well now." "You're looking good," Cindy told him. "Yeah, thanks, but if I could get all this stuff off and eat a decent meal, I'd be better," Jim replied, referring to the infernal "intermittent" pneumatic stockings he had to wear for his circulation.

Kobrine continued to keep Jim in bed for a week after the umbrella surgery, until a CAT scan showed just one small air bubble left in Jim's head. On May 11, he allowed Jim to sit up and move around in bed. "It looks like things are sealed," said Kobrine. "Whether this is forever or whether it changes when we move him around, we will have to see." The next day a huge truck arrived outside the hospital, driven from Florida by a restaurant owner with an enormous "Get Well, Bear" sign on it. Kobrine and Cathy maneuvered Jim to the window where he stood for two minutes—the longest he had been on his feet yet—and was seen by the public for the first time since the shooting. "He loved that," says Kobrine. "All of us were excited about his showing himself to the public for the first time," says Wynne. "Jim was smiling and waving—and wailing. It was real good timing for that truck to arrive." Jim wore his plaid tam-o'shanter cap sent to him by Senator Hayakawa. Jim would ask people, "Want to play with my fuzzy yellow ball [on the hat]?" "Oh, Jim, please. Forget it," Wynne would tell him.

Ed Kornel, who missed the truck and all the excitement, asked Jim later, "What did I miss?" Jim told him the truck was carrying dead people. "He couldn't separate his dreams from reality at that point," says Kornel. "And he really started to indicate his tremendous fear of death. He had this recurrent thing about witnessing his own funeral. He dreamed he had been out with his friends in a carriage, and he was wrapped in a sheet, and his friends threw him out of the carriage. He began to want to participate in his own care and wanted to be informed about everything. The CSF leaks became a big concern for him. He was afraid they'd start again and more surgery would be needed." He would say, "You can talk directly to me, you know. It's not like I'm a corpse." Jim also was terribly upset at the incontinence of bowel and bladder he was experiencing at this time.

"In the next few days Jim began getting out of bed, even taking a couple of steps, with maximum assistance," says Cathy Wynne, "with me and Dr. Kobrine on either side." Jim ventured out of his room for the first time in a wheelchair and chatted with other patients in the corridor. And a few days later he went downstairs to have physical therapy in the physical-therapy center on the ground floor.

His left arm was hurting and Jim would complain loudly about it when someone touched it. "Ow, ow, ow, ow." He was always trying to pull off the special stockings he wore, so he could get at his legs to scratch them (his many allergies to one medication or another kept him miserable from itching) or he would try to con someone into doing it for him. When Senator Charles Percy came to visit him again, Jim, out of nowhere, said to him: "You wear these things [the stockings], too, don't you?"

In physical therapy Jim began the hard work of making his left arm and leg work for him. "We did a lot of work," says Wynne, "working on his sitting balance, throwing the ball to get him to stretch his torso. We fitted him with a long leg brace to straighten his leg out of its flexion so he could stand, and his leg improved." Jim continued to run a low-grade temperature off and on. "We thought it was due to allergic reactions or not breathing enough to open up the lungs, or to tiny emboli," says Kobrine. "They were never life-threatening."

But on May 27 his temperature zoomed to 102.7. Kobrine started him back on "big time" antibiotics, but the next day he was wheezing, his temperature was up to 104, and "Flash" gave him alcohol baths. Nurse George Speese says, "I asked him a stupid question, like 'How are you feeling?' when any adult with a high temperature feels miserable, and Jim said, 'George, that's like asking Mary Todd Lincoln, "Except for the fact your husband was shot, Mrs. Lincoln, how did you like the play?" ' "

The next day he developed signs of pneumonia and an X ray confirmed it. It was an enormous relief to everybody that his temperature was not "head" related, and they assured Jim that he was going to be okay, that it was only pneumonia. Jim picked up on that irony immediately, telling everybody who came into his room, with great sarcasm, "Whoopee, have you heard the good news? I've got pneumonia. I'm not sick. I've only got pneumonia. Isn't that wonderful news?"

On the last day of May, with Jim's pneumonia clearing, Frank Slattery ordered pizza for Sarah, and a few close friends and some of the staff had a pizza party in Jim's room to celebrate his recovery, as well as the discovery that there was still some movement in his left elbow. Ed Kornel sang an original song he wrote for the occasion. Although Jim and Sarah did not know it, the end of May marked the end of the first series of near-fatal crises. They were about to begin a two-month hiatus of steady progress for Jim, and good times with their friends.

On May 27, John Hinckley took an overdose of a combination of Valium and Tylenol but was revived. He was despondent over a ruling that denied his plea that he be tried under the Youthful Defendants Act, which for him would expire when he turned twenty-six on May 29.

CHAPTER SIX

Summer 1981

On June 2 the recovered Ronald Reagan came to see Jim Brady in his hospital room. He had phoned Jim twice from the White House but this was his first visit to see him since they had both been wounded. Kobrine had suggested waiting until now. Nurse Susan Deyo was nervous about the visit, but Jim told her, "Don't worry, Flash. He's just an old shoe. Wait till you meet him. He's a great guy." "I'm glad I was able to come," Reagan told Jim when he saw him, in an oblique reference to his own close call. "Doesn't everyone get a visit by the president?" Brady joked from his bed. Reagan brought Jim a jigsaw puzzle depicting jelly beans, and a jar of the famous Reagan candy. In the puzzle box was a sheet of paper with the manufacturer's name. Sarah asked what that was for and Jim chimed in, "That's who you call if you can't finish it."

Reagan told Jim that he was holding his job open for him and scolded him, saying, "You've been on your back long enough, Jim, and work is piling up. It's about time you finished up this stuff and got back to the White House." It showed a nicely intuitive sense of what Jim needed to hear—that he was still needed. As he left, Reagan said, "We're waiting for you to get back. We need you." Jim replied, "I've been watching you on the television and reading newspapers and you're doing pretty well on your own." "Well, you rest and take care of yourself," said Reagan. "That's the first time you've said that to me," Brady joked back at him.

Several times during the visit Jim had trouble suppressing the emotion in his voice and he sounded as though he were crying—his "wailing," Sarah called it. And at one point Jim volunteered that Mrs. Reagan had sent him the Adolfo pajamas he was wearing—which she hadn't—and he wasn't. (No one was certain whether that was Jim's joke or his condition.) But overall Sarah and Kobrine were very pleased with the way Jim had handled himself during the president's visit. Dan Ruge, however, thought the visit had turned into a circus with more than a dozen people in Jim's room. It had been his idea that only Art Kobrine should accompany Mr. and Mrs. Reagan and he had pressed that idea on Mike Deaver. "The purpose was to treat the patient and not the visitor," says Ruge. "It just shows how important press events are to this administration. I don't recall anytime I've been more burned about anything than that."

Jim's wailing was the result of brain injury, possibly a combination of injury in several different locations—a little in the left frontal lobe, the limbic system, which coordinates one's emotional response, the right frontal lobe, and just the fact that there had been many places in the brain where there had been disconnections. "It's not really crying at all," says Kobrine. "It's a sign of a sort of stress, which tends to show up more when Jim is meeting with people less familiar to him than family and close friends. We all undergo that stress, but we have learned to control it, and more importantly, we have all the interconnecting brain cells we need to control it."

Jim's wailing was a very big problem in his recovery, however, because it alarmed people—they didn't know what it meant or how to handle it, when the truth is it meant almost nothing. Jim might do some wailing while telling a joke or just giving a straightforward answer to a straightforward question. Those closest to him learned to listen through the wailing, or to ask him to repeat what he said if it was hard to understand—which he very cheerfully would do. For the first couple of years Sarah often counseled him to "take a breath, Pooh," which seemed to help. As time went on he began to be more and more able to control it, but sometimes he was just eager to talk, and in effect, said, "the hell with it," in order to say what he wanted to say. "I can control it," he said to CBS's Charlie Rose in 1983. "It takes a lot of concentration to control it, but I can."

His injury caused other problems at the beginning. When the bullet severed the connections between the right parietal lobe of Jim's brain and his left side, it also, at first, caused him to be unable to recognize the left side of his body. He would look at his nearly lifeless left arm and not recognize it as his own. Asked how his arm was, he would say, "It's fine, but will you just take this other arm out of my bed and go put it on the windowsill?"

Another mental function that was impaired at first was the ability to identify faces, particularly new faces. Called prosopagnosia, this dysfunction points up the wonderful specialization of the brain. "It's almost as though there is a single brain cell for every face you will ever see in your whole life," says Kobrine. "It is what enables us to see a face once and never forget it." This ability is located in the right parietal lobe (for right-handed people), about where Hinckley's bullet wound up, and the injury caused Jim occasional confusion between two people who looked very much alike, particularly people he had met since the shooting. One of his best friends, U.S. Air Force Colonel Stuart Purviance, strongly resembled Norman Barr, an otolaryngologist on the staff at GWUH. Brady's nickname for Purviance was "Colonel Pervert." Dr. Barr knew Jim confused him with his old friend Stu Purviance, but he never could get used to being addressed as Colonel Pervert. Hospital name tags were a big help to Jim and helped him disguise his problem. For a long time, says Kobrine, "I saw Jim read my name tag before he addressed me by name." Sometimes Jim was adamant about what he thought he saw, and no amount of insisting on Sarah's part could dissuade him. "Well, to me, he's Colonel Pervert," he would say to her after she corrected him for the twentieth time.

Jim sometimes confused Ed Kornel with his friend Kenneth Adelman and would address Kornel as "Kenneth Lee," saying "Remember when we did this, or that?" "He would just ignore me when I said that wasn't me who did that with him," says Kornel.

From time to time Kobrine ordered lumbar punctures done on Jim to drain off excess CSF and reduce pressure. They were painful and Jim hated them. When he saw Kornel or Jacobson coming to perform the procedure, he railed at them as "sadists who were happy in their job."

Jim often amazed them all, however. When Pope John Paul II was shot and wounded in St. Peter's Square that summer, Ed Kornel suggested to Jim that maybe he should write the pope to commiserate with him. "Perhaps I could start out with 'Good Yontiff to the Pontiff,' " countered Jim, somewhat unimpressed with Kornel's suggestion. "Things like that made us confident that Jim would do well," says Kornel.

"In the beginning," says George Speese, "Jim only spoke when spoken to. Over time he began initiating conversation." When Speese began the Brady case, he had a full beard and moustache. In June he shaved it off and Jim greeted him with, "Oh, there's Jorge with his summer face," which particularly delighted Speese.

Recovery was the byword for Jim that summer, however. Problems with wailing, visual perception, prosopagnosia, and mental confusion seemed small and solvable. And everybody involved with Jim—doctors, nurses, therapists, and Sarah—felt that stimulation, social, mental, and physical, was crucial to his recovery. Sarah continued to spend every day with Jim, talking to him, bringing him back to reality, correcting his misimpressions. He sometimes made errors because his brain wasn't always receiving things straight, and his vision was altered and impaired. He didn't know he was taking things in wrong, he didn't want to make mistakes, he just couldn't help it. His heretofore trusty and nigh-brilliant brain was letting him down. Sarah, firmly and consistently, set him straight, but he didn't always accept her coaching. For a long time he didn't understand that he had specific gaps in his brainpower. It was only as he got better that he was able to begin to take that in, and then to try to work on the relearning he needed to do.

On the other hand, everything that Jim had learned or experienced before the shooting was still stored, almost perfectly, in his left hemisphere although he had considerable trouble with numbers, dates, time, keeping himself placed in the right day, month, and year, numerical figuring not being his strong suit in the first place. But most important, his gut political instincts were as sharp as ever. His assessment of what should be done in a PR sense in any given political situation was usually right on target. His ability to perceive correctly and to store new information was impaired—things that had happened since the shooting—but Jim Brady was the same man with the same personality and wit. If anything, he was as funny as ever because he was less inhibited. He just had specific brain injuries that prevented him from using his mind as effectively as he had in the past and interfered with his ability to take new information in correctly. "But," says Sarah, "I never for one moment felt after he was hurt that this man was not Jim Brady. His responses to everything were typical Jim Brady responses."

By June 10, Jim was off antibiotics and taking PT again in his room. He, Tim McCarthy, and Officer Delahanty were notified that they were being awarded the Distinguished Service Award by the Irish American Club. Irish Americans and Irishmen everywhere had taken note of the last names of those hit in the Hinckley assassination attempt—Reagan, Brady, McCarthy, Delahanty.

Through June and July, Jim and Sarah took a lot of pleasure and comfort from their friends. Bob Dahlgren gathered some of Jim's friends at Nathan's in Georgetown to film and record a luncheon given in his honor. All the guests were given Chicago Cubs baseball caps to wear. Lyn Nofziger dropped by to say, "I've known Jim Brady for a long time, and I want to apologize for that." Bartender Bill "Obie" O'Brien suggested Brady was an informant for the FBI. "No matter what bar I worked at . . . if you had to walk through an alley, up a flight of stairs, and into a back bar, Brady would show up within an hour after I started my first shift. He always found me." Bartender Brian Knight held up some phony checks for the camera, saying, "Jim, when you're released, I'd like you to pay these. The bookkeeper is quite upset." CBS's Bill Plante, acting as moderator, held the mike out to former White House Press Secretary Jody Powell. "Jody, as you know, we picked this gathering of sophisticates and intellectuals to consider Jim Brady." "Well, he certainly deserves consideration," Powell said. "I never realized what a handicap he had to deal with until I began to meet all of his friends and associates. I brought a rather scruffy-looking group aboard with me when I came to the White House, but this without a doubt is the worst-looking set of folks I've ever seen in my life. I just want to say that it is certainly a tribute to him that he has risen above all of them."

"It was a fun summer," remembers Sarah. Otto and Jan Wolff brought fried chicken by one night for the Bradys, and the Coles and the Wolffs brought lobster another. These evenings were such hits that they began to have happy hour regularly on Friday nights in Jim's room. The word leaked out and Washington restaurateurs, knowing of Jim's gourmet tastes, started sending special treats to the hospital for Friday Night Happy Hour. Dominique's sent lavish and exotic hors d'oeuvres served by a waiter in black tie every Friday night. Gary of Gary's cooked a steak dinner right in Jim's room. Germaine's sent Asian delicacies, Mel Krupin sent matzoh-ball soup. Mr. Kim of the Sorabol brought Korean food.

"Otto ordered food from Mr. Kim," says Jan Wolff, "but Sarah told him not to order Bim & Bob or kimchee—Jim's favorites—because they were too hot."

"I hope you have number seventeen," Jim said when Mr. Kim walked in. Then, "Where's the kimchee?" he asked.

"Mr. Wolff said you shouldn't have it," Kim told him.

"Next time tell Wolff to stay the hell out of it," said Jim. The Madison Hotel sent Mexican food and Jim's former boss at HUD, Jim Lynn, and his wife, sent a complete dinner from the elegant French restaurant Jean-Pierre. Friends and staff dropped by to imbibe from the Bradys' well-stocked bar and the refrigerator Dick Allen had sent. Jim would point out the new bears he had received and have a little story or quip about each one. One bear was so big Jim called it the "Sit Upon Bear," because it often served as an extra chair for visitors. One night Kobrine perched on the Sit Upon Bear to eat his supper while he talked to Jim and Sarah. One bear was dressed like a doctor; another bear was dressed like a nurse; another, as a policeman, sat in a chair outside Jim's room. "Then all the departments wanted to be represented," says Frank Slattery. "There was a Foods and Services bear; we had eight or nine bears hanging around outside Jim's room." "Jim was responding to all of this, too," says Deyo. "He always had a funny joke about the bears. There was an OT bear and a PT bear." Sarah's favorite was a well-worn teddy bear sent by a child who had put two Band Aids on its head.

Seeing Jim for the first time, most people were struck by how much weight he had lost—mainly on the hated pudding diet. People would come in and say, "Gee, Jim, you've lost a lot of weight. You look better than you did before you came in here." And Jim would reply, "Well, yes, I do. But of the number of ways available for losing weight, I wouldn't put getting shot in the head very high on the list."

Someone had started a "Free the Bear" petition, which sat on an easel. It was a reflection of Jim's intense desire to leave the hospital and to go home, and Jim required everybody who came into his room to sign it. He tried in vain to get Kobrine to sign it because he knew Kobrine was the one person who could "free" him. Kobrine said, "I'll sign it, J.B., when the time comes, but I can't do it yet." Every day, Jim would say to Kobrine, "I want you to sign my goddamn petition." Every day, Kobrine refused. Jim threatened Kobrine that he would have the Secret Service take him away; that he would give him a Bear Slug; that he would refuse to go to his therapy sessions if he didn't sign it. It was a running battle.

Although Jim enjoyed the Friday night soirées in his room, he was not yet initiating much conversation, only responding, and he was easily exhausted. Many first-time visitors were devastated by the change in his appearance, his being bedridden, and the emotion in his voice. Because some guests felt uncomfortable over what this might mean, there developed a tendency to talk over Jim, and around him. People would stand on either side of his bed and say to each other, "Gee, Jim looks good, doesn't he?" Bob Dahlgren observed this and it began to grate on him. Finally, one night, he said to Jim and everybody else in the room, "Dammit, we're all acting as though Jim isn't even here. I want us to start talking straight to him and not about him. He's still alive. He's not a corpse lying here." It was a needed therapeutic growl, and it addressed an issue that most disabled people deal with all the time—the inability of those who haven't had the experience to figure out that the disabled have the same feelings everybody else has, and that they need to be treated with the same kindness, consideration, and directness with which we treat everybody else.

"And Jim gradually became more involved in the Friday night parties, too," says Cathy Wynne. "He began participating more. At first he was so into himself he didn't pay much attention or he'd play with his puppet." Dahlgren began briefing visitors ahead of time on what to expect and to tell them to speak directly to Jim. "Some nights he was delighted everybody was there," says Jan Wolff. "Some nights he was in pain, and some nights he was whacked out on medicine."

Art and Cindy Kobrine brought their children Nicole, thirteen, and Steven, ten, to the hospital to meet Jim for the first time: Nicky, a gymnast, had broken her arm and Jim drew a picture of a bear on it—"A very good picture," says Cindy—and signed it. He teased her about their both having their left arms in casts. They were in awe of him, and Jim took over, asking them "What school do you go to?" and "Are you smart?"—making them feel right at home.

At the White House there was growing concern about the press-office operation. Karna Small's lack of experience had left her unprepared to do the press briefings, so Jim's absence had thrust his other deputy, Larry Speakes, to the fore. Although considered a good administrator and experienced in press relations, Speakes was not felt to have the background in and understanding of the broad scope of the American political system that Jim brought to the office—nor the enormous personal self-confidence and charm.

According to Alexander Haig, then secretary of state, it was Speakes's unsteady television performance on the day of the shooting, when Speakes was asked by the press whether or not the nation was on military alert, that led to Haig's running up the stairs from the Situation Room to appear live on television in the Press Room. He tried to calm the nation by proclaiming, looking a bit wild-eyed and out of breath," "As of now, I am in charge here in the White House pending the return of the vice-president." It was a gaffe on Haig's part, but Speakes had answered the question on the military alert by rolling his eyes to the ceiling and saying, "I just don't know about that." Understandably, there was unsteadiness in many quarters of the White House that day simply because the five most important people in the administration, Reagan, Deaver, Meese, Baker, and Brady were at GWU Hospital, two of them wounded by gunfire. The vice-president was in Texas, and Lyn Nofziger was handling press at the hospital. Those left knew little more than anybody else. The place was in turmoil. Although he grew to be very competent in the job, "Larry was a disaster in those early briefings after Jim was shot," says one top administration official, and they began to think about bringing in somebody else.

In mid-June Kobrine received a phone call from Chief of Staff Jim Baker at the White House. Baker asked Kobrine for an update on Jim and whether there was a realistic chance he could come back to work. "I won't know for a year," Kobrine told him. "My feeling was I could lie a little for the good of my patient," says Kobrine today. "Well," said Baker, "at some point we've got to consider what's best for the president. The question is: Do we continue on like this indefinitely or do we look to somebody else for the job? We have a problem in the press operation here," and he explained to Kobrine the problems that were developing in Brady's absence. "We may need to make some changes," said Baker. "We're thinking of asking David Gergen or someone from the outside to come in as press secretary. Could you help me get some indication of how Jim would react to that?" Kobrine agreed to test the waters with this proposal, and made a point of seeing Jim privately in his room the next day.

Kobrine began tentatively. "Tell me what you think of Speakes," he asked Jim. "Well," said Jim, giving his joking private assessment of Larry Speakes, "I gave him his job and I left a bottle of smart pills on my desk, but I don't know if he's taken them yet." "Well, who's this guy Gergen?" asked Kobrine. "How do you think it would work if he were brought into the job for the interim?"

Jim sat up, agitated. "Are you kidding?" he said. "That won't work. Catfish can do it till I get back." "Jim was terribly upset," says Kobrine. Brady and Gergen were rivals for power in the White House press operation, and before Brady was shot, Gergen as staff director under Baker had been trying to insist that the press secretary should report to Baker, Deaver, and Meese through him.

"Get me the drop [the White House signal phone]," Jim said. He called Sarah. "They're trying to take my job away from me," he told her. Kobrine was stunned. Here was his severely brain-injured patient taking the tiniest bit of information and immediately making the correct assumption from it—that his job was in danger—and then acting on it. Kobrine suddenly felt he was out of place as the middleman in this transaction. He tried to calm Jim down, assuring him that his job was not in danger, but when he got back to his office, Kobrine called Baker and told him how Jim had reacted. "I've got a doctor-patient relationship with this man. I may have to operate on him again and I don't think I should be in the middle like this," said Kobrine. "I don't think I should be in this position. And I believe that the hope of returning to his job is fundamental to his recovery—that hope is part of his therapy and it would be catastrophic for Jim to name anyone else to be press secretary." Baker was as surprised at Jim's strong reaction as Kobrine was. "You're right, you're absolutely right," Baker told him. "I'll come talk to Jim." "The minute I heard about Jim's reaction I closed down any further discussion of a change," says Baker. And when he saw Jim the next day, June 15, in his hospital bed he told him, "Bear, you don't have to worry about your job. It's going to be there when you get back." Baker arranged for a White House "squawk box" so Jim could listen to the daily briefings.

As a result David R. Gergen was made director of communications and Speakes was elevated to deputy assistant to the president and principal deputy press secretary, replacing Karna Small as number two to Brady.* Gergen was put in charge of the press office, the Office of Communications, which deals with news organizations outside Washington, and the speechwriting office. Most important, to the working press at least, Gergen and Speakes would share the briefings by alternating each day. The White House managed to convince reporters that the changes were not related to any dissatisfaction with Speakes. *The Washington Post* said, "Speakes who has been overworked while Brady convalesces at GWUH will share daily briefing duties with Gergen." Immediately reporters wondered out loud if the dual system would work. But, "Let's give it a try," Gergen told them. Time would prove that it wouldn't, and Gergen eventually left the White House. In the *Post* Lou Cannon wrote on July 18, "Reagan has pledged to hold the press secretary job for Brady . . . and Baker and Gergen reiterated that pledge, as they announced the press office changes."

On July 1 Kobrine gave an interview to Victor Cohn of *The Washington Post* saying that "James S. Brady was making ex-

*Even before the shooting Speakes had replaced Karna Small as Jim's backup briefer. As Small says, "Initially the understanding was that I would support Jim in giving out press guidance. But I'd had no experience in government, and as it evolved, Larry started doing some of the briefings as well. I didn't like to brief and didn't feel my experience had prepared me for it."

traordinary progress toward an essentially normal life," despite, wrote Cohn, "the bullet that irretrievably smashed more than a fifth of his brain." "We are very optimistic," Kobrine went on. "We plan if all goes well to let him go on an outing in the next few days, then start sending him home for some weekends sometime this month. The aim is to release Brady from the hospital by the end of the summer. He is still in the relatively early post-injury phase of neurological recovery that typically takes a full year. We're still not out of the woods," Kobrine emphasized. He pointed out that bullet fragments could still cause infection that could break out anytime. "Once we make it six or eight months down the pike, I'll feel a lot easier." Kobrine described the improvements he had been seeing in Brady as "dramatic. I think he gets more and more like the old Jim every day. . . . I'd say he's normal the overwhelming portion of the time."

And on the Fourth of July, as Kobrine had hinted, he allowed Jim to leave the hospital for a "Gay Nineties" picnic at the White House in the afternoon, and to watch the fireworks later from a room in the Hay-Adams Hotel just across Lafayette Park from the White House. "He was still having an occasional drop of fluid from his nose," says Kobrine, "but I was just sure it would go away." Art and Cindy Kobrine, their children, Nicole and Steven, nurse Flash Deyo, Officer Frank Slattery, Jim, Sarah, Sarah's mother, Frances Kemp, her brother, Bill Kemp, and two-and-a-half-year-old Scott Brady made up the party.* When they entered the White House, Jim, wearing a straw hat, said, "Hi, Rex," to White House Usher Rex Scouten who was flabbergasted Brady remembered him. "I had only met him a couple of times, and fleetingly," says Scouten. With Kobrine pushing Jim's wheelchair they toured the public rooms of the ground floor, then went upstairs to go through the Red Room, the Blue Room, and the Green Room. The White House was empty of people. President and Mrs. Reagan were at a birthday party in her honor at Mount Vernon.

Scott Brady was in heaven, running here and there in the mansion, trying out all the chairs. As his grandmother tried to corral him, White House butler Freddy Mayfield told Sarah, "That's all right, Mrs. Brady. This is *your* house. He can do

*The Dahlgrens, the Churches, the Wolffs, and the Ahearns were on the White House grounds and joined them later.

whatever he wants." Mayfield suggested they might want to go out on the balcony to get an overview of the party going on the White House lawn. As Kobrine pushed Jim outside, someone below caught sight of him, then someone else. People in the crowd of a thousand started pointing and as all heads turned toward the balcony, spontaneous applause broke out, then cheering, and tears. Jim gave them the thumbs-up sign. They burst into "For He's a Jolly Good Fellow." They shouted "We love you, Jim, we love you," and then yelled "Hip Hip Hurray" over and over, clutching their balloons to their chests. "It was one of the most emotionally heavy episodes that I've ever seen," says Kobrine. It was the first of many such emotional tributes the American people would pay to Jim Brady.

White House press aide Jeanne Winnick caught up with Jim as he was leaving. She climbed into the van with him. "Hey, Boss," she said as she hugged him and handed him her beer. "Here. Have a roadie."

Later, at the hotel, as he sat in his wheelchair watching Washington's spectacular national fireworks display, Jim said wryly from time to time, "Gee, they really didn't have to go to all this trouble just because it's my first day out."

The shooting of Jim Brady had evoked an outrage not only in Washington but throughout the country, and prompted a pouring out of love and concern for the man they perceived to be an all-American good guy. Mail and gifts poured in—and the flood of mail continued for years after the fact. Jim received seventy thousand pieces of mail just in the eight months he was in the hospital. Sarah was overwhelmed with the wave of well-wishing and said to Jim one day, "Gosh, doesn't it make you feel good to hear that all these wonderful people care about you?" "Yes, it does," said Jim, "but I'd a lot rather be getting all this tribute because of something I'd done than for something that was done to me."

Flash, looking at his room full of bears and the mountains of mail said, "It's a damn shame nobody cares, Jim." "Well," said Jim, "it's a hell of a way to test it."

"I was overwhelmed by how much Mrs. Reagan was doing," said Sarah. "Calling, sending gifts and food over from the White House."

The next day, July 5, back in his hospital room, Bill Crain from Centralia was visiting Jim when "down the hall came a black lady and her two aunties," says Crain, "looking for Jim. Sarah allowed them to come in, and Jim, by gosh, Jim entertained them. He made them feel better. That's typical Brady."

A few days later a telegram from Jack and JoAnn Hinckley arrived. "It said something to the effect," says Sarah, " 'We were thrilled to see you out. We pray for you every day.' I was surprised to see it," Sarah says. "It took me aback but I was pleased to see they cared. I feel sorry for them—as a mother I can empathize with their feelings."

On July 7 Jim's parents went to Chicago for a fund-raising dinner that was addressed by President Reagan. In his speech Reagan said, "Jim Brady should be here. Jim's parents are here. I talked to him just before I left. He's getting better every day. His job is waiting for him, and we miss him very much."

Two weeks later on July 21, for Jim's second outing from the hospital, Bob and Suzi Dahlgren gave a party celebrating Jim and Sarah's eighth wedding anniversary at their home in Georgetown. Restaurateur Germaine Swanson came to cook Southeast Asian delicacies, and Dahlgren alerted the White House so that, during dinner, the President and Mrs. Reagan called to congratulate them. Jim wailed badly throughout the conversation although, says Art Kobrine, "he didn't wail at all the whole rest of the day." "I felt so bad about it," says Cindy. "He'd been doing so well a minute earlier."

In physical therapy Cathy Wynne had Jim fitted for a full leg brace, which helped him with standing exercises away from the parallel bars. Jim continued to have intracranial pressure buildup and Kobrine ordered periodic spinal taps of excess CSF, which Jim hated. Jim and Sarah went out with friends again to their old haunt from campaign days, the Sorabol Restaurant in Arlington. As he was wheeled into the restaurant a newsman asked Jim what he thought of John Hinckley. "I'm sorry he wasn't a better shot," said Jim, meaning that he knew he wasn't the target.

As they entered the month of August, Sarah, Kobrine, and everybody around Jim took more and more hope from his steady progress. Art Kobrine felt confident enough about his patient that he rescheduled a previously postponed trip for a job interview at Northwestern University, his alma mater, in Chicago. Before leaving town, however, on August 3 he made early-morning rounds on his patients and when he stopped in to see

Jim, "I remember looking at him and thinking to myself, 'Hmmmm, he's having a seizure,' but I also thought, 'It'll pass,' " says Kobrine.

But the seizure didn't stop and after a minute or two Kobrine called for IV lines into Jim's arms and he mentally canceled his trip to Chicago. Jim's bad luck persisted, he thought. Susan Deyo was down the hall but she heard Jim's bed sides begin to rattle. He would often roll over on his left side and try to pull himself up. But the rattling went on and on. In the next five minutes Jim was given all the Valium he could safely have. By this time anesthesiologist Don Lee arrived and began giving him sodium pentothol. "You also can only give so much sodium pentothol," says Kobrine, "and in three or four minutes we gave him as much of it as he could have." Dr. Lee intubated Jim right in his bed. He was given the paralyzing drug Pavulon, and the seizures appeared to stop, but because of the Pavulon and pentothol, Jim could not breathe on his own. We had to "bag him to get him breathing," says Kobrine. An emergency CAT scan was done "and he looked fine but by the time the scan was finished, the Pavulon had worn off and Jim started seizing again. When EEG leads were applied to his head it was apparent to us that he hadn't stopped. He had gone into *status epilepticus*—which is constant, unrelenting, generalized seizing." It is rare for this to happen when a patient is on antiseizure medicine and there is a significant mortality rate.

Kobrine and Lee moved Jim to the recovery room and began pumping phenobarbital into the lines in Jim's arms. "We pushed phenobarb, phenobarb, phenobarb," says Kobrine. "We would stop and look at each other, and then keep on giving it and giving it. We were afraid of giving him too much because it could stop his heart—because it is a barbiturate—it lowers the blood pressure in high doses." But Jim kept on seizing and Kobrine and Lee had no choice but to keep pushing phenobarbital. "We just looked at each other, and said, 'We're just going to have to give it to him until he stops seizing or his heart gives out.' "

Sarah was at home. "My habit was to stay at the hospital until eleven-thirty at night; then when I got home I pulled the phone into bed with me. Before going to sleep I would always call to check on Jim and the first thing in the morning at six-thirty." But this morning, she didn't awaken until 8:45 and when she called, a Secret Service agent told her Jim was having a seizure. "When I got there his room was packed with people. Jim wasn't outwardly seizing. They told me his brain was seizing."

They kept pushing phenobarbital into Jim's veins and Jim seized all day long. Sarah paced the halls and Jim Baker came from the White House to check on the crisis.

"All cells were firing," says Kobrine. "Seizing uses up electrical power and energy and pours more acids into the bloodstream than the blood can neutralize. The heart can't beat when the pH is changed and a patient goes into cardiac arrest." All day Kobrine was thinking of the tiny bullet fragment he hadn't been able to get because it had gone straight back, deep into the left lobe. He always feared it might decompose and cause seizures before scar tissue encapsulated it, and he was pretty sure that Hinckley's bullet was coming close to killing Jim again.

Suddenly, at 7:30 P.M., the seizing stopped. "It just stopped," says Kobrine. "One minute the EEG was going wild and the next instant it was absolutely normal."

Jim slept all night, and the next morning, although exhausted, groggy, and half alert, he seemed fine. "But then," says Kobrine, "CSF started *pouring* out of his nose again. All the seizing had caused an increase of intracranial pressure and all the healing that had been going on so well was disturbed. I knew absolutely that I had to do more work on those leaks to get him well."

But Kobrine was sick at this development. He was sure the leak was coming from the same area as before—the shattered underside of the skull, through the connecting sinuses, near the bullet entry point. He began pondering and studying and consulting with his colleagues—trying to figure out how he could get at the leak without opening up Jim's head again. The flow of CSF had slowed to a matter of drops, but the danger was that infection might be transferred from his nasal passages to his brain. He talked to otolaryngologist Norman Barr and together they worked out a scheme to get at the leak through an inch and a half incision around the orbit of Jim's left eye and down partway along the left side of his nose. Jim heard a question asked about it during Speakes's briefing and was very upset. "No, no more surgery. They're not going to cut on me again." Two weeks later, under general anesthesia, in the operating room, they removed bone and bullet fragments from the ethmoid sinus in a three-hour operation, and in the sinus they saw a quarter-inch gap on the underside of the skull. They packed the cavity with fat taken from Jim's abdomen and crossed their fingers. "And it stopped," says Kobrine. "It enormously stopped—all but a few drops. And then completely."

In his amazing ability to come back from the assault of a deadly series of blows that threatened his life, Jim, the next day, was "alert and chattering," says Kobrine. Jim kept his spirits up in spite of all the pain and danger and the continued nagging insults accompanying all his major illnesses. He suffered from side effects from the many drugs being used—fever from drug allergies—collapsed lung sacs from all the anesthesia used during his daylong seizure. The contracted muscles in his left arm and leg were very painful. He could barely move. He had lost the ability to smell and taste. But still Jim was back on the mend. There had been one crisis after another, but he was fighting hard to come back in between them, and although he was fearful about his health, Jim Brady was very glad to be alive. Three days later, while Dick Church was visiting him, Jim had a brief "focal" seizure. "I thought it was Jim's joking at first," says Sarah. "It ended so quickly. He just kind of shook his head and right arm a little bit."

"Obviously it scared Jim," says Church. "Even his bad leg moved. His whole body stiffened and his legs came up."

In physical therapy he began using the parallel bars, working on standing, strength, and balance. His Secret Service policemen joined in his therapy, playing toss with him. And Jim's lifelong friend Mick Scheriger came out to spend a week with Jim. He watched him in his earliest days in physical therapy. "I saw the damn pain come over his face and he not knowing where the end of the road is. I saw some effort put forth there that you've got to admire. Just the *effort* he put forth. I don't know if I could have done it," says Scheriger. "You think you're that strong, but you don't know if you could do it."

Scheriger and Jim had a black friend they went to high school with—Nate Clay. He was a fine athlete, who, in the 1960s while playing baseball in college, slid into home plate and broke his neck, paralyzing him. Nate Clay, visiting in Washington that summer, came to GWU Hospital to see Jim—to cheer him up as Jim had done for him once. Years before, after Jim had moved to Chicago, he and Scheriger looked Clay up and took him out on a binge that ended with the two of them, roaring drunk, pushing Clay in his wheelchair down the middle of Michigan Avenue at four in the morning. It was typical of Jim to keep old ties alive, especially with those who had suffered bad luck or adversity.

A few days after this latest surgery, John W. Hinckley, Jr., was formally charged in a thirteen-count indictment that included the attempt to assassinate President Reagan, and the assault with intent to kill James Brady, Tim McCarthy, and Thomas K. Delahanty. A few days later, wearing a bulletproof vest in court, Hinckley pleaded not guilty to the charges. His attorney was told by Judge Barrington Parker he would have one month in which to notify the court whether or not he intended to argue that Hinckley was insane at the time of the shooting and therefore not guilty of the offense.

Jim had a lot of comments about Hinckley, says Ed Kornel. "He thought he was crazy but he also said he would like to get his hands on him. He would make understatements about Hinckley such as 'I don't think I'd like him for my roommate.' Jim hated him on the one hand and pitied him on the other. He'd say, 'He couldn't hit the side of a barn from the inside.' "

The scene of the shooting was played endlessly on television for the first year or two afterward. Never had an assassination attempt been filmed in progress so clearly and it was a riveting scene, which the nation relived over and over. Jim saw it on TV over and over again as well. He referred to his part in it as "the now famous scene of me lying facedown with my head bleeding into a grate in front of the Washington Hilton Hotel." Bill Plante offered to show Jim CBS's tapes of the day of the shooting, but "Jim didn't want to see them," says Kornel. "It was too upsetting to him. He became superstitious about it, as though if he talked about it, it might happen again." Kornel told him, "It's just incredible what you have gone through. Don't you want to talk about it?" "I know it," said Jim, "but there are a lot of things in there [his mind] I don't want to dredge up." He called his brain "gray fluff" as does Pooh Bear in *Winnie the Pooh*. But he had always done that.

Now "gray fluff" had more significance to him and to those who heard him use the term.

The day after Hinckley's plea, August 29, was Jim's forty-first birthday. President Reagan chatted with Jim by phone from his Santa Barbara ranch, then released this statement: "Jim Brady is a talented and dedicated public servant. He is my friend and I am proud to have him as my press secretary. Nancy and I salute the 'Bear' and Sarah today and we look forward to celebrating his next birthday in his office at the White House."

The White House press corps, led by Bill Plante, then took over the phone line and delivered birthday greetings and friendly insults. Walter Rodgers of the Associated Press offered up a perfect imitation of a loon (in honor of the "Call of the Loon" record Brady used to pipe into the press room). Dean Reynolds pointed out to Jim that his beloved Chicago Cubs this season, "for the first time have a chance to finish last twice [because of the baseball strike]." At the end, Sarah got on the line and said, "Jim has the biggest grin on his face he has ever had in his life."

With Jim in his room was Jeanne Winnick. She and Jim became friends during the Reagan campaign and Jim had brought her to the White House with him in January. "I'm so glad to see you, Bear," she said. It was her first visit. "Everybody sends his regards." "Even Admiral Avocado is thinking of me?" asked Jim. "Admiral Avocado" was the nickname Jeanne and Jim had devised for a former communications director in the campaign, a crony of Edwin Meese. He was a retired admiral with an avocado ranch in California, who tried to run the office like a battleship. Avoiding Admiral Avocado's vigilant eye had turned into a huge game—and ultimately into a huge joke between them.

In spite of extremely serious setbacks, "it was a fun summer," says Sarah. "We became so close to the staff, we were all so hopeful." "There was an overwhelming wish to help," remembers Cindy Kobrine. "Everybody was totally caught up in making this guy better. He was such a nice guy and Sarah, too. They were both so funny and appealing that everybody got emotionally attached to them. The better Jim got the harder they worked."

Happy hour on Friday night by this time had become a huge rollicking affair. Aside from hospital staff who came by, Bob and Suzi Dahlgren, Dick and Jeri Church if they were in town, and other friends stopped in. And there were the media regulars—Bill Plante, Gary Schuster, Steve Neal, and Lisa Myers—all great pals of Jim's on the 1980 Reagan campaign. Secretary of Defense Caspar Weinberger came one Friday and Secretary of the Treasury Donald Regan another. Roger Mudd dropped in and so did Bryant Gumbel, and Sarah's friend Pamela Jacovides. "We would stop by on Friday nights," says Cindy Kobrine, "and bring the kids and you could hardly get into his room it was so packed. You never knew who you were going to run into when you went." Jim looked contentedly around his crowded hospital room one night and remarked, "Where the Bear is, people get together."

Jeri Church says, "We thought it was just wild—having those Friday night parties. It was the kind of thing that was so important to Jim." "And to Sarah, too," adds Dick. "Sarah always managed to provide the stimulating atmosphere that would allow that sort of thing to happen."

"I took Jim a six-pack of Coors," says newsman Lou Cannon, "and he made some joke—called it ghetto Kool-Aid. But he could hardly talk. Sarah didn't want him to have any beer, but he drank two and a half of them. I was struck by the fact he still had a sense of humor—that he was still 'Brady.' I thought I'd meet someone who was unrecognizable, but it wasn't true. He was horribly wounded but he wasn't another person—or a changed person. He had the same personality." Old friend and mentor Bill Greener was amazed to hear Jim recite the entire "Jabberwocky" by Lewis Carroll one night.

Eddie Mahe, friend and former employer of both Jim and Sarah, visited Jim the night Jody Powell brought Jim some Pearl beer. "Jim knew my wife Fran was the nicest, most compliant person," says Mahe, "so he assessed the situation and told her, 'Go get me one of those beers, Fran.' "

Peter Hannaford from the Reagan campaign dropped in. "We talked politics," says Hannaford, "and Jim was up on the events of the day. He was having a hard time controlling his voice, but the TV was on and he was commenting on the news."

Senator Strom Thurmond and his wife, Nancy, "were two of the greatest people in wanting to help," says Sarah. "Strom came often to see us. He delivered two Easter baskets to us, sent a crate of oranges. Nancy would call to ask 'Can I take

Scott for the day?' or 'Can we have lunch?' They invited me constantly to things." And Carolyn and Michael Deaver took Sarah to Dumbarton Oaks for a picnic lunch.

"That summer was such a dramatic time, and even a sweet time in so many ways," says Sarah, "in terms of what was going on with our personal relationships. The Churches were in and out of town constantly. They were wonderful the way they were there for Jim. They just know him better than anybody."

Childhood friend Bernie Gross drove nonstop from Centralia to the hospital that August and got as far as his hospital-room door. He was so insistent on seeing Jim that Frank Slattery was alarmed and told Sarah, "There's some flake out here who claims he knows you." When Sarah came to the hospital, she cleared Bernie to see Jim. "Jim laughed so hard when he saw him," says Susan Deyo. " 'Bernie, how the hell are you?' he said."

It was in August, also, that Big Jim came to see his son for the first and what was to be his last time. He and "the Aunts" (Helen and Margaret) and brother, Ed Brady, drove out together from Illinois to see their "darling boy." All elderly by now, they drove 150 miles a day, taking five days to make the journey. "Big Jim's strokes had taken their toll," says Sarah. "He didn't visit very long; seeing Jim was hard on him."

"Sarah and Art became good friends—confidantes," says Cindy Kobrine. "They developed a strong relationship based on mutual trust and confidentiality. They made the decisions together. Jim was in on it, but not in on it, too. They would plan on how to tell Jim about the next difficult procedure. Jim objected to everything." Jim particularly hated the plastic balloonlike "intermittent stockings," which were hooked up to a pump. "If I just could have a pretty girl rub my legs it would be much better," he said. Jim tried to con the nurses into helping him take them off. To Flash he said, one day, "This is the best chance we have to get rid of these stockings. If you take 'em off quick before [Kobrine] has a chance to get in here, he'll never notice."

Two weeks later when there had been no further leaks, Kobrine thought it was safe for Jim to risk a visit home. Jim was increasing his lobbying to leave the hospital. His "Free the Bear" petition was covered with names. On Saturday of Labor Day weekend, shortly before noon, Jim Brady left GWUH for his first day's visit home. With press and photographers waiting, dressed in a plaid jacket and a yellow hat and wearing a cast on his left arm, Jim was wheeled into the waiting van for the short trip across the Potomac. "It was such a joyous day," says Sarah. "Our neighbors had made WELCOME HOME BEAR signs. Scott was so excited." As Jim came in the front door, however, Sarah saw fluid leaking from his nose. "It was the worst moment I have had from beginning to end of this whole thing," she says. She called Kobrine. "Oh, hell," he thought to himself. Kobrine thought the leaking problem was behind them.

The press was out in full force to cover Jim's homecoming. "They were so rude," says Susan Deyo, "even going around to the back of the house to call through the window." Jim remarked, " 'Coon's gonna give 'em hell now." But Sarah was overwhelmed by all the emotion and turmoil of the day and, in tears, she called Larry Speakes at home to ask for help. Speakes, who was on his way out for the evening with his wife, came over to talk to the press so the Bradys could have some semblance of a civilized dinner. It was the first time since the shooting that Sarah had talked to Larry Speakes and, except for a glimpse of Jim in the emergency room five months earlier, it was the first time Speakes had seen Jim since the shooting as well. As things quieted down, Jim offered his traditional toast: "Once again, we are gathered at the table with good friends."

By the time Speakes arrived, things were calmer and Sarah met Larry at the door, saying, "It's all right now. I probably overreacted." Larry told the throng gathered in the street, "Look, get your pictures, then respect their privacy."

"It was the first time I visited with Jim," says Speakes.

"Catfish, how are you doing?" asked Jim.

"These press getting under your skin?" asked Larry.

"No, they don't bother me," said Jim.

Jim went home each day over the three-day weekend, going back to his room on 5E at 10:30 each night. "I was scared to death," says Sarah. At the end of the holiday Sarah admitted she was exhausted "physically and emotionally." "Last weekend was a ten-pound weekend," Jim described it. Through September and October he began to go home for day visits every weekend, but Jim's first visit home raised a number of new problems to be faced.

"It was exciting to have him home on the weekends," said Sarah, "but he always had a GW nurse with him, so it was like a visit. When Kobrine started talking about Jim's coming home for good I was not mentally prepared for it. His home visits made it very clear to me how difficult it was going to be to have him home all the time. Above all, I was scared to death something might happen to him. I also realized our house wasn't set up for it. He needed a reclining lounger chair; our porch needed to be winterized so he would have a comfortable place to be on the main floor, where fortunately we had our bedroom, too. We needed an elevator to get him from the garage at street level to the main floor; and wheelchair ramps; we needed a bathroom that would accommodate his wheelchair; and we needed full-time nursing help.

"Emotionally, it was difficult for me. In fact, when Art first mentioned it, I got real mad. I thought it was a long time off. I thought he would remain in the hospital for rehabilitation like most patients. I did not want to face the fact Art was thinking of sending Jim home. The very thought made me panicky. I wanted him to be where I knew he was safe." But most rehabilitative patients had spinal cord or other injuries, not head injuries, and Kobrine felt he needed a different kind of rehabilitation—a mental kind, where he would have the stimulation of family, friends, colleagues, and public events. "But I was afraid for Jim's health—terrified that something would happen to him. At the hospital they watched him twenty-four hours a day.

"So Art said, 'Not yet, but we need to start thinking about it.' As we got further and further away from the seizure and Jim got better and better, I started realizing perhaps it was possible.

"I went to see Sandy Butcher as I always did when I was upset," says Sarah. "She understood completely, and said, 'Doctors don't realize how much it entails to send someone home. What we need to do is get a team together of his doctors, nurses, and therapists to discuss his home care.' Through her good help I was able to put my mind to getting ready to bring Jim home."

Cathy Wynne and Susan Marino made suggestions about ramps and Jim's bathroom. "I suggested they put in a hand shower," says Marino. "Jim agreed—'I'll be a funky bear without it.'"

"Jim Lynn helped me find an architect for the changes in the house," says Sarah, "and he and Jim Wilderotter helped me work with workmen's comp, who would be funding all of these things."

Over the next few weeks, while Sarah prepared for the adjustment to life with Jim at home, and Jim worked hard in his therapy sessions, Kobrine was busy conjuring up a new way to seal Jim's brain off from the contagion of outside bacteria. His ploy this time was to try to seal up the sinus passage at its small point of entry high up in Jim's left nostril. Anesthetizing Jim with cocaine again, Dr. Barr took silver nitrate sticks and touched them to the tissue around the pin-sized hole. "I thought if we roughed up the mucosa there, it would form scar tissue and close the hole," says Kobrine. Jim enjoyed the notion that he had been anesthetized with cocaine. "Don't bother me, Sarah," he told her. "I'm on a trip." Ed Kornel brought him a T-shirt that said I TOOT COKE. The procedure brought the leaking down almost to nothing, and a second application of silver nitrate in mid-October substantially did the trick. Kobrine wanted to watch him but at last he could really begin to think of sending Jim home.

In the meantime, he continued to go home for day visits on the weekend. On one of his visits home, Senator Bob Dole and his wife, Liddy, sent a champagne candlelight supper served by a tuxedoed waiter.

The news that Jim was able to go home for weekends was a cause for celebration in Centralia, and radio station WILY, declaring September 11 Jim Brady Day, opened its lines so Centralians could call in messages to Jim. Schools were dismissed for the afternoon, and there were scores of callers—friends, classmates, teachers, businesses, clubs, acquaintances, and admirers. Phyllis Alstat ("a heartthrob," says Jim,) said, "Remember, Jim, whenever you came over we messed up my mother's kitchen and got flour all over the place?" Kay Warner said, "I sure do miss those cheer-up calls from the White House, Jim." Stella Black, Betsey Kourdouvelis, and the Kesslers called in, as did Senator Percy, Ronnie Mann, Dick Mann, and Connie and Jack Parker. Nate Clay promised, "I'm going to take you out on the town as you did for me in Chicago." Aunt Louise and Uncle Sam Davidson called, and one of Jim's teachers said, "I used to tell you to quit talking and stop teasing those girls. But now I'm going to tell you to keep talking." Ruby Ryan said, "Hang in there, baby. We're all pulling for you." They were all reaching out to convey their deep concern and affection for their native son.

Jim greeted them in a taped message. "This is the First Bear. This is Jim Brady, and I want to thank you for honoring me with my own day at the radio station. It certainly humbles a person to know that he has the support of his hometown the way I do. I appreciate all your cards and letters folks, and all the little bears. I look forward to seeing everyone . . . soon. . . ."

CHAPTER SEVEN

Home for Thanksgiving

In October Cathy Wynne had a short leg brace made for Jim so he could bend his left knee and really begin to work on walking with the aids of an arm crutch on his good right arm, and Cathy steadying him on his left side. His mobility would be important to his returning home, but the first few steps were tentative. Jim had very little feeling in his left leg—it was stiff and clumsy and he was constantly afraid he would fall. His right side was weak from lack of exercise and not trustworthy either. But Kobrine came in to check on his patient in physical therapy one day and found him actually walking a few steps. "J.B., I love you!" he exclaimed exuberantly.

"Jim has better balance than he thinks he does," said Sue Marino, "but he's not getting full information on what his body is doing. That makes it hard for him to test it or push it to its limits." Marino had been seeing Jim regularly all along "to work on his muscle contractures, to inhibit the tone of his contractures so he doesn't get any tighter than he already is."

Jim was at last physically well enough to begin sessions in speech pathology, too—to work on improving the serious problems he had with the working of his brain. Speech pathologist Arlene Pietranton joined therapists Wynne and Marino. They would often confer with each other in order to coordinate the goals they had for Jim, and in turn, the three of them kept in touch with Kobrine, his residents, and Jim's nurses in order to stay on top of the case. "It's been a real different kind of case," says Wynne. "Everybody involved with Jim is emotionally involved—because of Jim's personality and because he has been through so many awful crises. There are phone calls back and forth, one of us telling the other, 'I think I see this—what do you think?' Kobrine has been on top of everything—final decisions always came down from Kobrine after he consulted with Sarah. He has a good grasp on the case in its wholeness—he can see the big picture and for that reason he makes the right decisions most of the time.

"Kobrine's reputation is for knowing what he wants done with his patients. If you happen to do something he doesn't want, he'll let you hear about it in a big way. He's a real perfectionist and very protective of his patients, and if there is a screwup, you know there is his wrath to face. I've had run-ins with him and he has upset me a few times. I've confronted him afterward and, dammit, if he hasn't apologized to me. Most people stay afraid of him because they don't confront him. But his heart and soul are in his case. And Jim's case is a complex one. That and Jim's fame increased the pressure on all of us."

Arlene Pietranton first examined Jim at his bedside on October 15, 1981, seven and a half months after the shooting, and for short periods over the next six working days. It took that long to evaluate him because there were conflicts between her schedule and Jim's and because she found Jim extremely "fatigued—his body tremendously stressed by the original insult and succeeding operations." She felt that he had never had the luxury of simply being a patient. He had more visitors and more demands made on him than most patients. Sometimes when she went upstairs to see him he was asleep—he was sleeping more during the day than at night at that point. But when he was awake she found him "consistently alert and responsive." When she asked him questions about his personal history, however, he was confused. He maintained that he lived in Centralia—he forgot about his previous marriage. "If I asked him what he was doing that day, he said he had an appointment in another part of the country as press secretary. Some confusion was understandable because he was getting visits from the White House staff and hearing about all these travels and events." She concluded that Jim's short-term memory was "moderately impaired." (Pietranton was using a five-step scale of impairment: minimal—hardly noticeable; mild—not extreme, but obvious, others would notice; moderate—reaches the point where use of skills is affected; moderately severe—most of the time it affects the use of skills; severe—all of the time, with a decrease in use of one's skills.)

She found him very impulsive in his responses, and she planned to include in her program for him the relearning of his inhibiting his first response—to make him wait. For instance, such exercises as telling Jim to "pick up the pen and put it in the cup, but before you do that, turn over the brush" would, at first, confuse him. He wanted to respond to her first words. She started slowly and gradually began adding exercises that were above his level of performance so they would be more and more challenging. "That gives the brain the chance to use healthy brain tissue in slightly different ways to develop new habits. There is some evidence that neurological tissue does not regenerate," she says, "but through exercise, areas of the brain can be stimulated to increase their connections into surrounding areas so that the brain is able to operate at higher levels."

Pietranton adjudged Jim's emotions to be *labile*—unstable—"they came to the surface more easily, showing up in his wailing and loss of pitch control—a condition," she says, "triggered by honest emotion. His ability to override that was damaged, probably by the rippling effect of one damaged area communicating with another damaged area."

As they started working together, Pietranton saw another very typical head-injury deficit—Jim's ability to analyze how well he had performed the task before him was poor. He couldn't see his mistakes.

She found problems with a number of Jim's language skills. He was capable of understanding everything said to him, but, she says, "he had a problem listening long enough to get the full message." She adjudged his "auditory comprehension to be 'mildly impaired.' " The left temporal lobe, where one receives auditory information, was not damaged, but the ability to respond to heard information is in the frontal lobes—both of which were damaged. Jim had the capability of understanding the message, but at first wasn't able to process it and act on it correctly.

Pietranton noted Jim's problem with perseveration—getting stuck—the broken-record syndrome. "Jim picked up on a lot of jargon while he was in therapy," says Pietranton, "and as time went on he would catch himself and say, 'I perseverated on this one, didn't I?' "

At first Pietranton thought Jim had symptoms of frontal-lobishness, the most glaring of which was initiation, or the lack of initiating anything—conversation, eating, bathing. As he got better the most noticeable symptoms of that aspect of his injury gradually disappeared. Jim's verbal expression, she observed, was within normal limits, but at times it showed up as "moderately impaired." He had the ability to use language appropriately and his syntax was correct. "Some of his answers weren't appropriate," she says, "but they were stated in good language. His reading comprehension was within normal limits but it was impaired because of his impulsiveness."

Pietranton, lastly, saw that Jim had impaired thought organization. He had trouble with getting things in the proper sequence, drawing analogies from a simple set of facts, and with abstract thinking. "As time went on," says Pietranton, "his awareness of his impairment was good," but he had trouble monitoring it from moment to moment. "He showed excellent insight into problem solving," says Pietranton, "and his ability to use his mental skills was quite good. It was just that his other problems got in the way." Pietranton and Jim began working together an hour a day on a program to improve his mental functioning. "At first I put a tremendous amount of emphasis on his taking initiative. I tried to structure our sessions in order to make him make choices. For instance, if I asked him to write something I wouldn't give him a pen until he asked for it."

In his moods Jim could alternate between being noncommunicative and depressed, or childish and demanding, or he could be right on target in his analysis and conversation. "When all circuits are wired together correctly," says surgeon Hugh Trout, "he is hilarious."

Jim started to want to talk, and he confided his concerns to Ed Kornel. He was worried about the welfare of Sarah and

Scott, and whether he would ever get home, and would they be taken care of if he didn't make it. He talked about his work—how badly he wanted to get back to it. "We used to talk about going places," says Kornel, "like barhopping in Ireland—just leaving everything behind and forgetting our troubles." At times, Jim was very low, even tearful, asking, "What good am I to anybody?" With the love and encouragement of Sarah and the hospital staff and friends, and his own amazing bounce, he was always able to pull himself out of the depths. Examining him one day when Jim was being particularly quick and talkative, Kobrine told him, "J.B., you're as sharp as a tack, you know that?" "I'd say more like as sharp as a marble," Jim answered.

Ed Kornel recalls watching television with Jim in November 1981 on the day it was revealed that Richard Allen had accepted some money and watches from Japanese businessmen on behalf of Mrs. Reagan, and had left them forgotten in his office safe. "Man, you have just chopped your own head off," Jim fumed at the televised picture of his friend Allen. "You won't be back."

Stuart Purviance remembers that someone announced to Jim during happy hour one night that he had a joke that would blow his mind. "Please—don't," said Jim, laughing. Another time Jim challenged Purviance, "Could you lie here for six months in this hospital bed?" he said. "Well, *you* did it," replied Purviance. "Well, you mean anybody can, then?" said Jim, somewhat disappointed.

On November 9 Jim went to preside over the reopening of the newly refurbished and enlarged press room in the White House. It was his first visit back to his own territory and he was warmly greeted. "Hello, good friends," he said from his wheelchair on the podium he was sharing with President and Mrs. Reagan. Reagan said, "As happy as we are about the reopening of the press room today, we are even happier, more elated, by the presence of a man who truly belongs in this room. A man whose courage has been an inspiration to all of us. I am proud that Jim Brady's my press secretary. Jim, we're all waiting for the day you're back for good." "I am, too, Mr. President," Jim replied.

"You know, of course," the president went on, "that the floor of this press room is built over the old swimming pool, but it isn't true that the floor has been hinged and will spring like a trap anytime you ask the wrong question." "Yes, it is," interjected Jim, gleefully. To laughter and applause, Reagan added, "I hope this room is always filled with as much good humor and integrity as today." Mrs. Reagan hugged and kissed Jim and stage-whispered in his ear, "You're still my youngest and handsomest, Jim," while the president looked on and said with mock injury, "The husband is always the last to know."

Helen Thomas of the Associated Press called out, "We miss you, Jim." "I miss you, too," he said, and, after a well-timed pause: "I miss *most* of you. We tried to run over Sam in the street." Jim earlier had spotted ABC's irrepressible Sam Donaldson outside with a camera crew filming his arrival.

As his nurse pushed his chair out the door, Jim called over his shoulder, "I'll come back." Jim spotted Sue Mathis whom he had hired to work with the out-of-town press. "Sue Mathis—aren't you even going to come over and say hello?" "It was the most amazing thing to me," says Mathis. "I had stayed in the back of the room because I was afraid he'd not know who I was." "Do you like your job?" Jim asked her. "I hope you're having a good time." "His voice broke," says Mathis. "I went back to my office and cried for half an hour."

On November 17, U.S. District Court Judge Barrington D. Parker ruled that John Hinckley, Jr.'s constitutional rights had been violated when FBI agents questioned him without a lawyer present shortly after his arrest, and later when prison administrators seized some of Hinckley's papers from his prison cell. Therefore, Parker ruled, those statements and papers could not be used as evidence during his trial. Prosecutors contended that the testimony of law-enforcement officials who talked with Hinckley the evening of the shooting would be vital to convincing a jury he was sane at that time, and that their questions were "standard biographical questions which the FBI routinely asks . . . and were not intended" to get incriminating evidence from him. Parker moved to suppress testimony that applied to a 7:00 to 7:30 P.M. time frame. Among other things, they had asked Hinckley what he had been doing during the year before the shooting. They also asked if he had a girlfriend. John Hinckley answered that he had a "one-sided" relationship with actress Jodie Foster.

The prosecution maintained that Hinckley's notes and diary were taken for "indications of his state of mind" to deter-nine how "serious a risk of suicide" he was since he had ttempted suicide twice since his arrest, once in May with an overdose of Tylenol he had saved up, and again in November, vhen he tried to hang himself from the bars in his window vith his jacket. He had begun to turn blue when he was cut lown. His writings included a fictional conspiracy plot to kill a president, written while he was incarcerated in the federal prison in Butner, North Carolina, pending the trial. Judge Parker's ruling was appealed twice to higher courts by the prosecution but it was upheld.

Back at George Washington University Hospital Jim was naking steady progress in physical therapy, occupational therapy, and speech pathology. He was increasingly restless for his reedom, and he and Sarah and Bob and Suzi Dahlgren went or steak dinner at Gary's restaurant for a fling. As he got better he role of "perfect patient" began to pall on him. One day Dahlgren tried to talk Jim into making a phone call to a youngster who had suffered brain damage after being accidently hit n the head with a baseball bat. Jim didn't want to do it. "Why don't I send him my Ernie Banks baseball instead?" said Jim wickedly. Dahlgren, who had already set up the phone call and knew the lad was eagerly waiting, broke into a cold sweat. 'C'mon, Jim, just a short phone call." "I think he'd much prefer my Ernie Banks baseball," repeated Jim, knowing full well the inappropriateness of the offer considering the injury. Dahlgren was visibly relieved when Jim made the call, chatted graciously with the boy and told him, "We're lucky to be where we are and getting well and getting good care."

At last, toward the end of November, Kobrine gave the word. Although occasionally there was a leak of cerebrospinal fluid, it was very slight and all other signs were good. Jim could go home for good, in time for Thanksgiving. The new home-care nurses came to the hospital for training during Jim's last week there. Sarah began doubling her efforts to get the house ready, although it wouldn't be completely finished until after Christmas.

Before Jim left the hospital he asked Kobrine to tell him exactly what, medically, had happened to him. "I spent an hour and a half going over everything," says Kobrine, "showing him X rays, CAT scans, going through his record." After hearing it all, Jim, adopting the current fad of Valley Girl talk, told

Kobrine, and anyone else who would listen, "This is a totally new head you gave me, A.K., totally."

At parties in Jim's room over the weekend, the Bradys and the staff said their emotional good-byes. Sarah handed out some of the hundreds of teddy bears as mementos. The rest she sent to a home for handicapped children. And on Monday, November 23, Art Kobrine finally signed Jim's "Free the Bear" petition. Before leaving his room Bob Dahlgren told Jim, "You weren't able to walk in on your own steam, but, by God, you should walk out of here." Jim immediately struggled to get out of his wheelchair. "Not yet, dummy," said Dahlgren. He told friends later, "The guy was actually ready to try it." Downstairs and outside, Cathy Wynne and Sarah helped Jim out of his wheelchair and walked him slowly the few steps to the waiting van. "One of the greatest experiences I've had in nursing," says Susan Deyo, "was the day Jim Brady walked out of the hospital. We all cried."

There was a crowd of reporters, hospital staff, and other well-wishers. The seventy-two-piece Washington-Lee High School Generals Band played "When Irish Eyes Are Smiling," then the University of Illinois fight song. Jim gave the crowd his thumbs-up sign. Kobrine and Brady shook hands, and in an interview with Victor Cohn of *The Washington Post,* Kobrine said that Jim's "intellectual capacity is fine," that it was too early to predict when he might go back to work, but that eventually he could hold "an intellectual white-collar job." Kobrine said that Jim would be returning to the hospital five days a week for four hours of therapy each day.

At home, Sarah uncorked a bottle of champagne first thing upon entering the house. Three-year-old Scott was there, of course, as well as Frances and Bill Kemp. Nineteen-year-old Missy would soon join them. Now the household included round-the-clock nursing care, too. After a week at home, to everyone's relief, the CSF leak stopped for good.

Home for Thanksgiving. It sounded so wonderful, and yet it was to be extremely difficult. Everything had changed, and even with all the preparations they had made, there was still a myriad of other adjustments to make.

Jim didn't speak to the press gathered to see him leave the hospital that day, but through his office at the White House he released a statement. He called it a "special day" and said he was "saddened to say good-bye to the hospital staff whose dedication, competence, and refusal to give up have made today possible." He offered a "sincere thank-you to so many wonderful people throughout the country and around the globe. Your prayers and words of support and encouragement were the greatest source of strength and courage I have ever known. We rejoin our friends and neighbors with a true spirit of optimism for the future. They say, 'The Bear will be back!' I am here to say, 'The Bear *is* back!' "

The most difficult part of Jim's coming home was having around-the-clock nursing care, but Jim needed help doing everything.

"The reality of working out how much and what kind of nursing care Jim needed, I found very difficult," says Sarah. "I wasn't accustomed to having live-in help and the complete lack of privacy that comes with it."

In addition, Sarah was expected to provide meals for everybody, launder the mountain of bed linen that piled up every day, and in general, run what had become a very complicated household. When the washing machine broke down, it loomed as a major catastrophe in Sarah's mind. "The sheer drudgery of it at first totally exhausted me."

As time went on, Sarah could see that she didn't need RNs for Jim. "The RNs, being professionals, tended to want to run our lives, and to run our house like a hospital," says Sarah. "I couldn't convince them we didn't need them right there with us every moment."

The night nurse particularly was a stickler for duty. "She disapproved of our drinking and my smoking," says Sarah. "In addition, she was a vegetarian and she spent a good deal of time reading her Bible in the living room.

"She also had the unnerving habit of creeping around the house at all hours of the night. She would come into our bedroom in the middle of the night and reach under the covers for Jim to use the urinal."

"She had the coldest hands," claims Jim.

After about two weeks of this routine, the Bradys went out in the evening for the first time. "When we got into the van it seemed like it was the first moment we had been alone together since Jim came home," says Sarah, "and, among other things, I asked Jim what he thought of our night nurse."

"You mean Hitler?" said Jim.

"Yes," laughed Sarah. "And we both decided we couldn't stand her. She had to go.

"We had the superconscientious RNs all day, and then Hitler would arrive and glare at us for having a drink. It was a zoo."

It would take a while to find the right people to help them, but Kay Ryan, director of the Americare Health Services, trained people for the Bradys until they found just the right combination. Ryan understood what the Bradys needed—Jim called her "Mother Superior." And by the end of the year Mother Superior had found nursing assistants Linda Day and Emmy Fox.

"My first concern was that whoever it was be kind and good to Jim," says Sarah, "and when I heard Jim and Linda laughing and talking downstairs as he showered and dressed, I knew we'd found the right person."*

Emmy Fox, a recent immigrant from the Philippines, was their other "find." Sweet-dispositioned and patient, "Emmy and Linda fit into our family situation so well, and we began to function very comfortably together," says Sarah—Linda helping Jim during the day; Emmy arriving at four to see him through the evening. (After the first few weeks it became clear they didn't need someone at the house all night, sleeping in, nor did they want that intrusion.)

In December Jim's father died of a heart attack. He was eighty-four but his family felt certain that Big Jim's ill health, already poor from a series of strokes, was worsened by the heartbreak of his only child's tragedy. "He just grieved himself to death," says Ed Brady. Sarah decided not to tell Jim right away. She was afraid the shock might bring on more seizures. She waited until he was safely at the hospital for his daily therapy, then met him there and, with Dr. Kobrine, broke the news to him. "He wept briefly," says Sarah.

Leaving Jim with Head Nurse Pam Campobianco and family, Sarah made the journey alone to Centralia for the funeral. But Jim has always refused to accept his father's death and, to this day, has not been able to internalize the concept that his

*Tragically, it was discovered that Linda Day had cancer and she died in 1985 at the age of forty-one. Since then, alternating with Emmy Fox have been, first, Paula James and Margaret Miller and then Darnell Hardy and Mary Dickerson.

Frank Johnston

Planning the Reagan Revolution, January 1981: from left, Vice-President George Bush, Jim Brady, Jim Baker, President Reagan, Secret Service men, and Tim McCarthy (far right)

Jim hosting fellow Sigma Chis
in the Roosevelt Room of the White House,
March 18, 1981

White House Pho

Jim in his Cubbies hat,
March 27, 1981,
three days
before the shooting

Seconds before the shooting: from left, Rick Ahearn, Jerry Parr, Jim Brady, President Reagan, Michael Deaver, policeman Herbert Granger, Walt Rodgers, policeman Thomas K. Delahanty, NBC cameraman Sheldon Fielman, Tim McCarthy (right foreground)

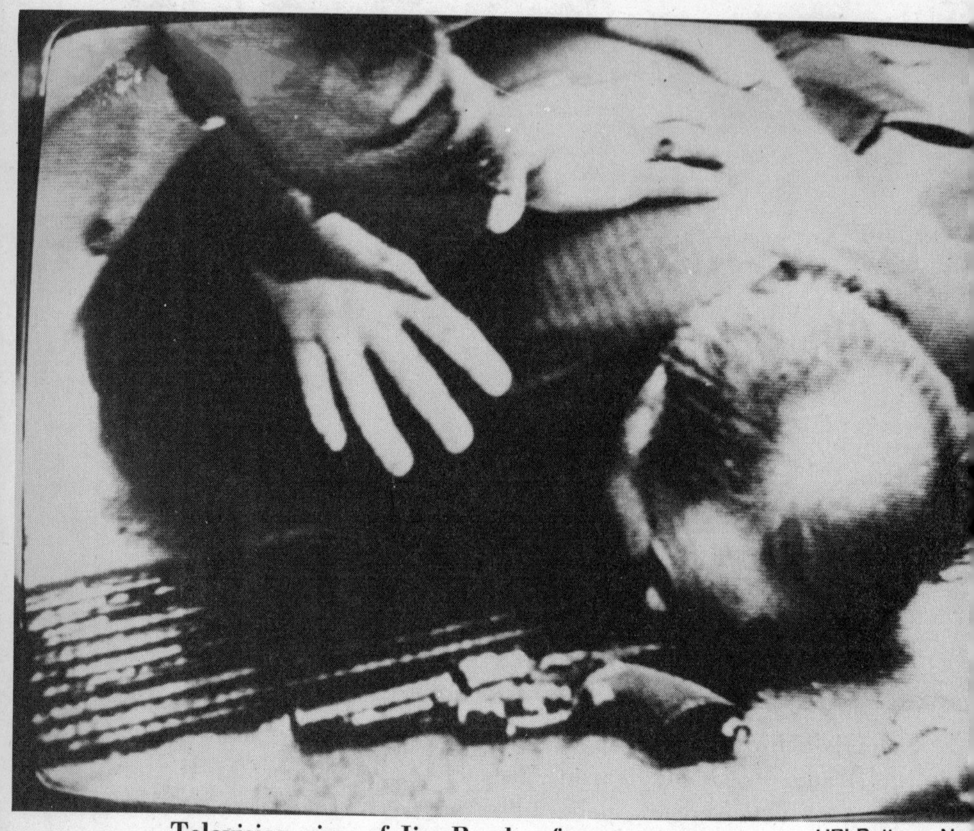

Television view of Jim Brady after the assassination attempt

UPI Bettman Ne

First time out of the hospital for the day, with Scott, July 4, 1981

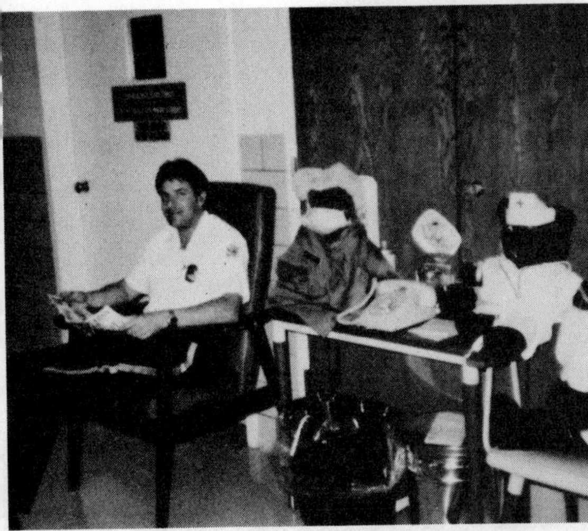

Officer and bears guarding Jim's hospital room, 1981

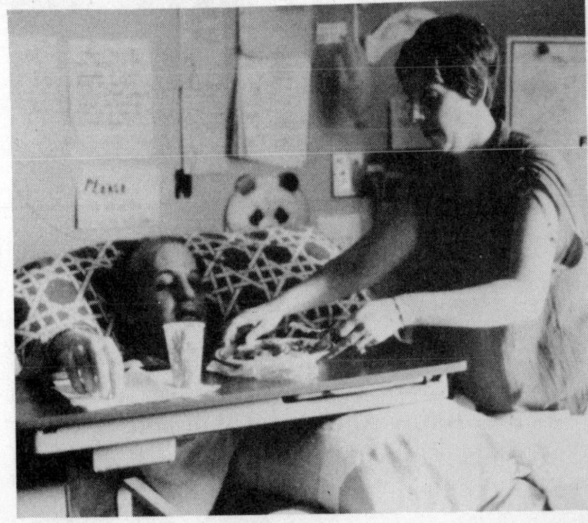

Sarah helping Jim with dinner, summer 1981

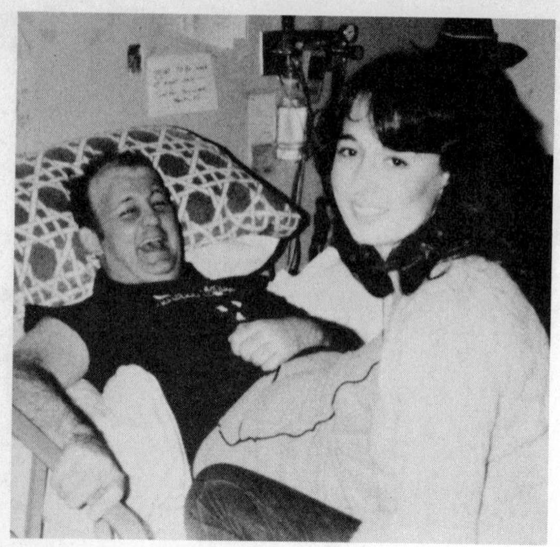

Jim in the hospital with nurse
Susan "Flash" Deyo, fall 1981

Tim and Kathy Ahern and Bob and
Suzi Dahlgren with the
"Free the Bear" petition, October 1981

White House Photo

the Oval Office
efore opening the press room,
ovember 9, 1981

White House Ph

Dedicating the refurbished White House press room, November 9, 1981. Jim claims a trapdoor has been installed over the old swimming pool.

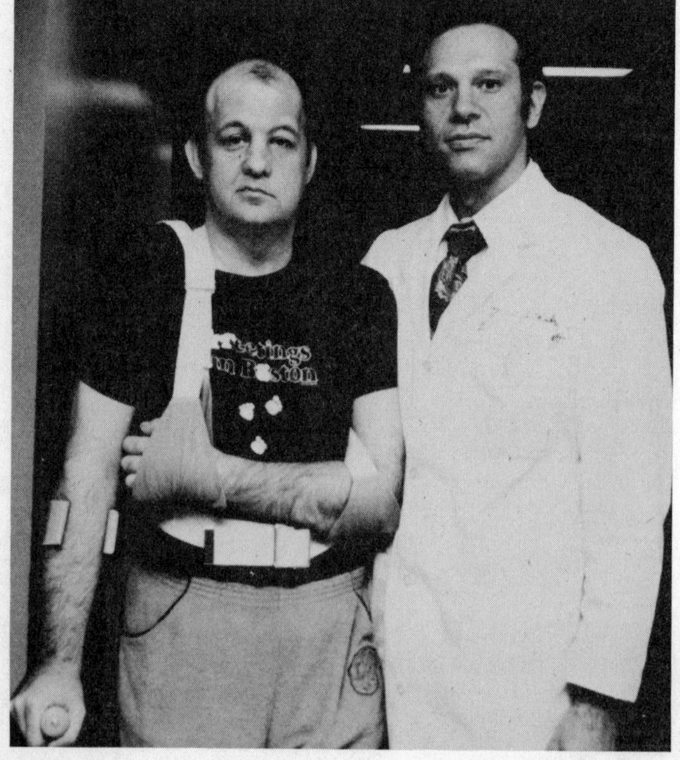

Jim and Dr. Arthur Kob November 23, 1 the day Jim left the hospital

father is gone. "I think that is because Big Jim died when Jim was still so injured," says Sarah.

Jim was plunged immediately into the regimen of therapy. There was no doubt in his mind that he was going to recover completely. He and Sarah started accepting some of the many invitations that were coming into his White House office. But their favorite evenings out were with friends for dinner. At first, people were taken aback at his lack of initiating conversation. But in December Arlene Pietranton and others noticed that Jim was beginning to initiate and anticipate things in his therapy. It was an enormously good sign that he would not retain that aspect of frontal-lobishness. Although he showed considerable sluggishness and some slurring of speech, much of it was due to the heavy doses of phenobarbital he was on to prevent seizures. And, of course, his brain was still recovering and beginning to develop new ways to handle old behaviors. Jim slept almost twelve hours a day, and he had little energy when he was awake. But he was at his best when he was socializing with his press and political friends.

That Christmas, Illinois friends Susan and Jay Bryant dedicated their Christmas card to Jim, with a poem, titled The 1981 Christmas Train, that ended:

Train that's bound for glory,
Clackin' on round the bend.
Flacking this year's Christmas story:
Brady's on the mend.

In January he and Sarah and Missy attended the annual Washington Press Club dinner, Jim taking his seat at the head table "to thunderous applause," said the *Post*. He was besieged by people wanting to shake his hand and said to one of them, "It's going to be a wonderful evening." The spontaneous and emotional ovation Jim received that night was typical of many such honors to come. In late February at the Kennedy Center's opening night performance of the Dance Theatre of Harlem, Jim was given an "Emergence Award" by the ballet company. He and Sarah accepted many chores as charity chairmen as well, starting with the D.C. Society for

Crippled Children campaign that spring. They came to be in great demand as patrons for many charities and fund-raisers.*

Sally McElroy brought Jim his White House mail and notes to sign twice a week. She reported happily, "He still dumps on me, just like he always did. I'll bring letters for him to sign and he'll notice a typo and say, 'I see you're up to your old tricks.' "

On February 23, the D.C. Court of Appeals upheld Judge Parker's ruling that denied the government its use of some testimony taken from Hinckley by the FBI following his arrest, as well as some writings taken from his prison cell. The skirmishing over the use of these materials had caused the trial to be delayed for several months as it was appealed to higher courts in North Carolina. Three days later, Jacob A. Stein, Jim Brady's lawyer, filed a $46 million civil suit against John W. Hinckley, Jr., in the U.S. District Court in Washington for his assault, which caused "severe and permanent injury" and for acting "willfully, wantonly and with a reckless disregard for human life." Tim McCarthy and Thomas Delahanty had already filed similar suits.

As the Washington winter wore on, close friends could see the gradual, steady improvement in Jim. In March he began to verbalize his feelings to Arlene Pietranton. It was another good sign. "In therapy, he was very cooperative, he never expressed dissatisfaction or bitterness about what had happened to him, but he was frustrated by having to come back to the hospital every day. 'I feel as though I'm in a bear pit (always using "Bear" metaphors whenever possible),' he would say, 'and that people are looking at me all the time.' " Pietranton felt keenly that "although Jim had the luxury of a tremendous amount of support, he never had the luxury of privately recovering, and that constantly being in the public eye was difficult. My reaction to his expressing his feelings was very positive. Until then, although he responded to me, he hadn't initiated any conversation with me."

Others noticed the improvement, too. Out for dinner one night in mid-February the table talk centered on a question

*Among them: the Hexagon Club, the Easter Seal Board, New Life (wheelchair athletics), the Wooly Mammoth Theater; the Mash Bash for Critical Care; the Ear Ball; the Hunt Ball for the National School for Therapeutic Riding.

asked during President Reagan's press conference that day by the ever unpredictable Lester Kinsolving. "Yes, who asked that wild question?" said Sarah, who hadn't heard all of the press conference. "Jimmy Dick did!" Jim called out gleefully, teasing *Washington Post* writer Jim Dickenson. Brady knew all about the story and was well acquainted with Kinsolving. He just wanted to twit Dickenson. At the same time, aspects of his brain injury were evident at mealtime. Jim would eat whatever was in front of him, nonstop, until it was gone, and then be too full to eat his main course. This was the *impulsiveness* described by Arlene Pietranton, which was slowly responding to therapy in all three of his therapy sessions, with Pietranton, Cathy Wynne, and Susan Marino. But Jim was so happy to be out of the hospital. His happiness was clearly visible on his face. And he was making good progress in his therapies, even though he endured a great deal of pain with every move he made. He just knew he was going to beat this thing. And as the first anniversary of the shooting drew near, Jim felt more and more as though he was putting it all behind him.

There had been many requests for first-anniversary interviews and Jim and Sarah agreed at last to an interview with Barbara Walters for the ABC news magazine *20/20*. "The *20/20* crew came in the morning and set up a real 'studio' in the house," says Sarah. Barbara Walters arrived at noon and interviewed them for a couple of hours. "I was highly impressed by her sensitivity," says Sarah. "She was very loving and lovely and extremely sensitive to the fact that Jim was still recovering, and conducted the interview so as to put as good a light on things as possible. She had done her homework and was well aware of how he was." Walters was wearing a pink cotton sweater, which both Jim and Sarah admired. "Three days later a pink Peter Pushbottom sweater arrived for each of us. She also brought with her a wonderful copper chili pot for Jim."

In the piece that appeared the next week, Walters began: "Jim's major emotional problem seems to be getting his thoughts into words. This will improve. And sometimes his voice turns into what sounds like crying or wailing—this embarrasses him. And although he remembers everything that happened before the shooting his memory of recent events is a little hazy. Still, considering where Jim Brady was a year ago this time, his recovery is indeed a joyous miracle."

Jim told Walters he didn't have any recollection of what had happened to him, and when asked if he had any feelings about John Hinckley, he said, "Just say he was a bad shot."

"Thank God," said Walters.

"He couldn't hit a bear in the back with a bull fiddle," Jim added, once again underlining the fact that he wasn't the target.

The pieced showed Jim in physical therapy and a brief episode of him wailing badly while reading a news item in speech pathology.

Art Kobrine described Jim's condition and said, "I think Jim Brady can return to an intellectual type of work in the White House, for instance. . . ." Jim told Walters his "near-term goal" was to go back to the White House and be press secretary.

"And the long-term goal?"

"To be a public-affairs director of a corporation."

"How would you describe Sarah Brady?" Walters asked Kobrine.

"Sarah has been the most positive influence in this whole affair," said Kobrine. "Sarah has helped me, has stood behind the physicians, the nurses, her husband, her friends. People have turned to Sarah for help, for support. She's a classy solid lady."

"Don't you ever get bitter?" she asked Sarah.

"No, I don't think I feel bitter. I'm sorry it happened, of course. I wish like anything that it never happened, and it's not anything I would ever wish on anyone. But I don't feel bitter at all."

"You said to me when we first met," said Walters, " 'If Jim never gets any better than now, it's enough.' "

"Oh, yes. Because he's so well now. He's got his mind, his personality, he's fun to be with. For me he's absolutely perfect; he's not happy with himself right now. He's such a fighter, I think that's what's going to make him get back to work."

"And in the final analysis, what have you learned?"

"How wonderful having the person you love with you is. Just how wonderful it is to have him. That made me appreciate all the people I love—just life itself. It's just wonderful to have it. 'Cause it's much better for him than the alternative."

In an interview for *Family Circle* magazine that spring, Jim said, when asked if Sarah had been strong for him, "If I had to go into this with anybody, I'm glad it was you, 'Coon."

"I'm glad to hear you say that, Pooh," said Sarah.

"You've been a tower of strength," Jim added.

"You've been pretty strong yourself, Pooh."

"It comes from you, 'Coon."

Jim admitted he sometimes felt angry at his lot, but "Thank heavens, his energies are directed toward other things," said Sarah, saying she had just seen Jim walk with a cane for the first time in physical therapy. "When you start with someone who couldn't sit up and now can walk with a cane, he's come a long way."

Jim also had begun swimming therapy. "You get movements in the water that you can't get out of water," he pointed out. But his water therapy was a short-lived experiment. "It was too cool to be therapeutic," says Wynne. Jim's extreme sensitivity to heat and cold on his skin made his immersion in a slightly chilly pool unbearable. The skin sensors on his left side had been scrambled by the bullet as had so many other connections. Temperatures that used to feel soothing to him were now extremely painful—they felt scalding or, on the other hand, freezing to him.

Even so, on swimming days, Jim kept up a steady patter of jokes. He would kid about being the leaky liner for the hull of the *Titanic*. He wanted nurse Emmy Fox (he called her Mongoose) to dive for pearls, always saying later, "The Mongoose never did get a pearl, did she?" Bob Dahlgren brought a rubber duck to the swimming sessions and had it talk to Jim.

Jim and Sarah went to the annual Gridiron Dinner that year on March 27. Once again there was an emotional standing ovation for Jim. Vernon Jordan, black activist, former Urban League president and now Washington attorney, saw Jim as he was being wheeled out of the men's room. "Hey, Jim," said Jordan. "How ya doing?" "Fine. How're you?" said Jim. " Vernon, they tried but they couldn't get us, could they?" Jordan himself had been shot on May 29, 1980, with a 30.06 rifle. He says one of the first telegrams he received was from former segregationist Governor George Wallace of Alabama, who was paralyzed from the waist down in an assassination attempt made by Arthur Bremmer.

The next day, March 28, Sarah and friend Barbara Greener were spray-painting the Bradys' porch furniture. "I walked into the living room," says Sarah, "and Jim, in his 'Bear Chair,' was having a seizure. I injected him with phenobarb and it stopped. I called Kobrine and he drove over to check Jim over, and decided he was okay."

Two days after Gridiron, on March 29, Jodie Foster was secretly spirited into Washington to have her testimony videotaped as a witness for the defense in the upcoming trial. Only a handful of people knew she was there and they were sworn to secrecy. Her lawyer, Nathan Lewin, had asked that her testimony be handled this way because, he said, Miss Foster was planning to be in Europe making a movie and would be unavailable to testify. Others thought the reason for the secret videotaping was to spare Foster the public circus that would surely have accompanied a public courtroom meeting between her and John Hinckley.

As it was, it was bad enough. Sitting in the witness box with Hinckley eyeing her (at one point he complained he couldn't see her and was allowed to move), she testified that two or three weeks after the beginning of classes at Yale University in September 1980, she started receiving handwritten communications from a John W. Hinckley, Jr.—either in her mailbox in her dorm or shoved under the door of the suite she shared with two other girls enrolled at Yale. In October she received some more. The first batch were "love type letters and poetry—like the fan mail I generally receive," said Foster. The second batch was the same type of material, she said. She placed no importance on it, she testified, and threw it away, although by then she had come to recognize Hinckley's handwriting.

In November, the FBI contacted her and told her "I had received a kidnapping threat apparently, or I had been told of a kidnapping threat that had been put upon me in November, so I was told to keep anything that looked at all suspicious." Now she was alert to danger. In early March 1981 she found a packet of more notes and letters from John Hinckley under her door, which "were a different type of letter," she testified, "so I gave it to my dean." Hinckley delivered his messages three days in a row, March 4, 5, and 6, the last one dated "One A.M., March 6." "I particularly remember," said Miss Foster, "I came in around fifteen or twenty minutes later." Foster said all the envelopes were hand-delivered but that she never saw Hinckley. The envelope on March 6 was addressed to "Jodie Foster, Superstar."

Inside was the message "Jodie Foster, love, just wait, I will rescue you very soon. Please cooperate. J.W.H." Miss Foster started to say, "I had never seen a message like this before, but of course in the—" "Objection," said the U.S. attorney, Robert Chapman. Foster was about to say that the same message was sent to Jodie Foster, or to Iris, the character she played, by Travis Bickel, played by Robert De Niro in the movie *Taxi Driver*, but the question of whether the movie was going to be allowed to be shown in the courtroom as evidence was still undecided, therefore the prosecution's objection. But in the version shown to the jury she said she had seen such a message when she played Iris in the film *Taxi Driver*. "The Travis Bickel character sends Iris a rescue letter," she said. Foster went on to say, "Also there was a reference to John Lennon, who had been shot, obviously, and that was another reason" that she was alarmed "and also because they . . . seemed more distressed than the other letters."

Defense attorney Gregory B. Craig asked Foster, "How would you describe your relationship with John Hinckley?" "I don't have any relationship with John Hinckley," she replied. Craig and Chapman went forward to confer with Judge Parker before the bench on a legal technicality when suddenly Chapman burst out in outrage and disbelief, "He just threw a pen up here," he said, pointing at Hinckley. "He just threw a pen and I looked around, and he threw a pen up here." Hinckley had thrown the pen at Foster. Judge Parker barked an order. "Let the defendant go in the cell block a second." As Hinckley was led out he growled, "Jodie, I am going to kill you, I swear to God."

Whether it was a calculated action designed to keep himself out of prison or a true emotional outburst is known only to Hinckley. But it was very upsetting to those in the courtroom and to Jodie Foster in particular. A nurse was called in to attend to her, but she soon regained her composure and the testimony was ended.

When Jim Brady was told of Hinckley's outburst, he said, "That won't get him a date with her. He hasn't learned his lesson, has he?" Jim told friends, "I think it's funny that after doing all that, Jodie Foster won't have anything to do with him."

Jim Brady, at home that evening, March 29, 1982, the very eve of the anniversary of the shooting, was having trouble again—this time catching his breath. Sarah, terribly worried, called Kobrine, who told her to get an ambulance to bring Jim to the emergency room at GWUH. "Jim was very aware that he was in the very same bay in the same emergency room he was in one year before," says Kobrine. "I was here a year ago to the day," Jim said. "I just wanted to stay out of that goddam emergency room as much as I could." "He got very frightened," says Kobrine. "I hope this doesn't mean I'm going to die," he said. Susan Deyo came downstairs to comfort him. "It'll be allright, Bear," she told him. He held on to her hand. "But from the X ray, once again everything looked fine," says Kobrine "and I sent him home." (As it happened, on the same day, President Reagan made his first visit back to the Washington Hilton Hotel since the shooting to give a speech. He came and left through the hotel garage and reporters were kept far away.)

Jim and Sarah were to leave by train for Chicago in a day or so. Jim had been invited to throw out the first ball at the season opener of his team, the Chicago Cubs. It was to be a triumphal homecoming for the Illinois boy whom Chicagoans were proud to call their native son.

But the next morning in physical therapy, says Cathy Wynne, "Jim came in having difficulty breathing. His color was very gray. I had him lie down and called Kobrine." But Kobrine was tied up and he sent resident Ed Kornel. "When we took off his trousers, his left leg was bright red and swollen," says Wynne. As Kornel started to do a physical, Kobrine and Dr. Hugh Trout came in to check Jim out, and after a lung scan showed a few pulmonary emboli had gotten through the umbrella, Kobrine decided to admit Jim to the hospital.

"It was spooky. Here he was, March thirtieth, 1982, one year later to the day, back in the very same room on Five-E. At the time," says Kobrine, "I was thinking of it as a lucky room, but on second thought I realized it brought back to Jim all the bad times, and reminded him of his longing to go home. Jim was very much aware that it was exactly one year later as though fate had determined this and he was very depressed." Kobrine treated the clots with bed rest with the legs elevated. As a result Jim developed reflex esophagitis and couldn't eat without vomiting. He lost sixty pounds in two months. Intravenous feeding was started. In addition, a lung infection from the clots made breathing difficult. Kobrine brought internist George Economos into Jim's case to oversee his general health, and to monitor and coordinate the many drugs he was taking. "Jim had thought everything bad was behind him and here he almost had to go through the same thing all over again," says Art Kobrine. "He was very ill. He must have asked himself, 'Is it worth it?' " Kept flat on his back, he had to stop therapy and his muscles lost strength; it was a serious setback.

Arlene Pietranton visited Jim in his hospital room. "He was disoriented and drowsy," she says. "His level of responsiveness had decreased dramatically at that time. I remember one time he just lay there. He did nothing and said nothing. I was just visiting him but there was no social initiative on his part and no response to mine." A week later she found him better but she felt he was recovering very slowly. "He was oriented and outgoing. He was verbally requesting things. But he continued to be drowsy. He may have had a lower oxygen level due to the pulmonary emboli. Everything together was serious enough to take its toll." Kobrine added another antiseizure drug, Clonopin, which further depressed Jim's system.

On April 20 Hugh Trout sent Jim home with the blood thinner heparin, and Sarah learned how to give it to him by injection. Trout chose heparin over the other most effective blood thinner, Coumadin. Kobrine had questions about the use of heparin, but on the other hand, "I felt that long-term Coumadin use was potentially dangerous, too, and I thought it unlikely Jim would *not* need long-term blood thinners in his life. And I thought heparin might work. The advantage of heparin is that it can be reversed easily, within four to six hours. The disadvantage is that on some rare occasions it washes calcium from the bones." Kobrine also had the thought in mind that if he had to operate on Jim again, he for absolutely certain didn't want him to have a bleeding problem in his head due to Coumadin. Heparin seemed the best of a bad choice, but the bone-wasting problem potentially inherent in heparin would come back to haunt them before the summer ended.

It was a very bad time for Jim and Sarah, and it coincided with a rash of news stories about the trial of John W. Hinckley, Jr., which was slated to begin soon. A week after Jodie Foster's testimony Judge Parker set the trial date for April 27. John W. Hinckley's father, John senior, earlier had criticized the Justice Department for dragging its feet, and said, "We've been ready to go to trial since November." But it was his son's defense attorneys' request for suppression of evidence that the prosecution was appealing, and then Hinckley lawyer Vincent Fuller asked for thirty more days to prepare. Assistant U.S. Attorney Roger M. Adelman, speaking for the United States government, opposed the request, saying, "We're ready for trial now." Judge Parker gave them three weeks.

Meanwhile, Jim's former employers Jim Lynn, Don Rumsfeld, and John Connally began work on establishing the James S. Brady Presidential Foundation, a nongovernment fund "to provide assistance to any needy individual wounded or killed in an assassination attempt on any senior federal official, presidential candidate, or on family members of the President and Vice-President of the United States and to provide assistance to the individual's family."*

"I don't know whether we will ever have to use it. We haven't yet, but it is reassuring to know it is there," says Sarah.

As a corollary, White House Counsel Fred Fielding asked Congress to pass legislation allowing federal workers wounded in any assassination attempt to accept private contributions for medical expenses while still receiving a government salary. Fielding had no trouble finding support for the measure; it was sponsored by Republicans Senator William Roth and Representative Robert Michel—and managed on the House floor by Democrat Tom Foley. The bill passed in four hours, start to finish, and President Reagan signed it on April 13, preparing the way for the proposed $5 million fund for future medical expenses and other needs such as Scott's education. Fielding, who kept a framed copy of it on his office wall, always pointed to it and said he wished he could get all legislation passed that

*Nancy Reagan is honorary chairman of the foundation; Donald Rumsfeld, chairman; James Lynn, president. The other members of the board are Joe M. Rodgers, Robert S. Strauss, James A. Wilderotter, S. Jackson Favis, Joe L. Albritton, Dr. James E. Cheek, John B. Connally, Katharine M. Graham, J. W. Marriott, Jr., C. Peter McColough, Donald S. MacNaughton, Dr. Dennis S. O'Leary, William M. Plante, Jack Valenti, and Lew R. Wasserman.

easily. Workmen's compensation had paid for most of Jim's medical expenses and for the modifications to his home, but workmen's comp had a ceiling, and Jim's expenses were enormous and ongoing.

As Hinckley's lawyers and the government's prosecuting attorneys wrangled over such questions as whether part of the earliest FBI interview of Hinckley was admissible evidence, whether the movie *Taxi Driver* and network videotapes of the shooting would be shown in the courtroom, and whether the victims of the shooting would be called to testify, Jim slowly recovered from the effects of the escaped blood clots. It was reported that Hinckley was going to claim that he was not trying to hit the president, but rather was trying to hit the president's limousine. Therefore, said the U.S. attorney's office, the films must be shown to show how Hinckley aimed his weapon and fired it and that he intended to commit the crime. Hinckley's lawyers said Hinckley would not claim to have been shooting at the limousine but that showing the videotape unedited "would inflame the passions of the jury."

In an important decision, Judge Parker reversed himself in deciding to allow the jury to remain unsequestered—that is, to allow them to go home each night instead of keeping them together in a hotel where their access to media reports of the trial would be monitored or denied. The prosecution was afraid jurors would inadvertently see news reports of the trial and be influenced by other people, instead of focusing on the evidence presented in court.

One by one the legal questions were resolved, the jury of five black men, six black women, and one white woman was chosen. Judge Parker had yet to rule on the question of whether the government would be allowed to split the charges in the case as to who had to accept the burden of proof of insanity—whether Hinckley's lawyers had to prove that Hinckley was insane, or whether the government had to prove he was sane. District of Columbia law dictated the former, but federal law dictated the latter. The question arose because the shootings of President Reagan and Secret Service man Tim McCarthy were legally considered federal offenses, and the shootings of Jim Brady and Thomas Delahanty considered local, or District of Columbia, offenses. The prosecution was asking that the burden of proving insanity be on the defense for Brady and

Delahanty, and the burden of proving sanity be on the prosecution for Reagan and McCarthy. Judge Parker ruled that federal law superseded local law, and since all the charges were presented in one indictment, federal law would apply across the board in this case. Judge Parker's ruling would make the government's case more difficult, but it was not an unexpected result. "It was important," says defense attorney Gregory Craig, "but had Parker ruled otherwise, I'm sure it would have been reversed on appeal."

The stage was set for trial. The burden of proof was upon the prosecution. It would have to prove that at the time of the crime John Hinckley was sane (that is, responsible) beyond a reasonable doubt. But that included a further test. To find Hinckley not guilty by reason of insanity (NGRI), the jury would have to find that as a result of a mental disorder he did not know that what he was doing was wrong, or that he was unable to conform his behavior to the law.

The problem, many thought, lay in the federal law, and after the trial, the Justice Department set about changing the law to put the burden of proof of insanity upon the admittedly guilty perpetrator of the crime—the defendant.

But for this case, the lines were drawn. The point was made by one of Hinckley's lawyers who said he "didn't expect any dispute during the trial over whether Hinckley suffers from a psychiatric disorder." Prosecutor Roger Adelman responded, "None of the government psychiatrists think there is any serious problem with Mr. Hinckley at all."

Three weeks after he entered GWUH, on April 20, Jim Brady went home to Arlington once again. "He's doing fine," Dr. Dennis O'Leary told the press, but friends who saw Jim soon after he left the hospital were stunned at his appearance. He was thin and subdued. For the first time, he appeared to have lost some of his optimism. It was going to be a much more difficult fight than he could ever have imagined, and that knowledge was written all over his face.

In addition, the Hinckley trial was at the top of the news every day and Jim, still the news junkie, was inevitably confronted with the story of his shooting day after day. On television the videotapes ran again and again.

In physical therapy, Cathy Wynne noticed the change. "Jim sort of did a downer. The trial was in the news all the time, hitting him in the face every day. He was quiet—lethargic."

But there were pleasures and honors coming along, too. This year Jim was able to attend the White House Correspondents' Dinner on April 21, receiving another thunderous ovation, and he threw out the first pitch at the Old Timers baseball game at Robert F. Kennedy Stadium. In May, Jim was awarded an honorary doctor of law degree by McKendree College in Lebanon, Illinois, an honor from his home territory he was very proud of. "We look for someone who has distinguished himself in his field," said McKendree's president Gerrit Tenbrink. "His strong will and courage were exemplary to our students and students across the country." Later that month, five hundred "friends of the Bear" discoed in the courtyard of the Department of Agriculture to raise money for the James S. Brady Foundation.

In Jim's absence the press office at the White House had become and unwieldy two-headed mess under the joint management of Larry Speakes and David Gergen. Their animosity over the turf increased by the day. "In a way, the press operation fell apart almost immediately," says Gergen. By all accounts the rivalry between Speakes and Gergen got serious and nasty. "It was truly awful," says Gergen. One press staffer says that Speakes order his staff: "If the tall man comes around don't tell him anything—don't give him any information." (Gergen is six feet six.)

"Everybody leaks like mad," said Judy Woodruff. "Their definition of a leak is whether it is in their interest or not. Nofziger and Clark (of the NSC) are always working on Reagan on right-wing issues. Deaver and Baker are always working on Reagan to moderate him. They all have their own little principalities and their own spokesmen and probably wouldn't want a strong person in the press secretary's position at this point."

Gergen left the White House in 1983, leaving Larry Speakes in charge of the press office.

PART FOUR

A Life in National Politics

CHAPTER EIGHT

To Washington and Sarah Jane Kemp

Sarah Jane Kemp was born February 6, 1942, in Kirksville, Missouri, but, except for her first six years, spent mostly in Buffalo, New York, she grew up in Alexandria, Virginia, a close-in suburb of Washington, D.C. She had been steeped in politics all her life.

Sarah's parents, Frances Louise Stufflebean and L. Stanley "Stan" Kemp were small-town midwesterners; she from Brookfield, Missouri, and he originally from Washington, Iowa, until his family moved to Brookfield, too. Although they knew each other all their lives, their romance began when they were both in summer school at Northeast Missouri State Teachers College in Kirksville. Married in 1939 they were living in Kirksville where Stan was teaching and coaching at the high school when Sarah was born. "But times were hard," says Frances Kemp, "and Stan wasn't making much money." The infusion of federal funds for World War II hadn't yet turned the economy around, and now, with a new baby, Stan Kemp went to St. Louis for an interview with the FBI. "I just about died when I heard his plans," says Frances. "But he got the job and it started the next month in Newark, New Jersey." "I'll send for you," he told her and she and baby Sarah joined him there in July. From Newark to Norfolk, Virginia, to Buffalo,

New York (for five years), they moved, and then to Washington, D.C., and the Virginia suburbs where Mrs. Kemp still lives today.

"Sarah was always very active and outgoing," says her mother. "She wanted friends over and wanted things happening!

"She started kindergarten at age four and a half and was always the youngest in her class. She was a good student, but she was a lot for having fun and didn't apply herself as well as she might have," her mother says fondly. But Sarah did well enough to be accepted at William and Mary College on the edge of the restored colonial village in Williamsburg, Virginia. ("Bill and Mary," Jim Brady calls it, displaying a little regional rivalry. "Is it accredited yet?" he always adds.)

Sarah played so much bridge and had such a good time her freshman year "that she didn't make her grades," says Frances. Academic year 1960–1961 she worked in her father's office. Stan Kemp had left the FBI in 1952 to work on Capitol Hill and was administrative assistant to Republican Congressman Walter Norblad from Oregon when Sarah joined him.

Sarah went back to William and Mary the next year, received an A.B. in education in 1964, and taught school in Virginia Beach for two years. "I went there because a lot of my friends from William and Mary were teaching there, and I loved the beach life. We just partied all the time. I dated a number of different people—mostly naval officers."

But a romance with one naval officer became serious, and when it failed Sarah was jolted into reassessing her life. She moved back to Arlington and taught in a formerly all-black school that had just been integrated. "I sort of went through a reversal stage," says Sarah. "I became almost puritanical and really threw myself into my teaching."

Midway through the school year a bizarre nerve disorder struck Sarah's left side. "I had gone on a diet that year and lost a lot of weight and wasn't taking care of my nutrition," she says. "I was five seven and had gone down to ninety-eight pounds. A virus attacked two cranial nerves in my brain," affecting her left arm and hand, but most dramatically, her left eye was pulled completely over to the outside corner of the socket so that her eye appeared white and pupilless. There were no guarantees that she would recover, and she wore an eye patch all spring. "I was almost resigned to living my life that way." But one morning in June, "I got up and looked in the mirror and saw that it had moved. Within one day it zoomed back into place," she says. "That was my growing-up year."

Sarah's younger brother, Bill Kemp, meanwhile was serving in Vietnam. He was there from 1967 to 1968 during the Tet offensive. "I didn't think it was right for us to be in Vietnam," says Sarah. "I wasn't part of the kids who were demonstrating; I disassociated myself from them totally. But I remember arguing with people about the war. I didn't have a lot of information or strong opinions. I just didn't think it was right to be there."

Sarah threw herself even more into her teaching the next year. "I loved that school and really put an awful lot into it those two years. It was a wonderful experience."

At the end of the second year, however, "I made the decision that I was a very intense person who would always get very deeply involved in what I was doing. I think I took teaching and my students too seriously and I felt I needed a more well-rounded life—and a job where it wasn't so hard to draw the line on the amount of effort I was going to put in. Plus, I always loved politics. We *lived* elections when I was growing up."

That summer, 1968, she worked as a volunteer at the Republican Congressional Committee in the finance division, and in the fall hired on with them full time.

In 1969, when Ed Terrill became director of the campaign division of the Republican Congressional Committee, Sarah asked for an interview with him for a job. "She was working in the financial part of the Republican Congressional Committee," says Terrill, "doing grunt work at a very low salary. She told me she wanted to improve herself."

As it turned out, Terrill had come from Brookfield, Missouri, as had the Kemps, and on top of that Sarah's mother's brother was best man in Terrill's wedding. "It never dawned on me who she was," he says. "But as she left my office it did and I ran after her." Terrill himself was a recent arrival in Washington. One of his first hires was Sarah.

In the sixties, Terrill, working for the RCC, oversaw the fieldmen in the races in fourteen or fifteen Midwest states. "I had worked with Jim Brady in Illinois in the Ogilvie campaign and knew him very well. He was a very competent operator. In those days, I worked out of my basement in Madison, Wisconsin. Republicans weren't very affluent then."

After a year on the committee, in February 1970 Sarah was asked to work on Ronald Reagan's gubernatorial campaign in California. "But Ed was against it," says Sarah. "And just a month later I met Jim."

In March, "we made Sarah the assistant campaign director for our annual conference of campaign managers," says Terrill. And among them was Jim Brady. "When Jim walked by and took an eye to Sarah," says Terrill, "he came to me and said, 'Hey, who is this assistant campaign manager you've got there?' " And he asked Ed to introduce him to her. At the evening cocktail party, "we met and talked and really hit it off," says Sarah. "I had heard of him. I knew he was a very sought-after bachelor. I had read about his races in the files and I knew the feeling at the RCC was 'We've got a bright young man working here.' "

"Because he had taken a shine to Sarah I invited Jim out to dinner with our staff," says Terrill. "It turned out that we didn't have enough room at our table for two people, so Jim and Sarah sat by themselves. So I feel a little responsible for their meeting."

"Ed told me the next day," says Sarah, " 'Now I want you to know that Jim Brady is a man of the world, Sarah.' "

"I'll be careful," she told him.

"Yes, I was a rake and a roué," confirms Jim.

But the truth was Sarah Kemp had fallen in love. She'd fallen head over heels for Jim Brady. It was love at first sight. At twenty-eight, she was ready to meet the love of her life, and she had met him. "I was totally taken with him," she says.

"Sarah was living in her own apartment then," says her mother, "and she'd had dates and dates and dates. But after every new date, she'd tell me, 'Oh, achh! I don't want to see him again.' But one day she told me, 'Boy, Mother, I met the grandest fella last night.' And it was Jim, of course. I think maybe in the beginning I wasn't all that thrilled about it. My first reaction was, 'Oh, Sarah, you don't want to marry someone who's been married before and has a child.' But she said, 'Mother, what do you mean? It doesn't matter.' "

After that first evening together, "we went out every night through the weekend; out to dinner alone the next night, then with Dick and Jeri Church who happened to be in Washington, too," says Sarah, "and to the Watkinses who lived here."

"Sarah wasn't a typical Brady broad," says Dick Church. "She was a sharp gal." "Until Sarah," says Jeri, "we had never met anyone we would have chosen for Jim. She was different and special. But Jim was becoming more serious, too, at that point in his life. He treated her differently—nicely—and didn't try to B.S. Sarah as much as he did other girls."

"Jim invited me to come to Chicago the next weekend," says Sarah.

"And, by God, she came," says Jim.

"I got in Friday night, March sixteenth, in time to celebrate Saint Paddy's Day the next day," says Sarah. And what a day it was. "First we went to Hobson's for beer and gumbo. Then to the Saint Patrick's Day parade. Then to Elfman's for potato pancakes and large pickles; to a German place for Austrian food; to Butch McGuire's for hot dogs and beer. Then Jim said, 'As long as we're downtown we might as well have dinner!'

"But first we went to Su Casa for nachos and margaritas; to a Polynesian restaurant for more hors d'oeuvres; we went to a party, then decided it was too late for dinner so we had pizza. It was the most fun I've ever had. He was so bright and so much fun; that combination I loved seeing. I hadn't run into too many people like that.

"And we had a lot of things in common; the same friends in politics; our careers; and we loved to eat. After knowing Jim for two months, I went from one-hundred-eight to one-hundred-twenty pounds. I became a real eater after that."

When Jim came to Washington, they went to Sunday night prayer services at Mr. Smith's restaurant, where they could order a beer and listen to live gospel music.

"I was in Chicago just before Christmas [1970] and Jim said, 'Let's go to Aspen for Christmas.' I couldn't believe I could be away from home for Christmas. But I borrowed ski gear from friends of Jim's and we went." The next Christmas they took Missy to Aspen with them.

And so began three years of a long-distance marathon of a romance with Sarah spending much of her salary flying to Chicago three weekends out of four, and Jim flying to Washington on the fourth weekend. "I think my mother thought I was crazy," says Sarah.

"Well, I knew Sarah was crazy about Jim," says Frances. "I knew she was in love with him, because whatever Jim said was all right with her, and that's not like Sarah. Even including the decoration of her living room!" she adds.

And Jim was in love with Sarah. "Before she even got home from Chicago," says Frances, "Jim was on the phone. 'Is the 'Coon there yet?' " (Frances wasn't at all sure she wanted her Sarah to be called Raccoon or 'Coon.)

"Jim is so generous, so good, and so thoughtful," says Frances. "I learned to love him. And he was always bringing something. For instance, Stan wanted me to have some new pans, and the next time Jim came he brought a copper skillet. He came down from Boston once bringing lobsters. The first thing Jim always did when he walked in the house was to look in the refrigerator to see what there was to eat. He always said there was nothing in there to eat. Which was funny because *their* refrigerator was *packed* with jars of exotic mustards and caviar. Nothing you could actually eat."

In May, Jim took Sarah to Centralia for the first time to meet Dorothy and Big Jim, and his friends. "Dorothy and I hit it off really well," says Sarah. "She was so cute. I remember she had written out the menu she was serving for Sunday breakfast and had it at each of our places."

"Jim got all his dad's good points, and all his mother's, too," says Sarah. "He got his drive and self-confidence from Dorothy, and his gregariousness and Irish part from his dad."

In June 1970 Jim brought Joe Anderson into the campaign business for about six months, making him coordinator with the Republican National Committee for the Dick Wathen campaign for the U.S. House of Representatives in the Ninth District of Indiana. And for Jay Wilkinson's campaign for a House seat from Oklahoma that same year.*

"The national Republican Congressional Committee decided," says Anderson, "that one of the wonderful things they could do for all their candidates at great expense was to set up this great information machine which supposedly would tell

*Anderson later started his own advertising agency in Davenport, Iowa, and handled Senator Jim Leach's campaigns in 1974 and 1976, among other things.

you everything you needed to know about your opponent—how he voted on thus and such, etcetera. It didn't work for dink."

What it did do, says Anderson, "was to turn out to be a communications link between the staffs in Washington and the rest of the country. We figured out how to send messages on it and we all adopted animal code names. I was the Walrus, Jim, the Bear, of course. There was Patty the Possum, and that is how Sarah became the Raccoon. I hardly ever call her Sarah—I almost always call her Raccoon.

"So that's what we did with this expensive machine—we sent animal messages back and forth on it."

"Some campaigns used it more than others," says Sarah, "and used it well. We put one in each of the key races around the country." Jim and his firm had one because they were handling several campaigns.

Governor Ogilvie had appointed Speaker of the House Ralph Tyler Smith to replace Senator Dirksen when he died in 1969. Illinois law dictated that he stand for proper election in 1970. His opponent was Democrat Adlai Stevenson III. Jim and his firm handled Smith's campaign. "Our motto—'Downstate needs a senator, too.' " (Smith was from Alton.)

They ran a law and order campaign and tried to tie Stevenson to Jerry Rubin and the critics of the Chicago police. And they indulged in a few tricks, too. "Stevenson was giving a 'come as you are' party," says Jim. "And we saw to it that a lot of their flyers were handed out to skid-row bums and street people. 'Where did those dirty people come from?' the Democrats were saying," Jim laughs. "We were rightfully blamed for it in the press."

In the Schlafly campaign, sharp conflicts had developed between Jim and Phyllis Schlafly. "I was running her campaign, hell," says Jim. "She was running it—she had a mind of her own. There's only room for one campaign manager and she was it." There was a crisis every day. There would be some outrageous quote in the paper and Jim would ask Schlafly, "You didn't say this, did you?" "Yes, I did," she'd answer. "I said it to the editor." "To the editor," says Jim. "It had to be to the editor."

The final straw came when Jim nixed Schlafly's plan to take two station wagons full of nuns to the state capitol to lobby against the abortion bill. "It was more than I could take," says Jim. "To incarcerate those poor nuns in those station wagons—saying the rosary all the way up to Springfield. I told her it was insane, that abortion wasn't a bread-and-butter issue, that it would hurt her chances."

Schlafly called Jim and his boss Tom Bertsche to a meeting at her home in Godfrey, Illinois. "Only I missed the plane," says Jim, "and Tom went alone, only to be met at the airport by one of Phyllis's minions who fired him and me. Tom swore I did it on purpose. Got his ass down there only to be fired."

"I was ready to kill him," says Bertsche.

"It was one of the nicest firings of my life," says Jim. "It was getting so that I was embarrassed to tell anybody I was working for Phyllis, because after they stopped laughing, then they wanted to know why."

And handling the Schlafly campaign had an impact on Jim's own personal political views. "Jim was a practical Republican, through and through," says Susan Bryant. "My guess is that on social issues he is moderate to liberal. He's not an ideologue on any issue. At that time he was probably against gun control. But the Schlafly campaign finished off any opposition he might have had to the Equal Rights Amendment."

"Schlafly took a drubbing," says Jim, and so did Wathen and Wilkinson. But Jim had learned he could make a good living running congressional campaigns. So far he had run nothing but long shots, and no winners. Mick Scheriger asked him, "Are you ever going to win an election, Brady?" But Jim did win the Republican Campaign Committee's office pool that year, says Sarah, "calling every single race right."

Meanwhile, back and forth Sarah and Jim were flying. "I managed most of the time to get youth fare on the airlines," says Sarah, "but in order to get it I had to make myself look like I was twenty-one. I took off all my makeup, wore a fall with a flip, and put a ribbon in my hair. So Jim, the sophisticated political operative, would pick me up at O'Hare and here would be this twenty-eight-year-old child," she laughs.

It was very important to Jim that he be up on everything in the culture. "He wanted me to wear my skirts shorter," says Sarah. "To wear hot pants and see-through blouses without a bra. He told me, 'You just let your mother dress you.' He read everything. He took *New York* magazine, among others. He was always in the know. When buffalo sandals were in style he had buffalo sandals. He shopped at Saks and wore Gucci shoes."

Sarah made several trips to Centralia during their three-year courtship—always to the now traditional Hambletonian trotting races and the accompanying birthday party for Jim in the Bradys' backyard. Sarah was a big hit with Jim's Centralia friends. They very soon felt Jim had found the right girl. "Sarah is well liked here," says Bill Crain. "Before Sarah, Jim had brought a number of women home," says Dorothy Mann. "Dorothy [Brady] would say, 'Oh, dear, some of these little girls he's bringing home.' When he brought Sarah here we were all rooting for her." But Jim had always brought all his friends to Centralia. It was just too great a place, his thinking went. He had to share it.

In January 1971 Sarah left the Congressional Committee and went to work for newly elected Republican Congressman James D. "Mike" McKevitt, the district attorney from Denver, Colorado. "I met Sarah when I came to Washington for help from the RNC for my campaign," says McKevitt, "and we hit it off right at the beginning. Even then she was unflappable. She was always very courteous and businesslike—very gracious, but she had a Virginia shyness about her. She was the first person I hired for my Washington staff.

"She was my executive assistant—eyes and ears. She taught me everything from the quickest way to get to my office, to the ins and outs of the personalities on the Hill. She was an all-around adviser. She had learned a lot from her father, and often she called him for counsel.

"Sarah did a large variety of things for me. It was a dog-and-pony show up there. She handled dignitaries, did my scheduling, made appointments. She was my personal confidante. Both of my top assistants keyed off of her. She could do anything and did.

"In effect, Sarah ran the office in a very quiet way; she was its soul. Everybody came to her with their problems. Yet there was never any overfamiliarity. She was Mother Bear."

The first thing Sarah advised Mike McKevitt to do was to throw a reception for his colleagues on the Hill immediately after he was sworn in. "It's an important thing to do," says McKevitt. "A lot of new congressmen don't have them. Then

Sarah asked me if I'd like a good bartender, and that's how I first met Jim Brady. It was a great party, and over in the corner, behind the bar, Jim was sort of the grand host of the event—the kind of guy who had befriended everybody before the evening was over.

"Jim is now very much like he was then. There was always a mystique about him—a little screen there—as he made observations on the subtleties of events, or threw out his cogent remarks. You never *really* knew what was going on in his head. Now, people think his pixieish way has something to do with his injury. But he's sitting there and the wheels are always turning. Jim's very unique, very difficult to read. He's one of these guys who is insurmountable. 'You can't beat me,' he is saying. 'You'll never destroy me.' There's a sureness about him; there's never a sign of insecurity, of ignorance, or inferiority. It's an amazing thing—the power of the personality and the human mind. He has a will of iron."

Over the next two years, McKevitt says, every Friday night as he left for Denver and his district, Sarah was leaving for Chicago and Jim. "She was devoted to him, utterly devoted. Some of her friends wondered, 'Does Brady really appreciate her? Does that guy realize what he is getting?' " The long-distance aspect of their romance was difficult. "But," says Sarah, "Jim called me every day, and usually more than once. We talked constantly when we weren't together."

Congressman McKevitt had settled on two issues he wanted to work on in his first term: immigration, and control of the Saturday-night special handgun. "As a former D.A., gun control was an important issue to me," he says, "and I still feel very strongly that way. We reported bills out of committee on both issues, but then we saw how the power of the National Rifle Association had worked subtly behind the scenes to defeat us." The importance of handgun control was underscored when a popular woman on McKevitt's staff, his caseworker Janet Dent, was shot to death by her estranged boyfriend with the very gun the boyfriend had given her for her own self-defense. "That brought the issue home to everyone in the office," says McKevitt. And it strengthened Sarah's own position, which had always been for strong handgun control. "It shocked me. Jim and I had double-dated with them and went out together on staff parties," says Sarah.

Sarah celebrated her thirtieth birthday in Chicago in February 1972. Jim threw a big champagne brunch for her. One member of the party then slipped out at intervals to buy more champagne. "It turned into a two-day party," says Jeri Church. "I remember having deep conversations sitting on the floor around Jim's coffee table." And Dick Church was moved to moon the party, knocking the milk punch onto Jim's alpaca rug. Joe Anderson had taken up painting and they all trekked up to his apartment to see his work. The Churches bought one—a huge one. "They left with it," says Sarah, "and an hour later they were back. They couldn't fit it into any of the cabs they'd hailed."

"I can't believe how many spontaneous things Jim and I did," says Sarah. "We went to Texas for the Texas-OU game. We went to Fort Lauderdale. We met once in Atlanta."

Sarah was with Jim in Chicago, however, when he decided it was time to javelin his needleless Christmas tree into the Chicago River from his Marina City balcony. "It was in May," she laughs.

That summer Jim brought Missy to Washington "and we took her camping to Assateague Island off the Maryland coast," says Sarah. "And we just ate. Jim inherited from his dad the ability to relax totally when he was on vacation. His eating habits were, that he'd just get up in the morning and start to cook."

"Fried 'Pooh-tatoes,' bacon, ham," says Jim.

"We'd eat, have a couple of beers and go back to bed. For dinner we'd have fresh corn. Jim would grill the steaks. And he made a reflector oven from foil and baked biscuits right on the beach. 'Bear's Beach Biscuits,' we called them. We were drinking gin and cream soda. When Jim fixed it for a party he called it 'Kettle of Gin.' "

"Jim and I had these dumb little stuffed bears," says Sarah. "There was Pooh, Poohford, and Pooh Belle. We took them everywhere with us. When we went to visit our friends Marianne and Herm Schmidt in Williamsburg, our bears had to be in the backseat. I made a tie for Jim once, and made one for Pooh, too."

Sarah always drove on their trips because Jim no longer had a driver's license. "By the time I knew him I never did see his car," says Sarah. "The city of Chicago had taken it and he could get it back only if he paid his parking tickets."

Nineteen seventy-two was another election year. With Watergate temporarily tamped down, Richard Nixon was running for reelection, and Jim's candidates that year were Bob Lambkin running in the Twenty-third, and two Missouri candidates, plus some other advertising accounts. Jim also kept his hand in numerous other races around the state, including Governor Ogilvie's reelection bid.

Daniel Kearney, who was director of the Illinois Housing Development Authority, says about Ogilvie's term: "There was always a little suspicion between the professionals who came in to run the agencies and the political types like Jim Brady and 'B' Oglesby who were interested in getting the governor reelected. Jim Brady had a fine appreciation of the policy side. Because he has this great sense of humor and could deliver pithy insights about various political personalities, it would be surprising to hear his insights on issues."

President Richard Nixon and Vice-President Spiro Agnew won reelection easily in 1972, defeating Senator George McGovern and Sargent Shriver, but in Illinois, Governor Richard Ogilvie lost his office after only one term—his bright political future done in, most people thought, by his putting a state income tax on Illinoisans for the first time. And Mike McKevitt was defeated by Democrat Pat Schroeder. Sarah spent two months in Denver working on McKevitt's campaign, and Jim met her there several times.

Sarah was as much in love with Jim as ever, but she was beginning to worry about the uncertainty of their relationship. Jim was still proving to be very good at playing the elusive bachelor, although once, two years into the romance, he playfully placed a Jaguar cigar band on her finger in lieu of an engagement ring.

After two and a half years, Jim and Sarah weren't seeing quite as much of each other as before, especially during the summer of the campaigning, although they talked on the phone every day.

However, in August, a friend told Sarah that Jim had been seen with someone he had met during the campaign. "I had planned a big party for Jim's birthday in Centralia at the Centralia House," says Sarah. "When I heard there was someone else in the picture, I was so upset I was about to die inside, but I decided I wasn't going to play the hysterical woman. I called Jim and said as coolly as I could—I had rehearsed it—'Jim, we've been seeing each other for a long time and maybe this has gone on long enough. And I understand there are other people in your life now, too. If you want to keep seeing me, fine. I want to, too. But I don't see how I can continue to see you if you're seeing someone else. So I'm not coming to Centralia next week for your birthday.' " Jim protested, but Sarah said, "You think it over and let me know."

"As far as I was concerned it was the biggest gamble I ever took in my life," she says. "Since he'd been married before I knew he wasn't exactly dying to remarry."

Two days later Jim called. "You have to come," he told her. "I promise I won't see her anymore, especially," he added, "if you're going to be that way about it."

"I think Jim thought that would calm me down for a while and he'd face the next step when he had to," says Sarah. Looking back on it, Jim always says, "She gave me an ultimatum." But Sarah doesn't see it that way. "I left it up to him."

And when they met at the end of September for a confab with one of Jim's congressional candidates in Kansas City, Missouri, Jim presented Sarah with an engagement ring. It was a very sentimental weekend as they pledged their love to each other. But, Sarah says, "the only hotel we could find was the one the National Malamute Convention was at. And in the middle of the night if one of them would bark, then ten thousand would bark. If one had to go out, twenty had to go out. We were awake all night," she laughs.

On their next visit to Centralia, after the election, says Dorothy Mann, "Betsey Kourdouvelis and I decided to have an engagement party for them so it would be very difficult for them to break up." "Well, it'll be the longest engagement in history," said Jim when he heard about it. "I was saving it for the Bicentennial," he says today.

The combination of their engagement, the slim political pickings left by Ogilvie's defeat by Democrat Dan Walker (not to mention the defeat of all of Jim's candidates), and the fact that he was ready for a bigger pond, all came together to inspire Jim's next move.

On December 31, 1972, after Sarah spent Christmas with him in Chicago, he moved to Washington to be with her. "This town was made for us," he told Mick Sheriger. "They're not going to blow us out of here." "I don't recall that we ever discussed my moving to Chicago," says Sarah. "It was always understood that Jim wanted to be in Washington."

As soon as the new Congress convened, Jim and Sarah both went to work for newly elected Joseph J. Maraziti, Republican congressman from the newly created (by redistricting) Thirteenth District of New Jersey. For Sarah it meant a large salary increase. She soon became Maraziti's administrative assistant and recruited most of Mike McKevitt's former staff for the office. For Jim, it was mostly a stopgap measure while he looked for something else. He worked as a consultant on a daily basis, and "I wrote his newsletter for him," he says.

While Jim was still working for Maraziti, a strange phone call came for him one day. "This is Jim Brady's fiancée," said the voice.

"Oh, no, you're not," said the secretary, Sarah's friend. "Sarah Kemp is Jim's fiancée and here she is right now," handing the phone to Sarah. Evidently, Brady, the not-so-sly fox, hadn't the heart to totally dampen the flames of his campaign fling.

"I talked to her very calmly," says Sarah, "and gave her my home phone number and told her she could call Jim there in the evening if she wanted to. But I was just livid when Jim came in that night."

Jim put on a wonderful show of obfuscation, telling Sarah, "That's the dumbest thing you ever did, giving her your number. She's a maniac. Now you'll never be safe." In an added embellishment, today Jim says, "She told me if I moved to Washington she'd shoot me, but someone beat her to the punch." When the young woman called, Sarah answered, "He's right here," and handed Jim the phone. "We had him between us and he couldn't appease either of us," says Sarah. "We had a huge fight and he ripped the phone out of the wall. I had a hard time explaining to my mother why my phone was out of order."

"I just don't know how this could have happened," Jim told Sarah, "but if you're going to be mad about it, I'll just leave." And he went off to stay in a hotel. "He had an amazing way of making it look like it was all my fault," says Sarah. "But I was just crushed. 'This is it,' I thought."

The next day Jim called. "Will you come pick me up?" he asked Sarah.

A few days later Sarah got a bill for Valentine's Day flowers Jim had sent both to her and to Fiancée II. The Yah-Hah years were having a lingering death.

"With a little time, things sort of smoothed over," says Sarah. "Jim could never, ever say he was sorry for something. But he soon started doing nice things for me—took me out to dinner. We went back to having good times."

David Cole, a colleague of Sarah's at the campaign committee, and his wife, Brandy, had dinner with them at Sarah's apartment. "I remember we talked and laughed and had an uproariously good time," says Brandy. "There was a long cocktail hour. I'm not sure we ever got around to eating dinner." "We had prime rib," says Sarah, "but we didn't eat till about eleven, because I forgot to turn the oven on." At the end of the evening, David Cole said, "Next time it's our turn," and they made a date for two months hence. "Of course it will be black tie," said Cole. Jim showed up two months later at the Coles' backyard barbecue in black tie.

In his job search, Jim, ever the operator, had quickly learned the ropes of job hunting in Washington. He got hold of the "Plum Book," which lists all the presidentially appointed jobs in the administration, and went through it looking for likely positions. The Illinois congressional delegation helped him, and he interviewed at the White House personnel office as well, making contacts wherever he went. He turned down several positions until the right one came along. And in March Jim secured a job at HUD and became part of the "Greener Group," William I. Greener, Jr.'s PR operation for James T. Lynn, secretary of Housing and Urban Development.

"Jim Lynn was an attorney in the Cleveland firm of Jones, Day, Reavis and Pogue," says Jim, "and was highly regarded in Ohio Republican politics." Lynn joined the government as general counsel to the Department of Commerce. "I promised my family it would be two years and we would leave," he says, "but at the end of two years they made me undersecretary. And after two more years, I was getting ready to leave when I was asked to take over HUD by President Nixon."

Bill Greener, assistant secretary for public affairs (as PR is termed in the government), wound up putting together a little group of men who were hardworking, sophisticated, and savvy on the one hand, and clever, funny, and freewheeling on the other. "Jim and Greener hit it off right away," says Sarah. "Jim even went to Greener's barber to have his hair cut that very day." "I liked him right off," says Greener. "I checked him out and got nothing but good recommendations." Thus began two years of intense associations and hard work.

Greener's group was Ronald Weber, "who was Deputy Dawg," says Jim; Dick McGraw; Jim Brady; Bob Dahlgren; and Hugh O'Neill. "I was the last to join the group," says Jim. His title was special assistant to the undersecretary of HUD for field operations. "I put him in charge of the advance people for Lynn and for preparing the briefing books," says Greener. His specialty was as political adviser to the public affairs operation. "Also, I could write," says Jim, "and most of those on the team could not." Dahlgren and O'Neill were his assistants.

Deputy Dawg Ron Weber had worked for Greener at the Cost of Living Council under former Illinois Congressman Don Rumsfeld, "and when that went out of business," and Rumsfeld became NATO ambassador in Belgium, he says, "Bob Haldeman told us we could pick our spot in the Cabinet. Bill Greener is one of the best media-contact people ever to hit Washington. He's a genius at knowing how to get good press, and we had heard good things about Jim Lynn." Bill Greener, a retired air-force lieutenant colonel, says, "We were a hardworking, hard-playing, hard-drinking crew. Jim had landed in the right place."

There were about thirty other Schedule C (presidential) appointees under Lynn: attorneys, special assistants, undersecretaries who headed other divisions. And they all pulled together to effect the policy changes Lynn was charged with making.

"There were the policy people," says Ron Weber, "who were in charge of drafting the new laws and administering them; the legislative people who explained the change to Congress; and the PR people who sold it to the public and HUD's constituencies." "They had a world of talent," says Jim.

"Everybody did everything," says Dick McGraw, who was director of field operations. "Everybody was in each other's pocket. That's the way Greener ran the shop. He gave people a lot of latitude."

"We had more fun than any group of people should have

had," says Weber. "The fun part of HUD was that there were people there who hadn't really worked for five or more years. We said, 'Let's see if we can get them to get back to work.' Greener wanted to fire them. But what he did was to layer in a handful of pros to do what was necessary. We determined who wanted to work and who didn't. Several were transferred to the newly formed Department of Energy. 'Thank you, God,' we said, 'for the DOE.' Others quit at our suggestion." Jim says the attitude was "We're the Bees. Bee here when you come. Bee here when you leave. We asked one guy what he did, and he said, 'I don't do anything.' And we said, 'You mean you keep working up these great ideas and they never get implemented?' And he said, 'No, I just don't do anything.' " "There were always enough good solid career types who really dove in and did a good job," says Weber.

"There were so many areas that needed attention," says Jim. "We rewrote the housing laws of the nation—no small accomplishment—taking some eighty or ninety narrow and categorical programs and combining them into fifteen or twenty programs. We had to train the field force. It was a lot of hard work—we often worked twelve hours a day." "On my first day at work," says Debby Jones Abbott, "I was leaving the office at seven-thirty and they said, 'What's going on, Jones? Taking the afternoon off?' We worked nights and Saturdays, too."

Attorney Jim Hedlund, who worked for Undersecretary Jim Mitchell in the legal division, recalls, "My first reaction to Jim Brady was bafflement. He was putting people on most of the time. Brady and Hugh O'Neill came down to talk to us and Brady was using these PR terms. After a while I figured out what he meant."

"We had a lot of fun at HUD, and we put in long hours," says Hedlund. "What had happened is that Nixon had suspended all subsidized housing, which had gone from zero dollars in 1968 to a huge budget. And he had charged Jim Lynn with a comprehensive review of what the federal government's role in public housing should be. The main premise was that the government was involved in an extremely expensive program which would surely get into the billions over a twenty-year span. The number-one purpose of HUD, of course, was to house the poor, but the second purpose was to prop up the housing industry. It was an unwritten law. And keeping the housing industry fat and happy was not deemed an appropriate role for government." On top of it they were building "these large buildings which didn't meet the needs of the poor who had all sorts of social problems attendant to that of poverty which those huge projects only made worse."

Ron Weber echoes Hedlund's reaction to Brady. "We didn't know what to do with him. He was so bright and so off the wall and irreverent. He was not shy; he always had an opinion. But his conclusions were always right even though his techniques weren't always. He'd sometimes come up with multimillion-dollar schemes. He was a quick study and good at detail in his own weird way, and good at making things happen as long as he had someone to do the paperwork."

Jim's main responsibility was to develop "marketing plans" to explain and sell the new housing law to its constituents: governors, mayors, and the housing industry. "He came up with brilliant plans for the secretary's tours," says Weber. And Jim used techniques he had used in politics, especially large flow charts to keep track of Lynn's schedule. "Jim told me on one of my visits to Washington," says Tom Bertsche, "that they thought the flow chart was the most amazing thing they'd ever seen. They thought he was a genius." "Don't tell anybody," Jim told Bertsche, "they think it's fantastic."

Bill Lilly, who left the magazine *National Journal* to join Lynn at HUD, says, "Nixon had suspended all housing funds—illegally. He impounded them. So there was a lot of tension among the various interest groups: the mortgage bankers, the builders, the mayors. And there was a real split in the black community. Lynn was always under attack. But we were presiding over failed programs.

"Brady did a very good job of developing relations with big-city mayors," says Lilly. "He was very good in an embattled situation. Brady and Greener were very much alike, and like the rest of us, Jim didn't care what the politics were. He was a completely free spirit. He, and we, used to laugh at the White House. They'd send all this stuff over and we'd throw it in the trash can.

"We got terrifically fair treatment by the press, and came to be known as not being part of the iron triangle (Nixon, Ehrlichman, and Haldeman). Brady was terrific at marketing the policy, and he really handled well the various black constituencies involved, including the employees at HUD. Jim is the least racist guy I've ever known. And we were never perceived as being antiblack.

"Lynn was a real taskmaster," adds Lilly, "but he worked as hard himself, and he was brilliant about shielding us from all the Watergate stuff. There was a great sense of idealism about what we were doing."

The long hours, the tension, Watergate, all led to late-night drinking bouts after work and on their many trips. Flying in late one night to a convention, two of Lynn's staff were so smashed they had to be taken off the plane in wheelchairs. "Brady covered it up so Lynn wouldn't know," says one who was on the trip.

Jim often traveled with attorney Jim Mitchell when, as undersecretary to Lynn, he was out giving speeches to realtors or mayors' associations. "We called him 'the Under,' " says Brady, "or 'the Under Walrus' because he had a moustache."

" 'Shape up, it's the Under,' they'd say with a salute," says Mitchell. "Jim also got involved with me when I had a reporter in, or when he had one he wanted me to see. We were smart enough to let them guide us in press matters. They tended to look at it from the press's side and encouraged us to tell more, rather than less. So we became known as open and responsive, although as lawyers, we were trained to do the opposite.

"They were really an incredible group. They all shared the same principles; all intensely loyal, all funny; they were thorough. And any one of them really would have been a first-rate person on your staff, but to have them all there together was special.

"HUD is one of the more interest-group-laden agencies of the government. There are half a dozen large organizations whose businesses depend on HUD dollars—the National Association of Home Builders (NAHB), the mayors' association, Realtors, other trade associations—multibillion-dollar organizations. We were expected to attend their meetings, and Jim's role was to facilitate those appearances. Often we would be on the road together."

There were many road trips, remembers Mitchell, "often with as many as twenty people along to explain the different aspects of the housing law. Much of Jim's time was taken up with that kind of thing. You were also expected to be at all these parties. There'd be a press conference or an exclusive interview. And Brady, Greener, and Dick McGraw were so good at this. The only people who never lobbied us were the poor people who lived in public housing. We almost never heard from them."

Jim advanced trips for many at HUD including Robert C. Odle, Jr. ("Oddly," Jim called him), who was deputy assistant secretary.

Working on the budget one Saturday, Odle says, "We got a call that the secretary was coming in. We'd been quaffing a few beers and didn't think he would approve, so we all herded into the undersecretary's bathroom and hid out until he was gone."

One time, "we got drunk," says Jim Brady, "and Jim Mitchell, the Under, tap-danced on top of Lynn's desk. Lynn heard about it and called Mitchell in. 'Mitchell, you're your own worst enemy,' Lynn told him, which became known as the 'your own worst enemy lecture,' " says Jim.

When Odle and his wife gave a black-tie dinner party one night, "the doorbell rang, and there's Jim in dungarees holding a rake saying he was Bosworth, the yardman. He thoroughly embarrassed everybody and then left." When Odle visited Jim in the hospital after the shooting, Jim's first question was, "How's your yard?"

"Greener's group became known for their efficiency," says Bill Rhatican, who was working in the White House communications office. Rhatican remembers a Florida meeting of all the Cabinet officers. "The best organized of all of them in a PR sense was Lynn. Lynn went from room to room to room, to do one-on-one TV interviews. Most of the other Cabinet officers had a lot of downtime. Brady and Greener, et al., took their jobs very seriously, but not themselves. And there are not many people who can make that distinction."

Dick McGraw remembers a trip he and Lynn made to Chicago. Jim had advanced the trip and from Chicago he called to warn the secretary that the director of Housing Region V wanted to confer with Lynn before he saw anybody else. "He may be going to try to sandbag you," Jim told him. "I think we oughta try to prevent the meeting."

But the man met Lynn's party at the airplane gate, and before Brady or McGraw knew it, he'd hustled Lynn and Jim Mitchell into separate waiting cars. "Dick, they're being kidnapped," said Jim. "C'mon, follow me." They jumped into Jim's rental car, "chased them through the damn city," says McGraw, to a private club where Lynn was nose-to-nose lobbied for two hours. "He was not happy," says McGraw. "He did not like being spirited off like that. And he told us not to let anybody pay for the twenty-dollar hamburgers we'd ordered." It was late at night when they finally got to their hotel. And then Lynn couldn't find the speech he was to deliver the next day. He dumped the contents of his briefcase out and threw it across the room.

"Lynn told the guy the next day in a public meeting," says McGraw, "if something like that ever happened again, he'd be in need of employment."

"That whole trip became the subject of a series of jokes," adds McGraw. "If, for instance, you want the secretary to be kidnapped, let Brady advance the trip. If you want everything to go wrong from the time you leave till the time you get home, let McGraw go with you."

Hugh O'Neill, who worked closely with and for Jim, says, "Jim Brady probably could get the overall PR and political aspects of the picture better and quicker than anybody I knew. That's what made him so good." The word about Jim, though, was, "that he talks in Sanskrit. He talks in allusions and he puts out incomplete thoughts because his mind is always racing ahead to his next thought."

Joan McEntee joined Lynn's staff in 1974 and found "an incredible group of people," she says. "It was a period of one's life never to be forgotten and Jim Brady was a big part of that. On the job he was brilliantly creative and witty. He had his own language; it was almost stream of consciousness. Everything we did went through the press operation. Jim could come up with a press release literally five minutes before our deadline."

With both of them employed and making good salaries, Jim and Sarah began house hunting. Their friend Brandy Cole, a real-estate agent, found a house near hers in Arlington. When Jim walked into the house he fell in love with it. "It was really the bar in the basement that did it," says Brandy. "Little did I know the retaining wall would fall down and they'd get water in the basement," she adds.

But Jim could imagine himself operating on his guests behind that bar. "Okay," he said, "we'll buy the house but that doesn't mean we have to get married." "But he knew in his heart of hearts," says Brandy, "what it meant if he bought a house with Sarah." An "action-forcing event," he and Sarah have always termed it.

And shortly thereafter they set their wedding day for July 21, and when the sale on the house became final, Jim moved in. Sarah kept her apartment at Southern Towers, and together they planned their wedding.

They joined historic Christ Church in Old Town Alexandria so they could be married there. "I, being a mere Presbyterian," says Sarah, "had to agree to go to special classes. Evidently, the Episcopalians and the Catholics have some arrangement with God, because Jim, a Catholic, didn't have to."

A hundred guests attended, including a contingent of family and friends from Illinois. Heber Pierce was Jim's best man. Joe Anderson, David Cole, and Bill Kemp were the other groomsmen. Brandy Cole was Sarah's maid of honor and her other attendants were Betsi Burkett, Mary Ann Venner Schmidt, and Missy, then twelve. Tom Bertsche was ushered into George Washington's pew, a place of honor. Many new friends from HUD were there, too. After the ceremony most guests walked to the reception, held at the nearby Anchorage House in Old Town. "We had two bars, and finger food," says Sarah. "And on the buffet table were cold salmon, shrimp, chicken puffs, and shrimp salad. A trio of piano, bass, and drums played a variety of music."

"It was a wonderful wedding," says Susan Bryant. Jim's friends were impressed with the elegance of the whole affair. Among them were Dick and Jeri Church. "You are always happy for Jim when something would go well, and we were thrilled for him because Sarah is obviously such a neat gal," says Jeri. "So there I am at this elegant wedding, chatting with Dorothy Brady, listening to chamber music, when all at once there is my husband mooning the reception from an upstairs window. Dorothy had the graciousness not to say anything." " 'B-r-a-a-d-y,' yelled Church in his squeaky little voice," says Jim, "and there in the fourth-floor window I see his rosy little red ass.

We knew it was Church, 'cause that was his trademark."

"Jim was right down below," says Church. " 'Hey, listen, please do it again,' he says. 'I want to get the photographer over here.' " "I'd have been disappointed if he didn't do it," claims Jim.

After the reception Jim and Sarah showed up unexpectedly at the party her mother was having for the family because she had neglected to take the skirt of her going-away suit to the reception at the Anchorage House. And then it was on to the newly infamous Watergate Hotel for the night. "First thing next morning," says Sarah, "Jim called and invited all our families to the hotel for brunch. And then we went home to our new house." They planned a wedding trip for the fall to St. Croix in the Virgin Islands.

Meanwhile, the Illinois crew, Joe Anderson, the Bryants, the Churches, the Pierces, and others, went on partying "for two days after the wedding," says Susan Bryant. "Just to give you an idea of how bad we were, I went to the wedding in one dress and went home in another. I bought one and threw the other away."

"I think Mom and Dad thought Jim was something of a rake," says Bill Kemp, "but after they got married Jim went out of his way to be a good son-in-law." Bill and his father had started building a sailboat in the backyard, and though Jim didn't work on it, he named it: "*The Backyard Bounty.*" And he and Sarah were present when it was launched on nearby Occoquan Reservoir. "We discovered immediately it had a leak," says Bill, "which took all summer to fix."

Stan Kemp was a Dixieland jazz fan, and Jim was always on the lookout for a record his father-in-law didn't have.

The first fall of their marriage the Bradys went to a Halloween party out in the Maryland countryside. "Two friends and I were the Three Bears," says Sarah, "in long underwear we had dyed brown. And Jim was Goldilocks. He was just classic. He had a blond wig, red leotards, and a doll in the pocket of his pinafore" (which he dropped in the toilet at some point of the evening because he wasn't used to hoisting a skirt up in the men's room.) "On the way to the party we got lost and Jim had to run into a farmhouse in his costume to get directions."

The major outcome of the evening, however, was the acquisition by the Bradys of a little gray kitty. The farm cat had

had a litter of kittens in the barn. Jim and Sarah named him Stutz Bearcat, and he became their darling.

Throughout all this time, Watergate revelations were beating on the door of the Nixon White House. Senator Sam Ervin's committee began its investigative hearings the summer of 1973. That fall Vice-President Spiro Agnew resigned in disgrace. Nineteen seventy-four brought the inexorable impeachment hearings of Representative Peter Rodino's House Judiciary Committee. "We had ringside seats for that," says Jim, "and it was terrifying to watch. There were people who had done the deed that you knew. I don't say that with pride, but it's true. Nixon made his bed, and he had to sleep in it, and he pulled his coverlet up." "The day McCord sang to Sirica," says Susan Bryant, "we looked at each other and said, 'What have we done?' The next four years were awful—a time of distress. We came to Washington because we thought we could have fun working in government without the pain of campaigning for somebody." During the Watergate hearings, Republican Senator Robert Dole characterized Haldeman, Ehrlichman, and Nixon as "See No Evil," "Hear No Evil," and "Evil," respectively, causing Jim thereafter always to refer privately to Nixon as "Evil." When some of Nixon's tapes were released, Jim and the bunch were particularly struck by an exchange Nixon had with Bob Haldeman about how a U.S. action would affect the Italian economy. "Fuck the lira," Nixon said.

"I guess he didn't care about Italian currency," Jim observed.

"We were looking for diversion from all that," says McGraw. "Lynn would come back from Cabinet meetings upset at Nixon's demeanor, and his inattention to Cabinet-meeting affairs."

"Yes, this was Watergate time," says Lynn, "and one thing that kept my sanity was that crew. There never could be a crew as good at what they do as Greener's crew—which included programming me to keep from doing dumb things—or rather, to have me doing things which were fraught with danger but which turned out well.

"Greener and Brady were a great team, with Greener the leader," says Lynn. "They reminded you of things you already knew: Never say something that isn't true. The best defense is a good offense. Include among your advisers people in the media who are intelligent and knowledgeable. (They're all frustrated and want to be running your business.) Self-deprecation is a wonderful thing. Don't make a five-week story out of one that will die overnight."

In the middle of his term at HUD, Lynn says, "Democratic Senator William Proxmire said that HUD should be renamed DUD, and that Jim Lynn was a wonderful fella, but he oughta resign. I was so darned fed up, and I hadn't had my legislation passed, and on Greener's advice I called the AP and told 'em, 'I will if he will.' I don't know if it's a coincidence or not, but he never went after me again in that way."

Lynn tells of receiving a speech written by his HUD speechwriters "that was the worst speech I'd ever seen. It was an important speech and I was furious. I called Greener, who told me, 'There's only one thing you can do, and that is—wing it.' I gave my speech from notes on a yellow pad, and the reaction to it was terrific. I never gave another prepared speech. I told Greener, 'If I didn't know you better I'd think this was a careful plot.'

"It was kind of nice having that crew along on my travels," he says. "At a convention of mayors at some watering hole in the west, Jim Mitchell showed up in a polo shirt, and I told him, 'It would be a good idea if you wore a shirt and tie. There are a lot of cameras down here.' That night I was sitting having some beers with some of them and down the hall comes Bill Lilly dressed in his Brooks Brothers pajamas and wearing a necktie around his neck.

"But the times you remember are the times you goof," says Lynn. Perhaps the best-remembered goof was a Brady-advanced trip to Ohio and Tennessee. "There'd been some tornadoes and lots of damage," says Lynn, "and the president told me to go down there. At that time, the federal emergency agency was under HUD. We landed at Chattanooga and got into our choppers to go inspect the damage in a little nearby town, but the only flat place to land was in a football field. The whole town, including the mayor, was expecting us and was there, and down comes my helicopter. I stride over to the gate—only there's one small problem. There's a padlock on the gate and the janitor can't be found. The crowd starts to laugh. But we weren't laughing. Finally, we just had to give up and bid adieu. So I strode back to my helicopter and took off," he laughs.

Jim's propensity for nicknames was shared by Bill Greener

and grew out of the intense working relationships and the ensuing fondness for each other. It was Dick "Quick Draw" McGraw, or "Dickie"; Bob "Boobie" Dahlgren, or "Irving Dahlquist." (Dahlgren once got an invitation addressed to him that way.) Bob "Oddly" Odle; Jim "Wild Rooter" Wilderotter; Jim "Head Loon" Hedlund; and on and on. Jim, of course, remained "the Bear," and he was variously called James, J.B., or just Brady. Dahlgren called him "Mr. Bradley" so consistently that others did too. Jim and the rest called Greener, "Perfessor," or "the Doctor," or "the Dean," or "the Green One." When Greener first saw Jim after the shooting Jim greeted him, "It's the Green One."

They had their own patois and in jokes. They could make jokes about sections of the federal housing code that only they thought were hilarious. They made up words they could use in public, which had private, mostly crude, meanings. A "lurkey" was "a cold rush of shit to the heart." A "blivet" meant "ten pounds of shit in a five pound bag." In the hyped atmosphere at HUD they found frequent and creative use for these terms.

"Brady, Greener, and I once played a terribly complex practical joke on Dahlgren," says Dick McGraw. "Lynn was up at Camp David one weekend, about to make a presentation to several senior people in the administration, and Dahlgren had the weekend duty back in Washington. We called Bob and told him to get the figures pertaining to the Better Communities Act—five years forward and five years back—and told him to call back and read them to us by year, and to do it quick. And he did. One hour later we called him back ranting and raving, saying he'd given the figures wrong, and they had been given out to the press. 'Your ass is on the line, Dahlgren,' we told him, 'and you'd better get back in there and get the numbers and call Lynn. He wants to talk to you personally.'

"Dahlgren was a worrywart and so impeccable in so many ways. To be accused of such an error, well, he was really, really scared. We let him stew for a while, and it was Brady," says McGraw, "who finally said, 'We'd better insert the cadmium rod—we're going critical. Dahlgren's about to blow.' "

Jim called Dahlgren, and told him, "I want you to follow my instructions, Boobie. Crook your little finger. Put it into the corner of your mouth, and pull." Dahlgren caught on; it was "the Hook."

"It was an unkind thing to do," says McGraw, "but we did it. Dahlgren's impeccability invited it—cried out for it."

But for all the fun, says Dick McGraw, "we accomplished more than we set out to do. The Better Communities Act took the pork barrel away from Congress and it remains in effect today. And, as a result of the National Housing Study, rent subsidies now go directly to the tenants so they can choose their own housing, rather than to the builder. There has been no new public housing built since then, although that which exists is still subsidized, of course." Lynn's crew planned an enormously successful Ten Cities Tour (which became legend to the HUD insiders) to sell the law. The National Housing Act of 1974 was termed "the most farreaching law in housing history," by Democratic Senator John Sparkman.

"The ten-cities tour went like this," says Greener. "We went to ten cities in two weeks. A typical day was that we'd land in Seattle, for instance, tonight, brief all the regional HUD people in the morning, have lunch with the senior elected officials of the region—mayors, governors—and brief them; then Lynn would introduce the new guidelines to county and state officials; at four o'clock, we did press interviews and met with newspaper editorial boards. The next morning we'd leave for San Francisco and repeat the procedure. It was a wonderful way to let all our officials know how the new act worked." Greener remembers the Seattle stop particularly because "Jim knocked on my door fifteen minutes too early that day." And after that everything went wrong, he claims; the briefing books were loaded into the airplane hold, and no telling what all else. "I was mad all day."

One night during the tour Greener had a few drinks and fell asleep on the couch while happy hour went on noisily around him. "I'd been working forty hours straight and had been sweatin' out my day," he says. "When I woke up Jim and the others had stuck a lily in my hand and piled about fifty briefing books around me."

The camaraderie that grew out of their intense hard work and accomplishment extended to their social lives. They often "just daily," says Greener, had lunch together at the Class Reunion, a bar-restaurant near the White House that became the hangout for journalists, government PR people, and security types. They met there after work as often as not and always on Friday nights. "They would take roll call," says Bill Rhatican. "If you weren't there the first question you'd get was, 'Where were you last night?' "

Bill O'Brien, bartender at the Class Reunion, pulled one on them one night, telling them he had a rare and exotic treat for them—imported vodka—the famed Russian Zelco vodka, in fact. "Finally he 'fessed up that it was really cheap stuff," says Ron Weber. But Zelco vodka thereafter became a code word for them. When leaving the office, they'd say, "I have to go see Dr. Zelco," or about a project, "I couldn't have done this without the help of Dr. Zelco."

"We'd play Liar's Poker," says Weber, "and Brady always saved dollar bills with a lot of sequential numbers on them. One day, Dahlgren caught on and said, 'Brady, you cheat!' Jim said, 'That's what this game is all about, isn't it?' "

Joan Grbach, co-owner of "the Class" (also called "the CR"), says, "Before Sarah had Scott, she and Jim often used to meet each other here after work. Sarah is so low-key, always sweet and nice. The staff always liked her because she took an interest in them."

But the long hours were hard on wives and marriages. "We had fun," says Sarah, "but Jim was always working. We never took vacations during that time. And as time went on, I'd get upset because Jim wanted to go out with the gang every night." Sarah was free to join them, and usually did, and it was probably easier on her than the wives at home with children, "because I was working fairly long hours, too."

HUD spouses became close friends, too, particularly everybody in the public-affairs group: Sarah, Bobbie McGraw, Suzi Dahlgren, Elizabeth O'Neill, Charlene Greener, and Stephanie Weber. They all got on as famously as their husbands. "We went on picnics and did a lot of outdoor stuff," says Sarah.

"We used to get together every weekend at a different house every time," says Hugh O'Neill, "for cocktails, dinner, and general conversation. The wives all got along together. It was unique. You don't usually find that closeness within an office staff like that. I think Greener was the glue, plus Jim's wanting to cook for us. Jim loves to be a host, and he loved to entertain at home, and used any excuse to do so, a birthday or whatever." O'Neill started making Jim's Chili, and "once I forgot to seed and chop the jalapeños," he says. "So Jim had to make a house call. He came over and diagnosed the problem. We removed the jalapeños, then sat around drinking beer and listening to Judy Collins sing 'Amazing Grace,' Jim's favorite song—Jim in his straw hat. I had my cowboy hat on." There was "total familiarity" among them, says O'Neill. "I helped paint the Bradys' house. Bobbie McGraw helped Sarah make curtains."

"What struck me about Jim and Sarah," says Bobbie McGraw, "was how generous they were with their friends. They entertained constantly." In 1974 Jim and Sarah instituted annual Saint Patrick's Day parties. "There were always large groups of people, and plenty of food—Mulligan stew. Everybody was sitting on the floor because there wasn't a stick of furniture. They had no money.

"We would have work parties at each other's houses, more the girls than the men. The men recognized work when they saw it, and we couldn't trust the men with the painting anyway. But they helped build a shed at the Greeners, and Jim pitched in when we landscaped our yard." Jim teased the McGraws about living in the farout suburb of Middleridge, Virginia. "The last stop before Richmond," he called it.

Jim brought wheelbarrow load after load of dirt up from the creek, says Dick McGraw, claiming after each one, à la Redd Foxx, "Get ready, Elizabeth, I'm comin'. This is the big one." Greener showed up six hours late to that work party. "I very cleverly went to the Gridiron Club that night," says Greener. "I did, however, stop by in my tails to wish them well and to have a boozeberry with them."

On Saturday mornings, says Greener, "Sarah and I used to take my son Tom fishing. The three of us would fish and clean the bluegills we'd caught. Sarah was a good fisherlady."

They all picked up on the word *egregious*. For a while, everything was egregious. " 'Oh, that's so egregious,' we would say," says Stephanie Weber. "Then we always burst out laughing."

Jim and Ron Weber usually drove in to work together. (Jim was newly relicensed.) "If Jim was driving, it was his terrible old green VW—which rarely got out of first gear," says Weber. "I'd say, 'Jim. Shift.' And he'd say, 'Shall I do that again?' Jim'd come roaring up in first gear to River House where we lived, and yell out, like a conductor calling stops, 'Here's the Brady-mobile, en route to the Class Reunion with an intermediate stop at HUD.' "

"He drove like a maniac," says Stephanie Weber, and Ron recalls the time "we were coming off a ramp into traffic and a car wouldn't give way to us. Brady blew his horn, but no go. So Jim gunned it and slammed right into it." "Fools," Jim shouted.

"It was the best collection of like personalities ever put together. We were all newly married," says Ron Weber.

When the O'Neills' house caught fire one night, and their dog took off, "Jim was the first person I called. Jim and Sarah and Liz and I drove around Old Town from twelve-thirty to three in the morning looking for the dog. We never told him it was a Doberman." They went back to the Bradys' and gathered the rest of the group there while Jim made dozens of potato pancakes, "his answer to everything," says Ron Weber. "But nobody ate 'em." The O'Neills lived with the Bradys for two weeks while their house was being repaired, "and the Doberman, too," says Sarah.

Chicagoan Dan Kearney, who had joined HUD when Ogilvie was defeated, says the HUD days "were the mini-equivalent to our days in Illinois in that there were awfully good people there. Brady and Greener both have a masterful insight into how to present the best aspects of a policy. And it was a politically hyped time. Nixon froze all these housing programs. Congress was up in arms, with reason, at times. A lot of people were left hanging while we worked out the new policy."

"Dan'l," as Jim called him, and his wife, Gloria, joined in some of the weekly HUD parties, where he says, "Jim always becomes the commanding person, raconteur, jokesman, storyteller, and cook. He'd have a beer in his hand and made sure you got one." The Kearneys were treated to Jim's Chief Illiniwek dance several times, too. "It was unbelievable," says Kearney. "You'd see this two hundred and fifty pound guy dancing for five, seven, ten minutes—all over the room. And it's not just the dance, it's the noises he makes. There's nothing like it to stop a party. As my wife said, 'I was always afraid he'd drop dead of a heart attack, to see this two hundred and fifty pounder doing this thing.' "

Gloria Kearney went to one Brady party when she was pregnant and overdue for delivery. "Wouldn't you know her labor started early the next morning," says her husband. "And when the doctors wanted to know what she had eaten in the last twelve hours, they were flabbergasted when they were told. It was smoked salmon, oysters on the half shell, stuffed baby eggplant, some kind of chili concoction, and more."

Missy visited Jim and Sarah every summer, and met them in Centralia each August, too, for Jim's birthday and the Hambletonian. "Jim and Missy always had so much fun together," says Frances Kemp. "They would roughhouse on the floor like a couple of kids."

While things were going so swimmingly in Jim's career, Sarah had found almost immediately that there were problems in Maraziti's office. As *The Almanac of American Politics* described it: "He had a woman on his congressional payroll who never showed up and whose relationship with the Congressman appeared to be less professional than personal. Some members of Congress can survive revelations of sexual peccadilloes. . . . But this story . . . considered in the context . . . of his less than boulevardier appearance, only made him look ridiculous."

The Almanac also pointed out that Maraziti sat on the Judiciary Committee, which decided later to impeach Richard Nixon. He "was the oldish junior Republican (he was 62 at the time) whose tongue-tied oratory always left him satisfied with the President's innocence. . . . He was known to be an idolator of Richard Nixon. Named by *New Times* magazine as one of the ten dumbest members of Congress, Maraziti did precious little to dispel that reputation." After working for the highly principled McKevitt, it was a confusing comedown for Sarah.

It was Sarah who discovered that the handwriting on the paycheck of an alleged member of Maraziti's New Jersey staff and that of a woman they all knew in Washington were exactly the same. "I went running into the congressman's office to tell him of my discovery and he pinched my cheek and said, 'You're a smart little girl.' We in the office just couldn't imagine him with this young girl. He was bald, out of shape, wore glasses—

he looked old. He wore rubbers all the time. If he were a woman you'd say he was matronly." Sarah sought the advice of an attorney to be assured that she and the staff weren't doing anything illegal.

"For a year and a half we were walking a tightrope—hating to be a part of hiding this affair from his wife, yet not wanting her to know about it for fear she'd be destroyed by it." And Sarah was guided by her father's advice: "Be loyal to your employer."

The congressman's girlfriend bought a townhouse on Capitol Hill, and Maraziti lived there unless his wife was in town, when he would check into the Capitol Hill Club. He asked staff members to cover his tracks and asked them to do personal favors—sending one of them over to spray the townhouse for roaches. All of this coincided with the steady revelations of Richard Nixon's Watergate illegalities.

Toward the end of 1973, says Sarah, "Maraziti became fanatical about his reelection." And he ordered his staff to put out a mailing before the end of the year. In order to do so they worked all night. "By this time we were all on the brink of insanity over the affair," says Sarah, "and had grown very close because we could only talk to each other. We felt beleaguered—incarcerated even. Along about midnight, we sent out for wine. We were giddy, and we started putting an M&M into each envelope, then occasionally a peanut. One staff member drew a picture of a little hand waving 'Hi!' and put it into one of the envelopes. A couple of days later we began to worry what the people who got those letters would think."

Finally, a disgruntled employee, whom Maraziti had fired, blew the whistle on him, and the New York and New Jersey press closed in on the scandal. They started calling the office for Maraziti and for Ann Le Claire (the pseudonym of his girlfriend). "We told the congressman," says Sarah, "who knew the jig was up. And he just quit coming to the office. He just hid out on the House floor all the time. He ordered us not to answer the phones. So we put all the lines on hold, and when anybody would walk in, there would be all these phones flashing. A day or so later when the *New York Post* said they were on their way down from New York to see him, he told us, 'Close up the office, and don't anybody make a noise.' It was three

P.M. This is the God's truth. So we were sitting there in the dark and tiptoeing around."

And it was Sarah, as administrative assistant, who was on the front line every day, braving the incoming fire from the press on the steadily increasing revelations about his love life. "That was Sarah's darkest hour," says McKevitt. "She was scared to death that in covering for him they'd get into trouble themselves. They had a wild man on their hands."

Sarah regaled Jim with what was going on in her office and he thought it was hilarious. "Don't tell me. I don't want to know," he said, à la Watergate, which was about to reach its climax. "I want complete deniability."

The story finally came out in the New Jersey papers with the headline: BEAUTIFUL NO-SHOW ADORNS MARAZITI'S STAFF. It was their own little Watergate and Sarah had to testify before a New Jersey grand jury. (There was no indictment.) Sarah later ran into the congressman's wife, who told her, "That woman is always getting him into trouble. She's been after him for years. In fact," said Mrs. Maraziti, "the last time I saw her I went up to her and just kicked her."

When Maraziti was mercifully defeated in 1974, Sarah wanted to leave the Hill. "It wasn't very satisfying working for just one man," she says. "My dad told me that Evans and Novak [syndicated Washington columnists] were looking for an AA. I interviewed for the job and was hired to work on their newsletter. It didn't pay very well, but I was ready to start the job when Eddie Mahe, executive director of the Republican National Committee,* called me. He said, 'What're you doing?' And I told him. 'Be over here in four minutes,' he said. And he offered me the job of coordinator of field services. It was a hard decision, but I took the RNC job."

*Mary Louise Smith was then Chairman of the Republican Party.

CHAPTER NINE

"The Five-sided Funny Farm"

In January 1975, his mission accomplished at HUD, Jim Lynn was called to the White House by President Gerald Ford to become director of management and budget. "Ford wanted him at OMB," says Jim Brady. "He wanted his own man, and he thought Lynn was a wunderkind of agency politics." Lynn handled a number of sensitive things for Ford, says Jim, along with overseeing the budget process. "He is an attorney's attorney." Bill Greener went over with Lynn as public affairs director, and took Pat Coyle and Jim along, too. "Jim was good, the best," says Greener. "I wanted him with me."

Greener called his two favorites, Jim and Pat Coyle, Laurel and Hardy, "because they were always doin' somethin'," he says. Twice in one day, he says, they activated the alarm system at OMB by touching some top-secret filing cabinets that were wired. "The next thing we saw was an officer with a revolver aimed at our heads" says Jim. "We had to do some fast talking the second time."

"Others of us at HUD were told to be patient a bit," says Alan Kranowitz. And Jim Mitchell, Joan McEntee, Dan Kearney, and Kranowitz followed later. "In my mind," says Kranowitz, "OMB is the most professional agency in the government. It's small and very lean—staffed by solid, capable, professional personnel, and frankly, there is far less time there for frivolity. I remember a staff meeting in which Jim asked, 'Do you know how many polyesters had to be killed to outfit this group?' "

Jim was delighted at the opportunity to leave HUD. Bill Greener was his mentor and he had learned a lot at HUD under him. He had worked hard, made many friends, and was satisfied with his accomplishments. "Jim wanted to move on and begin to make his mark on his own," says Sarah. "And no way was I going back to HUD," says Jim. "He thought of it as a funny farm," says Kent Watkins. Jim's title at OMB was special assistant to the director.

That summer Bobbie and Dick McGraw invited the Bradys down for the week at their cottage on the ocean at Bethany Beach, Delaware. But soon after they arrived, says Bobbie McGraw, "a phone call came from Sarah's mother. They had just learned that Sarah's father had lung cancer." The doctor said it was inoperable. "Sarah and I were close. We both cried a lot, and Sarah and Jim went home immediately. I was impressed with Jim's capacity to care, also. They both felt it was important to spend their limited vacation time with him. Sarah is very close to her family."

"I always felt so lucky for so many years that our family had had no tragedies," says Frances Kemp. "Our family was so close. And Stan was so warm with everybody. He'd never been sick in his life. He was just sixty when he died."

Stanley Kemp had oat-cell lung cancer—a very fast-moving and fatal kind. He received radiation and stayed at home as long as he could. But he was extremely uncomfortable and couldn't sleep well. "The first thing that Jim did, bless his heart," says Frances, "was to bring over a lounge chair for him. Stan'd sleep on that chair or on the couch. Toward the end, in the hospital, we started taking turns staying all night with him, Sarah, Bill, and I."

Something daffy always seemed to happen to the Bradys just when life was grimmest. Something they could laugh about years later. Coming home from the hospital late one night that fall, Sarah couldn't find her house key, the lights were all out, and Jim was sound asleep. She couldn't raise him. She started around the back of the house to knock on their bedroom window to waken him. With her arms laden with purse and packages, "I went racing around the corner of the house, when suddenly I just dropped six feet down." At first she couldn't imagine what had happened, but she'd fallen into a window well. "I was all banged up and it was cold and damp and full of wet leaves. I had hurt my knee and I couldn't get out. It was over my head. I started yelling and yelling, but nobody came, so I really started screaming, which brought the men who shared the house next door." "We've been hearing you," they told her, "but we thought it was a cat fight." They rousted Jim, "who just reached down and pulled me out by my shoulders," says Sarah. "What were you doing out there with those fellas anyway?" he asked her. He was annoyed at her. He couldn't imagine how she'd gotten herself into such a fix.

Sarah was with her father when he died at seven o'clock on November 20, 1975.

"Jim was almost as stricken as Sarah was," says Frances. "He was such a big help. He just took charge. Stan and Jim's relationship was very good, and we had a lot of good times together. They didn't last very long, but we were a happy family."

One week after Stan Kemp died, the day before Thanksgiving, Big Jim Brady had a heart attack, and Jim and Sarah rushed out to Centralia. "It was the saddest time for me," says Sarah, "to be leaving my mother." By the time they got to Centralia, Big Jim was out of danger, and the next day, amid the happiness about Big Jim's condition, Sarah told Jim, "I have to go home." She left him in Centralia, and drove their rental car through a snowstorm to the St. Louis airport, and arrived home in time to have Thanksgiving with her mother.

"When my mother died," says Ron Weber, "and we had the funeral in Pittsburgh, Jim was furious with me that I didn't let him know, so he and Sarah could be there. They are that kind of people."

"As a son-in-law, Jim has always been great, he really has," says Frances Kemp. "After Stan died, every Sunday he asked me to be over there. I told Sarah, 'I shouldn't be over there every Sunday—Jim probably wants to do other things.' But Sarah said, 'No, Mother, it's Jim who always brings it up.' Not many men want their mothers-in-law around but he just was thoughtful and kind. Twice, for Christmas, he gave me, and Sarah, too, a day at Elizabeth Arden. He would ask me to go out with them for dinner, and he was loads of fun to be with. After dinner at the King's Landing in Alexandria one night, Jim said, 'Let's go to Henry Africa's for a drink.' And after that, he said, 'I know what we'll do. We'll go to F. Scott's in Georgetown.' I'd never been there and I thought it was wonderful."

Sarah and Jim invited Frances to go with them to the Tidewater Inn in Easton, Maryland, one weekend. "We ate crabs one night and had dinner in the inn dining room the next. Jim and Sarah danced and danced. They were so much in love. Thinking about how they'll never dance again hurts me almost more than anything."

At OMB, at first Jim shared an office with Greener until Greener's patron, Don Rumsfeld, returned from his post as ambassador to NATO to become Ford's chief of staff. Greener went over to become deputy White House press secretary to White House Press Secretary Ron Nessen. Lynn hated to lose Greener. "Aw, you just parked him with me while you were in Europe, didn't you?" he chided Rumsfeld.

Office space was tight at OMB. The agency is in the Old Executive Office Building next to the White House. "I was put into Jim's office," says Joan McEntee, who was special assistant to Associate Director Jim Mitchell. "Two days later they built a wall down the middle of the room to make two offices. The men's room was next to my office. Brady had the air conditioner and I had the heater. In the winter he'd yell out to me, 'If you don't turn up the heat I'm going to die in here, goddamit!' "

"Jim went and talked to Lynn about the fact he hadn't been promoted to replace Greener," says McEntee. "And Lynn agreed. At that time, Jim started getting credit for his own good work. Jim's major responsibility was to explain the arcane workings of OMB to the press and public. He wrote a lot of Lynn's speeches, and translated others into understandable English. I've never known anyone other than Jim who can sit down at a typewriter and think and conceptualize while he's typing. He also recommended to Lynn what public appearances he should make and did a lot of the advance work for him. It was at OMB that Jim began to do both the creative broad-scale planning *and* the follow-through details he'd taken care of before."

"Also," says Jim, "Lynn asked me to help develop a marketing plan for the relocation of the Vietnamese refugees who were coming to this country."

"OMB was austere," says Jim. "All work and green eyeshades. There was a lot of budget cutting going on." And soon, another opportunity came along. Don Rumsfeld became Ford's secretary of defense. Bill Greener went to the Pentagon with Rumsfeld and, a month later, January 1976, with Greener's backing, Jim moved to the Pentagon to be assistant to the secretary of defense. Lynn told Greener, "Well, if you take Brady, you might as well just take everybody."

"I was Rumsfeld's scheduler and planner, and planned his trips. I did his calendar," says Jim. "Rumsfeld was a firm believer that the most important thing you could do was to use your time well." Rumsfeld was charged by Ford "with reversing the downward trend of real defense spending," which, they said, had been going down for twenty years.

"We had a calendar meeting every day to go over all his incoming invitations," says Jim. "I prepared the packets that were handed out at that meeting. We discussed them and made decisions on what he should accept and what to turn down." When Rumsfeld made up his mind on anything, that was it, says Jim. "Those opposed, signify by saying 'I resign.' " Jim reported to Greener, but his office was in the suite of offices used by Rumsfeld's relatively small personal staff of about seventy people. Greener oversaw his own staff of five hundred, which in turn dealt with the thirty thousand public-affairs people in the American armed services all over the world. Greener's office was nearby in Pentagon terms, about a block away. Even so, Jim and Bill worked closely together. "The lure of the Pentagon to Jim was strong," says Joan McEntee. "He loved the uniforms, the ships, the planes. They were catered to—waited on hand and foot. And he took some great trips while he was there."

"I'm a frustrated admiral," says Jim. "You go to the Pentacle [one of his names for the Pentagon], you get to live out your fantasies. If the president says, 'Move the Washington Monument three feet to the left,' you could get the One hundred first Airborne over there, and have it done by next morning. It's a can-do attitude. They never say, 'We can't do that.' "

"I'd known Jim over the years," says Don Rumsfeld, "from

his involvement in Illinois politics. At the Pentagon we worked long hours and there was always a good deal of potential for error. When you're working closely with Jim, everyone keeps their perspective better. He has a very constructive and refreshing sense of humor. It's a unique talent which contributed to making whatever we were doing better than it otherwise would have been."

Another talent Rumsfeld appreciated "was Jim's superb memory, and his way of dramatizing things orally, making them memorable and useful.

"He was very professional—a superb staff man. It wasn't a frivolousness he contributed. It was a balance, his humor being an additive, which only made our work more successful. He was irrepressible in his goodwill as well.

"He was a very hard worker with a lot of drive and energy—an upbeat hard worker with a contagious kind of enthusiasm that lifted others. He was always serious about his work when he was working, but all the while he kept that good humor."

Rumsfeld says Jim was "engaged substantively and administratively in all our meetings by virtue of being one of the small number of people involved in the three-hundred-sixty-degree circle around" him. "À la Everett Dirksen, Jim believed the oil can is mightier than the sword. He constantly provided that human kindness, and goodwill, and perspective about what it is people are doing, including the staff and the press, both of which always have the potential for miscommunication instead of a fuller understanding. Jim's the kind of person that anyone with any sense wants around him."

"Rumsfeld did not like sloppy work," says Rumsfeld staffer Robin West, "and Jim was well regarded. He dealt with people well."

There were hundreds of political appointees in the DOD but the coterie of appointees closest to Rumsfeld, who also became close to each other, were Alan Woods, chief of staff; Jim Brady; Bill Greener; Kenneth Adelman, Rumsfeld's speechwriter and policy man on economic and international affairs; Ty McCoy, Steve Herbits, and Robin West, who directed personnel. In addition, air force Lieutenant Colonel Stuart Purviance was assigned to the Protocol Office of the secretary of defense and he was Jim's assistant.

"I think Donald Rumsfeld has a talent to find top people," says Stuart Purviance. "He trains them and lets them go about their business. Jim was very disorganized but he was fun to work for. He was always forgetting messages, losing phone numbers. We'd get him organized when he went down the hall to see someone. He was basically an advance man for Rumsfeld, and he brought a creativity to the job—something the Pentagon was not used to. PR was a game to Brady, a serious game, but goddamit, he had fun at it, and he knew how to play it. He liked to push the system. I never saw him at a loss as to what to do."

"Purviance became our Mr. Fixit," says Woods, "but early on, Jim asked him if he could take care of his parking tickets, and later he discovered the only way Purviance could take care of them was to pay them himself."

Also, early on, Jim remarked to Purviance that his office windows were filthy. "In the Pentagon," said Purviance, "you just never open the windows." But when Jim got back from lunch that day, there was Purviance hanging outside Jim's window—washing it.

"The first thing Jim did," says Jan Wolff, "was put the 'red phone' from the Pentagon downstairs in his house. During parties he'd call Andrews Air Force Base to check on the weather, then do a funny imitation of the call."

Purviance and others were gathered into the Brady fold of friends, and became regulars at their parties. "I've never met anyone who had more friends than Jim Brady," says Purviance. "It was always an interesting group, a continual traveling salon. People from all walks of life. Married, single, it didn't matter, he enjoyed having people around him. You just knew he was a good guy."

Purviance and Brady occasionally went to a topless place near the Pentagon for lunch. Sally McElroy, Woods's secretary, always told him, "Just be sure there aren't any press there." "One day," she says, "Jim came back from lunch with a red garter on his arm. The dancing girls had bought *his* drinks."

"Adelman and I were sort of the two brats at the Pentagon," says Robin West. "I organized the personnel; Adelman handled economic and international affairs. From afar it looks all very noble, but up close it edges into being silly and that gets to you after a while. And Brady was always very ironic about that. Jim was just a very friendly, warm, generous man."

One of Jim's names for the Pentagon is "the five-sided funny farm."

"At the Pentagon," says West, "most people are trying to figure out how to kill other people on a cost-effective basis. They may be extraordinarily capable people, but when they acquire a vast knowledge of armor-piercing tanks, for example, that tends to affect them. Brady wasn't doing that. Political appointees have different skills and haven't spent the last fifteen years learning about armor-piercing tanks.

"The protocol surrounding the secretary of defense," West adds, "is the equivalent to that for a four-star general. We would travel very grandly, but none of us took it seriously." Including Rumsfeld, says Alan Woods. "He is very shrewd, but he's a man of simple tastes. He is not interested in pomp. But we had a protocol officer, and stewards, and little ceremonies all the time—when people were coming in or were leaving."

"The first time in the Pentagon I sent my secretary with something for Brady," says Kenneth Adelman, "she walked in and his chair had fallen over backward. He just stayed there. He said, 'Yes, may I help you?' 'I have a memo from Mr. Adelman,' she said. 'Thank you very much,' Brady said from the floor." It was a strong beginning to the Brady-Adelman friendship.

Alan Woods was Rumsfeld's chief of staff at the Pentagon, Rumsfeld's Rumsfeld, they called him, Rumsfeld having just been President Ford's chief of staff. "Jim and Bill Greener were a lot alike," says Woods. "Greener was an excellent PR planner. Jim wasn't as good a planner as Greener, but Jim was more laid back and comfortable. The interesting thing about Jim was that he remained laid back as his responsibilities grew. He was always comfortable with the mantle of responsibility.

"He was a good, hard worker who always got the job done but who believed in having fun. He is in the business of inspiring fun." As at HUD, they worked hard, "real hard," says Woods, "six-forty-five in the morning to nine-forty-five at night, five days a week." And they worked on weekends, too. "Working for Don Rumsfeld is a real experience because he is a very demanding individual in much the same way as Jim Lynn. He is a perfectionist with a precise idea of what he wants and sometimes he can express it and sometimes not. Jim might have to bring a scheduling idea to Rumsfeld six times before it would sell. Ken Adelman did fifteen drafts of speeches. In our minds there was not necessarily an improvement in the PR plans or speeches, but there was enough creativity in the group that the plan would *change.* There was, however, a lot of respect for Rumsfeld.

"It was the late 1970s," explains Woods, "and we had just been through Vietnam and Watergate, and President Ford had ordered the Defense and State departments to stay out of politics. Ford was desirous of moving the Department of Defense back to being nonpartisan.

"We, on the other hand, were always trying to think of political things we could do for the 1976 campaign—most of them marginal." One day the perfect political opportunity opened up, they thought. It seemed that Secretary Rumsfeld, "a well-known friend of Israel," had been nominated to receive the Scopus Award from the American Friends of Hebrew University. (Hebrew University in Israel has a campus that sits upon Mount Scopus.) Jim, Woods, and Adelman all urged Rumsfeld to accept this award. "The campaign was on, and we knew the president was eager to have Jewish votes," says Alan Woods, "so we were selling this plan like mad, and finally convinced Rumsfeld he should do this."

"After bringing it up and bringing it up, Jim had beaten Rumsfeld into giving a speech and accepting the award," says Kenneth Adelman. "He was to be 'Citizen of the Year.' "

On the appointed day, they all flew up to New York on a Pentagon plane, and once ensconced in the hotel, "I was going over his speech with him," says Adelman, "and Rumsfeld got grumpy. It was a black-tie, evening affair, and he asked, 'Why are we doing this again?' The only thing he's there for is to help Ford with the Jewish vote."

Meanwhile Jim went out to get a copy of the evening's program. But to his horror he saw that the winner of Citizen of the Year—the Scopus Award—was one Harry Schwartz. First Runner-Up—Secretary of Defense, Donald Rumsfeld.

"I'm dressing in a borrowed tuxedo," says Adelman, "when Jim pops in and says, 'Ken, you'd better change the speech.' 'Rumsfeld's doing that,' I told him. 'No,' says Jim, 'instead of Citizen of the Year, he's only the runner-up.' "

Adelman and Brady argued back and forth as to whose responsibility it was to deliver the bad news. "It was a bad scene," says Woods, "but one idea was to go into Rumsfeld's room and announce, 'Everybody in this room who's getting the Scopus Award, step forward one step. Not so fast there, Secretary Rumsfeld.' "

As it was "we both walked in together," says Adelman, "and I said, 'Mr. Secretary, Jim here has something to tell you.' Jim glared at me. 'Go on, Jim, say it,' I said. 'Well, here's the program,' said Jim, and Rumsfeld read it. 'Let me see. Harry Schwartz is Citizen of the Year?' 'Well, you see, you're in second place,' said Jim."

Then they noticed that Zbigniew Brzezinski, candidate Jimmy Carter's foreign-policy adviser, was also going to speak that evening. "Initially Rumsfeld was just silent. Then he said, 'Well, with Brzezinski on the program we've got to rewrite the speech.' Then he got heated. 'This is a hamburger operation,' he said, 'just a hamburger operation.' " ("As opposed to steak," says Jim.)

It turned out that Brzezinski spoke right after Rumsfeld spoke, "and he contradicted everything Rumsfeld had said, implying the Ford administration had been selling out Israel," says Adelman. "We both spoke too long that night," says Rumsfeld. "Or, I *know* Zbig did, and I may have, too."

On the plane ride home, "two of us had to sit up front with Rumsfeld in that little plane, and I lost that one," says Adelman. "Rumsfeld gave us a going over and asked whose idea was this thing, anyway? Of course, we blamed it all on Jim since he was nowhere in sight."

"In the end, Rumsfeld took it with great good humor," says Alan Woods. "He keeps the 'This Is Not the Scopus Award' plaque on his wall.

"It was probably the worst-planned event the whole time Jim was in the job," he adds.

But Jim was good at his job—very competent, says Adelman. "His advice to Rumsfeld was always good. Rumsfeld was not a freewheeling individual and Brady may have loosened him up a bit. Jim is very good when stimuli are coming at him, and he works his butt off when someone gives him responsibility."

It was while Jim was at the Pentagon that the Bradys, the Greeners, and the McGraws took several weekends in West

Virginia together. "We shared a love for West Virginia," says Bobbie McGraw. "Jim and Sarah both love the mountains." The McGraws were both originally from West Virginia, and they planned the group's trips. Bobbie says, "We first shared a cabin in Bluestone Park near Hinton."

"We drove out," says Bobbie, "but Jim and Sarah flew into Beckley, West Virginia. When they went to get the car they'd reserved, they were told, 'We let the car go, and it's in Pittsburgh.' What to do? What to do? The agent did know a crazy man, he said, 'who'll do anything for money,' and the Bradys hired him, thinking the trip would cost at least a hundred and fifty dollars. On the way, their driver pointed out the magnificent homes along the highway (the double mobile homes) and told them about his pet raccoon."

"A fog settled in," says Sarah, "and the foggier it got, the faster he drove around those mountain curves. When we got there, safely, he charged us twenty dollars."

"Our little bedrooms went off from the big living area," says Bill Greener. "We had a big fireplace and Jim did the cooking. We drove a pot of Jim's Chili up with us."

Jim says, "Greener is a great organizer. On these trips of ours, he'd say, 'Team A will play tennis at such and such a time; Team B will play golf at such and such a time.' Finally, we'd say, 'Shove it, Greener.' "

"The weekend after Ford was defeated, which was supposed to be our victory weekend, we went to Blackwater Falls. Jim always did the cooking, but I did the grocery shopping that time. I bought two kinds of pasta—there were to be two sauces—one was never enough," says Bobbie McGraw.

The same group gathered several times at the McGraws' Delaware coast beach house. "Jim has retained more of the child in him—that is, and is still a responsible person—than most people," says Bobbie. "He was always the first one to go get the kites at the beach, or the popcorn for the movie."

Over the year remaining to the Ford presidency, Rumsfeld, Brady, Greener, Adelman, Woods, and the others shared some memorable trips abroad and around the country. "It was the job Jim loved the most," says Sarah.

The NATO countries hold meetings several times each year, and there was a meeting in Hamburg, Germany, and two held in Brussels that year. A great deal of Jim's time was spent in overseeing the advance work for these trips. On Rumsfeld's most ambitious foreign trip they stopped first in Lisbon, "where we picked up Jim," says Greener. "We went to Portugal to do a little PR because there was a worry about their government's going communist. . . ." Jim had gone over first to be sure there was a minimum of pomp for Rumsfeld. "The advance man told me there would be twenty-five motorcyles there to pick us up. Rumsfeld did not like that—could not abide that. I went over to be sure everything was buttoned up." From Lisbon they flew to the NATO meeting in Brussels.

"Jim and I roomed together on Rumsfeld's foreign trips," says Kenneth Adelman. ("Ken Adelman is not a speechwriter," Jim would say. "He's a themist.")

In Brussels, says Adelman, "Jim and I were always fighting with Greener and his wife because they'd want to see eighteen cathedrals, and Jimbo and I would want to eat great food, and spend three and a half hours doing it."

Charlene Greener said, "I didn't come all this way to eat."

"Well, I certainly did," said Adelman, "and I know Jim did."

"In Brussels," says Robin West, "we were assigned a car, but after the airport we never saw it again. Adelman and Brady had it." "Years later Jim still remembered the name of our airport chauffeur," says Adelman.

From Brussels, they stopped briefly in Athens, then flew to Nairobi, Kenya, then to Kinshasa, Zaire.

"We had breakfast on Mobutu's yacht," says Jim. "They do deferred maintenance over there, and we landed on the yacht by helicopter. I swore if I landed I'd never get off."

The food in Africa left something to be desired, Jim thought. His recipe for Chicken Mwamba: "You get a chicken that has died from natural causes, like starvation. Put peanut butter on it. Grill it. And, yuck."

"I had lived in Zaire from 1972 to 1975," says Adelman, "and Brady and I had a wonderful time buying things, and ran around trying to change money on the black market."

Adelman taught Brady a few words in "Lingala—one of the tribal languages," he says. "*Ozali malamu.* Hello. How are you. *Malamu mingi.* Very well. When Adelman visited Jim a month after the shooting, "he still had tubes going here and there," says Adelman. "He was sleeping and I shook him a little and said, '*Ozali malamu.*' And Jim said, '*Malamu mingi.*' We were very happy to know there were things going on in there." Jim tried out his high school French in Zaire, too, says Adelman. *"J'ai une grand-mère et trois stylos rouges."*

On those long airplane flights, Jim wasn't one to curl up with a book, says Adelman. "I never saw him with a book in my life. He would B.S. for ten hours straight, standing up with a drink in his hand. He could talk about anything."

"A secretary of defense hadn't gone to Africa in a long time, if ever," says Alan Woods. "We were concerned about the rebels in Zaire, and Kenya was just in the process of purchasing some airplanes."

The last stop was an overnight rest stop in the Canary Islands, "where I spent the day writing the trip report," says Alan Woods. "You could see the beach from my window, but you never got *to* it." "The same night we arrived home," says Greener, "we had to rush back to the Pentagon to work on the evacuation of U.S. citizens from Lebanon because of a threatened attack."

"Jim and Ken always found time to get to the local market place to buy something to take home," says Alan Woods. "I always envied that quality on their part." Jim's propensity for buying things became a source of great amusement to his friends and colleagues, and a bit of a problem in his marriage. "Jim suffers from overconsumption," says Sarah, "and money was a big problem between us because Jim spent like wildfire. We had fights over money, and Jim had a very bad temper. It's an Irish temper. He once threw a burrito at me, and it landed sort of draped over my forehead," she laughs.

"When I picked Jim up at the airport after that big trip," says Sarah, "he was carrying two spears and a Masai war shield and a pot. He was so pleased with himself." About his shopping in Kenya, Jim says, "They were two Masai spears, a wildebeest-hide shield, and a cooking kettle that pygmies cook people in. You never know whether you were going into the bush and you might need these things."

"Jim took up pipe and cigar smoking," says Sarah. "He had six pipes, and bought the best cigars and tobacco. One day he came home with a little sack. He had bought an antler that had a cigar clipper in it." Greener called Sarah and asked what had become the usual question. "What did Jim buy today?" "Oh, just an antler," she said. "Oh, that's good," said Greener, "just an antler. That's good, an antler."

When they took a weekend with the Greeners and the McGraws in West Virginia, says Sarah, "Someone said, 'Oh, let's stop and look at antiques.' I'm thinking, 'I know it's going to be a disaster.' And pretty soon, Jim comes up. 'Look, Raccoon, look at this.' He had found some old biscuit boxes. 'And they say I can have three for the price of one,' he told me. We have some of the darnedest stuff. Wooden doors, a pair of oars. Dumb stuff."

Jim's new driving license proved a mixed blessing. Jim had forgotten some lessons from the past and he and Sarah occasionally had blowups about driving. "When I met Jim he didn't have a driver's license," says Sarah. "So I always drove. And on the road Jim could act violent. Once I was driving us on the beltway, and a truck came up behind us and honked—he wanted us to go faster, I guess. Then the guy pulled out and passed, and Jim put his foot on the gas pedal and grabbed the wheel. 'Go after him. Go after him,' Jim was shouting."

"Chicken wouldn't do it," says Jim.

About once a year Jim would get serious about losing weight and go on a diet. "He'd stop drinking and cut down on the food," says Sarah, "but it never lasted long." But he had high blood pressure and knew that his extra weight was hard on him. "I bought a new Brooks Brothers shirt and it ripped down the back on the first wearing," he told Jan Wolff. (The Wolffs were new Brady friends. Otto Wolff worked at the RNC with Sarah and Jan worked for the air force in the Pentagon.) He had gained so much his doctor sent him to a diet doctor who suggested Jim begin running. Jim told him, "First of all, I don't run. I belong to this club that if you feel like you want to run you call this number. It's like AA." "Okay," said the doc, "then start walking. Walk to work."

"That lasted about a week," says Jan Wolff. "It was only about a mile, but he hated it."

Rumsfeld traveled widely in the United States, visiting many of the major military commands. In addition, in an effort to sell the increase in the defense budget, he appeared before the editorial boards of numerous newspapers. To the same end, he went on Tom Snyder's late-night show, and on the Phil Donahue show, and he spent a lot of time lobbying members of Congress on Capitol Hill. Rumsfeld's every official move had to be choreographed by Jim and his aides in concert with the concerns of the rest of Rumsfeld's staff, primarily Greener.

It was on a NATO trip to London, then Scotland, says Jim, that Rumsfeld laid down the Danoon Doctrine. "I had lined up some nice shopping and sightseeing tours for the wives who came along," he says. "But Rumsfeld said, 'We don't go on these trips just to shop. We came to work.' You'll find the Danoon Doctrine right up there with the Monroe Doctrine," Jim says. Rumsfeld laid it down forcefully.

"We went to Hawaii to meet with the Korean minister of defense to discuss our mutual problems. At the big dinner at Hickam Air Force Base, the Korean minister got up and began his toast, 'South Korea resembles a standing rabbit. . . .' That about finished us off," says Jim. It sent Rumsfeld's staff into paroxysms of painful-to-conceal laughter.

In Hawaii, says Adelman, "Rumsfeld stayed in a private home and there were three cabins on the beach where we stayed and were served by Filipino stewards." It was on this trip that Jim charged a $1,798 bill for the "Luau Singers" to his personal credit card, only the bill got home before he did. "The bank called to say we were overdrawn," says Sarah.

In November 1976, Gerald Ford lost the White House to Democrat Jimmy Carter. "But the hard work kept up during the transition, too," says Alan Woods, "and someone like Jim was really helpful to the Carter people in getting their offices arranged so they could be effective.

Sarah was still working at the Republican National Committee and during the 1976 campaign, she says, "we had all this money for congressional campaigns, and we sent people out to work in them. I monitored all those kids and their expenses." That summer Eddie Mahe sent Sarah to New York City to be the Republican National Committee's presence at the Democratic Convention. "She went up there, got some work space, and ran a press operation for the week," says Mahe. After the election Sarah went on to become the director of administration, one of the senior staff at the RNC. "I oversaw the total maintenance of the building—which included the accounting division; the facilities division; security; printing;

phone services; parking. I was no longer directly involved in politics."

Bill Greener and Jim began to talk about forming their own PR firm. "We almost went into business together," says Greener. "Jim Lynn and Bill Seidman were willing to invest in it and we went a long way to getting it organized. But before it really got under way, Greener in April was offered a job as senior vice-president at Carl Byoir, "a worldwide PR firm," says Greener, "and I took it."

Meanwhile, says Adelman, although the Carter people had asked Jim to stay beyond January 20, Inauguration Day, "Jim decided to stick around the Pentagon even longer while he job hunted and until they found him. At the end, he was ducking around corners to avoid being found. He'd rush into his old office semidisguised and rush out. He'd take long lunch hours. One day they asked him, 'Aren't you about to leave?' Nothing happened and a few more weeks went by, and they said, 'Toodleoo, Mr. Brady. It's been great. You've served your country *so* well.' "

Jim found himself in limbo. Thinking he would be in business with Greener, he hadn't been looking very hard for employment. In fact, he had hung around the Pentagon longer than he wanted to, waiting. Now he was on the street, and jobs for recent Republican political appointees were hard to find in Washington in 1977. The public's backlash against Watergate continued with the 1976 elections. The Congress remained decidedly Democratic, and Jimmy Carter had taken over the federal government.

"Jim didn't handle being unemployed well at all," says Sarah. At a party at Greeners', "Greener was flaunting his new job; meanwhile Jim was talking about writing his résumé to get a job. He was having trouble writing it. Said he wanted to take a cross-country train ride and write it. 'I think that would relax me enough so I could write my résumé,' he said."

Well, that took the cake. "Greener and everybody were unmerciful to him," says Sarah. "And Jim got so mad he took off walking. He said he was going to walk home—which was about ten miles. Late that night I finally got upset when he didn't show up. He walked in very late with a smug look on his face."

From then on Greener put him on. "Jim, there's a good ball

game on the tube. Can't you just walk out here and watch it with me?" Or "Walk on out here, Jim. There's something I want to tell you."

"Jim had trouble getting a job," says Ken Adelman. "It was a bad time for him. He was depressed. And I was angry that people weren't coming through for him. Every time we would have lunch, I'd get fired up and call a few more people." Adelman was unemployed for a couple of months, too, before he went to the Stanford Research Institute in California. In fact, many Schedule C employees found themselves out of jobs. It was an accepted risk in the political game they were playing.

"Although it seemed at the time to last forever," says Sarah, "Jim was out of work only three months or so. He had put out a number of applications, and to a certain extent he was waiting for the right thing to come along. He was offered a job in the Alaska state government, and we talked over possibly moving to Alaska to take it."

Although he wasn't out of work long, he piled as much novelty into the time as he could. "Jim wore it well," says Jan Wolff. "Sarah was very distressed about it, but Jim was waiting for the right job."

One day Jim called Stephanie Weber at work. "Hi, it's Jim. Listen, I've written a poem," and he read it to her. It was titled "The Third Season" and was about fall. Illinois had already produced Carl Sandburg. Could it be his successor was standing in the wings?

He continued to spend money while he was out of work, much to Sarah's exasperation. "He'd take off and spend all his savings." Sarah called home one day to cheer Jim up. "What're you doing?" she asked. Jim, very pleased with himself, told her, "I'm bricking the kitchen." "You're what?" Sarah exploded. "I'm bricking the kitchen," he said. Jim and Bob Dahlgren had bought a case of beer and were happily drinking it, while putting up brick on one wall of the Brady kitchen. It was to be Brady's Trattoria—that was the idea. "Wasn't it marvelous he did that?" says Bill Greener. "Bricking the kitchen" went into the Brady lore.

While out of work Jim spent a lot of time planning dinner parties. "After a long lunch at Nathan's in Georgetown one day," says Sarah, "he went out and bought a set of wooden dishes and place mats for twelve for a party he was planning. Here he's out of work, and he spends three hundred dollars on the *dishes* for one party," she laughs. "He really felt guilty about it. He said, 'I promise I won't do this again,' but he couldn't go anywhere and not spend money."

One scheme Jim had was to start safari hunting tours to Africa with a friend of Kenneth Adelman he'd met in Zaire—Lawson Mooney, "who was a cross between Ernest Hemingway, Zorba the Greek, and a White Hunter," says Adelman. "Jim knew somebody from Chicago in the travel business who wanted to start safaris so we set it up so the three parties could talk to each other. Mooney had married a Frenchwoman and lived in France, and the Chicago travel agency brought Lawson and Lise over here to discuss the idea. It was a tradition that Lise Mooney cook a dinner while she visited us, and Jim drove her all around to specialty shops so she could get the right ingredients. We had the dinner, but it quickly disintegrated into tales of how Lawson had killed the Big Five of animals—elephant, lion, et cetera. Now and then somebody tried to interject questions about how the travel scheme would work but to no avail."

"Jim and I were both unemployed at the same time," says Alan Woods, "and we played in the afternoons. We went to the racetrack at Bowie. We went to Bobbie's Beef and Barbecue for lunch. That's when I introduced Jim to sleaze." Woods knew of all sorts of very cheap restaurants and Jim and Sarah dubbed him the "King of Sleaze."

"Jim would come over to my office," says Kent Watkins, "and we would sit on the floor—and talk about forming a partnership in PR, or about his becoming a lobbyist. I would drop in on him at home and he'd be making his tomato catsup—his apron on. But he was down, and I wondered, 'Is there any way he'll pull out of this?' "

On July 21 Jim and Sarah celebrated their fourth wedding anniversary. They had had an intense and happy four years, but for the last year or so Sarah had been disappointed she hadn't gotten pregnant. For now it was all right, with Jim out of a job, but she was beginning to worry. She was thirty-four and she wanted a child.

In August, Jim took a temporary consulting job to Averell Harriman's Committee of Americans for the Panama Canal

Treaties, which supported the United States' giving up control over the canal. It was made up of elected officials and private citizens—Democrats and Republicans, including ex-senators Hugh Scott, John Sherman Cooper, and Henry Cabot Lodge.

Jim's job was to help sell the transfer to important Americans. "I was welcome, of course, at the Pentagon. I had a lot of friends there. I contacted governors, mayors. I helped with strategy. The Panamanians threatened they'd blow the SOB up if it wasn't transferred, no idle threat."

Control of the canal had been a problem between the United States and Panama for years, and negotiations for a new treaty were begun by Richard Nixon. In 1974, Henry Kissinger signed "an agreement in principle" with the Panamanians. In 1975 Ford continued the negotiating as riots and demonstrations against Americans in Panama intensified and the issue came to a boil. Jimmy Carter finished the negotiations and signed the agreement seven months into his first year in office.

Giving up the canal was considered a sellout by right-wing Republicans, and during the 1976 Republican presidential-primaries campaign, Ronald Reagan had attacked President Ford's support for a new treaty, using the quip, "We bought it. We paid for it, and we intend to keep it." (Republican Senator S. I. Hayakawa had a variation on that theme: "It's our canal," he said, "We stole it fair and square.")

"Hell, I hadn't thought about the canal for thirty years," says Jim.

Senate minority leader Howard Baker, although originally opposed to it, helped get the treaty through the Senate, while Reagan's best friend, Paul Laxalt, led the opposition.

Jim invited his parents to Washington for the signing of the treaty in the White House by Jimmy Carter and Panamanian ruler Omar Torrijos on September 7, 1977. Dyed-in-the-wool Republican Dorothy Brady didn't think much of Carter's low-key, low-budget style. "They served store-bought cookies and iced tea," she says. "Now, Mother," Jim cautioned her, "he *is* the president."

Jim continued to serve as an adviser to Averell Harriman after the signing, "meeting Averell at Twenty-one and places like that," says Jim. "Twenty-one was his fast-food place." "He called the most incredible people to ask them to put up ten thousand here and ten thousand there. He was a hell of a man."

On their visit to Centralia, for Jim's thirty-seventh birthday celebration, Sarah, as a representative of the Republican Congressional Campaign Committee, addressed the Centralia Republican Women's Federation. "There wasn't one person there under seventy," she says. She was intrigued that they had developed a new system for raising money for the club. "If you didn't wear your elephant pin to the meeting you would be fined. They had a long discussion about whether the fine should be ten or fifteen cents. They even asked my opinion." After her speech one lady told her, "I know your speech was wonderful, and I'm real mad at myself for not putting my hearing aid in sooner."

CHAPTER TEN
"Roth-Roth"

Jim's work for the Canal Committee and Harriman was winding down and early in November he had a job interview with Dennis Thomas, who was Delaware Republican Senator William Roth's administrative assistant. Thomas was given Jim's name by Pete Teeley, communications director of the Republican National Committee, who knew that Jim was job hunting.* "When I talked to Thomas, Jim's name was first on my mind," says Teeley.

"We were looking to enhance our whole operation," says Thomas—to get some publicity for some of the tax-cut proposals Roth was making. "I called all of Jim's references, perhaps fifteen of them. Uniformly it came through that he had succeeded in his job without walking on people." Among them was Bill Greener, who told Thomas, "You couldn't do better than Brady." And Jim became Roth's executive assistant and press secretary.

"Jim was a good mixture—an engaging type who was a generator of ideas," says Thomas. "He knew the process. He'd been at HUD and Defense. He knew the people, and that the trick is not to get the press to write about us, but to generate

*Teeley had been traveling press secretary during Gerald Ford's 1976 presidential campaign.

what is written about us. Jim understands what to do in order to have attention brought to what we were doing."

The idea of cutting taxes to spur economic growth, says Senator Roth, "came to me from blue-collar workers in Delaware who were making twenty-five to thirty thousand dollars and were angry because inflation had forced them into higher and higher tax brackets. 'What are you going to do about it, Senator Roth?' they asked me." Out of this awakening Roth and Republican House member Jack Kemp developed the Kemp-Roth tax-reduction bill (or "Roth-Kemp" as everybody in Roth's office consistently calls it). They had introduced it at a press conference in July 1977. It called for a 10-percent tax cut each year for three years. "Two reporters showed up for our announcement," says Roth, "one from a Wilmington, Delaware, paper and one from the Buffalo, New York, paper, Jack Kemp's district. Nobody else came. It was two years before our tax program became center-stage material and it happened because Jim was with me. It was our one big effort to sell the party to a broader cross-section of Americans. Roth-Kemp became the centerpiece of Reaganomics, the tax cut, and indexing for inflation. But I always coupled it to a limitation on spending." Jim himself quickly became a believer in the tax-cut, supply-side theory, and would become one of the principal players in selling the policy to the country, which would eventually make possible the passage of the 1981 Reagan tax-cut bill.

"Before Jim arrived," says Thomas, "we were always skirting on the edge of disaster with our tax program." Roth and his staff didn't know it, but Jim Brady was about to put the little-known Senator Roth from the tiny state of Delaware on the map.

The first day Jim came to work, says Bill de Reuter, his assistant, "he took me to the Class Reunion where he knew everybody in the place. He introduced me to a lot of people, and gave the impression he was co-owner of the place. Jim started right in calling me 'Roto.' Even Roth began calling me Roto. People still call me that. He soon got to know everybody on the Hill—elevator operators, cooks, cafeteria workers. They would put extra cheese and bacon on his hamburger. He made people happy just by being around him.

"I learned more about PR in one week from Jim than I had

learned up to that point," says de Reuter. "That first week he was there we got an AP wire machine and stuck it in a closet." "It's a matter of seconds whether you make the papers or not," Brady told him. Brady had Roth responding to everything. As time went on "UPI and AP would be quoting Roth on a Supreme Court decision," says de Reuter, "when Roth wasn't even on the legislative committee!

"Jim would watch the wires for news, write something out, and say, 'Get this over to so-and-so journalist right away. Put it in front of them while they're writing.' Then he'd run in the office with the resultant news clipping."

"Jim quickly assessed the difficulties of promoting a minority senator from a small state," says Dennis Thomas. "If you work for the president, the question is: Who is he going to see? When it's a minority senator from a small state, you have to create the press."

One big problem Roth had was that all of the network television for the entire state of Delaware came out of Philadelphia. The only TV that originated in Delaware was public television. So it had to be national news to get into public TV. Jim would say, "I never thought I'd have to get into national television to get into a Delaware living room."

"The first thing we did with Jim," says Bruce Thompson, Roth's legislative assistant, "was to work on Roth's college-tuition tax-credit amendment to the new Social Security bill, which at that point was in Senate-House conference. The Senate conferees were for the tuition tax credit—the House conferees were against it." (It proposed a $250 tax credit for parents who had children in college.)

"It was a session late in December 1977, and there was a frenzy of activity. Jim was putting Roth into contact with reporters to explain his stance." Late in the afternoon there was a break in the activity, and they had a meeting in which Jim asked, "What's a tuition tax credit?" "I started explaining it," says Thompson, "and Jim says, 'No, no. Just give me two or three major points for the TV cameras.'" Jim gleaned from Thompson that the tuition tax credit was a $250 credit for parents of college students; that the new Social Security bill was going to hit middle-income people hard, and this tax credit would give them a little break; that they would be able to keep more of their own money. "Jim went to Roth," says Thompson, "and said, 'Here. Stick to these two or three points,' and he pushed Roth into the press conference—and this huge bank of TV cameras. Roth said exactly what Jim told him to say. Roth got major coverage on the nightly news and the next day he was on the front page of *The Washington Post*. We all learned from Brady to make a few points, and to say them over and over again. Most guys never learn it, and just go on explaining complicated bills to bored reporters."

When it became apparent that the amendment would not survive, however, Roth had to give up. But then Jim advised Roth to "do a George Aiken." (During the Vietnam War, Senator George Aiken said, "Why don't we just declare victory, and get out of there?") So Roth said, "We won. We spotlighted an important issue, but it is obviously not the time to pass it. We will withdraw it and bring it up again." "And Roth got all sorts of praise for his action," says Bruce Thompson, "whereas, if he had not withdrawn it, it would have lost, and Roth would have appeared defeated. And it got Roth on the front page of the *Post* again."

"Jim was such a quick study," says Dennis Thomas. "He could come in and make things happen. There are a lot of capable, bright people on the Hill, but there's not a lot of good chemistry. So much of it is the relationship between the principal people and the staff. It comes down to personality and finesse. Jim could go in and quickly put people at ease."

Just two weeks later, in January 1978, Jim readied Roth and the staff for a response to Carter's annual budget. The thousand-plus-page budget was made available to the press and to congressmen on Friday so they could study it for its official release date on Monday. "We worked all day Friday and all that night," says Thompson, "going over that thing. I was doing a budget analysis, and Jim, sitting there at his typewriter, was saying, 'I need good lines. Give me some good lines.' " ("Bruce Thompson makes dull figures sing," says Jim.) One they came up with was "Carter's budget is an economic road map to Cleveland." (The city of Cleveland had just declared bankruptcy.) "I resisted that one," says Thompson, "because I'm from Cleveland, but it got into our press release anyway."

"Hold on to your wallets, Mr. and Mrs. Taxpayer USA," they said. "Here comes another Carter budget." And they declared that Carter had adopted "the pickpocket theory of taxation." "Roth was a little reluctant and Jim had to talk him into releasing it," notes Thompson.

By Saturday morning it was snowing in Washington and hardly any newspeople were in the Senate press gallery, "so we drove around Washington delivering our releases to *The Washington Post, The New York Times, The Wall Street Journal*, the networks—all the major news organizations. Because of that, and the pithy way Jim phrased Roth's response, Roth was quoted in every budget story written," says Thompson.

A few days later Jimmy Carter addressed the Congress with his State of the Union message. "We had Roth's reaction ready six hours before he gave his speech," says Bill de Reuter.

AA Dennis Thomas and Brady worked well together, too. "Jim's really valuable contribution was in knowing how the process worked, knowing the press's orientation, and having the tenacity to stay there all night digesting the budget. And the next day we had a response. Jim was an executive assistant and not just a press secretary, because he made valuable contributions in all areas. He was involved in all discussions in which we developed policy and then, how to handle it. He's a damned intelligent person."

In February, at a Senate press secretaries' luncheon, Lou Gerig, Indiana Republican Senator Richard Lugar's new press secretary, met Jim Brady for the first time. "I had been in Washington one week, and had never been out of Indiana," says Gerig. "I arrived at the luncheon ten minutes late, and all the chairs were taken. Jim looked at me and said, 'Are you a rookie? Why don't you come over and sit down by me, Rookie.'" When Jim heard Lou Gerig's name, he said, "It could be worse. They could've named you after a Dodger."

"Jim invited me to come down to his office. 'If you need any help,' he said. And I did. I was scared—overwhelmed. I didn't know anybody else in town. Jim really made me feel at home. He was extremely, extremely kind to someone he'd never met before.

"'Pick a time,' Jim had said, so I called him the next day." Brady talked to Gerig about getting Senator Lugar to loosen up and to get to know the media better, especially those journalists in the Senate press gallery. "Sometimes you *develop* opportunities for your senator to be in the media," Jim told him. "Go over and meet the press people and see what they need from you."

Gerig soon learned that Jim was building up to getting Lugar in on a new scheme he had for Roth and other like-minded senators to respond again to Carter's budget. "It was like 'You've just taken two hours of my time, now do I have a deal for you!' " says Gerig.

"Well, what do you want Lugar to do?" Gerig asked.

"I want him to come over to the Senate press gallery," said Jim. "We're going to have a select group of senators there who will all be wearing green eyeshades and green armbands like bankers, and they'll be brandishing big hedge clippers to cut the budget." They hadn't come up with a name yet, "but that's what we're going to do." Soon, Roth himself came up with a name for the group—the SOBs. Save Our Bucks. Jim's outrageousness was infectious.

For the great event, Jim managed to put together Republican Senators Roth, Lugar, and John Danforth, and Democrats William Proxmire, Sam Nunn, and Richard Stone. They were the SOB Task Force.

"Our efforts were to focus attention on the spending cuts we were proposing," says Dennis Thomas. "But the funniest thing," says Bruce Thompson, "was to see the reaction of the other senators." By now Roth was a true believer, but the rest of them "all had bemused looks on their faces, as if to say, 'This is crazy. What am I doing here?' "

"They all had their green eyeshades on," says Thomas, "and their pencils with erasers on both ends. And Roth was holding up the budget and cutting at it with these huge shears.

"Everybody in the press showed up," says Gerig, "which impressed Lugar. Afterward, Lugar said, 'Well, we did it. Now we'll see what happens.' The next day it was all over *The New York Times*, the *Post* and the networks. It was as widespread coverage as he'd ever had, and was the first time he'd been in the national media. We started doing more of that type of thing with and without Brady. A lot of senators have been influenced by the way Jim Brady did things."

"Danforth just marveled at the publicity he got back home," says Thompson. "Brady changed the way people do press conferences on the Hill. Now they all have UPI wire machines.

The old way was—you'd hand the press one of your brilliant memos and it would sink without a trace. Jim's method was more than a gimmick. It got results.

"Within a year of Jim's arrival," he adds, "when we had a press conference there would be a hundred reporters. Republicans were pushing tax cuts and the Democrats were trying to take the issue back." "We all worked hand in glove," says Jim, "setting up Roth's hearings, getting his witnesses."

Jim tried to shape Roth up in other ways, too. "He had some suits I was trying to get hold of and burn," says Jim. "And he had a purple Aloha shirt" Jim was itching to get his hands on, too.

"Jim affected my thinking," says Roth. "I had never gone out to seek press coverage. Jim soon taught me the error of my ways. If you want to get something done you have to get the press behind you," or at least understanding what you're trying to do.

"We became known for our gimmickry. We'd go anywhere—we'd talk to three people if it would help. We had to try to put our program out in new clothes. And we took help from any quarter," says Roth, "if it meant across-the-board cuts in defense or social programs.

"Jim was very imaginative. At our first meeting, Jim came up with the idea of handing out pencils with erasers on both ends, so you could only erase, not add, things to the budget. He loved to be involved in the office—in tax matters, foreign policy. He was a key adviser. He liked to poke his nose into everything."

As at HUD and the Pentagon, Roth's staff worked long hours, and they often went out for a case of beer when it got to be 6:30 in the evening. "Jim came in early and stayed late," says Thompson. Jim asked Roth if they could make popcorn in the office. "I said, 'No, what would people think?' " says Roth. "But Jennings Randolph [D., W.Va.] moved in next door and every afternoon we smelled popcorn, so I said, 'Okay, go ahead.' "

The Gandy Dancer, a bar on Capitol Hill, became the after-hours spot for Jim and those of Roth's staff he could lure there. "It was his favorite haunt," says Thompson. " 'Let's go over and have *one* beer,' he'd say. I'd usually say, 'No, I can't.' After about four beers we'd leave. I could always tell my wife I was with Jim, and she'd forgive me."

Bill de Reuter had just been married when Jim talked him into going to the Gandy Dancer one night. "We'll just have one beer, I promise you." "No, I can't," said de Reuter.

"It'll only take ten minutes," said Jim.

"We started talking and having one beer after another until it was so late I'd missed all rides to my house in Reston [about thirty miles from the Hill]. 'Take my car,' said Jim. And I did, but I just couldn't make it. I pulled over and slept on the side of the road until five in the morning. My bride had been up most of the night and was worried, to say the least."

Jim's alibi to Sarah that night was: "I've been kidnapped. Have they called yet for the ransom money? I sneaked out the window while they were in the front room."

Jim occasionally persuaded the German chef at the Gandy Dancer to make his Goat Gap Chili. "On the menu there was a notice that you had to sign a waiver if you ordered it," says Thompson.

Jim was becoming more philosophical about his weight. "His theory on gaining weight," says de Reuter, "is that the earth neither gains nor loses mass. So once in a while some mass would drift toward him. Then he'd go for a week or two without eating much."

"Jim was loud, profane, and funny," says Thompson. "And he didn't curtail any of it around women. Roth had a sweet, kindly, very proper caseworker in her late fifties who was in the cubicle next to Jim's. After about a week or two she went to Dennis and said, 'I think I really ought to be moved.' It was never malicious on Jim's part, but he wasn't about to change or tone down.

"As much a genius as he is," says Thompson, "organization is not one of his strengths." In the office, Jim's desk became a cause for alarm. "Twice the fire marshal called to say Jim's office was a threat to the building." "He had no sense of filing anything," says de Reuter. "If I don't touch it for three months," Jim's theory went, "I'll just dump it."

"But he'd ask for the same thing two or three times and would scream and shout and swear he didn't have it until we'd look and there it was. I had to keep a duplicate file where I could find things for him."

"He was not mechanically inclined," says Thomas. "Nor was Roth. Jim came into Roth's office one day with a phone call and between the two of them, they cut the guy off and broke the phone. Jim was like an older and heavier Tom Sawyer. He was always getting others to put up his bookshelves or to repair something."

"Jim hated to drive and ride in a car," says Thompson. "He hated to drive to my house in Chevy Chase, and he razzed Dennis about living in the sticks." Thomas lived on a farm forty miles out near Mt. Airy, Maryland. "You need a six-pack and a picnic lunch to get to Dennis's," Jim said.

Jim and Sarah kept up with their friends from HUD, the Pentagon, and the RNC, incorporating their new friends from the Hill into the mix. At dinner with the Adelmans early that year, Sarah confided to Ken and Carol that she was upset that she wasn't yet pregnant. Whereupon Adelman bestowed upon her one of his statues from Zaire—a fertility fetish—called Baluba. "I told her to put it above their bed looking down on them, and to put some grass around it. A few months later she called to say, 'It worked.' " Sarah was due at Christmastime and she planned to continue working until her delivery.

The Adelmans sometimes did play readings for after-dinner entertainment. Ken cast Jim as the coach in *That Championship Season* one night. "He was terrific," says Adelman, "he really liked it. It didn't seem like he was reading it, but living it."

Sarah and Jan Wolff discovered they were pregnant about the same time and when Jan confided it to the Bradys, Jim said, "Are you guys pregnant?" "They made it sound so wonderful," says Jan. "Jim and Sarah were taking Lamaze classes and Jim would tell how they would take their blanket to class, and how Sarah would lie on the floor and pant, making it sound so funny. Jim loved it. They had a ball with the idea of having a baby."

"Through these years," says Sarah, "Jim always wanted to keep his ties to the church. We went to church pretty regularly before our baby was born. Jim signed himself up once to give Sunday afternoon tours of our church, Christ Church in Alexandria." Sarah and Jim served as hosts for coffee hour after church as well. "Jim decided one time we should have bloody Marys instead of coffee," says Sarah. "Our new minister and Jim really hit it off over that."

Through Republican politics, "Jim met a former priest, Phil

Guarino," says Sarah. Phil and Susan Guarino came to the Bradys for dinner, "and the men did the entire Catholic mass that night, and Jim played all his records of religious music."

That summer Jim, "B" Oglesby, and Hugh O'Neill went fishing and Jim decided to use their sizable catch to throw another party. "Jim spent the whole day breading the fish," says Jan Wolff, "and by the time everybody came he was exhausted. Jim invited maybe sixty or seventy people. By the time Senator Roth arrived the coleslaw was all gone. Jim chided Sarah, 'I can't believe this, 'Coon.' Then he'd announce periodically to the crowd, 'Coon and I are trying to cut expenses, and cabbage is all the way up to eleven cents a pound now. 'Coon thought that's where she'd cut corners.' "

"Jim used to do most of the cooking," says Jan. "Sarah and I almost resented all the credit he and Otto were getting. They were the showmen, and we got to do the uneventful things." For the second year Jim had signed up for cooking classes. Occasionally, "the devil would make me stop by F. Scott's, a Georgetown bar and restaurant, after class," he says. "Jim brought into the office a big box, full of Italian olive oil and other authentic stuff," says de Reuter.

In July, a small tragedy befell Jim and Sarah. After years of ill health, their beloved kitty, Stutz Bearcat, succumbed to congestive heart failure. "We just cried and cried," says Sarah, "and when Jim brought him home from the vet, we buried him in the backyard." That very afternoon they went out to the Maryland countryside to get two new cats, Sugar and Spice. And every now and then Jim'd put flowers on Stutz's grave.

To the great satisfaction of Roth and his office, in June of 1978 Californians voted for Howard Jarvis's Proposition 13, which curtailed the fast-rising, pegged-to-inflation property taxes in California. Inflation, which had taken off in Richard Nixon's term, was climbing steadily under Jimmy Carter, and Carter showed no ability to curb it. Roth and Kemp invited Jarvis to Washington and they held a press conference together in the Senate press gallery, and talked about the beauties of lowering taxes. "We told Jarvis that ABC and NBC and CBS would be there to cover it," says de Reuter, "and Jarvis said, 'You mean the local affiliates?' And we said, 'No, the nets, man, the nets!' "

Californian Arthur Laffer, designer of the Laffer curve, joined them, too, to add his theory that at a certain point heavy taxes cost the government more than they bring in, because they do away with the incentive to work hard, earn more money, and invest it in productive enterprises (as opposed to tax-shelter schemes). It was important support for Roth and Kemp's tax-cut bill.

Jim and de Reuter began to put out *The Tax Cut News* every Monday—a four-page paper "which generated interest on both sides and among reporters," says Bruce Thompson. They also did regular updates on the SOB Task Force's accomplishments.

In April, Jim's press release for Roth attacked Carter's planned anti-inflation message and accused Carter of adopting as his motto "When in danger or in doubt—run in circles, speak and shout."

"It was Jim's idea to carry the Roth-Kemp tax-cut plan to the entire country," says Roth. The Republican party had formally adopted the measure and in August 1978, during the recess, party officials rented a plane, which Jim dubbed "The Tax-Cut Clipper" and flew to seven major cities, where they held televised press conferences, just like the famous Ten Cities Tour at HUD. All the Republican candidates for the presidency joined them at some point and many congressional leaders as well. Starting in Washington, they went to New York, Philadelphia, Detroit, Chicago, Oklahoma City, and Los Angeles—the main TV centers of the country.

The tour, Roth says, "was an extraordinarily successful event. It was the first time in years Republicans had a positive program to offer to the people. Wherever we went we had tremendous coverage which was very important to the 1980 election. We made the tax cut our issue, and it came to characterize the need for a change in economic politics. It's nice to succeed and have fun in the process."

Brady and Thompson gave their spiel over and over to reporters on the tax blitz. "Jim and I would switch roles; he'd do the substance and I'd do the explaining to the press. We promoted our Republican tax cut and carried a big map of the United States that showed all the unemployment caused by the Carter people.

"Jim would tell Roth," says Thompson, " 'Don't talk about productivity or plant equipment and things like that. Talk about the average person and how government should tighten its belt.'

And he'd say, 'No, Senator, you don't want to say something new. You want to say the same thing over and over again.' "

In October, right before the off-year elections, "the Democrats tried to take the tax-cut issue back," says Thompson. Democratic Senators Sam Nunn and Lawton Chiles wrote a tax amendment calling for a 20 percent tax cut spread over four years, but only if federal spending was reduced to offset the cost of the tax cut. "We had two options," says Thompson. "Either oppose it or embrace it. And Roth voted for it. He had always supported cuts in federal spending as well." The amendment passed the Senate, 65 to 20, lost in the House, and went to the House-Senate conference.

But it was worry time for Roth, Jim, and other Republicans who, although they had voted for it, didn't want the Democrats to get credit for promoting a tax cut. They believed they had made tax cuts their issue. "Jim had been pondering this for days," says de Reuter, "in anticipation of its passage."

"Jim and I went to the Gandy Dancer that night," says Thompson, "and Jim suddenly said, 'Hell, this amendment is just the son of Roth-Kemp! We've had a live birth here. It's our baby.' " Brady, Thompson, and Thomas began to hatch a publicity scheme to take credit for it. "We decided we'd claim Nunn and Chiles's amendment for our own, call it 'Son of Roth-Kemp,' have Roth hand out cigars like a proud father."

"Get me a box of cigars. Get me a picture of an elephant," said Jim. And they went to work making up cigar bands. De Reuter says, "We Xeroxed a little picture of an elephant from the dictionary and wrote, 'It's a Roth-Kemp' under it. Jim wanted a sunrise on the label. We Xeroxed our creation over and over, making labels for all these cigars."

That afternoon Jim called a press conference, telling the press that Senator Roth had an important announcement to make. Accompanied by Republican Senators Howard Baker and Henry Bellmon, and Republican House members Bob Michel and John Rhodes, Roth stuck a big cigar in his mouth and announced "to Mr. and Mrs. Hard Pressed Taxpayer" that there had been "the birth of a healthy son of Roth-Kemp." And he passed out cigars to the reporters gathered around. "You oughta be ashamed of yourself, Brady," CBS's Phil Jones told him.

"The next day," says de Reuter, "the biggest picture of Bill Roth I've ever seen of anybody to this day appeared on the front page of *The Washington Post*. All day newspeople called us for cigars, so all day we had to keep Xeroxing elephants to make more cigar bands." At a later date, the *Post* editorialized against Roth's media stunts. "Something to the effect: 'Where has all the good old-fashioned honesty gone?' " says Jim. "Screw 'em," he adds, throwing caution to the wind. Jim's byword usually is that "you don't pick a quarrel with someone who buys ink by the barrelful," but "I also subscribe to Churchill's dictum," he says, "that there are some things people should not see being made in public; among them, sausage and laws."

As for the "Son of Roth-Kemp," says Bruce Thompson, "Carter came out against the tax cut and worked against its passage. When the bill went to conference, the Republican House conferees were instructed to accept it, but Carter sent Treasury Secretary Blumenthal to the Hill with the threat that Carter would veto it if they passed it. What was important to us was the perception of who was giving tax cuts to working people." It couldn't have worked out better.

In the 1978 elections, the Republicans picked up three Senate seats and fifteen House seats. Five liberal Senate Democrats lost, and though the party out of power usually gains seats in the off-year elections anyway, "we were encouraged by the '78 results," says Thompson. "We felt there was a movement in our direction by voters who wanted their taxes cut." (Other factors were involved of course, too. The liberals were targeted by single-issue groups, antiabortionists, particularly.)

"The old guard of the Republican party always fought against deficits," says Thompson, "and would oppose tax cuts and spending until the budget was balanced. It was the root-canal theory of government. No wonder we were the minority party.

Now Roth and others were beginning to embrace supply-side, tax-cut economics, which promised, they hoped, short-term deficits but long-term economic boom. "We began to be the party of ideas," says Thompson, "instead of the party of reaction."

"In former days," says de Reuter, "Roth would get an occasional little clipping, and be covered by two reporters at the most. We went from those lean days to fifteen hundred clippings a week. We didn't have time to look at 'em. Jim would paw through them, pull out a few, and laugh and laugh. Senator Roth wanted us to keep a scrapbook, but it was impossible; there were too many of them. *Sixty Minutes* was calling us, and NBC, everybody. But Jim was always looking ahead. 'What can we do next to keep the pressure on?' He was always pressing us for ideas, and then they became his ideas. He was a terrible plagiarist, but he'd just laugh at us over that.

"We'd run around town looking for another prop for the next Brady scheme," says de Reuter. "Jim would say, 'Get me some hedge clippers.' 'Go out and buy a basket full of food and compare it to a basketful you could buy before Carter.' 'Find out what a car cost when Carter came in, and what it costs now.' 'Find me an elephant!' We were beyond questioning Jim as to why he wanted this stuff. We just did it. He always went for the visual part and the message was always the difference between the Democrats and us."

"People in the press gallery would laugh and cheer when they saw de Reuter coming with a Brady press release—another Bradyism," says Thompson. "Jim always sent stuff by the photographers' gallery, too, announcing this or that photo opportunity. 'Those guys are bored,' he'd say, 'they're just sitting around.' I never thought it was possible to get somebody that much media exposure. Even the *National Enquirer* had a story on Roth with a coupon that said, 'Cut My Taxes, or You're Fired!' Bagfuls of those coupons were delivered to the Hill. The tax-cut issue just kept on growing.

"If credit is to be given, it has to be given to Jim for raising the tax cut as a national issue," he adds.

Jim would greet Thompson's memos with derision, and told him, "Before I leave here I'm going to teach you how to write. This is too boring. You're writing like a lawyer."

"He wasn't exactly tactful," says Thompson. "He'd lean under his desk and pretend to start a chain saw and cut your paper to shreds. He'd start snoring while you were talking to him, or say, 'MEGO [my eyes glaze over]! Give me a good line, Bruce. Don't go on and on!'

"He hated the word *that*. He had a pile of *that*s in his drawer that he cut from our prose—literally—with scissors.

"He thought international trade was boring and would try to steer us off of that. It was hard to boil international trade down to two or three sentences. He'd not bother with things he wasn't interested in."

"Dennis was a great part of that as far as ideas go, too," says Lou Gerig. "He was as crazy as Jim Brady but he wouldn't get out in front and be the clown." "Jim had his method of operation with the press, a concept he called 'trolling,' says Dennis Thomas. "He created it. He would grab me by the coat. 'Let's go trolling,' he'd say, and we would go over to the Senate press gallery and pass out our press releases. Then Jim would move in and out among the press, putting out his line. But he never abused his position. He was honest and never crossed the line. He knew the difference between being light and funny and being outrageous and absurd."

"The one thing Jim taught me," says Lou Gerig, "is how to make your senator available after a major address by the president of the opposite party—and how to hang around the press gallery. Jim was high-powered, but somewhat low-key. Media people always mentioned Jim Brady's name when they were talking about how to be a good press secretary. When the press saw Jim coming, they always enjoyed seeing him—he always drew a crowd. By talking to them he would be tipped as to what kinds of things they were after, and then he and Dennis worked up some usable information."

"And Roth opened up a lot more to the press because of Jim," says Bruce Thompson. "He was more accessible, more trusting. He got to know a lot of them and to like them."

Ted Carmody, who followed Brady as Roth's press secretary, says, "as his successor, I was overwhelmed by 'Bradyism.' " Roth was the intellectual leader of the Finance Committee, but because of Brady, when Roth sponsored the Trade Reorganization Act, some Democratic senators didn't want to testify. "They were afraid Roth would hit them over the head with a rubber chicken. But Roth could always get cosponsors for his projects because they knew he could get media coverage."

Sandra Evans, then married to Pete Teeley, was writing for the Bureau of National Affairs, an information service that gathers news for newspapers and lobbyists. They put out a daily tax report. Evans had met Jim before but "I had occasion to deal with him on a professional basis when he was working for Roth," she says. "He was wonderful at getting back to me, or getting me in to see the senator—when I worked for an organization no one had ever heard of. He made sure I knew what I needed to know for my readers.

"Jim had a good perspective on who he worked for. So many people who work for one man think he is the end all and be all. I once interviewed Roth, and later Jim called and asked how it went. I told him I just sort of let Roth talk about a lot of things he wanted to talk about. 'Oh, no. You didn't let him do that, did you?' said Jim. 'Did he commit news?'

"You have to be awfully ballsy to do the things Jim did, and Roth had to go along with it, too. He is an amiable sort of fellow."

Sue Mathis, a reporter for the Cox Newspapers, went to talk to Jim about "Kemp-Roth. (Roth-Kemp, I should say. Jim was very sensitive about that.) Jim was on fifteen phone lines. It was crazy. In all I spoke to him for about one minute. But I chuckle every time I think of that desk. I put my tape recorder on a corner of it, and Jim said, 'All right. Who's been messing around with my desk?' I thought, 'How the hell would you know?' But he assessed that something had been moved."

"I think Jim was the perfect press secretary in that he did not express his views," says Lou Gerig, "only those of the person he worked for. As press secretary, you can wind up in the media a lot, and it can be heady, you can get your ego inflated. Jim was always aware of whom he was working for, and it would be *their* views in print, not his views. He doesn't see his position as being the one having views." But Jim did become a believer in the value of tax cuts to stimulate the economy and to help low- and middle-income working people.

Sarah and Jim's baby was due on Christmas Day, and she worked until the weekend before Christmas. On December 29, now overdue, Sarah went in for a checkup. Her doctor examined her and took a blood sample and sent her home. But later that day he called to say, "You and your husband better come in to the hospital and bring a suitcase." "I threw some things in a bag, and Jim and I went to Alexandria Hospital. There, the doctor advised that I have a cesarean section, because the test showed the placenta was gradually losing its ability to nourish the baby. Jim and I, of course, immediately agreed." Sarah had had amniocentesis, but she and Jim didn't want to know what sex her baby was. As she was being wheeled in,

Jim told her, "Write down what you really think it is." "Twenty minutes after I went into the OR I had a baby boy." He was James Scott Brady, Jr., six pounds, nineteen inches long, and healthy. "He was the prettiest baby I ever saw," says Sarah. Jim told Otto Wolff about Sarah's C-section, "They put a zipper in so they won't have to do it next time."

That night, Jim and Missy, who had been with them for Christmas, dropped in on the O'Neills. "Well, I guess this is what life is all about," Jim told them.

On New Year's Eve, the Wolffs went to the hospital to see the new baby. "Jim was dressed up in a hospital gown, hat, and had a surgical mask hanging from one ear. 'Did you see Scott?' he asked. 'C'mon down and see him. He's going to be the one crying. He had his weenie whacked today and he's really pissed off.' "

"The baby's first checkup in January," says Sarah, "fell the day after we'd had a major snowstorm, and Jim called me to say he would be home to take us to the doctor." Jim showed up driving a brand new yellow CJ7 Jeep with a black top. "He bought it without a word to me," says Sarah.

"I just knew we had to have it to get Scott to the doctor through this snow," Jim told her.

Sarah and Jim had decided before Scott was born that she would not return to work but would stay home to care for him. In February, however, her old friend from the RNC, Eddie Mahe, now John Connally's presidential campaign director, persuaded Sarah to work part time as director of Volunteers for Connally. "That lasted three or four weeks," she says. "I didn't enjoy it. I found it too hard to leave Scott. As a wife and mother my interests were changing."

Mahe was also working on Jim to join the campaign as press secretary. "I want the best," he told Sarah, "and you know who that is."

"We talked about it," says Sarah. "Jim knew he wanted to be in on the '80 presidential campaign, but he wanted to wait and see how Connally was going to do."

In the Senate, Roth's campaign for Roth-Kemp continued. They were ready for Carter's new budget with Jim's press release made up of sixteen one- or two-liners. "An economic iceberg ready to sink the taxpayer." "It's like looking at the package of bacon in the supermarket. You don't see the fat until you open the package." "A Band Aid budget when we really need major surgery." "We can cut spending to fight inflation. At the same time we must cut taxes to get the country moving again. Carter is saying if you don't get well, you don't get your medicine."

The next day, Carter's State of the Union address was "warm milk before bedtime—rhetoric over reality. . . . Carter's New Foundation is built on economic quicksand. He talks less government while promising more. He wants to help the needy without weeding out the greedy."

In March, Jim and Roth issued a one-word press release in response to a proposal to provide a fifty-dollar-a-day tax break for Congress: "Stupid."* At the bottom of the page was the footnote: (*Strong message to follow.).

In May, the basic Roth-Kemp formula in a nutshell: "Cut spending, cut taxes, and you'll cut inflation."

To celebrate the first anniversary of the announcement of Kemp-Roth, and in the ongoing spirited but friendly battle to have people call the bill Roth-Kemp, not Kemp-Roth, that July Jim and the boys decided they would have a big birthday cake made. "We got Jack Kemp to join Senator Roth on the podium, and to help hold up the cake that said Roth-Kemp on it in big letters," laughs Bruce Thompson. "It was a running battle between our office and Kemp's. Sometimes we called it Roth-Roth, and I'm sure they called it Kemp-Kemp."

"Jim was always involved in planning office parties," says Roth. "We would play softball games between the Washington and Wilmington staffs, and the office in Wilmington would sometimes bring in ringers from the Philadelphia Phillies."

"Jim brought out Roth's sense of self-deprecating humor," says Thomas. "They had a warm and close relationship which continues to this day. Through humor Jim enjoyed a sense of confidentiality with him that others couldn't. That was true probably with Connally and others to follow. Complaining wasn't one of the things he did very much."

That summer, Jim, Sarah, and seven-month-old Scott went to Bethany Beach with Pete and Sandra Teeley. "We went out to dinner together and the Bradys brought Scott," says Sandra, "and Jim was playing with Scott throughout the whole meal.

It was just so nice to see him enjoying his son so much—making him laugh—talking to him—joking to him, just silly stuff."

That summer, too, Jim had two important and very different job offers he was considering. Eddie Mahe was still after him to join the Connally campaign, and Bill Greener, now public-affairs director of G. D. Searle Co. in Chicago, and Don Rumsfeld, chief executive officer of Searle, wanted Jim to join them. "It was a hard decision," says Sarah, "a choice between the Searle job that offered money and security, and a political job that offered no security and little money." But Jim just wasn't ready to go into the corporate world. And Sarah agreed with him. "He felt, if he got into the presidential campaign, he would have the chance to become spokesperson for the Department of Defense or, preferably, the Department of State."

"And," says Bill Greener, "it's a given in our business that the top job in PR is that of White House press secretary. Everybody knows that. Jim and I had talked about it, often." If Connally won, Jim undoubtedly would have the job.

And during the spring and summer of 1979, sixty-two-year-old John Connally had made a number of impressive appearances. He announced his candidacy in January, and in March in Indianapolis, the Mid-West Republican Leadership Conference provided one of what had come to be called "cattle shows," where the major Republican hopefuls showed up to give speeches. Connally and Reagan had, so far, snubbed these appearances, but this time Connally was there. CBS News distributed a straw ballot, and "Connally won easily after giving a characteristically forceful speech."

Later in the spring at a Republican state dinner in New Hampshire, Connally was the "star of the show," and after speeches, "the judges of the press declared Connally the 'winner' again." (Again, Reagan, who was leading in the polls, did not appear.)

It appeared that John Connally, twice governor of Texas, had a decent shot at the Republican nomination, perhaps better than most of the others. He was a conservative Democrat who had joined the Republican party in 1970 and had served in Nixon's cabinet as secretary of the treasury. He was tall, movie-star handsome, and an articulate and moving speaker. He had the support of much of big business, and support from the New Right as well. He was able to raise money for an expensive TV advertising campaign and, in fact, wound up raising $12.9 million. And in the spring of 1979, Americans' approval rating of President Jimmy Carter had sunk below 40 percent. Carter looked very vulnerable, and Connally seemed impressive.

One Sunday Jim drove over to talk to David Cole about the job offers, "a conversation I think about often," says Cole. "I told him, 'You know Rumsfeld well enough so that if it works out you'll be press secretary; if not you can go back with Rumsfeld.' I think Jim said to himself, 'If I go for the Searle job, I'll close this chapter of my life, so I'll go for the brass ring one more time.' "

There were many people Mahe wanted to bring into the Connally campaign, but he told Otto Wolff he would "hang out of an airplane by his fingernails if he thought he could get Jim to come on board." "Jim is just a funny human being who has a tremendous amount of talent—political and writing talent," says Mahe. "That's why I went after him. I determined he was the best one around."

And so, Jim signed up with "Big John" Connally from Texas.

"I was going for the big quinella," says Jim Brady. "And I thought John Connally was the best candidate on the horizon at that time."

Jim signed up David Cole as a volunteer, too. "Brady could get you to do anything he wanted you to do. 'Come, come, come. Volunteer,' he said. Well, I'm a political animal, and I thought Connally'd make an excellent president. If you live in the world of politics you know you have to volunteer now and then, so you'll wind up with that Schedule C appointment."

"I was madder than hell when he left to go with Connally," says Roth, only half kidding. "Yes, he didn't think he could win ever again without his charlatan there at his side," says Jim.

"We were happy for Jim," says Bruce Thompson, "but we were all upset and disappointed he was leaving. We *hated* to lose him. You're not working when you're working with Jim. You're stimulated, you're thinking of new ideas, you're having fun."

Otto Wolff, too, had joined the Connally campaign as director of administration in Connally's national headquarters in Arlington, Virginia. "I'm a party person," says Wolff. "In election years joining up with a candidate is the only game in town. I thought John Connally would make a respectable showing, carrying the Republican flag into the convention.

"On my first day, Jim stopped by my office," says Wolff. " 'Herr Wolff,' he said. 'This is a most egregious day.' "

"Jim began traveling with Connally most of the time," says Sarah, "but he was usually home on weekends at first." With baby Scott they were able to make their annual August trip to Centralia, where Dorothy Mann assured them, "If you are working for Connally, Jimmy, we'll support him, too." Bill Crain remembers seeing Jim walking around town wearing overalls, carrying nine-month-old Scott in his arms. "I always admired Jim's ability to handle his life so there seemed to be time enough for everything."

Jim and Sarah found time to throw a going-away party for Sarah's college friend Betsi Burkett and Madhav Raul, who were leaving to marry and live in his native India. "We fixed Tandoori Chicken," says Sarah, "but we colored it with beet juice. It was shocking pink, but delicious."

On one of Jim's weekends home they went out to eat in Alexandria. "I had been on the Scarsdale diet and not drinking for two weeks while Jim was out of town," says Sarah, "and the two or three drinks I had went straight to my head. On the way home Jim realized I almost wasn't able to drive, and he told me to stop the car so he could take over. I stopped and Jim got out to go around to the driver's side." But Sarah immediately took off—without Jim.

"The next morning I saw that Jim had slept in the basement, and was awfully grouchy about something," says Sarah. Then he told her she had left him on the streets of Alexandria the night before. "Well, who took the babysitter home, then?" she wanted to know. "Well, it wasn't me," said Jim.

"The Raccoon was apparently overserved," says Jim.

CHAPTER ELEVEN

"Big John"

For two years before Jim Brady joined John Connally's campaign, twenty-six-year-old Mike Crockett, who met Connally when he represented him in a real-estate transaction, had been traveling with the governor while he raised money and tested the waters. "Mike Crockett was the one constant in the campaign," says Eddie Mahe. "He was his traveling aide." Jim and I hit it off," says Crockett. "It was only me, a member of his political-action committee [the John Connally Citizens Forum], and his secretary. It was a real relief to have Jim Brady there. He gave real life support there during the campaign. With his great sense of humor he was able to entertain Connally during some hard, trying times. Jim and I hit it off."

Julian Reed, a close Connally friend and political consultant, was director of communications in the campaign. "Jim and I kind of split things up at first. He'd stay in town sometimes and I'd go out with Governor Connally. Jim was aware of all that was going on in the campaign, even though he'd had no involvement in it." As activity picked up, both Brady and Reed were out most of the time.

Jim's press office in Arlington included four young people: Mitchell Stanley, Margaret Nathan, Mark Weinberg, his secretary, Vash Brandenburg, and volunteer Kathy Ahern.

"Jim Brady had a reputation that preceded him," says Mark Weinberg, "for being clever, creative, and having a good sense of humor, and for not being detail oriented. But his 'not being detail oriented' was not to be mistaken for being unaware. He gave set instructions of the concept he wanted, and you were left on your own to develop it. He wasn't petty about how you did it, but he wasn't oblivious to what you were doing either."

Mitchell Stanley had left his job in the State Department because he was bored, and volunteered with the Connally campaign. "Connally really looked strong," he says. "I called up and asked, 'Where's the most interesting place to work?' 'The press office,' they told me. Jim's attitude was 'If it didn't cost anything he'd add you to the staff.'

"Connally was sort of an aberrant candidate. He couldn't seem to get good press coverage," says Stanley. "Jim asked me where I had worked. I told him the State Department and he wanted me to set up a press conference at headquarters for the foreign press. 'Get as many people as you can. Just do it.' We turned out about sixty people. Brady, Sam Hoskinson, and Julian Reed briefed them on Connally's foreign policy. I became the official unpaid assistant press secretary.

"I came in at six every morning, and Jim would call and ask, 'What's in *The Washington Post, The New York Times*?' so Connally could respond if he were asked. When it was time for me to go to my new job I told them I was having so much fun I wasn't going to join them. Brady is really an interesting character to work with because to him *nada es imposible*. It's just a matter of lining things up in the right way so it could be done. He always spoke authoritatively and confidently. I guess that's the essence of leadership."

Kathy Ahern, housewife, mother, and grandmother, volunteered in the Connally campaign and "got so interested I was going every day from nine to five doing anything and everything. I saw a sign on the bulletin board for a full-time volunteer in the press office and thought I'd just as soon work in one place." Ahern didn't meet Jim until he came home from one of his campaign trips, but she took a phone call one day from someone who said, "This is the Bear."

"I thought it was an obscene call, a kook," she says, "and I went to the girls with it. But everybody shot out of their offices saying, 'Oh, it's the Bear.' " As the campaign picked up, says

Kathy, "people in the press office complained they never got to see Jim, that it was like working for someone who wasn't there, so I went and bought a bear, and put a sign on it, 'The Bear Is Always with Us,' and put in in his chair." Kathy Ahern took Jim's phone messages for him. "I felt very protective toward him and tried to make things as easy for him as I could."

Margaret Nathan was working with a PR firm in Dallas, but she was dying to get on the Connally campaign. When Julian Reed hired her he told her to be in Washington in four days. "I walked into the Arlington headquarters and into this madhouse of craziness at eight in the morning or earlier. Jim was in his small office and was on the phone with all of his other lines lit up."

"Who the hell are you?" he asked Nathan.

"Margaret Nathan."

"So—?"

"I'm supposed to be working for you."

"Oh, yeah." He stood up. "Welcome to the NFL."

"And it was," she says. "Just the fact that every time you picked up the phone it was always someone whose name you already knew in the media.

" 'I don't know what to do with you,' Jim told me. I started doing press releases and mailings. We had thousands of names of press in every state and our office mass-produced all of Connally's speeches."

After a week of working from early morning to late at night, Jim and Hugh O'Neill tried to talk Nathan into going for a drink at Chadwick's in old Town Alexandria, the Connally afterhours bar-restaurant hangout. " 'Oh, no, I can't,' I said. 'I have too much work to do.' Then Jim and Hugh came and unplugged the typewriter and took me along. But we usually worked from seven-thirty in the morning to late in the night.

"Jim was real tough to work for. He demanded a lot from you but never let you know exactly what you were supposed to do. He just expected you to be responsible and to recognize what needed to be done and to get it done. If you made a mistake he would get really angry and let you hear about it for days. He'd make you figure out your own errors." Jim and Nathan had it out one day over a press release, she recalls. "He got you to the point where you could stand on your own two feet. 'Don't say, "I assume," ' he'd say. He hated that phrase.

'Say, "I don't know but I'll find out and call you back." ' He'd say, 'Don't be dumb. Figure it out for yourself.' And hang up. But when you got it right, he'd be the first one to tell you so.

"If he was on the road he'd call in with a thousand orders, from finding other people, to getting all the statements out, to letting us know what the day's statement was. It didn't take me long to figure out what I was supposed to do. Everybody pitched in and did whatever needed to be done and every day was different. When he was in, it was always a different experience. He had a million things he wanted us to do, and when you started one he'd pull you off and start you on something else. We were able to work that way. He created that energy that moved that side of the campaign.

"He rode us hard about really taking care of the media people. He didn't regard them as enemies. On the other hand, he'd not allow the media to beat us up. I think the press genuinely liked him and I think Jim regarded them almost as an ally. It was—'They've got a job to do, and we've got a job to do. And that is to make their job easier. So go do it.' "

"Jim Brady unlocks the potential in people to go out and do seemingly impossible things," says Mitchell Stanley. (Kathy Ahern, a southerner, pronounced his name "Mee-chell." He became Mee-chell to everybody.) "He could be impatient with people. He liked us to anticipate problems and he was a good tactician. He is limited only by the amount of ingenuity and resources available. There is no job too big if you just sit down and start it. He changed my whole life. Had I not met him I am sure I would have gone to live in some pesthole to labor there in obscurity."

Friday nights Jim's crew usually repaired to Chadwick's Tavern and George Bush's staff people met there, too. Jim's friend Pete Teeley was Bush's press secretary and there was a strong rivalry, usually cordial, between the two camps. But one night Teeley called Jim to tell him that his staff, wearing their Connally pins, had been loudly making fun of Bush at Chadwick's. The next day Jim chewed them out.

"Connally got a big ride in the press at first," says Pete Teeley. "His picture appeared on the cover of *Time*, and Jim asked me when I was going to get Bush's picture on the cover of *Time*. I told him, 'When a major stockholder of *Time* becomes finance chairman of our campaign.' " (As was Texan Arthur Temple for Connally.)

Soon Bill Rhatican joined the campaign to handle press inquiries in Connally's Arlington headquarters. "Jim Brady needed someone back here who could take press calls," says Rhatican, "about Connally's positions on issues, or about his latest statements."

"Rhatican became the contact guy between Brady and Arlington headquarters," says Mahe.

"There are very few people who have the personal presence that Connally has" says Rhatican. "But the Connally campaign was chaotic, although all campaigns are chaotic by their very nature. But in this campaign, the candidate *was* the campaign." Old cronies and colleagues popped in and out of the campaign when Connally summoned them. "The campaign entourage becomes a cocoon and nothing happens outside of it as far as they're concerned." Part of that was just the usual tug-of-war that goes on between the candidate and his staff on the road, and the managers back at headquarters. But "he wanted to make all of the decisions," says Jim Brady, "not just a few—all of them."

This led to all sorts of inner-circle arguments and second-guessing of the experts Connally had hired. And by all accounts, although brilliant and charming, Connally could also be difficult and stubborn, all too sure that he knew the best course his campaign should follow. He could be dictatorial and high-handed.

"In other campaigns, the candidate is the spokesman for the campaign," says Rhatican. "The candidate will articulate a particular point of view and turn to the staff to flesh out that viewpoint. That way information is always flowing back to the candidate. In the Connally campaign, the candidate didn't want that. He was out there campaigning in that cocoon and that was the way he wanted to operate. Which made Jim's role in the Connally campaign that much more critical."

Dave Parker, Connally's scheduler, had his work cut out for him. "Where are you sending us now?" Connally would demand. "He just didn't like to be organized and have other people order him around," says Parker. "He thought he could be anointed as president. But he knew he had to do it too. It's just that campaigning is tough, damned tough."

"Jim's reputation on the campaign was that he was the only guy who could argue with the governor and get away with it," says Rhatican. "When the governor would ask why he had to make this appearance or that appearance, Jim would say, 'Because you have to, Governor.' "

"Governor Connally relied heavily on Jim for advice. He was Connally's adviser in the broadest sense of the word," says Mark Weinberg.

"Our position was that we were there to help the governor," says Rhatican, "but there was a lot of unhappiness back at headquarters. The policy-development office found it difficult to get information through to the governor.

"One of the jokes of the campaign," he adds, "was that Jim was essentially unreachable, that the governor was easier to reach than Jim was."

None of these seemed like insurmountable problems in the fall of 1979, however. There was a presumption on the part of the Republican candidates who had already announced that aging actor Ronald Reagan, at sixty-eight, would somehow falter, and that the thing to do was to be in position to pick up the reins when he did. When Jim joined Connally, Reagan had not yet even announced his candidacy. "One of the most valuable assets Ronald Reagan has always had going for him," says *The Washington Post*'s Jim Dickenson, "is that he has been consistently underestimated."

But there was a wide range of people who thought that of all the Republicans John Connally was the best qualified to be president because of his experience in government. He had been governor of Texas, secretary of the treasury, and secretary of the navy. People were impressed by his bearing and demeanor, his brilliance and energy. He had "command presence."

Dickenson, previously with *The Washington Star,* had written during the drab Nixon administration that Connally was "like a peacock roosting with a flock of mudhens. . . . He is tall, handsome, intelligent, forceful, successful, well tailored, ambitious, and blessed with enough self-assurance for a regiment."

During the fall, Jim was on the campaign trail with the governor about three days a week. He and Julian Reed split up the duties at first. "From time to time you would see Jim in the office on a Sunday," says Rhatican. "Sarah was always with him and sometimes Scott, too. Jim's office desk had stacks of pink telephone messages on it, each one six inches high."

"Jim brought toys home to Scott from the campaign trail," says Jan Wolff, "among them a little yellow Jeep like his own."

"When he was home, however briefly," says Sarah, "he was great about forgetting the office. He separated the two. He was exhausted and he would eat, rest, and play with Scott."

Connally was scheduled to appear in Indianapolis to address a meeting of the National Republican Women's Clubs on September 29. "Brady was in the war room trying to think of something glitzy to attract attention," says Mahe aide Michele Davis, "and he said, 'Y'know, a big thing right now is roller skating.' And we all said, 'Oh, come on, Brady.' But he said, 'Why don't we have a whole bunch of people rolling around handing out Connally buttons and literature?'

"So we had about forty schoolkids who were dressed in white pants and T-shirts that said 'Connally is rolling.' Connally didn't know what was happening. All these kids were whirling around him. But that's where the cameras were, and we got the media coverage. That's Bear," she says.

"Jim broke into the inner circle quickly, which was a little unusual with John Connally," says Crockett, "and with most candidates, I believe. He was particularly good in pressure moments, when nobody else wanted to give Connally bad news. Jim had a good background in foreign affairs, political affairs, and a good feel for military affairs. He was able to use his knowledge in briefing Connally. Connally loved to talk about foreign affairs and loved to talk to Jim about them. They became good, close friends. Certainly it was more than an employer-employee relationship. John Connally trusted Jim and enjoyed being around him."

In October at the Washington Press Club, Governor Connally delivered a major foreign-policy address on the Middle East. It was widely advertised and extensively covered by the media. In it he called for establishing U.S. Air Force bases in the Sinai desert and putting a fleet in the Indian Ocean to guarantee a peace settlement based on the Israeli withdrawal from the West Bank, Gaza, and the Golan Heights and Arab recognition of Israel's borders. The result would be peace in an area torn by "constant tension and warfare," and a guarantee of the free flow of Middle East oil to the West, he said. He took a considerable amount of time reviewing it with others, says Crockett. "It was the right thing to do," says Jim, "but I told Connally it's like mentioning Social Security in a campaign. Never, Never. 'If it ain't broke, don't fix it.' " After the speech, two Jewish members of his national campaign committee resigned in protest, one of whom had signed off on the speech. Connally lost the financial support of a number of Wall Street and business people as well.

"It was one of the best-thought-through geopolitical speeches on the subject ever given," says Connally's son, John III. "And some Jewish leaders understood that, but said they couldn't overcome the perception that it was in some way anti-Semitic. Others refused to even read the speech, saying there were buzz words and hidden meanings in it."

"Whereas we used to have three events at every stop," says Crockett, "a press conference, a fund-raiser with fat cats, and a meeting with the general public, after 'the speech' we had to add a fourth meeting with the local Jewish leadership."

"Yes, we got the Jewish Defense League after him," says Jim. "At the Century Plaza in Los Angeles these guys were hiding in the stairwell, and they came out yelling and screaming. Scared the shit out of us."

"I think that speech was the turning point of the campaign, the beginning of the end," says Margaret Nathan. "I think Jim foresaw it, but I remember Jim giving Mark and me a passionate defense of it for purposes of answering phone calls after the speech. He made Mark answer all those press calls."

"If the governor made a mistake," says Reed, "it was that he was so sure of his analysis of the problem that he felt the reasonableness of his plan would be so clear, no one could mistake it. The irony is that many of the points in the speech were advocated by others, but piecemeal."

"The Mideast speech was to be the 'Bold Stroke,' " says Parker. "It was such a Bold Stroke it practically bowled him right out of the Republican party."

Early in November at a presidential forum in Portland, Maine, Connally and George Bush were "cheered with great enthusiasm." But still a poll among Republican voters showed Ronald Reagan to be the front-runner with 37 percent, John

Connally with 15 percent, and Senator Howard Baker with 13 percent.

"Sarah had rushed us to the airport for that trip." says Julian Reed, "and Scott was along. How Jim loved to hug that kid."

The next day, November 4, 1979, the country was shocked by the news that supporters of the new fundamentalist government of Iran had seized the U.S. embassy in Tehran and was holding 101 American hostages.

Three days later Senator Edward M. Kennedy announced he would challenge President Jimmy Carter for the Democratic nomination.

On November 13, 1979, Ronald Reagan in a low-key-speech announced his candidacy in New York City.* He advocated tax cuts to stimulate business activity as the key to economic recovery. In a press conference the next day on Capitol Hill, Reagan announced that Jack Kemp would be chairman of his campaign policy-development committee and his chief spokesman. Using the phrase that would outlive most other words uttered that day, Jack Kemp began, "It is an honor to be associated with the oldest and wisest of all the candidates who has embraced the youngest and freshest ideas on how to stimulate the economy." "Oldest and wisest" quickly became the "O and W," a nickname that went into the Reagan campaign lexicon.

"We kept close touch with Jim throughout the Connally campaign," says Bruce Thompson. "He was always trying to get Connally to talk about tax cuts. He'd send me a clipping where Connally had mentioned tax cuts, and say, 'See. I'm working on it.' "

The Connally campaign, meanwhile, was plotting a coup to knock Reagan out of the lead in the cattle-show–straw-vote game. At a Republican state convention in Orlando, Florida, on November 17, they believed they would come close to beating Reagan. Perhaps even win. They had put an enormous amount of money and effort into the scheme. But they committed a fatal political error.

"We had been saying that our goal was to keep Reagan below fifty percent in this straw vote," says Eddie Mahe. A win-

*The final roster of Republican candidates was Ronald Reagan, John Connally, George Bush, Philip Crane, Howard Baker, John Anderson, Benjamin Fernandez, and Harold Stassen.

nable goal. But John and Nellie Connally were so optimistic about the outcome they ordered their aides (who protested strongly) to tell the press they just might win it. "He went in there and raised the expectations so that if he'd gotten ninety-nine percent of the vote, he'd have still looked like he lost," says Jim Brady. It was Reagan, 36 percent, Connally, 27 percent, Bush, 21 percent.

To Mahe, this was the beginning of the end. "We needed more than we got. To me it was a disappointment." At the end of November, the polls showed Reagan at 50 percent, Bush 14 percent, Connally 12 percent, and Baker 11 percent.

But Connally would continue his quest for four more months, planning his final shootout to take place in the South Carolina primary in early March.

Back on the Hill, Senator Roth and others were holding President Carter's feet to the fire. "In January, with inflation inching up toward twenty percent, we made Carter take his budget back," says Bruce Thompson. "He had promised a balanced budget but when it wasn't balanced he had a big meeting with congressional Democrats and they laid on some taxes that would cover it." In retrospect, considering Reagan's two-trillion-dollar national debt, making Jimmy Carter take back his unbalanced budget is an irony to say the least. "Carter called Senator Roth. 'Can't we talk?' he asked. And Roth met with him three times."

Over the Christmas holidays the Soviet Union invaded Afghanistan, and in response Jimmy Carter imposed a grain embargo on the Soviets and later canceled United States participation in the Olympics.

Those incidents and the hostages in Iran had dominated every day's news, but in February the country began focusing on the upcoming string of precinct caucuses and primaries.

One Thursday night Jim found himself alone in California, the candidate having gone home to Texas. He called Sarah. "Hi. I'm out here in California," he told her. "Why don't you get on a plane and I'll meet you in Hawaii for the weekend?"

"So I did," says Sarah, and we had a wonderful three days."

For the Connally campaign, there were still the Iowa caucuses to get through. And Jim started traveling full time. Although Connally was directing almost all his effort toward South Carolina, they had heard of the huge effort George Bush was putting into Iowa. It became clear at the last minute that he couldn't just write off the state. "Connally came up with the idea of campaigning through Iowa around the clock for forty-eight hours. It was an idea born of desperation," says Eric Engberg of CBS News. "We almost died, the press and the staff, that is. Connally said he *liked* it, and just might do it in every state."

It was on the "Iowa Death March," as it was dubbed, that Connally felt moved to bring up his milk producers bribery trial. "We were in Iowa at a dairy cattle auction (a real cattle auction)," says Jim, "and Connally says, 'A lot of people don't know this, but I know a great deal about milk producers. I damn near went to jail for the milk producers.' " Eyes rolled back in heads, notably Jim's. "Here I'm out there twenty-four hours a day, saying 'You're innocent' when I can get more'n ten people together, that is. Then you plead guilty. He was such a bad boy that day."

"Brady didn't try to put spin control on the matter. He would just disappear when his candidate did something horrible," says Engberg. (Connally was acquitted in the 1975 trial.)

Says Michele Davis, "I never saw Jim Brady cower before anybody. Connally would get this set to his jaw, and Jim would put him in his place because of his straightforwardness. The night of the Iowa debate everyone felt reasonably good about how Connally had done, but Jim said, in front of Connally, "He was good enough to be a third-choice candidate."

In Iowa, Connally polled just under 10 percent of the vote, and George Bush shocked Reagan with his upset vote of 33 percent as opposed to Reagan's 29 percent. Reagan neither campaigned in Iowa, nor did he appear at the Iowa debate, but when he arrived in New Hampshire he debated twice, the second time being the famous Nashua debate in which he shouted, after *Nashua Telegraph* editor Jon Breen told a technician to turn off Mr. Reagan's microphone, "I paid for this microphone, Mr. Green," getting the name wrong, but his gut reaction right. It accelerated the turnaround Reagan's polls already showed.

"I'll never forget," says Mitch Stanley, "the top leadership of the campaign sitting around Connally headquarters, and Connally saying, about the Nashua debate, 'I'm not going up there with all those goddamned ninnies. I'll stop Bush right here in South Carolina.' "

Mary Leonard covered the Connally campaign full time for the *Detroit News* from mid-1979 through the convention. "On the forced march through Iowa," she says, "we went out to farms and Jim was out in these muddy fields in his pinstripe suit, his Guccis, and his Burberry coat. We arrived at a fraternity at Iowa State University in Ames at midnight. And all the kids were drunk or stoned—it was practically a toga party. Connally gave his stump speech, but the kids were mocking him, saying, 'Who is this guy? Why is he here?' Poor Jim's eyes really rolled around.

"Connally was a difficult person," says Leonard. "He wanted to be his own campaign manager. He's a take-charge kind of person who always thought he was right in everything he did. He was his own worst enemy, and never did much to dispel the image he was a rich man's candidate. 'I've been rich and I've been poor, and I'd rather be rich,' he would say. His strategy to run a fifty-state campaign was a bad one. They spent a lot of money to no avail."

Reagan won New Hampshire with 50 percent of the vote to Bush's 23 percent. Connally was hardly a blip on the screen, but he had spent little time there campaigning. On the day of the primary Reagan fired his three top aides: campaign manager John Sears, political director Charles Black, and press secretary Jim Lake. Losing Lake set the stage for the appearance of Jim Brady in the Reagan campaign.

In the meantime, as things began unraveling for Connally, his campaign staff took small comfort and perverse pleasure in the inevitable stories of campaign goofs and tales of feuding between Connally and his managers. "I was sort of watching over Jim's interests as the campaign came down around our ears," says Mitchell Stanley, a man with a droll, acerbic wit. "At the end it was sort of like being in the bunker in Germany. I think the whole Connally campaign began with a bunch of guys sitting around with Connally, and one of them saying to him, 'I think you ought to be president.' 'Well, hell, why not,' Connally probably answered. Unfortunately, in the Republican party you just can't do that.

"Campaign stories became such daily fodder of life on the road," says Stanley. "In Arkansas they arranged to have the Republican delegates bused into a huge fund-raising event, and they all lined up to shake John Connally's hand. One old guy shook Connally's hand, had a heart attack, and died right there."

"He went down like a Leviathan," says Jim, "took about three chairs with him. Then Connally led everybody in prayer."

"Another time Jim called in to tell about Connally's being at a little fudge stand in New Hampshire. Jim thought finally the governor was going to get some good press. He goes up to the stand and pulls out a wad of hundred-dollar bills. The little woman had no change and Connally turned around and asked, 'Who has change for a hundred?' Which just emphasized the perception he was the candidate of big-money boys.

"It all ended in ashes. I used to wear bow ties, and Jim told me not to. 'People won't take you seriously,' he said. I said, 'Are you kidding? On the Connally campaign?' "

"John Connally was a commanding figure and every bit as good a stump performer as Reagan," says Engberg. "He could get up and really capture a crowd. He rarely looked at a note. But he wasn't very good with common people. The gag was that if there were two thousand voters in an industrial plant, for instance, he would head immediately for the executive office to meet the president and vice-president. The line was that he peaked the day he announced.

"When he gave his geopolitical speech he would roll off the trouble spots of the world, the Strait of Hormuz, Yemen, the docks of Yokohama, Canada, whatever. One day Brady says, 'This guy oughta be the Rand-McNally candidate for president.' Jim had a lot of regard for Connally, but he wasn't above cracking jokes behind his back."

(Jim had a lot of respect for Mrs. Connally too. "She's a sharp lady," says Jim. The Connallys have a relationship like the Reagans—demonstrably close. They often hold hands.)

The culmination of the geopolitical speech went: "I believe in free trade, but I believe in fair trade. We sit here—the largest market in the world—access to or the denial of access to our markets can make or break a manufacturing nation. I want a leader who will stand up to the Japanese and tell them unless they open their markets to us, they better be prepared to sit in their Toyotas on the docks of Yokohama, eating their Mandarin oranges and watching their Sony television sets. CUZ THEY AIN'T ACOMIN' IN HERE!"

"That always brought the house down," says Jim. "He was almost like Elmer Gantry."

"We reporters would repeat parts of this speech like a Greek chorus," says Mary Leonard.

"Jim was always of very good cheer," says Engberg. "He knew how to take his licks. He never turned against the reporters." Jim often went out to dinner with them on the road. "He always ordered on the expensive side of the menu," says Engberg, "and waited for the press to pick up the tab. Dinner was for having a good time, and laughing about the day's events."

On the campaign plane, "in North Carolina," says Jim, "we had a chatty pilot who kept pointing out the Snake River so many times it became a joke." Brady began to do a takeoff of a "Bob and Ray" routine with Jim Dickenson in which a bored radio interviewer keeps asking the same questions of a long-winded zoology professor. Brady would begin: "Ladies and gentlemen, I'd like to call your attention to the fact we are now passing over the southern [or northwestern, or Empire State] branch of the Snake River, the world's longest waterway, which flows through or touches on no fewer than some twenty-three states and some fourteen provinces as it wends its majestic way from the polar ice cap to the Gulf of Mexico."

Then the questions, all designed to show that the interviewer hadn't been listening: "Perfesser, this is a pretty long waterway, isn't it?"

"That's right. It's the world's longest waterway."

"I suppose it flows through a lot of states and provinces, doesn't it?"

"That's right. It flows through no fewer than twenty-three states and fourteen provinces." And so on.

When Engberg first saw Jim Brady about a year after the shooting he was concerned about how to approach him. He didn't know how much damage Jim had sustained. "I went up to him and said, 'Jim, I don't know whether you remember me, but I covered the Connally campaign.' "

"I sure do," Jim interrupted him. "You're Eric Engberg."

"Then," says Engberg "I asked, 'By the way, Jim, what's that body of water outside there?' "

"That's the Snake River," Jim said.

"Then I knew he was gonna be okay," says Engberg. "That he had the same faculties and sense of humor as before."

"In retrospect," says John Connally, "when Ronald Reagan announced, it was over. He had the support of the Republican party at the working precinct level. People forget that Reagan almost took the nomination in 1976—that's how powerful he was."

They thought they had a good chance to stop the Reagan juggernaut in South Carolina, and they poured all their resources into that effort. "Those were great days," said Connally. "It was an open primary, anybody could vote. We thought it was a good testing ground. We had more support than Reagan did—that of the governor, of Senator Strom Thurmond. We were treated enormously well by the people of South Carolina. We had no complaints. But for the last fifteen years Reagan had become more than a candidate. He was a symbol. I had no choice but to try to appeal to the same constituency he had. No matter how hard we worked we couldn't prevail. And Reagan had the same amount of effort going in all fifty states."

Connally intended to be a one-term president. "There isn't going to be any second term for me," he told Engberg. "I'm going to put in the kinds of policies this country needs." "He proposed a stronger defense, a pro-business program with tax incentives, but with a lot of federal regulation. Connally is not a hands-off guy," notes Engberg.

"Jim Brady had a good background," says John Connally. "He was well schooled in government and had a vast store of knowledge. We asked him his judgment constantly, and his judgment was unerringly good. We depended on him a great deal. He was my press secretary, but also an adviser.

"Everyone who traveled with him was fond of him. Nellie and I particularly appreciated his talents. He was always in good humor. He has a tremendous wit and political instincts.

"The press liked him and if there was a difficulty with a policy they would express themselves about it to Jim. His antennae were long and sensitive to the needs of the press. And that is extremely important. The candidate gets tired and the press covering him gets equally tired, because the candidate tends to repeat himself day after day. It's difficult to write favorably about the candidate in that situation. So you try to see that members of the press are as comfortable as possible. One of the great values Jim had was he was always sensitive to their physical well-being, and aware of their professional needs. He unfailingly met their needs with sympathy and a high sense of good humor.

"He worked with his peers in exemplary fashion. I never saw him off balance or disturbed. He had an amazing mental equilibrium. If he was ever angry he didn't show it. All in all he absolutely did a superior job. My lack of success was in no way the fault of Jim Brady."

After Connally was shot and wounded in 1963, he took a fatalistic view, and he refused the Secret Service protection he could have had during his presidential campaign. "I just think if people want to commit a crime they'll find a way to do it. Hinckley could just as easily have dropped a hand grenade."

But, "not having Secret Service protection created problems," says Engberg, "because for one thing the Secret Service sort of provides a skeleton of organization for a candidate.* Connally's motorcade was stopped by Reagan's Secret Service at a North Carolina airport once, and we had to wait while Reagan's entourage rolled right past us. Connally got out of his car and stood, watching, hands on his hips, with his ten-gallon Stetson on, and his jaw thrust about four feet beyond his nose. 'Where were they in Dallas?' he'd say. Others thought it was partly a political decision, to show how brave and strong he was, and how weak and old was Reagan."

In addition, the campaign labored under a public perception of Connally his aides never could change: that he was a wealthy wheeler-dealer, a Texan in the mode of Lyndon Johnson. That he had been acquitted of taking a bribe from the Milk Producers' Association while he was governor didn't help. Connally announced he wouldn't take matching federal campaign funds, "which reinforced the idea he was a wealthy fat cat who didn't need the funds," says Rhatican. "In addition," says Republican political consultant Ron Walker, "there was no party infrastructure out there supporting Connally." The Republican party infrastructure was for Reagan.

John Connally III, who worked full time in the campaign and sometimes served as his father's surrogate at events, says,

*"The Secret Service provides vehicles and drivers," says Jim Dickenson. "They handle press credentials, help with advance work, and share the pro rata cost of the campaign plane."

"Jim Brady was a wonderful guy to deal with. He was so terribly smart—bright and intuitive. He was a big bundle of feelings—a real emotional type in the sense he was able to grasp the sensitive issues of the people in politics. The commitment the staff makes to a candidate is almost Herculean, and people take what they do very seriously. It's like a quest for the Holy Grail. This produces a tinderbox situation.

"The job of the press secretary is that of trying to translate internal positions of the campaign to an external expression that is consistent and appropriate. That's why the press secretary is so important. And Jim was not only a press functionary. He was a member of the inner circle and was consulted about most issues in the campaign and was an adviser. He was particularly helpful because he was such a sensitive man—his mental acuity was tremendous.

"And he had a great sense of humor which is just absolutely critical when things take on such an aura of importance even when they're not, and people become ponderous about matters that aren't. Jim helped keep us on an even keel.

"Jim's attempts to pick up the staff, I think, were attempts to pick himself up at the same time. He had, during the campaign, moments of depression—when he questioned his contributions. We all had them when we wondered if what we were doing was right. There were times at the very end Jim was concerned he wasn't able to help my father more. There was a great frustration on the part of people who believed in my father—wanting to contribute to his victory—and the level of their anxiety was directly related to their ability to contribute."

One problem they picked away at was how to "communicate to people how sensitive my father is to people," he says. "So once Jim shows up with this whole bagful of little animals. He called them 'wuppets.' The idea was to hand them out with little messages on them. 'Connally for President,' for instance. 'How about "Connally loves you?" ' Jim suggested, in jest, of course. I thought it was great, it was hilarious. Although we never did figure out how to translate the idea to public use."

But wuppets started appearing everywhere, in the office, on the plane. "Their gestation time is three days," says Jim. "Put three of them in a drawer and before you know it you'll have a drawerful of wuppets." "Jim always had such a way with children," says Dave Parker. "My children still refer to him as 'the wuppet man.' "

Howell Raines of *The New York Times* wrote, "Connally's principal campaign contribution to South Carolina was to introduce Gucci shoes to South Carolina villages that knew them not." He was referring to Jim. "Jim Wooten [ABC News] dubbed him 'Diamond Jim' because of that and because he had that quality of enjoying himself," says Mary Leonard.

A few days before the South Carolina primary was Texas Independence Day and Jim cooked his chili for the campaign crew in the kitchen of the Capitol Inn Motel. "It was near the end and we needed that uplifting," says Mike Crockett. "Jim was wearing this T-shirt that was two sizes too small, dishing out his chili. We asked him, 'Where are the beans?,' and he was astonished that somebody would even mention beans."

"On primary day when the returns came in, it was a deep disappointment," says young Connally. "Our concern was how my father would view it. We were wondering how are we going to tell him, 'We've got to get out of this.' He came in and said, 'Well, fellows, I guess that's it.' Then he said, 'We took on the champ and he licked us.' I was extremely proud of him at that moment—as proud as I've ever been of him, and there have been many times I have been very proud of him. The way he accepted it without bitterness or rancor. It was a question of whether to continue this as an ego trip, or to face the facts and get out. It was us or Reagan, and Reagan beat us."

Reagan won the primary with 54 percent of the vote to Connally's 30 percent. "Connally won one convention delegate," says Mary Leonard, "The twelve-million-dollar delegate' they called her. She voted for John Anderson at the convention." "Twelve million for one delegate is excessive," says Jim.

"Those last days of the campaign were good," says Connally "and it was sad when I had to withdraw. I immediately called Reagan to recommend he take Jim on."

When John Kolbe, old friend from the Ogilvie days, read that Connally had dropped out, "I thought, 'Oh, poor Jim. He's out of a job again. What is he going to do now?' I don't think it was more than three days later that I saw some little item attributed to Reagan spokesman Jim Brady. I was just stunned.

'Boy, does he move fast,' I said to myself."

"What I remember most about Jim was his professionalism in doing his job," says Julian Reed. "Even when things began to look less promising, particularly in South Carolina in our last days as we were closing down our campaign. He was a very good source of strength and comfort to Connally himself. His demeanor and good humor helped keep Connally on course during a difficult period."

"Jim left a poem for Governor Connally when he left," says Katherine Williams, Connally's secretary. "He told him to read it that night."

On a trip to Mexico when Reagan was president-elect, Eric Engberg asked Jim how he was getting along. "Well, I think this president will get as much done, but it won't be as much fun."

CHAPTER TWELVE

"The O and W"

"Jim came home from South Carolina and the Connally campaign by way of Texas the next week, wearing his new Lucchese boots and a Stetson," says Sarah.

"Let's go to the Eastern Shore," he greeted her. "I need to get away." While Sarah got a babysitter and packed up, Jim went shopping and brought home two mopeds to take on their trip. He was up to his old tricks. "Here we were down to our last penny," says Sarah, "and Jim spends twelve hundred dollars on two mopeds."

"When Connally dropped out," says Don Rumsfeld, "I tried to get Jim to come to Searle again—and he was close to coming, too."

But on the third day at the shore, Jim got a call from Edwin Meese, Ronald Reagan's longtime aide, now campaign chief of staff, "asking him if he were interested in working for the Reagan campaign," says Sarah, "saying they needed someone on the plane to handle press queries. Of course, Jim *was* interested, and we cut our weekend short so Jim could fly out to California the next day to meet with Reagan and Meese."

"I thought Reagan was inordinately nice," says Jim. "My question was, 'Is this for real?' "

"I heard from Governor Connally about a number of people," says Ed Meese. "And he mentioned that Jim Brady was a top-flight person. Jim met with me and Bill Casey at our office on Century Boulevard in L.A. I knew immediately that here was someone I'd enjoy working with. Jim had done so many different things. He was a versatile person who could help out on our press policy, policy development, and policy research."

Jim says that he, Casey, Meese, and Nofziger went to dinner and the next morning Meese told him, "We are prepared to offer you a job." "As what?" Jim claims he said. "Paint the house? Sweep up after the convention? I kept waiting for the words 'press secretary' to come tripping across his tongue, but they didn't." "That will evolve," said Meese. "Here you've been the commander of a destroyer, then all of a sudden you're a laundry boy," Jim told *The Washington Post*'s Bill Peterson. But Jim accepted the offer and went home "to brief the KGB [Sarah]," he says.

"Jim started traveling three or four days a week," says Sarah. "He was always home on weekends." They used their mopeds to visit friends in the neighborhood on those weekends, like the Coles. "They rode around on them together," says Brandy Cole. "Papa Bear, Momma Bear, and Baby Bear."

"Jim was really hired for a new position of briefing the press on various issues," says Meese, "and he pepped things up out there [on the campaign]." (His title was director of public affairs and research.) "He had a tremendous knowledge of Washington, the Hill, the executive branch. And he was able to recall anecdotes about his experiences in those places that were helpful for us who hadn't had the Washington experience. He was a valuable resource."

"The firing of Jim Lake created a vacuum and the necessity for a Jim Brady," says newsman David Hoffman. "They needed someone to deal with press who knew the issues and could explain Reagan's positions in detail. Jim was advertised as a traveling press person."

CBS's Bill Plante had been covering Ronald Reagan since October 1979. "Jim came in to brief on foreign policy but his role grew and he wound up being a traveling spokesman. After Sears and Lake left they floundered around bringing on board old pals from California.

"On the campaign you never felt Jim was an adversary. We

viewed him as somewhat detached by virtue of working for Connally and others. He qualified as a pro, rather than a rabid partisan. There's a tendency to trust the pros to a far greater degree than the true believers."

"I was the new wunderkind," says Jim. "Finally there was someone coming aboard who knew what was going on presswise. There was a childishness about the campaign. When Reagan didn't want to answer a question, nobody pushed him. I could get him to answer things he didn't want to answer. I'd say, 'It ain't in the bag yet, sir. It's winnable, but we've got to play at one hundred percent of our ability.' "

On the campaign plane, Jim, and Plante, a wine connoisseur, established "a wine cellar" in the compartment above Plante's seat, "always with three or four bottles of wine in it." And on Saturday mornings back in Washington, Plante took Jim by Eagle Wine and Liquor for wine tastings with wine consultant Doug Burdette, "until it was time to go to Nathan's for lunch," says Burdette.

Peter Hannaford, Mike Deaver's PR-firm partner, dipped in and out of the campaign and first met Jim in Michigan during the primary. "I didn't think I was going to like him. I regarded the Connally campaign as quixotic and so disdained Connally and anybody who had the bad sense to hire on to his campaign.* But I had known Jim all but two minutes and I liked him immediately. We were bouncing around in some funny van which was in the motorcade going into Detroit. Jim started reminiscing about party activists and I was in stitches. We had the best time laughing all the way to the hotel.

"My impression came to be that Jim thought of the Connally campaign as an assignment—a good professional opportunity. I was always puzzled as to how he could have made the transfer overnight. It was as though he'd been a Reaganite forever." Jim's message, says Hannaford, "is that you have to have a sense of humor about yourself. He was so realistic—so realistic. He fit in very easily. He had a serious mind, too, which came through."

Lou Cannon of *The Washington Post,* and author of *Rea-*

*Hannaford and the other Reaganites had read the polls that showed John Connally to have so many negatives as to be unelectable. "He couldn't spend enough money to overcome them," says Hannaford. "And he continually sent his message to the wrong people—to the Fortune Five Hundred and to his Wall Street friends."

gan, met Brady on Jim's first trip. "Someone said to me, because I was reporting all the time on staff, that Brady was pretty good. I got him aside to talk to and I remember he was appalled by the loosey-goosey way they ran the press operation and the lack of substantive information. Also the way the candidate liked to wing things. He was a little wide-eyed at the way the place operated. Here Jim has just come from the losing Connally campaign where he had a lot of professionals around him, and here's this guy on a roll. He'd never encountered someone quite like Reagan."

Cannon once wrote, "Ronald Reagan never met a statistic he didn't like." Reagan had this fey collection of statistics and stories and examples, many of which just didn't stand up to close examination at all. But he believed in them and repeated them often. "What was frustrating in covering the campaign," Cannon says, "was that they'd have what they wanted to say. Then a question would be raised and they couldn't substantiate it to us. Sometimes because it was wrong, but even when it was right they couldn't back things up.

"Brady was wary of me, but what impressed me was that he did try to get information to me. And he knew it had to be in the same news cycle, not a day later as the staff had operated before. I was impressed with his answering me within an hour. And I got more than the statement—I got the meaning behind it. He generally somewhat improved the statement. What he provided was basic information. He was pretty professional and they didn't have a lot of that. On the Reagan campaign, there was no idea of what you needed—what constitutes a news story. Getting substantive information was a problem and Brady improved that and beefed that up."

"Jim could articulate the official line of the Reagan campaign," says Howell Raines, "in a way the others couldn't."

Says Jim, "There's nothing more dangerous than an idle reporter with a typewriter, who has a certain amount of space to fill. A stop at my desk on the plane was compulsory if you were going to write about the event. I'd tell them why we were going to stop in this town, what the political significance of the stop was, and maybe weave in a story Reagan had told. God, he could tell stories."

Jim was not immediately accepted by all the Reaganites. "There was resentment about Brady," says Cannon, "but this was a group of people who'd been with Ronald Reagan a long time. Brady's from the outside, and he has good relationships with some of the reporters. Their having been the guardians of access to the candidate, it was natural."

The arrival of Brady on the scene also coincided with an increasing number of negative news stories about Reagan. Some insiders who weren't thrilled about widening their circle to include anybody, especially a newcomer fresh from the camp of a competing candidate, tended to blame Jim for this turn of events. But what was happening at this time was that it was becoming startlingly clear to reporters that Ronald Reagan, much to their amazement, was very probably going to become the Republican nominee and they began to take a closer, harder look at him. "It was just about this time," says Cannon, "that everyone was writing articles about Reagan's screwups. In April and May Reagan got quite hot about it. And there was the initial suspicion that Jim was somehow responsible." "What I think we're seeing in what's going on is a little journalistic incest," Reagan said.

Political reporter David Hoffman, who was then with Knight-Ridder, now with *The Washington Post*, says, "There began to be stories questioning Reagan's facts. CBS did a spot comparing what Reagan said with the facts. My assignment was to do long pieces about the issues he was raising. 'What would Reagan do—what kind of president would he be?' " Two very bright young men were on the plane and assigned to handle questions about the issues, "but their answers were unsatisfactory. They weren't press people. And the longtime Reaganites were sycophants. They gave soft advice. Jim was an outsider and a professional. He understood exactly what our needs were.

"That's where Jim Brady was valuable. He brought the needed texture and his Roth background. The main question about Reagan was: Can he reconcile cutting taxes, a buildup of defense, and a balanced budget. As the campaign went on, there was a big question about whether that was possible. Everybody said it couldn't be done. But the supply-side school said, yes, it could be. If you cut taxes you'd gain revenue rather than lose it because there'd be more prosperity and that would pour money into the tax coffers. Suddenly a tax cut doesn't cost anything. It's the politics of a free lunch."

George Bush called it "voodoo economics," words he later dined on as Reagan's vice-president.

"At least Jim could plausibly explain how it would work," says Hoffmann. "He believed it and still does. 'Here's how it will work,' he said, and he sold the tax-cut idea." On one trip, says Hoffman, "Jim had spent the day with me explaining this stuff and that night he and I had a long drinking session. We spent until two in the morning talking about the Republicans and Reagan.

"Now I can see how wrong they were. The analysis was correct, but the solution was wrong. At a crucial point Jim was the explainer of the theoretical tax-cut policy. It wasn't his fault; it was his role to tell a bunch of reporters how it would work."

But Jim says today, "Supply-side has been working. It really doesn't have much to do with the deficit. The Congress is responsible for that."

"Jim understands public versus private information," says Hoffman. "He was always performing a defining function. He was always the spokesman. Jim constantly disseminated information as long as you were with him. He understood a lot of levels to play on."

About this time there was a small battle brewing within the campaign on whether to come out for going back to using the gold standard. "They decided not to and I think wisely," says Hoffman. "Reagan was already perceived as a right-winger. They needed to downplay extremist things." At a time when Reagan was said to still be considering the gold standard, Hoffman quoted Brady as saying, "It's not going to be an issue—not even a peripheral issue—in this campaign."

"After Jim came on the campaign," adds Hoffman, "I told him naïvely, 'I have yet to see Ronald Reagan up close in a private session.' In May at a private, off-the-record reception at the Crystal Country Club in Michigan, Jim told me I would be at Reagan's table. I thought it would be swell! We'll get an up-close look at him. But the funny thing is, Reagan is no different in private than the anecdotal storyteller he is out on the stump. He's a back-and-forth kind of guy who loves small talk—not a strong intellectual bent there. He was just telling stories. He didn't ask us what we thought about the campaign or what we thought his chances were. He was charming and genial, sincere and personable; and he didn't want to engage any of us in any way. There is no real private Ronald Reagan that is different than the public Ronald Reagan."

"Oh, my," says Ronald Reagan, "Jim came aboard and he was immediately front and center and very much a part of the team, and, yes, first of all he had a great sense of humor, but he also had that great gift of knowing whether to push on something or let it die, you know—that twenty-four-hour story that you wanted to correct and you found it was just better if you didn't say anything, it would go away. He had a great instinct for that. We were all a tight little team in the front of the campaign plane, and when he came aboard I immediately met him and he was in the inner circle from then on." Jim's sense of humor was not irreverent, says Reagan. "It was always good humor and always fit the occasion.

"I can visualize him there on the campaign plane . . . when something broke that we had to discuss. . . . And he was a great voice of reason on how to handle it, and we all turned to him for his analysis of what should be the procedure."

By June, when Missy was to graduate from high school in Chicago, Jim was immersed with Reagan in California. "So Scott and I went to Chicago," says Sarah. "Missy was so disappointed that Jim couldn't be there, so she told her mother that she really wanted me and Scott to come."

Jim's little press team, Mitchell Stanley, Mark Weinberg and Kathy Ahern, had closed down the Connally shop, and in May Jim pressed them into service as volunteers for Reagan.

"After Jim Lake was fired and Bill Casey came on as campaign manager, the headquarters in Washington was dismantled, and we moved to Alexandria," says Kim Hoggard. "I was the only press-office person on the ground at the time. I was answering press questions, arranging press travel, running a news-clipping service. When Jim came on he called and suggested we have a luncheon meeting. At the appointed hour up drives Jim Brady in this Jeep, with Mitchell Stanley, Mark Weinberg, and Kathy Ahern. There was no way we could all get into the Jeep, so Jim says, 'Well, we'll meet you at Chadwick's.' Jim sat there all through lunch and cracked jokes the entire time. I said to myself, 'I don't get this. Who is this guy?' The purpose of the lunch was to introduce me to his three volunteers who were to help shore me up with all the press responsibility I had." "Yes, we were the pariahs from the Connally campaign," says Stanley.

After South Carolina Reagan still had a number of primaries to go through, but after his 48 percent win in the Illinois primary on March 18, it was almost a walk to the Republican nomination. Bush won the Connecticut primary on March 25, but Reagan won the New York primary the same day. And in April Reagan won most of the delegates in the Pennsylvania primary. In May, Bush won the Michigan primary, but Reagan added enough delegates to his total there to assure winning the nomination, and Bush withdrew several days later before the Ohio, New Jersey, and California primaries on June 3.

> On June 18 in Lubbock, Texas, John W. Hinckley, Jr., bought two boxes of .22-caliber ammunition for $9.75 from Leon Langford, owner of the Empire Pawn Shop. One of them contained twelve Devastator bullets, which were designed, it said on the box, "to deliver maximum energy at normal shooting ranges."

In June Lyn Nofziger rejoined Reagan and was press secretary through the convention and the general-election campaign. "When Nofziger returned to the campaign he was greeted well by the press," says David Hoffman, "because he was an insider. Jim was never considered an insider. In the fall campaign, Jim was more the research director and less of a press guy. Reagan's advisers were confident that Lyn would be discreet. With Nofziger there Brady never had a chance" to prove himself as press secretary.

"There was a certain sense of rivalry between Jim and Lyn," says Doug Bandow. "There was some tension there. Jim was at first the interloper." Nofziger was also the "key political person on the plane," says Meese.

In *The Washington Post*, Myra MacPherson wrote on June 5: "There has been an attempt to add more Washington experience to the campaign with James Brady, a veteran press and public relations adviser who has worked for former budget director James T. Lynn, Delaware Sen. William Roth Jr. and John B. Connally during his unsuccessful try this year. Brady appears easygoing, gets along well with the press and coins some good one-liners that sometimes find a way into a Reagan speech. One of them this week was 'The Jimmy Carter dollar has become the J.C. Penny.' "

"Yes, I finally got that one in after three tries," says Jim. Other Reagan lines he provided: "It takes the Congress two months to make minute rice." And—"We've got to weed out the greedy in order to help the needy."

But, says Jim, "Reagan was the best writer for himself." And one of his best was "It's a recession when your neighbor loses his job; it's a depression when you lose your job; and it's recovery when Jimmy Carter loses his job."

"That's vintage Reagan," says Jim. "Just leave him alone with his three by five cards and he comes up with the best stuff. He'd say, 'I gotta write a get-off line now,' harking back to his days as an actor."

About a dozen people worked in Reagan's headquarters at first. That spring Jim was instrumental in getting the Reagan operation to move its small Alexandria headquarters to the one Connally was just vacating in Arlington. Now that the primaries were over they were no longer constricted to the federal matching-fund spending ceiling and they could spend money again. They needed more space. Upon Jim's recommendation Otto Wolff became the administrator of the building as he had done for Connally. As time went on the number of workers increased, and after the convention the national headquarters was moved from California to Arlington.

"I next saw Jim at Arlington headquarters after the primaries," says Kim Hoggard. "He was as crazy as ever—blowing his horn. There was some panic situation and he said the only thing he could do was to talk to Governor Reagan to get the straight story on the matter. I'm dialing the ranch and it's busy, busy. Meanwhile, Jim starts telling me a story. I get Joe Holmes on the other line, then I hear, 'This is Ronald Reagan.' I told Jim and he looked at me, his eyes wide open."

But, says Jim, "I was very comfortable with the governor. I wasn't in awe of him." And Jim had learned that Reagan's amiable temperament was for real. "He got mad and threw a tantrum on the plane once," says Jim. "All the old-timers said, 'Jesus, that's the maddest we've ever seen him.' But it didn't even raise a hair on the back of my neck. I thought, 'There's more anger in Connally's little finger than in the whole man.' "

Martin Anderson, who was Reagan's senior political adviser on domestic and economic matters, had worked for Ronald Reagan since 1975. He met Jim on Jim's first trip out with Reagan—to Dallas. "On the plane came Jim Brady, who sat down and explained to me all the ins and outs of cowboy boots and the fact that Lucchese boots were the only ones to consider buying. Brady came into the campaign," says Anderson, "and was regarded as a Connally legacy. But within a few days Jim adapted very well, and very rapidly built up trust among the Reagan people. It was very difficult to be accepted in that situation where most of the senior people had been with Reagan for years, and Jim did an enormously effective job in forming good working relations. He was trustworthy and he was smart about research and policy developments, which was very unusual for a press secretary. It was unusual in that Jim was participating in developing the policies he was explaining to the press. In trying to develop ideas, I would go to him early. He was a great source of information and he knew what the implication of the policy would be—how the press would receive it. Because the press would say, 'Really, you're going to do that. How interesting.' Meanwhile, they're writing it all down. In the evenings, we did what Ronald Reagan did. We worked on yellow legal pads—through the evening. Brady was a hard worker. Our nights out were rare—memorable, but rare."

"It is grueling on the road, pretty arduous," says Michele Davis. "For three months we had no creature comforts."

"The scene on the campaign plane," says Anderson, "was tense. It was one third hard work, one third holy crusade, and one third circus. As the plane took off, Jim would play 'On the Road Again,' and either Nancy Reagan or, if she wasn't on board, a stewardess would roll an orange down the aisle, attempting to bowl it all the way to the back of the plane. It was very difficult." Sometimes Reagan himself did the honors. "I hate to say this but I think one of the very few people who did it was Ronald Reagan, with a little flip of his arm." "I did it, too," says Jim. "When the orange had been bowled, and the plane was still on takeoff, a couple of TV cameramen usually surfed down the aisle on the plane's plastic safety-instruction cards."

"I never saw Jim and Reagan sitting and talking about ponderous issues," says Michele Davis, "But there were many times when he'd go to the front cabin to talk to Reagan. He and Ronald Reagan liked each other. When the president would roll an orange down the aisle, Jim would be cracking one-liners at him." (Davis followed Jim to the Reagan campaign.)

"Leadership '80" was a 727 United charter. "The food was excellent," says Anderson. "It was a happy place. There was a real spirit of independence on that plane. I never saw anyone wear a seat belt. On takeoff everyone was sitting on the arms of their seats or standing in the aisle having a drink. One stewardess tried in vain to put some order back into the plane, but after one raucous takeoff, she finally gave up."

Richard Allen, Reagan's foreign-policy adviser, met Jim on the same Texas trip. "I remember meeting him and liking him instantly. His humor is arcane and there's always some meaning in it. It turned out we lived around the corner from each other in Arlington. He had these boots on and he'd tell me why I'd be a spiritually better person if I had boots.

"Jim kinda came on and just blended in—a gear that meshed without a sound. I was watching him to see how he'd behave. The first day we had a foreign policy or defense statement we were working on, and Jim said, 'If I were you I'd do it this way.' And it was better.

"Jim had a very natural relationship with Reagan. Neither one of them has any pretensions—there's no mask there. What you see is what you get. Jim saw a lot of him. There was an almost total absence of jockeying around Reagan, even the times he'd be alone on the bus. Jim knew there were times he should be left alone."

Because of Jim, says Allen, "we wound up at some improbable places for awful food. He always wanted to go out to some wild and crazy place, which always turned out to be average."

Reagan spent the hiatus between the last primary and the Republican convention "healing some party wounds" by holding fund-raisers so the losers could pay off their campaign debts. And he made up with Gerald Ford who believed that "Reagan's reluctant campaigning had cost him the election in 1976."

At the convention in Detroit Reagan's major piece of business was choosing his vice-president, and although Reagan said he really wanted his friend Senator Paul Laxalt, the choice had boiled down to George Bush and Gerald Ford. His advisers had reservations about Bush, but they were worried about the problems raised by having a former president in the job. Already the jokes were making the rounds: "Ford would be president before nine, after five and on weekends." In an interview with Walter Cronkite in which Ford appeared to be setting the terms, Ford said he would "have to play a meaningful role." In the end Ford took himself out of it, leaving the way for Reagan to choose Bush. While Cronkite was interviewing Ford, Sarah, at home, saw Tom Brokaw interviewing Jim, calling him a "key figure in the campaign." Brokaw said, "Jim tells me not to believe everything I've heard. I'm going to go with Jim and not jump to any conclusion."

"Jim was in the room with Reagan when these discussions were going on," says Sarah. "I could tell he was in the midst of things."

"Ford the co-president," says Jim. "I said, 'Be serious, Governor. We don't need it to win. And you don't want a co-president, nor does Ford want to be co-president.' "

"I remember seeing Jim at the convention," says John Kolbe, Jim's Illinois political friend, now political editor at the *Phoenix Gazette.* "I finally found him in the press center of the RenCen [Reagan's headquarters hotel, the Renaissance Center]. We chatted for about twenty minutes and people were coming up to him all the time. It was clear to me he was already well settled into the job and seemed to be enjoying it, just by the way reporters came up to him. It was clear he was trusted and liked from the banter and repartee that passed between them.

"I asked him what was going to happen after the convention. Were they going to broaden the campaign to include a wider political base? And Jim made a very wise remark. 'You gotta dance with the girl who brung ya,' he said."

"There was a rumor at the convention that Nofziger was trying to put Brady in my job," says Pete Teeley. "I can't believe it wasn't true. But Bush made it clear I was his press secretary. From Jim's standpoint I know his druthers would have been to stay on the presidential campaign."

"At the convention," laughs Bruce Thompson, "Jim and I labored hard behind the scenes to make sure that the Kemp-Roth part of the Republican party platform was rewritten to become Roth-Kemp. And when it was endorsed it *was*

Roth-Kemp. During the Reagan campaign and during the convention Jim would call me about Reagan's tax policy. 'They're saying it would only help the rich,' he'd say. I'd start out explaining and he'd say, 'No, no, no. Give me two sentences.' Two days later you'd see it pop up. These calls were made on the run. He was always on the run." Jim Brady had no converting of Reagan to do re the Roth-Kemp tax-cut proposals. Although not a tax cutter in 1976, in 1978 he was sold on it by Jack Kemp as an incentive and balm to the economy.

After the convention Jim and Sarah spent a weekend at the beach with Pete and Sandy Teeley. "Jim had his new Jeep along and we took a ride down the beach but he didn't let enough air out of the tires and we got stuck," says Teeley. "By the time we got some guys to help dig us out the incoming tide was about a foot from the wheels."

In August the Reagan campaign took on Joe Canzeri "the popular longtime travel aide for Nelson Rockefeller." "I was the tour director," says Canzeri, "in charge of the whole road show—moving people around according to the schedule." Canzeri went out of his way to arrange for special treats from time to time: Lobsters once, and in Erie, Pennsylvania, he ordered thirty large pizzas from Bernice's—each one individually inspected by the Secret Service.

After the convention, a residence for the Reagans was established at Wexford, Virginia, in the home Jacqueline Kennedy had refurbished for the Kennedys' getaway in 1962. The Reagans began weekending there, instead of California, so they could more easily campaign in the Northeast, the South and the upper Midwest—their targeted areas.

"There was a certain amount of general grumbling about the influx of Bush people into the campaign after the convention," says David Hoffman, although Doug Bandow feels that "Jim Baker was recognized as being a very bright person and a good organizer."

"Most of the work of the campaign was done on the ground," says Meese, who was second in command to Bill Casey. And indeed it was—the nitty-gritty, boring stuff, that is: the administration of the campaign, paying salaries and bills; gathering information and writing speeches; strategizing; planning the events at which Reagan would appear; making sure there were phones and work spaces for the press. But as in the Connally campaign, those at headquarters thought they were controlling the "flying circus"; those with the candidate tended to regard those on the ground as somewhat irrelevant. After all, they were handling things moment to moment—press crises usually. Reactions to the day's news and Ronald Reagan's frequent gaffes and gaps in knowledge, in particular. They had the candidate and that was where the excitement was.

"It was the plane against Arlington," says Cannon. "The people on 'Leadership '80' thought the people in Arlington were a bunch of boobs—who were always sending them strange messages. Bill Casey ('Mumbles') was considered a bumblewit. And Meese was as sweet and disorganized as ever.

"But the view from Arlington was that the plane bunch was just a bunch of leakers. Arlington was infuriated about negative stories that would come out about Ronald Reagan. And they were jealous because we all treated Arlington as though it were irrelevant, which it largely was. Casey complained periodically about 'too many leaks.' Casey wasn't on the plane because everybody except Reagan thought he was hopeless," says Cannon. "And they wanted layers around him. Casey did one thing, though. He got the campaign back on an even keel financially. He was merciless in firing people but he did get the campaign in shape."

One reporter remembers that occasionally Casey would meet Reagan at some airport. "Casey'd be driven out on the tarmac in a big, black limousine and Reagan would get off the plane to talk to him about God knows what."

"They had the misconception they were running the campaign," says Canzeri, "whereas anybody who knows—knows who's got the body's got the power. Once the primaries are over and you go into the general election, it's a whole different ball game. The psychology flip-flops. Now you're really running for the big enchilada."

"They'd call us from Arlington," says Jim, "and say, 'You have to do this or you have to do that.' We'd ignore them."

On the ground in Arlington, a crony and aide to Ed Meese, retired Admiral Robert Garrick, was named director of research and policy information and was trying to run Jim's hapless press volunteers as well. "That lunkhead," sputters one reporter.

The first day Jeanne Winnick walked into Arlington headquarters to take a job in the research and writing division under Garrick, she ran into Jim Brady, who told her, "You can't be working here. You're tanned." "I'd been told that before I started work to go to the beach, 'because when you start work you'll not see the sun again.' It was true," she says.

Garrick was in charge of circulating materials so that all the top campaign people would have input into Reagan's speeches.

There began to be a running battle between Garrick and Brady. Garrick thought he should also control Jim, and Jim had turned the avoidance of Garrick into a science. With Jim on the plane most of the time and Garrick in Arlington, it wasn't too difficult.

"Brady was most elusive," says Winnick, "especially if he knew Garrick was trying to get hold of him. Jim, having been in the Washington mix for years, really had no use for this fellow from California. It became a real tug-of-war between them." Garrick had an avocado farm in California and this was when Winnick and Jim started calling him "Admiral Avocado."

"Garrick wanted to be called 'Admiral' and he thought he was commanding a ship. If he couldn't find you at your desk, he'd doubt your sincerity and loyalty. I'd go to the ladies' room and over the loudspeaker would come 'Jeanne Winnick. Report to your office.' But Brady was not about to kowtow to him. So Garrick began to track the campaign plane using the twenty-four-hour tracking system we had so he could get Brady on the phone. In addition, using his military training he was actually calling airport towers to track the plane. Even then, Jim was sometimes 'unavailable.' "

Almost self-appointed, Admiral Garrick was "running a subterranean communications operation," says Mitchell Stanley. "When no one would tell him he was not press secretary, he became in his own mind communications czar. He was actually czar for the area around his own desk."

As the country began to focus on the upcoming Democratic convention, Reagan, out on the campaign trail, began committing the gaffes for which he was so famous. Says Lou Cannon, "Following a pattern which the Reagan team had established for doing worst when things were going best, the candidate and his staff then went out and almost blew the election before the campaign formally began."

Reagan insisted on going through with a speech in Philadelphia, Mississippi, where three civil-rights activists were murdered in 1964, telling the crowd he believed in states' rights, when the next day he was due to address a civil-rights organization, the Urban League, in New York. Speaking to the VFW in August, Reagan characterized the Vietnam War as "a noble cause," which had the effect of picking open the barely healed wounds the war had inflicted upon the country.

He sent George Bush to China to show the ticket's foreign-policy expertise, but at the same time said he would, as president, establish an official U.S. office in Taiwan, Nationalist China, an act prohibited by U.S. law.

On Labor Day, the day he and Carter both opened their campaigns for the general election ("the day we came out of the chute," says Canzeri), Reagan, who was at the Michigan State Fair, said of Carter who was in Tuscumbia, Alabama, "Now I'm happy to be here while he is opening his campaign down there in the city that gave birth to and is the parent body of the Ku Klux Klan," an untrue statement. Reagan had to apologize to Tuscumbia and Alabamians, but, says Lou Cannon, "Lyn Nofziger made matters worse, blaming the press for overplaying the story." "Nofziger literally physically shoved members of the press," says Howell Raines, "to prevent Reagan from being questioned about these subjects."

Stuart Spencer, a respected Republican campaign manager, who had managed Jerry Ford's campaign against Reagan in 1976, was brought into the campaign to calm things down and to steady Ronald Reagan for the heavy national campaign ahead. This he did, first by controlling the press's access to Reagan; then by doing everything possible to promote the nice-guy image that served Reagan so well when Carter began to make attacks on him. Carter predicted Reagan would polarize the country, separating "black from white, Jews from Christian, North from South, rural from urban." The election would decide "whether we have peace or war," he said. Reagan adopted an injured tone, saying he was "saddened" by the remarks. "I think he's a badly misinformed and prejudiced man," Reagan said.

On September 21, Reagan held a debate with John Anderson and polls showed he had helped himself with those who viewed it. Jimmy Carter declined to participate.

Five days later, on September 26, the campaign flew into Portland, Oregon, where Bill Kemp was working for the U.S. Bureau of Land Management. "I hadn't been in contact with Jim, but I took off work to go out to the hotel near the airport to see if I could see him. I was early and I found a little balcony where I could view them all when they came in. But it was such a visible spot that the Secret Service took me out of my good position to a nearby corridor, and they frisked me. I have always wished they had frisked Hinckley as they did me." Reagan's plane was delayed coming in and Bill never did get to see him that day.

It was on September 26 also that John Hinckley bought two .22-caliber pistols from Snidely Whiplash's Pawn Shop in Lubbock. The next day he flew to Washington. Then, tracking President Carter's campaign schedule, he flew to Columbus, then bused to Dayton. On October 9, when Carter was in Nashville, so was Hinckley, and he was arrested as he ran to catch a plane because the security X ray showed he was carrying three guns. After his guns were checked out and confiscated, he was fined $62.50, and released.

Two days later, while visiting his sister in Dallas, he replenished his arsenal with the purchase of two more .22-caliber Röhm revolvers and two boxes of shells, which he bought for $98.80 from Rocky's Police Equipment and Pawn Shop, owned by Isaac Goldstein. On October 17, he was in Washington again.

When California attorney Ken Khachigian came on the campaign as speechwriter in early September, he had heard of Brady. "He seemed to be getting high marks from the people in the campaign. The first time I met him he was standing by himself waiting for the campaign bus. He had a facility for being the first one out there in the morning. Within hours we hit it off. We palled around a lot. I had to work at night on speeches for the next day and wasn't as free as he was, but we had opportunities to get to the bar at night.

"We'd team up in briefing the candidate. We'd tag-team

when he would hold press conferences. Stu Spencer said, 'You two do good work.' Jim had a good PR sense and I had a good sense of issues.

"Jim was very skillful at helping reporters with their stories," says Khachigian. "He gave little political lectures on why we were where we were and what was at stake in this area. One radio reporter had to give a five-minute report three times a day. And Jim would chuckle, 'I can write her stories three times a day.' He felt pride in his control of what was being reported. Every hour he had to have fresh material. Jim was very skillful—a good propagandist. He was much more comfortable with the press than I was."

"There are no rules to the care and feeding of the press," says Jim. "You try to 'shape' their stories—now they call it 'managing the news'—but you sit down with them and show them what you're about—why we're going into this town. Then you have a pop quiz to see if they got it."

Brady told Khachigian, "Rule number one: We get them to buy us dinner every night, so at least we can eat good. And if we do it right, they won't get much out of us." "So we'd be vague, say things 'not for attribution' or 'off the record.' We were living on twenty-five dollars per diem. When a reporter pulled his notebook out one night we said, 'Sorry, we have to get back for a staff meeting.' But in between times they got a lot of stuff out of us and tons from Brady."

"The only release you get on the campaign," says Bill Plante, "is to go out every night for that, hopefully, good meal, and you just might get a little shitfaced every night but you have to get up and get going five or six hours later so you couldn't overdo too much."

Jim treated his colleagues to his Indian dancing. "He'd break into this thirty-second Indian dance," says Khachigian, "bouncing all over the place. And you always had to survive being cut to ribbons by Jim all the time. He respected people who gave as good as they got. He loved to tease.

"I never knew a guy who didn't have to work as hard as everybody else in order to make it all work. I'd be looking through the papers for speech material and Jim'd have *Bon Appétit* open, checking recipes to cook for the next time he was home. He was very serious and businesslike and professional when it was business, however."

Jim called Khachigian, who is Armenian, "The 'Menian."

" 'Hey, 'Menian,' he'd say to me." "Ken Khachigian's coming on was the greatest thing that ever happened to us," says Jim. "Hell, I thought the Armenians had all starved. I grew up eating all my Brussels sprouts because of the starving Armenians."

"Jim got along especially well with the press," says Khachigian. "By and large you enjoy them as people—you just wish you could sever the relationship with them as reporters. They can also be petty and mean. Jim would say very candid things about the governor, then chuckle. He was open even with the new guys. I don't know why he never got burned."

Plante says, "Jim went all the way in joking with us. He would join us in kidding about Reagan when Reagan got in trouble."

"Jim had a Sony Walkman—he loved those gadgets," says Khachigian. "He'd pop in a tape and be sitting back there looking past you, boogieing a little bit. He'd do his routines. He had memorized long passages of dialogue from *Semi-Tough* by Dan Jenkins. It was his way of intellectually testing you.

"Jim was constantly on. When we were in New York he dragged me to Twenty-one. 'You have to go to Twenty-one when you're in New York,' he told me. He wanted to live life to the fullest and did."

Khachigian remembers, "We were in Ohio in an awful club, just awful, and Jim accused the waiter of storing the wine next to the refrigerator coils. It was Ziggy's Continental Restaurant and it was a twenty-five-dollar cab ride to get there. After we were in the White House it all seemed so unpresidential."

Dean Reynolds recalls going with Jim and newsman Steve Neal to a Mexican restaurant. "I remember being struck by his habit of salting plain tortilla chips. Jim adopted all of Steve Neal's oddities. Neal walks around dribbling a basketball that doesn't exist, and Brady would start dribbling a nonexistent basketball. They would pass it back and forth. They presented a rather peculiar pair."

Jim had told Eddie Mahe aide Michele Davis in April, "I think something may open up on the Reagan campaign." "And after about three weeks," says Davis, "he called and said, 'C'mon over.' I interviewed with Lyn Nofziger and started as a Nofziger aide.

"Brady was sort of an information tank," continues Davis. "He was the one who would read things off the wires and would

Sarah, Jim, and Cathy Wynne on the day Jim left the hospital for good

The Washington Post

Missy, Jim, and Sarah, Christmas 1981

Jim in the bear chair with three-year-old Scott, March 1982

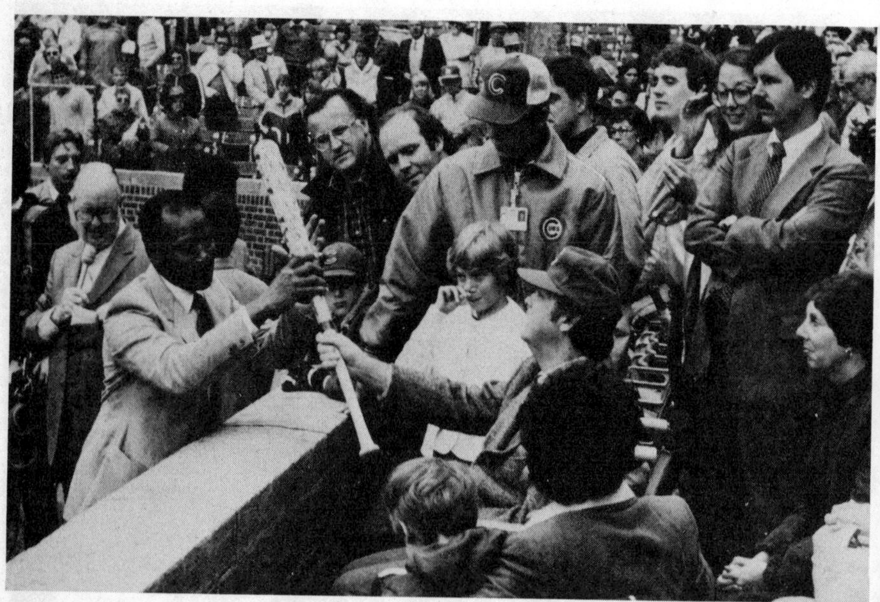

Michael Doss

Jim at Wrigley Field receiving a bat from Chicago Cub Ernie Banks, September 1982

Jim returning
to the White House,
November 1982

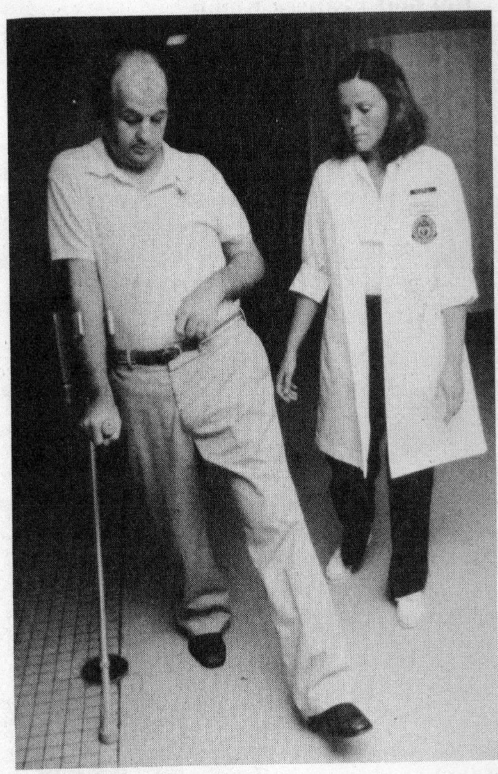

Pain and Torture
with Cathy Wynne,
1982

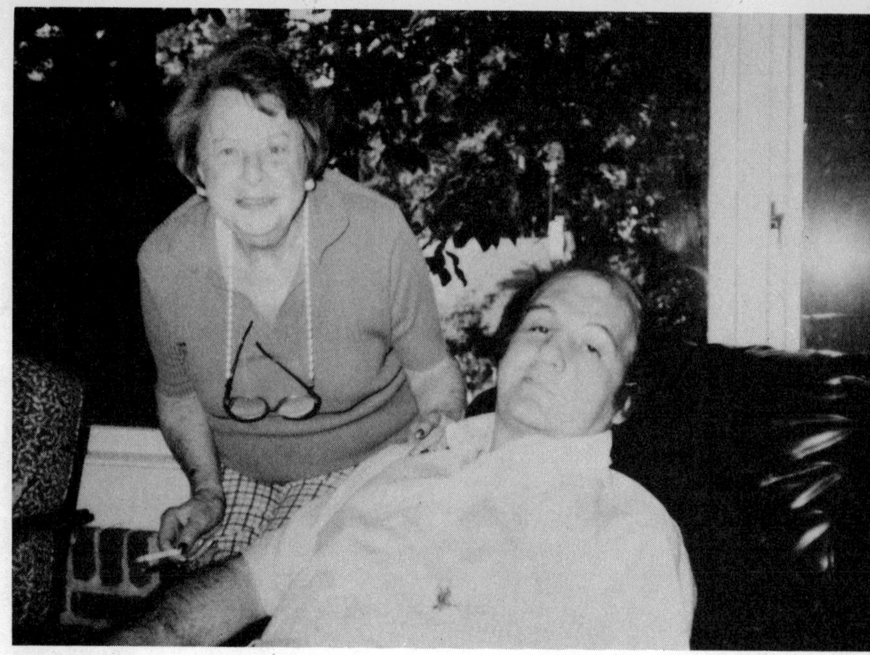

Jim and Frances Kemp
in his bear chair in "Pooh Corner,"
summer 1983

Welcome home to
Centralia,
October 1983

White House Photo by Mary Anne Fackelman

Jim at his White House desk, with Sarah, November 19, 1984

Jim, receiving the first annual
Will Rogers Humanitarian Award,
flanked by Sarah and Bob Dahlgren,
February 27, 1985

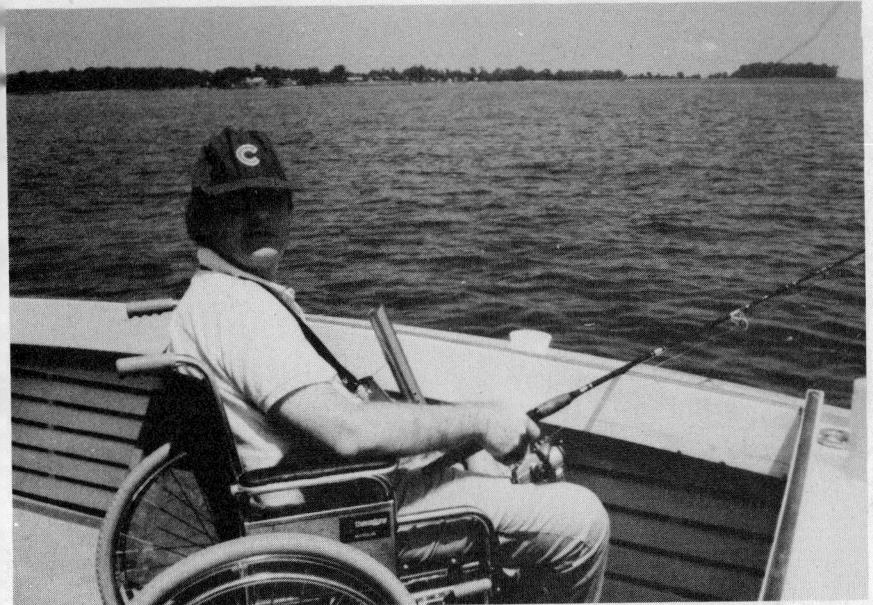

Fishing (for sharks?) on Chesapeake Bay, 1985

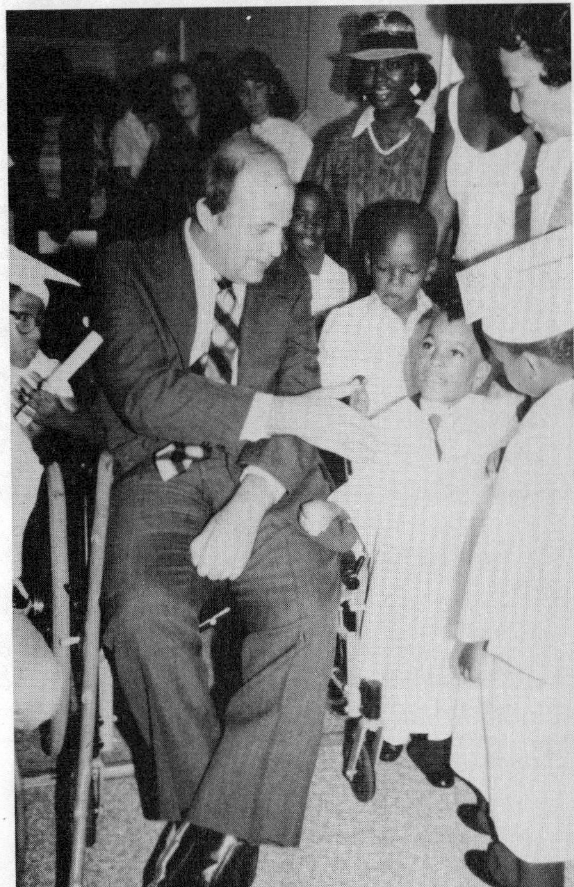

Jim greeting children at the Hospital for Sick Children, Washington, D.C., 1986

Carolou Marquet

Jim in his White House office, 1984

Bernie Boston, *Los Angeles Times*

flag them—'Hey, this will be a problem, this won't be a problem.' He would sit in on these sessions and he would always have the pithy phrase that would invariably be picked up on by the press. He was just kind of a conduit—the lofty thoughts of Marty Anderson were brought down to earth in practical terms by Brady.

"Jim would say, 'I think what Marty is trying to say is—boom!—see?' Then Ken would say, 'Here's my speech. What do you think?' And Jim'd help boil that down. He was the one to watch the news the most. He always was the person who kept us timely. He was always calling to the Arlington office to get the latest.

"On their bus tours, Brady would have on his Walkman. He would sing out 'On the Road Again.' He listened to the oddest mix of music. He loved country and western." On a bus tour through Illinois, "he broke the whole place up with his stories of what it was like to grow up in southern Illinois. He said he had the best memories of haystacks and they weren't culinary or for the cows. He began naming all the haystacks after alleged girlfriends. That one was Betty Sue, this one is Gladys Jean.

"He was saying he was the embodiment of midwestern values. Everybody, of course, guffawed. But it came through that he was at home in rural America. We went to a pig farm, I recall, and the Reagans walked through these pig stalls. Following behind them Brady would go up and snort and get the pigs squealing. We had a fun, fun time on the campaign. We were the challengers. We were the rebels. We could be outlandish," says Davis. "You could always guarantee that if you were around Brady, you'd laugh.

" 'Don't give me anything substantive that would clutter my mind,' Jim would say. He was all PR and smoke-filled rooms—the political gut work. He had great guts, he really did. And innate political sense. Working with our communications bunch, he'd say, 'What's the line of the day? This is the problem today. How can we counter it?' "

In September Jim flew home briefly to cook his chili for the 5th Annual Chili Bull, begun originally by PR consultant Susan Davis in her backyard to raise money for Children's Hospital. He had won first prize the first three years of the contest, and then was inducted into the "Chili Hall of Flame." "He came home, cooked his chili, and left it on the stove with a note for me," says Sarah. " 'Be sure to clean around the sides of the pot,' it said. 'A clean pot is a winning pot.' " He won first prize again—the use of a limousine for a night.

Marty Anderson had two young research assistants—Kevin Hopkins and Doug Bandow—who alternated on the plane. "Tweedledum and Tweedledee they called us," says Hopkins. "Or the Twins," says Bandow. They worked on the excerpts that were put into Reagan's set speech for the five or six stops they made every day. "Jim and Ken did that as well," says Hopkins. "We all did what was necessary. Jim's main responsibility was talking directly to the press as a policy expert. Jim was bothered at first that he didn't have a defined niche, but he went about the job cheerily without stepping on Lyn's or Marty's roles. He helped me personally by introducing me to people who produced a lot of economic information to us." (These included Bruce Thompson and others on Senator Roth's staff.)

"Jim took Doug and me under his wing and tried to get us involved, for which we were both grateful. He gave us challenges, and things we could learn. Things you don't learn in textbooks. Jim was often in the bars at night talking to the press, to socialize and to make sure they got their stories right.

"Nofziger and Brady were often referred to as 'the Twins,' too," says Hopkins. "When Lyn grew his beard he said he did it to distinguish himself from Brady. Everybody on the campaign was somewhat good-humored but Jim was more so than anybody. He brought his wuppets along from the Connally campaign, his little fuzzy creatures. They were about an inch high and had stickum on the bottom. They would have a ribbon on them with a message like 'Vote for Reagan.' People would wear them or put them on their desks. One morning Jim came in and found little wuppets all over his office. I did it, but never admitted it to him."

One thing Bandow and Hopkins researched was Reagan's quotations of "facts" that were coming under fire. "We found he was mostly accurate on most of his statements," avers Bandow. "Most people in the press were friendly, if cantankerous, but fair. The major problems arose when they didn't understand something—not because they were trying to screw us.

Some of them were quite perceptive, and asked questions that would put us on the spot. We needed Brady to keep the misunderstandings to a minimum.

"Jim was the one who recognized the timeliness of issues—the importance of addressing issues quickly as they arose. He always listened to an early-morning radio show and gave me a hard time when I slept in. He told me, 'That's when there's a good opportunity for you to see how things work.' Jim didn't sit back and wait for the press to show up. He went out to work with them.

"Jim was the prime originator of what we called 'the Ed Gray Award.' " Gray, it seems, although fondly regarded as "a real gentleman," says Bandow, had a penchant for doing silly, out-of-it things. "He once backed up and sat down on a tray of Baked Alaska pies. When Reagan was governor of California, Ed Gray managed to get all of the allotted state cars parked at L.A. airport. Then he couldn't remember where he had left them. He was the one who left his briefcase on the tarmac."

Jim's favorite Ed Gray story is about the time Gray took the elevator to the basement parking lot of the State Capitol in Sacramento, even though there was a sign there stating clearly "Do Not Take Elevator to Basement." The basement had been flooded by a rainstorm. Mike Deaver found Gray, hours later, waist deep in water, calling "Help me, help me!" "We all got the Ed Gray Award on occasion," says Bandow.

"Jim tried to maintain the Scarsdale diet for a while on the campaign. He had his book along with him," says Bandow, "and the stewardesses tried to cook his special things. Jim had an awful lot of charm with women. But it was a failure. There was too much temptation. We'd go to lots of receptions where the food was piled high. Jim was often out to dinner with the press and the press room always had cold cuts laid out, and so forth."

"Jim was constantly guzzling Tabs," says David Prosperi. "The joke was that Marty Anderson's two aides would invariably knock Jim's soda can over. 'Don't sit next to those guys,' he'd say. At the end of the day Jim might have one drink, and later after the news was secured at night he'd be in the hotel bar because that was the best way to find out what was going on. A lot of times, and in the general election, Jim had no time for that. He'd be working at the Xerox machine or with a typewriter making sure the next day's speech was correct vis-à-vis the place or checking facts with Marty Anderson or Nofziger.

"You could usually find Jim in the press section of the plane finding out what was going on, feeling them out. They liked him because he was honest and funny.

"Jim taught me a lot about deadlines and the individual reporters—if it was a financial speech to call *The Wall Street Journal.* He made me aware of the machinations of the media. He was like a teacher. And we got along well. We could make light of Reagan and the press knew it was not in malice. Both Jim and I felt the campaign was not the end all of life."

On October 7, in Steubenville, Ohio, Reagan proved he was still fully capable of getting himself into trouble even with his improved team. After a rally of a group of steel company executives and workers and community leaders, S.O.S. (Save Our Steel), Reagan met privately with the leaders of the group. They were concerned with foreign dumping of cheap, subsidized steel, and federal environmental regulations. Reagan commiserated with them and said that for the sake of the environment, some people in Washington believed in "no growth." "I have flown twice over Mount Saint Helens out on our West Coast," he said. "I'm not a scientist and I don't know the figures, but I just have a suspicion that that one little mountain out there in these past several months has probably released more sulfur dioxide into the atmosphere of the world than has been released in the last ten years of automobile driving or things of that kind that people are so concerned about."

Downstairs in the press room, Reagan's remarks were being played over a loudspeaker "by accident," says David Hoffman, and that had reporters perking up their ears and turning on their tape recorders. "Suddenly we were hearing this incredible monologue," says Hoffman.

"He was loose again," says Howell Raines.

Reagan went on: "Indeed there is a very eminent scientist associated with Texas A and M who has written about nature laughing at us and according to his research, if we totally eliminated all the man-made sulfur dioxide in the air today, we would still have two-thirds as much as we have because that's how much nature is releasing. I know Teddy Kennedy had fun at the Democratic Convention when he said that I had said our trees and vegetation cause eighty percent of the air pollution in this country. Well, now, he was a little wrong about what I said. First of all, I didn't say eighty percent, I said ninety-two percent, ninety-three percent, pardon me. And I didn't say air pollution. I said oxides of nitrogen. And I am right. Growing and decaying vegetation in this land are responsible for ninety-three percent of the oxides of nitrogen."*

But that was not the end. He said that the Great Smoky Mountains are so named because "that haze over those mountains are oxides of nitrogen. I think it's kind of interesting that there are some doctors that are lately investigating and experimenting that they believe that the atmosphere up there in those mountains might be beneficial to tubercular patients."

And yet there was more. He went on to talk about Santa Barbara harbor, "where we have some oil wells being drilled out in the harbor and a great organization formed to stop that. . . . There have been sixteen permanent oil slicks in the Santa Barbara Channel as long as the memory of man and far back beyond any development of oil or drilling of oil anyplace before we even knew about such things. And an English sea captain back in the 1700s anchored off the shore, woke up in the morning and wrote in his logbook, 'The sea was covered with a viscous material that when the waves moved it gave off iridescent hues.' But around the turn of the century when we did know something about oil, Santa Barbara was a great health spa. . . . And one of their advertisements at that time said in addition to salubrious climate, that the southwesterly prevailing winds blowing across a large oil slick off the coast of Santa Barbara purified the air and prevented the spread of infectious diseases."

" 'My God,' everybody around him said," says Jim. " 'Sir, you didn't have to say that.' But he believed it."

*Free nitrogen (N_2) makes up 80 percent of the air we breathe, but growing vegetation does not release nitrogen or nitrogen compounds; and except for ammonia (NH_4), decaying vegetation releases only water-soluble nitrates and nitrites into the soil. They are beneficial. Nitrogen oxide (NO) and nitrogen dioxide (NO_2) are gases emitted from autos and industrial plants. They are noxious, and are totally different from naturally existing nitrogen and nitrogen compounds. And as Lou Cannon writes in *Reagan*, Reagan "wasn't even close to being right in his guess about the volcanic Mount Saint Helens, which at its peak activity was producing 2,000 tons of sulfur dioxide a day compared to 81,000 tons of sulfur dioxide each day by automobiles." "He was off as usual," says Hoffman. "Close, but no cigar."

"Ronald Reagan had been making that statement for years," says Peter Hannaford. But perhaps only to oil-company executives and other true believers.

Adding more grist to the mill, the next day campaign aides handed out a proposed speech that included the statement that "air pollution has been substantially controlled." Bemused stories were written; the *San Jose Mercury* editorialized that "only Ronald Reagan could say trees cause pollution." But the reaction to this odd performance was only beginning to gather steam. Los Angeles coincidentally was experiencing its worst smog pollution in twenty years and Reagan was due to speak at a rally in Burbank at the end of the week. His plane had to be diverted to LAX because the Burbank Airport was closed down by smog. "It was a wonderful irony," says Hoffman. "Finally, reality was intruding on Reagan in spades."

Speaking at Claremont College the next day, Reagan was met by students chanting, "Smog. Smog. Smog." Attached to an enormous eucalyptus tree was a banner that said, "Chop me down before I kill again." "The 'Killer Trees' thing took root at that rally," says Hoffman.

A few days later as "Leadership '80" was flying across the country, Ken Khachigian looked down and noticed they were flying over a forest fire. " 'Look, Jim,' " I said, " 'that's proof that trees cause pollution.' And we laughed. 'Hey, let's go back there and tell the guys that the governor is right and they're wrong. Trees do actually cause pollution.' " Brady and Khachigian walked down the aisle into the press area, saying, " 'Hey, look, there's proof you guys are wrong.' I don't remember either of us saying 'Killer Trees,' although Killer Trees was already in the lexicon." But members of the press do, and they remember that it was the boisterous Brady who was pointing and yelling, "See, Killer Trees. Killer Trees."

On the campaign charter, "there was a very raucous atmosphere," says Hoffman. "On every takeoff, Brady played his tape of Willie Nelson's 'On the Road Again.' Every river we crossed was announced by Brady to be the north fork of the Snake River. ("We even got Reagan to do it," says Jim.) Every time we saw a little smoke it was 'Killer Trees.' It permeated the news coverage and was a major embarrassment in many ways. These things have a rhythm and it went on for several days. We reporters made jokes all the time. When the schedule said 'staff time,' we knew that was nap time for the Old Ruler."

The Reagan plane had a semiprivate area up front for the Reagans, Deaver, Nofziger, and other senior people who came in and out of the campaign; it had a couch, comfortable chairs, a desk, tables, and lamps. Behind it was an office area where Jim, Marty Anderson, one of "the twins," and Ken Khachigian worked across from each other at a table. In this area also were a Xerox machine, electric typewriters, and the teleprinter through which Arlington sent its speeches and messages to the plane and vice versa. There were two air-to-ground phones. "We had a large stuffed bear that was sort of a surrogate Brady," says Michele Davis. Behind the "office" were seats for about eighty press people. This area was decorated with red, white and blue bunting and American flags. A stuffed monkey and somebody's stuffed canary hung from the ceiling. At times there was loud rock music blaring.*

Joe Canzeri had spirited a piano on board, which Mike Deaver played all the way from Dulles to San Antonio on its first trip. "Was that a piano I saw go by?" Mrs. Reagan was heard to ask. Whenever the campaign made a stop the stewardess at the door would proclaim, "It's show-time!" to people as they filed off the plane.

"Killer Trees" had only heightened the atmosphere inside the plane. In October another press plane was added, called the "zoo plane," which carried mostly TV cameramen and technicians (known to reporters as "the Visigoths"). Three days after "Killer Trees," a toga party was held on the zoo plane. Costumes were put together from purloined hotel sheets. A food fight began thirty minutes into the party. "You've got to have things that make it easier to bear," Jim was quoted as saying. One stewardess noted, "It's difficult to soar like eagles when you're dealing with turkeys."

When Jim's clowning was finally written about by *The New York Times*'s Howell Raines, "I'll never forget someone calling me up and saying it was in the paper," says Khachigian. "I was very remorseful. I called Brady and he chuckled. He had this way of chuckling after every sentence. It didn't seem to bother him. 'I don't know why we ever did that,' he said. It was really eating at me but Jim was not remotely concerned."

*Stewardesses on board were: Beth McCall, Jan Hamlett, Jan Ericson, Trish Hoffman, Betsy Strong, Dana Miller, CeCe Kramer.

"The press suggested putting Ronald Reagan in a sealed room with a running automobile, and Jimmy Carter in a room with a tree and see who would survive," says Khachigian. "It was awful. They just had us."

But Meese and Casey did not chuckle. It appeared to Reagan operatives that the campaign had stopped dead in the water, and this they thought did not help. "It was illustrative of the kinds of things we'd be nitpicked about through the last days of the campaign," says Khachigian. Although they were divided about it they decided they would try to get Carter to agree to debate: The next time the plane came back to Washington, Casey told Brady, "You're not going back out." "And there was a meeting," says Peter Hannaford, "in which Jim was told to do less talking."

"Jim came home that night with the funniest expression on his face," says Sarah, but he didn't tell her what had happened.

"All that hoopla ended when we accepted the debate," says Khachigian. "Jim was grounded and the cover story was that they needed him at headquarters to get ready for the debate on October twenty-eighth. He was only off the plane for about four days because we returned to Washington on the twenty-second to get ready for the debate. Jim was half philosophical about it, but he was resentful and angry after he was pulled off. He got the brunt of it. Nobody remonstrated with me." Jim told Khachigian, "I must have been smoking dope or something. I want to be out there where the rubber meets the road!"

"That's where the excitement is, and the fun," says Khachigian.

"The Killer Trees incident brought to a head the unhappiness over what they thought were leaks from Brady," says Lou Cannon. "On at least two occasions they blamed Brady for leaks that appeared in my stories, when they came from another person on that plane."

"We were appalled and angry about it," says Hoffman. "We gave the staff a lot of grief on it. We really rallied around Jim."

And some on the staff lobbied to get Jim back; the speechwriting contingent felt Reagan's remarks were their fault. "It was clear we made a real mistake," says Bandow, "because we hadn't written remarks for him. It was the worst kind of situation for Reagan, because he just had to extemporize. I called Kevin and said, 'We need to find out about natural oil slicks and trees causing air pollution and the rest.' Virtually every one of them had some accuracy."

"Stu Spencer told me," says Cannon, " 'Aw, we'll get him back here in about a week.' Brady had to go along with the cock-and-bull story about how he'd always planned to go back to Arlington. But Stu realized that Jim was very good for Reagan. Deaver and Spencer worked very closely together and complemented each other. Deaver has good ideas and knows how to handle the Reagans. Brady was a little more a free-wheeler than they really wanted, but in that narrow compass he worked in okay."

"We were wearing armbands—Free the Bear," says Michele Davis. "When he came back he did act a little embarrassed—which lasted about twelve hours."

"I thought it was hilariously funny," says Reagan's photographer, Michael Evans. "It was exactly the kind of attitude the Reagan people needed to take toward that disastrous blunder."

"I said, 'Where's Brady?' " says Michael Deaver, "when I didn't see him. And I called him. 'Casey took me off the plane,' Jim told me, and I said, 'Nobody takes anybody off this plane but Deaver. Meet us at the next stop.' "

"After Killer Trees, and Jim was grounded that week," says Jeanne Winnick, "Garrick was really on him. Even though Jim was unhappy to be there, the presence of an insider from the plane was definitely uplifting to the rest of us at headquarters. Everyone was glad to see him as he breezed through the halls, which I think disturbed Garrick. He smelled possible insubordination 'on his watch.' And rightfully so. The last day of Jim's grounding, I broke all rules, took a pizza count, and jumped into Jim's jeep to help him bring back a dozen 'destroyers.' The entire policy-research division was enjoying a great lunch when Garrick stormed into the office and demanded, 'Who's behind this?' and there's Brady stuffing his face. Garrick was looking for him the next day, but Jim was back on the plane."

Howell Raines told Jim, "I had no idea Casey would go around the bend on this." And Jim said, "Oh, don't worry about it. It's all been worked out."

For his part, Reagan apparently still believes his information was correct.

"I thought it was funny," said Reagan in 1985 about Killer Trees. "This was after I had cited this very eminent scientist—I think it was Texas A and M—who had cited, with all the furor about air pollution and so forth, he gave the facts and figures on how much of it was pure nature; that if you could wipe out all the man-made sulfur dioxide in the air, you'd still have over a third as much as we presently have that is just coming daily from nature. And then I remembered the other one—the fact that that haze over the Blue Ridge Mountains* they talk about—that haze is what is known in smog as oxides of nitrogen and that the trees emit it.

"And so it was one day when the press was after us on things of that kind, I cited the need to be—to have some common sense about environmental problems and not go off in a panic about everything and cited some of these things. Well, some of the press started in on me, that I called the trees killers, the killer trees, and so forth. So Jim was just responding to them and their charge. . . . I didn't think anything about it."

"The chemistry on the plane was good," says Cannon. "Deaver kept Reagan relaxed. And my impression is that Reagan liked Jim Brady, but he doesn't pay a whole helluva lot of attention to staff.

"Brady is willing to lose something for the sake of a good one-liner. He's like Reagan himself in that respect. Jim loved Reagan's deficit remark, that 'it was big enough to take care of itself.' [In answer to the question "What are you going to do about the deficit?"] In that sense, Jim was right for Ronald Reagan. There's that streak of irreverence in Jim Brady that I believe people like."

"Jim always said the worst flaps he wasn't responsible for," says Bandow. "There were a lot of accusations directed at him on the sort of quotes that said, 'A campaign insider said, "Oh, yes, we really blew that," or "We have a problem on this." ' "

It was in October, also, that *Parade* magazine quoted Richard Nixon as saying he had been advising Reagan and he would be consulting with him when he became president. Dean Reynolds asked Joe Canzeri about it and Canzeri said, "He's hallucinating." Reynolds reported that in his story that night.

"Reagan had to call Nixon and smooth it over," says Canzeri. "I went to him and offered to resign, but he laughed and said, 'Absolutely not. Don't worry about it.' "

"Jim Brady (who calls Canzeri the Mini-Guinea) told me," says Reynolds, "that if I'd come to him he would have said,

*Reagan had said Smoky Mountains in his Steubenville remarks.

'He's fuckin' hallucinating.' That way he would've kept me from using it."

On October 31 there was a Halloween party on the plane. People outdid themselves on their costumes. "I believe I was a rabbit," says Jim, who procured a Yoda mask for their guru, Marty Anderson, and Reagan bowled a pumpkin down the aisle on takeoff.

"I get so nostalgic about this period," says Hoffman. "It was the most fun I'd ever had. I had started with Reagan back in February and we went to places I'd never been to. I spent eight months away from home. It was that kind of investment I had in this enterprise.

"The final days were hectic. Dick Wirthlin's polls showed a landslide, and they could hardly restrain their euphoria. Seeing their faces I knew they thought they were going to win."

On November 3, the day before election day, "Leadership '80" flew from Cleveland to Peoria to Portland to San Diego to Los Angeles. Bob Hope was on the plane with the Reagans.

"On election day," says Sarah, who had flown to Los Angeles, for the great event, "I got to the hotel [the Century Plaza] at four o'clock. Jim came up to the room to see me, but by then I knew it was going to be a winner. It took some of the excitement away. I hadn't even gotten to the election-night party. I remember thinking, 'How can these Californians stand this? No wonder they're so laid back. The world has been all decided by the time they get up in the morning.' "

"I spent the day getting the Reagan people to various broadcast booths," says Jim. "At five-fifteen NBC declared Reagan the winner. The 'Coon got there just in time for the gong to go off."

"On election day," says Hoffman, "all things change. Now the 'Big Feet' in journalism show up. Suddenly all bets are off and you start with a clean slate again.

> John Hinckley watched the election returns with his parents in Evergreen, Colorado. "As Reagan's totals mounted," wrote Jack Hinckley, "John seemed as elated as I was. 'Maybe there's hope for the country yet,' he said."*

*Jack and JoAnn Hinckley with Elizabeth Sherrill, *Breaking Points* (Grand Rapids, Mich.: Chosen/Zondervan, 1985).

CHAPTER THIRTEEN

"The House"

Jim and Sarah flew home from Los Angeles separately. "But somehow, even with a morning press conference in L.A., Jim beat me home," says Sarah. "I brought back the big black stuffed bear that had flown as mascot on the campaign plane. The next morning Jim went right to work at transition headquarters* handling press as the East Coast spokesman." Lyn Nofziger was West Coast spokesman, and was in California with the Reagans.

For the next two months Jim and Nofziger would dribble out what precious little news there was—mostly Cabinet appointments. Because there was so little news the press pored over these appointments endlessly. There was intense competition to get them first. For Jim the pace was furious. And underlying all his activity was the suspense and tension over whether or not he would be named White House press secretary.

"For the most part," says David Hoffman, "the transition briefings were completely useless. It's an unstable period for the press. And Jim was beseiged with press requests.

"Good morning, Breakfast Clubbers," said Jim at his first briefing on November 4. Reporters Gary Schuster and Jim

*1726 M Street N.W., Washington, D.C.

Dickenson asked the all-important question, "What are you going to do about the Snake River, Jim?"

"The Snake River we'll cover later on," said Jim, who was all business that day.

"Meese sometimes joined Jim in the briefings. He was sloppy, bright, and funny. He's the Pillsbury Dough Boy," says Hoffman. "He *also* knew if you didn't want to answer questions you could answer with humor."

The next morning Ed Meese observed at the briefing that Reagan pollster "Dick Wirthlin has been working all night rewriting our strategy to conform to the results."

On November 17, Jim told the press there would be open coverage at the beginning of state dinners. "You can go in and look at the tables and take a pat of butter and some bread, or whatever you want."

The next day he announced the menu for a dinner with senators and their wives. "Sherried consommé, veal piccata, salad with *fromage,* and raspberries. Not only that, they're going to have cheese," he said.

Just before Thanksgiving, Jim announced that Reagan was to be presented with a turkey by the Turkey Growers Association. "All right!" said the press, thrilled to have some news. "This same turkey bit President Nixon, and messed up the carpet when it was presented to President Ford. So we'll see what this one does." As it turned out, the turkey was frozen. Jim announced the president-elect's visit to his allergist ("Is he allergic to turkeys, Jim?") and to his dentist ("I don't know which tooth it is" he said). Jim commiserated with the press about Reagan's having had no press conferences except at curbside because before when they yelled questions at Reagan they only had to yell, "Governor, Governor, Governor." "And now it's 'President-elect, President-elect, President-elect.' It's more difficult for you. I understand that."

"During the transition," says Bill Rhatican, "Jim put a group together to review candidates for the public-affairs offices in the different agencies. It included David Gergen, Larry Speakes, Mike Baroody, and me. It was fascinating. Between us we had worked for every agency.

"We did the first cut on literally hundreds and hundreds and hundreds of résumés coming into the transition office. There were six to twelve résumés per job."

Rhatican himself had worked in the White House and government long enough, he felt. "It was fun and incredibly interesting, but there really is a world outside those gates. I missed Little League baseball games and Little League soccer games that I'd rather I had not missed."

Larry Speakes had called to see if Jim wanted any help, and Jim told him, "Be here tomorrow at seven A.M."

"Jim feigned studied casualness about hiring Speakes, but he had made inquiries about him before he showed up," says Lou Cannon.

"When is a decision going to be made on the staffing of the press office?" Jim was asked at his November 17 briefing. "I don't know. I keep reading about that," Jim said.

"In Jim's office during the transition," says Bruce Thompson, "first he had a regular desk, then he got another desk, then a long table. All were piled high. Finally he operated from a little desk in the corner."

"Brady felt strongly that he had to help staff out the government," says Thompson. "My job was to get lists of people for the job of assistant secretary for public affairs at Treasury. We had Jim down for the job. Reagan wanted him and they talked. The State Department wanted him, too. I think in his own mind, he'd have gone to State if he hadn't been picked for the White House. We told him, 'You don't want to go to the White House. You'll have a heart attack and it'll kill you.' We all knew how anxious he was for the job, and we were anxious for him."

Jim and Sarah took a victory weekend at Bethany Beach with their friends—Cathy and Bruce Thompson, Dawn and Dennis Thomas, Jan and Otto Wolff, and Susan and "B" Oglesby. Oglesby brought his pasta machine along, and he and Jim made pasta. There had been an article in the *Post* saying it was a possibility that "Jim Brady, a relative unknown," would be named press secretary. The next morning Jim awoke to see that Dennis Thomas had written "THE RELATIVE UNKNOWN" in huge letters in a sand dune visible from their deck.

On November 30, John Hinckley flew to Washington and stalked President-elect Reagan as he came and went from his temporary quarters in Blair House, just across

Pennsylvania Avenue from the White House. Once he had a gun with him.

He also asked someone to take a snapshot of him with his own camera in front of Ford's Theater where President Lincoln was assassinated by John Wilkes Booth.

As November gave way to December there was still no appointment of a press secretary. But none of the Cabinet appointments had been made either, and there was lots of press speculation about them. In his December 3 briefing, Jim said that Reagan was adding to his list of occupations: radio announcer, actor, and now "cabinetmaker." Meese told them, "Whoever is talking to you about Cabinet appointments doesn't know and isn't telling the truth. The people who do know are not talking." "How do you know?" he was asked. "Because I know who knows." "How do you know *they're* not talking?" "Because we have them followed day and night and all their phones are tapped," Meese replied.

Jim had opened the briefing with the announcement that an item in *The Washington Post* was correct. That's "where Brady gets most of his briefing material in the mornings," said Meese.

As the days wore on and still no announcements, Jim told the press, "This isn't any more fun for me than it is for you, I can assure you." On December 8, Jim countered the press charge that Reagan was slow in making Cabinet announcements by comparing his pace to that of Kennedy, Nixon, and Carter. Then he introduced Bush's press secretary, Pete Teeley, by poking fun at George Bush's preppy image, saying, "There is no truth to the rumor that Bush is trying to change the eagle on the vice-presidential seal to an alligator."

"During the transition, Jim had me over to do some briefings," says Pete Teeley. "It was a very, very tough time for Jim at that point. He was briefing daily and was being told very little by Meese. Fortunately, the press quickly realized it and understood it, and Jim made light of it, telling them that if they took him out to lunch and put down 'informed source' they might get audited by the IRS.

"He was philosophical about being in limbo. 'If I get selected I get selected,' he said. I remember talking to Jim Baker about the fact they were having such a big discussion about it.

I told Baker, 'I think you oughta hire Brady.' Baker was in a sensitive position himself, not being a Reaganite. They were considering several women—Lisa Myers, among them, as well as Jim Doyle, Gerry Lubenow, and Jerry Friedheim, who'd been at Defense.*

"But Jim knew Reagan better than anybody else. He'd been on the campaign and knew the issues. He was respected by the press. I thought he was the natural choice."

"I told Jim I'd come out for him or against him, whichever would do the most good," says Lou Cannon.

"What Jim was really good at was his repartee with the press," says Ken Khachigian. "He wanted that job so bad. He wasn't coy about it. 'I don't know why I want this thing. Getting it could be the second worst thing that could happen to me, the first being not getting it.' I called Baker and Deaver and urged them to take Jim. I thought it was humiliating the way they made him wait."

"I talked to Nofziger about Jim's being White House press secretary," says Senator Roth, "and wrote a letter to Meese urging it, too. I thought he was the right man for the job. I can't remember a press secretary having greater respect from and rapport with the press." But Roth was somewhat irritated at the Reagan administration's taking all his good staff. "I had a great little team and they all left me," he says.

Not only did Jim have to parry all the speculation about his becoming, or *not* becoming, press secretary, but when Nofziger resigned on November 30 he had the minor irritation of coming officially under the command of Admiral Garrick.

"At the end of the campaign, Garrick left for California," says Jeanne Winnick, "and we thought he'd not return. So we threw an elaborate good-bye party thanking him for his campaign efforts, thinking he'd be gone forever. But he was soon back as deputy director of public affairs for the transition. The only time Jim and I went out to lunch during the transition, and it hadn't been two minutes after I returned and I get a call from Garrick in California. 'I know who you went to lunch with

*Myers is with NBC News, Jim Doyle formerly with *Newsweek*, Lubenow with *Newsweek*, and Friedheim, a former newsman, who had been in Public Affairs at the Pentagon. "Pat Buchanan [conservative columnist] was seriously considered," says David Gergen, who said he himself did not want to be considered for the post.

and I don't appreciate it. Look, you work for me!' So the battle continued. At every briefing Garrick would stand to Jim's left, looking over his shoulder as though he was his supervisor. When Jim got the nod, he said, 'Hey, come work for me.' 'Where do I sign?' I said. Jim started laughing and said, 'It's going to be one hell of an Armageddon but I'm going to steal you away from Garrick.' 'Oh, please do,' I said. 'I've paid my dues.' "

On December 8, John Lennon was murdered and John Hinckley left Washington for New York to mourn him with hundreds of thousands of others. Ronald Reagan was in New York on December 10, and flew back to Washington the same day. While he was still at the Waldorf in New York, the press asked him whether *now*, after the Lennon murder, he was for gun control. "No. If you shoot someone in California," he replied, "you automatically get five years in prison." Soon after that Mrs. Reagan volunteered that she had a tiny little gun she kept in her nightstand.

Over the next ten days, Jim at last announced and introduced all the major figures in Reagan's cabinet.* "Come on over at two o'clock," he told the press at one point, "and we'll parade them out for you."

On December 16, it was noted by the press that Reagan, now in Los Angeles, was going to visit the Sherman Oaks Meat Locker Plant. "Why?" they wanted to know. "I give up," said Jim. "Someone earlier asked me if that was a singles bar and I don't think it is." Lester Kinsolving wanted to know why Reagan found time to have dinner with Kay Graham, owner of *The Washington Post*, who supported Carter, and hadn't found time

*On December 11, Jim announced that Donald T. Regan had been nominated secretary of the treasury; Caspar Weinberger, secretary of defense; William French Smith, attorney general; Malcolm Baldrige, secretary of commerce; Richard Schweiker, secretary of health and human services; Andrew Lewis, Jr., secretary of transportation; David Stockman, head of OMB; William J. Casey, director of the CIA.

On December 16, Alexander Haig, Jr., secretary of state; and Raymond J. Donovan, secretary of labor.

On December 17, Mike Deaver, assistant to the president; Max Friedersdorf, assistant to the president for legislative affairs.

On December 19, James G. Watt, secretary of the interior; Samuel R. Pierce, Jr., secretary of HUD; James B. Edwards, secretary of energy; Jeane J. Kirkpatrick, U.S. representative to the United Nations.

to visit his loyal supporters at the conservative magazine *Human Events.*

Two days later there was a great deal of going back and forth by Jim and reporters about the request by President-elect Reagan that senators and congressmen wear formal morning attire at his swearing-in. "I think actually what happened," said Jim, "was that the OSHA inspector for swearing-ins went up there and feared there'd be a concentration of polyester and it would be a fire hazard." When a reporter misspoke and said "transmission" when he meant "transition," Jim said, "Don't clutch."

Don Rumsfeld tried once again to get Jim to join him and Greener at Searle in Chicago. "But it wasn't surprising to me he wanted to try for the top job. He had been a deputy and had learned all he needed to learn." says Rumsfeld.

On December 30, when still there was no press secretary, came the question "Jim, since you have said that Reagan is his own best speechwriter, are we to look to the possibility that he is going to be his own press secretary? This is alarming. What about this?"

Kent and Linda Watkins had a party for Jim late in December. "We billed it as a pre–press secretary party," says Kent. "Jim was very apprehensive. But we had a toast. 'Here's to the new press secretary.' Later he told me, 'It must have been all that goodwill at your party that did it, Kent.' Jim had all sorts of interesting preparation for what could have been his tenure as a great press secretary," says Watkins.

"Jim lived through that period gracefully," says David Hoffman, "and no one else really emerged for the job. We in the press wanted to influence the choice. The Reagan people had to have received dozens of supporting calls for Jim. To the press the overriding question was who was going to be press secretary. We all knew it wouldn't be Nofziger because Nancy was sensitive to appearances in spite of her loyalty to those who work for Ronnie.

"The great tragedy was that Jim had weathered so much in the sense of patiently waiting. He had to earn it. Whereas Meese, Baker, and Deaver and the rest all knew on election day they were in."

"I was the only one who auditioned for the job," said Jim.

"I was a strong proponent of Jim's getting the job," says

Dick Allen. "I have a rule which is to go all the way to support my friends. I intended to go back to my business—I didn't want to go back to that snakepit—but I was appointed December twentieth. I thought it could be fun, depending on the combination of people there."

"There were rumors around and Jim's name was not on that short list," says David Prosperi. "Outwardly, Jim was not showing signs of wanting the job that much. He was just running the transition press office and handling the introductions of the Cabinet. The press already knew him and liked him. In my opinion, he earned it."

The word was that Ed Meese opposed Jim's appointment because he thought Jim talked too much to the press. And Reagan's top advisers, particularly Ed Meese, had several schemes to downgrade the importance of the press secretary. They were leery of sharing their power with an outsider. In November *The Washington Star* quoted Meese as saying, "I don't think the press secretary is the only guy who ought to brief the press." But Jim had no problem with that. He said, "I'm not going to put myself up as someone with a world view of everything that is going on in the government." He said he encouraged administration officials, including Reagan, to take part in the briefings. "Politics is addition, not subtraction," Jim always says and he also subscribes to the view that press *is* policy. Meese also had earlier suggested having four press secretaries, each with expertise in a different area, an idea that others thought unworkable.

"It was my thought that we should have a woman," says Jim Baker, "but we never came up with anyone we thought had the qualifications who had an interest in the job. I never offered it to anybody else. All the while, Jim was acting press secretary, and he endured the period of limbo with wit and grace and courage."

But "Deaver liked Jim," says Joe Canzeri, "and was responsible for his becoming press secretary."

"The story of his getting the appointment," says Bandow, "is that it was Reagan who finally cut through the process and said, 'You haven't shown me anybody better. He did a good job for me on the campaign, so let's do it.' "

"When he was recommended for that position," says Reagan, "I didn't have to think twice." He agreed that it suddenly became clear that Jim was the right person for the job.

"Most of us felt this was one of the most important jobs we were selecting a person for," says Ed Meese, "and we felt that in fairness to the president we should not limit ourselves in our search. We were looking for someone who was knowledgeable in the ways of Washington and who got along with the president and the press. Finally, both Jim Baker and I agreed that there was nobody better than Jim, and the president was favorably inclined toward Jim."

The warring between the right-wing faction headed by Meese and the moderate faction headed by Baker and Deaver, which was to rage on for the next four years, also extended into the choice of press secretary. Neither side wanted another strong player to develop in the press office. Karna Small was recommended by Pat Buchanan among others, and the duo of Brady and Small, announced on the same day, was originally intended to mollify both sides (as well as to put a woman in a visible position). It appeared that Small was the candidate of the conservatives and Brady that of the moderates.

"The day I called him and asked would he take the job" says Jim Baker, "I told him Karna Small would be his deputy, and he took that well. He knew her. He talked about access and the importance of access and it's safe to say in the two months he was here he had good access. He had fourth best access." (After Meese, Baker, and Deaver.)

Jim had twice been a guest on Small's NBC radio show during the campaign. "He was one of the best guests I ever had. He was not only factual, but hilarious," says Small. "After we were appointed, Jim and I had a two-hour conversation about how we would work together; how we would structure the press office."

"This is probably the most important conversation we'll ever have," Jim told her.

In retrospect, in what appeared to be an ironic portent of the tragedy to come, on January 6, the same day Jim's appointment was announced, Larry Speakes was asked in the briefing, "Larry, why would the president-elect give [President of Mexico] Lopez Portillo a rifle at a time when guns are a particularly sensitive issue in this country?" He was referring to John Lennon's murder.

"Well," said Speakes, "this was a rifle from his own gun collection and he knew of President Lopez Portillo's gun collection, so he thought it would be a gift [he could] give him."

In *The Washington Post,* Elisabeth Bumiller chronicled Jim's first full day as press secretary to President-elect Reagan, beginning at six A.M. on a snowy January 7 when Jim took the subway to transition headquarters, reading the accounts of his appointment in the papers on the way. "Hmmmmmmm," he smiled at his front-page picture, "Brady above the fold," and reading through the story sighed, "I guess 'pudgy' is going to stick."

In the next four hours, wrote Bumiller, Jim met with two dozen people, received fifty calls, held one press briefing, and accepted congratulations "that flowed like the Dom Perignon he opened" when Reagan offered him the job. Out on the street, people recognized him and called out to him. "Hey, Mr. Secretary," yelled one. "Well, look who this is," said another who was buying lunch at the same hot-dog stand. "You know this whole thing's all right—if you don't inhale it," Jim laughed. Bumiller described Jim's laugh as "a low, deep laugh that eventually turns to giggle. His eyebrows are continually arched, his cheeks full, his chin doubled. His expression . . . is one of pleasant bemusement at the world around him."

"He caught me in the hall that day," says Jeanne Winnick. "He had a diagram of the press room—and he described my job to me. 'You'll do a lot of running around, and traveling,' he told me. I had no idea what I was getting into."

At 2:00 P.M. Jim met with Reagan and his economic advisers at Blair House, where he took notes on seven pages of legal paper.

At 5:00, he was back at headquarters talking to Larry Speakes and Mark Weinberg about the fact that David Stockman had "committed news" after the meeting with Reagan.

" 'Factoids,' we call them," said Jim and then told Speakes he was to do the briefing the next day. Speakes looked "slightly ill," wrote Bumiller. Jim elaborated on the perils of press briefings. "The chances of being held up to nationwide ridicule and scorn are indeed great," he laughed. And he quoted former White House press aide Jerry Warren, "Well, if I run this red light and I have an accident and I go to the hospital, I won't have to do the briefing tomorrow."

By six o'clock three dozen congratulatory telegrams were on Jim's desk and he began returning phone calls. "Fast," wrote Bumiller. At this early stage Jim had managed to make the job "look like nothing but fun." "Well, it is," Jim said with unconcealed joy.

In his briefing that day, Jim was asked if the Department of Energy would be once again moved around and scattered instead of dismantled as had been proposed. Jim said, "For years we had eight baboons out there but no one knew we had eight until they brought them all together in the same cage."

Home at 9:00 P.M. Sarah was waiting with a rum and tonic.

Home at 9:00 P.M. Sarah was waiting with a rum and tonic. "If Jim ever came home at six o'clock," she said, "I wouldn't know what to do." Jim changed from his impeccable three-piece suit into Levis, moccasins, and an L. L. Bean flannel shirt. The Christmas tree still stood in one corner. Dinner was "Bear's Goat Gap Texas Chili."

Sarah told Bumiller, "If something like Jim's job is going to come at a certain time in life, I suppose the perfect time is now. We waited until late to have a child, and now that he's two, I like being home with him." She said she was excited about Jim's job, "although I may, just six months from now, say, 'God, I was really naïve.' "

The next day Reagan told the press at curbside about a meeting at the State Department, which was "about establishing the routine and how we're going to function, and I told them how to be courteous and kind to the press."

"Good. Starting when?" they wanted to know.

"Oh, starting right away," Reagan said.

By January 12, Speakes had briefed three times since Jim's appointment. Jim confessed that he'd been having too much access, "and that's why I haven't been returning your phone calls and haven't been down here to brief. Maybe moderate access or semi-access would work a lot better."

There was a question about the Arabian stallion that President Lopez Portillo sent to Reagan, and Jim said it would be taken to the ranch, and that Reagan would be riding while he was in Washington but "we don't know where or on what." "You're right," said a newsman about this trivia. "You have too much access." Jim then introduced Sheila Tate, the newly appointed press secretary to Mrs. Reagan.

"Jim and I had a one-hour meeting," says Tate. Among other things, they talked about planning a press event that would "humanize" Mrs. Reagan. "Jim made an extraordinary effort to put an end to the traditional warfare between the First Lady's East Wing and the President's West Wing press operations," she says. " 'Let's make sure this doesn't happen,' " he said." And he invited her to attend the morning press-office briefings, "which are invaluable because we make sure we aren't competing for press attention at the same time. That may seem elementary, but it wasn't happening before. And thereafter we never had a problem.

"I came away from that first meeting knowing he was going to be so much fun to work with. A lot of men get involved with policy and forget the human touches.

"I was crazy about him. If we were overly concerned with something, he would put it right back into perspective with a wry comment or joke.

"Early in the administration," she says, "I was having trouble getting the things approved that the press wanted in terms of coverage for state dinners. I went to Jim and he said, "Let's go see Deaver,' and we got the approval. Jim said to me, 'You know, Sheila, almost every event in the White House is put on with the expectation that the press will cover it. We lose sight of that. Sometimes I have to say, 'What the——do you think we are doing this for?' "

During her tenure as Mrs. Reagan's press secretary, "I often said," remarks Tate, "in the words of the great Jim Brady, 'What the——do you think we're doing this for?' "

Jim quickly began assembling his staff. He asked Larry Speakes to be his deputy and pulled many others in from the Reagan campaign staff. "My management style is to get good people and let them run their department," says Baker. That described Jim's style as well. "Jim hired the people, running their names by me, all except Karna Small."

Flying to Juarez, Mexico, for Reagan's meeting with Lopez Portillo, after the word came out that he was press secretary, "Jim came up to me," says David Prosperi, "and said, 'I just want you to know you are on my team. I have a role for you—I want you to be my TV guy.' A few days later, 'Oh, by the way, you're assistant press secretary.' I appreciated that Jim had confidence in me and let me make the majority of decisions without input from him."

"Jim wanted Kevin or me to handle issues in the press office, but we both decided we wanted to be involved in making policy, not explaining it," said Doug Bandow.

On January 13, "Jim called me from Air Force One," says Sally McElroy, who knew him from Pentagon days, "on his way 'out to California to get the man' as he put it." Jim wanted Sally to come to the White House and they had been leaving messages all over, trying to get in touch with each other to no avail, and now Jim was saying, "Did you mean what you said?" "Sure," said McElroy. "Well, then, pack, because I want you to come over and work for me."

On that same flight, Jim typed a letter to his two-year-old son on Air Force One stationery.

> January 13, 1981
> Tuesday
> Dear Scott,
>
> I am flying aboard Air Force One to the West Coast to pick up President Elect and Mrs. Reagan and bring everyone back to Washington for the Inauguration.
>
> Only three of us are taking this big bird on the flight which takes us over St. Louis (probably Centralia and Gram's and Pop's house), Kansas City (where your mommy and I got engaged) and Gallup, New Mexico (where there are a lot of Indians) . . . all at an altitude of 31,000 feet. Departed at 6:59 A.M.
>
> We had a big breakfast and I have begun to work on press coverage of all the events to come in the next week when we get a new President.
>
> I have so many things on my mind. I have only a few days left to staff up the White House Press Office, decide when to have the first press conference, develop a press plan for the first 90 days, and have time to keep current on everything I must know to brief. (The briefings, I notice for the first time yesterday, are getting harder. I had an uneasy feeling when I didn't know all of the answers . . .)
>
> I haven't really come to grips with it yet but I'm sure it will all work out. It always does. (Remember, The harder you work, the luckier you get. . . .) When I left the office yesterday, we had gone over the Public Affairs

slots for the entire administration. I made my choices and there was general agreement although I will watch closely to see that people I can work with are installed. Also up in the air is a White House Communications office. You are lucky that all you have to worry about now is your moon car, bike, blackie bear, and Sugar & Spice. (Mommy has to take them to the vet for their shots and to have their shots . . .

I just read the last line and I am not typing with a "full deck" this morning. I meant to say to have their claws clipped (Spice doesn't like that!).

I am going to call Mommy and you soon from the plane. I hope you are awake now and having waffleswaffleswaffles. The Creep-mouse is going to get your feetfeetfeet. . . .

I miss seeing you because you are asleep when I leave for the office and asleep when Daddy gets home. Last night I had the flu and didn't even get to ask what you did while I was at the office.

I keep worrying about staffing and the so little time to do so much. If I get through these next few weeks I think everything will be fine. I have to find a Secretary quick.

Well, son. I have not written you the most interesting letter but I feel better getting my worries off my chest and thinking of you and mommy at home with the nice kitties. It was cold this morning when I left and dark too. There will be a lot more days like that.

I love you truly,

Daddy—/s/ Daddy

P.S. Won't it be fun to have Missy come and visit you!

"On election night in L.A.," says Michele Davis, "I had bailed out of town. I flew back to Washington and loaded up my pickup truck and drove home to Oregon. When he was named press secretary, I got a phone call from Brady. 'You're missing the opportunity of your life,' he told me. 'Get back here.' I argued with him and he told me, 'There is no reality,

Michele. You can fake it better back here.' On Inaugural Day I was being pulled over in Utah for speeding. I went back to work for him, but that lasted about five days; then Nofziger made me a better offer, as assistant to the president for political affairs. I took it only because I consider myself more a political person than a press person.

"He kicked doors open for me. He allowed me opportunities for whatever reason. It was his doing that got me on the Reagan campaign and his pushing that got me to come back. I am beholden to him.

"Oregon looked good, it looked really good. But it *was* a little boring after a week. I had difficulty getting the news. I'd read this little, tiny newspaper. Jim said, 'You're a fool if you pass up this opportunity. You'll kick yourself.' He was combative about it. 'Think about what you're doing,' he said. Jim has taken care of a lot of people. There's a string of people Jim Brady has cajoled into reaching their heights. He is such a liver, he didn't like to see others not living up to their potential. He was almost abrasive in challenging you to do your very best."*

Kathy Ahern had kept track of Jim's phone messages all through the Connally and Reagan campaigns. "I was blessed with a good memory and saw he got all of them," she says. At the end of the transition, "I was keeping his appointment and social calendar. Some of the press tried to walk right in and I used to throw myself against the door and wouldn't let them in. I was hoping to go to the White House with him, but I didn't think I'd get to go.

"But the day he was named, Jim called me from Blair House to say, 'Go upstairs and see Mr. Baker's assistant. You are going to the White House.' I was a basket case. I didn't even care what I was going to do."

The day before the inauguration, Jim told Karna Small, "I'm going to be tied up with the president and traveling with the press corps. You take copies of the inaugural address (the first paper of this administration) and go over to the White House and open it up. Take over."

"What was that you said?" said Karna.

"I said, 'You go over to the White House and take charge.' "

"I thought that was rather an interesting order of business,"

*Michele Davis is now executive director of the Republican Governors Association at the Republican National Committee.

she says. "Thank goodness Larry was there as well as Mark Weinberg and Kim Hoggard. We set out from the transition office with the trunk full of speeches to drive to the White House to take over the government. That's a little dramatic, but that's the way we saw it."

They got through the first and second checkpoints, but at the third they were turned back. "We had to double back and find a police escort who believed us. We trudged across the mall in the cold and the mud carrying the boxes of speeches to take over the government."

The press was there with cameras and microphones. And they surged in. "How does it feel," they asked, "on your first day?" "I think I said, 'Give me a minute to warm up and get the mud off my shoes." Overshadowing the normal excitement of the president's inauguration was the dramatic fact that the Americans held hostage for fourteen months by Iranian radicals, which had contributed to Jimmy Carter's defeat, were being released on Inauguration Day.

"The tension that day was so great because the Iranians wouldn't let the plane take off until they received word that Mr. Reagan had been sworn in," says Small.

Similarly, Jim had asked Kathy Ahern to pack up his papers for the move to the White House, "but don't put them on the truck," he told her. Kathy and her husband, Tim, moved Jim's things in their car, "and as soon as the swearing-in was over, my husband and I drove over the Theodore Roosevelt Bridge—I took the stuffed bear with me—and all the streets were closed. I went up to a policeman and showed him my White House pass and told him my mission. We were the only car on Constitution Avenue. My husband let me out and I took some things for the top of Jim's desk and walked up to the White House gate.

"It was eleven-thirty. The Carter people were still there. I was embarrassed, but Connie Gerrard (secretary to the press office) couldn't have been nicer. I wouldn't go into Jody Powell's office, although he wasn't there. A bunch of the working press were sitting there, waiting for the hostage situation to break. And they were coming in the office all the time. After President Reagan was sworn in, I no longer felt like an outsider. I took Jim's things into the office. I was the first one from the transition to come into the White House. I always thought I'd seen enough that I wouldn't be impressed by the White House, but I stood there and tears just rolled down my cheeks. And I never got over that feeling of awe at being there."

The day before the inauguration Susan Bryant read in the paper that a man in her church choir was killed while building the scaffolding for the inauguration ceremonies. "I mentioned it to Bill Greener, who called Brady," she says, "and when I went to the wake the man's wife met me at the door, saying, 'Do you know that President Reagan called and I talked to him and Mrs. Reagan, too?' It's a measure of Jim, and the man he worked for. It's the midwestern ethic, but it's Jim, too."

On Inauguration Day, David Hoffman asked Jim for some color for his story. "Jim recognized instantly what we needed. And he came back out and read off exactly the sort of detail we needed."

Dorothy Brady and Missy came to town for the festivities of inaugural week, along with Dorothy Mann and Betsey Kourdouvelis and their families from Centralia.

"We were assigned a military aide, a marine," says Sarah, "and a car and driver. I wondered what they thought of this madhouse with sleeping bags everywhere and a twenty-four-hour party going on. But one day I came home and the driver was chasing Scott, and the military aide was ironing Jim's trousers. By the end of the week, they fit right into our household.

"There were parties every day, some given by people in the press; columnists Joseph Kraft and Bob Novak each gave one."

On Inauguration Day Sarah joined Jim at the swearing-in on the Capitol steps and at the exclusive brunch inside afterward. "Then," says Sarah, "Jim went with Reagan and I went to the parade and sat with Mrs. Reagan's friends and the wives of senior staff and the cabinet. Dick and Pat Allen and I dropped in on Jim in his office afterward. He was madly working, but we looked around his office and discovered in the closet the bottle of champagne and the bulletproof vest Jody Powell left for Jim." "He really got a kick out of the bulletproof vest," says Hugh O'Neill. "He showed it to me and said how much he appreciated the touch. Jody Powell left with a very good reputation."

At 5:00 P.M., National Security Adviser Dick Allen briefed

the press on the release of the hostages. And Jim was pressed on whether or not Reagan would honor the agreement Carter had worked out with the Iranians. "You know," said Jim, "we've been here just a little less than twenty-four hours and they're extremely complex."

"Forty-eight hours," argued a reporter erroneously.

"Okay, all right—we've been here a lifetime, and I've been here a lifetime today."

That night Sarah went to the ball at the Smithsonian with family and friends, while Jim worked in his new office on his overdue communications plans.

"The first day I came in at seven-fifteen, "says Karna Small, and people started asking me questions before I'd even read the paper. I went down to the mess and Jim said, 'Where have you been? It's the middle of the day already.' And I understood that he really meant it." Reagan and Bush joined Jim on the podium at the briefing the next day.

As time went on Larry Speakes filled in for Jim in the briefing room more often than Small did. "I did not like to brief," she says, "and didn't feel that my background and experience had prepared me for it."

"The first morning I started at seven-thirty and Helen Thomas was already here," says Sally McElroy. "And there are always people here until late—seven-thirty. Jim told me, 'If you're involved in PR and public affairs, this is the top job.' He always said, 'I'm working for the leader of the free world.' He was so honored he was like a little kid about it. He liked parrying with the press.

"It was really hard for Jim at first. He had cut a deal where he would be in on all meetings and he'd do the press briefing after being filled in briefly. We were flying blind half the time. At six or seven o'clock, Jim would start returning phone calls. His press buddies, Bill Plante and Gary Schuster, would come up to shoot the breeze. Both of us felt a lot was falling through the cracks, but it really didn't. Jim had the idea that he wanted a personal letter to answer all his mail. He was never able to get around to it. He rejected the form letter made up for him, but he didn't have time to personalize the letters I worked up.

"But we were getting much more on top of things. I didn't know the system either. Every day I'd learn a new name of somebody else I could send problems to. I soon learned I could just get an answer from Jim about a lot of stuff and handle it right away."

Being named so late, Jim had had only two weeks to recruit and organize his staff, and by Inauguration Day he had only half of them in place. Nor had he spent enough time with Reagan and his advisers to be up to speed on major policy decisions. "But I spent six months as an issues adviser on the campaign with him. I know how he thinks," says Jim. He was more worried about the perception than the access.

Florence Taussig had worked in Bush's advance office during the campaign and heard about a job in the press office. "But I couldn't reach Jim until I called Kathy Ahern, who told me to call him on his private line at seven in the morning."

"Don't take any other job, don't do anything," Jim told her and made an appointment to meet her the next day.

"I waited for an hour while reporters went in and out of Jim's office, and finally he came out and apologized for making me wait."

"Around every corner there was somebody else putting in a good word for you," Jim told her. "Well, when can you start?" And they agreed on eight o'clock the next morning. "The hours are terrible, the pay is not good. You'll be giving up any private life and having any time to yourself," Jim warned her, "but the benefits for the future are really great. You'll get to travel and you'll be close to the Oval Office."

"We were just two months into it," says Taussig, and everything was just beginning to fall into place and get organized. I remember how busy Jim was. I just hardly ever saw him. But I went on the first foreign trip to Canada, and one night while there, Larry, Sally McElroy and I had a beer in his room."

"Once in the White House, I didn't see him much," says Pete Teeley. When Bush flew to Germany for Hostage Day, "Jim asked me to take notes on it, and to get some color, as well as at another meeting we had with the hostage families."

"Jim had access. He did," says Sally McElroy. "He tried to work it so that he and Larry and Karna all had it but that didn't work. There was one period when he wasn't able to brief for a week because he was in so many meetings. They almost mutinied in the press room. After the first month he said to me,

'Are you having fun?' I said, 'Fun? Once I stop being scared maybe I'll start having fun.' "

"You get a lot of crazy calls," says Jeanne Winnick, "and TV producers wanting to know minute details. Even a simple speech in a Washington hotel—there are a lot of things to coordinate. But you find you can handle twenty out of twenty-four calls."

In Jim's briefing on January 26, he said that "about a dozen of the hostages had serious problems, mostly mental," which got him into hot water with his old friend Ken Adelman, because Jim was wrong.

"I'm sorry," Jim told him. "I really blew it."

On January 30, the press wanted to know why Reagan was going to Camp David. "To case the joint?" one asked. "Well, yesterday," Jim responded, "when we walked across West Executive Avenue from the press conference he said, 'This is outside, isn't it?' Other than the inaugural ceremonies and a brief walk to the Treasury he hasn't been outside. And it's something that he really likes."

On January 29, Ronald Reagan held his first press conference as president amid a firestorm of worry in the White House press corps about the changes Jim was instituting.* The first was that reporters were to remain seated and were to raise their hands for recognition instead of leaping about and shouting to get the president's attention. The second change—to be tried later—was a lottery to pick who would be allowed to ask questions. It was the lottery that had the regulars in the press in turmoil. But for now, the insistence on decorum was all that was asked, and they were merely sullen, not yet mutinous. Jim opened the press conference and said, "It is the president's hope that his press conferences will serve as a helpful means of communicating to the American public. In the process of informing the public, he expects and hopes that he can enter into a partnership with the press, recognizing that while you and he have different responsibilities in our society, we all share the same goals. . . . Like many of you, we have been concerned about some of the more hectic characteristics of the presidential press conference. Today I'm asking you to join us in an effort to restore confidence, dignity, and decorum to this

*These changes were recommendations from a committee assembled by the White Burkett Miller Center of Public Affairs at the University of Virginia.

institution. . . . To this end, we are respectfully requesting that members of the press wishing to ask questions remain seated, raise their hands, and wait to be called upon."

The first stage of this experiment was viewed as an enormous success by the press and the White House alike. About the proposed lottery, however, there was anguish. "We cover the president every minute of every day; this is impossible," they said. "Why should the people manning the barricades twenty-four hours a day, seven days a week, *not* have first crack at examining the president versus people who only come in when they hear there's going to be a news conference? This is impossible!"

Jim said, "I'll let Karna Small brief the day we announce the rules for the lottery."

"Jim was so busy, coming in and out of his office all day," says Kathy Ahern. "Their social schedule was pretty heavy, too, and he had to change his clothes right there in the office. Sarah brought his clothes in or he brought them in the morning.

"I was responsible for having that fire in his fireplace going all the time. I would do anything to make his job easier. It was a high-pressure job with so much activity all the time. But my first love was the press office in the campaign. A campaign is like a family, so close-knit. It's more fun than the aftermath."

"After the inauguration we were out almost every night, it seemed," says Sarah. "There was a dinner at the Irish embassy and one at the embassy of Cyprus. There was an elegant luncheon at the British embassy for Margaret Thatcher to which the president came, and a White House luncheon for the president of Korea."

In an interview with Gary Schuster, Jim said that he believed "in the libertarian theory of the press—that in the marketplace of ideas, that truth will emerge. . . ." He also asserted, "I weigh in on policy in the White House," and as press secretary it was ingrained in him to ask, "Why are you doing this?" "I think that's an important question," he says. Jim subscribes to the view that press *is* policy; that the way policies are presented to the public inevitably alters the policy, and done intelligently, improves it.

In February, out for dinner at the House of Hunan with Gary and Barbara Schuster and Steve and Sue Neal, "I remember Jim arrived and left in a White House car," says Sarah. "It was the coldest night of the year and I'd parked two blocks away. As Jim got into his car, I flipped him the bird. I was kidding—mostly.

"In February also, we and the Schusters went to the Tidewater Inn together and had a wonderful time pigging out," says Sarah. "Jim and Gary had an oyster-eating contest, which Jim won, but not by much."

In the February 4 briefing, Jim was asked how his administration described a poor person. ("Scripps-Howard employee," said one.) "Well, I'll stand on your definition of needy," said Jim, then added, "Reagan feels by getting rid of waste in programs that he will actually be able to increase benefits for the truly needy."

After working very late following Reagan's first Oval Office speech on February 6, says Jeanne Winnick, "we all went back to Jim's office and he opened up his refrigerator and passed out beers to all of us. I thought to myself, 'This is the way it should be.' "

One part of the job Jim was finding easy. Reagan "is totally accessible and very quotable," he said. He always carried a notebook to record Reagan's first reactions. "These quotes are invaluable aids in dealing with the media because they reflect the president and not a speechwriter or press aide."

On February 12, Jim said Reagan "*hopes* that the budget will be balanced in 1983." The press remembered that Reagan said it would be in 1982. Said Jim, "The economy's in the worst shape it's been in since the Great Depression . . . the economic inheritance [from Carter] being much worse than anyone thought it would be."

"Jim started getting some negative criticism from the press because he wasn't briefing as much," says Jeanne Winnick. "He was really trying to work his way inside with the Reagan people. Larry was managing us, really, giving Jim the space to get inside. A common complaint from the press was that his door was closed a lot. He was briefing perhaps only two out of five times. I went in and told him, 'You've gotta be around more, more accessible.' 'Yeah, I know,' Jim told me. 'If you hear stuff like that, then it's good to take note of it.' We all knew what he was trying to do, and that the access was well guarded since he came from the Connally campaign. It was all so new to everybody and we were all trying to feel our way.

" 'You want to bring something in to me,' Jim said, 'you bring it right in.'

"He was just on the curve of his grace period. But the basic thrust was that Jim was trying to work full time at getting into the inner circle. Everybody was still trying to get their ducks in a row. Jim was setting himself up to strategize and work out policy statements. I think it's what he really wanted to do. He didn't want to worry about the nuts and bolts of the press office, vacations and so forth. Larry was the management person Jim never wanted to be."

After only three weeks in office there appeared a story in *The Washington Post* critical of Jim for his unavailability to the press, although he had given fourteen out of the first twenty-two briefings. Jim said his first priority was to get to know the president better by observing him in all sorts of situations. "It's working itself out now," he said. "I have found it hard to find time to be press secretary." But the story gave Jim high marks for his ability and humor when he did brief. "It's not full disclosure, folks," he said, explaining why he would not give further details of a Cabinet meeting. And it was noted that Jim had announced that the budget-cutting sessions of Reagan and the Cabinet had "tested to the limit the principle of the mind's ability to absorb what the seat can endure."

But, says Sarah, "Jim told me the press was beginning to play hardball."

After that article on his inaccessibility, Jim Mitchell sent Jim a recording of loon calls. "Jim would play it to the press over the intercom," says Sally McElroy. "He would call reporters in selectively to hear it. Not that the tape is funny," she says, "it's just so unexpected."

Several reporters taped the calls and would play them when certain overly serious reporters started to ask Jim a question in the briefings.

Jim played the loon calls for John Kolbe, visiting from Arizona. "He turned it up full volume and sat back with his hands behind his head and a big smile on his face. 'It's comforting to the jackals of journalism,' Jim said."

"On Saturday mornings," says David Gergen, Jim actively worked the press who were looking for 'raisins' [a Bradyism meaning angles, bits of news, inside personality items] for their

Sunday stories. If Jim wanted to bury something he would announce it late on a Friday afternoon for the Saturday papers."

"Larry had briefed often during the transition," says Mark Weinberg. "Brady believed in having a strong staff available and that's exactly what he had in mind when he had Speakes brief and sent his deputy to staff briefings. He allowed other members on his staff to be quoted, although on important matters he would put things in his name. He had the helpful tendency of saying, 'Next time maybe this would be good,' or 'This has worked for me in the past.' He had an amazing ability to predict how the press would react. 'The *Times* will do this, the wires will do this, the networks, et cetera.' He never lied; he believed the press is a worthy adversary. He'd only get angry if he was told something untrue. There are always those in the administration who feel you can't tell the press secretary something—or he'd be angry if people tried to take his territory over."

"Briefing was easy for him—to deal with the back and forth in the briefings," says Khachigian. "The anger and excitement inherent in press briefings didn't shake him up. He gave as good as he got. And he was totally at home in the White House.

"Once in the residence," says Khachigian, "Jim was sitting on a sofa going over a speech with the president, and Jim is just uncontrollable. He was eating all the damn jelly beans—he was pounding his hand into the jelly-bean jar. Talk about being laid back—I couldn't believe it. He was eating them like peanuts, practically tossing them into the air."

> John Hinckley was back in town for two days, February 15 and 16. He toured the White House to see if there were metal detectors there. He went to Senator Edward Kennedy's Capitol Hill office, his second visit. With his gun in his pocket he waited for him, but he never saw Kennedy.

The next day in the briefing there was a tough question to Jim asking whether, no matter what questions the press asked him, he would talk only about the budget. "Now that is news management and news control as I see it," said the questioner, "unless you can persuade me otherwise." "I'll try to persuade you otherwise," said Jim. "We have a timetable where we will make announcements when they're ready to be made."

On February 23, the press tried for forty minutes to get Jim to say more about Brezhnev's suggestion that there be a summit conference, but to no avail.

In Jim's briefings late in February and into the first weeks of March, the pressure and tough questions continued. On February 25, there was a back and forth on whether there was covert activity in El Salvador. And there was cynicism about what Jim was going to say about a meeting of economic advisers, with the press predicting sarcastically that he would say, "It was a good meeting; a free, frank discussion on a wide range of topics."

The next day they asked, "Since each of Reagan's trips to California costs two hundred and fifty thousand dollars, will he cut down on these weekends and sacrifice along with the rest of the people? Also, how involved is Reagan in the decision-making process, or is he just informed as to the best way to go?"

"The decision was made consistent with his views and his guidelines," said Jim.

On March 2— "Is the president going to get the budget cuts and tax plan he proposed?" "Everybody agrees we should have a smaller government," said Jim, "until it comes time to cut their program. The saying on the Hill is 'Don't cut you, don't cut me, cut that program behind the tree.' There's always someone behind the tree, an infrastructure that's built up around that program, and until we realize that all of us will have to look at a reduced budget, we'll never get over that schizophrenia."

Jim said about Weinberger: "Cap the Knife is going to have an opportunity to live up to his name, by reducing overhead, reducing administrative costs, reducing programs that have nothing to do with . . . our readiness capability or our fighting ability."

On March 5—Jim explained the hated lottery to the dubious press. "The president will draw the questions [out of a jelly-bean jar] and there will be a photo opportunity at that time." "Hasn't he got anything better to do?" said one. "I don't like your reform," said another. "Are you sorry you're doing this, Jim?" "Soon it will be over," said Jim. "Can I vote twice?" said another pressie, "I'm from Chicago." Jim said, "If you only voted twice in Chicago you weren't doing your duty." "Will this be done again?" they asked. "Only on overwhelming recommendation of this body shall this be attempted again," said Jim. "Does the president listen to these briefings?" "I hope not," said Jim. "He has better things to do." "Like throw a lottery," said another.

In the White House, says Rhatican, "Jim maintained this great sense of self-confidence. He knows he's good at what he does, and is able to make good decisions and to carry them out and still never be full of himself. Most people sensed this and liked it.

"Jim had the ability to walk into a senior staff meeting and say, 'Now, look, goddam it.' He would carry the press's water, and vice versa—present the president's views to the press. I've seen him work and it's a sight to behold. When a line of questioning becomes close to hostile, Jim can turn it aside with a one-liner that snaps the tension. When a reporter has talked with Brady, you can see the Brady light touch leap off the page of his copy."

In mid-March when Jimmy Carter criticized Reagan's cuts in social programs, Jim said, "We've contended all along that the best social program is a job. . . . You can try to spend yourself to prosperity, or you can try to unleash the private sector. We are opting for the latter."

On March 18 Jim hosted a group of visiting Sigma Chis in his office. In the briefing that day a reporter suggested that Reagan seemed to be coming down on both sides of the automobile-import policy. "Squarely," cracked Jim.

The next day, responding to some saber rattling over Nicaragua by Alexander Haig, Jim said, "Well, there are still democratic elements in the government, and we are hopeful that that will lead Nicaragua to stop the shipments of arms to El Salvador and to take a more moderate course of action."

"I'd see him a lot at the White House," says Bruce Thompson. "Dennis and I'd go over and stop and have a beer in his office. Or I'd be sitting in my office, and I'd get a call from Jim. 'What's the distribution of the tax policy? Okay, 'bye.' "

On March 21, a coterie of Brady friends and colleagues held a Brady roast at the Georgetown Club in Washington, which drew President and Mrs. Reagan on down. "A babble of Brady buddies," said the invitation. Jim had had a bad week, coming under fire at his briefings over a State Department statement about El Salvador, and the release of a Gallup poll showing Reagan had a low approval rating. Reagan cautioned the roasters to "be gentle." And to Jim he said, "You're not to take seriously anything they say." "I never do," replied Jim. Jim Baker started off, "You know, roasts are supposed to be events where you say things about people you wouldn't normally say. But in Brady's case, I suppose this could be just another day at the office." Then Baker purported to quote Ed Meese saying to Reagan, "You know, Mr. President, if it weren't for Jim Brady, John Connally wouldn't be where he is today." But, said Baker, "He's ours. We bought him, we paid for him—and we're going to keep him."

Ed Meese addressed the matter of Jim's access to Reagan. "Just the other morning," he said, "Brady solved the question of access for all time. Because while the president was taking a shower, Jim Brady showed up in a wet suit."

"The honeymoon for the president will be a lot longer than the one for me," Jim answered. "My honeymoon ended about a week after I got there." But it was an evening filled with laughs and affection for Jim. On the way out someone asked Nancy Reagan if she still didn't think Jim was handsome enough. "First of all, I never said that; and secondly, I think he's divine," she said.

On March 26, Jim went to the Radio and Television Correspondents Dinner after first speaking to a William and Mary College alumni dinner that Sarah had booked him for.

"The last time I saw Jim he had even cut his hair," says Kevin Hopkins. "It was at a press conference right before he was shot. We were riding up in a freight elevator in the OEOB. Jim was very preoccupied, but we exchanged a few words. He was no longer the good-humored, happy-go-lucky guy. The job was weighing on him, and it was no easy task although he was coping with it, but I thought he was excellent."

"I really wanted the first interview with Reagan," says Lou Cannon, "and was told that Nofziger opposed it. Nofziger wanted to give it to a friend, not to the liberal *Washington Post.* Jim told me, 'You hang in there, we'll get it.'

"I got the interview on March twenty-seventh and it ran the twenty-ninth and Jim was shot on Monday the thirtieth. I remember then that he had told me on the twenty-eighth, 'Well, you got your interview.' It made me feel bad to think of it. The truth of the matter is it took a lot of the fun out of it for me and did for a long time. It reminded everybody of their own mortality and that none of this stuff is as important as we may think it is. Brady is a visible reminder of how close we are to losing it all."

Jim Baker keeps a needlepoint pillow on the couch in his office, which says, "When you're up to your ass in alligators, it is difficult to remember that your original purpose was to drain the swamp." "Jim's tenure was a short period, but it was an extremely important time," says Jim Baker. "He had to deal with important presidential decisions and conflicts."

"In our senior staff meetings," says Baker, "we hadn't really gotten our organization together. He was one of the principal players and came up with substantive ideas but from a different angle than on the campaign. In the White House the press secretary has to know it all. And Jim was aggressive about having access. He'd say, 'I have to be in that meeting,' and I never, of course, argued about it, ever."

But, says a former senior staffer, "Jim did not have total access, and Meese was the critical player discouraging this."

Former Director of Communications David Gergen* says, "My view is that the press secretary ought to have unquestioned access to any meeting he wants to come to, so that he knows the nuances and disagreements and where the lines are drawn—so he knows better what to say and how to say it. Meese's theory was that you tell the press secretary after the fact, and Baker always gave Jim a good briefing, but it's not the same thing as being in on the small intimate meetings with the president and the National Security Council."

"But Jim was really amazingly detached from his White House job," says Brian Whelan. "When I talked to him on the phone it came through to me that somehow he had resolved in himself that the stage was a little bigger than Springfield or Illinois, but that he had seen all the players before, and he could handle the larger stage. He would do his best and beyond that, some things would work and some wouldn't. And as far as his own fame went, he would enjoy it, but he knew someday he would be out of the White House, and he would be dealing with the same people in a different role."

*Gergen is now editor of *U.S. News and World Report*.

Jim was on guard against the hubris that infects many people when they attain high position. He liked to quote General Joe Stilwell, "The higher the monkey climbs, the more you see of his behind." And he adopted singer Pearl Bailey's name for the White House. "The House," he always calls it.

"Jim was having a wonderful time at the White House," says Ted Carmody, who followed Jim as Roth's press secretary. "When you think about Jim Brady you think about missed opportunities."

"Brady was sensational," says Dick Allen. "He was a jewel. You have to have brains, depth and reach and grasp of substance. Jim understood the substance. All he had to do was hear it once, and it was his. He's the kind of guy who has the unusual facility of dealing well with both camps."

"What a loss," says newswoman Mary Leonard. "He would have been such a great press secretary, and it was the culmination of his dreams."

> On March 29 John Hinckley arrived in Washington about noon, after an all-night bus ride. He checked into the Park Lane Hotel two blocks away from the White House.

"I think of how it might have been," says Dave Prosperi. "He would have helped the White House have better relations with the media. I don't think we would have had as many credibility problems, such as Grenada. Jim would have tried hard to avoid that. He was a hardworking guy from day one. He didn't have time to sit down with me, but he'd say, 'This is how it works.' He knew what his job was. Early on in the administration there were a lot of meetings to formulate policy, and Jim found it very hard to do the briefings and attend the meetings, too. The press knew that Larry wasn't in the loop and didn't speak for the president, so it was a waste of time listening to Larry—a few phone calls would serve better. It was hard. After two or three times of unanswered phone calls the word was that 'Jim is not accessible.' It is a much faster pace in the White House than anywhere else. Jim would have been one of the best."

Lou Cannon says, "Brady was very good at substance but he was not made for the bureaucracy because he tends to operate as a freewheeler. He would have been a stormy character over there. The press operation would have been more important and not divided as it was between Gergen and Speakes. The communications shop might have been a bigger player. Brady was an outsider but he was steadily insinuating himself into the inner circle.

"But the way they have kept their power is by keeping others out. I think Jim had a chance. His incapacity left them with a big problem. Speakes is a lot more able than others think, but he was not prepared. And he and Gergen never got along."

"When Jim was shot it wasn't fun anymore," says Susan Bryant.* "We had worked for Republicans all over the country, and it was a 'new beginning,' just like magic. Everyone we knew from Illinois was on an upper. But the fun went out of life, and now it's work.

"All those setbacks. That's when you knew what he is made of. If you asked which of the group loves life the most we'd have said—Brady. He lived it to its fullest.

"Jim represented the little kid that's in all of us, and his ability to display those qualities and to still be an important part of government was just wonderful. It's so boring and stodgy to be part of government. People have to have all these perks—security, a driver, their office. They become so self-important. And here is someone who came along and says these things aren't all that important. It was his irreverence—he wasn't disrespectful—but irreverent. It's a fine line but he knew where it was."

"When you think of where he had come from, from no job to press secretary, then to being brutally wounded," says Robin West. "It's just not fair. When he became press secretary it was with unflagging humor. Most of those guys took themselves so seriously. If ever you needed something, he might have three hundred phone calls waiting, but he took the time to have a drink with a friend of mine from *The New York Times*. His strength is his humanity."

Lou Cannon says, "What Jim has done is that he has given the lie to the easy things people say—'Oh, it's better you die if you can't really live.' Those clichés really aren't true. I'll never think that again."

*Susan Bryant is now a Republican campaign consultant.

The other thing it's done, says Cannon, is to put things into perspective. "What he had done is very inspirational, and has brought a sense of perspective to a lot of us. So I'm grateful to him."

"In a short period of time he had a large influence," says Bruce Thompson. "I think he would have been an enormously positive influence on the White House. Jim would have been more of an adviser than a press spokesman."

"I watched him walk out those doors that day onto the Rose Garden," says Jeanne Winnick. "He gave me the high sign. And later, when I found myself having all these wonderful new experiences I would think, 'This isn't right. This wasn't the deal. Jim is supposed to be here.' That was the hardest thing for Sally McElroy and me."

"It's an unfinished story," says Hoffman. "Whenever I give speeches around the country I'm always asked about Jim Brady. There is a reservoir of caring and goodwill for him. People don't ask me about Reagan, but they ask about Jim."

Five years after the shooting, Helen Thomas, White House correspondent for United Press International and dean of the White House press corps, gave an assessment of Jim Brady—the man, the press secretary, and the press secretary he would have been.

"Whenever I look at the picture of Jim on Inauguration Day, I think of President Kennedy. There is nothing to match the high hopes—the happiness pervading the White House on that day. Their joy knows no bounds.

"John Kennedy and Jim Brady. These were two people who should have been there in the White House, because of their great wonderful Irish minds which always had that saving grace of wit and humor—understanding that life is not easy, but at times it is very, very funny.

"To meet Jim is to know him. He is always the same. Open and friendly. There's not a sinister bone in his body. And yet you know where he stands. He is definitely a Republican, and for Reagan. Although I don't think he is as far to the right as Reagan is.

"I think he would have handled some of the more controversial issues with ease and the proper amount of cynicism. He would have kept the White House from getting out of kilter and obsessed. He'd have been a great leavening agent. The way he would have expressed himself would have had the effect of moderating things.

"I think he would have softened this administration. Jim would have cajoled the president, 'C'mon, get off this ideology. You and I are two boys from the Midwest.' That sort of thing. He and Reagan would have had great rapport. As it is there's a kind of lack of compassion, a dried-out atmosphere, like a squeezed lemon.

"I think it is inevitable that Jim would have made mistakes—not catastrophic mistakes. But he would have rolled with the punches and would always have created an atmosphere of tolerance, and would have made the White House a friendlier place."

One thing Jim did that particularly pleased Helen Thomas was to visit the press room early in the morning to "troll," as he put it, for what the press's questions were going to be that day. "Jim would actually come into the press room in those early morning hours," says Helen. "He subscribed to the press view that 'while we are sleeping, *half* of the world is making trouble.' It was in those early morning visits that Jim took many, many queries from us. What a joy that was! It was that extra something—that attempt to get us official information. He was someone you could work with. He'd always tell you the truth or at least steer you in the right direction.

"He handled everyone kindly. I never heard him say a mean thing to anybody, ever, which takes some doing because I admit we are obnoxious in doing our job. I didn't see in this man any pettiness or vindictiveness. I think he lived basically by the Golden Rule. He's the All-American boy—baseball, Mom, and apple pie, or, in his case, Chili.

"We can be very obnoxious and demanding," says Helen, "But as the saying goes, 'If you can't stand the heat, et cetera.' It's the second most important job in the White House. It takes infinite patience, agility of mind, and stamina. But the rewards are great.

"A press secretary can't help but learn a hundred new things every day. Jim had the proper amount of ambition. He wasn't avaricious. He was a whole person in every sense. There was an affection for this press secretary I have never seen for a press secretary—ever.

"He was a real man. He has the kind of strength you look for and expect to find in people.

"And he has proved that in ten thousand ways, the way he has accepted his fate and fought against the odds to live, when nobody could believe he'd survive.

"I really think Jim is brilliant—the way his mind has withstood this incredible assault. He still has an agility of mind, and the wit he has is evidence of a quick trigger. He hasn't lost that. I've never seen anyone with such an indomitable will to live—and to live in the best sense. It is inspiring.

"Jim is not going to be counted out. He's like a great tree standing by the river. He's a role model and that's what life is all about. He realizes life is to be lived—that we should give our all—that we're lucky to be alive.

"Jim's example is the greatest testimony to human courage and a belief in life I have ever seen—the fact that he believes life is still worth living.

"He will always be there because life is a personification of *you*. And Jim knows he has to fulfill his destiny."

PART FIVE

The Bear Is Back

CHAPTER FOURTEEN

After the Trial

The Hinckley trial was grinding to its conclusion. The Bradys and their friends who were following it closely feared that Hinckley would escape punishment, and rightly so, for on June 21, 1982, the verdict of not guilty by reason of insanity was handed down by the jury. Publicly Jim was keeping a stiff upper lip, and during the trial he told an interviewer, "I have no feeling for Hinckley one way or another, except for pity." In a joking aside, he added, "and the fact that he's a fruitcake." But Gary Schuster was watching television with Jim one night when news of the trial came on. "Jim looked over at me, and I could see tears in his eyes. He said nothing."

In his final argument Hinckley's lawyer Vincent Fuller said he didn't think a fact like the "use of Devastator bullets is particularly significant. . . . I submit these are the acts of a totally irrational individual" locked away "from the real world because of his total isolation" and that the victims were mere bit players in his troubled mind.

"How dare he say to you . . . to forget the Devastator bullets?" rejoined prosecuting attorney Roger Adelman. "How dare he say . . . 'Jim Brady, forget the Devastator bullets'? I defy him. . . . Mr. Hinckley has been avoiding responsibility all his life. . . . All the evidence shows he appreciated what he was doing was wrong. . . . It would be nice if Jim Brady could hear this morning that he is a bit player." Tim McCarthy, Tom Delahanty, and President Reagan too, he said. "I'm going to ask you . . . ladies and gentlemen," to return guilty verdicts on each of the thirteen counts of the indictment. "The time has come for John Hinckley, Jr., for the first time in his life, to take responsibility for what he has done."

Jim and Sarah decided not to make any comment on the verdict. But the next day their lawyer, Jacob Stein, filed a $100 million lawsuit against R. G. Industries, the assemblers of the handgun.

Kobrine was worried about his patient. "He had lost strength and weight during the trial. He was down in the dumps. He saw the possibility that this guy who doesn't care about anybody might go free."

And Jim had a great fear of Hinckley. On the one hand, he viewed him rationally as a very disturbed man, but on the other hand Jim felt an irrational vulnerability to him. One of Jim's lifelong friends from Centralia assured Jim that if Hinckley ever was released, he would "take care of him. And I mean that," says the friend. "Jim was really afraid," says Kobrine. Jim told Kobrine, "He's gonna come for me and finish the job." "Jim wailed the most he had ever done during the trial," says Kobrine.

A week after the trial ended Jim had another flareup of phlebitis, but it was quickly detected, and after three days of bed rest in the hospital, Jim was back on his schedule of daily therapy. But privately Kobrine wasn't satisfied with the progress of his patient. He continued to be very lethargic. And Arlene Pietranton found Jim to be "very drowsy" in her therapy sessions, even though at the same time "he was responsive and he initiated social interaction."

A group of new friends who hadn't seen Jim for a while were stunned at his decline from earlier in the spring. After one dinner party Jim asked Sarah, "Who *were* those people?" He was confused. Kobrine and Sarah were having to wage a constant battle between the welfare of Jim's legs and the well-being of his head. To keep blood from pooling and clotting in his legs, the foot of their bed was raised; and to keep fluid from accumulating in his brain, the head of the bed was raised. And Jim was having short focal seizures every three or four weeks. On Jim's CAT scan Kobrine could see that the ventricles of the brain, where cerebrospinal fluid forms, were overly large. Actually they had been that way since Jim's March rehospitalization, and Kobrine knew there were only two reasons for it. Either the fluid was just filling up increased space created by the loss of brain tissue, or the absorption process wasn't working. Kobrine thought the latter might be the case and that the excess fluid was exerting pressure on Jim's brain.

"I had always been throwing around in my mind the idea of putting a shunt into Jim's cerebrospinal system to siphon off excess fluid," says Kobrine. "And when he didn't seem to be improving at the same rate, even given all his recent setbacks, I thought the lack of improvement might be related to excess CSF. My feeling was that if you don't try it you'll never know."

On July 6 Kobrine brought Jim back into GWUH for the operation. Under local anesthesia Kobrine inserted a one-eighth-inch-diameter pliable tube through the fat and muscle of his back into his spinal column at the level of his waist. Then, tunneling around to the front through the layer of Jim's fatty tissue, he fed the other end of it into the peritoneal cavity in his abdomen, where the excess fluid could flow and be readily absorbed into the bloodstream. "It made an enormous difference," says Kobrine. "The whole look he had about him changed. He woke up earlier—his alertness improved. There is no way to prove it for sure, but there's no doubt in my mind it helped."

In speech pathology, says Arlene Pietranton, after the shunt was installed, "Jim was alert, outgoing, witty, and very responsive." In early August, three weeks after Jim left the hospital, a friend who called the Brady household was greeted by an exuberantly happy Sarah. "We're celebrating here today. Jim walked a hundred twenty-five feet by himself!"

But just ten days later Jim's bad luck resurfaced, and the blood thinner heparin Jim had been taking since the blood clots in March lived up to the down side of its reputation, that of robbing bones of calcium. Jim suffered compression fractures of four of his vertebrae (two lumbar and two thoracic vertebrae). This added a burden of pain to Jim's load of discomfort that continues to some degree to this day. "It is a very rare side effect of heparin," says Kobrine. "Everybody was very surprised to see it, but in Jim's case, true to form, everything bad that could happen seemed to happen to him." Trout and Kobrine changed to the blood thinner Coumadin and put Jim into a full-body brace, which Jim hated. A twelve-inch band of heavy plastic laced up around his middle and supported two thick pieces of metal that ran up his back and curved over each shoulder to his chest. Jim wore this device for over a year, loathing every minute of it.

The next summer at a bluegrass-music party given by ABC's Hal Bruno, Jim, still wearing the brace, insisted toward the end of the evening that he had to get the thing off his body. With Sarah embarrassed, protesting, when the monstrous contraption was finally off, Jim looked around at those near him and said, "How would *you* like to wear that goddamned thing?" He called it the Iron Maiden and it did indeed resemble some sort of medieval torture device.

But it was to be the last major setback for Jim, although of course, he did not know it, except for seizures every four to six weeks. He could at last concentrate in a sustained way on his therapy. Late in August there was another scare and Jim was hospitalized for "bronchial wheezing," but it proved to be his asthma acting up and not a clot in his lung as they feared.

He was up and about before the month was out, and went to a performance of the uplifting musical *Sound of Music* at Wolf Trap, the outdoor summer theater in the suburban Virginia countryside. When Bob Dahlgren wheeled Jim in, the audience spontaneously arose to give him a cheering ovation. He was doing so well that Kobrine okayed a long weekend at one of their favorite spots in Bethany Beach on the Atlantic coast. Sarah was so looking forward to the trip, but "it was one of the saddest times for me," she said. "You can't go home again, as they say. I really saw the difference between what Jim used to be able to do and now could not do."

David and Brandy Cole, along on the trip with them, said, "Jim was in real agony. It is the only time I have seen Sarah really upset. It was their first visit back to the sea. Sarah cried and really let go among her close friends. 'This was our place,' she wept, 'the beach, the water.' " Beach time had always revolved around Jim's planning and cooking fabulous meals. Now he was unable to do any of it.

In September Kobrine and George Economos pronounced

Jim well enough to travel by train to Chicago where he was awarded the Lincoln Award by the Illinois Republican party. (Airplane travel was out of the question for the foreseeable future. Kobrine was afraid a sudden drop in cabin pressure might cause some of the healing inside Jim's head to come unglued.) The Bradys saw old friends—the Churches, Greeners, and Whelans. The Churches had a big party for them, and they had lunch at Jim's favorite, the Cape Cod Room in the Drake Hotel. And Jim threw out the ball at Wrigley Field when his beloved Cubs played the Pittsburgh Pirates.

Chicago welcomed Jim Brady back with many emotional displays. Bob Dahlgren, who accompanied them on the trip, said, "Even the concierge was weeping as we left. After that trip I think I could cry at an underdone grilled-cheese sandwich." "Jim so loved that trip," says Sarah. "We went out in a private railway car once owned by the brewer Augustus Busch. It was such a fun trip." At the award banquet in the Palmer House, Centralia attorney Jim Wham eulogized Jim. "A gallant man is with us tonight by the grace of Almighty God."

On October 19 Jim returned again to the White House press room. It was a momentous occasion for him. He was to go before his press constituency—to field their questions. And he took it all very much in stride. Deputy Press Secretary Larry Speakes joined Jim on the podium. "How are you doing?" Jim opened.

> **Speakes:** This whole gang needs straightening out. I want you to put it on them. [Laughter] They give me a hard time. Go; get them.
>
> **Brady:** That is what you are supposed to do.
>
> **Speakes:** No; that is why I have got you here. The whole gang needs straightening out.
>
> **Brady:** Mr. Good Guy; Mr. Bad Guy. [Laughter] Me, Good Guy. He, Bad Guy. [Laughter]
>
> **Q:** You have got to tell the president we need more access.
>
> **Brady:** Is that what you have been telling him? [Laughter]
>
> **Speakes:** Yes; I am telling you they have been giving me a hard time. I am beat down.

Q: Do you know we had a briefing here yesterday, and only Helen came?

Brady: I can't believe that. I wish I had been here. [Laughter]

Q: How do you think the president is doing?

Brady: I think he is doing fine.

Q: Why? [Laughter]

Q: Do you think he's doing great, or just brilliant?

Brady: I'll use your words. I think he's doing brilliant.

Q: Do you see any similarity in the campaign style—now, and two years ago?

Brady: Some.

Q: Like what? Like shielding him from the press?

Brady: Boy, oh boy, the Catfish has been doing that? [Laughter] I watched him drinking a glass of water today; and it didn't come out of his body, though. [Laughter] So, evidently, you haven't been too rough on him. [Laughter]

Q: Oh, you'd be surprised.

Q: Did you watch the World Series?

Brady: Oh, I've watched part of it. I think those damn pesty Cardinals are going to win. [Laughter] They have always been my second team.

Q: How is the president going to do in Illinois?

Brady: He will do all right in Illinois.

Q: Peoria?

Brady: Yes.

Q: Jim, I was on a program out in the Midwest, and your aunt came on, and talked about you and your mama. And—isn't it—one time your mama was— [Laughter]

Brady: [Laughter]

Q: I think you own Illinois.

Brady: Well, I put people in the right places when I've got big-city journalists out there on the air to hear what she has to say. [Laughter] Aunt Louise is on every call-in show in the nation. [Laughter]

Q: Make a prediction for us. Is the president going to run again in '84?

Brady: Well, I'll let him make that announcement.

Q: Do you think he should?

Brady: Sure. Why not? You all don't want me moping around here unemployed, do you? [Laughter] One of the biggest hazards of running in '84 is that you'll get beat. [Laughter]

Q: Do you think he ought to change his style?

Brady: No. He is pretty successful with the style that he's got.

Q: Jim, when did you name [Speakes] Catfish?

Brady: Day one. Don't you think he's an old catfish?

Q: We think he's a Mississippi boy.

Q: Sometimes, a shark. [Laughter]

Brady: There have been a few things said here I don't know about if you've turned into a shark from a catfish. [Laughter] I am going to have to go back and read your briefings.

Q: Even the Yankees are learning how to eat catfish now, Jim. They are selling it at the stores around here.

Brady: I'll be damned.

Q: Are you still listening to those briefings?

Brady: I sure do.

Speakes: Can't you tell—he's got all the guidance. Sometimes it elevates my blood pressure. [Laughter]

Q: Sometimes it puts you to sleep.

Brady: That depends on who asks the question. [Laughter]

Q: Do you see room for improvement?

Brady: I would not criticize the Catfish with him sitting right down here.

Speakes: Should I leave the room?

Brady: No. He knows the worst thing that you can do is try to answer a question if you don't know the answer. [Laughter]

Speakes: That's the truth.

Brady: You can get in more trouble that way.

Q: Did you see the president?

Brady: Yes; I sure did.

Q: What did he say?

Brady: Which time?

Q: Ah-hah; all times—this time.

Brady: Well, I think he knew the answers.

Q: This is about the second anniversary of the Killer Trees quote, isn't it? [Laughter]

Q: Yes; right. [Laughter]

Brady: We'll get Howell Raines to write it again. [Laughter] I haven't seen any Killer Trees since I've been out here.

Q: Yes; but Khachigian has.

Brady: We'll take that up with Ken. Maybe Deukmejian is seeing them out in California.

Q: Yes; right.

Q: How do you think the Republicans are going to do in this election?

Brady: President Reagan could wear purple tights and be a flaming homosexual and he would still be elected. Do you want to get up here, and take the rest of this briefing? [Laughter]

Q: What about the Senate? Is he going to gain in the Senate?

Brady: He could. He could very well gain in the Senate.

Q: How many; one, two?

Brady: I don't have my pad here with me where I figured it out. [Laughter]

Q: Will you come back to see us?

Brady: I sure will.

Q: Listen, this was fun. You sound just great.

Brady: Well, thank you very much, Sarah, really.

Q: We need a sense of humor around here.

Brady: Yes; and how. [Laughter] You take care.

The Press: Thank you. Good-bye.

The White House press corps had greeted Jim warmly, and when the briefing was over they followed him down the hall to greet him personally. When Jim went into his old office he took note that Larry Speakes had put up his own pictures and moved Jim's bear from the mantel. "Well, Catfish," he said, "I see you've changed some things around." "Just making things more comfortable," said Speakes, "but when you come back we'll change it right back. I'll leave you here in your office," said Speakes as he left. "He was very gracious about it," says Cindy Kobrine. Then the Kobrines and the Bradys had lunch together in the mess. "All the waiters came to the table," says Cindy Kobrine. "They all wanted to make a special point of telling Jim how happy they were to see him."

A week later Doug Burdette took Jim to a Harlem Globetrotters basketball game. "When they announced Jim was there," says Burdette, "seventeen thousand people went bananas. Jim must have signed fifty autographs, and although he got weary, he personalized every one."

When Jim's old friend Ken Adelman was appointed director of the Arms Control and Disarmament Agency that year, he invited Jim to his swearing-in in the Roosevelt Room of the White House. Jim told Reagan, "I never thought Ken would amount to a thing myself."

That fall Sarah pondered a request to become involved in the fight for the passage of California's Proposition 15, which would strengthen California's already-stronger-than-most-states' handgun laws.* The request ironically came from Peter Hannaford, ex-partner of Michael Deaver and a longtime associate of President Reagan.† Sarah very much wanted to do it and she sought the advice of friends. Bill Plante pointed out that it could look bad for Jim as the president's press secretary, because she would be campaigning in Reagan's home state on an issue he had long opposed.

In the end she decided against it, "but it killed me to turn them down," says Sarah. "I really wanted to help." As the daughter of an FBI agent, responsible use of handguns was something she had always felt strongly about, and now her life had been shattered by someone who had lied on his federal form (Hinckley had lied about his address, a felony), and who told psychiatrists he would not have purchased guns had there been a waiting period for checking him out.

*Proposition 15 required the registration of all existing handguns, and put a freeze on the sale of new handguns. California already had a fifteen-day waiting period for anyone seeking to buy handguns. In 1986 the NRA claimed that Hinckley had purchased guns in California, but that is untrue.

†Doug Bailey of the Republican political-consulting firm Bailey, Deardourff called Hannaford for help in attracting Republicans to work on it. Reagan's wealthy friend and supporter Justin Dart was among those who agreed to help.

CHAPTER FIFTEEN
Facing Reality

Jim and Sarah's social schedule became busier and busier that fall, 1982. Besides the many press and charitable functions they went to, they also kept up with old friends, going out for dinner. They spent an evening at Charlie's Georgetown as guests of owners Bob and Betty Martin, listening to nightclub singer Sylvia Syms. Syms came down from the stage to sing to Jim:

> **From this moment on,**
> **You and I, babe,**
> **We'll be riding high, babe.**
> **Every care is gone.**
> **From this moment on.**

"Cole Porter would be proud of you tonight," Jim told her.

Bob Dahlgren got together a stag luncheon at Jim's old Saturday haunt, Nathan's restaurant in Georgetown. When it was over Dahlgren said to him, "Get your money up on the table, Brady." "I don't have to," Jim said. "Whaddaya mean, you don't have to?" asked Dahlgren. "Well," said Jim, "I don't recommend it, but first you have to go out and get yourself shot." Dahlgren began to refer to Jim as "The Nation's Guest," and often Jim did, too. He found it amusing.

When Dr. George Economos and his wife, Lou, gave a dinner party of Greek food in Jim's honor that fall, the Economos's daughters, Themis and Demes, performed some Greek dances for their guests. "Hey, Brady," Dahlgren called out from across the room, "why aren't you out there dancing?" "I can't, I'm a cripple, you know," said Jim, trying out his latest line.

Kristi Coombs and Arlene Kulis from the cast of *Annie* came to Washington with their families for an evening of music in the White House theater. When Jim missed throwing out the ball for the Cubs' first game that April, he also missed their singing of "The Sun'll Come Out Tomorrow" in his honor. "They sang twelve songs from the show," said Sarah, "and we were all, audience and cast, in tears."

Out for dinner with Steve Neal at the House of Hunan one night, Jim told the waiter, "If you need any help cleaning the woks—just take this guy into the kitchen with you," pointing to Neal, whose kinky, Brillo-pad hair was an old joke between them.

The Bradys became regulars for hamburgers and bluegrass music at the Birchmere in Alexandria, and they went back to the Sorabol for Korean food. Dining there one night, Sarah asked the chef about a particular dish. "Is it made with peanut oil?"

Quipped Brady, "Where have you been, 'Coon? Peanut oil was the last administration."

New displays of Jim's wit and political acumen thrilled Sarah beyond words. She was always on the alert for tiny nuances of improvement. She above everybody else had the most confidence in Jim's ability to recover. She knew him the best. He would continue to get better and better, but that in itself would cause a crisis of its own the next summer.

Sarah, Art Kobrine, and Bob Dahlgren had begun to think that Jim needed the stimulation of being back with his colleagues regularly at the White House. Sarah called Jim Baker who told her, "Anything we can do for Jim we want to do," and he suggested she work it out with Larry Speakes, who was still sharing the briefings with David Gergen but running day-to-day affairs in the press office. "What I had in mind," says Sarah, "was for Jim to go in once a week for a few hours, which would include the lunch hour."

"I called Larry," she says. "It is the only talk I've had with him since the shooting. He was just very matter-of-fact about my request. He had been alerted by Jim Baker. He wasn't solicitous, just very matter-of-fact. I told him I didn't want it to interfere with the briefings or the regular working of the press operation."

"You know, Sarah," Speakes told her, "I want to hold this job open for Jim."

And what came out of the phone call was that Jim would spend a few hours each Friday in his White House office. "I made a point of never going in with him," says Sarah.

On November 5, his first day back, Jim Baker asked him, "Jim, how should we handle the unemployment story?"

"Your resignation would knock it off the front page," cracked Jim.

In his office Jim listened over the intercom while Speakes did the press briefing. "It was a tower of babble," he punned.

"He's going to work with us," said Speakes, "and be part of the team. I am, more than anyone, glad to see him back. I think it's the greatest thing for him and for us."

But pleased as Jim was about his return to the White House, it was not to be the reentry he had envisioned.

Thanksgiving of 1982 marked a year out of the hospital for Jim and the Bradys celebrated. Dorothy Brady came from Centralia and they all gathered at Sarah's mother's house. Frances Kemp gave her annual champagne toast adding, "We have more to be grateful for than usual this year." Scott, almost four, asked the blessing. "Thank you, Lord, for this wonderful food." He added, "Snack, snack, snack. Now it's time to snack. Amen." "Where he got that, I never will know," said Sarah.

Before dinner they had a picture-taking session, "and my mother, without thinking, asked Jim to back up a little for the camera," says Sarah. "I started to say, 'Why, Mother—' then we all laughed." They laughed joyously at the unspoken acknowledgment of how much better Jim was than when he left the hospital a year earlier, that they could even forget momentarily about his injuries. "Jim walked to the table for the first time ever that day," says Sarah, "and, in fact, walked all over Mother's house. His progress renewed the holiday of Thanksgiving for all of us and gave it a good connotation again." Since her father had died at age sixty in 1975, family gatherings had been subdued because of his absence, but Jim's recovery marked a new beginning.

It had not been an easy year; it had been filled with both hope and disappointment, a year of hard-won physical and mental progress on the one hand, and debilitating physical setbacks and rehospitalization on the other. But mainly it was a year in which Jim's progress had been on a steady upward climb. The jury wasn't in yet as far as his ultimate recovery went, but as Sarah said, "for someone who couldn't even sit up by himself, and who now can walk with a cane, he has come a long way. The worst things that could have happened to Jim did not happen and his progress has not plateaued yet." That was the most exciting sign of all. As long as Jim kept on making progress, not leveling off, there was hope for more and more recovery.

At the 1982 White House Christmas party Jim astounded NBC's Chris Wallace by remembering that his wife, Elizabeth, was from Rhode Island. They had met very briefly at the Kennedy Center Honors Gala in 1980 and had "a less than two-minute conversation," says Wallace. "Oh, sure, she's from Rhode Island," said Jim. "We talked about that at the Kennedy Center."

One seriously life-threatening problem persisted—Jim's seizures—still caused, Kobrine was sure, by that unreachable bullet fragment deep in his left frontal lobe. And Jim had a seizure in December. But nothing stopped the Bradys from enjoying life as much as they could.

Jim continued to have brief and relatively mild focal seizures from time to time. They all involved his right arm and right leg. He could feel them coming on and he feared and hated them. He didn't lose consciousness, and in the middle of them he could say, "I'm having a seizure." Kobrine told Jim that alcohol probably would contribute to bringing them on, and Jim acted on that information immediately. "Jim will order a drink and hold it, but not drink it," says Kobrine. Jim had a seizure in physical therapy while walking the halls with Cathy Wynne one day. She eased him to the floor so he wouldn't hurt himself and when he stopped convulsing, Jim, sweating and exhausted, said to her, "It's not a pretty sight, is it?" He always needed to sleep long and heavily after a seizure.

In January 1983 Jim and Sarah tried going back to another favorite spot—one where they had established many wonderful memories. They took a long weekend at the Tidewater Inn in Easton, Maryland, located on what is called the Eastern Shore on the Chesapeake Bay.

Once checked in, they took the elevator to their floor, but Sarah was almost unable to get Jim and his wheelchair through the narrow hallway of their room. Sarah's struggles with his wheelchair brought home to Jim the physical helplessness he felt, and for the first time since his injury he broke down and wept in front of Sarah. Sarah wept, too, and comforted Jim, then went about getting them a more conveniently arranged room. "It hit me then that we had to start new traditions," says Sarah, "and not try to do everything we had done in the past."

On Valentine's Day, 1983, John Hinckley made his third attempt at suicide while in custody, by drinking a toxic cleaning compound. Over breakfast Sarah told Jim that Hinckley had tried it again.

"How'd he do?" asked Jim.

"Well, it looks like he flunked again, Jim," said Sarah.

"Maybe we should send him a how-to kit," Jim suggested, "with a razor blade in it."

Through January and February Kobrine and George Economos had Jim heavily sedated with phenobarbital, which slowed him down in every way and made him constantly sleepy. Kobrine decided to try lightening the dose a bit at the end of February.

On March 8 he had a light focal seizure. "He remembers having them," says Sarah. "While in the midst of a seizure he would stare very hard to his right, and tell me later he felt like every muscle in his body was strained. He would have a seizure every two or three weeks."

The next day, however, the Bradys were on tap to fulfill their roles as chairmen of the first annual March of Dimes Gourmet Gala benefit where Sarah and Jim cooked his Goat Gap Chili. "Well, we really started out to make spaghetti sauce," he explained. Called to the dais for the second time as a prize winner, he announced, "I think I'm on a roll." About somebody else's carrot cake that won a prize, he asked, "Is that twenty-four-carrot cake?" His wit and attention to detail thrilled Sarah and close friends, who were seeing constant improvement in Jim's mental functioning.

On Saint Patrick's Day Jim became an honorary member of

the Friendly Sons of Saint Patrick, invited by Ed Hickey of the White House military office, and he went to the annual stag dinner with Bob Dahlgren and Sam Sampsell.

On March 30, there was a celebration of "two-years-of-life-after-the shooting" at a party Stuart Purviance had put together at the elegant supper club Pisces, in Georgetown.

Also on the occasion of the second anniversary, Judy Woodruff interviewed Jim for *NBC Nightly News* in a piece titled "The Man They Call the Bear." "What can we tell people about how the Bear is?" asked Woodruff. "Tell them the Bear is fine," said Jim. "The Bear has some pain but that's to be expected."

"And to what do you attribute your miraculous recovery?"

"I've had good therapists," said Jim, "and the Raccoon."

"I think he's always been that way," said Sarah. "His mom is that way. He was a hard worker and tenacious as a little boy."

"Yes," said Jim, "and I think of the alternative."

Asked how he felt about John Hinckley, Jim said, "Every day as I drag my pain-ridden body around that gymnasium down there, it's pretty difficult not to think of why I'm in this situation I'm in. But I think dwelling on it is counterproductive. On the other hand, I hope he doesn't win the Irish Sweepstakes either.

"When I think they're going to let him go—," Jim trailed off.

"When did the enormity of this thing hit you?" he was asked in another interview.

"I don't know whether it has yet," Jim replied.

Jim was the Grand Marshal of the Cherry Blossom Parade that spring, getting a huge response from the crowds as he passed by. He told friends he really wanted to be in the Gross National Parade, held the same day, and would have entered the "Female Head-of-Household Brigade."

That spring Art Kobrine asked Jim if he would be chairman of a twenty-million-dollar fund-raising effort to build a five-story addition on to the hospital. "No," said Jim, "but I'll be Chair Bear."

In the summer the Bradys went to opening night at the National Theatre to see *Same Time Next Year*. After the show they went to the Class Reunion for a bite. Sarah remembered all the good times she and Jim had had there, and a sudden vision flooded over her of how vital and vibrant Jim had been then. "It was the first time I have cried in a long, long time," she told a friend.

A few days later Jim and Sarah celebrated their tenth anniversary. Bob Dahlgren alerted the White House and the Reagans telegraphed them, "I hope you have a hundred more."

The seizures finally ended in May (although, of course, no one knew it was the end) when Jim had his last episode while out to dinner with Chicago friend Brian Whelan. "It was almost imperceptible," says Whelan. "He just went listless. Sarah got out a syringe and give him a shot." Kobrine kept Jim on phenobarbital. "All things being equal," says Kobrine, "it'd be better if he weren't on it. It makes his tongue a little thick. That's phenobarb language. But one has to weigh that against the disaster of his having a major seizure again." Kobrine looked forward to reducing Jim's dosage. "Everything will improve," he said.

Later Sarah told Brian, "I'm almost glad it happened in public. It's not as bad as Jim has feared."

When David Hartman interviewed Jim in 1985 for *Good Morning America*, he asked him, "What does it do to you, mentally and emotionally, Jim, when you were so capable, obviously, not to be able to do the things physically you'd been used to doing all your life?"

Jim paused. "It's humiliating," he said. "That's one word that comes to mind."

Having seizures in public was humiliating. Being barely able to walk was humiliating. Being in a wheelchair most of the time was humiliating. Being dependent on others for almost everything was humiliating.

If Jim feared and hated having seizures in public, there was another mean trick his body was playing on him that was even worse for his self-esteem. For the first several years of his recovery, Jim wasn't always able to tell when he needed to urinate. Although the accidents became fewer and fewer, the ones in public undid Jim completely. He was devastated by them—the shame over incontinence rooted so deeply in the human psychology as it is. After all, he felt, if you can't control that, what can you control?

Leaving a restaurant in his wheelchair one night, Jim's bladder suddenly let go with no warning. Although no one else was aware of it, Jim, of course, was, and on the trip home he wept and railed at Sarah in helpless frustration over the unfairness of it. But even that humiliation Jim learned to handle with humor, telling his doctor that his soaking of his office carpet "would build character into it."

Little by little his control improved until it ceased almost completely to be a problem—to Jim's immense relief.

Little by little Jim was getting better in many subtle ways. And a corollary of that was that he was more and more aware of his disabilities and his difficult life. Seeing him leave for physical therapy one morning, a friend called out, "Have a good day." "Yeah," snorted Jim, "as good a day as you can have at the hospital." He was having to deal with more pain, too, because as his nerves healed the pain became worse.

"The part of the brain that registers normal sensation was injured," says Kobrine, "and he has altered sensation. The brain decides what hurts and in Jim's case interprets the sensation wrongly. It's a matter of your brain tricking your mind.

"He was subject to psychological ups and downs, too," says Kobrine, "because of the injury to the brain tissue that moderates those defense mechanisms."

But Jim was increasingly able to put in longer days without tiring as readily. Increasing his endurance was very important to him. As he worked harder and harder, however, it started to become painfully clear to him that he was no longer able to see the light at the end of the tunnel. Up until the summer of 1983 he was just positive that he was going to be able to beat this thing and recover completely. In a Father's Day interview with CBS's Bill Plante, Jim said, "I will not be a cripple. I will not have it." Intellectually and emotionally he was wrestling with the inevitable handwriting on the wall—denying to himself that he was going to have to make major adjustments in his thinking about his condition. In occupational therapy one day he told a visitor, "It ain't dead yet," referring to his left arm for which his therapists privately held out no chance of functioning.

But in August that year, it all came crashing down for Jim one day in physical therapy. He complained to Cathy Wynne of vague abdominal pain and refused to work on his exercises.

Wynne, worried, called Kobrine, who came over to find Jim lying on one of the exercise tables looking very morose. Kobrine checked him over. "It doesn't look like there's anything organically wrong with you, Jim, but it looks like you're pretty down in the dumps."

"Yes, I am," admitted Jim, tears beginning to roll down his face.

"Well, there's nothing the matter with that. Everybody gets down in the dumps sometimes."

Jim broke into loud sobbing, and between his sobs, his sorrow poured out.

"Here I am," said Jim, "some fucker has shot half my brain away, and maybe he'll be out on the streets someday soon. Meanwhile, I piss in my pants, I can't remember things, I'm here at the hospital every day. Wouldn't you be depressed?"

"You're right, goddamit," Kobrine came back at him. "That fucker oughta be taken out behind the barn and shot. I agree with you, Jim. But that's the fact of it. You're shot in the brain. You're never going to be as good as you were. You've just got to be tough, Jim. You've just got to be tough."

"I know, I know," sobbed Jim. "The Bear is tough, but you're not the one whose back aches, and who can't get out of your chair."

"But you've got to be tough, Jim," Kobrine repeated. He could cajole Jim no longer. "You've gotta be tough."

"North American brown bears are tough," said Jim, his sobs subsiding. "The Bear is tough. The Bear is tough."

"Soon he was over it and was joking and throwing off his one-liners," said Kobrine. But Jim had hit rock-bottom. At last he had faced his tragedy and knew for a fact that only small victories lay ahead—not the complete recovery he had dreamed about.

"He thought if he worked hard he'd be perfect," says Kobrine, "and I didn't dissuade him from that. I felt I needed to hold that out to him to make him work it out and to keep him working hard."

It was the beginning of Jim's gradual acceptance that he had permanently entered the world of the disabled, and it was the beginning of his reaching out a helping hand in a more serious way to the many Americans who have suffered disabilities of all kinds.

The good news was that his cognitive skills were improving and would continue to improve for at least ten years after the shooting. But that wasn't a big comfort to Jim at that point. Coming to grips with the loss of his mobility was almost unbearable to him.

Jim began to talk about "levitating." He desperately wanted to "levitate." And he wasn't just kidding either. Or was he? Like talking about going shark fishing with dynamite, it was hard to tell. In an interview with Bill Plante, Jim announced that he'd been working on trying to levitate. "Are you going to levitate on the air for us?" asked Plante. "No. I'm saving it for NBC," said Brady. "NBC [in 1983] is in third place," he said, "and dropping quickly. My levitating would put it over the top."

Someone has to be the first one to levitate, he always said. "Why shouldn't it be me?" He was kidding, of course, but levitating was an idea he liked—loved, rather. He sat in his Bear Chair at home, barely able to move, and imagined himself levitating out to the kitchen, to the refrigerator, to the deck out back, to the swing set in the yard to play with Scott. Being able to move with ease was an idyll, an obsession, that was never far from his thoughts. "I'm going to give levitating a hell of a try."

He mourned the loss of his mobility. He spoke sorrowfully about his paralyzed left hand. "It's my little dead hand," he will say, patting it protectively. "It just lies there." "Don't hurt my paw," he will warn people, about his hand or his lame left foot and leg, which were also tremendously tender.

"I anticipate no new motor function," said Jim's "physical terrorist," Cathy Wynne, in 1983, "but he'll be able to use what he's got. It's been a long time coming but now he is independent in getting into and out of a chair. The quality of his gait is improving. I expect him to walk better and his endurance to improve."

Wynne said she expected Jim to get rid of the wheelchair except for long distances. But it was not to be. "For a year I pushed him," said Wynne in 1984. "After a year you're not going to get a new muscle back. I didn't accomplish some of the things I wanted to, and I feel bad about that. But when I think about the amount of mobility he has—he really has movement in his left hip only—so it is amazing what he does with that little bit of movement. His being able to get out of a chair is due to his perseverance and mine. I wish the pain element somehow could have been out of the picture so he would have been freer to move. Also the phenobarbital; he would lie down and fall asleep so I had to treat him sitting or standing."

Wynne used electric stimuli to help decrease Jim's pain, especially after his vertebrae fractures. "It helps release the body's own chemicals which anesthetize the pain. But he is not easily convinced that the pain of therapy is worth it.

"Jim has a very stubborn nature," said Wynne. "I learned early on that I would get nowhere in treating him in a conventional manner. I learned to joke with him. Once he could see I wasn't taking this all that seriously, and I let his personality come through by drawing him out on things he was interested in, his sense of humor has been the lifesaver through the whole mess. He taught us all drinking songs—'I Used to Work in Chicago' and 'The Lady in Red.'

"He's such a bright person it is hard to stay on his level for any length of time. I found I would have to rise to his level or lose him. With Jim I had to adapt to a large degree. There was always something new. He has started initiating a lot more. For instance, the other day we couldn't find him. He was on his way to the elevator to get himself up to speech pathology.

"One time he really sat me on my chair. The phone rang in the clinic and when I came to answer it, Jim was on the phone saying, 'It's your mother.' She was so excited. 'Was that Jim Brady?' 'Tell her bears can answer the telephone,' said Jim.

"Jim still has a tremendous lack of function in his left leg except for his hip and some of his thigh muscles," said Wynne. "He has no voluntary control over his left foot and ankle and needs the brace which holds his ankle and knee. His high muscle tone helps him walk [because it makes his leg stiff]. At the same time he has pain from these flexed muscles. He still spends a lot of time just standing to work out the flexion."

Wynne often had Jim stand on one leg—the Whooping Crane position, Jim thought of it, and he supplied the whoops—sometimes perseverating on them to Wynne's complete distraction.

"Jim, you're perseverating on those whoops."

"Yes, I'm perseverating," Jim would answer. But Jim, before and after his injury, was also not above attempting to try the patience of those around him.

For a long time Wynne didn't know there was a precedent to Jim's whooping-crane act, but Jim had once or twice been the guest of a fey little group of Washingtonians who call themselves the Cogswell Society. This group had discovered an obscure sculpture in a tiny city park dedicated to Temperance. It was built by one James Cogswell and features a crane standing on one leg at the top. A totally irreverent bunch, they would begin their monthly lunch meetings by standing on one leg, raising their wine glasses high, and shouting, "To Temperance!"

"This working with Jim Brady can be so damn crazy at times," said Wynne, because she was never quite sure when he was being his playful, outrageous self or if it was his injury cutting in, and Wynne cited his ability to imitate funny accents, such as the classic Canadian accent, which he mimicked saying, "Throw me downstairs the ball." "He's a very unusual man, incredibly unusual."

In 1984, Jim's "wailing" was still a problem, too. "It is off-putting to too many people," said Wynne at the time. "It's the saddest thing because the intellect is there. I tell him, 'Turn that soprano into a baritone.' " Jim told CBS's Charlie Rose, in an interview, "I can control it, but it is difficult." But by 1986 it almost never happened anymore. Jim had it almost completely under control.

After three years of therapy, Cathy and Jim had developed an easy bantering relationship. "She saw me at my darkest hour," said Jim. "I sure did," said Wynne, "and it has been a rocky course. I have had to hurt him so much and he will tell you so, too. The amount of pain Jim has to endure is really awful. It's a tragedy."

Jim, almost from the beginning, claimed that PT (physical therapy) stood for Pain and Torture; and that OT (occupational therapy) stood for Obvious Torture, "and is a black art," Jim likes to add.

"Going back to the White House helped him a lot," said Wynne. "He is happier and more alert on those days. Jim rarely says anything about what has happened to him, but he has a normal resentment of what happened. If he didn't I would *really* worry about him. He keeps a lot inside. It's his sense of humor that keeps him going—and all the rest of us, too."

"Stop trying to kick my legs out from under me," Brady told her one day as Wynne tried to position his left foot with her foot, and he threatened her with the "salmon paw," raising his right arm as he went into his Bear routine.

"Jim, will you work on your quads, please?"

"I thought you told me I have dead quads and therefore couldn't move them."

"No, I never told you that and you know it."

"I'm crippled, you know, and you've got to be nice to me," Jim said protectively.

"Keep working."

Later as Jim was walking for therapy, Wynne told him he was walking so well he needed longer walks. "I suppose you're going to put me out on the street and make me manage all the trucks and cabs and traffic, aren't you?"

"Hang on," she said as Jim got a little ahead of her.

"Hang on, whaddya mean, hang on? Do you think I'm Peter Pan and am going to fly out of here?"

"First, she told me I was going to go through life looking like a question mark," said Jim. "Now she calls me 'Mr. Posture.' "

From time to time Jim's therapists asked Jim to list what he thought his strengths and weaknesses were. In 1983, playing it mainly for laughs, he named as strengths that he was "a good bear, a great chef, good with children, handsome, friendly, remembers names. I'll purr if treated right."

His weaknesses? "Don't call Wynne [he called her Winnie] a twit or a bimbo; don't hit said twit with my cane." He couldn't think of any other faults but Wynne, Marino, and Pietranton could, and they were working every day on them. He wanted, he said, "to be more easily ambulatory. I can walk but it takes great pain and a lot of trouble, and I can't do that as easily as I want to do it." When friend Steve Neal complimented him on walking up steps with Wynne's help, Jim said, "Yeah, especially when you consider that I have to drag *her* around with me."

Part of Jim's injury and a classic head-injury problem was that he had lost a little bit of social inhibition. "He is too candid," says Sarah. It was a difficult problem to attack because for a very long time Jim couldn't recognize some of his behavior as being inappropriate. He was particularly wicked with his cane, using it as an extension of himself. It was one of few avenues of self-assertion he had, and he liked to threaten people with it, harmlessly and jokingly in most instances. And he also used it to reach out, to make contact, to get someone's attention. Occasionally, however, he threatened to bull's-eye a friend's backside, and he made a few direct hits on them, too.

Some of his friends, too, encouraged Jim in the behavior therapists term "inappropriate." One night in 1983 while crossing the deserted top floor of the Kennedy Center, a friend pushed Jim madly around the Atrium, chasing first one, then another member of the Brady party—Jim brandishing his cane, calling out, "Make way. Make way for His Poohship." "The Imperial Pooh" was another moniker bestowed on him for the evening.

Men friends kept him abundantly supplied with the latest dirty jokes. Dahlgren always addressed him as "Asshole" or "Dipshit." It was the male way of stimulating Jim and he enjoyed it enormously and needed the macho context. At the same time, it didn't fit into what his female therapists considered "appropriate behavior," especially when Jim then failed to make the distinction between his buddies and people in the therapy office.

His language was always colorful, but now occasionally he was a little off as to when it was appropriate to use locker-room language or tell dirty jokes. For a while he told a raunchy sheep joke to everybody he met,* including a church lady who came up to him at a restaurant and told him she had been praying ceaselessly for him. "He was probably a little more selective before," says his daughter. "However, sometimes he just can't resist an opportunity like that. Like the Killer Trees. He knew it'd get him in trouble, but he did it anyway." And Jim still did have the latest jokes in town—his delivery of them, especially the shorter ones, was impeccable, and hilarious. "Jim has never told me the same joke twice," says Doug Burdette.

Once again, sometimes it was hard to tell what was Jim Brady and what was the injury, because it had always been Jim's personality to let fly with risqué language and jokes when he was around his colleagues and friends, women included. And now he considered the hospital staff to be colleagues and

*Why did God make women? Because sheep can't cook.

friends. As much as he wanted to get back to his work, the hospital had become the major focus of his world. None of these things were very much out of character for Jim, they were just nuances of behavior. He often before liked to teeter on the outrageous edge of social norms. Now he occasionally stepped over that fine line. The most effective relearning of "socially appropriate behavior" took place when someone he had offended confronted him with his insensitivity. Jim's innate kindness couldn't bear that accusation. He took it very personally and would usually not repeat the behavior. "I threw him out of the department a couple of times," says Wynne. "He could be a real latrine lips when he was pushed too far."

"All through it, and even to this day," says Art Kobrine, "he was so witty that it sometimes took me a minute to figure out whether he was off the wall or right on target."

Little by little he became resensitized to the fine tuning his therapists thought was important, with occasional, some thought deliberate, relapses. So much of Jim's life was now beyond his control, it would be unnatural for him not to lash out now and then. In fact, Jim had to learn to restrain himself more than he had to before the shooting because people assumed some of his antics were the result of brain injury, when in fact, they were not.

Cathy Wynne felt one of Jim's best strengths was his ability to remember every single therapy patient's name. "He really developed rapport with a large number of patients here," she says. "Many are really disabled. They can be poor, sick, old, or young. But he makes up funny names for them. And his interaction with patients is constant. There was a librarian in for therapy who was afraid to approach Jim because she was a Democrat. But once they got together they would recite poetry together, particularly 'The Cremation of Sam McGee.' If one would falter with the lines the other would pick it up. They had this place in stitches."

"Jim never had typical frontal-lobishness," says Kobrine, "but at various times he had various aspects of it, including: inattentiveness, short attention span, seemingly flat affect, difficulty with initiation—he wouldn't initiate the next behavior until someone told him to—for instance, at first he would chew and chew and chew until someone reminded him to swallow."

Initiation remains perhaps Jim's biggest problem today, his

therapists feel. Although it improved enormously over the first six years, getting started on a project and staying on course are still difficult for him. With the help of a well-trained assistant, however, therapists feel that he can put his marvelous public-relations abilities back to work very successfully. And, for that matter, Jim's working strengths were always in the realm of trouble-shooting, of handling his candidate's image and issues, all of which he did on the spur of the moment out of his vest pocket. "He never worked with reports and papers in his life," says Sarah. "It bored him then and it bores him now." Sarah is not worried about Jim's inability to sit down and write an outline of a project and carry it out. "That is just not the way he has ever worked."

After six years, Jim had nearly beaten his "wailing" problem. "When he's laid back and with friends he doesn't wail," says Kobrine. "I have seen it on his face when he just starts to wail and then I can see him consciously suppress that. That's learned behavior. Jim's way of diffusing tension is to crack jokes. It is a very deep-rooted way of his to cope with his stress."

"This isn't exactly your cup of tea, is it?" Wynne asked him one day. "Well, whose cup of tea is it?" answered Jim. "He's such an independent cuss," she says, "but he can't call the shots anymore."

Jim is often very hard on himself, referring to himself as a "gimp" or a "half-wit." And there were days in therapy when he got very down and depressed indeed, particularly in OT and SP, where his mental problems were much more evident to him.

It was always clear, however, that Jim's fine qualities far outweigh his deficits. His political instincts are as sharp as ever. He knows exactly how things are going to play to the public, and he knows what to do and say to defuse touchy political situations. In public, he has been unfailingly loyal to the Reagan administration. When asked how he viewed the U.S. air strikes on Libya after the Gulf of Sidra "Line of Death" incident (and before the air raid on Qaddafi's headquarters), he said, "It was time to flex our muscle a little bit"—a perfectly defensible low-key political evaluation.

"Jim is around people constantly," says Kobrine, "and the higher up you are and the more you have achieved, the less you can lose brain and not seem different. Everything Jim did was right up front and public, and therefore was so highly noticeable."

From the beginning Jim was aware that he was very important to his fellow therapy patients at the hospital. He brought them signed photos from the White House, encouraged them in their therapy, sympathized with their pain, and joked with them.

He also accompanied Kobrine on his rounds on 5E from time to time, bucking up the spirits of the neurosurgeon's patients.

One who went through the GWUH therapy shop the summer and fall of 1982 was Tim Wyngaard, executive director of the House Republican Committee. Wyngaard had a stroke that July. "At first I couldn't comprehend what had happened to me," he said. While still almost comatose, Wyngaard overheard conversations between doctors and others in which his chances for ever returning to work were given no hope; in fact, they said he would need total residential care for the rest of his life. "Interestingly enough," he said, "it was these conversations that made me come out fighting. They told me I had severe brain damage and would be physically handicapped. I clawed my way back up by my fingernails.

"I owe my existence to Jim Brady," he said, "and to a couple of other people." [Susan Marino was one of them.] "The first day in therapy I met Jim. He and I had had previous contact when I was on the Republican Congressional Committee. He gave me an extremely friendly greeting—told me, 'Get those pegs in those holes.' " (A reference to the basic test he was about to undertake to see what he could and couldn't do.) The therapist also had Wyngaard copy the phrase "Today is Tuesday, August 10, 1982." "It took me twenty-five minutes to copy it. That and the pegboard so exhausted me I spent the rest of the hour sleeping.

"The great thing about Jim was that every day he had a different greeting—a new nickname—which was often tied to current events. He was reaching out and being very careful not to let me wall myself off. He actually reaches out and embraces you, and says, in effect, 'We can be whole.'

"The relationship I admired Jim for was the relationship between himself and other patients down there. He clearly set out for himself the role of reaching out to them and making them feel important—making them feel like worthwhile human beings. There were a lot of welfare patients, for example, but it didn't matter who they were. Every elderly woman got a personal greeting every day. And he singled out the younger patients. There was a young black girl, about fourteen, who'd had a stroke, amazingly. From the first day Jim talked and joked privately with her, telling her to 'line those therapists up and threaten them with her stick [her cane] and make sure they worked with her.' She would laugh, and say, 'Yes, sir, Mr. Brady.' He spent three or four minutes with her every time she came. He always had a few minutes for everybody in the workroom."

In an emotionally eloquent accolade to Jim, Wyngaard said, "He is a magnificent, brave, strong, and good man. I thought, 'If he can make it this far with an injury much greater than mine, then I can make it, too.' Jim Brady epitomizes that no matter what happens to you, it's what you do with what you've got that counts.

"Bear is the right name for him. He is big and soft and loving. Just by his presence he reaches out and puts his arms around you, so you can have the comfort of 'The Bear.' You can take care of your problems by hugging into him, as you can with all good teddy bears.

"He is one of the strongest people I have ever known in my life. All the strength underneath all of that—to be able to come through as compassionate, as caring, as genuine, as understanding as he does. And to grow and continue to grow in spite of everything. He is more a man today than he ever was in his life. To have him there just as an example with his comradeship, the laughter, the joking, the political chitchat. It was enough to turn my life around. I love him like a brother.

"Jim had the same sort of damage I had, which means that he clearly had difficulty in sitting down and developing a thought all the way through. He (and I) had visual and spatial and lineal (putting things in order) problems.

"At first, it doesn't mean anything to be told your IQ has been lowered, or this part of your brain isn't functioning. It was hard to believe that the organ that was going to help me has been damaged in such a way that I couldn't understand I needed help. It doesn't make any sense until therapy puts you in touch with your deficits. There was no comprehension on my part until therapy tested what my problems were.

"I was well into therapy before this realization hit me—that I had any deficits. Therapy can be helpful and it can be demoralizing. The GW therapists are the most professional group of people I've ever worked with in my life. They did more for me than any other person there. But they are organized to deal with what your deficits are. So you are constantly being slapped in the face with them. I didn't realize I had severe visual damage (as did Jim), so I'd read just the right-hand page of a book, or the right side of a newspaper. I'd finish the paper in minutes. The vision comes in but there is nothing back there to make sense of it."

Wyngaard recovered quickly, and left the hospital in October and eventually returned to his job, but, he said, "When something like this happens to you, I describe it as having fallen inside your head. You know the world is out there, but eventually you realize you can't get back to the world you see and know is out there. That's the only way I can describe what happened to me."

While Wyngaard was in therapy, he and Jim were both doing the same sort of work: putting pegs in the pegboard, putting square shapes in square holes. "At first," said Wyngaard, "it was maddening, absolutely maddening. One of my first bits of therapy was a modified erector set. They would give you a book on how to build a farm truck. Mine turned out to look like a 747. Your vision and comprehension prevented you from doing it."

Jim called Wyngaard "Admiral" or "Professor." They would joke about building farm trucks and then building farm wives. "How's the old farm wife coming?" Brady would shout out, then "Ee-eye, ee-eye, oh."

"We talked about going fishing. We'd talk politics. Jim'd sit there and laugh at the screwups in the White House. We were both feeling negative about the image the White House was creating for itself at that time." After Richard Schweiker's disastrous explanation of the Reagan plan to reduce Social Security benefits, Wyngaard and Brady would joke about: "How John Block loses the farm vote"; "How Malcolm Baldridge loses the business vote"; "How William Brock loses the overseas-industry vote." "We indulged ourselves with that kind of black humor."

While Wyngaard was still in therapy, Ed Rollins, Reagan's political adviser, a member of the White House senior staff, had a mild stroke, and he wound up in therapy as well. "One more down here," Brady and Wyngaard joked, "and we can organize this place into a Republican precinct, take over the place, and run it the way we want to." "We got into jokes about who'd be next," said Wyngaard.

While Rollins was in the hospital, President Reagan came to see him. "Jim was there that day, too," said Wyngaard, "and I asked him if the president came to see him."

"No, he's got different priorities today," said Jim.*

In addition to reaching out to his fellow patients, Jim also served as counsel to Cathy Wynne on such things as where she could meet a friend after work. He sent her to Nathan's where his friend Bill "Obie" O'Brien tended bar. "And it's a wonderful bar," says Wynne, "a lot of fun. You can actually have an intellectual conversation there." Obie wrote notes on napkins for Wynne to deliver to Jim, which cheered him up.

"Obie doesn't like to overserve you," Jim told her, "and he steers girls away from the jerks and on to the good guys," says Wynne.

When Wynne was taking lifesaving classes to become a senior swim instructor, Jim said to her, "You're learning it in a pool. I taught it on a lake." And he told her, "You've got to get really aggressive, really assertive. Don't try to think it through. Just get angry. Just get out there and save that guy." "I found those tips enormously helpful," says Wynne.

Cathy Wynne left GWUH in 1984, and Jim began having physical "terrorism" with Tom Welsh, and then, in 1986, with Noreen O'Kane. O'Kane tried a new approach to therapy, that of using a relaxation technique—trying not to cause Jim any pain—doing gentle oscillating movements. It was a new theory and Cathy Wynne had told Jim about it. "He thought it was a swell idea," she says. But he also said, "I'll believe it when I see it." Wynne tried the new technique on Jim before she left, "but he gets so sleepy he yawns, which just increases his muscle tone," she said.

*On August 17, 1986, Wyngaard suffered a second stroke and died of complications.

Jim loved it, however. He had had enough of pain and torture, and to a certain extent his injury prevented him from being fully able to see the value of enduring the pain and the resultant payoff.

That September Jim addressed volunteers at the March of Dimes Gourmet Gala. "We need to raise a hundred twenty thousand dollars," he said. Then looking around the room, said, "Hell, Germaine [a Washington restaurateur] has that much around her neck."

In October 1983 the Ford Motor Company loaned the Bradys a car that was equipped to hold Jim's wheelchair. After their first trial run, Sarah called Kobrine. She was flying, she was so happy. "This is the first time we have operated as a family unit since Jim was hurt," she told Kobrine. Later that month Jim and Sarah were able to make their long-awaited pilgrimage home to Centralia. In their Ford LTD, they set out with Emmy Fox to make the journey. It was such a treat for them to be by themselves on the open road that "by noon," says Sarah, "we weren't even a hundred miles out. Jim wanted to stop every thirty minutes to get an ice-cream cone. We had a two-hour lunch, then stopped again. We barely made it that night to White Sulphur Springs, West Virginia, only two hundred miles away."

On the third day out, Jim and Sarah picked Scott and a Brady friend up at the Louisville, Kentucky, airport to drive the last 180 miles toward the homecoming in Centralia. In Evansville, Indiana, just across the Illinois line, the cook in the truck stop came out to say, "You're Jim Brady, aren't you? I was just sure it was you. I just want you to know how much I admire you." "Thank you very much," said Jim. At the next stop, now in Illinois, his home state, the proprietor offered ice-cream bars to the travelers—fellow Illini making their gestures toward Bear Brady from Centralia.

In Jim's honor Governor Jim Thompson had proclaimed Monday, October 10, 1983, "Welcome Home to Illinois Day." After they crossed the Illinois state line, more and more people recognized him on their stops—their faces often crossed with emotion. They were expecting him and were moved by the sight of the familiar face. Most of them approached him, but many didn't want to interject themselves and spoke only to members of his party. "Is he heading for Centralia?" said one man, his eyes filling up momentarily. "Yes, he is." The man nodded slowly in approval. Native son returning to the heartland and native soil.

Native son began reminiscing about all the friends he expected to see, and all the hijinks of his youth. With particular amusement he recalled Peno Castelari's restaurant. Jim claimed that three counties cornered in the middle of the place so the owners could move their slot machines around to whichever county they were legal in at the moment.

The plan was that Jim and Sarah were to meet Dorothy and homecoming organizers Red Schwartz and Ruby Ryan at the John Deere dealership just south of Centralia. As Dorothy Brady came wheeling up in the backseat of a police car, Jim greeted her with "I saw you sitting up straight in the police chief's car. I didn't know whether they arrested you or not." Seeing attorney and fellow Sigma Chi Jim Wham, Jim said, "Brother Wham. Are you still on that Ferris wheel of life?"

Now in a Ford convertible, Jim, Sarah, Scott, and Dorothy rode to the intersection where the Centralia High School Marching Showcase waited to lead them into town. On Poplar, the major north-south avenue, they began making their way north to Broadway, the main street. Centralians waving homemade signs lined the streets all the way. "One-deep," noted Jim. WE LOVE YOU, the signs said. WE'RE GLAD YOU'RE BACK. WE ALL LOVE YOU, BEAR. WELCOME HOME JIM. ENJOY YOUR VISIT, one said modestly. WELCOME JIM BRADY FROM ALL OF US ON LAKEWOOD DRIVE. One youngster sported a T-shirt saying, "Centralia, Illinois. Home of Jim Brady." People dashed out to the car to shake Jim's hand. "I shook his hand, I shook his hand," one lad said excitedly to his friend. Church bells rang out as the procession passed by.

"You know what," said Jim, "it's so good to be a Bear."

At the corner of Broadway and Elm, on the steps of the Home Federal Savings and Loan, Centralian, and Illinois State Comptroller, Roland Burris officially welcomed Jim. A message from Governor Thompson was read, and Thompson added that Jim's visit was "just the lucky charm needed for our victory over Ohio State." Mayor Jack Sligar gave Jim the "key to our city," and Sarah was praised for being an "inspiration to all the women in America."

Just two blocks away the parade ended at Dorothy's house where well-wishers and friends packed the front lawn. Jim walked slowly through them for a brief press conference.

"I think Thomas Wolfe was wrong when he said you can't go home again," Jim said. Asked what was the first thing he wanted to do? "I want to spend some time with the old war-horse," he said.

"That's his mother," said Sarah, laughing.

"I hope there'll be a pot of homemade vegetable soup on the stove," Jim went on. "And I'll make my annual pilgrimage to the Centralia House for some good Creole cooking." Asked what he thought about the resignation the day before of James Watt, the controversial secretary of the interior, Jim refused to comment, but said he would have advised him "not to be so loose with the lip, because loose lips sink ships."

As to whether Reagan would seek another term, Jim said, "My educated guess is that this time next year we'll see him on the campaign trail."

When the Bradys retired inside Dorothy braced her son. "Old warhorse? Old warhorse?" she said.

Not backing down for a minute, Jim said, "I meant it as a compliment." But Dorothy wasn't totally convinced.

That night old friends Bill and Lyla Crain, and Jo and Dewey Kessler served up a sumptuous meal for the household and close friends. It was the first of several nights of good eating. They had a Creole dinner at the Centralia House the next night, and on Wednesday, after a big reception at the Elks Club, Jim and Sarah and friends went on to dinner at the Bigger Jigger. Thursday night was potluck supper at Ronny Mann's "lake house," and on Friday the Bradys headed north for Champaign-Urbana, the home of the fighting Illini, and the University of Illinois. On Saturday, for the first time in sixteen years, Illinois defeated Ohio State 17 to 13. Jim joined Illini fans shouting "Chief, Chief, Chief, Chief."

Back home Jim took an increasing interest in current events. His visit home seemed to give him a needed boost in his recovery.

Jim and Sarah went by train to Columbia, South Carolina, to be patrons for a Children's Hospital benefit early in November, at which Barbara Mandrell and the Oak Ridge Boys performed. The Bradys were given the key to the city and people lined up to get Jim's autograph. Asked at a press conference, "How are you?," Jim said, "I'm doing better. I've worked through a lot of the pain but I'm not as steady as I used to be. Sometimes I'll take a header. If I think I'm going to take a header I always look around for a good place to land." Getting expansive with the idea, he added, "For instance, if I see Dolly Parton is sitting there, I'll head for her."

Asked if Reagan was going to run, Jim said, "My guess is that he will run. Mommy wants him to." Political questions to Jim made Sarah nervous at this point, and she hoped Jim's remark wouldn't make the wires.

In December 1983, Ed Meese got into hot water when he said that most people standing in soup lines didn't really need to be there, they chose to be there. Jim, hearing it on television, said, "Good God, Ed, have you lost your head?" When he saw Meese at a White House Christmas party a few days later, Jim said to him, "Been standing in any soup lines lately, Ed?" Meese laughed and said he'd been hearing a number of comments like that.

In February, when Soviet Premier Yuri Andropov died, Jim told friends he thought Reagan should go to Moscow for the funeral. "Hell, it's a golden opportunity," said Jim. "It may never happen again in twenty years."

In early 1984, Sarah and Jim's close friends felt they could see important improvements in Jim after his down periods from the summer of 1982 through the summer of 1983. Friend and PR colleague Ron Weber said, "He's the old Jim today. If I had a PR problem and, I'm not dumb, but if I really couldn't get a handle on it, I'd call Jim and talk to him about it."

Similarly, Alan Woods said of Jim at that point, "Jim is the same person he always was and always will be. His essence as a human being hasn't changed one whit. My greatest concern is his delivery of the language. His memory has never faded. I think he could do sustained work depending on his ability to communicate. He's a creative person and still has good ideas about PR. It's a matter of finding a stream of activity he can enter—a PR consulting business or lobbying."

In an interview with Bill Plante in March 1984 for Charles Kuralt's *Sunday Morning*, on the third anniversary of the shooting, Jim acknowledged he was bored. "Physical therapy quickly gets old," he said, "but I'm an obedient Bear . . . and Kobrine said they'd pull my number off the wall," if he didn't keep going.

"Is it kind of a drag?" asked Plante.

"It *is* a drag. Sometimes you say to yourself, 'Omigod, I can't do that,' and then Poof! You do it and it wasn't all that hard after all."

Jim said he was walking without a cane now, although "it's dangerous," and the next step would be levitating. "I can't levitate yet, but it can't be that Byzantine. . . . I ain't a cripple. I won't have it," he added.

Plante asked Jim several times how he could be so tough as to go through what he had endured. "If anybody else can do it, I can do it," he said. "And partly it was because they've told me I can't do it. . . . The better you get the tougher it is, that's the way it works out."

Plante asked him how he had been able to keep any discernible bitterness out. "I've never had a session of 'Why me, God?' " said Jim. Plante pressed him on the subject.

"That wasn't in the leaves," Jim said cryptically. And later in answer to the same question, "It's just the way this unit has always been set up." It was a difficult question to answer, and Jim wasn't about to wax glowingly about his own personal qualities. "Bears by their nature are humble animals," he had said on previous occasions. "It goes with the territory."

When Plante asked Jim what he viewed himself as doing in the future, Jim said he could see himself joining a Republican think tank such as Herman Kahn's Hudson Institute, or doing PR for a corporation.

And for the immediate future? Jim said he'd like to be "a communications adviser to the 'Old Man.' Have them make me an offer," he said. "I want them to focus on a role for me. Bears know what they're about and what they can do." The next thing he looked forward to? "To be invited on the plane with the Old Man."

"What do you miss the most that you used to do?" asked Plante.

"My meeting I had every day with the 'O and W.' " And, Jim added, "if I continue on in any capacity, it'll be as an adviser."

For public consumption Jim maintained the fiction that he

saw Reagan regularly. When he was asked what he and Reagan talked about, Jim would say, "Well, I talk to 'Dutch' like a Dutch uncle, and tell him that he needs to do this or that."

Plante said, "A lot of people in the high-pressure, ambition-oriented West Wing don't quite know what to make of Brady anymore, or how to deal with him without being just a little patronizing; but there is no question that there is also a tremendous feeling of goodwill toward him."

Mike Deaver was shown saying, "Well, having been there that day when all of them were shot. . . . I think it's something short of a miracle to see him walking about this White House. It's an absolute inspiration to all of us, not the least of whom, the President." Deaver added that Jim could continue to serve as press secretary "as long as he wants to and he does."

Jim told Plante he would like to do more than just answer his mail. He'd like to be involved "to make certain that the open line of communication is kept between the president and the American public."

In the same piece Kobrine said, "He had a devastating injury, lost a lot of brain substance." His remarkable recovery "is because he's a fighter. . . . He's a little bit lazy at times, too," and alternates between his fierce fighting, "and then getting tired out and lazy and a tiny bit bitter . . . but that's all overcome by fighting."

Jim, watching at home, was a little bit hurt. "I'm not a lazy Bear," he said.

Jim's philosophy, then? asked Plante, closing the interview.

"Even though you get knocked on your keister, you keep getting up and go back into the line, back into the line, back into the line."

Jim was privately bemused by the annual specials the networks did on him. He knew he was newsworthy and he didn't want to be forgotten, but, he told Kobrine, "next year they're going to do a special on the manufacturer of the bullet that blew my brain apart. And the year after that they'll do a special on the handgun that held the bullet that blew my brain apart."

Jim knew that the public was still focusing on the bullet and the brain injury. It seemed to him he just couldn't get beyond that and he wanted to. He himself tried not to think about what had happened.

Friends at the networks offered to set up a screening to

show Jim all the tapes from the day of the shooting. Pressed to remember what happened that day Jim said, "I purposely have tried not to go over it in excruciating detail, because that's exactly what it is, excruciating." The TV films of the shooting, he said, for him "have the sense of the macabre, and I just don't want to see them.

"It doesn't do any good to have any anger because that leads to recriminations, and revenge and other counterproductive thoughts." That was for public consumption, however. In private he did have such thoughts, but he fought against having them. He knew they were hard on him. For a long time after the shooting, he was convinced that Teamster President Jackie Presser was in Reagan's car in the motorcade that day. (He wasn't.) Not a fan of Presser's, Jim would say, "Why didn't they tell me that shlep was going to be around? I know I wouldn't have gone then."

That same spring Jim talked further about his disabilities. "Getting out of my chair ain't easy," he said, "but I can do it; the same with getting out of bed. I've relearned how to walk. You have to learn it all over again. The right leg does okay, but the left leg has a mind of its own. It does what it wants to do. You have to hunker down and reason with it. Stairs and throw rugs are the true bane of my existence. Throw rugs are there to throw you on the floor."

Likewise, he said, "my left arm will move when it wants to move, and surprise me. There's a signal up here," pointing to his head, "that only goes so far." About his walking, Jim said, "My gyroscope doesn't work. It's supposed to keep you from falling on your frigging face. You'll be trying to walk and all of a sudden your scuppers are in the water, and you're taking on water. They're on this kick to get me to walk without a cane, but it's dangerous. I could easily fall. It has to do with your posture. You feel anxious—uneasy—about it. Part of it is not having any feeling in my left leg."

About the cognitive side of his injury he said his mind was playing tricks on him. "It does that with figures and dates. You *know* what the day is—and you go to say it—and," he said incredulously, "it ain't that date. That's not a very nice mind to do that to me. Now you *don't* know what the date is and you feel like an idiot. That's one problem I haven't solved." But he was continuing to improve, he said. "Kobrine told me he hadn't seen such improvement this far away from the trauma.

But the ultimate improvement will be when I levitate. I get so tired of being the product of somebody else and not of myself. It's about time I assert myself." And levitate! he meant.

Jim didn't mention to Plante that his walking without a cane had been the result of an incident he initiated. At home ten days earlier, he had ordered nurse Paula James, "Get my cane so I can beat you with it." By now well used to Jim's frequent and overblown threats, James retorted, "If that's what you want it for, get it yourself."

At that Jim walked without any support the thirty feet to get it. It was a first for him. He had never walked without his cane before.

"I didn't know you could do that," said James.

"I knew I could do that," Jim replied.

"Brady, you've been malingering," Otto Wolff accused him, when he heard about it.

In 1984 Jim was still seeing Sue Baylis Marino three times a week. In occupational therapy he had progressed from the simplest, most rudimentary exercises—the pegboard—to playing games and solving puzzles on a computer Control Data had donated to the hospital in Jim's name. "The Confuser," Jim always called it. Marino's aim "was to make Jim independent in such areas as bathing, dressing—'activities of daily living' as they are called. We have also tried to figure out how to control the pain and are doing pretty well with that." Originally, Jim virtually ignored anything that appeared to the left of his center. But now, Jim's left-sided neglect had receded enormously. "For a while he insisted there were two Sue Marinos," she said. Early on one day, she appeared first on his right, then went behind him and appeared on his left. "There's someone impersonating you," Jim would tell her in all seriousness. "You'd better get hold of her."

"It is the right side of the brain where visual perceptual skills are located," said Marino. "Each half of the eye sees half of what is there." And Jim's vision in the left half had virtually been knocked out. "He has come a long way to appreciating the totality of a picture. At first, working on a puzzle he would focus on one tiny part and be unable to complete the whole puzzle. Nor was he able to use clues or my guidance to finish it.

"His left-sided neglect, severe at first, is still there, but much less so. Using the computer he is quicker to touch figures on the right side of the screen, or will miss one on the left side altogether. In cooking he will stir the right side of the pot much better than the left side. At first, if he were making cookies he would only cut out cookies from the right half of the rolled-out dough.

"His improvement is partly recovery, partly learned. He knows when he can't find something, he has to look over to the left. He used to bump into things on the left of his wheelchair, but that happens very seldom now.

"Jim had difficulty in finding his way around the hospital," said Marino, " 'route finding,' which was related to his problems in spatial relations. For instance, he had difficulty in looking at a geometric design and being able to copy it.

"In art therapy he enjoys drawing pictures of cowboys with bullet holes in their hats, but doesn't always see it as being part of what happened to him."

At first, Jim had trouble with "body scheme"—remembering how the human body is organized. "He had difficulty looking at an eye piece of a puzzle and putting it into the right place, for example. This problem is related to his early difficulty of recognizing new faces. This doesn't get in his way anymore," said Marino.

Marino had Jim working on the simplest sorts of puzzles to improve his memory, his concentration and organization. "You'd think he would be resistant to them," she said, "but he has been good about it all along. He does realize he has difficulty and now he sees how he has improved. 'This is to work on my visual memory,' he will say. I try to relate it to him—'This will help you remember news events, faces and things like that.' "

"Jim knew he perseverated," said Marino, mentioning another old problem. "Perseverating is indicative of generalized brain injury, sort of like a reverberating circuit. At first, if he would say something, for instance, whatever it was that made him say it in the first place keeps triggering and he repeats and repeats it. If I point it out to him he recognizes it, but being aware of it doesn't necessarily make it possible to stop. He is getting much better though."

Another problem they were working on, said Marino, was the difficulty he had following procedure and getting things in the right sequence. "If something is given to him out of order he has difficulty putting it in order." Knowing that cooking was one of Jim's interests, Marino used it in Jim's therapy. The kitchen in the hospital's therapy wing is adapted for people in wheelchairs, "a gimp-proof kitchen," Jim called it. "With his difficulties, cooking became a weeklong activity—figuring out what to do next.

"He always wanted something gourmetish," noted Marino. "Chili, of course. Then there was New Orleans jambalaya, Mexican cucumber soup, James Beard's tomato bisque, recipes from Marian Burros's cookbook *Keep It Simple*."

Marino would have Jim write down what ingredients and equipment he needed, and she would order them from the hospital cafeteria. "We usually had to split up a recipe; cut up the vegetables one day, for instance, and assemble everything the next. He needed a lot of structure and cues but he was able to draw on his old skills.

"The first time Jim made his famous chili," said Marino, "he wanted to put in the whole can of chili powder, and I wouldn't let him do it. Later I found out he was right. We had a few disasters—the tomato bisque curdled—but Jim still enjoyed eating them."

Jim's problems were lessening. By 1984, said Marino, he needed much less cueing and he perseverated less. "Quite often he enjoys the activity and gets caught up in it. Sometimes he will get stuck on chopping up two or three tiny pieces of onion. When I point it out to him he never appears to be embarrassed. 'Oh, that's that perseverating again, isn't it?' he'll say."

"Cooking is not easy," said Marino. "There is a lot to learn and to integrate."

One problem that seemed to stick was that of initiation. By now Jim had no trouble initiating conversation and most other things, but when it came time to put his mind seriously to work, he needed some nudging to take the first step, then the next one. "It is easier to verbalize that something needs to be done than to initiate something physically, like reaching over and picking up a pen and starting to write, or to pick up the phone and make a call.

"I am continually impressed," said Marino, "with how when someone comes in to see Jim here, he sits straighter, he can always think of something chitchatty about the person to say. He is doing really well with new things happening in the news—showing more abstract thought and opinion and drawing on old opinions to bear on new happenings. He will often come up with new funny responses I've never heard before."

Marino let Jim know he could talk about what was bothering him—Hinckley, his injury, whatever. "Usually he didn't take me up on it, but there are days when he really gets 'bummed' as he says. And it happens more lately as he is more aware of his limitations."

Sometimes in the privacy of the therapy room Jim wept and wailed and talked about being a "crippled Bear." "Sometimes he talked about it's not being fair," said Marino. "He has become more aware of the finality of it. And yet he doesn't have the full cognitive awareness of his limitations. It's a little like being drunk. You don't realize how drunk you are. It takes a lot of insight to see where your difficulties lie." But for his family and the rest of the world, Jim kept a stiff upper lip. He told his Uncle Ed, as they prepared to go to physical therapy, "they'll probably kill me this afternoon." "That's the way Jimmy handles it," said Ed Brady. "I know he gets down, but he doesn't show it."

During a cooking session in early 1983 Jim prepared to cut the root ends off a bunch of green onions for the jambalaya he and Marino were making. "Now I'm just going to perform a little rabbinical procedure here," he informed her. Jim was as irreverent with Marino as he was with Cathy Wynne. "Jim likes to give us a hard time," said Marino, "but he is basically very cooperative and also offers support and encouragement to the other patients. He is really a role model around here."

Talking about her goals for Jim, Marino said her efforts "were geared toward things which contribute to Jim's feelings of self-worth."

"Which are immense," said the listening Brady.

To Marino fell the task of working with Jim's left hand—trying to stretch it and exercise it so the contractures wouldn't be so painful. "He called it 'bone-crunching time' and begged me not to bone-crunch, accusing me of taking lessons from the Marquis de Sade." And Jim used his standard threats on Marino. The Bear paw, pretending he would maul her like a bear. He occasionally tricked her into shaking hands with him, and then gave her a bone-crunching handshake in return.

Marino also observed Jim's interactions with the other patients. "I often introduced them to him and they enjoyed meeting him. He was always very receptive to meeting people." Ed Brady observed his nephew comforting a patient, "a woman in her fifties who had both legs off above the knee. She started to cry and Jimmy said to her, 'Better things are going to happen and they're worth waiting for.' "

"Jim quite often was able to pick up on their difficulties—sometimes being very concerned about other patients' feelings. We had one patient with head trauma, who was going through a very agitated phase. Jim said, 'That person has two personality traits—disagreeable and unpleasant.' What pleased me," said Marino, "is that he would say it in a very quiet way, so only I could hear.

"Jim was a good influence on this patient. He'd be able to calm her right down by saying something funny to her.

"A quadriplegic patient here gets a big kick out of Jim—she lights up when she sees him. A lot of higher-level patients knew him and benefited from talking to him.

"He named everybody: 'Deke the Greek,' 'Lou the Sioux,' 'The Gerbil.' And the names stuck."

Jim and Marino listened to the news together and to presidential press conferences. "After a press conference Jim would imply that Ronald Reagan could use his advice. 'I would've warned him not to pick on So-and-So to ask a question,' he'd say." Jim liked to answer back to television news. "It gives him a chance to use his one-liners."

By 1983 speech pathologist Arlene Pietranton said of Jim, "I have seen him make dramatic improvement and there hasn't been anything to make me feel he is plateauing yet. He is quick-witted, he has a high level of abstracted and integrated thinking. My goal right now is to increase the speed at which he accomplishes tasks, and to increase the thoroughness of his responses."

Brady, listening, said, "Their goal is to see that you never speak again and so can't testify against them."

"Half of what we do in here is sparring with each other," laughed Pietranton.

"From the beginning," she said, "Jim was capable of understanding everything." In other words, he could receive information perfectly well; where he had trouble was in organizing that information and sending a message back. He himself recognized the problem when he heard things come out of his mouth that he didn't intend. Even though he knew what he wanted to say, sometimes his brain scrambled the message before it reached his mouth. With persistence he was able to overcome this and to get out what he had originally meant to say.

In 1984, after two and a half years of working with Jim, Pietranton contrasted the early days of therapy with Jim's progress. "Now he takes initiative. He will turn the computer on, for instance, to get the session started. One day last week the cafeteria sent up a dish of liver for his lunch. Jim had the meal sent back. If he needs help with his wheelchair he will directly request it. He will ask the reasons for whatever activity I have planned. Some of the things we were doing on the computer were too simple and Jim said he thought they were not worth his time."

Sarah says, "For the first two years he would answer any question directed at him beautifully, but he would never initiate any conversation. But that has all changed."

"When we first started he would have just sat there and not asked what we were going to do," said Pietranton. "He ate whatever meal was sent to him. Now he is more back to his own personality. He is very direct and frank about his feelings and preferences. Now Jim is much more involved. He actively follows through on activity and tasks. He is much more aware of what's going on in the world than I am. He is very, very current."

Pietranton, too, mentioned Jim's involvement with the other patients. "He has been a real strong advocate in helping other patients here. He is very giving of his time. He realizes patients regard him as a celebrity and is gracious about autographs and picture taking. He inquires after them and extends himself to them."

Pietranton said that she had never "observed Jim telling risqué jokes to those who would not appreciate hearing them. He is definitely more aware of what is appropriate behavior. But Jim likes to fool around. For instance, one day after having watermelon for lunch, he was flipping the seeds around. I told him, 'No food fights in my office.' I was very firm about it."

Pietranton cited an earlier incident when Jim had thrown

an ice cube at Sandy, an aide in the office. "That is rude, Jim," Pietranton told him. "Over the weekend, he must have thought about it because on Monday he said to her, 'I hope I didn't offend you, Sandy.' That kind of sensitivity really amazed me at the time," said Pietranton.

When Pietranton first began working with Jim she devised very structured tasks for him. "Gradually the tasks became less structured and more demanding. For example, in the beginning I couldn't have given him a piece of paper and had him write out how one makes popcorn. Now he can make a good stab at working it out on his own.

"Initially it was important to keep responses similar. Now different responses are possible—such as on the computer. Before, if it asked him to respond in different ways he would perseverate on the previous answer.

"There have been times when there have been obvious changes. There was a period of time—within a week—when Jim was all of a sudden giving opinions, taking initiative, being able to speak up about things."

Jim picked up on Pietranton's husband's Italian name and called her "Guinea Fowl." "He will read anything," she said. "He will pick memos out of the wastebasket. 'Did you get back to this person?' he will ask me. Or if I'm busy working on something before our session begins, he'll say, 'Are you saying you're not going to be civil till you get that memo done?' He teases me because I come from a long line of Rhode Island Democrats. But I can tease him right back about his political attitudes and candidates. He doesn't get overly defensive, although he is very loyal to the Republicans."

In April 1983 Jim's therapists had a team meeting to discuss his progress. "Jim knew about it and was very concerned," said Pietranton.

"You're going to be talking about me, aren't you?" he said. "Are you going to keep me coming for therapy, or are you *not* going to keep working with me? You're not going to turn the poor Bear out onto the street, are you?"

"I was surprised at his reaction," said Pietranton, "in the sense with which he is really connected to this place."

But for his part, Jim was displaying how deeply he had internalized Kobrine's prescription: that Jim would receive therapy as long as he kept improving. Jim did not want to hear that he had stopped improving, had "plateaued," as therapists termed it. He wanted to get much better.

At the same time, as a result of their meeting, Pietranton, Marino, and Wynne realized that Jim was getting tired of the same routine. "His attention to his tasks was not being well focused. He was very bored by what we were doing and we started making some changes," said Pietranton.

Instead of having Jim write answers to questions she had posed, Pietranton started asking Jim his opinion about newspaper or magazine articles. "He has a good perspective on the news. He knows what is going on and has reasonable opinions."

At that time Jim started working on the computer, and Cathy Wynne tried Jim out on a stationary exercycle. "That turned out to be a disaster," says Jim. "They had to call a proctologist to get me off the damn thing."

A year later Jim claimed he was so good on the "Confuser," "if I went any quicker you couldn't see my fingers move. I'm as quick as a Tasmanian devil."

The next spring Pietranton assessed Jim's overall progress. "I think the amount of progress he has made has been excellent. The extent of injury and the deficits he had were really incapacitating. The quality of his life without therapy would be as different as day and night.

"Now he can actually be part of his environment, he can interact with people. And he is clearly able to influence people. Certainly he is not leading the life he was before, but socially he can enjoy people and they him.

"Jim continues to make changes at this level where he has an increased use of his cognitive skills. So he is increasingly able to use those skills to monitor himself and modify his responses. He is able to alter his behavior in response to other people as well. His brain has more resources available to him, and although it is unlikely he will ever recover to where he was before, there is no indication he has stopped making progress. He is still changing."

Jim had had more therapy than most people are able to get, said Pietranton, "but he has certainly benefited. He is a good example of what therapy can do. There's a lesson to be learned from this. It is always the cruel issue of money versus benefits.

Jim would not have been able to reach this level of recovery without therapy.

"Everybody with a head injury is different. Our attitude is: This is a person who is unique and who deserves treatment as long as he gets better."

In January 1984 Sarah's assessment of Jim's difficulties coincided exactly with that of his therapists. "I have seen the most dramatic improvement in Jim in the last two months," she said, and she felt very hopeful about that. As for his deficits, "The biggest difference I see is that Jim doesn't have the same inhibitions as before. His judgment on saying things, for instance, telling a racial joke to a black person. Another problem is that he will get an incident happening today mixed up with the past and he relates things to the past. But he is living more and more in the present. He has a big interest in everything and he sees the significance of events much quicker than I do. He probably gets most of his news from television and has taken an interest in light TV entertainment.

"Jim gets upset about his arm or that he can't get up and do things, and when he used to think people were talking *about* him and not *to* him." She knew that Jim's playful nature raised eyebrows on some people. "Jim always had a childlike quality about him. He called himself the Bear, as everybody knows, and would hold up his hands for approval. From time to time people see it and it bothers me when they mistake it for his injury. And Jim picks that up right away."

In October 1983 Cathy Wynne had said, "The biggest problem I see right now is that I'd like to see Jim's cognitive stuff organized better."

Six months later Art Kobrine said, "I see a brightness that wasn't there before. He is more symmetrical. Here we were yesterday talking about the primary, about Hart and Mondale. And he was so absolutely on target. Then he turns to me and says, 'Whose campaign is Deaver working on this year?' Things aren't wired exactly right. But he knew he had made an error and he quickly and coolly covered it."

CHAPTER SIXTEEN

Looking for a New Direction

Sally McElroy at the White House also felt there had been a great deal of progress. "His speaking, as far as expressing himself, is so much better. Before, he'd say a few words then there'd be a long pause. I really think he's made a lot of progress. He's starting to get a little bored with the things I have for him. The novelty of coming back to the White House has worn off, and he tends to get bored with what he does here." Jim was mainly answering his own mail and giving Sally some input into his responses. Jim's attention span was improving all the time, and now, he was beginning to be willing to get involved with disabled groups. "Initially he wanted no part of anything like that," says McElroy. "In that respect he's come a long, long way."

Twelve-year-old Mike Beatrice of Swampscott, Massachusetts, became one of Jim's pen pals. He sent Jim bear posters and other bear things and came to Washington to have lunch with Jim in the White House mess. "A woman in Illinois wrote Jim every week," says Sally McElroy. "A lot of people write of someone who has had a similar accident and ask us to write them. Jim says, 'I guess it helps, so let's keep answering.' "

But most of all, Jim wanted to be involved in the White House and the upcoming 1984 campaign. In a television interview he announced, "I am making myself available for the 1984 campaign." He told everybody he ran into who was working on the campaign that he wanted a job. "Put me to work," he told Michele Davis. "You know what my strengths and talents are." "I would have hoped," said Otto Wolff, "they'd give him something in the campaign. I talked to "B" Oglesby about it."

But nothing came of Jim's attempts to get involved more in the White House and in Reagan's reelection campaign. The truth was that Jim needed help to carry through on any project. Just what sort of help he needed would slowly emerge over the next three years. But there's no doubt Jim could have made effective campaign appearances for the Reagan-Bush ticket.

Jim, however, was making many nonpolitical appearances, and every appearance caused a minor sensation in terms of the emotional and appreciative reception he got. "I think it's hard for the campaign to go on and he not be a part of it, but I think he's campaigning in his own way," said his daughter. "He knows what will produce what in a PR sense."

Missy, who hadn't seen her dad for ten months, saw many changes for the better that fall. "It's the fine points I am seeing now," she said. "Before, it was leaps and bounds. Before, he was totally unrealistic. Now he is a lot more realistic. But he has always been a great exaggerator and storyteller. You always have to take Dad with a grain of salt."

Seeing him in August, and then again in September, she even saw improvement in that one month. "In August his speech wasn't so good. Now he is keeping it more level."

For Jim, being involved in the campaign was his overriding concern. Jim knew he could make a contribution there, but no effort was made by the campaign to give him a role. Nor, it seemed, was Jim able to get more involved in the White House.

After Jim's return to the White House in November 1982, "Jim Baker came by occasionally," says one staff member. Not many others on the senior staff took the time to visit Jim during his Friday office hours. Neither did Reagan. Many of them ran into Jim in the mess at lunchtime, however, and the Reagans ran across Jim and Sarah occasionally at official White House functions, or at the large annual press parties. But Reagan never summoned Jim to the Oval Office for a talk to hash over, one on one, their mutually terrible experience at the hand of John Hinckley, as one might expect of two comrades-in-arms.

"If it had been put on his schedule, he would have gladly done it," says a staffer. But somehow, over the years, it never was. "I wish he would," says one.

The White House, of course, was going full blast, with all throttles open, and pressures were intense. Perhaps they could be forgiven for largely ignoring Jim's return. Although there is no doubt that Jim was regarded with great affection, the truth was that the president had long since recovered from his gunshot wound and everybody in the White House, except Jim, had moved on. And in 1982 when he first returned to the White House, Jim had not achieved the degree of recovery he enjoys today. Sometimes he would let down and let go emotionally in the privacy of his White House office. The staff there sometimes saw him at his worst. His wailing put many people off. But at the same time, Jim was looking for—longing for—some involvement in the process he knew so well. No one, it seemed, had the time to figure out how he could be useful; nor was figuring that out an easy task, either. But one insider says it was possible that more could have been done by the press office to utilize Jim's marvelous PR instincts.

But, says Sarah, "I really never felt or noticed anything like that."

As it was, Jim spent his one morning a week dictating and signing letters with his secretary and friend Sally McElroy. "And," says Jeanne Winnick, "I always made a point of running by Jim whatever press release I was working on that day. And he caught some errors I made, too." He usually lunched with friends or fans. It would be a while before Jim would begin to accept the chairmanships of the many organizations for the handicapped that were seeking his help. He was still clinging tightly to the hope that he would get well enough to resume his old job.

Whenever Kobrine asked Jim what he had done at the White House that day Jim would indicate by a well-known male gesture that it was just another day of—doing nothing.

One thing Jim and Sarah hadn't partaken of before Jim was shot, the most delectable plum that came with being close to the White House, was a White House state dinner, an event where all the sacrifices of attaining the pinnacle are forgotten and only the pleasures remain. Attending a state dinner makes the invited guests feel they are participating in a special moment of history, and it was a special dream of Sarah's. "Jim and I were invited to a state luncheon for the president of Korea early in 1981, and the British embassy invited us to a dinner for Prime Minister Margaret Thatcher to which the President came," she says.

In the fall of 1981, Sarah was invited to the state dinner for Hosni Mubarak, Egypt's new president. "I turned it down," she says, "because Jim wasn't invited, and in my heart of hearts I thought he could have gone, even though he was still in the hospital." Neither Sarah nor Jim has been invited to a state dinner since, although they attended a luncheon for the Irish ambassador in 1983.

Cindy Kobrine says, "They're probably afraid he'll wail and be conspicuous and be an embarrassment, whereas if any of them spent any time with him they'd know he can be the most delightful, witty person." Sarah feels, however, that it is due to staff turnover and perhaps to the departure of chief of protocol Lenore Annenberg, "who always took such careful pains to see that we were included, having worked with Jim on the campaign. I don't believe it is personal." It was not something the Bradys worried about at all. It was their friends who felt Jim and Sarah deserved a little more attention.

"This points up the transient and fragile nature of friendships made in politics," says one political reporter. "It is an intense experience you share together, but when it is over people tend to go their own ways and often those friendships do not survive. But Jim ought to get the Purple Heart and veterans' benefits for what he's been through."

On *Washington Week in Review*, the correspondents were talking about how Reagan is able to shut out things he doesn't want to think or talk about, when Jack Nelson of the *L.A. Times* recounted this anecdote: "One day the White House called a number of people to come over for a little ceremony to give Brady a mug with Reagan's likeness on it. The idea was to use the mug as a gift to raise money for the Jim Brady Foundation to take care of people injured in the line of duty. Brady was sitting in his wheelchair, and Reagan came in and said, "Hi, Jim," stepped up to the microphone, pulled out his index cards, read from them for about a minute, turned around, and went back into the Oval Office. He never even talked to Brady. I stood there dumbfounded."

Others who witnessed the same scene were equally shocked. Jim got off a couple of funny lines that went completely by the president. Reagan said he would probably fill his mug with jelly beans, and Jim said, "I'm going to put Mount Gay rum in mine."

"Jim Brady took a bullet for the president," says Jack Nelson. "It might have been any one of us." And FBI officials believe that the bullet that hit Jim would have hit Ronald Reagan had it not hit Jim first.

One Friday as he was leaving the White House after lunch in the mess, Jim remarked to his nurse's aide, Paula James, "Do you get the feeling they don't want me around here?" "Why, no, Jim," she said supportively. "Well, I do," he said. "People don't take me seriously anymore."

On ABC's *20/20* in 1985, Jim was shown chatting with a group of other disabled people. One little girl in a wheelchair asked him, "Do you like the White House?" "Yes, I do," said Jim. "I hope it likes me, too."

Publicly Jim often claimed that he spent two or three days a week at the White House. He didn't want people to know how little time he put in there.

A penetrating article about Jim's restlessness appeared in the *Los Angeles Times* on September 23, 1984. Headlined, BRADY BORED, WOULD LIKE ROLE IN REAGAN CAMPAIGN, it quoted Jim as saying, "I'm somewhat bored." Sarah worried about the timing of the piece, coming as it did just six weeks before the presidential election.

The article suggested problems between Larry Speakes and Jim, calling their relationship "cool but cordial," and quoted a White House official who said he occasionally sensed "a ripple of resentment" on Brady's part over the "delicate" job arrangement, that of Brady's taking over his old office every Friday morning.

When asked how "gracious" Speakes had been about turning over his office each week, Jim replied, "It's my goddam office—he doesn't turn it over to me. I'm the one who's being gracious."

And, the story went on, "Speakes admitted that he no longer tries to involve Brady in White House affairs."

"I see Jim very briefly," Speakes said. "He comes at a time when I'm moving and hopping around. We're busy, so we don't sit down and have a long conversation. But we do talk back and forth as I prepare for briefings, and at various times I do keep him informed. Jim is sharp, his humor is there and he is up to the minute on news events."

Speakes said that he does not covet the press secretary's job title even though he performs the job. "The title is his," he said.

Jim told Marlene Cimons, "I'd like to be a communications adviser; I'd like to get Reagan ready for big press conferences, or for the times he has to go on the tube." But he said he had not talked with members of the White House inner circle about such a possibility.

And he wanted to be involved in the campaign. "I want to be going with the flying circus. I'd like to do the same thing I did last time; the care and feeding of the press."

The story went on:

> Ed Rollins, director of the Reagan-Bush reelection campaign, told Brady that he would very much like to use him in the campaign. Brady was enthusiastic about the idea but Rollins has not yet followed up on his offer.
>
> Dr. Arthur Kobrine said he sees no reason why Brady could not be given a limited campaign role.
>
> "There's no question he is bored now," Kobrine said. "We talk about it all the time. Physically, it might be difficult—a political campaign is hectic. He can't run and catch airplanes. But his political insight and nuances are extraordinary. He is able to see situations accurately in a way other people can't see. It would be a shame not to utilize such a resource."
>
> Brady's wife, Sarah, agreed but said she thinks that her husband realizes he will never be able to assume his former duties again. "It's coming at him now that it's the campaign and he'd love to be doing those things again," she said. "But I think he knows deep down inside that he's just not able to."
>
> Kobrine said that he intends to talk to White House Chief of Staff James A. Baker III and his deputy, Michael K. Deaver, after the election about getting a more substantive job for Brady.
>
> "I hope there isn't any reluctance to provide a job en-

vironment," Kobrine said. "After all, his injury was in the line of duty. It's not like he got drunk one Saturday night and ran his car into a tree. He took a bullet meant for the President of the United States."

Kobrine said that some of Brady's White House colleagues "don't know how to handle it when he does the wailing. They don't listen through it—if they did, they would see he's still right on target."

Kobrine talked about Jim's sense of humor and his amazing progress and said, "He's been frustrated. I've been with him when he's cried. He gets tired and depressed in March. Every March since I've known him has been a terrible month. But he has never quit."

The article mentioned the "cool but cordial" relationship between Jim and Speakes. During the eight months Jim was in the hospital Larry Speakes had not visited him. Nor had he called Sarah to inquire after them. The first time he saw Jim after the shooting was on Labor Day 1981 when Sarah called for help in handling the press outside during Jim's first visit home. "I had a hard time seeing Jim," says Speakes. "It took a long time before I could see him."

"And," says Sarah, "for a long time I discouraged any visits to see Jim except for our closest friends." Sally McElroy kept the press office informed on Jim's progress.

But still, it seemed curious behavior for someone who owed his job to Jim Brady in the first place, and would continue to hold it because of Jim's strong reaction to the plan to replace Speakes and appoint a new press secretary. But it was consistent with Speakes's image among his staffers as a social loner and someone who found reaching out to others very difficult. "It would have been nice if Larry had encouraged us to do something for Jim as a group," says one press office staffer.

Back in 1980 during the transition, when Jim was East Coast press secretary, Speakes had tried a number of times to reach Jim to ask if there was a place for him in the press operation. And Jim needed experienced help. Speakes, who was then working for the public-relations firm of Hill and Knowlton, had worked in the Nixon and Ford White House press offices, and had been press secretary to Senator Eastland. "I knew anybody who labored in that vineyard couldn't be all bad," says

Brady, referring to the Ford White House.

After Jim returned to the White House for his few hours each week, there were rumors as time passed that Larry Speakes sometimes found it hard to turn his office over to Jim for that time, perhaps understandably. As time went on the rumors were that he wanted to have the title of press secretary for himself.

"But I never pushed for anything," said Speakes in March 1984. "I am the deputy press secretary. I have not ever felt I was any less effective because I had that one word before my title and I still don't. As long as it's important to Jim, I want it to remain the same. So it doesn't bother me."

As to why he hadn't gone to see Jim, "I felt," added Speakes, "that after Jim was shot, my job, number one, was to step in and serve the president; and, number two, to protect this job for Brady. I didn't feel it was proper for me to move into Jim's office. I stayed in my little office for several months until they hired Pete Roussel, and then Jim Baker told me I should and I must move. So I did.

"I still feel it's important that Jim realize I'm sitting in this seat for him and that, when, if he were ever able, that he could come back to this office. . . . It was important to Jim and his recovery to realize he was the press secretary, and this job was his and he had something to come back to. . . . Speakes told his staff the same thing.

However, says a White House staff member, later in 1984, "at the end of Reagan's term, Larry made an effort to try to solicit support for his having the title, and for giving Jim the title press secretary emeritus and an office in the Executive Office Building. He equated the title with an elevated role and thought it would give him more importance with the reporters." But Jim Baker told Speakes, "I just don't see how we can do that," in the light of his commitment to Kobrine. Privately he said that as long as he was chief of staff, Jim would have the title because it was the one thing that gave Jim encouragement.

Sarah and Jim were not contacted about these proposals—a breakdown in communications—because Sarah had often wondered aloud to friends if she and Jim should make the first move to give up the title or to work out a better arrangement for the White House and the Bradys alike. "We would have been open to such a discussion," she says.

Tim Wyngaard, who went through therapy at GWUH with Jim, said in 1984, "I am personally convinced that if Jim loses that title, it will kill him. Not overnight, but in time.

"The words *sensitivity* and *politics* are mutually exclusive," Wyngaard added.

Shortly after the 1984 election, Jim Baker and Donald Regan exchanged jobs and Regan became chief of staff at the White House. Speakes was quoted as saying how "much better it is now than in the previous administration." He felt things would be better for him under Regan, and reportedly he did gain more access to the president. Jim's view of that, however, is that he "had as much access as he wanted." Jim believes that access is something you have to fight for.

But Speakes and the others at the White House were new associates of Jim's, and not the only ones to take a slightly distant approach. One of the most painful facts of Jim's trauma was that a number of good friends and old colleagues cut themselves off from him—some immediately—others more gradually. It is a common phenomenon suffered by almost everyone who has a serious illness or injury that permanently alters them. "They lose their friends," says Cathy Wynne. Most people have not had the exposure to those who have one disability or another, and so, perhaps it wasn't surprising that people in the White House weren't any better at dealing with Jim at first than anybody else. (If as good, says one insider.) In most cases those who fell away had a fear of not knowing "how Jim was," and no confidence in their ability to deal with him. "It's so ironic," says Jan Wolff, "because if it had happened to someone else, Jim would be taking care of them, having them over."

Among those who dropped away was one of Jim's oldest Washington friends, who just never contacted the Bradys again after his first and only visit to the hospital. He explained it by saying that when his own father had a stroke he hadn't been able to handle seeing him, and he felt he couldn't handle the changes in Jim. But Jim grieved over that loss in particular. It was a bitter pill for him, and an agony for Sarah to see him unhappy about it. A number of other associates used the same phrase—they "just couldn't handle it," meaning the changes from the brilliant, rollicking raconteur they knew to the struggling man whose flashes of wit and brilliance were, at first, few and far between. To most others, the fact that the basic man was still there was enough.

"Jim Brady has one of the best brains still that I have ever run across," says Ron Weber. "There are others who get from point A to point B by deductive reasoning. Jim gets from point A to point B and nobody knows how he does it. His attention span is short, but it always was short. He'd start a conversation and then he'd go away and come back and change the subject because he was bored with it. He'll talk about something else briefly and come right back to it. It's just that he had another thought about it. Jim's mental process has never changed. He was always off the wall. Now people attribute it to the shooting. But I am telling you he is the same guy."

Bob Dahlgren thought Jim was as funny as ever and liked to tell about asking Jim, after his appearance in November 1984 at the Good Shepherd Home, a rehabilitation center in Pennsylvania, "Can you imagine what the world would be like without organizations like Good Shepherd?"

"Yeah, it'd be ass deep in gimps," said Jim.

The next year the Bradys lost a new friend, a television producer and wife of one of Jim's doctors, when they wouldn't give her the go-ahead to make a docudrama of Jim's life. The Bradys and the couple had become, Sarah thought, good friends, eating out together, even taking some weekend trips together. At one point, Sarah made what she thought was a casual remark to the effect, "Wouldn't it be fun if someday we could work together on Jim's story for a movie?" The TV producer evidently took the remark as a go-ahead and she and her agent shopped the story around to the networks in New York and told Sarah that the film had to be made soon, any delay was out of the question. After much discussion, Sarah finally wrote the woman that they weren't ready to do a movie quite yet. A few days later she received a very unpleasant phone call. "I have never been treated in such an insulting way in my life," said the woman. She went on, "I'll have you know that my husband saved your husband's life." (He had performed minor surgery on Jim.) "And," she shrilled on, "I'll have you know that my husband has never even submitted a bill for the care he has given to your husband." (Jim's medical care was completely covered by Worker's Compensation so her point was moot.)

Sarah was aghast at the attack. Was it her fault? Had she unwittingly led the woman on? She didn't think so, nor did her close friends. The proof of the "friendship" became clear when the television producer never contacted Jim and Sarah again. Sarah discounts all the other rumors and stories, however. "It is natural for friendships to wax and wane over time," she says. "And since the shooting we have made so many new friends, better friends even than we had before." There were many people who needed them, too, and who took great hope from the way the Bradys handled their crisis.

Many new friends stepped into their lives. Marian and Don Burros, Wendy and Ernie Baynard, Debbie and Jerry File, Robin Smith and Bill Plante, Dick and Germaine Swanson, and Lou and George Economos. Don Burros arranged to have zippers put into Jim's beloved Lucchese boots so he could get them on. The Burroses and others formed "The Eating Club" with the Bradys and held potluck suppers several times a year. Debbie File and Wendy Baynard were neighbor-friends of Sarah's and they began doing many things together as families.

In 1985 Bob Dahlgren died suddenly and unexpectedly. His death left a big hole in Jim's life. "The only nonmedical person who had a more important impact in Jim's recovery was Sarah," says Art Kobrine. "If a person can have one friend in his life who is as good a friend as Bob Dahlgren has been to Jim Brady, he is indeed fortunate."

Ernie Baynard, Jerry File, and Jim have become good friends. Jerry File has gone shopping with Jim for birthday presents for Sarah and Scott, and Baynard and Jim meet regularly for lunch, "and share a fondness for those ghastly sheep jokes," says Wendy. "Jim in many respects is the closest friend I've got," says Baynard. "If I were in trouble Jim would stop at nothing to help me. He is our son William's godfather, or god-bear as he insists, and Sarah is his godmother." Jim and Baynard have taken several short fishing trips together.

"Physically Jim's stamina is improving. His mind is good and his speech has improved dramatically. I think he could occasionally brief the press. He is very careful about what he says about the White House." As for Sarah, Baynard says, "She has the faith of the martyrs. There is an awful lot of love involved."

"Our relationship with Jim and Sarah has been very special for Jerry and me," says Debbie File. "We feel they are part of our family. We feel we have all grown so much as individuals ourselves because of the relationship. Jerry has such respect for Jim, and I just feel that Sarah has been the most positive, caring, loving person I've ever known. She and Jim are never bitter, discouraged, or negative. They both are always upbeat and have so much empathy for other people's problems."

When Sarah was out of town on a speaking tour in 1985, Debbie accompanied Jim to several events and was mistaken for Sarah by many people. "No, but they wear the same shoe size," Jim told everybody.

"I have had such support throughout this whole thing," says Sarah. "The whole neighborhood has been awfully good to us—the Coles, the Veldes, Mrs. Hanson, and Anne Marie Tighe. We weren't really a close neighborhood before, but since this happened we've had a lot of gatherings. Our good friends, the Dahlgrens, the Wolffs, the Webers, Bill and Charlene Greener, the Baynards, have all been with us all along the way. Bobbie McGraw came and stayed at the house with Scott for two weeks after the shooting.

"My mother lives about a mile from us." Sarah pauses, then says emotionally, "I can't say enough about my mother. She has done everything possible she could do. There's no way I can describe how good she has been to us. She took care of Scott practically full time for two years. And my brother, Bill, gave up his job and transferred from the West Coast to be here for us." ("Bill Kemp is one of the unsung heroes in all of this," says Stuart Purviance. "He's a nice, quiet guy who really came through for his family.")

"Debbie File organized the Alexandria hospital auxiliary, called TWIG, to send a casserole for two every night for Mother and Scott, and our minister and assistant minister (the 'alleged ministers') have given me a lot of upbeat support.

"Members of the press particularly turned out to be among our staunchest friends: Bill Plante, Steve Neal, Gary Schuster, and even the press just doing its job of covering us has been kind and sensitive. I don't know whether it was because of Jim's being so active with the press, or because of the accident, but they have been so very supportive—not just in their writing but as friends. We have made so many new friends in the press, and it's been fun for me.

"President and Mrs. Reagan were so nice to us on a personal basis," says Sarah, "remembering us on special occasions." The Reagans always called Jim on his birthday, the White House switchboard tracking him down wherever he was. And Mrs. Reagan has involved herself in several events for the disabled in which Jim played a major part.

Public support has been extremely important to the Bradys, too. "It really gives Jim a boost to be recognized and remembered," says one friend.

"Jim needs his male friends," says Cathy Wynne, and she cited the lift it gave Jim when Steve Neal occasionally brought hamburgers to the hospital to have lunch with him. "They had a language all their own," says Wynne. Neal was the source of many of Jim's latest jokes. An old favorite was the pope joke. Brady would claim that Neal just quite possibly was the pope. "Well, did you ever see him and the pope in the same room at the same time?" he'd ask slyly.

Above all, it was Art Kobrine who became the rock in the Bradys' lives. "From the beginning," says Sarah, "Kobrine has been open and honest, telling me what all the dangerous possibilities are, but holding out hope, too." Indeed, from the beginning he told her what Jim's physical problems would be, that he would not have the use of his left arm, but probably could learn how to walk by himself, and perhaps even drive a car. "If I ever needed to get my act together, I called Kobrine. He feels that Jim can return to a meaningful job. He told me the road would be generally up, but with ups and downs along the way." Those assurances and honest assessments have been extremely important to Sarah's ability to cope with the difficult days that lay ahead for her.

The admiration between Art Kobrine and Sarah was mutual. Kobrine and his wife gradually became intimate friends with the Bradys as they struggled together along the road to recovery. Art says of Sarah Brady, "Sarah is an extraordinary person. A first-rate human being and mother. A lot of people who are strong, as she is, don't see themselves as having strength. But I have dealt with many, many families in similar circumstances and she is extraordinary. She is a strong-willed, tough-minded person who has faced squarely every crisis. She does what needs to be done, time after time after time."

Kobrine would have the opportunity to say in public how he felt about both Jim and Sarah. In April 1984 Kobrine presented to Jim the second annual Ernie Banks Positivism Award given by the Emil Verban Society. (A slightly tongue-in-cheek organization in Washington, made up of displaced Illinoisians who are Chicago Cubs fans.) Reagan had received the award the year before, but Jim, "is perhaps in a class by himself," said Kobrine. "The optimism of other individuals pales in comparison with the degree of optimism, enthusiasm, and gusto for life that our present recipient demonstrates on a daily basis. I know. I have watched him almost every day for over three years, accomplishing goals few thought were possible, constantly setting new goals, seemingly out of reach, only to grab for them and succeed, time after time. When those around him were discouraged and depressed it was his jokes, his irreverent sense of humor that saved the day." Jim is "always able to laugh at himself, to make light of his situation, to poke fun at others in a loving way, but never—I repeat—never, willing to quit."

That September, Kobrine was asked to present to Sarah the USO Woman of the Year Award given to outstanding volunteers at a ceremony at Ft. McNair Army Base in Washington. Sarah shared the day with actress Elizabeth Taylor, who also received the award. "There are few who know Sarah better than I do," said Kobrine, and he chronicled the crisis-ridden eight months Jim was in the hospital, when he and Sarah shared their hopes and fears, "in fact, shared our innermost feelings." Throughout it all, Sarah also "found time and energy to get involved with the other patients on the neurosurgical floor, providing much needed support and strength for situations often not as grave as her own. . . ." And, he said, "bitterness has never crept into her being. . . . I have heard her explain on more than one occasion, simply, that bitterness is nonproductive and one must move ahead and not dwell on the past, not waste precious energy in nonproductive emotion. . . . I can think of no one more fitting than Sarah Brady to share this year's USO Woman of the Year Award, and it is an honor and privilege for me to present this award to her."

At one point Sarah assessed what they all had been through together. "I guess I have a certain amount of strength to handle the big problems of life," she said. "It's the little details that get me down, like when the washing machine breaks down." She felt she hadn't done any more than any other wife would have done. "Maybe I had to be strong just to make it through the whole thing—and now I just try not to compare our lives with before. I was luckier than a lot of people who have lived through this sort of thing. I received so much support from family, old friends, and new friends, and people around the country. I was able to deal with things a little bit at a time because things evolved slowly. First, you're just grateful for life itself—that Jim survived—and then you're thankful for all the small signs of progress along the way. For a long time I didn't believe that Jim's left arm might be disabled, but little by little I have been able to accept it. On the other hand, I feel confident that Jim will regain a lot of his former ability. The way he thinks is no different, his judgment, his reactions to events are the same as they ever were."

Early in 1983, Art Kobrine had said of his famous patient, "I just admire the hell out of Jim Brady. The recovery of patients with brain injury, whether it be from a stroke, a gunshot, or a stabbing, all depends on the same three things: how much viable tissue is left; how adaptable the system is to taking over functions previously controlled by now-missing brain tissue; and how willing the patient is to work. Jim shows a tremendous amount of dedication. He is here at the hospital four and a half days a week, working five or six hours a day. A bilateral injury like Jim's is more difficult than a one-sided injury, but recovery is highly individual. He is still making progress, he is working hard, and he is getting the positive reinforcement he needs from Sarah, the rest of his family, and his friends."

Bruce Thompson, who saw Jim in December 1984 after seeing him in August, said, "Even in that one period of time he seemed to have progressed. He was less tired, more alert, very funny. I'm convinced he'll come back. That's just the kind of drive he has."

"Sometimes he's just great and sometimes he's not on track," said Sarah at that point. "There are some real gaps and limitations which may always be there."

Jim was at his best out in public. At the Kennedy Center

Honors Gala that same month, Walter Cronkite came up to Jim and said, "Do you remember, Jim, you asked me what recommendations I would have for changes in the White House press operations, and I said, 'I'd like to go back to the days of FDR where once a day they'd grab the regular members of the press for a session with the president in the Oval Office—not for attribution—but just to get to know each other'?" Cronkite added, "Jim, I wish you'd get back in that press room."

After the election, hard-line conservative and political columnist Patrick Buchanan was brought into the White House as director of communications (David Gergen's former job). Privately, Jim disapproved of the move and perhaps felt a little competitive about it. "We didn't need Pat Buchanan in there," he said. And in the White House mess that fall, when Jim saw the equally-to-the-right Paul Weyrich lunching with Buchanan, he said, "Oh, you're bringing them all in, aren't you?"

During inauguration week in 1985, Jim was awarded the first *USA TODAY* Unity Award. "Jim Brady represents the spirit and courage of the USA," said Allen H. Neuharth, chairman of Gannett Company, Inc., which publishes *USA TODAY*. "He has helped bring together people of all persuasions and backgrounds."

The next month Jim was awarded the first annual Will Rogers Humanitarian Award for his courage—and for his chili. It was a fund-raising banquet for the James S. Brady Foundation.

Jim started a new therapy in 1984—art therapy—with Wendy Maiorana. Jim told Maiorana it was the only place he went where no one hurt him. Jim slowly began turning out a few pieces, the first one, done in tempera, he titled *Novak's Beach House*. In their first session Maiorana asked Jim what he wanted to paint, and he said, "I think I'll paint Novak's beach house." He was harking back to the summers he and Sarah had vacationed with the McGraws, whose beach house in Bethany Beach was right next to syndicated columnist Robert Novak's beach house.

Jim loved the Washington stories about Bob Novak who, on television, at least, affects a vicious temperament and is apt to verbally attack anybody who crosses his path whose politics are to the left of center. "The Prince of Darkness," Washington political writers call him, mostly affectionately. Jim says that on those beach vacations, "Our lights would flicker at night when Novak walked up and down the beach."

"Jim sketched it in by pencil with a flourish, then began painting," says Maiorana. "Right toward the end he added a raccoon scrounging around in Novak's garbage can."

Jim's next painting was an impressionistic montage of his home in Centralia, painted in brilliant happy colors. "You're never quite sure," says Maiorana "what is happening during the process, but you know that something has been worked through. That's a lot of what art therapy is—the subconscious working through of subconscious issues and concerns. There is a putting to rest of them—and letting go. And the art itself is therapy as well."

In her home where she teaches, Maiorana has an eclectic collection of art, stuffed animals, her three cats—interesting things at every turn. All the things Jim loves. "How the heck are we ever going to get him out of here?" Cathy Wynne asked when she saw the setting.

Jim told Maiorana his goal in life was to have a hot-dog stand down on Washington's Mall. So in a collaborative effort she and Jim made a little wooden hot-dog stand. Jim glued it together and painted its wheels in bright colors.

Then Jim began working on an acrylic snow scene inspired by one painted by former President Eisenhower titled *The Forked Road.* He told Maiorana the scene reminded him of winter in Illinois.

Jim's contacts at GWU Hospital, particularly Kobrine and Wynne, felt Jim should be more involved in some aspect of the press operation at the White House—felt especially that it was needed therapy for Jim. Above all, they could see how not being involved was wearing on him. The more the White House ignored him, the more his self-worth suffered. It was a relentless circle.

After the 1984 election, when Kobrine read that Mike Deaver and Jim Baker were both going to be leaving the White House (Deaver to start up his own consulting firm, and Baker to become secretary of treasury), he called both of them.

"I talked to them about getting Jim involved in something—that he needed the involvement in order to keep on getting better. And I told them that it had to be someone at that end to bring him back into some participation, however peripheral. I thought everyone owed Jim that chance."

Kobrine said to Deaver, "You know, Mike, you've said before, 'There but for the grace of God go I.' " Deaver said, "I know it, I know it," and he would talk to former treasury secretary Don Regan who was taking over Jim Baker's job as chief of staff. Soon a call came to Jim at home from Regan's office, saying that the chief of staff would be calling soon, that he wanted to talk to Jim. Two days went by while the Bradys wondered and worried what the message would be. "I hope he's not going to fire me," Jim said.

But there was more stirring around the press office in the new order than Kobrine was aware of. When Regan donned the mantle of chief of staff, Speakes also lobbied him for the title of press secretary, as well as for better access. And he had the support of at least one member of the White House press corps, ABC's Sam Donaldson, who said, "Speakes is doing the job; and it's difficult to present to the public what his position is without the title." Of course Speakes was doing the job, and a difficult job it was, too. But it wasn't that Jim felt he could handle being press secretary full time again. He knew he could not. At the same time he felt he still had something to contribute, and in his heart he also knew that it was right that he keep his title and his entrée to the White House. He needed it. It was his only link to the world of politics he knew and loved so well.

When Regan's call came, it was to ask Jim to stay on as press secretary. If Regan had considered giving Speakes the title, the idea had been squelched by the Messrs. Reagan and Baker.

More important, nothing came of Kobrine's entreaties to Deaver and Baker, either. But in 1985, from another direction, Jim's good friend Brian Whelan tried again to get Jim involved in the White House. Whelan started by calling Kobrine, who told him, "I agree that's what Jim needs. But I've tried and nothing came of it. If you think you can get something done, go ahead." Whelan decided to go through old Brady friend "B" Oglesby, who was head of congressional liaison in the White House. Whelan thought that together they could work on Don Regan's right-hand man, Dennis Thomas, another old pal of Jim's. Whelan thought that for starters Jim could sit in on some monthly planning meetings. There were numerous discussions and ideas put forth, but this effort, too, sputtered away on the back burner for another year.

In May 1986, Bill Plante decided to check into whether Jim couldn't be doing something more substantive and he called Kobrine who, of course, and with some exasperation, said, "Yes, I've been trying to get something started for two years but to no avail." Plante went to see Don Regan with his concern and the next week Jim had an appointment at last with the chief of staff. Chalk it up possibly to the power of the press, Jim at last had his toe in the door.

Vocational counselor Cynthia Potesta tried to prompt Jim for the meeting. "Is there anything you need to take along?"

"I've got an office there," he said, a little annoyed. "I can get a pencil and a piece of paper if I need them."

Potesta tried to prepare him further, but Jim brushed her aside. "Don't worry. I'm not going to fall asleep on them."

"I saw the Chief today," Jim told several friends happily, "and it's given me a new lease on life."

The outcome of their meeting was that Jim began attending the senior staff meetings chaired by his old friend, and Regan's top aide, Dennis Thomas. But it wasn't what he had hoped it might be. "Boring," he told friends, "boring, boring, boring." He said, "My job in those meetings is to make sure nothing that's brought up actually happens."

In July 1986 Jim and Sarah were invited by Washington PR man Paul D'Armiento to appear together before the Washington Industrial Round Table, Jim to talk about his career and his recovery, and Sarah to talk about gun control. Jim spoke about the honor and pleasure he felt it had been to work for Jim Lynn, Don Rumsfeld, William Roth, John Connally, and Ronald Reagan. "The words of Don Rumsfeld come to mind," he said. " 'The harder I work the luckier I get.' Since the unfortunate incident I have been working very hard . . . and I have been lucky. Now the words come a little easier to me, it's a little easier to get around, and I still make a good pot of Goat Gap Chili. More importantly, I have started going into the office more often. My hope is to be able to take on Sam Donaldson and the rest. But in the meantime I have to put up with a little Pain and Torture. And I do as much as I can to speak about the National Head Injury Foundation, to help Mary Doremus, chairman of Challenge,* and to help my wife, the Raccoon, who, believe me, needs a lot of help.

"Notice how she took the microphone away," he added. "That's called, 'Shut up the Bear.' "

The crowd loved it.

In November 1986, at its national conference in Washington, the Public Relations Society of America gave Jim an award for his contributions to its profession. "His capacity for hard work and sense of humor have earned both respect and affection from his colleagues," said conference chairman Jack Felton. "He is a person who attained the most visible public-relations position in the world by the time he was forty-one years old. He is a person who, then, came very, very close to paying the ultimate sacrifice in service to his country. Since that terrible day in March of 1981, he has been a person whose daily battle with pain and whose determination to regain normal life have inspired millions. Yet he is a man who never asks, 'Why me?' Instead his resolve is to play the hand that's dealt you. Our recipient is a man whose professionalism and whose profound courage reflect the most admirable character traits possible. We are indeed proud to call him 'one of us.' "

"Thank you very much, ladies and gentlemen, for honoring me this way," said Jim, somewhat at a loss for words. "I appreciate it. My son Scott will appreciate it. My daughter Melissa will appreciate it. And my wife Sarah already appreciates it."

Later, Washington PR man Tom Mason who shared Jim's table and who hadn't seen him for two years, told Jim how very much better he seemed to him. "I'm gonna live," said Jim. "I'm getting better."

On November 24, the day before the White House's shocking revelations that money from the Iran arms sale had been diverted to the Nicaraguan Contras, Jim lunched with the graduate journalism students of American University in Washington. They asked him if the already revealed Iranian arms

*Jim is honorary chairman of Challenge, an organization that makes available to employers the names of skilled people who are also handicapped.

sales were going to harm Reagan and his administration.

"I don't think it's good, but I don't think it's fatal," said Jim. And of Reagan, "He's like a cat, and he always lands on his feet." Jim said that if Reagan "doesn't think the arms sales to Iran was a mistake, then it wasn't a mistake. . . . We listen to him very closely, then follow his lead." Asked if there should be a shakeup in the White House staff, Jim said, "Perhaps there should. As long as I'm not in it."

Asked about the relationship of press secretaries to the chief of staff, Jim said, "They have press secretaries for breakfast, and they use catsup on them."

And how is the White House feeling about the press? "I tell them, 'You vill like the press,'" claimed Jim. "'Ve haf ways of making you like the press.' They are honest people who have to call 'em the way they see 'em," he added. He said the most important quality of a press secretary is "honesty. Your word is your bond."

Ronald Reagan, he added, "is a man true to his word. He will go down in history as a thoroughly likable nice guy."

As Irangate heated up in the fall, Jim, in Houston for a neurotrauma conference at the University of Texas, was asked about it on television. "Well, I picked a good time to be in Houston," he said. When it was noted that Jim and Sarah were going to go to the rodeo while they were there, Jim said, "There's so much bull being flung in Washington I thought as long as I'm here I'd go and see how the professionals do it."

"I can't help thinking how things would have been different if Jim had been there," says Susan Bryant. "He never would have stood for this, and he'd have weighed in strongly on it, too."*

In March 1987, when Larry Speakes left the White House for a job at Merrill Lynch, seasoned government PR man Marlin Fitzwater was appointed in his place. His title is assistant to the president for media relations and White House spokesman. "Jim is thrilled that Marlin was appointed," said Sarah. "He's a professional," said Jim. He approved. And in a

*Since 1978, Susan Bryant has been a Republican political consultant in Washington and her husband, Jay Bryant, a political media consultant. Together they've formed RSM (Research Strategy Management).

thoughtful gesture, Fitzwater called Jim to say how pleased he was to be working under him.

That same month Jim was invited by Mayor Harold Washington of Chicago to be grand marshal of the St. Patrick's Day parade, the first time a Republican had been so honored. "Mayor Daley must be turning over in his grave," said Jim but he was thrilled to be honored by his fellow Chicagoans.

After Reagan's reelection, the handgun-control advocates had come looking for Sarah again. They wanted her to join their fight against a bill coming up for a vote in the Congress. Republican Senator James McClure of Idaho and Democratic Representative Harold L. Volkmer of Missouri had joined forces in 1979 to author a bill that would, if passed, go a long way to nullifying the already weak National Handgun Bill passed in 1968 after the assassinations of Robert F. Kennedy and Martin Luther King, Jr. The bill had languished in the House Judiciary Committee until 1986, when it was discharged and allowed to come before the Senate.

But this time, the anti-handgun movement had the backing of every major law-enforcement group in the United States—an important breakthrough. And this time Sarah felt there was nothing to keep her from getting involved, but she called White House congressional liaison "B" Oglesby to make sure she was right—that it was not a priority bill of the administration. Oglesby confirmed her impression, that although they were for the bill, they were not lobbying for it.

Sarah also touched base with Donald Regan, "to tell him I was going to join the board of Handgun Control, Inc.,* and start speaking out," says Sarah.

Regan told her, "I can understand how you feel, Sarah. Ann [his wife] has been after me to take a strong position on it as well."

Sarah told him she didn't want to create a sensation, but that she had written a personal letter to every senator on the Hill. "Well, Sarah, you've been around long enough to know that it will not remain a personal letter," replied Regan.

And of course, it did not. Her letter marked the beginning

*Handgun Control, Inc., 1400 K Street N.W., Washington, D.C. 20005 (202) 898-0792 of Sarah's national anti-handgun campaign, a fight, she says, "I am in for the long haul."

In addition to the White House's lukewarm interest in the McClure-Volkmer Bill, Sarah also noted that Attorney General Edwin Meese has "himself admitted there are problems with the bill."

Sarah began writing editorials and speaking out against the bill. Newspapers and magazines such as *The New York Times* and *Newsweek* carried her editorials, and she launched a speaking campaign, which took her to more than twenty states. In October 1985 she testified before the House Judiciary Committee. She appeared on *Hour Magazine* with Gary Collins, and in May 1986, just before the vote in the Senate, she flew to Dallas to appear on the Phil Donahue show along with Joseph McNamara, chief of police of San Jose, California. Together they countered the arguments of National Rifle Association representative Wayne LaPierre and an Atlanta, Georgia, gunshop owner.

"Our happy lives were changed forever," she said in her first fund-raising letter. But she has tried to keep emotional appeals out of her campaign. "I'm not asking for your sympathy," her ads say, "I'm asking for your help."

Even though she still considers herself a conservative Republican, "I have always thought we as Americans have too cavalier an attitude about handguns and the problems they cause. I am trying to say, 'Look, nobody is trying to take your guns away, or your right to have one for protection, as long as you know how to use it, how to store it, and how to take care of it.' "

But the McClure-Volkmer Bill, she says, "mocked my husband's suffering. And it mocked the survivors of those twenty thousand handgun victims each year who were not as fortunate as Jim was."

At one congressional hearing Sarah attended, Democratic representative Tom Robinson from Arkansas talked about the inconvenience that gun laws cause law-abiding citizens, and he told the story of how his own little boy went to a gun sale, bid on a gun, and because of gun laws had to wait two days before he could get his gun. "Can you imagine the agony of that little boy?" said Robinson. "He cried all the way home."

Sarah tells this story out on the lecture trail and says, "I can tell you about inconvenience, and my husband can tell you about inconvenience. And I've never heard our little eight-year-old boy whine about anything so insignificant."

Gun control was an issue with Sarah long before Jim was shot, too. Growing up she had always been aware of the care her FBI agent father took with his service revolver—locking it in a briefcase, then locking that in a closet when he came home at night.

There had been her co-worker, who was shot to death with her own revolver. And just recently, in 1984, on a visit to Centralia, Scott, then five, picked up what looked like a toy pistol on the seat of a friend's pickup. "It turned out to be a Saturday-night special," she says, "And it was loaded," she adds with horror.

So this is not an effort born out of a need solely for catharsis for what has happened to them. "I've never felt angry, or I've tried not to. I don't know if I've repressed it or not, but right away I decided that I knew Jim wouldn't have wanted me to be angry. I knew we had to get on with our lives."

As for Hinckley, says Sarah, "I just think of him as a sick young man who is locked away in a mental hospital. I don't think looking back on that part of it is helpful at all."

Jim, however, is more and more willing to admit his anger. "The longer I go, the angrier I get. That little twit over there . . ." (Across the river in St. Elizabeth's Hospital, he means. He can almost see it from his den window.) Jim believes Hinckley may be insane but he knew what he was doing. "Publicly, Jim won't speak out for gun control," says Sarah, "because of his loyalty to the White House, but he gets furious at the NRA guys when he listens to them on television."

"But," says Jim, "I can't spend a lot of time being angry. Those are negative vibes and I have a helluva lot of work ahead of me"

The NRA took note of Sarah Brady's activities, and began calling her "the tool" of the anti-gun lobbies, and of using emotion on an issue "that should be discussed intellectually." But Sarah, accusing the NRA of using scare tactics, relished taking on one of the most powerful lobbies in Washington, and she began referring to herself as Sarah "the tool" Brady.

When the final vote was taken, the handgun-control lobbies and Sarah felt that overall they had won. Although several controls on long-gun sales had been weakened, they had staved off the most noxious elements of McClure-Volkmer, and had added some new strictures on handguns as well. The most important victories were: the banning of imported parts to make Saturday-night specials (such as John Hinckley's gun); the banning of the sale or transfer of machine guns not lawfully owned as of the date of the signing; and the reaffirmation of the ban on interstate sales of handguns.

The one defeat that they all lamented was that the penalty for record-keeping violations (by gun-shop owners) was reduced from a felony to a misdemeanor, and they set about working to reinstate that requirement. They began lobbying again, also, for a waiting period and background checks for purchasers of handguns.

"It was the combination of having Sarah Brady and every major law-enforcement group in the country getting out front on this issue that was responsible for winning as much as we did," says Barbara Lautman, spokesperson for Handgun Control, Inc. "What Sarah was able to do was to motivate people to get involved." In May, before the vote, Handgun Control purchased full-page ads in major newspapers, which pictured Sarah and brought 250,000 responses. In September 1986, through ads in major newspapers and magazines, membership in Handgun Control, Inc., and donations to them, reached an all-time high.

The NRA claimed it had won the fight, but the day after the bill passed, it fired its entire public-education division. And it fired its executive director the morning the bill was signed.

When Ronald Reagan signed the bill on May 19, 1986, there were no photographs, no television, and no press allowed in to view the signing. "Can we get the president's feelings on signing the gun bill today, since we're not allowed to cover it? And it is legislation of real importance to the American people," asked Helen Thomas of Larry Speakes.

Then Sam Donaldson asked, "The Bradys are not invited today for the ceremony, I take it?"

"If I was you, Sam, I wouldn't want my name attached to those words," said Speakes. "I think it's an out-of-place question by far."

"Sarah Brady has opposed this bill," said Donaldson, pushing the issue. "And I take it that Jim also opposes it, although I haven't heard him say that."

"The shooting did affect Jim's views on gun control," says Sarah, although he has said nothing publicly about it. "It's your show," he has told Sarah. At first, he would ask her, "Well, are you going to let *me* have a gun to defend myself against Hinckley?" Gradually, however, he came around to supporting her views on the subject. And he is very proud of her visibility on the issue. "Besides," he says, "it's better than having her hang around the house."

Ronald Reagan, of course, has for years campaigned against gun control. The pro-gun people are part of his basic constituency. They, along with others like anti-abortionists, the prayer-in-the-school people, those fervent single-issue groups, were part of his political base; they can provide that winning fraction of a percent of the vote in states where the election is close. It is the sort of political compromise that presidential candidates are criticized for making. In Reagan's case, to his very good political fortune, he is credited with believing in these far-right views, views that seem antithetical to his amiable personality.

The bill was not a victory for the NRA and the gun people. Did Reagan not want to be seen signing a weak bill, or did he not want to be so closely associated with the gun issue any longer? Especially now that Sarah Brady had lined up against him on the issue? Reagan himself is a member of the NRA, as is Vice-President George Bush.

"In my mind," says Sarah, "I kind of equate President Reagan with a lot of the NRA members. They are fine people who if they knew more about what their lobby was doing maybe they wouldn't agree with the lobby themselves." Sarah often meets members of the NRA who want the same things she does; mandatory safety training, a waiting period, and a background check before a person is allowed to purchase a handgun.

Old friend from Pentagon days, Lieutenant Colonel Stuart Purviance, was stationed in Germany with the air force when he heard that Jim had been shot. "You realize when you're in Europe that you can shuck this protective thing you have in the States," he says. "Women can safely walk the streets of Europe. I think we should register handguns. I just don't see the problem."

As Sarah made more and more public appearances for gun control, and became a national figure in her own right, she bought some new clothes and changed her hairstyle. When Ernie Baynard complimented her on her new look, Jim said, "Yes, she's out of mourning."

In January 1987 it was revealed by St. Elizabeth's Hospital that John Hinckley had been allowed to leave the hospital grounds on December 28, 1986, for a twelve-hour supervised day trip to a Christian halfway house for prisoners, where he lunched with his parents and the director. Sarah and Jim learned about it while they were watching TV. "I was disturbed to hear about it, and surprised to learn about it after the fact," she says. "Jim was very upset about it."

"I am furious," he told her. "Just furious."

The Secret Service was furious about it too. They were not formally given notice but instead received a tip about the release, and as a result, they covered Hinckley on his outing.

As the sixth anniversary of the shooting drew near, St. Elizabeth's hospital petitioned the U.S. district court that John W. Hinckley, Jr., be allowed an unescorted visit with his parents, who live in nearby Arlington, Virginia, over the Easter holidays. The government opposed the hospital's application and in its filing included an affidavit given by Sarah, which included these points: 1.) that because of Hinckley Jim is "confined to a wheelchair"; 2.) that Hinckley's "request had no restraints and if he were to confront" Jim, Jim "would be completely vulnerable"; 3.) that Jim and Sarah have a suit pending against Hinckley, which he is defending vigorously, "raising every defense"; 4.) that Hinckley shows no remorse and "if he has recovered from his alleged mental disorder, one would have thought he would have demonstrated some acknowledgment of the terrible injury he caused. Under the circumstances we are apprehensive. His behavior is unpredictable. It may cause us further harm."

"It seems that every year around this time he does something like this," said Sarah to friends. And Jim was totally pessimistic about it. "He's gonna get out, and first he's going to go looking for Jodie Foster," he said presciently. "Then he's going to come after me." Jim worried that Sarah might be a Hinckley target now, too, because of her visibility on the gun-control issue.

On the day of the hearing Sarah was in the courtroom prepared to testify against the release. She was extremely nervous about finally seeing in person the man who had shot her husband and turned their lives upside down. "But I felt almost nothing," she says, "no anger, no bitterness, just curiosity at seeing him walk into the room. And I felt sadness and hurt at the thought of what he had done. I felt amazement at the fact that there he sat, and there I sat in the same room."

As Sarah sat in the front row on one side of the courtroom and Jack and JoAnn Hinckley sat on the other, Dr. Glenn H. Miller described what he called Hinckley's dramatic improvement. He said Hinckley now believes his wounding of Brady was a "horrendous act," and whenever he is asked about Brady he feels he has done something wrong, something he should not have done and he remembers Brady in his prayers and "wants to make restitution" when he gets out of the hospital. Miller testified Hinckley is no longer obsessed with Jodie Foster, that he has a girlfriend and has hopes ultimately of getting married to her.

Then Miller said, Hinckley's judgment is not perfect, and that he is "naïve" to have become involved with the characters who write to him. When asked to name these characters, Miller shocked the courtroom when he said that Hinckley had written letters recently to serial killer Theodore Bundy expressing his "sorrow . . . and his feelings of the awful position that Bundy must be in." (Bundy is on death row in Florida for the murders of three young women, and is believed by authorities to have murdered as many as forty young women.) Hinckley initiated the correspondence and Bundy wrote to Hinckley several times.

Miller also said that several years ago Hinckley had requested Charles Manson's address so he could write to him, and he had received a letter from Squeaky Fromme, a follower of Manson who is in jail for firing on Gerald Ford in 1975.

Judge Barrington Parker abruptly adjourned the hearing after saying that despite the government's subpoena for "all correspondence and available records" on Hinckley, no record of those letters was provided, and he ordered that they be produced. In the next week it came out that Hinckley's hospital psychiatrist, Joan Turkus, had learned of the Bundy correspondence on April 7, but had not noted it in Hinckley's record, nor had she told Miller until the evening before the hearing, and the government not at all.

On *The Today Show* that week Jack Hinckley said that his son wrote to Ted Bundy "as one human being to another. It may not be something that you or I would do, but because John did write him does not mean that he is still dangerous. We've been hearing all week long that John is still dangerous and all sorts of other terrible things and a certain hysteria has developed that we feel is not necessary, not pertinent to the case." He said they would try for release again "as soon as they think the hysteria has subsided and it's an appropriate time to do it."

Upon the seizure of Hinckley's letters, however, the hospital also found twenty pictures of Jodie Foster, which caused the hospital to withdraw its request for Hinckley's release.

In another revelation the U.S. Attorney's Office said that psychiatrist Miller was being paid to testify by Jack Hinckley, although Hinckley's lawyer, Vincent Fuller, said in court that Miller "was hired" by the hospital "as a consultant." An attempt to clear this matter up was met by silence from the Hinckleys and Fuller.

Jim and Sarah's relationship has withstood the difficult years. "You don't know how much you love someone until something like this happens," says Sarah. But Jim was the great love of Sarah's life, and Sarah of Jim's. That foundation of love had forged a tie that inextricably united them. "There is no doubt in my mind," says one of Jim's doctors, "that if there had been a choice between a slightly damaged Jim Brady and no Jim Brady at all, that Sarah would have chosen the Jim she has."

"The thought that our marriage might not survive never crossed my mind," says Sarah. "I still loved Jim. I never saw anything that made me think he wasn't the same person." Talking about it one day early on, in 1982, Sarah said, "Sometimes I have worried that our roles have been somewhat reversed and that Jim may resent that."

"No, I don't," said Jim. "If I had to go into this with anybody, I'm glad it was you, 'Coon. She has been a tower of strength," he told his interviewer.

"You've been pretty strong yourself, Pooh."

Sarah said, "I think it comes from Jim's mother who is a wonderful combination of Scotch-Irish and Pennsylvania Dutch, who has worked all her life and worked to put Jim through school."

As time went on, Sarah realized she would be running things at home. "I am more in charge now, whereas before Jim liked to feel he was. But he is getting less and less willing for me to make all the decisions. Now he has a view about where he wants to go and with whom he wants to be."

"Jim is funny and fun," says Sarah. "We have Scott and our home together. We have a lot of ties holding us together."

But that doesn't mean Jim and Sarah haven't each struggled with the enormous stress Jim's injury has put on their marriage. "I try not to dwell on what we could be doing if it hadn't happened," says Sarah. "Lots of times I wish that Jim could handle Scott and give me a little break. I feel the total responsibility for the decision making as to Jim and Scott's welfare and their future. So I feel all the mistakes are mine. And I doubt that I'm doing a good job. My time is so tightly scheduled I feel I almost never have time to myself." But Jim gives Sarah as much support as he can. "I talk everything over with him," she says. "He is my best adviser."

Sarah has rarely left Jim alone in the house for more than a couple of minutes. She worries about fire and the fact Jim might not be able to get out. "But now I can leave him a little more, to run to the store—things like that."

Jim and Sarah don't pretend they have a storybook marriage, but their sense of humor saves them every time. And luckily they both feel free to tell each other what's on their minds. They disagree and they bicker. A friend told them their bickering reminded him of Cybill Shepherd and Bruce Willis in the TV show *Moonlighting*. They indulge in creative bickering. A friend who was late meeting them for dinner one night said, "Sorry I'm late."

"Oh, it just gave us a chance to talk to each other," said Sarah.

"Yeah," said Jim, "we've gone ten minutes without hitting each other over the head."

Sarah doesn't protect Jim from his errors, nor does Jim hesitate to complain about Sarah's corrections. In an interview with David Hartman on *Good Morning America*, Jim described

Sarah: "She's a cheerleader. She stands back and pushes when I need to be pushed. And," he said turning to Sarah, "you do have a tendency to nag."

When he gets fed up with her corrections, Jim shakes his fist at Sarah à la Jackie Gleason, "You wanta go to the moon?" "No," Sarah always says. "Pow. Right in the kisser," Jim finishes the routine.

Sometimes Jim is a bit hard on Sarah in private. It comes out of his understandable frustration and inability to get control back over his own life. Sarah understands this, but it hurts her sometimes, too. "Dr. Frankel told me it is a sign of misplaced anger. We all do this sometimes when we're frustrated and unhappy—lash out at those nearest and dearest to us." And Sarah, too, gets angry with Jim sometimes when the burdens of her responsibilities overwhelm her. But their deep attraction for each other and the ensuing love that developed have carried them through. In the fall of 1984, Sarah wept as she confided to her closest friends that she and Jim had resumed making love.

"I think the only ongoing thing now that I find difficult at all is when I see Jim hurting," says Sarah. "He goes through a lot of pain, and that bothers me. Everything else has seemed, over time, to get better."

Sarah has consistently used the euphemism "when Jim was hurt" to refer to the shooting, until recently when Jim challenged her on it. "I wasn't hurt, I was shot," he said, "and it still hurts."

As Jim gets better, life is smoothing out. An important breakthrough occurred in July 1986 when doctors told the Bradys that Jim at last could start flying again. This news cheered Jim immeasurably. It gave him back some of the mobility he had lost. It had been hard on them not to be able to travel more easily. Jim and Sarah took their first trip by air on July 25, to Centralia, to surprise Dorothy on her eightieth birthday. "Where's the old warhorse," Jim called out as he walked through the house looking for his mother. "Where's the old warhorse?"

Scott Brady, almost eight, went along, too, of course. Now he was old enough to enjoy the pleasures and freedoms a small boy can have in a town like Centralia, where everything is so accessible.

Scott is an extremely bright, inquiring boy with boundless

energy. Not being at an age of reason when his daddy was injured it is impossible to tell how it has affected him over the years. "I think he has handled it beautifully," says Sarah. "Children adapt to these things almost easier than adults."

"Let's hope so," says Jim, "because he has to play the hand he was dealt, too."

"You have to play the hand you're dealt." It was an expression Jim had used over and over and applied to himself many times throughout his recovery.

There is no doubt Jim's fate did prey on Scott's mind from time to time, however. In 1984 on one of the many TV news blurbs related to the shooting, Scott saw a photograph of John Hinckley as a little boy, dressed in a cowboy outfit complete with holster and guns. Now here was something very close to something Scott could identify with—a little boy like himself who grew up to shoot his daddy. "I just hate that Hinckley," he cried angrily. "He's bad. He shot my daddy. I want my daddy to be like he was before. I'd like to shoot that Hinckley," Scott paused and finished lamely, "in the toe." It was as extreme a threat as he felt he could express. "Scott is not one of Mr. Hinckley's biggest fans," Jim has remarked.

With age will come acceptance and Scott will come to understand the great courage and spirit his father and mother have shown to the world in the magnificent way they have handled themselves in the face of tragedy. For now, it is hard for him to fully understand the unfairness of it. He just knows he loves his mommy and daddy fiercely and feels defenseless in the face of an unjust act.

But Scott has the wonderful sense of humor his parents have—making puckish remarks, playing with the language as does his father. Jim and Sarah are teaching him to love the things they love: their families, their friends, their animals, good times, travel and adventure.

"One thing," says Jim, "he's all boy." Scott could keep several people busy answering questions, keeping track of his play. From ages four to seven, he specialized in taking things apart: lamps, clocks, the home computer. If it was complex, Scott wanted to see what was inside. "When he's quiet, he's dangerous," Jim pronounced one day when an uncommon stillness settled over the household.

At a fund-raising auction for the Brady Foundation, ABC's

Thumbs Up

Sander Vanocur bought a ride on a Ringling Brothers elephant with the proviso that David Gergen use it. Gergen, in turn invited Scott Brady to join him. On the appointed day, Scott, who'd been briefed and was excited about his ride, ran toward the elephant as it was walking toward him. "I screamed," says Sarah, "and the elephant stopped—but Scott didn't." Scott, who is fearless to a fault, went right up to the monstrous animal. But the ride went off without a hitch.

EPILOGUE

March 1987

On this, the sixth anniversary of the shooting, Jim is still White House press secretary, and he continues to go to his office in the White House on Fridays.* He also continues in his therapies and continues to make progress. By mid-1984 he had made most of the significant progress he was expected to make. Now he is making small, subtle, but important refinements of his mental skills. His physical condition has not changed much, nor is it expected to, his dreams of "levitating" notwithstanding. However, he can become stronger, increase his endurance and his flexibility, as long as he continues to work at it. Every year on the anniversary of the shooting, the Bradys, the Kobrines, and others go out on the town to "celebrate life."

Jim's original team of therapists has moved on to other places, and he has been working with a new group—"Physical Terrorists" Tom Welsh and Nora O'Kane, speech pathologist Nancy Shafer and vocational rehabilitation counselor Cynthia Potesta. The purpose of Cynthia Potesta's involvement with

*When Donald Regan was unceremoniously dumped as chief of staff in the wake of the Iran-Contra scandal, so was his top aide, Jim's friend Dennis Thomas, and the additional senior staff meetings Jim was attending were stopped.

Jim was to help him "reenter out there into the real world." It had been a problem that wasn't yielding to any easy solutions. Although he could function very well as the very social human being he had always been, his problems were evident when it came to putting his mind seriously to work. She began by looking for interesting activities for him to do. "Initially I had thought of his doing free volunteer PR work." But her main purpose, she says, "was to get him to do things where he could feel productive."

Potesta and Jim did a lot of talking together, and she talked to Jim's therapists, "so I could understand his memory and distractability problems."

There had been one organization in particular that had been seeking Jim's help for several years. It was the National Head Injury Foundation. After researching it thoroughly Potesta thought that getting Jim to handle its PR might be a good first step for him back into the real world. But did Jim want to do it? Potesta herself had misgivings about his getting involved in it, as did others, including Kobrine. Perhaps it was too directly related to his own problems, but on the other hand, she thought, "it might help him adjust to what had happened to him. Because although he had made remarkable progress, his own head injuries were going to be a continuing problem for him.

"But Jim wanted to do it from the beginning," she says. When she asked him why, Jim said, "Because it goes to my strength, which is PR. Yes," he said. He wanted to be the Spokes Bear for the Head Injury Foundation. "I don't want to be thought of as a gimp, but I want to do that."

Jim and Marilyn Spivak, president of NHIF, then had several meetings. "I hooked them up," says Potesta, "and Jim came up with lists of ways to promote the foundation—one of them was to make a public-service announcement for National Head Injury Month coming up in October 1986. And Jim agreed to appear in it."

Jim and Potesta then brainstormed about how to get the announcement made. "Jim said he would call Porter and Novelli, Republican media consultants, to ask them to make the TV spot. He just picked up the phone and made that contact," says Potesta. "He had no problem in communicating." Potesta was amazed to see Jim perform so confidently.

Then, Jim said, "PSAs are fine but they don't raise money. They only establish name recognition. I'm going to go to Richard Viguerie for the fund raising." (Viguerie is a politically conservative mass-mail fund-raiser.) "We'll try it. Let's just see. He can only say no." And Jim called another friend to get Viguerie's number.

Both Novelli and Viguerie said they would help. "Jim was very charming in the way he got it across to them," says Potesta. "He wailed a tiny bit with Viguerie, then caught himself and stopped it. All that stuff—that political savvy—is all there. Because of his problem with initiating, he needs prompting to do the next thing, but he knows what the next thing to do is. Sometimes I hold my breath. Jim will take a moment to focus and then he comes back on the right track."

Once involved with NHIF, Jim started teasing Potesta. "He accused me of hooking him up with a liberal organization," she says.

"I can't believe you did this to me," Jim says. "We've got to get their headquarters out of Framingham, Massachusetts."

Jim and Potesta also met with the National Barrier Awareness Day Committee. This group asked, and Jim promised, that he would get its material directly to the president, and in fact, have a press conference with him. When Potesta suggested perhaps they had better check that out, Jim got angry with her for countermanding his decision. He was tired of being out of control. It seemed reasonable to him that he could ask for a few minutes of Reagan's time to support this cause.

It was a rare display of anger, however. "Before I met Jim," says Potesta, "I'd heard about him, and I asked myself, 'Well, just how nice can somebody be?' I have never met anybody I liked better. He is incredibly warm and empathetic, very sensitive, always kind."

She cited an incident when a woman came up to Jim gushing, "Oh, Mr. Brady, how wonderful to see you." Jim greeted her warmly, but then in a joking aside to Potesta said, "Maybe I should run for office."

More and more disabled groups sought Jim's help and Potesta always questioned Jim. "These are all disabled groups," she'd say. "Do you really want to do that?"

"Yes, I want to do that," Jim would answer. Jim very much wanted to be involved with something real, even though at first this very involvement brought it nearer home to him that he, too, is disabled. "He would get discouraged, calling himself 'damaged goods,'" says Potesta. "But now he is dealing with it beautifully."

Jim continues to deal with lingering problems of lack of initiating, perseveration, and short-term memory. "But," says Potesta, "you also see the sheer force of Jim Brady's personality coming out of all of that. And his kindness. I was totally unprepared for the depth of his kindness to people."

Since 1984, says Tom Welsh, when he took over from Cathy Wynne, "Jim's biggest progress has been mental. But I have seen dramatic differences in the way he handles things over this time. He is so quick-witted. He remembers some little joke about everybody he has met here at the hospital, and he is even quicker to make them laugh now. His memory has improved—he can really handle things now.

"Physically Jim is doing different things, including dancing (just swaying to the music, but dancing nevertheless). His endurance has improved as well as his balance and coordination. And he will be able to gain more strength in his leg and develop new skills. I can see him getting out of that wheelchair more and more. He is able to walk farther and farther. And that's difficult. He is a big man who carries around about two hundred pounds.

"Jim still has pain in his contracted left hand and entire left leg," says Welsh. "All pain is in the brain, and it is possible that the pain he feels is misperceived. But it is real to him. The chances that there will be any return of function in his hand are very poor and Jim still takes it very hard. I've seen him break into tears about it." On the other hand, Jim never complained about pain when he fell and broke several ribs the year before, says Welsh.

"Mentally, he's made leaps and bounds of progress. He is better motivated now and is much more receptive to doing new things because he thinks it will make him better. He has a schedule—more places to go. He's not out in limbo anymore. He has a purpose.

"Jim Brady is a pretty gritty guy," says Welsh. "A real likable 'brainy' guy. I still think he is. I can just imagine how he must have been before. He must have been so exceptional—

just an amazing man. He must have just had it all at his fingertips."

In 1984, says Welsh, Jim's behavior wasn't as appropriate as it is now. "The man needed more activity. He was bored stiff. It wasn't surprising he would come in here and swing his cane around. The man is all action—he likes to be involved in things."

And Tom Welsh asked Jim to get involved in raising money for starting a school to train physical therapists at GWUH. Jim told Welsh he'd be glad to be part of helping to train "physical terrorists."

Today physical therapist Nora O'Kane continues to work with Jim half an hour a day, Monday through Friday, having taken over from Welsh in 1985. She and Jim work at keeping him flexible, keeping his contractures from becoming too painful, maintaining and increasing his strength, balance, and coordination.

O'Kane knew Jim, having seen him in the therapy clinic for the prior three years. "Cathy Wynne," she says, "always stressed having Jim interacting with staff and patients. He has such a good public face and air about him that I wasn't really aware of what his cognitive and neurological problems were until I started working with him." One problem that stood out to O'Kane was Jim's almost complete lack of ability to recognize time, a result of the injury to his right temporal lobe. "If you have no concept of time, you can see how difficult it would be." That, and Jim's initiating problem, she sees as the biggest hurdles before him. But not insurmountable ones considering the progress he has made. "As long as he has a stimulating, positive environment, he is going to continue to change. An enriched environment makes all the difference in the world.

"Frequently, it is impressive how well he does," says O'Kane. She tells of being in the hospital lobby with Jim and seeing two little old ladies looking at Jim, obviously talking about him. Then they approached him. Jim, who was always up for public recognition, readied himself for the usual laudatory words but then was stunned to hear one of them say, "Say, aren't you the man who shot President Reagan in that assassination attempt?" Jim reared back in his wheelchair, looked back at them, and said, "No, I'm the man who was also *shot* in the assassination attempt made on President Reagan."

Not totally believing, they asked him, "Well, where did *you* get shot then?"

Jim, still gracious, pointed to his head. "You see this scar here? This is where I was shot."

Now the women were embarrassed and they backed off, apologizing. As they disappeared, Jim said to O'Kane, "Well, how do you think I handled *that* one?"

Another day O'Kane and Jim were out walking through the halls for therapy and a woman came up to Jim and made the remarks Jim had become accustomed to hearing. "Oh, Mr. Brady, it's just wonderful to see you doing so well. You are such an inspiration."

"You know," Jim said as the lady passed by, "I just wish I could get past this inspiration phase and get better."

A number of people Jim ran into assumed that Jim wasn't "all there." They would talk over his head to Sarah, asking "How is he?" "And I'm sitting right there," says Jim, chortling. The Bradys went to many receptions where Jim, in his wheelchair, was the only person in the room who was sitting down. It created difficulties for him because everybody else was working the room, schmoozing at eye level, and Jim was stationary, looking everybody in the belt buckle. "When you're in a group of people, you become the third person invisible," he says. But he would bide his time at these functions, graciously greeting those who came up to him with a handshake and a witticism. Jim was learning infinite patience.

In 1985 Jim acquired a new wheelchair—called a "Quickie." Made of light-weight graphite, it had been designed and manufactured by Marilyn Hamilton of Fresno, California, who became a quadriplegic in a hang-glide accident. For a time Jim went around with a big button on his lapel: "Get a Quickie," causing some double takes, which he enjoyed. He began calling his chair the Bumblebee because it was painted yellow and black. (Sarah ordered it in the colors of his beloved Jeep.) Sometimes he called it "the Mercedes," or "the Rolls."

In 1982 Jim himself came up with a new therapy—horseback riding. It came about when Jim ran into Bob Douglas, executive director of the National Center for Therapeutic Riding, at a Gridiron banquet. "Jim looked at me and said, 'Mack and Duke,' " says Douglas. Mack and Duke were the two horses

Jim and Sarah had ridden on the occasions they went riding in Rock Creek Park in the early years of their marriage.

Douglas, who has alleviated the symptoms of his own disabilities resulting from multiple sclerosis through horseback riding, talked up the idea for Jim. Jim was enthusiastic and so was everybody else, but Kobrine, Wynne, and Douglas wanted Jim to be seizure-free for at least a year before he began, to negate the chance of any accident. The bottom line in therapeutic riding is safety. Jim was disappointed, but he said, "I can still pet the horses, can't I?"

In March 1985, seizure-free for a year and a half, Jim began his twice-weekly adventures with Berney, a "skewbald of very mixed breeding," according to Susan Haque, who, with Douglas, alternates in instructing Jim. Jim has called his steed "Berney Babes" ever since he learned that Berney was a filly.

At first, as much as he loved it, Jim found a number of things about riding very difficult and painful, particularly mounting and dismounting Berney. "He would weep and claim he couldn't do it," says Douglas. But Douglas ignored Jim's complaints and Jim stopped making them.

At first, also, Jim refused to do any walking at the stable. "In three or four months," says Douglas, "he was walking the length of the riding ring—two hundred fifty feet in the soft dust to his chair. His basic self-confidence improved."

"Jim's bad days are much less common now and his physical discomfort is less and less," says Susan Haque. "Once he is up on the horse, he is quite comfortable—ready to work and to go have fun on the horse."

Jim has learned a lot of riding technique and knows how to use his "legs, hands, back, seat, and voice," the keys to handling a horse. "He has some trouble putting them all together at the same time," says Haque, "but there is steady improvement."

"He has the disadvantage of having only one hand to steer, but he is learning to balance on the horse now without holding on," says Douglas. Along with all the other therapeutic aspects of riding, it was helping Jim strengthen his back and stomach muscles, as well as stretch out his contracted left leg. And "riding helps his circulation all around," says Haque.

Douglas says, "Jim likes horses even if he's not riding. When he broke his ribs he still came to the stables, even though he couldn't ride." Susan Haque says Jim wants to know all about Berney and what Berney likes and dislikes and what she has been doing.

One of Jim's goals is to be able to go riding with Scott, who will soon be old enough to take riding lessons. The other is to "ride like the Duke" (John Wayne, of course). "And I think he will be able to get there," says Douglas, who has seen Jim improve in so many ways. "The biggest change I've seen is that he is able to handle things a lot better. His attention span has improved, too. He doesn't get upset if he can't do what I ask him to do."

"Mentally, Jim is much more alert," says Haque. "He is very witty and sharp. His humor has always been there; now it is more finely tuned and sophisticated. Jim is the most interesting pupil I have ever had," says Haque. "He's so complex. He is two people in one—the public Jim and the private Jim. He's very much a showman—he rides much better when someone is watching him on the rail. He really likes to meet and talk to people."

In June 1985 Nancy Reagan came to ride with Jim and other disabled students of the center to give a boost to the program. "Jim sat bolt upright throughout his exercises—no slouching at all," says Haque.

Occasionally there is a trail ride, which is Jim's favorite. "He enjoys the camaraderie and participates a lot in our chatter about our families and other things," says Haque. "Being in a wheelchair most of the time, it's a wonderful feeling to be up higher than everybody else, for once. It provides him with the freedom and mobility he doesn't usually have. It's just us, the horses, and the woods."

Douglas, too, has marked the improvement in Jim's mental progress. "At first, his attention span was very limited. You'd ask him a question and he would think a long time before giving an answer. Now he goes right along with the flow of conversation and jokes." Bob recently asked Jim to fill in for him by reading a speech at a ceremony at the Potomac Polo Field. "A year and a half ago it would have been impossible for him to do. But he did it fine. Perfect, in fact. Just judging from the gains he's made in this short period of time, I expect him to make a lot of changes and progress."

Riding Berney has been important to Jim, believes Douglas, because "Jim has to do some of the things *he* wants to do, and riding was a decision *he* made because he wanted to do it."

Douglas tells of taking Jim to the Alexandria waterfront to inspect a tall ship from Denmark. But seeing the foot-wide gangplank, Douglas said, "I don't believe we can get on this thing, Jim."

"Oh, yes, we can," said Jim.

After a few beers, they had an even rougher time getting off the ship. "But if there is something Jim really wants to do, he'll do it," says Douglas.

Douglas himself found that working with other disabled riders enabled him to "sort of get rid of how *I* am and get into how somebody else is." And he feels Jim will receive the same reward as he gets more and more involved in doing things for others.

Speech pathologist Nancy Shafer picked Jim's case up from Arlene Pietranton in September 1984. Two years later she too was working toward getting Jim involved as a volunteer where his strongest skills—his social skills—could be used.

Jim is still adjusting to his losses, says Shafer, and although he is able most of the time to treat them with humor, privately he succumbs to despair about them from time to time. "It's such a hard process to go through—the loss of an arm—his other problems," she says. " 'I'm a half-wit. I need a lot of help,' Jim sometimes says, again privately." But Jim has many, many strengths, his therapists agree.

"Jim's pre-injury memory is incredible," says Shafer, "and beyond that he is now able to remember and use new information very well." Occasionally his memory fails him, but less and less as time goes on. He has no trouble remembering what interests him and his memory for new faces has been almost completely restored. He is far better at it than most people. Jim still has some difficulty sequencing events in their proper order, but his ability to monitor his mistakes continues to improve. His impulsiveness has gone, and except on the rare occasion, Jim has really mastered his wailing. Incidents of "inappropriate behavior" become fewer and fewer. Usually they are provoked when someone argues with Jim or goads him. He won't let that alone and will be sure to have the last word.

When Nancy Shafer asked Jim recently to list what he considered his biggest problems, in the order of their importance to him, this time he had a very realistic grasp of what they are: First, not surprisingly, was "mobility"; then "speech with confidence"; "physical therapy"; "long-term memory"; "short-term memory." Never able to stay serious for long, Jim then wrote, "gimp-footed, withered-arm father," who "falls." He has taken a few spills lately and in 1985 Jim fell and broke several ribs. He still feels very insecure on his feet and probably always will.

"Speech with confidence" is important to Jim because he is often asked to say a few words at the many benefits he and Sarah are asked to sponsor. "He knows it is a problem," says Shafer. "Sometimes he loses his train of thought, or pauses for a long time, or goes off on a tangent."

But he was also beginning to perform better and better on the podium, not an easy thing for anyone to master. After becoming involved with the National Head Injury Foundation, Jim agreed to be its honorary chairman and to direct its public-relations campaign. It was the first truly constructive work he would do, and when he accepted the honorary chairmanship and the accompanying plaque at the NHIF meeting in April 1986, he gave an amusing little response that was typically Jim Brady.

"Thank you very much," he said, "but is that 'honorary' or 'ornery' chairman? One never knows—the nuances of our language being infinite. And in my case you have to use semaphores to get me to understand. I will say, 'Brain. Move leg.' And my right arm will move.

"You'd better get used to not being listened to, too," he added.

Then Jim told a Don Regan joke. "Have you heard Don Regan's written a book? *Presidents Who Have Known Me.*"

"Just kidding, Don," said Jim, pretending to look for a hidden microphone, and then in an aside to the audience, "in which case you won't have the Bear to kick around anymore."

Jim mentioned that his chili recipe would be in the NHIF cookbook. "That certainly would propel people along" he said, thinking of his handicapped compatriots. And he said he was going to have the Barrier Committee* come over to the hotel

*That same month, Jim had also been named national chairman of Barrier Awareness Week. "Who better to talk about barriers," he said, "than the

and look at the two-story, rapidly running escalators in the lobby. "I'm sure Sir Edmund Hillary would have trouble getting up that thing."

"Well, I'm told by my keeper," said Jim looking at Sarah, "that I can finish up now. (Marilyn Spivak, chairman of NHIF, had said in her opening remarks, "We often become not only caretakers of our head-injured loved ones, but their persecutors as well. And Jim agrees.")

Then Sarah stood up to address the group. "That's a hard act to follow," she began. She told them that this was the first opportunity she had had to be with families of head-injured members, and that although she had "felt very sheltered and safe" by the marvelous care Jim had received, she had "come to understand the importance of having a loving, caring support system like the members of the Head Injury Foundation." Sarah was speaking to a group who thoroughly understood what she and Jim had been through and as she finished, her eyes filled up with tears, as did those of everyone in the room.

And the byword from the Bear himself from the very beginning, which he expressed in 1986 in an *NBC Nightly News* interview, was: "You've got to persevere. Persevere, and keep your sense of humor. They couldn't shoot that away."

Bear himself?" "Get those barriers down" was his motto. To promote "barrier awareness," celebrities and community leaders were paired with disabled people, and the pairs spent one day with each other—the nondisabled simulating whatever disability his partner had, confinement to a wheelchair, blindness, cerebral palsy, etc. Bobby Burgess and Karen Pendleton of *The Mickey Mouse Club* were among the celebrities there. And Allyce Beasley of *Moonlighting*. In their closing press conference, they all sat on the stage in wheelchairs, and told about their day. In most cases, until the disabled person identified himself, it was impossible to tell who was disabled and who was not. Hearing someone remark on that phenomenon, Jim Brady said, "Well, I'm the real article."

[illegible]

NOTES

CHAPTER ONE

Page 23
Personal interview, January 28, 1985.

Newsweek, April 13, 1981.

Page 24
Marian Burros, *The Washington Post*, March 26, 1981.

Godfrey Sperling, *Christian Science Monitor*, March 17, 1981.

Page 29
Lee Lescaze, *The Washington Post*, December 1, 1980.

Page 58
Judy Woodruff, *The Making of a Woman Reporter* (Reading, Mass.: Addison-Wesley, 1982).

Page 60
Information on security procedures from *The Making of a Woman Reporter*.

Page 61
Quote from *Chicago Tribune*, April 1, 1981.

Page 65
From an interview for this book, May 23, 1985.

CHAPTER FIVE

Page 199
John Pekkanen, "The Saving of the President," *Washingtonian*, August 1981.

Page 220
The Washington Post, April 27, 1981.

Page 233
Quotes from Joe Mastrangelo, *The Washington Post*, July 6, 1981.

CHAPTER SEVEN

Page 272
Garry Clifford, *People*, March 8, 1982.

CHAPTER TEN

Page 358
Jack W. Germond and Jules Witcover, *Blue Smoke and Mirrors* (New York; Viking Press, 1981), p. 101.

Ibid., p. 102.

CHAPTER ELEVEN

Page 366
The Washington Star, April 1, 1975.

CHAPTER TWELVE

Page 381
The Washington Post, November 7, 1981.

Page 382
Marian Burros, *The Washington Post*, March 26, 1981.

Page 384
Lou Cannon, *Reagan* (New York: Putnam, 1982), p. 260.

Page 386
From personal interview, May 23, 1985.

Page 390
Cannon, *Reagan*, p. 261.

Ibid., p. 262.

Page 391
Ibid., p. 266.

Page 411
Reagan's quotes on "Killer Trees" taken from Ibid.

Page 413
Marlene Cimons, *Los Angeles Times*, October 1980.

Page 416
Personal interview, May 23, 1985.

CHAPTER THIRTEEN

Page 425
Dick Kirschten, *National Journal*, January 31, 1981.

Page 427
The Washington Post, January 12, 1981.

Page 438
Washington Journalism Review, March 1981.

Page 439
Quotes from *The Illinois Sig,* April 1981.

Page 440
Lee Lescaze, *The Washington Post,* February 15, 1981.

Page 444
Elisabeth Bumiller, *The Washington Post,* March 25, 1981.

CHAPTER FIFTEEN

Page 464
Quotes from David Hoffman, *The Washington Post,* November 6, 1982.

CHAPTER SIXTEEN

Page 502
Marlene Cimons, *Los Angles Times,* September 23, 1984.

Page 505
Personal interview, March 12, 1984.

Page 508
Rudy Abramson, *Los Angeles Times,* February 6, 1982.

Page 521
Quotes from Betty Cuniberti, *Los Angeles Times,* September 7, 1986.

Index

Index

Index